Reserved Words

and	**array**	**begin**	**case**
const	**div**	**do**	**downto**
else	**end**	**file**	**for**
forward	**function**	**goto**	**if**
in	**label**	**mod**	**nil**
not	**of**	**or**	**packed**
procedure	**program**	**record**	**repeat**
set	**then**	**to**	**type**
until	**var**	**while**	**with**

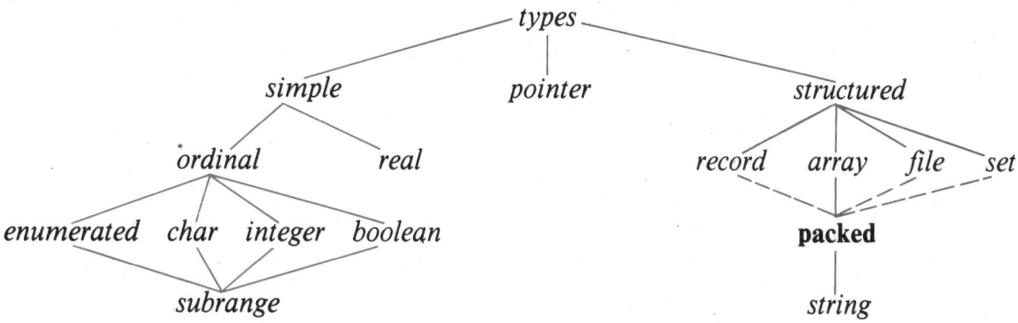

Operator Precedence

not						
*	/	**div**	**mod**	**and**		
+	−	**or**				
=	<>	<	<=	>	>=	**in**

Required Types

real	*integer*	*char*	*boolean*	*text*

Required Functions

abs(x)	*sqr(x)*	*sqrt(x)*	*sin(x)*	*Arithmetic*
cos(x)	*arctan(x)*	*ln(x)*	*exp(x)*	
trunc(x)	*round(x)*			*Transfer*
ord(x)	*chr(x)*	*succ(x)*	*pred(x)*	*Ordinal*
odd(x)	*eoln(f)*	*eof(f)*		*boolean*

Required Procedures

read	*readln*	*write*	*writeln*	*Input and Output*
rewrite(f)	*reset(f)*	*put(f)*	*get(f)*	*File Handling*
page(f)				
new(p)	*dispose(p)*			*Dynamic Allocation*
pack	*unpack*			*Transfer*

(*model program inside back cover*)

Oh! Pascal!

SECOND EDITION

For my grandparents, Molly and Sam Brecher.

D.C.

Oh! Pascal!

SECOND EDITION

by Doug Cooper and Michael Clancy
UNIVERSITY OF CALIFORNIA, BERKELEY

W·W· NORTON & COMPANY
New York and London

Oh! Pascal! was designed and typeset by Doug Cooper.

Printed in the United States of America

Acknowledgments

Intro: *Coney Island*, 1938–39, by Arthur Fellig (Weegee). Collection, The Museum of Modern Art, New York.
Cha. 1: UPI (top two photos).
Cha. 2: *Bed Amagansett, 1977*, by Lilo Raymond.
Cha. 4: © Sidney Harris.
Cha. 5: Rube Goldberg © King Features Syndicate.
Cha. 6: Museum of Modern Art Film Still Archives.
Cha. 7: *Self-Portrait of Maurits Cornelis Escher*, 1898. Collection of Cornelius van S. Roosevelt, Wash., D.C.
Cha. 8: *Typewriter*, 1965, by Robert Arnason. Courtesy University Art Museum, Berkeley. Gift of the artist.
Cha. 9: Phototeque.
Cha. 10: Courtesy George C. Page Museum.
Cha. 11: *100 Soup Cans*, 1962, by Andy Warhol. Photo courtesy Leo Castelli Gallery, N.Y.
Cha. 12: Collection H. Vever.
Cha. 13: Sara Krulwich/NYT Pictures.
Cha. 14: Charles Phillips.
Cha. 15: BIPS.
Cha. 16: Bettmann Archive, Inc.
Appendix A: Benno Friedman. © Push Pin Studios

W. W. Norton & Company, Inc. 500 Fifth Avenue, New York, N.Y. 10110
W. W. Norton & Company, Ltd., 37 Great Russell Street, London WC1B 3NU

ISBN 0 393 95445-5

6 7 8 9 0

Table of Contents

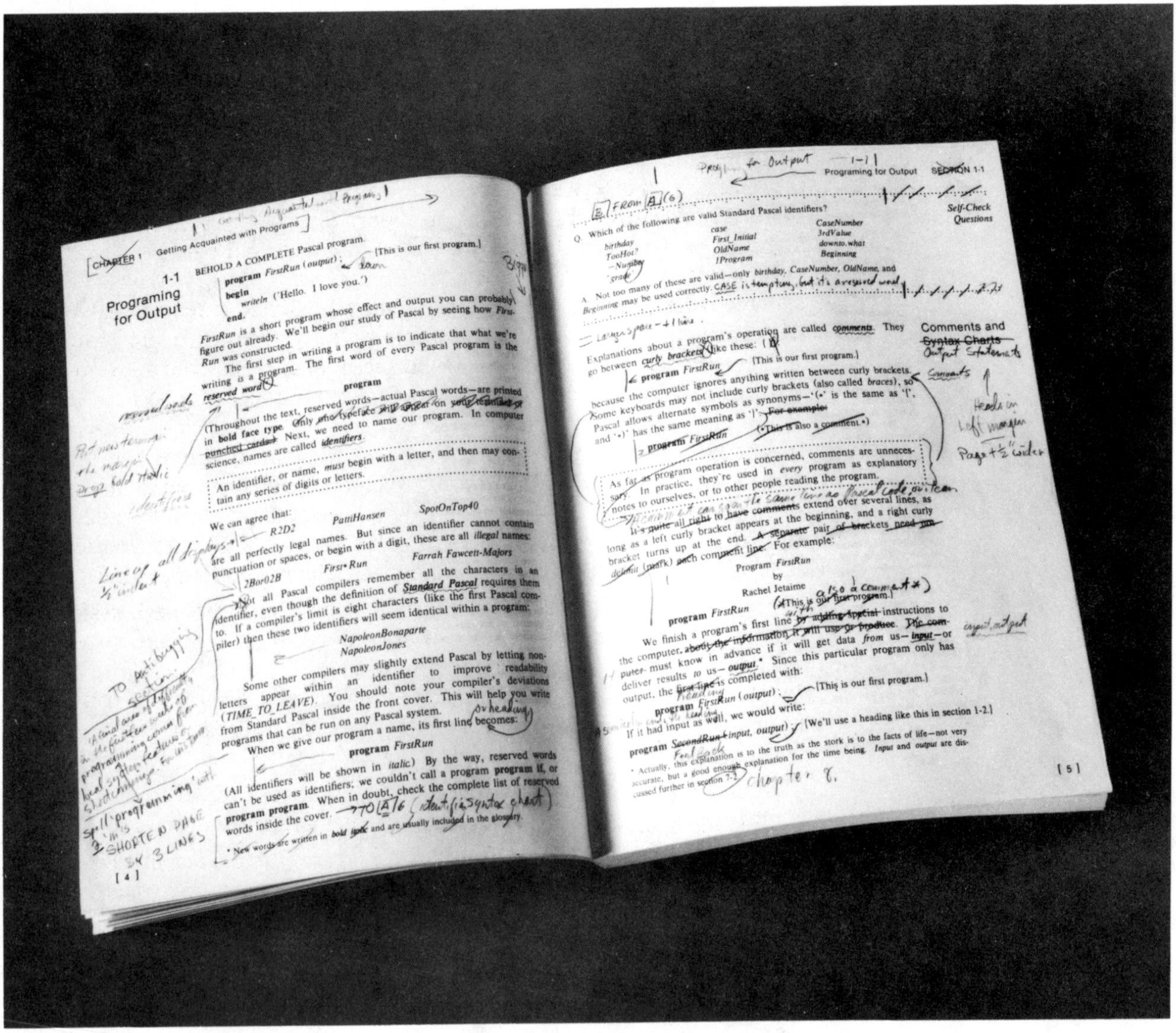
CHAPTER 1 Getting Acquainted with Programs

1-1 Programing for Output

BEHOLD A COMPLETE Pascal program.

```
program FirstRun (output);   {This is our first program.}
begin
   writeln ('Hello. I love you.')
end.
```

FirstRun is a short program whose effect and output you can probably figure out already. We'll begin our study of Pascal by seeing how *FirstRun* was constructed.

The first step in writing a program is to indicate that what we're writing is a program. The first word of every Pascal program is the reserved word

program

(Throughout the text, reserved words—actual Pascal words—are printed in **bold face type**. Only the typeface will appear on your terminal or punched cards.) Next, we need to name our program. In computer science, names are called *identifiers*.

An identifier, or name, *must* begin with a letter, and then may contain any series of digits or letters.

We can agree that:

R2D2 *PattiHansen* *SpotOnTop40*

are all perfectly legal names. But since an identifier cannot contain punctuation or spaces, or begin with a digit, these are all *illegal* names:

2Bor02B *First•Run* *Farrah Fawcett-Majors*

Not all Pascal compilers remember all the characters in an identifier, even though the definition of *Standard Pascal* requires them to. If a compiler's limit is eight characters (like the first Pascal compiler) then these two identifiers will seem identical within a program:

NapoleonBonaparte
NapoleonJones

Some other compilers may slightly extend Pascal by letting non-letters appear within an identifier to improve readability (*TIME_TO_LEAVE*). You should note your compiler's deviations from Standard Pascal inside the front cover. This will help you write programs that can be run on any Pascal system.

When we give our program a name, its first line becomes:

program *FirstRun*

(All identifiers will be shown in *italic*.) By the way, reserved words can't be used as identifiers; we couldn't call a program **program** if, or **program program**. When in doubt, check the complete list of reserved words inside the cover.

* New words are written in ***bold italic*** and are usually included in the glossary.

[4]

Programing for Output SECTION 1-1

Self-Check Questions

Q. Which of the following are valid Standard Pascal identifiers?

birthday	*case*	*CaseNumber*
TooHot?	*First_Initial*	*3rdValue*
—Number	*OldName*	*downto.what*
'grade'	*1Program*	*Beginning*

A. Not too many of these are valid—only *birthday*, *CaseNumber*, *OldName*, and *Beginning* may be used correctly.

Comments and Syntax Charts

Explanations about a program's operation are called *comments*. They go between *curly brackets* like these: { }.

```
program FirstRun   {This is our first program.}
```

because the computer ignores anything written between curly brackets. Some keyboards may not include curly brackets (also called *braces*), so Pascal allows alternate symbols as synonyms—'(•' is the same as '{', and '•)' has the same meaning as '}'. For example:

```
program FirstRun   (•This is also a comment.•)
```

As far as program operation is concerned, comments are unnecessary. In practice, they're used in *every* program as explanatory notes to ourselves, or to other people reading the program.

It's quite all right to have comments extend over several lines, as long as a left curly bracket appears at the beginning, and a right curly bracket turns up at the end. A separate pair of brackets need not delimit (mark) each comment line. For example:

```
{ Program FirstRun
        by
  Rachel Jetaime
program FirstRun   This is our first program.}
```

We finish a program's first line by adding special instructions to the computer about the information it will use or produce. The computer must know in advance if it will get data *from* us—*input*—or deliver results *to* us—*output*.* Since this particular program only has output, the first line is completed with:

```
program FirstRun (output);   {This is our first program.}
```

If it had input as well, we would write:

```
program SecondRun (input, output);   {We'll use a heading like this in section 1-2.}
```

* Actually, this explanation is to the truth as the stork is to the facts of life—not very accurate, but a good enough explanation for the time being. *Input* and *output* are discussed further in section 7-2.

[5]

Preface to the Second Edition

I approached this revision of *Oh! Pascal* with some trepidation. Since it was first published in 1982, I've received much advice on *Oh! Pascal!*, including suggestions that it be longer, shorter, harder, easier, funnier yet more serious, with fewer and additional example programs, and problems that are simpler and more difficult to do, as well as more but less mathematically oriented. I'm pleased to report that all of these comments were found to be useful, and are incorporated in the second edition.

Of course, there are some cosmetic changes as well. My main goals, though, have been to make the book easier to use, and to extend its coverage. It's suitable for any college-level course on programming using Pascal, and has enough material for the ETS Advanced Placement course as well. This edition is about 25% longer than the first, mainly because of new sections.

In addition to the new material and rearrangement, there has been extensive rewriting. In brief, the first five chapters have been tightened up, the middle five have had their hard example programs clarified and/or rewritten, and the last five chapters (particularly arrays, files, and pointers) have acquired a variety of additional examples. The major changes are:

- New Material: There are new sections on hardware and system software (Introduction), analysis of algorithms (5-2), program correctness and verification (9-2), software engineering (10-1), recursion (7-3, 11-3), and an entirely new Chapter 16 on advanced topics in sorting (including Quicksort), searching (including binary search and hashing), and string matching.
- Optional Early Coverage: There are new optional early introductions to one-dimensional arrays (4-2), and textfiles and file windows (8-2).
- Reordered for Easier Use: Procedures and parameters are introduced together in Chapter 3—no more side-effects. Functions are covered in 3-3. Arrays now come before records, rather than vice versa. The chapter summaries now collect all new Pascal syntax and rules presented in the chapter.
- More Accessible: Overall there's less concentration on syntax details. Chapters 1 and 2 have been condensed considerably. The **for** and **case** statements now have separate chapters (4 and 5), as does text processing (Chapter 8).
- Recursion: Recursion has a much greater emphasis. The expanded recursion section includes Towers of Hanoi and exponentiation prob-

lems. Advanced chapters include recursive array manipulation, recursive binary search, and Quicksort.

- New Examples: The more complicated examples in the middle chapters have been given extended developments, and difficult code has been rewritten. There are a variety of additional examples in the advanced chapters.
- Antibugging and Debugging: These sections have been expanded where appropriate, with additional emphasis on semantic (rather than syntactic) bugs, and greater development of antibugging tools (stub procedures, embedded debugging code, etc.).
- Spelling: Programmer, programmed, programming, etc. are now spelled with two m's, in conformance with the English language.
- Miscellaneous: Syntax charts are collected in an appendix. There is an index to programs. The page design has been changed; the page is shorter and lighter. Many small errors fixed in earlier printings have been corrected in this edition. The program layout style has been improved. (I've adopted the *Software Tools* layout rules.)

In any event, I hope you'll find that the book speaks for itself. If you're an instructor returning to *Oh! Pascal!* for yet another term, there are some new pictures to help you along. And, if you're a student learning Pascal for the first time, you may find that Computer Science is a little more fun than you thought. Thanks go to Mike Clancy and Jim Jordan for their comments on the draft, Ruth Mandel for help with the pictures, and especially to David Lichtenstein for his friendship. See you in the terminal room!

Doug Cooper
March, 1985

Preface to the First Edition

We wrote *Oh! Pascal!* to provide a clear, non-mathematically oriented introduction to programming and Pascal. We take it for granted that Pascal is a superior instructional language, that the way to learn programming is to write programs, and that problem solving should be taught in the first programming course. Our book is aimed at students who, although otherwise sober and upright, seem to lack an intuitive feel for computer science. We try to anticipate and answer questions, as well as to explain the facts in a friendly, refreshing manner.

Most of all, we've tried to make *Oh! Pascal!* a self-teaching book (as opposed to a reference manual that sticks to very small words). We've attempted a presentation that's detailed enough for people studying on their own, yet lucid, readable, and enjoyable enough for more traditional students to read before lecture. Most of *Oh! Pascal!'s* innovations, as described below, are motivated by this goal.

1) We emphasize general problem-solving techniques.

Most books begin and end their discussion of problem solving with stepwise refinement. However, many other methods that good problem-solvers (and programmers) take for granted have never been formalized in the student's mind, and need to be presented explicitly. A host of techniques for dealing with problems—massaging them, lateral thinking, examining solution spaces, etc.—are employed frequently throughout the book. We've been greatly influenced by people like James Adams (*Conceptual Blockbusting*, W.W. Norton), and Richard Skemp (*Psychology of Learning Mathematics*, Penguin), and we know that solving programming problems, per se, is often the least of a novice's woes.

2) An early discussion of procedures.

Pascal has to be taught in a way that encourages good programming. Thus, procedures are introduced when a conceptual need for them arises—during the first discussion of top-down design—even before the basic control statements have been defined. Our experience has been that this approach encourages modular program design, well-defined algorithms, and makes large-scale programs much easier to tackle later on.

3) Interactive programs are shown in action—the reader isn't forced to infer their differences from batch.

Like many other teachers, we struggled for years with texts that were designed for batch-oriented Pascal systems. These texts really penalize interactive programmers, because some techniques that are easily motivated in batch programs (especially the use of *eof*) greatly confuse interactive programs.

In *Oh! Pascal!* we started by writing all examples for interactive use, then modified and added until a sufficient set was suited for batch systems.* Throughout the book we point out features (or lack of features) that make specific programs more suited to batch or interactive use. As a result, we think that both groups of programmers get the impression that the book was aimed at them, rather than at the others. All programs show typical input and output.

4) Antibugging and debugging sections follow each chapter.

Every chapter is followed by a discussion of the potential hazards it has introduced. Especially difficult points are reiterated, typical error messages are deciphered, and general programming advice is dispensed. A special advantage of these sections is the opportunity to present *incorrect* examples, while carefully isolating them from the main text.

5) The **for** and **case** statements are introduced before the others.

This lets the student practice developing algorithms, and writing programs, before dealing with the brand-new notion of *boolean* expressions. Students gain experience with some of Pascal's bug-prone, but crucial, syntax details (like compound and empty statements) before they get to have fun writing infinite loops.

6) Every chapter includes self-check questions, and a self-test.

Numerous self-check questions, complete with answers, are scattered throughout the text. Each chapter is followed by 10-20 exercises and brief programming problems that are answered at the end of the book, as well as harder exercises for assignment. All in all, there are about 500 exercises in *Oh! Pascal!*

A number of other features were suggested by shortcomings we've found in other Pascal texts. Since long programs seem to be fundamentally different from short ones, we've included several lengthy examples; the longest (and last) runs five pages. At the same time, we emphasize the pseudocode development of all example programs, long or short.

We try to demystify and humanize Pascal and programming. Many students are intimidated by computers, and have little confidence in their own ability. We try to point out limitations of Pascal, and the reasons for them. We motivate the language through the requirements of programming and problem solving, instead of presenting it as a limited, but nontheless arbitrary, set of commands.

We're proud of the visual appearance of the book. Programming textbooks usually suffer terribly at the hands of compositers who force the reader to lose her place while she finds a program 'figure', or make pro-

* We use 'lazy I/O', as widely implemented, and allowed by the current draft standard.

grams break arbitrarily from one page to the next to keep each page's length the same.* By producing camera copy ourselves, we were able to show every example in-line with the text. Example programs longer than one page are almost invariably on facing pages, and are always broken at procedure boundaries.

A second advantage of doing our own typesetting is the accuracy it allows. Every program, and most subprograms, have been run without error or warning messages using the -s option (Standard Pascal only) of the Berkeley Pascal compiler (pc) and interpreter (pi). All program output displayed was produced by the actual source program shown in the text as it was being typeset. All examples and definitions conform to the ISO and ANSI Pascal standards.

We've included a glossary, chapter reviews, and reference matter inside the front and back covers. Space has been left for noting local system characteristics. We've also provided greatly simplified syntax charts. Although they don't constitute a formal definition of Pascal, they're a good reference for beginning programmers.

Finally, the title. It seems that bookstores shelve Pascal books inconsistently; some list by title, and others by subject. Lest a Pascal book escape notice, publishing wisdom requires that its title begin with the letter 'p'. As a result, the world has acquired *Pascal, Pascal Programming, Programming Standard Pascal, Programming For Poets (Using Pascal), Pascal Programming Structures, Practical Introduction To Pascal, Problem Solving and Programming in Pascal*, etc.

Wishing to dissent, but unwilling to make too radical a departure from the established norm, we decided that our title should start with one of two alternative letters—either 'o' or 'q.' To make a long story short, *Oh! Pascal!* was finally chosen. The alternatives (*O.K. Pascal, Quest For Pascal*, etc.) were too ridiculous to merit serious consideration.

Grateful thanks for early encouragement must go to Michael Spivak. We would also like to acknowledge the help, inspiration, and current or former existence of (carefully randomized using the 52 card pickup algorithm) Patti Hansen, Rachel M. Silverman, Michael Powell, Bruce Char, Phyllis Stern, Diane McNichol, David Lichtenstein, the Who, Neil Patterson, Dave Presotto, Andy Warhol, Barry Smith, John Foderaro, the Computer Science Division of U.C. Berkeley, Joanna Boudreaux, Dick Fateman's Sufferance, Gia Carangi, Joseph Ossanna, the MIT/SAIL jargon file, W.P.O.D., Bill Karjane, Thomas McGuane, Peter Kessler and Kirk McKusick (the Kompiler Kids), Unsung Contributors and Reviewers, and, naturally, Ernie K.

* Incidentally, all personal pronouns in *Oh! Pascal!* are feminine. After hundreds of years of 'he' and 'his', a few decades of 'she' and 'her' shouldn't bother anyone.

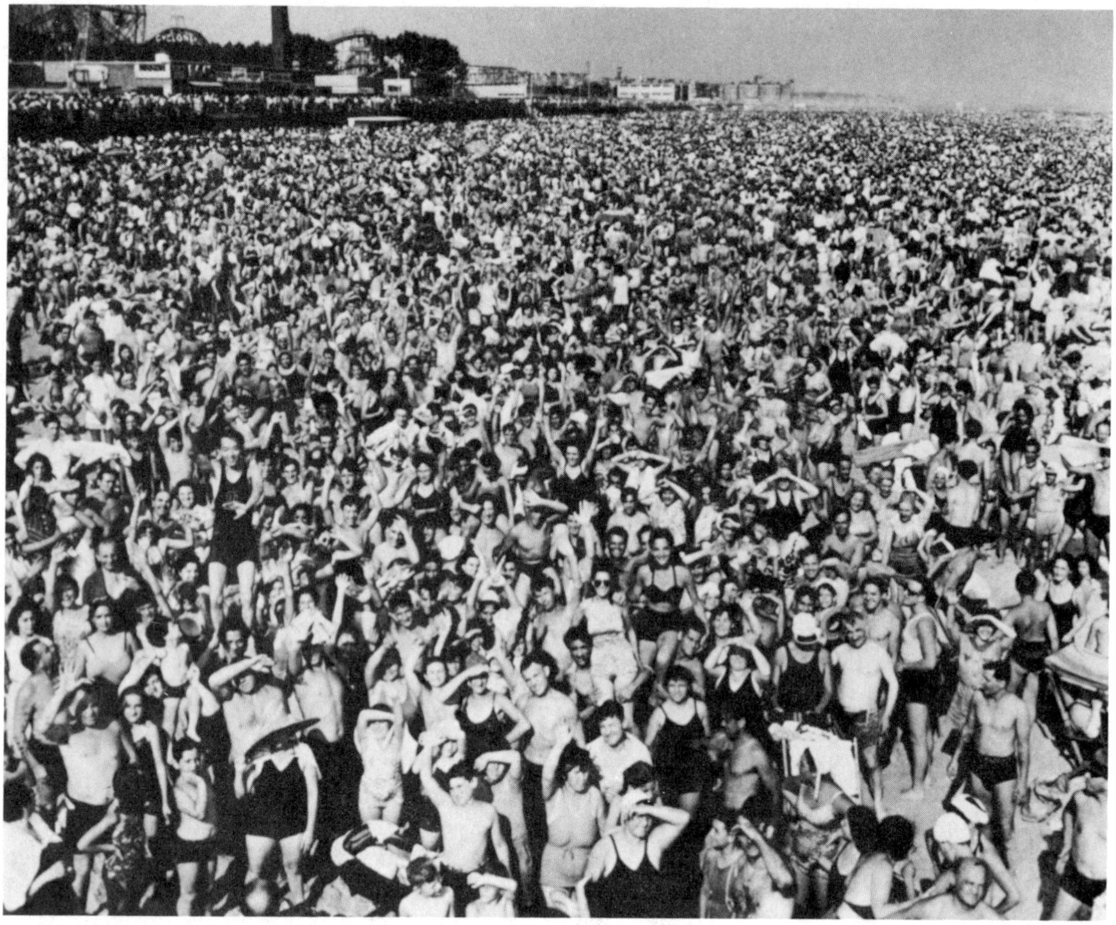

Introduction

WELCOME TO *OH! PASCAL!*, AND WELCOME to computer science. Let's begin with an introduction to the basics. We'll start out with some of the history of programming languages, and of Pascal. Then, we'll talk about devising algorithms and solving problems, and learn what we can do to get better at both. We'll round out our discussion with a quick guided tour of computer systems hardware. Finally, we'll close by saying a few words about the software that every system needs.

Programming Languages

There's an old story about an untutored bumpkin who listened to some students as they talked about the stars. Although the concepts they discussed were strange and new, he felt he could understand how astronomers used telescopes to measure the distance from the earth to the celestial bodies. It even seemed reasonable that they could predict the stars' relative positions and motions. What totally puzzled him, though, was how the devil they were able to find out the stars' *names!*

People sometimes approach programming languages in the same way—as though they're complicated mathematical codes that the first computer scientists were lucky enough to break. Well, they are ciphers of a sort, but they're not so hard to crack. Let's look at the three basic kinds of programming languages—low-level *machine* languages, intermediate *assembly* languages, and, finally, *high-level* languages like Pascal.

instruction sets

The most basic programming codes belong to an *instruction set*. These are the computer's built-in commands, and they aren't much more sophisticated than the operations we can punch into a programmable hand calculator. There are instructions for doing simple arithmetic, of course, and for saving answers and values as we go along. There are usually a variety of instructions available for comparing values, and for deciding what to do next. A special set of instructions store and retrieve things from the computer's memory. The fanciest instructions usually deal with getting more instructions.

machine language

A *machine language*—the simplest programming code—is defined by numbering the basic instructions. When we do this, each instruction's number becomes its code name. If we use eight-digit binary values for numbering (as computers often do), we can name 256 different instructions, starting with 00000000 and ending with 11111111. A machine language program is nothing but a long series of eight-digit numbers.

assembly language

Machine language programming is easy, but it's incredibly tedious. Fortunately, one of the earliest programmers had a bright idea. Why not write a machine language program that could recognize short sequences of English letters, and would automatically translate the English into the proper machine language instructions? Why not, indeed! Such programs were called *assemblers*; they understood *assembly language*, and were soon found on every computer.

Assembly language programming is a bit more palatable. An assembly language program is a sequence of two-to-four-letter assembly language commands, often accompanied by an additional shorthand that identifies locations in the computer's memory. For instance, the assembly language command **ADD R2, R4** means 'add the contents of memory location R2 to memory location R4, and save the sum in R4.' It isn't hard to imagine carrying out the same kind of command on any hand calculator that has a built-in memory.

Although assembly language was a convenience, it hardly exhausted the limits of human ingenuity. Why be limited to three-letter words? Programmers wanted to express themselves in relatively English sentences, rather than in the computer-oriented terms of machine and assembly languages. In response, research teams did the obvious. They repeated the same step that had led to assemblers, and wrote more complicated programs, called *interpreters* and *compilers*. The new programs translated increasingly sophisticated sequences of letters into a form the computer could understand. The letters, and the words they formed, were called *high-level* languages.

interpreters, compilers

High-level languages, like FORTRAN, BASIC, and Pascal, are consciously designed to help solve problems. In contrast, low-level machine and assembly languages, were expressly intended to operate computers. Programmers who use high-level languages don't have to worry about getting instructions, or keeping track of numbered memory locations. Instead, they give commands in a language that usually resembles a terse English. A typical high-level language program consists of phrases that are liable to be found in the statement of a solution—**if** a condition is met **then** we take an action or **else** do something different.

high-level languages

Many programming languages have been designed in response to different problem-solving requirements. Just as there are several types of hand calculators (statistical, business, scientific), there are also job-specific computer languages. You can write most programs using any language, in the same way that you *could* use a financial calculator to solve a statistics problem. However, it makes sense to use the most appropriate tool. We can discover the original purpose of some languages from their names:

some popular programming languages

FORTRAN: FORmula TRANslator is one of the earliest and most widespread languages. It's intended mainly for scientific applications.

COBOL: COmmon Business Oriented Language was developed as a standard for business computing. Many COBOL instructions are designed specifically for payroll or accounting applications.

BASIC: Beginner's All-purpose Symbolic Instruction Code is a simple language that's used to teach basic computer applications. Although it's easy to learn, BASIC doesn't go very far. It's a poor basis for understanding programming, and is no longer widely taught in college-level programming courses.

LISP: LISt Processing language is widely used in programs that involve processing of symbols, from mathematical symbols to the symbols that form natural (spoken) languages. It's one of the main languages used in artificial intelligence research.

Pascal

Pascal was named after the 17th century mathematician and religious zealot Blaise Pascal. Since it's not an acronym (it doesn't stand for anything) only the first letter is capitalized. Pascal was created with two main goals:

1. To provide a teaching language that would bring out concepts common to all languages, while avoiding inconsistencies and unnecessary detail.
2. To define a truly standard language that would be cheap and easy to implement on any computer.

In a sense, Pascal is a *lingua franca*, or common tongue, of programming. It's easy to learn, and provides an excellent foundation for learning other languages. We've found that people who know Pascal can master BASIC in an afternoon, and pick up FORTRAN in a week or two.

But what does Pascal *look* like? Niklaus Wirth, the Swiss professor who designed the language, intended that Pascal be as clear, readable, and unambiguous as possible. The displays inside the covers show all the reserved words that are the bare bones Pascal language. Clearly, Pascal isn't written in binary code. In fact, we're reminded of the famous ad:

If u cn rd ths ad, u cn gt a gd jb—Learn Speedwriting!

One of Pascal's big advantages over some earlier languages is that it lets us write a program using almost exactly the same terms we used to state the original problem's solution. Some day soon we expect to be seeing this sign in the subways:

```
if YouCanReadThis then begin
  StartWork (Soon);
  Earn (BigBucks)
end;
```

newer languages

Is Pascal the ultimate programming language? No. An eventual successor to Pascal may be Modula-2, which was also developed by Wirth. Don't worry that you're studying the wrong language, though, because the first term's worth of Modula-2 is almost exactly like Pascal. Modula-2 contains some additional features that make it attractive for later programming courses, particularly those that involve writing large programs that translate languages (the *compiler* course) or control computers (the *operating systems* course). Within a few years, Modula-2 may become a language widely used for undergraduate coursework.*

* Is this a plug for *Oh My! Modula-2!*?

Another potential Pascal successor, the Ada programming language, was commissioned by the U.S. Department of Defense. The DoD hoped to create a language that would be more reliable for the control of weapons systems, as well as less expensive to program in, than FORTRAN and the others. At the time of this writing it is not clear that either goal has been met, nor that the language will be widely used outside of defense contractors' programming shops.

Algorithms and Problem Solving

Before we can write a program we have to develop its *algorithm*. An algorithm is an outline of the steps that solving a problem will require. It's usually detailed enough to be the basis of a computer program, but it isn't written in a computer language. Instead, the algorithm is expressed in English. A good programmer will be able to *implement*, or realize, the algorithm in almost any programming language.

what are algorithms?

Is a recipe an algorithm? If it were, a Pascal textbook would consist of chapter after chapter of standard programs. A recipe is a highly restricted algorithm at best, because it only solves one specific instance of a problem—how to bake a chocolate fudge cake, say, rather than how to bake a cake in general. Algorithms tend to be less special-purpose; an algorithm is a set of rules to follow to solve a certain kind of problem, rather than one particular example of it.

dividing fractions

Suppose that we want to divide one fraction by another. If we knew the particular fractions involved we might be tempted to supply a recipe, rather than a broader algorithm. For instance, 1/4 divided by 1/2 can be solved by applying the specific rule 'divide the denominators,' which gives a correct answer: 1/(4/2), or 1/2. However, this is just a special case! The general algorithm we should follow—exchange the numerator and denominator of one fraction, then multiply the two fractions—is an algorithm that solves *all* fraction divisions.

Computer algorithms usually include some details that take machine limitations into account. For instance, if we were going to add two numbers by hand we'd just specify one step—add the numbers. A computer algorithm has extra operations for the computer's benefit:

get the numbers
add them up
print the answer

exchanging numbers

What about exchanging two numbers, a job we might have to do in a program that divided fractions? It's tempting to say that our algorithm is:

get the numerator and denominator
give the numerator the value of the denominator
give the denominator the value of the numerator

But can you spot the error that will occur if we follow these instructions exactly, the way a computer would? Both of our 'variables' (the numerator and denominator) will end up representing the original denominator, because we didn't save the value of the original numerator. A computer algorithm has to take this step explicitly:

get the numerator and denominator
save the numerator
give the numerator the denominator's value
give the denominator the saved value

Now, we know that some readers are beginning to panic already! The reason is that most people assume that their skill at developing algorithms is a given that can't be changed. During the first week of class, we often hear students express fears that, while they can understand algorithms, they won't be able to think logically enough to make up good algorithms on their own. Don't worry—problem-solving ability can be improved.

How can a rudimentary natural talent be sharpened? Well, let's consider what athletes do. They practice for hours, and employ coaches to watch for flaws in form. They read about their sports, talk to other participants, watch films of themselves in action, and mentally rehearse their moves. Nowadays, some athletes even use computers to analyze their performance, and suggest improvements. It all seems to help.

Build-up	*Display*	*Simulate*
Eliminate	*Organize*	*Test*
Work Forward	*List*	*Play*
Work Backward	*Check*	*Manipulate*
Associate	*Diagram*	*Copy*
Classify	*Chart*	*Interpret*
Generalize	*Verbalize*	*Transform*
Exemplify	*Visualize*	*Translate*
Compare	*Memorize*	*Expand*
Relate	*Recall*	*Reduce*
Commit	*Record*	*Exaggerate*
Defer	*Retrieve*	*Understate*
Leap In	*Search*	*Adapt*
Hold Back	*Select*	*Substitute*
Focus	*Plan*	*Combine*
Release	*Predict*	*Separate*
Force	*Assume*	*Change*
Relax	*Question*	*Vary*
Dream	*Hypothesize*	*Cycle*
Imagine	*Guess*	*Repeat*
Purge	*Define*	*Systemize*
Incubate	*Symbolize*	*Randomize*

Some Problem-Solving Strategies

Can we improve our ability to think? Well, as James Adams, author of *Conceptual Blockbusting—A Guide to Better Ideas* points out, most people view 'improving the mind' as acquiring more knowledge. Since our aim is to produce algorithms, though, we'll concentrate on practice, and on learning new ways of solving problems.

improving thinking

The first step in solving a problem is always the hardest. The table of strategies above is a list of suggestions to help you get unstuck. As we start to work on algorithms, we'll introduce several other general problem-solving methods. There are different thinking approaches—*visual* and *lateral* thinking are two that we'll discuss. There are also techniques (like *massage*) that aim at making problems more manageable.

Some other methods are particularly well-suited for the development of program algorithms. Throughout the text we'll be discussing ideas of *top-down* and *bottom-up* algorithm design. We'll see how an algorithm's *elegance* affects a program, and debate the merits of *efficiency*. We'll also find out about some solution methods that were largely impractical before the advent of computers—*exhaustive search* and *brute force* approaches.

Once we've figured out how to solve a problem, and have an algorithm in hand (or in head), it's time to write a program. Now, programming is a field that's undergone drastic changes in the past two decades. In contrast to the early days of computing, it is programs, rather than hardware, that are expensive. Studies have consistently shown that considerably more time and effort goes into patching and improving *existing* programs than is devoted to writing new ones. As a result, interest has focused on methods of writing programs that not only work, but can also be understood by others. The new field of *software engineering*—the study of producing programs—is one of the hottest areas in computing today.

Nowadays, for instance, there's a great deal of emphasis on things like program *style*. This is a far cry from the old days, when programs were judged by whether or not they ran, rather than how well they were put together. A well-written program doesn't just outwit the computer. It's put together in a way that someone who may have to read it two or ten years hence can understand. It implements the detailed sequence of steps that a computer requires, without losing or confusing a human reader who deals in concepts. It's also *robust* enough to continue working in a real world that's full of errors, both human and computer.

program style

Can stylish programming be taught? Again, in the bad old days, there was a notion that the ability to program was a mystical talent that couldn't be analyzed. But programming, like thinking, can be practiced and improved. Throughout the text we'll be raising many small points about software engineering, and making suggestions to help you create good programs. Programming problems are divergent—they usually have many solutions. Let's hope (for the sake of those who may one day have to read *your* code) that you learn the difference between good solutions and bad ones!

Computer Systems

It may be somewhat disconcerting to find that even though this text is devoted to the subject of computer programming, computers themselves are almost never mentioned. In practice, programmers don't *have* to know much about the internal workings of a computer, any more than typists need to understand the mechanical underpinnings of an electric typewriter. But rather than succumb to this appeal for ignorance, let's get an overview of what goes on behind the keyboard.

By now everybody must know that computers are systems with two sides: hardware and software. Neither is of much use without the other, and the programs we'll learn to write depend on both. A very simple picture of a computer system might look something like this:

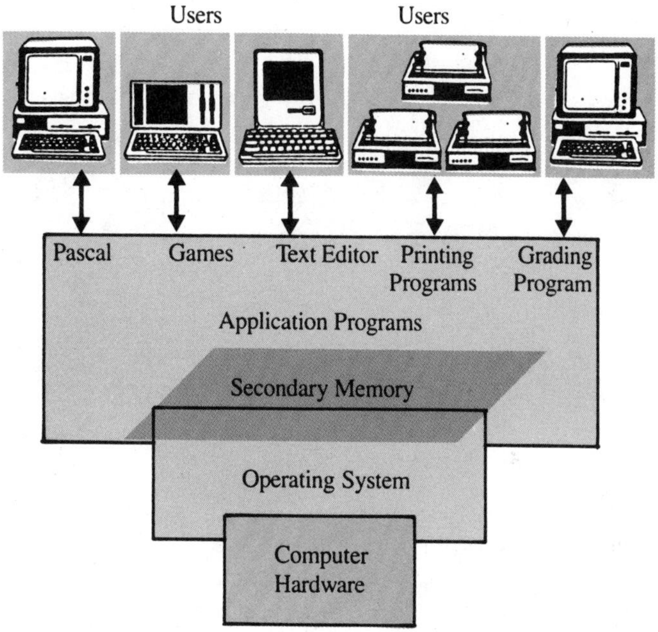

Hardware components are shaded in red. They include the computer, as well as machines that are connected to it: terminals, printers, secondary memory, and so on. Software components are given in gray, and include applications programs and the operating system.

It's difficult to separate hardware and software, since even the simplest tasks rely on both. We need hardware to enter data, but we need software to make sure that the computer can communicate with a terminal. We need hardware to print a hard copy of stored information, but we must have software to transfer the letters, one at a time, from the computer to the printer. We need hardware to actually compute figures, but we need software to prepare our figures for computation. Let's look at each part of the system in turn.

Hardware

A computer's hardware can be divided into three groups of electronics. The *CPU*, or central processing unit, is the heart of every computer. It runs programs, performs calculations, and manages the operation of the computer's other parts. *Memory* is the second essential component. It stores almost all information the computer uses, from the data needed for program steps that will take place a microsecond hence, to database information that might not be used for years. Finally, *I/O*, or input/output, devices are necessary for communication between a computer and its human users, or other electronic devices.

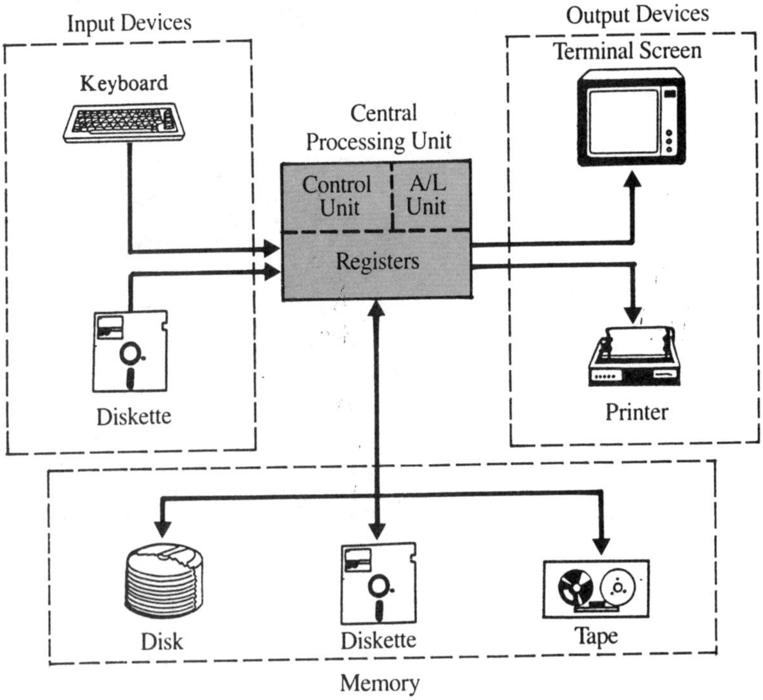

the CPU

The CPU provides what people think of as the brains of the computer. The CPU has several parts that work together closely. The *execution registers* hold program instructions while they are being executed, or carried out. Typically, only the current instruction will be held, which means that from the viewpoint of the execution registers, there is no difference between big programs and little ones, or hard programs and easy ones.

execution registers

The execution registers are also in charge of keeping track of current information—values that are in the process of being changed, currently active locations in memory, and the like.

the ALU

Determining the effect of each program step is largely the province of the *ALU*, or arithmetic and logic unit. The ALU is the CPU's decision-making unit. Its primary task is to make small comparisons (are these values equal? which is greater?) that, when taken in great number, seem to be reasoned decisions. To support its decision-making capability, the ALU also carries out elementary arithmetic operations like addition and subtraction. Again, each small step may be insignificant in itself, but they can eventually add up to give the computer the illusion of sophisticated mathematical ability.

The execution registers and ALU work hand-in-hand, with the registers posing the questions and the ALU supplying the answers. The *CU*, or control unit, keeps them in touch with each other, and also with the rest of the computer (the memory and input/output devices described below). In effect, the control unit serves as the machine's traffic controller.

control unit

Together, the execution registers, arithmetic and logic unit, and control unit largely determine how 'powerful' a given computer appears to be. One basic difference between computers is the speed at which the control unit is able to transfer information between the ALU and registers. A second is the amount of time required for the ALU to actually make a computation. A third is the amount of overlap that can occur—expensive systems will have additional execution registers and ALU's so that work can begin on a new program step before the old one is completely finished. A final power-enhancement mechanism is only found in the most advanced computers. They let operations take place in parallel—several program steps are carried out simultaneously.

computer power

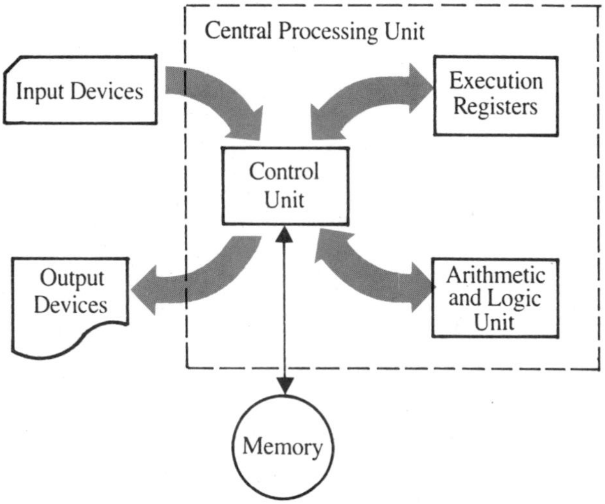

The CPU stands poised to carry out any single step of a computer program. To do useful work, though, the CPU must work with a computer's other components. *Memory* is the most important. It's needed to store programs that govern a computer's operation, along with data needed when programs are run, partial results that are derived and must be maintained during the course of a program's operation, and any final results that are saved for perusal later.

memory

Memory is usually divided into two varieties—*main* or *primary* memory and *secondary* memory. Main memory comes with the computer;

main memory

secondary memory

it's built in, but can usually be increased by purchase of additional 'memory boards' or 'memory chips.' Simply stated, main memory stores running programs and the information they currently use. It is directly in the service of the CPU, which means that the CPU (which is very fast) can go to and from main memory to get new program steps, and to store or retrieve data. Main memory is usually one of the more expensive hardware components, so computers will typically have just enough to meet the requirements of the largest programs they're liable to encounter.

Secondary memory holds programs and information that are not currently being used. Most people have seen the floppy disks that serve as secondary memory for personal computers. Typically, each floppy disk will store the instructions for (and have room for the results of) a single program. The computer user has to physically insert the disk in order to transfer its contents to main memory, and run the program it holds.

Secondary memory for bigger, shared, computers is generally made from large, rigid disks that are permanently mounted alongside the computer. Each user has a share of this common secondary storage, and doesn't have to divide her programs, or results, amongst floppy disks. Multi-user computers automatically carry out any transfers between secondary and main memory for the benefit of the computer user.

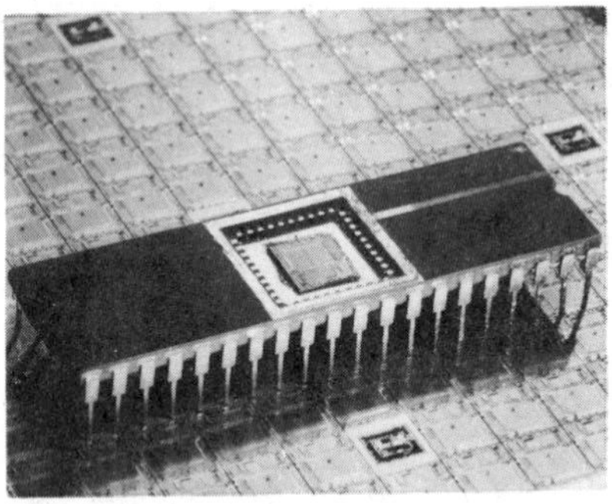

MAIN MEMORY

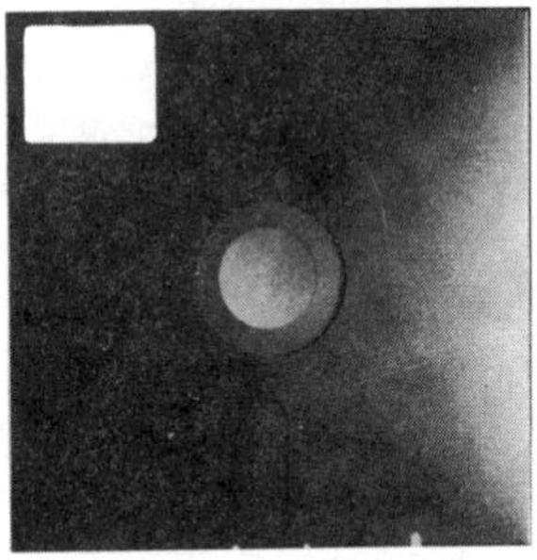

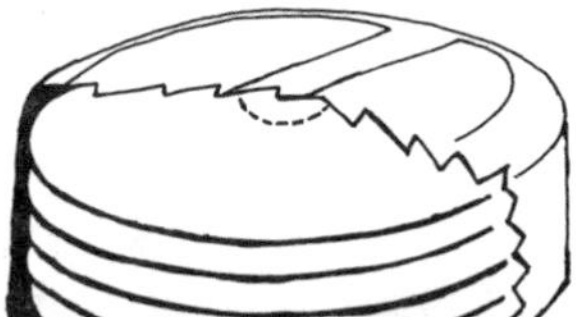

SECONDARY MEMORY

I/O devices

I/O (for input and output) devices form the third major component of computer hardware. I/O devices are specialized machines for communication between computer and people, or other computers. Without I/O devices, we'd have no way to store programs, or to supply data when they ran, or to receive results when they were through. An output device, like a printer, can be used to get the results of running a program, or to inspect data stored in another computer component—say, the main memory. Input devices serve a complementary purpose; we use them to supply the CPU (or memory, through the CPU) with new information.

networks

Network connections are a relatively new addition to the I/O family. They allow extremely high-speed communication between different computer systems. Networks are most commonly used to let computer systems share access to certain components, like printers or terminals. However, experimental networks can let the CPU on one computer interact with the memory of an entirely different machine, or give two different users the illusion of being on the same system.

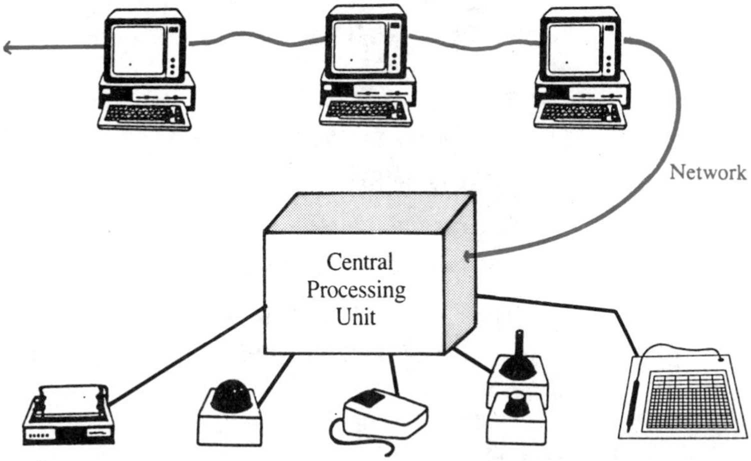

comparing computers

How do we compare the hardware of two different computers? The *speed* of a computer's CPU is a convenient reference because, regardless of the computer's price or its programmer's ability, its programs are almost invariably still executed one step at a time. Since a computer's actual computing is completed in the give and take of its control unit, execution registers, and ALU, the amount of time a single step takes provides a reasonable basis of comparison for two computers that will be expected to run the same sort of programs.

We can also compare two computers by their *size*. This measurement is usually concerned with the amount of primary memory the computer has, or is capable of having. This can be important, because some programs may require very large amounts of primary memory to run effectively, or to run at all. Finally, we can compare computers on the basis of *peripherals*. These include secondary memory, as well as input and output devices.

All the measures described above have their uses. However, we generally find that criteria like CPU speed, memory size, and peripherals alone are best used for comparisons of smaller computers intended for personal use. For larger computers that will probably be shared between a number of users, though, these measurements are often too simple. The prospective purchaser must try to determine just how harmoniously the separate hardware components work together. Ultimately, this will often turn out to depend on our next topic—software.

Software

Computer software falls into two major categories: applications programs, and operating systems. *Applications programs* are specific; each program does one particular job when (and only when) a computer user requests it. The *operating system*, in contrast, is a general piece of software. It runs continuously to coordinate the operation of the computer's hardware and software resources. In effect, computer users interact directly with applications programs, while the operating system is more closely associated with actual hardware.

When we think about software we usually imagine applications programs—programs that do some specific task. Some typical applications programs are:

applications programs

- Programs for word processing and text editing.
- Programs for game playing.
- Programs that handle accounting or arrange spreadsheets.
- Programs that help with instruction.
- Programs that prepare programs to run on the computer.

A look at any computer magazine will provide dozens of additional examples. In fact, a look through this text will provide plenty of examples too, since every sample program in *Oh! Pascal!* is some sort of application program.

By itself, though, computer hardware isn't sophisticated enough to run applications programs. Even though the control unit coordinates hardware operation in a low-level way, there must still be a connection between applications programs and the actual computer hardware. Why? Well, a typical applications program needs more than just raw computational power. It will undoubtedly require the services of different input and output devices. It may be stored with other programs in the computer's memory, and have to be retrieved before it can be run. It might even need hardware that's currently being used by another programmer.

operating system

This is where operating system software comes in. The operating system is a very large program that controls and coordinates the operation of computer hardware for the benefit of individual users and their programs. Now, if a computer just ran one program and had no peripheral equipment—like the microprocessor found in a toaster or carburetor—it wouldn't really need an operating system. The point of an operating system is to create an environment in which different applications programs, which use the computer system in a variety of ways, can be run. Since the operating system is so necessary, it is almost invariably supplied with the computer directly from the hardware manufacturer.

controlling access

What are some of the practical problems that an operating system deals with? For one thing, the operating system *controls computer access*. When you enter a password to log onto a computer, you do so at the operating system's request. The operating system organizes users; it, rather than you, is responsible for keeping stored programs and information that belongs to dozens or hundreds of computer users separate and retrievable.

allocating resources

The operating system also *allocates independent resources*. Suppose that several computer users want to use a single printer. Each user might independently request that some stored information be printed; it is the operating system's job to form a waiting list so that requests can automatically be handled in turn.

sharing resources

Not all resources are independent, so the operating system must also *schedule shared resources*. Although a printer can only handle one job at a time, faster resources (like the CPU) can be shared between users. The result of resource sharing is that each system user gets the illusion that she is working on her own personal computer. Behind the scenes, though, the operating system must work furiously to ensure that individual users' programs don't get mixed up as each takes its turn at using the CPU and main memory.

managing the environment

From our point of view as computer programmers, the operating system's main job is *managing the programming environment*. It supplies the tools we need to write programs, then arranges for our programs to run. As a result, we don't have to worry about the myriad details that are involved in computer operation.

Conclusion

Enough background—let's learn Pascal! Good luck in your study of programming. Chapter 1 begins in a page or two, and with it will come a whole new kind of understanding. We hope that you enjoy Pascal, and that you find your study of computer science exciting. If you have any suggestions for making *Oh! Pascal!* a better book, or if you spot an error to correct in the next printing, please write me directly at:

Doug Cooper
Computer Science Division
University of California
Berkeley, Ca. 94720
(*dbcooper@BERKELEY, ucbvax\!dbcooper*)

I'd appreciate it if you'd enclose a self-addressed, stamped envelope. Thanks to all those who helped spot bugs in the first edition, and for the many multiple submissions that didn't get answered.

'Bugs serious enough to cause a program crash are called run-time errors...'

1

Getting Acquainted With Programs

What makes computers tick? Well, they need a little electricity, a lot of patience, plenty of air conditioning or ventilation, and (finally) a program. In this chapter we'll see what Pascal programs look like, and start learning how to use Pascal to get things done.

From the programmer's point of view, *output*—showing or printing information—is the simplest job a computer can do. The output programs we'll write in section 1-1 won't compute anything, but they'll let us begin to put the hardware through its paces. In section 1-2 we'll reconsider information more formally as *data*. We'll see how Pascal breaks values into different *types*, and learn how to declare *variables* for data storage. We'll also write programs that accept *input* from a program user. Finally, section 1-3 revisits output, and explains how to program basic arithmetic calculations.

Out of necessity, this chapter contains a lot of information—probably more than any other chapter. It's important to avoid being overwhelmed. A couple of tricks may help make things easier. First, read the chapter twice. Don't try to learn or memorize everything at once because there's just too much. Skimming the chapter first will give you an idea of what's really important, and what's just a complicated (but small) detail.

Second, try to understand Pascal as it fits together, rather than as an arbitrary collection of separate facts. Don't be afraid to question the language designer's wisdom ('Why'd he do it that way?'), or our method of explanation. Pascal was largely designed as a teaching language, and as students you're the final arbiters of its success or failure.

Third, use the tools built into the text. The *self-check questions* supplied every few pages, like the *self-test exercises* found at the end of each chapter, contain questions with answers. If you can answer all of them, you've probably mastered the most important points of each chapter. All new Pascal, and assorted important facts, are summarized just before the exercises.

The last section of this chapter is the first in a series of special sections on *antibugging* and *debugging*—avoiding programming mistakes, and fixing the ones that slip by. We recommend that you read these sections before tackling the additional exercises.

Programming For Output 1-1

BEHOLD A COMPLETE Pascal program.

```
program FirstRun (output);
   {This is our first program.}
begin
   writeln ('Hello. I love you.')
end.
```

FirstRun is a short program whose effect and output you can probably figure out already. We'll begin our study of Pascal by seeing how *FirstRun* was constructed.

reserved words

The first step is to indicate that what we're writing is a program. The first word of every Pascal program is the *reserved word*:

program

Throughout the text, reserved words—actual Pascal words—are printed in **bold face type**.

Next, we need to name our program. In computer science terminology, names are *identifiers*.

identifiers

> An identifier, or name, *must* begin with a letter, and then may contain any series of digits or letters.

We can agree that:

R2D2   *PattiHansen*   *SpotOnTop40*

are all perfectly legal names. But since an identifier cannot contain punctuation or spaces, or begin with a digit, these names are all illegal:

2Bor02B   *First*Run*   *Farrah Fawcett-Majors*

program heading

When we give our program a name, its first line, or *heading*, becomes:

program *FirstRun*

(All identifiers will be shown in *italic*.) Reserved words can't be used as identifiers; we couldn't call a program **program if**, or **program program**. When in doubt, check the complete list of reserved words inside the cover.

syntax charts

Now, we already have two things to remember—the proper sequence of words in the program heading, and the rules for correct identifiers. The wary reader will anticipate having to remember quite a few of these rules for putting Pascal programs together. You might memorize as we go along, or mark particularly good examples to serve as patterns. We'll help by supplying *syntax charts* when appropriate. The chart of an identifier is:

identifier

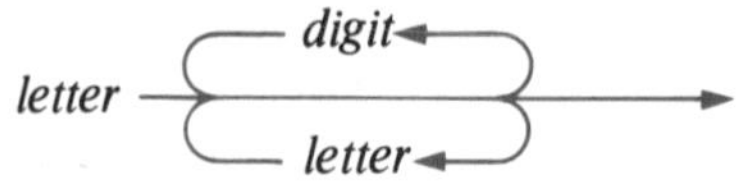

As long as we start on the left and follow the arrows, we'll have an identifier that satisfies Pascal's rules: it must start with a letter and can be followed by as many letters or digits as we wish. If we follow the shortest possible path, we'll have a perfectly legal one-letter identifier.

As you can see, the chart of an identifier almost seems to be more trouble than it's worth. Still, some people like to use syntax charts to clarify complicated rules. Others won't find charts useful at all, and can ignore them and remember the rules some other way. We've simplified some syntax charts (in comparison to the charts that accompany Pascal reference books) to make them easier to follow. All our syntax charts are collected in Appendix B.

Self-Check Questions

Q. Which of the following are valid Standard Pascal identifiers?

birthday	*case*	*CaseNumber*
TooHot?	*First_Initial*	*3rdValue*
–Number	*OldName*	*downto.what*
´grade´	*1Program*	*Beginning*

A. Not too many of these are valid—only *birthday, CaseNumber, OldName*, and *Beginning* may be used correctly. **case** is tempting, but it's a reserved word.

Comments and Output Statements

Explanations about a program's operation are called *comments*. They go between *curly brackets* like these: { }:

program *FirstRun*
    {This is our first program.}

because the computer ignores anything written between curly brackets.

> As far as program operation is concerned, comments are unnecessary. In practice, they're used in *every* program as explanatory notes to ourselves, or to other people reading the program.

alternative comments

Some keyboards may not include curly brackets (also called *braces*), so Pascal allows alternate symbols as synonyms—'(*' is the same as '{', and '*)' has the same meaning as '}'. A comment can go on the same line as Pascal code, or it can extend over several lines, as long as a left comment bracket appears at the beginning, and a right comment bracket turns up at the end. For example:

```
{                    Program FirstRun
                           by
                     Rachel Jetaime              }
program FirstRun          (*This is also a comment.*)
```

program heading

We finish a program's heading with instructions to the computer. It must know in advance if it will get data from us—*input*—or deliver results to us—*output*.* Since this particular program only has output, the heading is completed with:

```
program FirstRun (output);
    {This is our first program.}
```

A semicolon ends the heading. If it had input as well, we would write:

```
program FeedBack (input, output);
    {We'll use a heading like this in section 1-2.}
```

statement part

Since program *FirstRun* won't make any decisions or computations, we can get right to work on the *statement part*, where the program's business will take place. It always begins with the reserved word **begin**. (This is all pretty reasonable, no?)

```
program FirstRun (output);
    {This is our first program.}
begin
```

The statement part contains a series of instructions, called *statements*, for the computer to *execute*, or carry out.

standard procedures

Printing output in Pascal is taken care of by special statements called *standard procedures*. A standard procedure is essentially a built-in command. In a couple of chapters we'll see that we can invent new procedures to supplement the standard ones. Like most Pascal identifiers, procedure names give some indication of their purpose. Procedure *writeln* (pronounced 'write line') works like this:

```
writeln ('Everything between the quote marks will get printed.')
```

writeln

> To write a line of output, use the standard output procedure *writeln*. The *text*, or words, in an output line go between single quote marks. They may *not* contain a carriage return.

(We'll write procedure names in italic because they're identifiers.) To get us off to a friendly start, our program will print 'Hello. I love you.'

```
program FirstRun (output);
    {This is our first program.}
begin
  writeln ('Hello. I love you.')
```

* Actually, this explanation is to the truth as the stork is to the facts of life—not very accurate, but a good enough explanation for the time being. *Input* and *output* are discussed in detail in Chapter 8.

Only one thing is missing from *FirstRun*—the reserved word **end**, which is always followed by a period. It tells the computer that no more statements remain to be executed and that the program is through.

```
program FirstRun (output);
    {This is our first program.}
begin
    writeln ('Hello.  I love you.')
end.
```

Program *FirstRun* is complete—on paper! Actually running the program will generally involve using a few of the computer's applications programs. We typically face a three-step process:

1. *Editing*. First, the Pascal program (like the one we just wrote) is stored in a computer file. This step scarcely differs from using a word processor to store a business letter.
2. *Compilation*. Second, the file is read, but not changed in any way, by a compiler or interpreter. These special programs translate the stored Pascal program we wrote into a machine-oriented version the computer can run. The new version is usually stored in a new file automatically. The compiler or interpreter will spot, and complain about, many kinds of errors in our original program. These must be fixed (by a return to step 1) before the program can be compiled.

steps for running programs

3. *Execution*. Third, a command is given to execute the machine-oriented version of our original Pascal program. This step is sometimes joined with step 2.

The editor, compiler, and program execution commands you give will depend on your particular computer system, since they're not specified by Pascal. In any case, when the program is run something like this will appear as output:

↓ ↓ ↓ ↓ ↓

```
Hello.  I love you.
```

(The downward arrows (↓ ↓) mean 'The program's output would look like this.' The funny typeface is used for printing program output.)

Although the output above isn't too exciting, the idea of what we've just done is very much so. We've written a program, and made a computer follow our commands. A language that last week was barely conceivable (and totally incomprehensible), is suddenly starting to mean something. A certain amount of mystery, and a little magic as well, have left our lives forever.

Let's complicate matters by using two *writeln* statements.

separating statements

> In Pascal, the semicolon (;) is used as a statement separator. It belongs between any two statements or parts of a program.

Two or more statements in a program are executed in the order they appear in. Our new program looks like this:

```
program SecondRun (output);
  {Demonstrates the statement separator.}
begin
  writeln ('Hello.  I love you.');
  writeln ('How about lunch?')
end.
```

```
Hello.  I love you.
How about lunch?
```

write vs. *writeln*

The *writeln* procedure puts each line of output on a separate line, as above. Another standard procedure, called *write*, prints its output without putting a carriage return at the end of the line. As a result, the output of two or more *write* procedures will wind up on a single line. Eventually, when a *writeln* is encountered, a carriage return is printed to end the line. Any output that belongs to the *writeln* goes on the same line, of course. If there's no partial line or new output, the *writeln* prints a blank line. For example:

```
program SeveralLines (output);
  {Demonstrates procedures write and writeln.}
begin
  write ('A fine ');                  {These lines are printed...}
  write ('romance, ');
  writeln ('with no kisses.');        {...on the same output line.}
  writeln;              {These put two blank lines in the output,}
  writeln;              {since there's no earlier output or new output.}
  write ('A fine romance, ');
  writeln ('my friend, this is!')
end.
```

```
A fine romance, with no kisses.


A fine romance, my friend, this is!
```

Not all Pascal systems will immediately print the output of a *write*. Some systems collect the partial line internally, without printing, until a *writeln* is encountered. As a result, it may be impossible to actually print anything without putting a carriage return (through *writeln*) at the end of the line.

printing single quotes

'How do I print a carriage return?' is always one of the first questions to ask when you learn a new programming language. 'How do I print a quote mark?' is another. In Pascal, the single quote, or apostrophe, is itself quoted by being entered twice:

```
writeln ('You wouldn''t, I couldn''t, and she won''t!');
```

```
You wouldn't, I couldn't, and she won't!
```

This coding trick is used in a number of other languages as well.

Self-Check Questions

Q. There are errors on each line of this program. Find them.

```
program Print.Paper (output;)                          {line 1}
begin;                                                 {line 2
   write ('To think that two and two are four, );      {line 3}
   writln (and neither five or three, ');              {line 4}
   write ('The heart of man has long been sore ';      (line 5)
   write ('and long 'tis like to be.')                 {line 6}
end                                                    {line 7.}
```

A. Written correctly, the program would be:

```
program PrintPaper (output);                           {line 1}
begin                                                  {line 2}
   write ('To think that two and two are four, ');     {line 3}
   writeln ('and neither five or three, ');            {line 4}
   write ('The heart of man has long been sore ');     {line 5}
   writeln ('and long ''tis like to be.')              {line 6}
end.                                                   {line 7}
```

Variables and Input 1-2

THIS PROGRAM USES A *variable*, and has *input* as well as output.

```
program FeedBack (input, output);
    {Reads and prints the value of a variable.}
var QuakeYear: integer;
    {This declares a variable called QuakeYear.}
begin
    writeln ('When was the San Francisco earthquake?');
        {After printing this message, the computer waits for the program
         user to enter a value, or reads it from a data file.}
    readln (QuakeYear);
    write ('The Great Quake occurred in');
    writeln (QuakeYear)
end.
```

```
        ↓        ↓        ↓        ↓        ↓
When was the San Francisco earthquake?
1906
The Great Quake occurred in        1906
```

You can probably figure out everything that *FeedBack* does already. We'll begin our discussion of variables by learning about the values they can hold.

The Simple Value Types

The variables we use in programs are like the memory keys of hand calculators—they store values—but they're much more powerful and convenient. First of all, we can create as many variables as a job calls for. We're not limited by the handful of storage spaces most calculators have. Second, we're not stuck with unenlightening names like *MEM1* and *MEM2*. Variables can have any names that meet the rules for identifiers.

Finally, we aren't restricted to storing numbers. Variables can hold different *types* of values, including whole numbers, characters, and decimal or real numbers. We can even make up entirely new categories (which we'll learn about in Chapter 9). However, we always have to specify the type of values a variable is going to hold.

> Four commonly used types of values are predefined as the *standard simple types*. Their official names, used in writing programs, are *integer, char, boolean*, and *real*.

standard types

integer: *integer* variables store integers—the positive and negative counting numbers (e.g. −2,−1, 0, 1, 2).

char: *char* variables can hold any of the characters—letters, punctuation marks, or digit characters—that appear on the keyboard.

boolean: *boolean* (boo´-lee-an) variables, sometimes called logical variables, have one of two values—*false* or *true*. They're used with the control statements shown inside the cover.

real: Positive and negative numbers that include decimal points, or are expressed as powers of 10, must be stored in *real* variables (e.g. −3.55, 0.0, 187E−02, 35.997E+11).

(In the text, Pascal type names are printed in italic to distinguish them from the integers and reals of mathematics.)

ordinal types

> Types *integer, char*, and *boolean* are called *ordinal* types.

We'll use the term 'ordinal type' when we want to exclude type *real* from the other simple types, but the distinction isn't critical now.

Grouping values into different types helps protect the programmer from the internal code the computer uses to store *all* values. Since the computer stores values of all types as binary numbers, it would be perfectly content to add an *integer* to a character, or to subtract *true* from 45.378. Errors of this sort (for example, where a programmer forgot that she was using a variable to store characters, and instead treated the stored value as a number), used to cause serious errors in large programs. Pascal's type separation provides a scorecard that helps prevent such nonsensical activity. If the compiler spots a problem, it prints an error message that points out the imminent *type clash*. We can fix the mistake before trying to run the program.

why have types?

Type checking also goes on while the program is running. The result of all this checking is one of the more important rules of Pascal programming.

The Golden Rule of Types

Give unto variables only values *of the same type*. Values *must* be of the same type as the variables they go to.

type clashes

The most common type clash occurs when the programmer forgets that *integer* variables must receive positive or negative values that obey the form of Pascal *integers*. They can't include commas (like 1,000,000), because a comma is a *char* value. Similarly, they can't include decimals or exponents (such as 5.0 or 13E+05), because that makes them Pascal *reals*.

There is only one exception to the strict type rule: *integer* values may be given to *real* variables. However, the values are converted into *reals* when they're stored, and won't be retrieved as *integers*. If 4 is stored in a *real* variable, we'll get it back as 4.000000000000000E+00.

crashing

Aside from this exception, the type rule is inviolable. When it's broken, the program ignominiously *crashes*—stops running. While this is no great shame (it happens to everybody once in a while), it's no particular honor, either.

The syntax chart of a *real* value is:

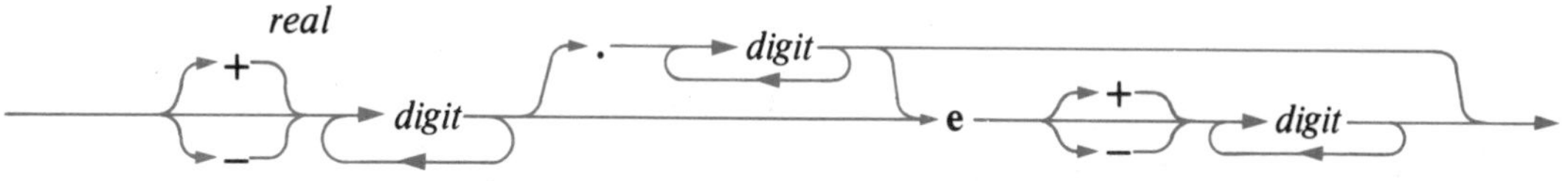

floating-point notation

Pascal *reals* are given in a shorthand called *floating-point notation* (or sometimes *scientific notation*). The number is expressed as a power of 10—the letter 'E' stands for 'times 10 to the power of.' A *real* given as a power of 10 need not contain a decimal point, but if it has one, there must always be a digit—even a zero—to the left of the decimal. Thus, the fraction ½ is thought of as 0.5, and not an unadorned .5, and a negative fourth is −0.25, instead of −.25. We'll see some examples below.

The smallest and largest *real* and *integer* values are allowed to vary from system to system, because they are *system-defined*. When you find the limits of your system, note them inside the front cover.

Self-Check Questions

Q. Write these numbers as Pascal *reals.*

a) 341,234	*b*) .234	*c*) 234.73456
d) 88	*e*) .008562	*f*) −9427.003
g) 10^{14}	*h*) −50	*i*) 12.500

A. Notice that conventionally there's only one digit before the decimal in floating-point notation.

a) 3.41234E+05	*b*) 2.34E−01	*c*) 2.3473456E+02
d) 8.8E+01	*e*) 8.562E−03	*f*) −9.427003E+03
g) 1.0E+14	*h*) −5.0E+01	*i*) 1.25E+01

The Variable Declaration

Variables get their names and types in the *variable declaration part* of a Pascal program. The declaration part comes after the heading, and before the statement part. It begins with the reserved word **var** (rhymes with 'car', or 'air'), which is a shorthand for 'variable.' Then, each identifier is listed along with its type—the kind of value the variable will hold. There's a semicolon after each declaration. Notice the position of the colon (:) in the declarations below:

```
program Variables (input, output);
  {Demonstrates variable declarations.}
var AptNumber: integer;
    ShoeSize: real;
    FirstInitial: char;
    OutToLunch: boolean;
begin
  ... {statement part}
end.
```

The syntax chart of a variable declaration part looks like this:

variable declaration

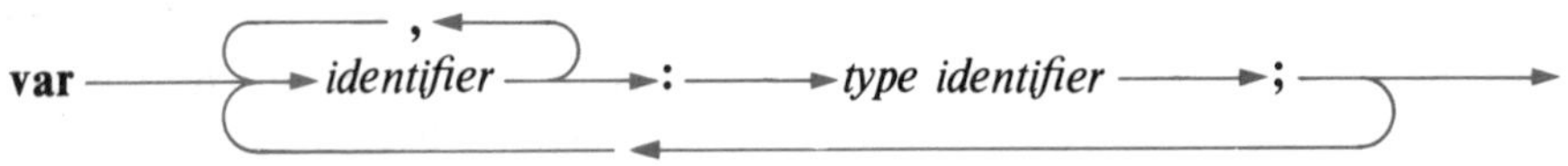

We needn't declare variables of every type, nor is the order of declaration important. To create more than one variable of a given type, separate the variable identifiers with commas, just like a list in a regular sentence. Make sure to include the colon right before the type.

```
var TVchannel: integer;          {One integer variable.}
    GPA, BattingAverage: real;
    Pagenumber, age: integer;    {More integer variables.}
```

Let's pause to make an important point about the way programs are typed in and stored.

program format

> Pascal programs are considered to be *free format.* The position of words in a program ('on the page,' so to speak) is generally unimportant, as long as they are in the right order, and no words or words and numbers, are run together (like **program***FirstRun*).

We can make a declaration that has minimal spacing (just one blank to keep **var** from running into *GPA*):

```
var GPA,BattingAverage:real;Pagenumber,age,TVchannel:integer;
```

Or, we can put in a zillion unnecessary spaces:

```
var              GPA          , BattingAverage
:       real     ;    Pagenumber
    ,age      ,TVchannel:    integer ;
```

> When you write programs, try to approximate the format of programs shown in this book. Above all, *be consistent.*

We *could* write entire programs as single, awfully long lines, or place just one word or symbol on each page or card. We won't, though, because such programs are awkward to read and modify. The form our examples use—indentation, with only one thought per line, etc.—makes programs easier to correct and understand.

Self-Check Questions

Q. Are these both valid variable declarations?

```
var day, month: integer;          var time: real;
    time: real;                       day: integer;
                                      month: integer;
```

A. Yes. The syntax chart shows that the exact order and grouping of declarations is unimportant.

Q. Match the variables with the values they may represent. Which values may not be given to *any* variable? Assume we've made this declaration:

```
var IntegerValue: integer; Letter: char; RealValue: real;
```

a) 7	*b*) 0.0	*c*) T	*d*) .3519
e) −52	*f*) 0	*g*) 5.E+22	*h*) ;
i) .9E−3	*j*) 35.2E−17	*k*) −18E+6.0	*l*) dd
m) −667.3	*n*) 1,387	*o*) −7	*p*) −12E−7

A. *IntegerValue* may be 7, −52, 0, or −7.
Letter may be '7', 'T', '0', or ';' .
RealValue may be 7, 0.0, −52, 0, 35.2E−17, −667.3, −7, or −12E−7.
The values .3519, 5.E+22, .9E−3, −18E+6.0, dd, and 1,387 aren't legal Pascal, and can't be given to any variables at all.

Input to Variables: *readln* and *read*

A variable can get a value in two ways: the value can be obtained while the program runs, or it can be given to the variable when the program is written. In this section, we'll concentrate on the first method, which lets the program user supply a value during program execution.

Now, you'll recall from our discussion of output that two procedures, *write* and *writeln*, shared responsibility for printing partial and full lines of output. Two more standard procedures, *read* and *readln* (pronounced 'read line'), serve a like role for program *input*. They 'read' values for variables.

> When one or more variable identifiers are put in parentheses after a call of *read* or *readln*, the computer will pause to read in values for them.

For example:

```
program Interactive (input, output);
   {Demonstrates interactive program input and output.}
var Number: integer;
begin
   writeln ('Please enter an integer value.');
   readln (Number);
   write ('The number you entered was:');
   writeln (Number)        {Print the value of Number.}
end.
```

↓ ↓ ↓ ↓ ↓

```
Please enter an integer value.
237
The number you entered was:        237
```

(We'll always print values supplied as program input in **bold.**)

When a running program encounters a *read* or *readln*, it stops to get input for the variable or variables given within parentheses. It doesn't announce that it has halted, though—the programmer must include a *writeln* to *prompt* the user to enter a value. Thus, the prompt 'Please enter an integer value' is essential to *Interactive's* successful operation. Without

prompting for data

it, the user wouldn't know that she was supposed to enter a number, and the computer (unable to complete the *readln*) couldn't move on to subsequent statements.

In chart form *read* and *readln* look like this:

readln and read

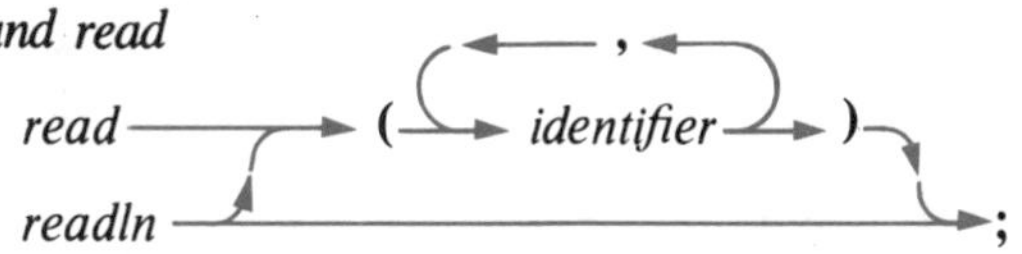

Note that, according to the chart, *readln* can appear by itself, without anything in parentheses, just as *writeln* could. We'll see why in a moment.

What is the difference between *read* and *readln*? Well, just because a user is asked to supply a single value doesn't mean that she can't provide more than one. The difference between *read* and *readln* lies in the way they deal with extra values on a line of input.

read vs. *readln*

> *readln* discards any extra values left on a line of input. When given without any variables in parentheses, *readln* removes the entire line. *read*, in contrast, leaves remaining values, even if a carriage return is the only value left.

It might be easier to imagine that input comes in the old-fashioned way—on a stack of punched cards placed in the computer's input hopper. Each card is equivalent to a line of input. *readln* always ejects the current card (and gets the next) as part of its action. *read*, in contrast, leaves the current card in the hopper, even if it has just read the last data value on the card.

Let's look at some examples. We'll declare some *char* variables:

var *C1, C2, C3, C4, C5, C6*: *char*;

return is read as a blank

and assume that each input statement below gets the sample input shown. A carriage return ends the input. The carriage return is always read as a blank.

Sample input to each statement: **ABCDE**

Statement	*Last value read*	*Value about to be read*
1. *read* (*C1*);	**A**	**B**
2. *read* (*C1*); *read* (*C2*);	**B**	**C**
3. *read* (*C1,C2,C3*);	**C**	**D**
4. *read* (*C1, C2, C3, C4, C5*);	**E**	*blank* (*the return*)
5. *read* (*C1, C2, C3, C4, C5, C6*);	*blank*	*start of next line*
6. *read*;	*illegal—read must*	*actually get values*
7. *readln*;	*none*	*start of next line*
8. *readln* (*C1*);	**A**	*start of next line*
9. *readln* (*C1,C2,C3*);	**C**	*start of next line*
10. *readln* (*C1, C2, C3, C4, C5*);	**E**	*start of next line*

If you compare the effects of statements 1 and 8, and 3 and 9, you'll see that although they both obtain the same values, the *readlns* remove the rest of the line as well. Statement 5 mimics statement 7 because it reads all input values *including* the carriage return that ends the line.

In practice, we will almost invariably use *readln* for ordinary input. We don't use *read* because it doesn't automatically get rid of the carriage return that ends each line—and that could be inadvertently read as a space character later (as in statement 6).

The exact meaning of *start of next line* depends on how input is being provided. Program *Interactive*, above, assumed that input was being typed into a keyboard during program execution. This is called *interactive* program operation because the user and computer interact with each other. Interactive programs usually have only one line of input (entered in response to the most recent prompt) ready at any time.

interactive programs

Not all programs run interactively, though. Those that don't are sometimes called *batch-oriented* programs. They get their input from stored *data files*, rather than from the terminal keyboard. Since all program input is prepared in advance, we can actually say what value is about to be read.

data-file programs

Occasionally, computer systems will require that input be typed into punched cards, and supplied along with the punched cards that hold the program. However, data-file input programs are often written for systems that can be used interactively. It may simply be more convenient to use a data file than to type input interactively. We'll provide examples of both interactive and data file programs throughout the text.

A special rule must be observed whether input is being supplied interactively or via data file.

> The Golden Rule of Input
> Always make sure that there's enough input.

If a program expects to read in eight characters or numbers, there had better be at least eight values waiting to be read in. If an interactive program is given too few values, it will hang without informing the user that more input is expected. A program that tries to read past the end of its data file comes to a worse fate—it will crash.

Self-Check Questions

Q. Suppose that we have a program that starts like this:

```
program ReadCharacters (input, output);
var C1, C2, C3, C4, C5, C6: char;
begin
    readln (C1, C2, C3, C4, C5, C6);
    writeln (C1, C2, C3, C4, C5, C6);
        ...         {This statement prints the variables' values.}
```

Match the inputs on the left with the outputs on the right. Blanks in output are shown with an underline.

a) **Hi there**	*a*) A1_B2_
b) **Hi** **there**	*b*) 57_4_3
c) **694** **827**	*c*) Hi_the
d) **57 4** **329**	*d*) Hi_the
e) **A1** **B2 C3**	*e*) 694_82

A. *a–c, b–d, c–e, d–b, e–a*

Numerical Input

A final area of detail involves the input of numerical values.

> Spaces and carriage returns *separate* numbers. Any non-numerical character *ends* a number.

In our earlier examples of *char* input, spaces (and, implicitly, carriage returns) were characters in their own right. When we read in *integer* or *real* values, though, spaces and carriage returns are ignored except as value separators. If it is seeking to read a number, the computer will skip over spaces (or carriage returns) as though they weren't there.

For example, suppose that *First* and *Second* are *integer* variables. The statement: *readln (First, Second)* treats the three inputs below identically, even though the first separates the numbers by a single space, the second by many spaces, and the third by many spaces and a carriage return.

a) **53 174**
b) **53   174**
c) **53**
174

where do numbers end?

Concern about where a numerical value ends develops when character and numerical values are intermingled. After a number is read, what value is *about* to be read? It's the character that ended the number—a space, letter, or punctuation mark.*

* We can't just say it's a non-digit because of *real* input, which may include a period or letter 'E' as part of a number in floating-point notation.

Self-Check Questions

Q. Assume these declarations:

var *C1, C2: char; N1, N2: integer;*

and this input to each statement below:

123 A45B

What values are supplied to *C1, C2, N1*, and *N2* by each statement? What value is about to be read?

a) read (C1);
b) read (C1, N1);
c) read (C1, C2, N1);
d) read (N1, C1);
e) read (N1, C1, C2, N2);
f) read (N1, N2);
g) read (N1, C1, N2);

A. A blank is shown as an underline:

	C1	*C2*	*N1*	*N2*	*About to be read*
a)	'1'				'2', or 23
b)	'1'		23		'_'
c)	'1'	'2'	3		'_'
d)	'_'		123		'A'
e)	'_'	'A'	123	45	'B'
f)			123		crash! *N2* can't be 'A'
g)	'_'		123		crash! *N2* can't be 'A'

Variables and Output 1-3

BY NOW, EVERYBODY CAN PROBABLY GUESS that the standard procedures *write* and *writeln* are used to print the value of variables. Commas separate variables from each other, or from text output. Variable identifiers aren't put between single quote marks, because that would make them text output.

simple I/O demonstration program

```
program TheBoss (input, output);
  {Demonstrates simple input and output.}
var Year, ChartPosition: integer;
begin
  writeln ('When was Born to Run released?  How high did it go?');
  readln (Year, ChartPosition);
  writeln ('Born to Run came out in', Year,  and hit #', ChartPosition);

end. {TheBoss}
```

```
When was Born to Run released?  How high did it go?
1973  3
Born to Run came out in    1973 and hit #       3
```

computer arithmetic

Mathematical operations like addition, subtraction, multiplication, and division may be performed within output statements. The symbols that represent some of the arithmetic operations are shown below. Only the multiplication symbol (*) is unusual. An asterisk is used instead of a cross (×) to avoid possible confusion with a variable named *X*.

Symbol	*Operation*	*Example*
+	addition	*Salary + Graft*
–	subtraction	*Score – Penalty*
/	division	*Height / Weight*
*	multiplication	*Bet * Odds*

Program *EasyCalculations*, below, has statements that print the value, sum, difference, quotient, and product of two *integer* variables. Note that the '/' division operator produces *real* output. We'll see some operators for *integer* division in Chapter 2.

calculations in output statements

```
program EasyCalculations (input, output);
   {Shows that expressions are evaluated before output.}
var Cat, Rat: integer;
begin
   writeln ('Enter two integer values.');
   readln (Cat, Rat);
   writeln (Cat, Rat);
   writeln (Cat+Rat, Cat-Rat);
   writeln (Cat/Rat, Cat*Rat)
end.
```

```
Enter two integer values.
21 3
         21          3
         24         18
  7.00000000000000E+00         63
```

Self-Check Questions

Q. Write output statements that:

a) print two variable identifiers (say, *NoseLength* and *TruthIndex*);

b) print their values;

c) multiply them by each other;

d) divide each of them by 5.3.

e) Combine these operations in a coherent series of statements.

```
A. {a} writeln ('NoseLength, TruthIndex');
   {b} writeln (NoseLength, TruthIndex);
   {c} writeln (NoseLength * TruthIndex);
   {d} writeln (NoseLength/5.3, TruthIndex/5.3);

   {e} write ('The value of NoseLength is ', NoseLength, 'while ');
       writeln ('the TruthIndex is ', TruthIndex, '. Their product is ');
       write (NoseLength*TruthIndex, ', and divided by 5.3 they give us');
       writeln (NoseLength/5.3, 'and ', TruthIndex/5.3);
```

Output Format

Printing of numerical values is a little bit strange in Pascal.

> When they're printed as output by a Pascal program, *integer* and *real* values are *right aligned*, or aligned with the right margin of, a space known as the number's *printing field*. Its size is called the *field width*.

printing fields

Right alignment and printing fields are a part of Pascal for a reason that anyone with the soul of an accountant will find obvious: they make it easy to print and read columns of figures. In the example below, the values of the *integer* variables *a, b, c*, etc. vary, but they are always printed in 10-space fields.

```
writeln (a, b, c);
writeln (d, e, f);
writeln (g, h, i);
```

3141	6626175	855
29979245	9	17321
60	1414	728

As frequently happens in computer science, though, the solution to one problem can cause another. The *default* field width is often too big—extra space will be left if an *integer* is printed in the midst of text output.

default values

Default values and actions are set or taken unless we explicitly specify otherwise. The printing of *real* values in floating-point notation is another Pascal default: the *real* value 255.0 is output as 2.55000000000000E+02. This is a horrible-looking shorthand for '2.55 times 10 to the power 2.' Note that there's a subtle danger inherent in this, since an impressive string of digits to the right of a decimal point implies an accuracy that doesn't necessarily exist.

Field widths and the number of digits in floating-point notation are system-defined values. You should note your system-defined values inside the front cover. Your computer may also ignore the minor Standard Pascal requirement that a blank space precede all positive floating-point *real* output (to leave room for a minus sign).

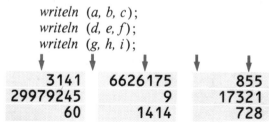

Fortunately, the programmer can choose her own output format by changing the default field widths. She can get rid of excess space by diminishing the field width, or provide extra room by increasing it.

Follow the value being output with a colon, and the *integer* number of spaces in the field. You will never lose digits of an integer variable, or digits to the left of the decimal point of a real variable.

As this example shows, field widths can be specified for the output of text as well as variables.

specifying field widths

```
writeln ('WOW':10, 'MOM':10, 'WOW':10);
writeln ('In', Year:1, ', Columbus sailed the ocean blue.');
writeln ('In', Year:5, ', Columbus sailed the ocean blue.');
writeln ('In', Year, ', Columbus sailed the ocean blue.');
```

```
       WOW       MOM       WOW
In1492, Columbus sailed the ocean blue.
In 1492, Columbus sailed the ocean blue.
In      1492, Columbus sailed the ocean blue.
```

Note that, if the new field width is greater than the number of characters in the value, blanks are printed on the left. If we accidentally, or deliberately, specify a field width that is too small for an *integer* or text value, the field automatically expands to accommodate the entire value. As a result, programmers often give a field width of one when they want *integer* values printed in the smallest possible space. The final digit of shortened *real* values is rounded.

Here's a syntax chart for *write* and *writeln* that shows the option of setting output field width.

write and writeln

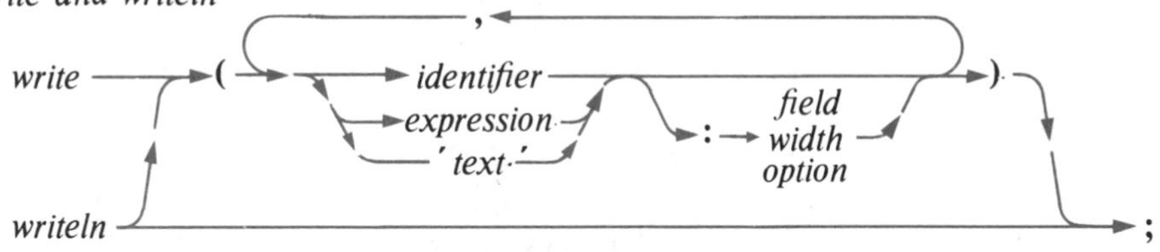

Self-Check Questions

Q. Is this a valid Pascal statement? What is its effect?

writeln (*Length*+*Width*:1);

A. The statement is perfectly legal, since field widths can be specified for expressions. Its effect is to print the sum of *Length* and *Width* in the least space required.

Antibugging and Debugging 1-4

LOOKING FOR (AND FIXING) PROGRAM *bugs*, or mistakes, is called *debugging*. Most debugging should take place while a program is still on paper, well before it's edited, compiled, and run. But since it's always possible to introduce bugs (like misspellings) while typing in a program, even the best-planned programs may require a trial run or two before they're completely debugged. You should allow time for debugging as part of the normal programming process.

Antibugging means programming in a way that helps avoid making bugs in the first place. Further along we'll see how some different programming techniques can help protect programs against bugs. For now, though, just reading these sections is probably antibugging enough.

Are bugs inevitable? We'd hate to think that they *have* to happen, but mistakes sometimes creep into computer programs because people don't think in the literal way that machines operate. Misplaced semicolons and spelling errors aren't very important to us, but they hopelessly confuse automatons. People have a remarkable, automatic, ability to fix problems that is miles beyond anything computers can do.

What is wrong with
with this sentence?

compilation bugs

Bugs fall into two general categories. First, there are *syntax* bugs—mistakes made with the 'grammar' rules of Pascal. Second are *semantic* bugs—errors made in the meaning or effect of Pascal programs. Syntax bugs can often be diagnosed by the computer as it compiles a program. Bugs caught like this are called *compile-time* errors. For example, the compiler spots certain mistakes by applying simple rules about correct Pascal. Some words invariably occur in pairs—every **begin** must be matched by an **end** later in the program. If a program is completely compiled and winds up short an **end**, you'll receive an error message that points out the omission.

```
"END" EXPECTED -- END OF PROGRAM NOT FOUND
```

This says that the computer expected the program to be longer, and to contain another **end**.

Syntax errors that involve punctuation are caught in a similar manner. For example, since the semicolon is Pascal's statement separator, the compiler expects to find a semicolon right before every statement. If two consecutive statements aren't separated by a semicolon (like *writeln writeln*), the compiler prints an error message. Some compilers are smarter than others, and will even temporarily patch the program. A compile-time message from the computer keeps the programmer informed.

```
writeln
writeln
↑ INSERTED ";"
```

This is just a temporary fix, because the original program isn't changed at all. It will work this time, but unless you fix the bug you'll get the same error message each time the program is compiled and run.

Incidentally, the error messages you see here probably won't be identical to the messages on your computer.

> *Oh! Pascal!* uses a set of error messages that are explicit enough to enlighten even the most baffled programmer.

The exact wording of error messages is implementation defined, just as the smartness of compilers varies from system to system. The error messages in our examples may be more detailed and exact than the ones you'll get, but they'll be a lot easier to understand.

Besides checking reserved words and punctuation, the compiler makes sure that all identifiers are legal. In effect, it checks names against a built-in syntax chart. It also examines each statement to make sure that all values involved are of the proper type. The example below errs by requesting a field width of 5.0 instead of 5.

```
writeln (23E-3:5.0);

                    ↑FIELD WIDTH MUST BE AN INTEGER
```

spurious bugs

Now, an unexpected side-effect of compile-time error-checking is that a real error early in the program may cause the computer to diagnose many apparent, but non-existent, mistakes further on. This can be terribly intimidating, and makes you feel like a total idiot. Suppose we've entered the following sequence of statements, with **begin** misspelled.

```
program ErrorProne (input, output);

   {Contains a misspelled reserved word.}

var Data: integer;

begn
   writeln ('Please enter a number.');
   readln (Data);
   writeln (Data)
end.
```

The program only contains a minor syntax bug, but it produces a sheaf of error messages. If you can decipher the mess below, you'll see that the misspelled **begn** makes the compiler treat the entire program as a long **var** declaration. As far as the compiler is concerned, we are attempting to declare a variable named **begn.** The bug throws the whole program out of kilter, so we get a string of error messages a mile long.

```
PROGRAM ERRORPRONE (INPUT, OUTPUT);
VAR DATA:  INTEGER;
BEGN
    ↑INSERTED ","
  WRITELN  ( PLEASE ENTER A NUMBER );
         ↑INSERTED ":"
          ↑INVALID TYPE IDENTIFIER
  READLN  (DATA);
        ↑INSERTED ":"
  WRITELN  (DATA);
         ↑INSERTED ":"
   "DATA" IS DEFINED MORE THAN ONCE IN THIS BLOCK
   ↑MALFORMED VARIABLE DECLARATION
END.
↑UNEXPECTED "END" -- END OF PROGRAM NOT FOUND
```

> Don't fix what isn't broken. Don't make random changes.

get a listing

When you're debugging a program, read the error messages first. Then, get a *listing*, or hard-copy printout, of the program and try to find the actual mistakes. When a short program produces a long series of error messages, look for a simple reason—a misspelled word, or misused feature. Don't despair. As you gain more experience, you'll become adept at separating the real bugs from spurious ones.

A common syntax bug is to include a carriage return in the middle of text output, like this:

```
writeln ('This is illegal because a carriage return
          can''t go between single quote marks.');

{However, this is perfectly all right, because
 a comment can extend over several lines.}
```

Another minor bug that has disastrous results is to forget one of the single quote marks that surrounds text output.

run-time bugs

Bugs serious enough to cause a program crash are called *run-time* errors—they occur or manifest themselves while the program is running. They're not syntax bugs, because the programs they're in obeyed the technical rules of Pascal well enough to compile. What do you think caused this run-time error message:

```
ABNORMAL TERMINATION --
IMPROPER DATA FOUND AT INTEGER READ, LINE 32
```

Apparently, program line 32 was a *read* or *readln* statement that tried to get the value of an *integer* variable. The program user entered a value of the wrong type (perhaps it was *char* or *real*) and the program crashed.

Be sure that interactive prompts ask for appropriate input.

order of input

The ordering of input data may cause unexpected errors. When the computer reads *integer* or *real* values, it ignores spaces and carriage returns except as value separators. Thus:

readln (*CharVariable, IntegerVariable, RealVariable*);

will accept as input the sequence:

L 16 2.83

But if we re-order the input statement to be:

readln (*IntegerVariable, CharVariable, RealVariable*);

and then enter values like this:

16 L 2.83

we'll run into trouble. Although space characters are ignored when we're thinking arithmetically, they're legitimate *char* values. After 16 is correctly given in to *IntegerVariable*, the blank following it is stored in *CharVariable*. What value does *RealVariable* take on? The computer tries to give it the letter 'L'—a type clash—and the program crashes.

local variations

A final area of difficulty in the first few weeks of programming comes from local system features or shortcomings. For instance, not all Pascal compilers remember all the characters in an identifier, even though the definition of *Standard Pascal* requires them to. If a compiler's limit is eight characters (like the first Pascal compiler) then these two identifiers will seem identical within a program:

NapoleonBonaparte
NapoleonJones

Some other compilers may slightly extend Pascal by letting non-letters appear within an identifier to improve readability (*TIME_TO_LEAVE*). You should note your compiler's deviations from Standard Pascal inside the front cover. This will help you write programs that can be run on any Pascal system.

Another detail associated with identifiers is that case is supposed to be irrelevant. These three identifiers are identical in Standard Pascal.

highnumber *HIGHNUMBER* *HighNumber*

This rule lets a program written on a computer with upper- and lower-case characters work equally well on a machine with only upper-case. However, it's a rule that's ignored in many implementations of Pascal. They'll treat the above as three completely different identifiers.

write test programs

In conclusion, the best way to clarify confusing points of syntax, semantics, or system peculiarity (if thinking about it for a while doesn't work) is to experiment. The computer won't blow up or break down if you make a mistake, so don't worry about causing the entire system to crash. It's also a good idea to *echo*, or immediately reprint, all input, to help make sure that input is what you think it is.

> If you don't understand a bug or feature, write a four or five line program that tests only the point in question. If your original program turns out to be based on a mistaken premise, it's best to start over from the beginning.

The best tip of all is to ask somebody for help, and to be willing to help somebody yourself. Practice in spotting and explaining bugs is beneficial to everyone.

Pascal Summary

• comment: program documentation, given between curly brackets:

{This is a comment. You will fail if your programs don't have them!}

• identifier: a name, any sequence of letters and digits that starts with a letter:

ThisIsAnIdentifier   *A2ndExample*

• program heading: the reserved word **program**, its identifier, and the *input, output* information:

program *Sample* (*input, output*); {program with both input and output}

• variable declaration part: the reserved word **var**, the variable identifiers, and their types:

```
var ANumber: integer;                {integer, char, and real are}
    Char1, Char2, Char3: char;       {predefined simple type identifiers}
    RealValue: real;
```

• statement part: the program's actions, separated by semicolons, all between a **begin** and an **end**:

```
begin
   statement;
      ...
   statement
end.
```

• input statements: *read* or *readln* accompanied by variable identifiers in parentheses. *readln* discards all values left on the input line, and need not be used to read a value:

```
read (Char1, Char2);
readln; {discard any remaining values from this line of input.}
readln (RealValue);
```

• output statements: *write* and *writeln* accompanied by text (between single quotes), identifiers, or mathematical expressions, all between parentheses. Commas separate these values. *write* prints (or readies for printing) without a carriage return. *writeln* does print a carriage return, forcing output of any previous *writes*:

```
write ('Here''s some text with an internal quote mark.');
writeln ('Everything so far will be on the same line.');
write ('Intermingled text', Char1, 'and variables', Num1 *2);
writeln;        {prints the previous line}
writeln;        {prints a blank line}
```

• printing field: the space an *integer, real*, or *char* value is printed in, aligned to the right-hand side. For *reals*, this size determines the number of digits given in floating-point notation. The computer's default field width is changed by following the value with a colon and an *integer*-valued field:

```
writeln (RealValue:5, ANumber:1, Char1:3);
```

Important Facts

• The carriage return is read as a space.

• When reading *integer* or *real* values, multiple spaces and carriage returns are ignored. The value about to be read is the character that ended the number.

• Interactive programs communicate with the user, and must always prompt her for input.

• The standard simple types are *integer, real, char*, and *boolean*. All except *real* are also known as ordinal types.

• A variable can only be given a value of the same type. A type clash, or mismatch, will cause a program crash.

• A compile-time, or syntax, error will be recognized by the compiler, but must be fixed by the programmer. A run-time error will cause a program crash. Semantic errors cause bugs that show up as incorrect results.

• Pascal programs are free format, but they should be written with indenting and spacing that makes them easy to read.

- When you're debugging a program, don't fix what isn't broken. Get a program listing to help you spot the real bugs, and avoid trying to correct spurious bugs.
- The Golden Rule of Types: Give unto variables only values of the same type.
- The Golden Rule of Input: Always make sure that there's enough input.

Self-test Exercises

1-1 When doesn't the identifier *input* have to appear in a program heading?

1-2 What would happen if the following line were inserted into a program?

{EXECUTION PROHIBITED WITHOUT OVERRIDE PERMISSION!!!}

1-3 Why are there blanks before some of the output words here? Did we make any mistakes?

writeln ('No', ',no,', ' you can''t', ' take that ', 'away', 'from me.');

1-4 Write a program that asks for a five-letter palindrome (a word that's spelled the same backward and forward), then prints the letters out in this pattern.

```
1 2 3 4 5
2 3 4 5 2
3 4 5 2 3
4 5 2 3 4
1 2 3 4 5
```

Try to figure out how many different ways you can spell the word according to this rule: start any place the first letter ('1' in the illustration) appears, then spell the word by moving to adjacent squares.

1-5 What are the four standard types? What is a type clash?

1-6 What is the value of an *integer* variable before we make any assignments to it? What about undefined *char* variables?

1-7 Explain the difference between a value or rule that is system defined, and one that's system dependent.

1-8 English sentences are supposed to obey syntactic and semantic rules, just like Pascal statements. Do these sentences contain syntax errors, or possible semantic errors?

a) What is this thing called, love?
b) To)be. or(not to be"
c) I should say not?
d) Green ideas sleep furiously.
e) I have to unequivocally say no.
f) Woman without her man is nothing.

1-9 The delicious recipe below is supposed to be supplied to a program. However, the program only has *integer* variables. How can the numerical data be read in?

32 onions
12 heads of lettuce
15 cloves garlic
99 roly poly fish heads

1-10 What is the output of this statement?

writeln ('A':1, 5:3+2, 6:4-1, 'D':2*2);

1-11 What kind of program errors can't be caught at compile time? Show an error that can't be found by the computer either at run-time or compile-time.

1-12 Suppose that these statements are going to be executed.

read (*Number, Count*);
readln;
readln (*Letter, Fraction*);

Show input that will give *Count* the value 17, *Fraction* the value 0.618, *Letter* the value '=', and *Number* the value 0.

1-13 Get values for the *integer* variables *Month, Date*, and *Year* given the input **10/19/85**.

More Exercises

1-13 The price of stocks is commonly given to the nearest eighth; e.g. 77 3/8, or 23 1/2. Write a program that determines the value of a stock holding by reading in the number of shares held, and the whole portion, and numerator and denominator of the fractional portion, of the price per share.

1-14 Suppose that electricity costs 4.75 cents per kilowatt hour, and that a surcharge of 10% is added to the bill. A city utility tax of 3% is also levied; however, no tax is put on the surcharge, and no surcharge is placed on the tax. Write a program that computes an electric bill.

1-15 Write a program to print a standard business form. Find out how many usable lines a single sheet of output can contain (the printer will usually skip a few lines at the top and bottom of each page), and then print two or more forms on a single page. Use every available line, so that no paper will be wasted if the program is run twice.

1-16 One of the hardest, yet simplest, formulas in the world is Einstein's equation $E=mc^2$. Write a program that accepts as input an amount of mass in grams, and prints the amount of energy produced (in joules) when the matter is converted to energy. In the same program, find out how far light travels in a number of years the user enters. Assume that the speed of light, *c*, is 3.0E+08 meters/second (it's not just a good idea... it's the law!).

1-17 When *integer* or *real* values are input, they don't have to be followed by blank spaces. The computer assumes that any input number ends when the first non-digit is encountered. Write a program that takes as input the month, day, and year in American form (e.g. 8/17/83 means August 17, 1983), and echoes the date in European form (e.g. 17,8,83 for the same date).

1-18 Ask a user to enter some digit that she particularly dislikes. Multiply it by 9, then multiply that by 12345679 (note that 8 is missing). What do you find? Modify the program to print out the entire multiplication as though you'd done it by hand.

1-19 Because a program user can't actually look inside the computer to see exactly what a program does, it's possible to make a program seem more intelligent than it really is. Write a program that appears to engage in small talk (by asking the user questions), but which in reality ignores her answers (because *everybody's* answers will be more or less the same). You can create a more convincing sense of interaction by periodically prompting for and echoing *integer* or single *char* data, like the user's street number or number of brothers and sisters.

1-20 How long can a single *write* or *writeln* be? How many words or characters can it contain? What happens if you type past the 'edge' of your screen, or past the end of a card? Will the line 'wrap-around' to the next line?

1-21 Can a *write* or *writeln* statement include a carriage return as part of its output? (This is aside from the normal advance caused by a *writeln*.) Are any other special characters, such as a backspace character, available?

1-22 What happens when you try to execute this statement?

```
writeln ('');          {There's no space between the quotes.}
```

1-23 Write a program that prints the figures shown below one above the other. Modify your program to print them side-by-side. (If they're smart, batch users will just have to shuffle their punched cards, and interactive programmers only use their text editors to move lines around.) Does knowing about the modification you'll have to make change the way you might write the original program?

```
     *                        * * * * *
    * *                       * * * * *
   * * *                      * * * * *
  * * * * *                   * * * * *
 * * * * * *                  * * * * *
```

1-24 Write a program that writes your name in block letters. Is it easier to print the letters vertically or horizontally?

1-25 In *cryptarithmetic*, letters take the place of digits. However, all other mathematical symbols are used normally, e.g.:

```
SEND + MORE = MONEY
```

Write a program that prints cryptarithmetic problems horizontally (as above) and vertically (as in grade school arithmetic books—a horizontal line replaces the equals sign). Let the user enter two four-letter terms, a five-letter result, and the operation that is to be performed. You may want to modify your program to print special-case operations, like square roots or divisions.

1-26 A popular breakfast cereal's main ingredients are sugar, corn syrup, and sucrose. Write a program that reads in the amounts of each ingredient in a 50-gram serving (assume *integer* amounts), then prints out the amount of each, the average amount of the three ingredients, and the percentage of the entire serving that consists of sugar products.

1-27 The Rabbitski sequence of numbers is formed by following this rule: each number is the product of the two previous numbers. Write a program that accepts two numbers, and prints the first three members of the Rabbitski sequence they generate.

1-28 Here's a problem to test your powers of observation. Compute and print the fractions 1/7, 2/7, 3/7, 4/7, 5/7, and 6/7. What similarity do they have? (Hint: look at them with numerators in order 1, 3, 2, 6, 4, and 5.)

1-29 In a recent election for dog catcher, Mary won by 74 votes over Peter, 23 votes over Paul, and 86 votes over Joan. Unfortunately, the computer that tabulated the votes had a bug in it, and only printed out the total number of votes cast—9,485. How many votes did each candidate receive? (Hint: try using the *integer* division operator **div** instead of the *real* operator /.)

1-30 Monica Marin and her friend Nadine decided to have a pot-luck dinner, to which Monica brought three different dishes, and Nadine five. Just as they were about to begin dining, Claire showed up. Naturally, she was invited to join the meal. In thanks, Claire paid Monica $3 and Nadine $5—one dollar per dish. Monica protested, however, feeling that she had gotten too much. How should the $8 have been divided to pay for the eight plates of food?

1-31 A problem we'll continue throughout the text is that of defining a new programming language. Make up a new language, and name it after yourself. For Chapter 1, choose reserved words to replace **program**, **var**, **begin**, and **end**. Predefine identifiers to replace the ones listed in the chapter summary. Draft rules of syntax that will make your new language's semantics equivalent to Pascal's.

'However, an unitialized variable is like an unmade bed--you can never be sure . . . '

2

Programming Calculations

It's time to stop using the computer as a glorified electric typewriter. In Chapter 1 we concentrated on moving values into and out of programs with the input and output procedures. In this chapter, we'll see how the *assignment* statement helps manipulate and store values within programs.

Section 2-1 introduces the *assignment operator*, which is used to give values to variables. We'll compute values with the arithmetic operators as we did before, but this time we'll look at *expressions* in detail, and learn more about the distinctions computers draw between values of different types.

Naturally, the programs we write will begin to get longer. Section 2-2 demonstrates some ways of ensuring that they don't get unnecessarily complicated as well. This section's main concern is with the style and *elegance* of programs. On the technical side, we'll see how to declare program *constants*.

Section 2-3 describes Pascal's *standard functions*. These are analogous to the function keys on a calculator (with some extras), and they compute values for assignment to variables. Section 2-3 is mostly for reference and review. This is a good time to find out about any nonstandard functions your system may support. As always, potential bugs and problems are described in the final section.

Before we begin, we'll repeat some advice from the last chapter. Start out by getting an overview of the material. Read through each section quickly, then go back and concentrate on the harder points. Try to figure out the 'why?' behind a rule, instead of just memorizing it. You'll find that getting into the habit of writing short test programs will vastly increase your confidence in your ability to figure things out.

Assignments and Expressions 2-1

ONCE AGAIN WE'LL BEGIN WITH AN example. Program *TailorSeries*, below, is an indispensable tailor's aid that determines all sorts of measurements from a male customer's waistline and weight. (You may be familiar with this series from your calculus courses.) Values for *Waistline* and *Weight* are prompted for, and then entered by the program user. The other variables are given values in the shaded *assignment statements*.

```
program TailorSeries (input, output);
   {Demonstrates the assignment statement.}
var NeckSize, HatSize, ShoeSize, ArmLength: real;
    Waistline, Weight: integer;
begin
   writeln ('This program computes sizes for a male customer.');
   writeln ('Please enter the customer''s waistline, in inches.');
   readln (Waistline);
   writeln ('Please enter the customer''s weight, in pounds.');
   readln (Weight);
   NeckSize := 3.0*(Weight / Waistline);
   HatSize := NeckSize /2.125;
   ShoeSize := 50.0*(Waistline / Weight);
   ArmLength := Waistline /2.0;
   writeln ('Neck size is ', NeckSize:2:2);
   writeln ('Hat size is ', HatSize:2:2);
   writeln ('Shoe size is ', ShoeSize:2:2);
   writeln ('Arm length is ', ArmLength:2:2)
end. {TailorSeries}
```

```
This program computes sizes for a male customer.
Please enter the customer's waistline, in inches.
32
Please enter the customer's weight, in pounds.
174
Neck size is 16.31
Hat size is 7.68
Shoe size is 9.20
Arm length is 16.00
```

assignment statements

The assignment statement is the most frequently used statement in programming. In Pascal it takes the form:

variable identifier := *the value represented by an expression*;

> The *assignment operator* (:=) changes the value of a variable within a program—to give it a starting value, or to alter its current value.

evaluating expressions

The computer first performs a calculation by *evaluating* the *expression* ('figuring it out') on the right-hand side of the assignment. Then the *result*, or computed value, is given to the variable on the left-hand side. For example, this assignment gives *LuckyNumber* the value 12—the sum of 7 and 5:

LuckyNumber := 7+5;

The colon distinguishes the assignment operator from an ordinary equals sign, which has a wholly different purpose in Pascal. We're best off reading the assignment operator as 'gets.' For example, the assignment above would be read as: 'the variable *LuckyNumber* gets assigned the sum of 7 and 5,' or, more tersely, '*LuckyNumber* gets 7 plus 5.'

Once they have values, variables can be used in expressions too. However...

A variable must be *initialized*, or given a starting value, before it can appear in an expression. The variable is *undefined* until it is initialized.

Age := 17; {Once *Age* is initialized...}
LuckyNumber := 2 * *Age*; {...it can appear in an expression.}

initializing variables

Many Pascal systems will automatically initialize variables to zero, or an equivalent null value. However, an uninitialized variable is like an unmade bed—you can never be sure of what you'll find there. No program that presumes to be written in Standard Pascal will use variables that are uninitialized and undefined.

The Golden Rule of types applies just as strongly to assignments as it did to input statements.

Variables may only be assigned values of the same Pascal type.

If *Age* is an *integer* variable, and *Fraction* is of type *real*, then these are valid assignments:

Age := 16; *Fraction* := 16.5; {legal assignments}

numerical assignments

The assignments below are no good because there's a clash between the types of *Age*, 16.5, and *Fraction*:

Age := 16.5; *Age* := *Fraction*; {illegal assignments}

It is legal to assign an *integer* value to a *real* variable, since the assignment can be made exactly. Such assignments should be avoided if possible, though, because they are confusing—the value can only be retrieved as a *real*.

character assignments

Assignments to *char* variables pose a special problem. We need to avoid confusion between, say, the letter 'E' and a variable named *E*; or between the character '6' and the *integer* value 6.

> When a character is used as a value of type *char*, it must be enclosed within single quote marks.

Initial := ´E´; *SeventhDigitCharacter* := ´6´;

This is similar to our use of quote marks to distinguish text values in output statements. A *char* variable, however, can only represent a single character value. The assignment:

Monogram := ´RMS´;

is in error, because it tries to give three different values ('R', 'M', and 'S') to the *char* variable *Monogram*.

Self-Check Questions

Q. Correct these assignment statements.

a) *2nd* := *1st*+*Correction*;
b) 5+7 = *Sum*;
c) *FirstLetter* := A;
d) *StartingCount* := *Initial* := 0;
e) *Efficiency* := .35;
f) *Initial* := ´WS´;
g) *Sum* := 9 **and** 13;
h) *TaxRate* := 5%;

A. The rewritten assignments:

a) *Second* := *First*+*Correction*;
b) *Sum* := 5+7;
c) *FirstLetter* := ´A´;
d) *StartingCount* := 0; *Initial* := 0;
e) *Efficiency* := 0.35;
f) A *char* variable represents just one letter.
g) *Sum* := 9+13;
h) *TaxRate* := 0.05;

Representing Values As Expressions

Somewhere in the course of every program, each declared variable takes on a value. In Pascal, two important ideas are associated with values: their types, and their *representations*. We're familiar with the basic types *integer, char* and so on. But no matter what its type is, a value must have some way of being shown. This brings us to the representation of a value—the symbol, or collection of symbols, that display it. These are representations of the value we call 'seven' (but could just as easily call 'hobgoblin,' 'Brobdingnagian,' or 'Rumplestiltskin'):

7 seven VII $|-7|$ 9–2 3+4 $49^{½}$

In Pascal, the legal representations of values are more restrained. An *integer* value, for instance, may be shown with numerals (12), a variable identifier (*RollOfDice*), or a combination of numerals, identifiers, and operation signs (*RollOfDice*+2). A Pascal function call (we'll encounter these in a few pages) might also express an *integer* value—*sqr*(7) calls the squaring function, and calculates the square of 7. Thus, it is a valid representation of the value 'forty-nine.'

In Pascal, any representation of a value is an expression, whether it's a numeral, variable identifier, function call, or sequence of operation signs and more basic expressions (called *operators* and *operands*).

Let's nail down the definitions that relate to expressions. Expressions are *stated*. Saying 'two plus two' states an arithmetic expression. The value the expression represents is computed by *evaluating* the expression. The answer obtained is the expression's *result*. Thus, in an assignment statement an expression is stated and evaluated. Its result value is assigned to a variable.

terminology of expressions

Self-Check Questions

Q. State each of these as a Pascal expression.

a) the sum of 5 and 9
b) the character P
c) the *real* representation of six
d) the character that represents six
e) the *integer* value six
f) negative 1 times *Value*

A. Here are some of the simplest expressions that do the job.

a) 5+9
b) 'P'
c) 6.0, 6E+00, or 6.0E+00
d) '6'
e) 6
f) −*Value*

The *integer* and *real* Operators

The *integer* and *real* operators are rules for combining operand values into new expressions. This is just a formal way of saying that these operators perform addition, subtraction, multiplication, and division. We have to distinguish between *integer* and *real* operators because they have some differences in most computer languages. For example, we can take two *integers* and add them, subtract them, or multiply them, and the result, or answer, will always be an *integer*:

4+3 *is* 7   4−3 *is* 1   4*3 *is* 12

But division gives us two sorts of results—*real*, and *integer*:

4 *divided by* 3 *is* 1.3333333333E+00	This is a *real* result
4 *divided by* 3 *is* 1, *and remainder* 1	This is an *integer* result

The second form of division, which you probably haven't seen since grade school, is as useful as the first. For instance, if we're dividing non-metric units of measure, like feet or pounds, fractional remainders don't do us much good. We want both the whole parts and remainders to both be expressed as *integers*; so many full feet and inches, or pounds and ounces.

real operators

The *real* arithmetic operators are:

Real Operators

+	addition	*Price* + *Surcharge*
–	subtraction	*Tuition* – *Scholarship*
*	multiplication	32.87 * 6.5E–02
/	division	*Spoils* / 2.0

integer division

The *integer* operators are the same except that the slash has been replaced by two special operators for *integer* division—**div**, and **mod**. The first, **div**, gives us the quotient of a division *without any remainder*. In practice, it's as though the quotient had been rounded toward zero. **mod** does just the opposite. It ignores the 'whole' part of the quotient, and provides only the remainder.

9 **div** 5 *is* 1	24 **div** 9 *is* 2	–9 **div** 5 *is* –1
9 **mod** 5 *is* 4	24 **mod** 9 *is* 6	9 **mod** 24 *is* 9

Although **div** and **mod** are reserved words in Pascal, they're thought of as symbols that represent operations, just like + and –.

integer operators

Integer Operators

+	addition	*FamilySize* + 2
–	subtraction	*ShoppingDays* – 1
*	multiplication	*Fine* * *DaysLate*
div	'whole number' division	10 **div** 3 (is 3)
mod	'remainder' division	10 **mod** 3 (is 1)

Since they're *integer* operators, **div** and **mod** may only be used with *integer*-valued operands. We can't use *real* operands with **div** and **mod** even when it seems perfectly reasonable. The expressions shown below are both invalid, because 2.0 and 1E+02 are *real* values.

4 **div** 2.0   1E+02 **mod** 50   {illegal expressions}

mixed expressions

> If an expression contains both *reals* and *integers* (or only *reals*), then the result of evaluating the expression will be of type *real*. The result of any expression that uses the *real* division operator (/) is also of type *real*.

3+1.0 *is* 4.0000000000E+00	2E+02–87 *is* 1.1300000000E+02
–0.1*5 *is* –5.0000000000E–01	4/2 *is* 2.0000000000E+00

Self-Check Questions

Q. Evaluate these expressions. Assume that the following assignments have been made: *Channel* := 6; and *Frequency* := 3.5. What is the type of each of the expressions?

a) 102 **div** 25	*b*) *Channel*∗*Frequency*
c) *Frequency*−*Channel*	*d*) 69 **mod** *Channel*
e) *Channel* **mod** 69	*f*) *Channel* **mod** *Frequency*
g) 12E+02+*Frequency*	*h*) 12E+02+*Channel*
i) *Channel*/1	*j*) *Channel*∗1.0

A. Note the mismatched types in *f*.

a) 4 *integer*	*b*) 21.0 *real*
c) −2.5 *real*	*d*) 3 *integer*
e) 6 *integer*	*f*) Type clash—invalid expression
g) 1203.5 *real*	*h*) 1206.0 *real*
i) 6.0 *real*	*j*) 6.0 *real*

Q. Which of these expressions can be assigned to *integer* variables? To *reals*?

A. Expressions *a, d,* and *e* represent *integer* values, and should be assigned to *integer* variables. Although *any* of the expressions shown here (with the exception of *f*) may be assigned to *real* variables, it's sloppy, potentially confusing type handling that should be avoided. Only *real*-valued expressions should be assigned to *real* variables.

Operator Precedence

In Pascal, as in ordinary arithmetic, we can combine several small expressions in a chain of operations. As long as the type rules are obeyed, we can make expressions as long and complicated as we desire.* However, a question arises: what part of an expression is evaluated first? How many different result values can you come up with for the following expression?

5 ∗ 20 + 8 **mod** 50 −3 ∗ 6 **div** 4 + 9

Completing the operations as they appear—5 times 20, plus 8, **mod** 50, etc.—gives 16 as the result. But we might just as reasonably work from right to left, and get 140. We've arrived at the problem of *operator precedence*—which operations should take place first? Stop reading for a moment, and try to come up with a few plausible solutions to this problem.

Two options come to mind. We can say that some operations are more important than others, and proceed from the most important operations to the least important. On the other hand, we might want to continue a standard practice of arithmetic and algebra—use parentheses to indicate the sequence of operations. Pascal takes both of these ideas.

* If you want people to think you know something about computer science, say 'We can state expressions of *arbitrary complexity*.'

1. There is a *hierarchy*, or ordering, of precedence of operations. Expressions that contain more than one operator from a given level of the hierarchy are evaluated from left to right.
2. Parentheses can change the order of evaluation, or make it clearer.

operator hierarchy

The arithmetic operations exist on two levels. Addition and subtraction have less precedence than the other operations.

The hierarchical rule of precedence is:

* / **div** **mod**	these operations are completed...
+ −	...before these operations.

Thus, we see that:

8.0/2.0 + 6.0	*evaluates to* 10.0, *not* 1.0
3−4*2	*is equal to* −5, *not* −2
5+25 **mod** 6	*equals* 6, *not* 0
3.5−1.25/0.5	*is* 1.0, *not* 4.5

When an expression contains more than a single operator from any one level, we do the multiplications and divisions first, then perform the lower level additions or subtractions.

5.5−3.375/1.125	*is* 5.5−3.0	*is* 2.5
5*3+14 **mod** 4	*is* 15+2	*is* 17
4.5/1.125−3.325*6.5	*is* 4.0−21.6125	*is* −17.6125
7−6*2−33 **div** 4−3	*is* 7−12−8−3	*is* −16

parentheses

Parentheses change this order of evaluation, because a subexpression within parentheses gets evaluated before the rest of the expression.

(5+3)*(8−2)	*is equivalent to* 8*6
(6/3)*(2−4)	*is the same as* 2.0*(−2)
2.5*(1.25+0.25)	*is like* 2.5*1.5

When we *nest* parentheses—use multiple levels of parentheses—calculations are done from the inside out, e.g.:

(8 **mod** (2 * (5 − 3 * (4 + 6 * (5 **div** 2)) **div** 10)))
(8 **mod** (2 * (5 − 3 * (4 + 6 * 2) **div** 10)))
(8 **mod** (2 * (5 − 3 * (4 + 12) **div** 10)))
(8 **mod** (2 * (5 − 3 * 16 **div** 10)))
(8 **mod** (2 * (5 − 48 **div** 10)))
(8 **mod** (2 * (5 − 4)))
(8 **mod** (2 * 1))
(8 **mod** 2)
0 {*as* 8 **div** 2 *equals* 4 *exactly*}

expressions should be clear

You can appreciate that there is often more than one way to write a particular expression. Sometimes we have to choose between using parentheses, and relying on the operator precedence rules. The main rule of thumb to follow is this:

> Figuring out what an expression means (to say nothing of evaluating it) should not bring great anguish to someone who is reading your program.

A string of operations can sometimes be confusing or ambiguous, even though it accomplishes exactly what you intend. Compare:

PartialResult / CompleteData − Correction
{*vs.*}
(*PartialResult / CompleteData*) − *Correction*

The first expression is correct, but unclear. The second is unambiguous. Write assignment statements and expressions that can be understood by human beings, and the computers will take care of themselves.

Self-Check Questions

Q. In what order are these operations done: **div**, *, **mod**, / ?

A. Because these operators are all on the same level of the operator hierarchy, they have equal precedence. They are carried out as they appear, working from left to right.

Q. These expressions are evaluated in a certain sequence by the rules of Pascal. Insert parentheses to make the order more explicit.

a) 5−9*3+2
b) 0.09/1.394*8.6/5.004E+02
c) 7*8−9+12 **div** 5
d) 1E+04/2.5E−01+350.0*−0.10
e) 1+3*9 **div** −6 **div** 7
f) 5.9E+07+(−18E+03)−0.6/5.9E−02−8.1

A. All other things being equal, evaluation goes from left to right.

a) 5−(9*3)+2
b) ((0.09/1.394)*8.6)/5.004E+02
c) (7*8)−9+(12 **div** 5)
d) (1E+04/2.5E−01)+(350.0*(−0.10))
e) 1+(((3*9) **div** (−6)) **div** 7)
f) 5.9E+07+(−18E+03)−(0.6/5.9E−02)−8.1

Focus On Programming: Constants, Style and Elegance 2-2

THERE'S NO RECIPE FOR A PERFECT program. A dollop of variables and a dash of comments are proper ingredients, but good programming (like good cooking) takes talent that doesn't come with the cookbook. Instructors at restaurant schools realize this, and begin their courses by teaching prospective chefs the Zen of boiling water or breaking eggs. We, in turn, will introduce the finer points of programming by considering the many ways of naming a variable.

We'll begin with the programming equivalent of making ice cubes—we'll write a program that takes a circle's diameter and computes its circumference. Only one algorithm really makes sense: get the facts, use the circumference formula, and print the results.

Request information
Perform calculations
Print output

A working program is barely longer than the algorithm:

```
program C (input, output); var X,Y: real;
begin readln (X); Y := 3.14*X; writeln (Y) end.
```

Simple as program *C* is, it's unacceptable because of poor style. The identifiers we've chosen, and the way the program is laid out, violate a basic precept of good programming.

> The Golden Rule of Style
>
> A program should be as easy for a human being to read and understand as it is for a computer to execute.

meaningful identifiers

Now, William Shakespeare ('A rose, by any other name, would smell as sweet') and Gertrude Stein ('A rose is a rose is a rose') didn't think names were especially important. Computers agree with them entirely, because as long as an identifier is formed in accordance with Pascal's syntax rules, anything goes. However, Abbott and Costello knew better, as we've shown in a selection from their famous routine *Who's On First*? A name can carry a tremendous amount of information (or misinformation), and identifiers should be as meaningful as possible.

For example, suppose that a program does a series of geometry calculations. We *could* have a variable declaration like:

```
var a, b, c, d, e, f, g: integer;
```

But contrast that with:

```
var area, base, circumference, depth, elevation, frustum, girth: integer;
```

The second set of identifiers is *mnemonic* (nih-mahn´-ick). Every identifier is a memory aid that clarifies the purpose of each variable.

One might argue that it's easy to remember the meanings of shorthand variable names (like *a*, *b*, and *c*) in a brief program. Unfortunately, although computers never forget, people do. In time, you'll have occasion to dig up a program written weeks or months earlier, and try to rewrite it, or include it in a larger program. You may find to your dismay that convenient shorthands have turned into unbreakable codes.

(Lou Costello is considering becoming a ballplayer. Bud Abbott wants to make sure he knows what he's getting into).

Abbott: Strange as it may seem, they give ball players nowadays very peculiar names.
Costello: Funny names?
Abbott: Nicknames, nicknames. Now, on the St. Louis team we have Who's on first, What's on second, I Don't Know is on third—
Costello: That's what I want to find out. I want you to tell me the names of the fellows on the St. Louis team.
Abbott: I'm telling you. Who's on first, What's on second, I Don't Know is on third—
Costello: You know the fellows' names?
Abbott: Yes.
Costello: Well, then who's playing first?
Abbott: Yes.
Costello: I mean the fellow's name on first base.
Abbott: Who.
Costello: The fellow playin' first base.
Abbott: Who.
Costello: The guy on first base.
Abbott: Who is on first.
Costello: Well, what are you askin' me for?
Abbott: I'm not asking you—I'm telling you. Who is on first.
Costello: I'm asking you—who's on first?
Abbott: That's the man's name.
Costello: That's who's name?
Abbott: Yes.

~ ~ ~ ~ ~ ~

Costello: When you pay off the first baseman every month, who gets the money?
Abbott: Every dollar of it. And why not, the man's entitled to it.
Costello: Who is?
Abbott: Yes.
Costello: So who gets it?
Abbott: Why shouldn't he? Sometimes his wife comes down and collects it.
Costello: Who's wife?
Abbott: Yes. After all, the man earns it.
Costello: Who does?
Abbott: Absolutely.
Costello: Well, all I'm trying to find out is what's the guy's name on first base?
Abbott: Oh, no, no. What is on second base.
Costello: I'm not asking you who's on second.
Abbott: Who's on first!

~ ~ ~ ~ ~ ~

Costello: St. Louis has a good outfield?
Abbott: Oh, absolutely.
Costello: The left fielder's name?
Abbott: Why.
Costello: I don't know, I just thought I'd ask.
Abbott: Well, I just thought I'd tell you.
Costello: Then tell me who's playing left field?
Abbott: Who's playing first.
Costello: Stay out of the infield! The left fielder's name?
Abbott: Why.
Costello: Because.
Abbott: Oh, he's center field.
Costello: Wait a minute. You got a pitcher on the team?
Abbott: Wouldn't this be a fine team *without* a pitcher?
Costello: Tell me the pitcher's name.
Abbott: Tomorrow.

~ ~ ~ ~ ~ ~

Costello: Now, when the guy at bat bunts the ball—me being a good catcher—I want to throw the guy out at first base, so I pick up the ball and throw it to who?
Abbott: Now, that's the first thing you've said right.
Costello: I DON'T EVEN KNOW WHAT I'M TALKING ABOUT!
Abbott: Don't get excited. Take it easy.
Costello: I throw the ball to first base, whoever it is grabs the ball, so the guy runs to second. Who picks up the ball and throws it to what. What throws it to I don't know. I don't know throws it back to tomorrow—a triple play.
Abbott: Yeah, it could be.
Costello: Another guy gets up and it's a long ball to center.
Abbott: Because.
Costello: Why? I don't know. And I don't care.
Abbott: What was that?
Costello: I said, I DON'T CARE!
Abbott: Oh, that's our shortstop!

Furthermore, although *you* may know what your shorthand means, nobody else does. If your program won't work, the person you ask for help

the moral

has to be able to figure out what's going on in the program. Imagine yourself in the position of an instructor or manager inundated with hordes of buggy programs filled with variables named *x, y*, and *z*!

> You're much more likely to get help if you use meaningful, self-explanatory variable names. Be sure that your identifiers mean something to *people* as well as to computers.

defining constants

Mnemonic names can be given to particular values by defining them as *constants.* Once it has been defined, a constant's value *cannot* be changed during the course of a program. The syntax chart of a constant definition looks like this:

constant definition

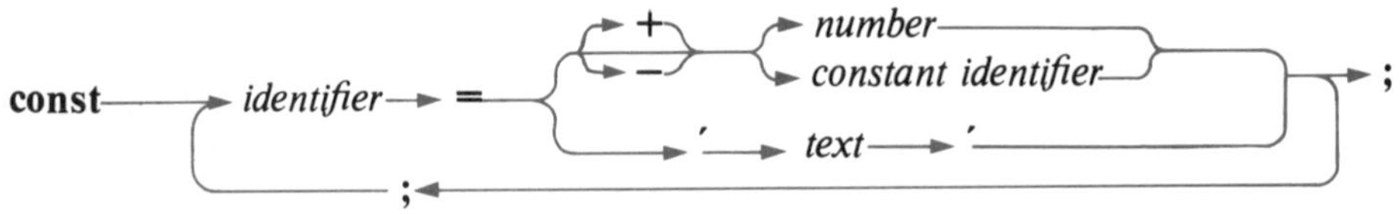

Constants are especially convenient for renaming long numbers—there's no need to use an approximation (3.14) just to avoid repeatedly typing 3.141592654. Constant definitions come just after the program heading:

program heading;
constant definitions;
variable declarations;
statement part;

In these examples, note that an equals sign (=), and not the assignment operator (:=), is used in the constant definition. In addition, it's obvious that we capitalize all constant identifiers. We do this as a matter of programming style, to make constants instantly distinguishable from variables.

```
const PLANCK = 6.63E-34;          {The constant's type isn't given.}
      LASTLETTER = 'Z';
      THISYEAR = 1986;
```

A special application of constants is the representation of a whole string of characters—what we've referred to as the text of output statements. The *text constant* must be enclosed by single quotes:

text constants

```
const TRUELOVE = 'Nicole';
      FIVEBLANKS = '     ';
      LICENSEPLATE = '973 UBK';
      DOTTEDLINE = '..........';
```

Although none of these text constants can be assigned to variables of type *char* (because they all include two or more character values), we can print the values of text constants with output statements.

```
writeln ('I wish ', TRUELOVE, ' would call me up!');
   ↓        ↓         ↓         ↓        ↓
I wish Nicole would call me up!
```

MAXINT

The constant *MAXINT* is predefined in every Pascal installation. It represents the maximum *integer* the compiler allows. You should note its value inside the front cover. *MAXINT* is the *only* standard predefined constant. In some systems, you may have to type it in lower-case letters.

An important restriction of constant definitions is that they be specific values, or previously defined constants. A constant declaration can't contain variables or arithmetic operations. This means that the value of a constant can't depend on program execution. These:

```
const HALF = 1/2;
      ROOT = sqrt(4);        {Illegal constant definitions.}
      RATE = InputRate;
```

are all illegal definitions. They require that a value be computed, or supplied by a variable identifier (like *InputRate*).

We can easily rewrite program *C* using mnemonic identifiers and defined constants. Although *FindCircumference* is longer than *C*, it can be understood more quickly.

constant demonstration program

```
program FindCircumference (input, output);
   {Computes the circumference of a circle.}
const PI = 3.141592654;
var Circumference, Diameter: real;
begin
   writeln ('What is the diameter of the circle?');
   readln (Diameter);
   Circumference := PI * Diameter;
   writeln ('The circle''s circumference is', Circumference)
end.
   ↓        ↓         ↓         ↓        ↓
What is the diameter of the circle?
8.25
The circle's circumference is 2.59181393955000E+01
```

Fixed-Point Notation

A common application of constants involves controlling the way that *real* values are printed. *Fixed-point* notation is the way that people (and not computers) usually write *reals*. The decimal point is fixed between the 'ones' and 'tenths' columns of the *real*, and there's no exponent. In contrast, floating-point notation puts the decimal to the right of the first digit, and an exponent must change to compensate for the floating decimal. For example:

Fixed-point	*Floating-point*
1.0	1.0E+00
10.0	1.00E+01
100.0	1.000E+02

Now, we've already seen that any value ready for output can be given a particular field width, or printing size, by the programmer. *real* values get one additional privilege.

> When they're output, *real* values may be given a second field 'argument,' in addition to the field size. The second argument tells the computer to use fixed-point notation, and specifies the exact number of decimal places (the *real's decimal accuracy*) that should appear. Remaining decimals are rounded.

field width and decimal accuracy

In the example below, the field width accorded each expression (100/8) is always ten spaces. However, the result values printed have progressively greater (and therefore better) decimal accuracy: 1, 2, and 5 places.

writeln (100/8:10:1, 100/8:10:2, 100/8:10:5)

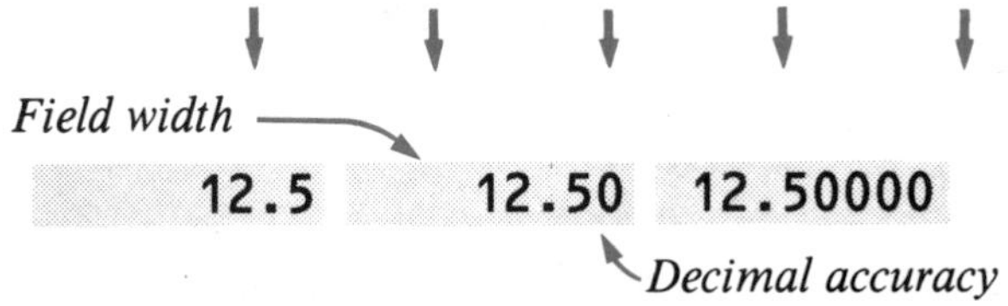

Programs that handle money are obvious candidates for fixed-point notation. A program like *SalesTax*, below, needs neither the sometime convenience of floating-point arithmetic (what would you make of a price tag that read $3.9899E+02?), nor the extreme accuracy of computer arithmetic ('With tax, that comes to one dollar and 5.86382547791 cents.').

decimal accuracy demonstration program

```
program SalesTax (input, output);
    {Asks for a price and amount tendered. Computes sales tax and change.}
const TAXRATE = 0.065;          {The local tax rate—6.5%.}
      FIELD = 5;
      DECIMALS = 2;             {Print output to two decimal places.}
var Price, AmountTendered, Tax, SalesPrice, Change: real;
begin
    writeln ('Please enter the price.');
    readln (Price);
    Tax := TAXRATE*Price;
    SalesPrice := Price+Tax;
    writeln ('The sales price is $', SalesPrice:FIELD:DECIMALS);
    writeln ('What do you need change for?');
    readln (AmountTendered);
    Change := AmountTendered-SalesPrice;
    writeln ('Your change is $', Change:FIELD:DECIMALS)
end. {SalesTax}
```

```
Please enter the price.
15.75
The sales price is $16.77
What do you need change for?
20.00
Your change is $ 3.23
```

why use constants?

Using constants is a matter of programming style. *FindCircumference* and *SalesTax* will both run without constants; in fact, no program needs defined constants in order to work. Yet, programs often require constants in order to be good programs. Suppose that a 2000-line program calculates property taxes like clockwork for a few years, and then—horrors! the tax rate changes. Must we search the entire program to update every instance of the old tax rate? Not if we had made the definition:

const *TAXRATE* = 0.003

for style

Changing the value of the constant *TAXRATE* updates the whole program. Could *TAXRATE* have been declared as a variable? Yes, but that would open the possibility of accidentally changing its value within the program. It's also misleading to call *TAXRATE* a variable instead of a constant, because declaring something as a variable implies that its value will change frequently, or be obtained from the program's user.

A second style motivation for using constants is less obvious. Writing a program is a little like writing an instruction booklet. Just including all the facts isn't enough—they have to be presented in a manner that even a casual reader can follow. Now, comments (between curly brackets) provide a running commentary, called *documentation*, that explains what's happening in a program. Defined constants go further. Like mnemonic variable identifiers, they help make a program *self-documenting*. For example, this statement doesn't say much:

as documentation

a := *b*−5;

Better variable names, and a comment, help it out:

Speed2 := *Speed1*−5;
{Find true speed by subtracting the fixed speedometer error.}

But mnemonic identifiers and a defined constant manage to do no-hands commenting—they document *without* additional comments. They're the best of all.

CorrectedSpeed := *IndicatedSpeed*−*SPEEDOMETERERROR*;

Self-Check Questions

Q. What types do each of these constants represent?

a) *WIDTH* = 5; *b*) *YEAR* = 1981;
c) *NUMBER* = ´5´; *d*) *SIZE* = 5E+02;
e) *DATE* = ´1981´; *f*) *SPACE* = ´´;
g) *MASS* = 1.79E−02; *h*) *TENSPACES* = ´   ´;
i) *WEIGHT* = *MASS*; *j*) *CENTURY* = *YEAR* **div** 100;

A. Note that *i* is legal if *MASS* has already been declared as a constant.

a) *integer* *b*) *integer*
c) *char* *d*) *real*
e) text constant *f*) *char*
g) *real* *h*) text constant
i) *real* *j*) invalid declaration

Elegance In Problem Solving

An *elegant* solution is one you wish you'd thought of yourself. A program is elegant if its algorithm is simple and concise, and solves a problem in a clear and complete manner. However, elegance isn't restricted to programming. It's an attribute of many kinds of solutions, and even some problems. A particularly elegant mathematical problem is the four-color theorem, which even first graders can understand. Much to the dismay of the sales department at Crayola, it states that any map can be colored with only four different colors.

The *proof* of the four-color theorem, which evaded mathematicians for centuries, is another matter entirely. Recently, a team at the University of Illinois came up with a proof several hundred pages long through extensive computer research. Its validity, though, met with resistance from parts of the academic community who felt that the new proof was too long, too unwieldy, too complicated, *too inelegant*.

word problems

Now, exercises found in textbooks usually have elegant solutions. In some cases, the problems merely need to be restated in a more elegant manner to be solved. 'Word' problems (that algebra and calculus students universally hate) are a perfect example. The problem is deliberately stated in the most confusing, complicated, *inelegant* manner possible. For example:

> A cyclist is exactly one-third of a mile from home. She is riding toward her front door at precisely 10 miles per hour.
>
> A fly has been traveling back and forth between the cyclist and the aforementioned door at the constant speed of thirty miles per hour, never stopping for rest. As our problem begins, the fly has just left the front wheel of the bicycle, and is heading toward the rider's door. When it reaches the house, the fly will turn back and fly to the bicycle again. It will continue this backward-and-forward motion between the onrushing cyclist and her door until it meets a horrifying death as they crash head on!
>
> The question is this: How far will the fly travel before it dies?

problem: the manic fly

Try to solve the problem before you read on.*

As you might expect, understanding the manic behavior of the fly (to say nothing of the suicidal tendencies of the cyclist) isn't a crucial part of the problem's solution. Furthermore, although the distance flown by the fly could be found by summing some ridiculous infinite geometric series, that isn't necessary either. Instead, we have to determine how long it takes the bicycle to reach the door—*Time*. Then, since we know the *Rate* at which the fly is flitting (30 *mph*), we can use everybody's favorite formula—*Distance* equals *Rate* times *Time*—to find out how far the fly goes.

> Since the bike travels at 10 miles per hour, it will plow into the front door (and the fly) in two minutes, or 1/30 of an hour.
>
> *Distance* = *Rate* * *Time*
> 1 *mile* = 30 *mph* * 1/30 *hour*

The fly travels exactly one mile. Had the problem been stated like this from the beginning—if a fly travels at 30 *mph*, how far will it go in 2 minutes?—there would have been no problem at all. It has an elegant solution—a simple, clear restatement.

* We grant that some readers, mindful of Zeno's paradox, will maintain that the fly never gets crushed at all.

A word that's used to describe the process of restating a problem is *massage*. Massaging a problem means rearranging its facts to get a better idea of what we're trying to find out, and to get rid of the clutter of irrelevant information. Indeed, learning how to massage problems is essentially the content of a high-school algebra course. A classic example of a problem that can be massaged into an elegant solution is:

massaging

Add together all the numbers from 1 through 100.

Again, try to solve this problem before you read on.

At this point, we see four possible solutions:

1. Write a program that contains an incredibly long assignment statement (or a hundred shorter ones).
2. Be adventurous! Look inside the cover for a control statement that looks appropriate, and learn how to use it.
3. Give up computer science, and go back to work on the novel. (Quitting is *always* a solution.)
4. Be clever.

It happens that this particular problem was given to the mathematician Carl Friedrich Gauss in 1786, when he was 9. His teacher, attempting to keep the class busy one morning, told them to add a long series of numbers. He had barely finished giving the assignment when Gauss stood up and handed in his slate, which contained a single number—the correct answer. How did he do it? Once more, try to figure it out if you haven't already.

What Gauss did involved looking *at* the *problem*, as well as *for* the *solution*. Were we to take the problem statement at face value, we'd be stuck trying to figure out a way to add a long sequence of numbers:

$$1 + 2 + 3 \cdots + 98 + 99 + 100$$

We might be able to think of a way of adding them quickly and painlessly—especially if we figured out how to use one of the control statements we'll meet a few chapters hence—but we'd still be adding them one by one.

But suppose that we massage the problem as Gauss did:

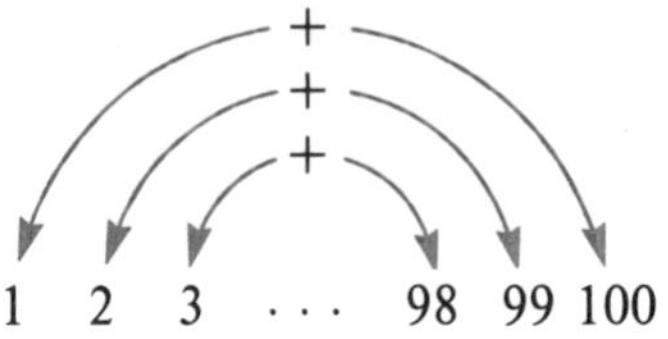

When numbers are added in this fashion, the sum is always 101. How many similar pairs are there? Well, every number from 1 to 50 has a matching number between 100 and 51, so there must be 50 pairs. Thus, the sum of all the numbers from 1 to 100 is 50 * 101, or 5050.

Granted, this is the sort of trick—easy to understand, but not so easy to think up—that students dread. Nonetheless, taking the first step toward elegance by wondering 'Is there a formula that might solve this problem, *and others like it*?' isn't hard at all. Don't just follow the old problem-solving saw 'State the problem.' Instead, state the facts, and see if you can massage them into a problem that you *do* know how to solve.

the moral

The Standard Functions 2-3

LOOK AT ANY POCKET CALCULATOR. ALONG with the keys that represent the arithmetic operators, we'll almost invariably find function keys for more complex figuring. A typical calculator has keys that find squares (x^2), square roots ($x^{1/2}$), reciprocals ($1/x$), and percentages. More expensive scientific or business calculators may include many others. Function keys save us from the death of a thousand cuts—a single keystroke completes what might otherwise require a long series of calculations.

Now, it's reasonable to expect a written computer language to be at least as powerful as the 'touch' language of a hand calculator. Pascal contains built-in functions, and lets us write our own functions to deal with new situations as well. For now, though, we'll be content to study the *standard functions* that are predefined in every Pascal implementation.

Arithmetic Functions

sqr	*sqrt*		{Square and square root}
sin	*cos*	*arctan*	{Standard trigonometric functions}
exp	*ln*		{Exponential and natural log functions}
abs			{Absolute value}
round			{Rounding}
trunc			{Truncation}

Ordering Functions

succ	{Successor—the next ordinal value}
pred	{Predecessor—the previous ordinal value}
ord	{Position of an ordinal value}
chr	{*char* value in a given ordinal position}

Boolean Functions

odd	{Is an *integer* odd?}
eoln	{Are we at the end of an input line?}
eof	{Are we at the end of the input file?}

function calls

> We use a Pascal function by making a *function call*. A function call usually has two parts—the name of the function, followed by the function's *argument* in parentheses.

arguments

We briefly mentioned earlier that *sqr*(7) is a call of the squaring function. Its argument is 7, and the entire function call represents the value 49. Thus, a function call is an expression that can appear as the argument of another function, or as part of an output statement. A function's argument can be an expression of any length:

```
writeln (sqr(7));                    {Will print '      49'}
writeln (sqr(7)+3);                  {Will print '      52'}
writeln (sqr(7+3));                  {Will print '     100'}
Root := sqrt(16-7);                  {Root gets 3.0}
HypotenuseSquared := sqr(3)+sqr(4);
NoChange := sqrt(sqr(7));            {NoChange gets 7}
```

The *result* of a function is the value it (and its argument) represents. It has a Pascal type—the function's *result-type*.

function terminology

To spout all these new terms at once, we'll say that a function (call it '*f*'), receives an argument (which we'll usually call '*x*'). The value that the function call represents is the result of evaluating the expression $f(x)$, and has the function's result-type.

Self-Check Questions

Q. What value will the following program segment print out?

```
Side := 4;
sqr (Side);
writeln ('The square of the side is ', Side);
```

A. The segment won't run at all, because the function call in the second line of the segment—*sqr (Side)*—is just a representation of the value 4 squared, or 16. It's as though we had written:

```
Side := 4;          {incorrect code}
16;          {The value sqr(Side) represents.}
writeln ('The square of the side is ', Side);
```

To get the desired effect, we should write:

```
Side := 4;          {the corrected segment}
SquaredSide := sqr(Side);
writeln ('The square of the side is ', SquaredSide);
```

Arithmetic Functions

The first group of functions take numerical values as arguments. Most are like the functions found on calculators, but Pascal includes a few extras. The square root and squaring functions are easy to understand.

sqr(*x*) Squaring function. Represents the square of its argument *x*. The argument may be either a *real* or *integer* value; the function's result has the same type as its argument.

sqrt(*x*) Square root function. It finds, and represents as a *real*, the square root of its *real* or *integer* argument.

sin(*x*), *cos*(*x*) Sine and cosine functions. They represent the sine and cosine of the argument *x* (given in radians), respectively.

arctan(*x*) Arctangent function. Represents the inverse tangent of *x*; the *real* result is in radians.

Although the result of *sqr* has the same type as its argument, *sqrt* is always a *real*. Thus:

sqr(3.0) *is* 9.0000000000E+00	*sqr*(3) *is* 9
sqrt(4.0) *is* 2.0000000000E+00	*sqrt*(4) *is* 2.0000000000E+00

trig review

The trigonometric functions also have *real* results. Their arguments may be either *real* or *integer*, but the argument is given in *radians*, rather than degrees.* In these examples, assume that the identifier *PI* represents the value 3.141592654.

sin(*PI*/2) is 1.0	*sin*(*PI* /4) is 7.07106781E−01
cos(0) is 1.0	*cos*(*PI* /3) is 5.00000000E−01
arctan(0) is 0	*arctan*(1) is 7.85398163E−01

You may wonder why functions like tangent, arcsine, and arccosine aren't built into Pascal. The answer is economy; any trigonometry or calculus text has a table that yields all the trigonometric relationships from *sin, cos*, and *arctan*. Predefining extra functions in Pascal would be redundant, and make the language less streamlined and compact.

Self-Check Questions

Q. Write expressions that make these assignments:

a) *RightAngle* gets half the sine of twice *PI*.
b) *FourthRoot* gets the fourth root of 4.7458321E07.
c) *FifthPower* gets nine to the fifth power.
d) *CosineSquared* gets the square of the cosine of 33.7.
e) *InverseSquared* gets the inverse of 97 squared.
f) *TangentSquaredPi* gets the square of the tangent of *PI*.

A. Assume that *PI* is a defined constant.

a) *RightAngle* := *sin*(2∗*PI*)/2;	*b*) *FourthRoot* := *sqrt*(*sqrt*(4.7458321E+07));
c) *FifthPower* := 9∗*sqr*(*sqr*(9));	*d*) *CosineSquared* := *sqr*(*cos*(33.7));
e) *InverseSquared* := 1/*sqr*(97);	*f*) *TangentSquaredPi* := *sqr*(*sin*(*PI*)/*cos*(*PI*));

* For reference, 180°=π radians (3.141592654 radians), 360°=2π radians, 90°=$\pi/2$ radians, etc.

Log, Absolute Value, and Transfer Functions

The next arithmetic functions we'll consider are the natural logarithm ('log' for short) functions. Both their result types are *real* whether their arguments are *real* or *integer.* Note that we're working with natural logarithms (base e), and not *common* logs (base 10).

$ln(x)$ *Natural log* function. Represents the natural logarithm (log to the base e) of its *integer* or *real* argument x. The argument must be greater than 0.

$exp(x)$ *Exponential* function. The result of this function represents e (the base of the natural log system), raised to the *real* or *integer* power x (i.e. e^x).

figuring exponents

We won't bother with a review of logarithms. However, they're handy because they help overcome a shortcoming in Pascal that often annoys programmers—the lack of a specific *exponentiation* operator. There's no predefined function for raising a number (call it a) to some power (call it n), as in a^n. Incidentally, the number a is known as the *base*, while n is called the *exponent*.* This formula can be used for exponentiation in Pascal:

$$a^n = exp\,(n * ln(a))$$

It is subject to the following restriction: the base, a, must be a positive *real* or *integer* value. (We pointed this out in the definition of $ln(x)$.)

Math	*Pascal*
5^8	$exp(8*ln(5))$
$9.87^{-3.51}$	$exp(-3.51*ln(9.87))$
$4.3^{1/2}$	$exp(1/2*ln(4.3))$
$(-5)^{0.15}$	Negative base; can't be done.

The last three arithmetic functions do jobs that are trivial on paper, but require some specialization in the computer.

$abs(x)$ *Absolute value.* This function shows the absolute value $|x|$ of its *integer* or *real* argument x. The result type of the function matches the type of its argument.

$abs(-10)$ is 10 $abs(-3.5)$ is 3.500000000000000E+00

transfer functions

$round(x)$ The rounding function represents its *real* argument, x, rounded to the nearest *integer* according to this rule:

If x is positive, rounding is *up* for fractions including and greater than .5, and *down* for fractions less than .5.

If x is negative, the result is rounded *down*—away from zero—when the fractional part is greater than or equal to .5, and *up*—

* Exponentiation is usually handled on calculators by the y^x key, and in many programming languages by a special exponentiation operator: '**'.

toward zero—otherwise. This makes *round*($-x$) equal to $-$*round*(x).

round(1.6) *is* 2 *round*(1.5) *is* 2
round(−2.6) *is* −3 *round*(−1.5) *is* −2

trunc(x) The *truncating* function represents the 'whole' part of its *real* argument x as an *integer*. Any portion of the argument that is a fraction less than 1 is truncated—cut off. In effect, the argument is rounded to the nearest *integer* toward zero.

trunc(4.8) *is* 4 *trunc*(−3.9) *is* −3 *trunc*(0.22573E+02) *is* 22

Functions like *round* and *trunc* are called *transfer functions*, because they provide a temporary means of 'transferring' a value from one type to another.

Self-Check Questions

Q. Write these mathematical expressions as Pascal expressions. Assume that *pi* equals π.

a) $8^{9.4}$ *b*) e^0 *c*) *sine* 45° *d*) *cosine* $3.0672^{2\pi}$

e) $\ln \frac{1+a}{1-a}$ *f*) $\frac{e^x}{2}$ *g*) $\ln(\frac{\pi}{2})$ *h*) $\frac{e^u - e^{-u}}{2}$

A. Answers:

a) *exp*(9.4**ln*(8)) *b*) 1 (any number to the zero power is 1)
c) *sin*(*pi*/4) *d*) *cos*(*exp*(2**pi***ln*(3.0672)))
e) *ln*((1+*a*)/(1−*a*)) *f*) *exp*(*x*)/2
g) *ln*(3.141592654/2) *h*) (*exp*(*u*)−*exp*(−*u*))/2

Q. Can the *trunc* function be persuaded to round off a *real* value (call it x) according to the rules of the rounding function?

A. It can be done, but we have to know if x is greater or less than zero.

round(x) is *trunc*(x+0.5) if $x \geq 0$
round(x) is *trunc*(x−0.5) if $x < 0$

Ordering Functions

Lest you start to think that computing is all numbers, we hasten to introduce four functions—*pred, succ, ord*, and *chr*—that are used to juggle other values. We'll relate the ordinal functions to *char* values for now, and find more applications when we discuss enumerated ordinal types in Chapter 9. A bit of background about computer character sets is needed to begin our discussion.

collating sequence

The computer's *character set*—all the letters, numerals, punctuation it can input or output—are in a certain order, called the *collating sequence*. Every key on a terminal or keypunch keyboard has a specific place in this ordering.

The concept of character ordering is nothing unusual—kids memorize the alphabet in a certain order, and learn the digits in numerical order. But defining a collating sequence is necessary to clarify some relationships—Does lower-case come before upper-case? Do punctuation marks precede numerals?—we wouldn't normally worry about.

control characters

The most common character set-up is the ASCII* (ask´-ee) character set, of 95 printable characters, as well as many 'control', or special characters, that cannot be printed. Control characters are generally used internally by the computer, and we won't worry about them. The standard order of the printable characters is:

    ! ″ # $ % & ´ ( ) * + − , . / 0 1 2 3 4 5 6 7 8 9 : ; < = > ? @
    A B C D E F G H I J K L M N O P Q R S T U V W X Y Z [\ ] ∧ _
    a b c d e f g h i j k l m n o p q r s t u v w x y z { | } ~

Note that the very first character is a space. Another character set, used on IBM computers, is the EBCDIC** (eb´-sih-dick´) set. Although most of the characters are the same as those in the ASCII set, their ordering is considerably different. Neither the upper nor lower-case letters are entirely contiguous (j doesn't immediately follow i, for instance), but the gaps in each set of letters are the same (j is the same distance from i as J is from I).

    ¢ . < (+ | & ! $ *) ; ¬ − / ∧ , % _ : # @ ´ = ″
    a b c d e f g h i j k l m n o p q r s t u v w x y z \ { } [ ]
    A B C D E F G H I J K L M N O P Q R S T U V W X Y Z
    0 1 2 3 4 5 6 7 8 9

A shorter set of characters, with only 64 members, is common on the CDC 6000 series of computers.

    : A B C D E F G H I J K L M N O P Q R S T U V W X Y Z
    0 1 2 3 4 5 6 7 8 9
    + − * / ( ) $ =   , . ≡ [ ] % ≠ → ∨ ∧ ↑ ↓ < > ≤ ≥ ¬ ;

The lower-case characters are the most obvious omissions from the CDC 'scientific' set, as are curly brackets { } (which is why CDC Pascal users must enclose program comments in the alternative symbols (* and *)). The space character falls between the equals sign and comma. However, . . .

* That's the American Standard Code for Information Interchange.
** Extended Binary Coded Decimal Interchange Code.

caveat emptor

Just because we show these character sets in a certain order does *not* mean that they're implemented in the same way on all systems. Check your computer before you rely on the ordering we've given.

The ordering functions (except *chr*) may take arguments of any ordinal type, we'll confine our examples to arguments of type *char.* The first two functions, *pred* and *succ,* can be used to tell us something about the relative positioning of characters.

pred(x) The *predecessor* function represents the value that comes immediately before its argument:

pred('d') is 'c'   *pred*('6') is '5'

relative ordering functions

succ(x) The *successor* function represents the successor to its argument:

succ('y') *is* 'z'   *succ*('3') *is* '4'

Those of you who are inclined to keep a lookout for trivia will recognize *pred* and *succ* as inverse functions—what one does, the other one undoes. What is the effect of this assignment?

SomeLetter := *pred*(*succ*('R'));

First the computer finds the character after 'R', which is, of course, 'S'. The predecessor of 'S', naturally, is 'R'; and 'R' is assigned to *SomeLetter*. A slightly (but not much) trickier assignment is

SomeLetter := *succ*(*succ*(*succ*(*succ*(*succ*(*succ*('A')))))) ;

If our parentheses match, the function call represents the successor to the successor to the successor to the successor to the successor to the successor to the letter 'A', and *SomeLetter* gets 'G'.

ord(x) The *ordinal position* function represents the 'place number' of a value within its entire type. If its argument is a *char* value, *ord*(x) represents x's position within the computer's collating sequence.

ord('A') *is* 65   *ord*('0') *is* 48

positional functions

chr(x) The *character position* function represents the *char* value in a particular ordinal position. Its argument must be an *integer* value.

chr(67) is 'C'   *chr*(57) = '9'

The examples reflect ASCII character ordering, used throughout this text. Numbers may seem high because non-printing characters precede the visible ones. Incidentally, the initial value in an ordinal sequence is the 'zeroth' value—not the first.

It's apparent from inspection that *ord* and *chr* are transfer functions (just as *trunc* and *round* are), and may be inverse functions as well. This is converting digits to numbers

useful, because sometimes we'll want to treat *integer* input as though it were a string of characters instead of a number. Suppose we try a simple example. Assume that the value of a *char* variable *InputCharacter* is '0', '1', '2', '3', '4', '5', '6', '7', '8', or '9'. How can we convert *InputCharacter* to the *integer* it represents? The obvious assignment is tempting:

ConvertedToInteger := *ord*(*InputCharacter*);

But if you look at the ASCII, EBCDIC, and CDC character sets, the numeral '5' never occupies the fifth position. On the other hand, all three sequences show the digits in order from '0' through '9'. Thus, this assignment solves our problem:

ConvertedToInteger := *ord*(*InputCharacter*) – *ord*('0');

boundary conditions

A test case or two (in particular, '0' and '9'), should convince you that the new assignment does just what we want it to. The trick of testing only the outside cases is called *boundary condition* testing. We assume that if an algorithm works for the highest and lowest numbers, it is well-behaved and will work for all the in-between numbers too.

Self-Check Questions

Q. Can you write expressions that use the *ord* and *chr* functions to duplicate the effects of *pred* and *succ* with *char* arguments?

A. Assume that *Symbol* is a *char* variable.

pred(*Symbol*) is *chr*(*ord*(*Symbol*)–1)
succ(*Symbol*) is *chr*(*ord*(*Symbol*)+1)

boolean Functions

Let's take a brief look at the last group of standard functions. When one of the functions in the first two groups was evaluated, the result was usually *integer, real*, or *char*. The final three standard functions have *boolean* results. They indicate whether some situation is *true* or *false*.

For example, the function call *odd*(*Number*) represents the *boolean* value *true* or *false*, depending on whether the variable *Number* represents an odd or an even *integer*.

The other two functions are used when we're reading input into a program—*eoln* stands for 'end of line', and *eof* means 'end of file'. For example, if we weren't sure how much data a program was supposed to get, we could tell the computer to keep reading input until either *eoln* or *eof* was *true*, i.e. until it was at the end of an input line, or had exhausted the entire 'file' of input data. We'll start to use *boolean* values in Chapter 6, and learn about *eof* and *eoln* in Chapter 8.

Antibugging and Debugging 2-4

AT THIS POINT MOST PEOPLE START TO make hopeful (but illegal) additions to Pascal. A common bug is the self-initializing variable. (If constants are initialized when they're declared, why not variables?) For example:

```
var Trial:=7: integer;
    Test: char; Test:='A';
    BigNumber:=124E+63;
```

These are all nice tries, but none of them is legal Pascal, and none of them may be used in a program. Variables are only given identifiers and types when they're declared. Their values must be assigned with the program. Confusion probably arises because constants are just the reverse—they're given values when they're defined, and they *can't* be assigned to. Don't forget that constants are defined with an equals sign =, while variables are assigned values with the assignment operator :=.

Another popular (and unauthorized) extension to Pascal is the chain assignment. For example:

```
A:=B:=C:=D:=E:=0;
```

It seems like a good idea, and is certainly a fast way to initialize several variables to a single value. (In fact, it's even allowed in some other programming languages.) Unfortunately, the chain assignment *isn't* part of Pascal, and assignments must be made one at a time.

```
A:=0; B:=0; C:=0; D:=0; E:=0;
```

The notion of type can cause trouble. A variable can represent an *integer* value, or a *real* value, or a *char* value, or a *boolean* value, but it may never represent values of the wrong type. Similarly, operators and functions usually are restricted to operands or arguments of some particular type. Many type problems are picayune; for example, the expression 4.0 **div** 2 is illegal because both operands of **div** must be *integer.* Steer clear of these minor problems by remembering:

types of expressions

1. If **div** or **mod** are used in an expression, all of the values in the expression must be *integer.*
2. If / or any *real* values are used in an expression, the result of the expression will be a *real* value.
3. The value a function call represents sometimes belongs to a different type than the function's argument.
4. The types of a variable, and a value being assigned to it, must be identical.

As we pointed out earlier, the fourth rule is a bit inconsistent. An *integer* value may be assigned to a *real* variable, but the opposite is not allowed. An ounce of prevention—using arithmetic values of the proper type rather than relying on Pascal's laxness—is worth a lot of program debugging.

run-time errors

Pascal deals with potential type clashes by performing run-time checks on data as it is entered, while the program is running. If data of the wrong type is encountered, a run-time error occurs, and the program halts—it crashes with an error message like:

```
ABNORMAL TERMINATION --
IMPROPER DATA FOUND AT INTEGER READ, LINE 27
```

A crash, in this case, is the lesser of two evils. It's preferable to have the program stop running than to have it produce results that are absurd, but may not be caught. Cases where this did *not* happen—$200,000 auto license fees, and doghouses with million-dollar property tax evaluations—are well known.*

Another kind of run-time error is caused by improperly using the standard functions. The most obvious is an attempt to find the *real* square root of a negative number—it simply isn't defined. The program crashes with a message like:

```
ABNORMAL TERMINATION --
ARGUMENT OF "SQRT" MUST BE POSITIVE
```

Certain other undefined values may or may not provoke run-time errors. For example, the character before the first character, *pred*(*chr*(0)), may turn out to be the *last* character in the computer's collating sequence. This means that we can't always rely on a run-time error to stop a program for us.

misusing functions

Using a function call as a statement, instead of as the representation of a value, is a common error. If we want to set *Side* equal to its own square root, this won't work:

```
readln (Side);
sqrt(Side);
```

Instead, we have to make a full assignment:

```
readln (Side);
Side := sqrt(Side);
```

Run-time errors are not restricted to problems of type. A shortage of program data can cause a crash as well, particularly when programs get their input from data files. An error message along the lines of:

```
ABNORMAL TERMINATION --
ATTEMPT TO READ PAST END OF FILE
```

* In Chapter 9 we'll see how to extend the idea of type checking even further. An *integer* variable, for example, can be declared in a way that limits its possible values—we might restrict it to representing integers between 0 and 100. Attempting to give it a value outside of these bounds (or a value of a different type) causes a run-time error.

'not enough data' bugs

implies that the user did not provide enough data for her program—there are more *reads* and *readlns* than input values. Although we know that data comes from punched cards, files, or keyboards, the computer thinks that its input comes in a 'file.' If the program tries to read in information after its file of data is exhausted, the program crashes. Incidentally, a special control character is usually set aside to mark the end of an input file. As a result, accidentally entering this character from the keyboard will occasionally cause a crash.

Clever use of the absolute value function can help prevent some inadvertent program bugs. For example, the following program segment is expected to update a user's savings account balance. Try to spot the bug it contains.

```
writeln ('How much do you wish to withdraw?');
readln (AmountWithdrawn);
Balance := Balance-AmountWithdrawn;
```

Suppose the customer enters a negative number, like '−100,' as the amount she wishes to withdraw. Instead of being subtracted from her balance, $100 will be *added* to *Balance*! This is clearly a profitable transaction for the customer. The bank, being a spoilsport, should rewrite the assignment statement like this:

```
Balance := Balance-abs(AmountWithdrawn);
```

The change keeps a perfectly understandable user mistake from ruining an otherwise working program.

Pascal Summary

• assignment statement: gives a variable the value an expression represents. The variable and value must have the same type.

Variable := *Value*; *IntegerVariable* := 3*4; *RealVariable* := 5/2

• *integer, real* operators: used with numerical operands to state expressions:

+	addition
−	subtraction
*	multiplication
/	*real* decimal division
div	*integer* whole division
mod	*integer* remainder division

• operator precedence: the order in which operators are evaluated in expressions. When two operators have the same precedence, evaluation goes from left to right. Parentheses can change the order of evaluation.

* / **div** **mod** *come before* + −

• function call: with its argument, represents a value. The standard functions are:

Arithmetic	*abs*(*x*)	*sqr*(*x*)	*sqrt*(*x*)	*sin*(*x*)
	cos(*x*)	*arctan*(*x*)	*ln*(*x*)	*exp*(*x*)
Transfer	*trunc*(*x*)	*round*(*x*)		
Ordinal	*ord*(*x*)	*chr*(*x*)	*succ*(*x*)	*pred*(*x*)
boolean	*odd*(*x*)	*eoln*(*f*)	*eof*(*f*)	

• constant definition part: the reserved word **const**, the constant identifiers and their values. The value of the constant must be known when the program is written, and cannot be computed or changed during program operation.

```
const NUMBER = 17;
      TEXTCONSTANT = 'Anything between quotes';
      SMALLREAL = 1.0E-9;
```

• fixed-point notation: a way of printing *real* values. A *real* in an output statement can be followed by ':*number*:*number*'. The first number gives the printing field, the second specifies the number of places to print to the right of the decimal:

```
writeln (GPA:10:2); {Print GPA to two places in a 10-space field.}
```

Important Facts

• Expressions represent values. The simplest expressions are constant or variable identifiers, numbers, characters, and function calls. More complicated expressions can be stated as a sequence of operators and operands. A result is obtained by evaluating the expression.

• A variable must be initialized before it can appear in an expression, and is undefined before then.

• Variables can only be assigned values of the same type. The exception is *real* variables, which can be assigned *integer* values.

• When an expression contains both *real* and *integer* operands (e.g. 1.0 + 1) the expression's result type is *real*.

• Parentheses can change the order in which expressions are evaluated, but should be used whenever an expression is potentially confusing.

• Identifiers should be mnemonic, and give an indication of the variable or constant's purpose. This helps make a program self-documenting.

• When a problem is stated in a confusing, inelegant manner, massaging or restating it can help you find a solution.

• A function call usually consists of the function's name, followed by an argument value in parentheses. Make sure that the argument has the proper type, and that the function's result type is what you expect it to be.

• The computer's character set is in a particular collating sequence that will vary from system to system.

• Translate a digit character to the number that it represents with: *ord*(*TheDigitChar*)–*ord*('0')

• Compute *a* to the *n*th power with: *exp*(*n***ln*(*a*))

• The Golden Rule of Style: A program should be as easy for a human being to read and understand as it is for a computer to execute.

Self-test Exercises

2-1 Is this a valid assignment statement? Assume that *Bonzo* is an *integer* variable.

```
Bonzo        :=
                74        ;
```

2-2 What are the types of these expressions when evaluated? *a*) 5*7; *b*) 10/2; *c*) 10.0 **div** 2.

2-3 How could you find the remainder of dividing 55.55 by 7?

2-4 Can variables be negative? Is this a valid assignment?

```
Whole := 77;
Opposite := -Whole;
```

What is the value of *Opposite*? What would it be if the starting value of *Whole* were –99?

2-5 How many levels of precedence are there for the arithmetic operators? Which operators have the lowest precedence? (Disregard unary negation.)

2-6 The square root function *sqrt* may be given either an *integer* or a *real* argument. What is the type of its result value in the calls *sqrt*(25) and *sqrt*(2.5E01)?

2-7 Does Pascal have a standard constant *PI*? What are its other standard constants?

2-8 What is Pascal's exponentiation operator? How can we raise *a* to the *b* power?

2-9 How can you find the cube root of a number in Pascal? The *n*th root?

2-10 Is –*abs*(*SomeNumber*) positive or negative?

2-11 How can you tell if the upper-case characters in your computer's character set are *contiguous* (which means they have no other characters interspersed with them)?

2-12 Pascal has only four standard types. However, we can define constants that are not *real, integer, char*, or *boolean*. What are these constants called?

2-13 In making numerical calculations, it's a good idea to remember that the result of a sequence of operations is no more accurate than its least accurate operand. Suppose that this assignment appears in a Pascal program. What should a statement to output the value of *Product* look like?

```
Product := 1.20775E-03 * 9.87 + 1.6666 / 9.0;
```

2-14 How many statements are required to initialize five different *integer* variables?

2-15 Suppose that *Letter* and *Number* are *char* and *integer* variables. Given an input statement:

```
read (Number, Letter);
```

show input that makes *Number* equal 73, and *Letter* equal 'T'.

More Exercises

2-15 In consideration of all the business programs that compute retail prices, write a consumer's program that figures out wholesale prices. Given a purchase price, it should deduct a 40% markup, and a 5.5% sales tax. Be sure to make the deductions in the right order.

2-16 Nowadays people often give credit card numbers over the phone. To stop people from making up numbers at random, credit card issuers embed codes within the number that depend on the number itself. A simple approach is to add the individual digits of the number, then tack on a 0 or 1, as required, to make the number odd. Thus, 49921 would be legitimate, but 52771 wouldn't.

Write a program that computes an add-on letter for an 8-digit number. The letter should be arrived at by adding the four pairs of digits in the number, finding the *integer* remainder of a division by 26, and then determining the character in that position in the computer's collating sequence.

2-17 Write a program that gauges inflation. It should take two prices as input, and print their cash difference, as well as the percentage increase to two decimal places. Then, modify the program so that, given the number of weeks between price quotes, it computes the yearly rate of inflation. Finally, upgrade the program to make it estimate a price a given number of weeks hence.

2-18 Three pairs of assignment statements are shown below. Write three individual assignments that take the place of the three pairs.

```
{a} l := a+5;
    l := b-2;
{b} m := a+5;
    m := m*2;
{c} n := 2*n-2;
    n := n div 2 - 3;
```

2-19 Here's a little number-juggling program. Ask a user for the year of her birth, and her age. Then double the birth year, add five, multiply by fifty, add her age, subtract 250, and divide by 100. Write the answer out with two digits of decimal accuracy. What is it? Don't forget to use constants where possible.

2-20 Write a program to carry out the following chain of calculations: Begin by entering a number. Multiply it by 5, add 6 to the product, multiply by 4, add 9, multiply by 5. Now, cancel the last two digits of the final number, and subtract 1. What have you got?

2-21 The amount of illumination provided by a light source decreases by the inverse square of distance to it. Write a program that lets the user enter the brightness of a light at distance x, then computes the brightness at distance y.

2-22 The common field cricket chirps in direct proportion to the current temperature. Adding 40 to the number of times a cricket chirps in a minute, then dividing by 4, gives us the temperature. Write a program that outputs the current temperature (given a count of cricket chirps in fifteen seconds) to the nearest half degree.

2-23 As electronic stopwatches become cheaper and more accurate, we will no doubt be deluged with impossibly accurate measurements of time. Write a program that takes a time period given in seconds, and prints out the number of hours, minutes, and seconds it represents.

2-24 The planet Mercury seems to have begun rotating in the years since the authors were taught otherwise in grade school. Nevertheless, Mercurian clocks (called Mercurichrones) are still not divided into periods of day and night. Instead, they break each rotation into 15 periods of 40 sub-periods each.

As we join this problem, Ziggy Stardust (just back from Mars) is about to land on Mercury. Suppose that he touches down at 19:56, Earth time. Write a program that finds out the current time on Mercury and the number of minutes in a Mercurian sub-period (you can define these as constants if you want), and then computes the time on Ziggy's 24-hour clock *and* on his new Mercurichrone after a given number of hours and minutes (entered as program data) have elapsed.

2-25 In the future, if there is one, there may be widespread use of electric cars. Naturally, this will render all programs that compute miles per gallon obsolete. Write a program that asks a user for the number of miles per watt (a basic unit of electricity consumption) her car gets, the distance she has traveled in miles, and the amount of time it took her in hours. Print out the distance traveled in kilometers, the amount of electricity consumed in kilowatts, her car's mileage in kilowatts per kilometer, and her average speed in kilometers per minute.

2-26 The field width specification given in a output statement can be an expression as well as a constant *integer* value. This is convenient because it lets us compute field widths when programs are run, as well as when they're written.

Write a program that prints the pattern shown below. Note that space is always evenly distributed between the symbols of any given line. The program user should enter the width of a piece of paper and the output symbol. The first and last symbols of the widest lines of the pattern should be against the edge of the page.

```
*                   *                   *
                    *
             *             *
*            *             *            *
          *         *         *
```

2-27 Write a program that accepts a number between 7 and 9 digits long, then echoes the same number written in a conventional way, i.e. with commas between every three digits from the right.

2-28 In many states, license plates contain three letters and three numbers, e.g. UBK 878. Naturally, license plates are manufactured in sequence, starting with AAA 000, AAA 001, and going to AAB 000, and eventually ZZZ 999. Write a program that takes as input a license plate's numbers and letters, and outputs the contents of the next plate to be manufactured.

2-29 Expressing a fraction as a decimal is easy—we just divide. But what about reversing the process? How can we express a decimal as a fraction? (We'll assume that the decimal is *rational* and *repeating*, like 0.333... or 0.646464..., and *can* be written as a fraction.) It can be done with the following formula:

Fraction = the repeating portion / 1–the ratio between repeats

In the examples above, .3 and .64 are the 'repeating' portions, and the ratios between repeats are .1 and .01. We're really thinking about the numbers as sums—that is:

```
 .3                    .64
 .03                   .0064
 .003                  .000064
 -------               ----------
 .333...               .646464...
```

Write a program that asks for the repeating portion of a decimal, and the ratio between repeats, and then tries to express the decimal as a fraction. Improve the program to *a*) show the fraction as a division of *integers*; *b*) allow the decimal to have a 'whole' portion to the left of the decimal. What do we mean when we say that the computer's method of representing *real* values may make certain decimal fractions impossible to attain?

2-30 Extend your personal high-level computer language to include the definition of constants. Do you want to modify your rule for creating identifiers to allow alternative characters (that might help make them more mnemonic)? What functions and operators do you think your language should have?

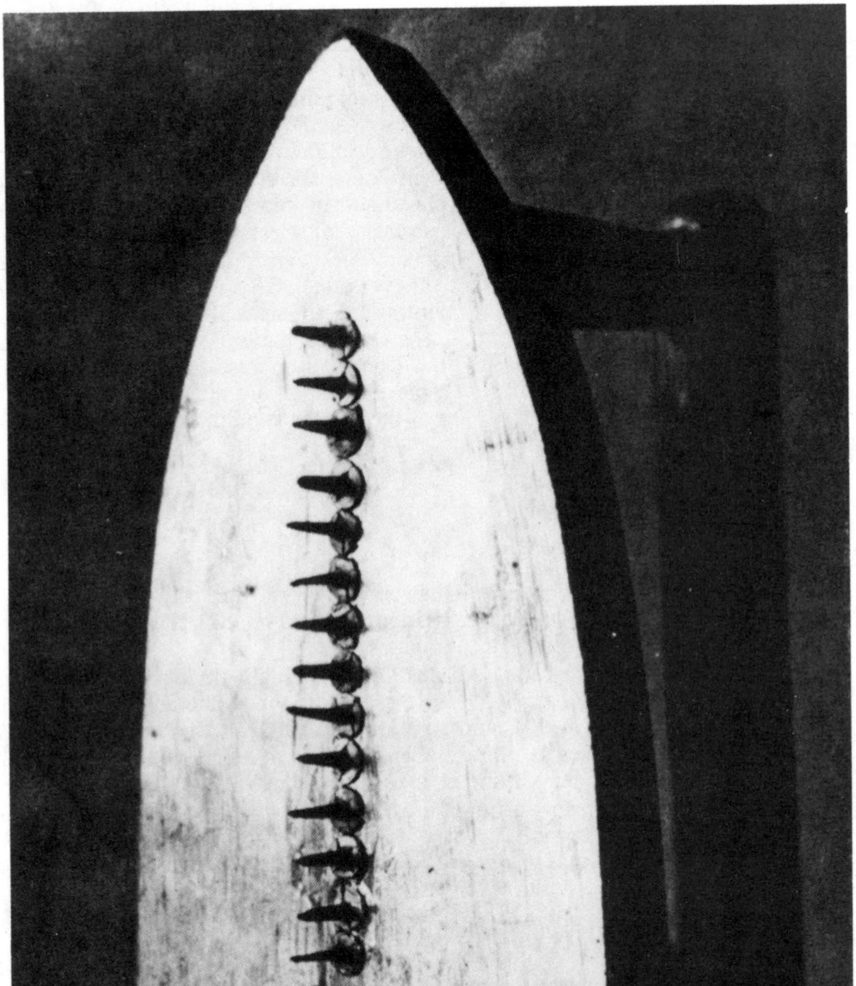

'[side-effects are] as incongrous and unsettling as a nail protruding...'

3

Procedures and Functions for Problem Solving

Have you ever had a lot on your mind? Well, just how many things were you really thinking about? Two? Five? Ten? Some researchers went to work on precisely this question—how many distinct things can a person think about at once—and came up with an answer, given in the title of their paper—*The Magic Number Seven* (*Plus or Minus Two*).* On the average, people can keep 7 (plus or minus 2) facts in their active minds at any one time.

Does this limit cause problems in life? You bet it does! How long could you remember this sequence of numbers?

1 0 3 4 4 8 4 8 0 4 1 5 5 2 4 6 6 7 8

Fortunately, people automatically come up with a way around the '7' limit by dividing long sequences into shorter number units.

103-44-8480 (415) 524-6678

It's not hard to recognize these as Social Security and telephone numbers.

Programmers have the same difficulty in dealing with the long sequences of tasks a program is required to do. As a result, Pascal (like most programming languages) has a facility for creating *subprograms* that divide programs into distinct *procedures* and *functions*. A procedure or function can be called, when necessary, to carry out a particular task. We'll see that most Pascal programs longer than twenty or thirty lines are usually broken down into subprograms.

A subprogram may need to get a main program value, or it might have to change the value of a main program variable. Section 3-1 is devoted to a discussion of the *arguments, value parameters*, and *variable parameters* that make this communication possible. In section 3-2, we'll get to work on procedures, while 3-3 covers the mechanics and applications of functions.

Section 3-4 looks at problem solving. We'll see how an approach to problem solving called *stepwise refinement* relies on subprograms, and how *top-down design* takes advantage of their *modularity*. The anti- and debugging section, 3-5, contains the usual hints for preventing and fixing bugs.

This chapter is important, since it's the beginning of our study of *programming*, as opposed to mere coding. Dig in.

* G.A. Miller, Psych. Review 1963, No. 2, 3/56, pp. 81—97.

Programming with Subprograms 3-1

ANYTHING THAT MAKES A BOOK OR MOVIE HARD to follow is also liable to complicate a program. The length and number of characters (or statements and variables) don't create confusion in and of themselves. Instead, the way they're put together causes trouble. Few people will settle down and study a program as though it were *A la Recherche des Temps Perdus*, but programs *do* have plots. A program isn't a mystery, though, and a program filled with devious twists and turns will never make the best seller list.*

Most programming languages help keep *main* programs understandable with *subprograms*. Pascal has two sorts of subprograms—*functions*, and *procedures*. The subprogram's name *calls*, or invokes, the subprogram, and gives us an idea of what it does. Since a single name can initiate long or complex code segments, subprograms make main programs programs easier to read and understand. The interested browser (as well as the computer) are referred to another part of the program that is set aside for the detailed code of the subprogram's *declaration*.

A procedure call is a statement that represents a sequence of actions. As a preview of section 3-2, here's the code of a procedure that reads two numbers and prints their sum. We'll assume that the numbers are prompted for before the procedure is called:

a typical procedure

```
procedure AddInput;
   {Read two numbers, print their sum.}
   var First, Second:  integer;  {local variable declarations}
   begin
      readln (First, Second);
      writeln (First + Second)
   end;  {AddInput}
```

Functions, which we'll learn about in 3-3, are declared in a similar manner. A function call is an expression that represents a value. The short example below is given two numbers when it's called, and represents their sum rather than printing it out:

a typical function

```
function Add (First, Second: integer): integer;
   {Represents the sum of its arguments.}
   begin
      Add := First + Second  {assign the function its value}
   end;  {Add}
```

Subprograms are declared one at a time, after program variables, but before the statement part:

* But books and movies certainly do. The film **The Big Sleep** (from the Raymond Chandler novel) contains a murder even the director, Howard Hawks, never understood.

program outline

program heading
constant definitions
variable declarations
procedure and function declarations
statements

nesting definitions

The outline of a subprogram is almost identical (except for the heading) to the outline of a program, which means that subprograms can have subprograms declared within themselves. In large programs this *nesting* of declarations can go four or five layers deep.

local identifiers are temporary

Subprograms can include the definition of constants, as well as the declaration of variables and other subprograms. These are called *local* definitions and declarations. They only exist during a call of the subprogram.

modularity

We can appreciate that letting a subprogram contain all the definitions and declarations it needs helps make subprograms *modular*, or self-contained. Everything that a subprogram requires, but that isn't used elsewhere in the program, can be created within the confines of the subprogram declaration. The local identifiers only have meaning when their subprogram is actually running.

Scope of Identifiers

local precedence

Suppose that the main program and a procedure both have a constant named *Current*. When we're in the main program, *Current* refers to the main program constant (since local declarations don't exist there). When we're in the procedure, though, *Current* means the local constant. The local identifier is said to take *precedence* over a like-named, but relatively global, identifier.

scope

The word *scope* describes the realm of an identifier that names a constant, variable, or subprogram. The scope of an identifier is the portion of a program—called a *block*—in which it continues to represent a particular value or action.

block structure

A block consists of a definition part, declaration part, and statement part. In the illustration below, each block is shown as a box. The scope of a global constant is the entire program—the largest block. A local identifier's scope is limited to the block it's declared in—'its' subprogram, and other subprograms declared within that subprogram. As far as the internal subprograms are concerned, an outer local identifier might as well be global. Not all languages have a *block structure* like Pascal's; some have only local identifiers, some only globals, and some don't allow subprogram declarations at all.

```
program A
procedure B
   function D
      begin {D}
         ...
      end; {D}
   begin {B}
      ...
   end; {B}
procedure C
   procedure E
      begin {E}
         ...
      end; {E}
   function F
      begin {F}
         ...
      end; {F}
   begin {C}
      ...
   end; {C}
begin {A}
   ...
end. {A}
```

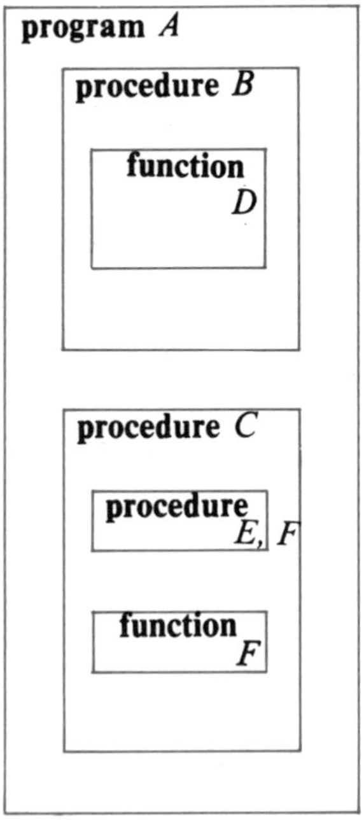

Identifiers defined in:	*Their scope is blocks*:
program *A*	*A, B, C, D, E, F*
procedure *B*	*B, D*
procedure *C*	*C, E, F*
function *D*	*D*
procedure *E*	*E*
function *F*	*F*

So far our concern with the scope of identifiers has been limited to potential problems of using the same name twice. We have said that the locally defined identifier takes precedence in a potentially ambiguous situation. But what if there isn't any ambiguity? Can an identifier defined in the main program be used in a procedure or function?

main-program constants

The answer is yes. Typically, we will only take advantage of this when a subprogram uses a main-program constant. This is one reason that we always capitalize the identifiers we use to name constants—so that they immediately stand out to the program reader.

A more interesting question is whether or not we can make an assignment directly to a global variable from within a subprogram.

side effects

> Technically, there is nothing in Pascal that prohibits making a direct assignment to a global variable from within a procedure or function. However, this sort of assignment is known as a *side-effect*, and is strongly discouraged.

Side-effects are responsible for some of the most difficult-to-find bugs in programming. Several programming languages developed since Pascal contain mechanisms designed to make side-effects impossible.

subprogram scope

How about calling subprograms from places other than the main program's statement part? Like variable and constant identifiers, procedure identifiers also follow the rules of scope. Once a procedure or function has been declared, its name has meaning in other parts of the program. These include:

1. The main program's statement part.
2. The statement parts of subprograms declared after the procedure or function we're concerned with.
3. The statement part of the procedure or function itself.

Typically we'll invoke procedures or functions from the main program, or from subprograms declared later on. The third case, in which a subprogram calls itself, won't concern us until we explore recursion in Chapter 7. We'll also see how a **forward** declaration lets two subprograms call each other.

We could devise some horribly complicated examples of identifier scope if we wanted to; programs with constants, variables, and subprograms all named *x*, *y*, and *z*. Our aim, though, is to write programs that make obvious sense, rather than the kind that are obscurely correct. *Parameters*, our next topic, help us avoid problems with scope. Let's see how they're used for communication between the main program, and individual functions and procedures.

Parameters

A subprogram call will usually be accompanied by the subprogram's arguments, given between parentheses. In these statements, 7 is the argument of the call of the *sqrt* function, while *Root* serves as the argument of the *writeln* procedure:

```
Root := sqrt(7);
writeln (Root);
```

Arguments are used for communication between subprograms and the main program that calls them. Sometimes subprograms will use arguments, and sometimes they'll change them. On various occasions, procedures and functions...

1. may need to get values from the main program—they may need 'value input,' just as *sqrt* 'needs' 7, or *writeln* 'needs' *Root*; or,

2. may have to return values to the main program—they may have 'value output' that involves changing the value of main program variables.

We can arrange for the transfer of values between the main program and its subprograms by declaring *parameters* in the procedure or function heading.

value parameters

A *value parameter* is a local variable, used only in the subprogram, whose starting value is given by an argument in the subprogram call. Changing the value parameter has no effect on its argument.

variable parameters

A *variable parameter* is an alternate name, meaningful only in the subprogram, for the variable that's supplied as its argument in the subprogram call. Changing the variable parameter *does* affect its argument, since they're the exact same variable.

Any expression can be the argument of a value parameter. Only a variable, though, can be a variable parameter's argument. As you might imagine, there has to be exactly one value or variable parameter declared in the subprogram heading for every argument in the subprogram call.

Using the standard functions has given us many examples of value parameters. The arguments that accompany a function call don't get changed during the call. They're just used by the function in the course of computing its value.

We haven't encountered any variable parameters yet, but it's easy to imagine a situation that requires them. Suppose that we want to read two values, then have a procedure exchange them. A call would look like this:

```
readln (First, Second);   {get the values}
Switch (First, Second);   {exchange them}
writeln (First, Second);  {print them in reversed order}
```

In the call of procedure *Switch*, *First* and *Second* have to be variables. Within the procedure, their values are transferred by exchanging the values of the variable parameters they correspond to.

Let's summarize the concepts introduced so far.

1. We can define subprograms—procedures and functions—in the main program, or in subprograms.

summary of subprogram concepts

2. A procedure represents a sequence of actions and can take the place of a program statement. A function represents a value, and can take the place of an expression.

3. Each subprogram's block, or body, can contain the same sort of definitions, declarations, and statements as the main program.

4. The identifiers defined in a subprogram have local scope, and can't be used from the main program. Within a subprogram, though, a local identifier has precedence over a global identifier with the same name.
5. If a subprogram variable needs to get its starting value from the main program, it's declared as a value parameter. An argument supplied in the subprogram call initializes the value parameter.
6. If a subprogram needs to make assignments to a main program variable, the variable is renamed in the subprogram with a variable parameter. Assignments to the variable parameter are just like assignments to the global variable supplied as its argument.

Programming With Procedures 3-2

AS ALWAYS, AN EXAMPLE. Program *Song*, below, uses subprograms in their most basic form—to print output.

```
program Song (output);

  {Demonstrates declaration of procedures without parameters.}

procedure Chorus;          {Print the chorus.}
  begin
    writeln ('Oh, I don''t care too much for Army life!');
    writeln ('Gee Mom, I wanna go back where the roses grow');
    writeln ('But they won''t let me go home.')
  end; {Chorus}

procedure FirstVerse;          {Print the first verse.}
  begin
    writeln ('They say that in the Army, the coffee''s mighty fine.');
    writeln ('It''s good for cuts and bruises, and tastes like iodine.');
  end; {FirstVerse}

procedure SecondVerse;          {Print the second verse.}
  begin
    writeln ('They say that in the Army, the biscuits are real fine.');
    writeln ('One rolled off a table, and killed a pal of mine.');
  end; {SecondVerse}

begin {Song}
  FirstVerse;
  Chorus;
  writeln;
  SecondVerse;
  Chorus
end. {Song}
```

```
They say that in the Army, the coffee's mighty fine.
It's good for cuts and bruises, and tastes like iodine.
Oh, I don't care too much for Army life!
Gee Mom, I wanna go back where the roses grow
But they won't let me go home.

They say that in the Army, the biscuits are real fine.
One rolled off a table, and killed a pal of mine.
Oh, I don't care too much for Army life!
Gee Mom, I wanna go back where the roses grow
But they won't let me go home.
```

order of calls

Each procedure's name serves to call, or invoke, the procedure's action. After the procedure is completed, we return to the next statement in the main program. The order of procedure calls in *Song* doesn't depend on the order that *FirstVerse, SecondVerse*, and *Chorus* are defined in.

> In general, procedures are declared in any order that makes sense to the program reader. They can be called in any sequence, for any number of times. There is only one rule to follow—a procedure must be declared before it can be called.

We won't be too concerned with this rule until we write procedures that call other procedures.

syntax rules

The syntax of a procedure declaration is similar to that of a program, with two small exceptions:

1. The heading uses the reserved word **procedure** rather than **program**.
2. The procedure definition ends with a semicolon, and not a period.

The heading is also the place where value and variable parameters are declared. The syntax chart of a procedure heading is:

procedure heading

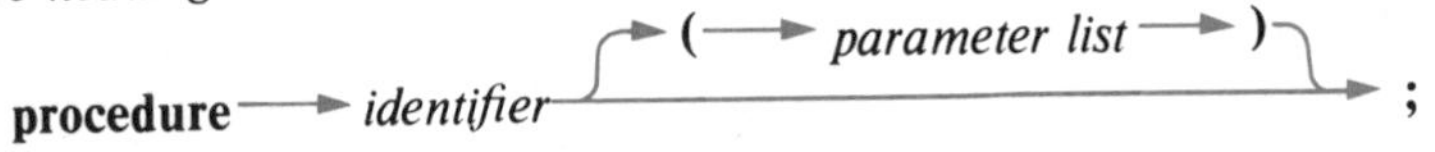

The *parameter list* syntax is:

parameter list

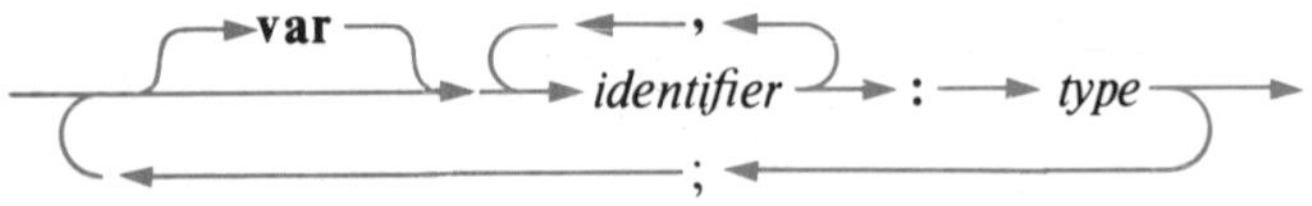

After the heading, a procedure block (or body) contains definition, declaration, and statement parts, just like a main program.

local definitions

Program *Song* was pleasantly uncomplicated because none of its procedures contained constants or variables. However, we can make definitions and declarations in procedures just as we would in programs. These are known as *local* definitions, as opposed to the *global* definitions found in the main program. As discussed in section 3-1, the potential problem of using the same identifier twice, once globally, and once locally, is easily resolved—the local definition takes precedence.

For example, program *Music*, below, uses the identifiers *SCALE* and *JohnnyOneNote* twice. When they appear within procedure *Tune*, only the local definitions are recognized. In particular, notice that the assignment of 'A' to the local *JohnnyOneNote* has no effect on the value of the global variable with the same name.

identifier scope demonstration program

```
program Music (output);

   {Illustrates scope of identifiers.}

const SCALE = 'Bass clef '; {This is a text constant.}

var JohnnyOneNote: char;

procedure Tune; {Note the identically named local identifiers.}
   const SCALE = 'Treble clef ';
   var JohnnyOneNote: char;
   begin
      JohnnyOneNote := 'A';
      writeln (SCALE, JohnnyOneNote)
   end; {Tune}

begin {Music}
   JohnnyOneNote := 'D';
   writeln (SCALE, JohnnyOneNote);
   Tune;
   writeln (SCALE, JohnnyOneNote)
end. {Music}
```

```
Bass clef D
Treble clef A
Bass clef D
```

Local variables are strictly temporary. If they are initialized on one call of the procedure, their values will be removed when the procedure ends. Were we to call *Tune* once more, *JohnnyOneNote* would have to be reinitialized.

Value Parameters and Variable Parameters

Our first sample procedures didn't change from call to call. Most of the time, though, we'll find that the action a subprogram takes depends, somehow, on a value or variable provided when it is invoked. We'll use value and variable parameters to let values or variables be 'passed' to the subprogram. Parameter declarations are like plain variable declarations, except:

syntax of parameters

1. The parameter list goes between parentheses.
2. **var** only precedes declarations of variable parameters.

> Parameter declarations are usually ordered to produce a procedure call that, with arguments, is self-documenting and not prone to argument-ordering errors.

There is a story about the procedure call *AddGin (ToVermouth, MakingMartini)*, but we're not going to tell it here.

value parameters

Let's look at some examples. The headings below declare only value parameters, because **var** doesn't appear in the parameter list. It's all right (and sometimes advisable) to extend long headings over two or more lines.

```
procedure GiveInstructions (Question: char; Difficulty: integer);
procedure ShowInterval (Argument: real; UpperBound, LowerBound: integer);
procedure Debugging (CompleteTest, Antibugging: boolean;
                     Message: char; {This is a good place for comments.}
                     Value1, Value2: integer);
```

The next set of parameter lists only contain variable parameters, because **var** appears before every group of identifiers.

variable parameters

```
procedure AdjustTerms (var FirstTerm, SecondTerm: real);
procedure Increment (var Initial, Monogram: char;
                     var From, Until: integer);
```

mixed headings

Finally, these headings are mixed. A distinct declaration, with its own type, is needed to separate value and variable parameter declarations. In all these examples, *Huey* and *Dewey* are variable parameters, while *Louie* is a value parameter. In terms of the kinds of parameters created, each heading is identical. However, each procedure gets its arguments in a different order.

```
procedure Able (var Huey, Dewey: integer; Louie: integer);
procedure Baker (Louie: integer; var Huey, Dewey: integer);
procedure Charlie (var Huey: integer; Louie: integer; var Dewey: integer);
```

Let's look at some parameters in action. As we've said before, a value parameter is a local variable that's initialized when the subprogram is called. Program *TestValue*, below, shows that modifying value parameters has no effect on their main program arguments.

value parameter example program

```
program TestValue (output);
   {Demonstrates value parameters.}
var x, y: integer;
procedure NoEffect (x, y: integer);
   {Shows that assignments to value parameters don't affect arguments.}
   begin
      x := y;
      y := 0;
      writeln (x, y)
   end; {NoEffect}
begin
   x := 1;
   y := 2;
   writeln (x, y);
   NoEffect (x, y);
   writeln (x, y)
end.
```

```
1    2
2    0
1    2
```

Procedure *SumSquares* throws an ordinary local variable into the works. It uses value parameters to obtain starting values for *First* and *Second* from the main program. Unlike *First* and *Second*, *Sum* isn't initialized as part of the call of *SumSquares*.

```
procedure SumSquares (First, Second: integer);
   {Squares, and sums, its value parameters.}
   var Sum: integer;
   begin
      First := sqr (First);
      Second := sqr (Second);
      Sum := First + Second; {initialize Sum}
      writeln (Sum)
   end; {SumSquares}
```

We can call *SumSquares* with any two arguments that represent *integer* values—numbers, function calls, expressions, variables, etc. Any similarity between names is purely coincidental.

value parameter arguments

```
SumSquares (5, 9);
SumSquares (3 + 2, 9 mod 8);
SumSquares (First, Second);
SumSquares (Second, First);
SumSquares (sqr(3), SomeValue);
```

Let's move on to variable parameters. Procedure 'output' is needed when a procedure is expected to modify a main-program variable. For instance, imagine a procedure that exchanges the values of two variables from the calling program. We don't know what variables to exchange; indeed, the pair may change with every call.

If we arrange for the variables that accompany the call to be temporarily renamed with variable parameters, though, there's no problem in making the switch. Since the variable parameter names become temporary aliases for their arguments, switching the variable parameters is the same thing as switching the arguments. An assignment to a variable parameter is just like an assignment to its argument. Suppose that we declare this procedure:

using variable parameters

```
procedure Double (var Parameter: real);
   {Demonstrates a variable parameter.}
   begin
      Parameter := Parameter * 2.0
   end; {Double}
```

Imagine that *Income* is a variable of type *real*. The call:

```
Double (Income);
```

is exactly equivalent to the main-program assignment:

```
Income := Income * 2.0;
```

Program *Exchanges*, below, provides another demonstration of variable parameters. Procedure *Switch* trades the value of its two variable parameters:

variable parameter exchange program

```
program Exchanges (output);
   {Demonstrates the use of variable parameters.}
var Little, Big: integer;
procedure Switch (var First, Second: integer);
   {Exchanges the values of First and Second.}
   var Temporary: integer;
   begin
      Temporary := First;
      First := Second;
      Second := Temporary
   end; {Switch}
begin
   Big := 5;
   Little := 10;
   writeln (Big, Little);
   Switch (Big, Little);
   writeln (Big, Little)
end. {Exchanges}
```

Let's look at an example that uses both value parameters and variable parameters. We'll write a procedure like our *SumSquares* example, but instead of printing the value we compute, we'll return the sum of the squares of the value parameters to the main program.

mixed examples

```
procedure FindSquareSum (First, Second: integer; var Sum: integer);
  {Uses value parameters to help compute a variable parameter.}
  begin
    First := sqr (First);
    Second := sqr (Second);
    Sum := First + Second;
  end; {FindSquareSum}
```

In this procedure, assignments to *First* and *Second* last only for the duration of the call, but the assignment to *Sum* has a permanent effect. The variable supplied as the third argument to a call of *FindSquareSum* will have its value altered within the procedure. The first two arguments can be any *integer*-valued expressions, but the third argument must always be an *integer* variable:

variable parameter arguments

```
FindSquareSum (5, 9, Answer);
FindSquareSum (3 + 2, 9 mod 8, Result);
FindSquareSum (First, Second, Sum);
FindSquareSum (Second, First, Total);
FindSquareSum (sqr(3), SomeValue, Solution);
```

Let's try a slightly more complicated example. Program *ParameterCrazy*, below, contains nothing but procedures and calls. It's an interesting example because the global variables *First* and *Second* are neither assigned to, nor inspected, in the main program—procedures do all the work. The variables must be declared in the main program since they are repeatedly used as arguments to value and variable parameters. In this manner, the information they carry is shared between procedures *GetTheNumbers*, *SwitchThem*, and *PrintTheResults*.

```
program ParameterCrazy (input, output);
    {Reverses two input integers.}
var First, Second: integer;
procedure GetTheNumbers (var First, Second: integer);
    {Reads values for the variable parameters First and Second.}
    begin
        writeln ('This program reverses two integers.');
        writeln ('What is the first number?');
        readln (First);
        writeln ('What is the second number?');
        readln (Second);
    end; {GetTheNumbers}
procedure SwitchThem (var First, Second: integer);
    {Swaps the values of two variable parameters.}
    var Temporary: integer;
    begin
        Temporary := First;
        First := Second;
        Second := Temporary
    end; {SwitchThem}
procedure PrintTheResults (First, Second: integer);
    {Prints its value parameters.}
    const PRINTSPACE = 1;        {Provide the minimum output field.}
    begin
        write ('In reversed order, the numbers are ');
        writeln (First:PRINTSPACE, ' and ', Second:PRINTSPACE, '.')
    end; {PrintTheResults}
begin {The main program, ParameterCrazy}
    GetTheNumbers (First, Second);
    SwitchThem (First, Second);
    PrintTheResults (First, Second)
end. {ParameterCrazy}
```

↓ ↓ ↓ ↓ ↓

```
This program reverses two integers.
What is the first number?
27
What is the second number?
935
In reversed order, the numbers are 935 and 27.
```

Let's summarize the rules that pertain to using arguments and parameters. First, there must always be the same number of arguments in a procedure call as there are parameters in the procedure heading. There's always a one-to-one correspondence between arguments and parameters.

arguments and parameters

Second, a value parameter's argument can be any value that could ordinarily be assigned to the value parameter. The value can be supplied as any sort of expression—an actual number or letter, constant, variable, function call, etc. This expression is evaluated right at the beginning of the procedure call, and initializes the value parameter.

Finally, a variable parameter's argument must be a variable. Furthermore, the variable parameter and its argument must have the exact same type. This rule comes as no surprise, since the variable parameter merely renames its argument.

Self-Check Questions

Q. The following procedure declaration contains an error that should be easy to spot. What is it?

```
procedure Wrong (A: integer; var B: integer);
   var A: integer; B: real;        etc.
```

A. Declared parameters share the scope of local variables. Procedure *Wrong* tries to use two identifiers (*A* and *B*) in equally local places. Whether the parameters and local variables are of identical or different types is irrelevant. It's as incorrect a pair of declarations as this would be:

```
var A: integer; A: real;
```

Q. What will the output of this program be?

```
program Confusion (input, output);
   {Comments? Nope—that would be telling.}
var A, B, C, D: integer;
procedure Confuse (C,A: integer; var D: integer);
   var B: integer;
   begin
      A := 5;   B := 6;   C := 7;   D := 8;
      writeln (A,B,C,D)
   end; {Confuse}
begin
   A := 1;   B := 2;   C := 3;   D := 4;
   writeln (A,B,C,D);
   Confuse (B,A,D);
   writeln (A,B,C,D)
end. {Confusion}
```

A. This deliberately muddled program deliberately tries to confuse value parameters, variable parameters, and local variables. Its output is:

```
1        2        3        4
5        6        7        8
1        2        3        8
```

Functions As Subprograms 3-3

PASCAL FUNCTIONS COMPUTE AND REPRESENT values. Functions that programmers declare are more interesting than the standard functions, because we can name them as we wish, tell them what to compute, and give them as many arguments as are necessary. In the assignment below, a call of function *Distance* (with its arguments *SpeedometerReading* and *ElapsedTime*) provides a value for the variable *AmountTraveled*:

AmountTraveled := *Distance*(*SpeedometerReading, ElapsedTime*);

Functions are subprograms, just like procedures. The appearance of a function's name in a program is a call that signals the computer to suspend regular program operations while it executes, or runs, the function subprogram's code. After the function's value has been determined, the program picks up from where it left off.

Naturally, a function must be declared before it can be used. In the declaration of *Distance*, below, note the specification of the function's type, and the assignment of its value.

```
function Distance (Rate: integer; Time: real): real;
  {Calculates Distance given Rate and Time.}
  begin
    Distance := Rate*Time {This statement assigns the function its value}
  end; {Distance}
```

The syntax chart of a function heading is:

function heading

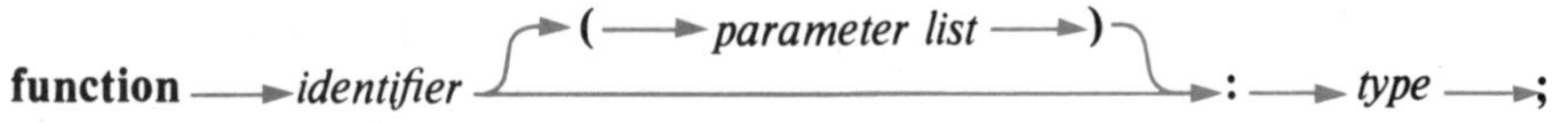

special function rules

Function declarations are intermingled with procedure declarations at the end of a program or subprogram's declaration part. As we've pointed out before, a function (unlike a procedure) represents a value. This has two consequences:

1. Since the function represents a value, we have to specify its type.
2. The function has to contain an assignment statement that gives it the value.

function type

> A function call may represent any simple type of value, ordinal or *real*. The function's *result type* is specified at the end of the function heading—a colon is followed by the type identifier.

Our example function, *Distance*, was of type *real*. Having set the stage by giving the function a type, we have to actually assign the function a value.

assigning function values

> The statement part of a function must contain an assignment that gives the function its value. This assignment can only take place within the function itself.

In *Distance* this assignment formed the function's entire statement part. Naturally, a function can take care of other business as well. A function's last action, however, is to give itself a value.

Self-Check Questions

Q. May a function call be an argument of a procedure? Another function?

A. Since it represents a value, a function call, complete with arguments, may be an argument of another function or procedure. It provides the initial value of a value parameter.

Focus on Programming: Functions

Almost invariably, we'll find that functions use one or more value parameters to compute a value—a value that the function then represents. Some typical function headings are:

> **function** *Cube* (*Number*: *real*): *real*;
>
> **function** *Decode* (*Letter*: *char*; *CodeKey*: *integer*): *char*;
>
> **function** *Highest* (*First, Second, Third*: *integer*): *integer*;
>
> **function** *NoArguments*: *integer*;

In each case, notice that the heading ends with a colon and the function's type.

arguments and parameters

As with procedure calls, there must always be a one-to-one correspondence between the arguments of a function *call*, and the parameters of a function *declaration*. Thus, any given function will always be called with the same number of arguments.

> **function** *Yield*(*Investment*: *integer*; *Interest*: *real*; *Days*: *integer*): *real*;
>
> (Function heading—value parameters)
>
> *Income* := *Yield* (1000, 0.097, 365);
>
> (Function call—arguments)

Variable parameters are seldom declared in function headings, because the avowed purpose of a function is to compute and return a *single* value. If a function has variable parameters, it will wind up returning more than just one value. This creates a situation that can confuse an unwary program rewriter.

> **The Golden Rule of Functions**
>
> If a subprogram is supposed to calculate more than one value for the main program, write it as a procedure.

Let's warm up by writing a few calculating functions that are standard in some other computer languages (and even some Pascal implementations). A function to do exponentiation is a must.

exponentiation

```
function Power (Base, Exponent: real): real;
  {Raises Base to the Exponent power.}
  begin
    Power := exp (Exponent * ln (Base))
  end; {Power}
```

A function that figures reciprocals is found on most hand calculators:

reciprocals

```
function Reciprocal (Number: integer): real;
  {Represents the reciprocal of Number.}
  begin
    Reciprocal := 1 /Number
  end; {Reciprocal}
```

A routine that's easy to write (and is useful for anyone who can't remember trigonometry) is a tangent function. We make use of the fact that tangent ϕ = (sine ϕ / cosine ϕ) in writing function *RadianTan*.

tangents

```
function RadianTan (AngleInRadians: real): real;
  {Represents the tangent of its argument.}
  begin
    RadianTan := sin(AngleInRadians)/cos(AngleInRadians)
  end; {RadianTan}
```

RadianTan's value parameter, *AngleInRadians*, clearly documents the fact that *RadianTan's* argument should be supplied in radians, rather than degrees. Unfortunately, the most familiar measurement of angles works the other way around, in degrees rather than radians. We can modify *RadianTan* to work with a degree-valued argument by including a radian conversion function *within the declaration of RadianTan*. The conversion function uses the equation $1° = \pi/180$ radians.

radian conversion

```
function tan (AngleInDegrees: real): real;
  {Represents the tangent of its degree-valued argument.}
  var Angle: real;          {This variable is local to tan.}
  function ConvertToRadians (Angle: real): real;
    const PI = 3.1415926;
    begin
      ConvertToRadians := Angle*(PI/180)
    end; {ConvertToRadians}
  begin
    Angle := ConvertToRadians(AngleInDegrees);
    tan := sin(Angle)/cos(Angle)
  end; {tan}
```

Our code is overly detailed, but it shows that a function can be declared within a function. It also gives an example of a value parameter taking precedence over a like-named variable that is relatively global.

driver programs

The operation of *tan* can be checked by including it in a *driver* program, as we've done in *TestFunctions*, below. This ploy lets us test the function in an environment that isn't cluttered with extraneous function or procedure declarations. Once we're sure the function works, it's easy to transfer it elsewhere. There are small mathematical inconsistencies in *TestFunctions'* output because of inaccuracies in the computer's arithmetic.

function driver program

```
program TestFunctions (input, output);
   {A driver program that tests function Tan.}
function tan (AngleInDegrees: real): real;
   var Angle: real;
   function ConvertToRadians (Angle: real): real;
      const PI = 3.1415926;
      begin
         ConvertToRadians := Angle *(PI / 180)
      end; {ConvertToRadians}
   begin
      Angle := ConvertToRadians (AngleInDegrees);
      tan := sin (Angle)/cos (Angle)
   end; {tan}
begin
   writeln ('The tangent of 0.0 degrees is ', tan(0.0));
   writeln ('The tangent of 45.0 degrees is ', tan(45.0));
   writeln ('The tangent of 60.0 degrees is ', tan(60.0));
   writeln ('The tangent of 120.0 degrees is ', tan(120.0));
   writeln ('The tangent of 135.0 degrees is ', tan(135.0))
end. {TestFunctions}
```

```
The tangent of 0.0 degrees is  0.00000000000000E+00
The tangent of 45.0 degrees is  9.99999973205104E-01
The tangent of 60.0 degrees is  1.73205073611582E+00
The tangent of 120.0 degrees is -1.73205095047500E+00
The tangent of 135.0 degrees is -1.00000008038469E+00
```

Top-Down Design and Stepwise Refinement 3-4

AS WE'VE MENTIONED EARLIER, PROCEDURES AND functions help make programs easier to understand. We'll often find that even relatively simple programs are broken into a sequence of procedure calls like this:

```
begin
   GetInput (parameters... );
   ProcessTheData (parameters... );
   PrintResults (parameters... )
end.
```

transparency

because procedure calls make the program's inner operations *transparent*. We know *what* the program does, but we can ignore *how* it does it. The detailed code that forms the body of the procedure is invisible unless we go looking for it.

The main reason we teach the use of procedures and functions early in your programming careers is their importance for problem solving. Two related techniques, called stepwise refinement and top-down design, rely heavily on the programmer's ability to write a program as a collection of smaller subprograms.

> Breaking a problem down into precisely stated subproblems is part of the *top-down* method of writing programs. It's called *stepwise refinement*.

stepwise refinement

In stepwise refinement, a problem is stated as a collection of obvious subproblems in the hope that some of them will be easy enough to encode in Pascal. If none are, the problem statement is refined. Each subproblem is decomposed, or restated as a collection of even more elemental subproblems.

Outline of a Problem

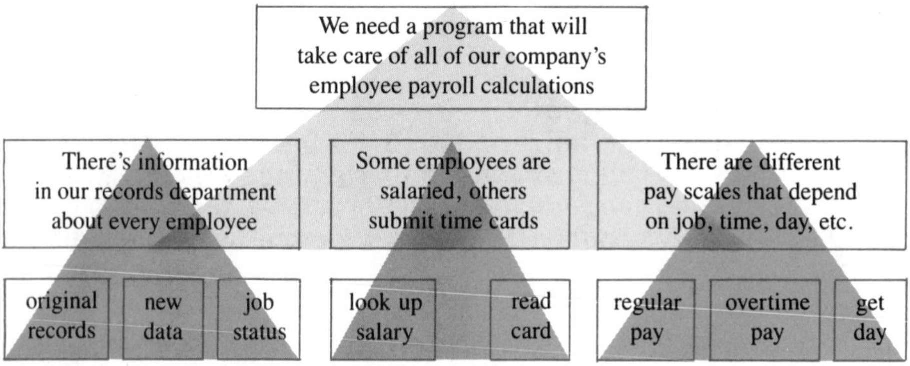
We need a program that will take care of all of our company's employee payroll calculations
There's information in our records department about every employee
Some employees are salaried, others submit time cards
There are different pay scales that depend on job, time, day, etc.
original records
new data
job status
look up salary
read card
regular pay
overtime pay
get day

The refinement proceeds from the general to the particular; from the abstract statement of a problem to a precise specification that may even include specific coding suggestions. Note that if a subproblem is particularly truculent, the refinement step may need to be repeated several times. 'Stepwise refinement' is a stilted and unnatural phrase—'relentless massage' might be better. Still, it accurately describes what we're doing—refining a problem, one step at a time, into its most basic description. Its best consequence is that...

> In exploring a problem through stepwise refinement, a program's algorithm is considered at all levels well before the details of its Pascal coding are dealt with.

top-down design

Top-down design describes our methodology for working on programs, rather than problems. Top-down programming starts with planning with the big decisions that have to be made in writing a programs' main procedures. Eventually, we work our way down to the small choices that are faced in implementing small procedures and functions. Major coding decisions are made first, and lesser ones are delayed for as long as possible.

Outline of a Program

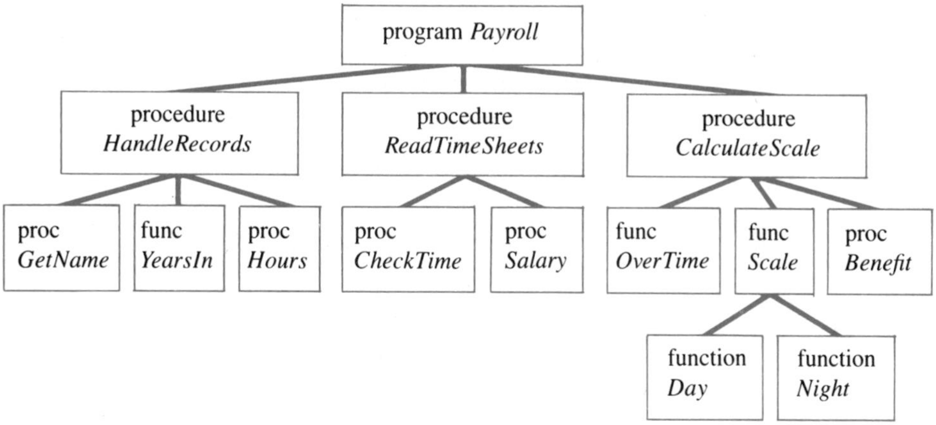

Once again we're going from the general to the particular. We design a program's main subprograms first. Small procedures and functions that are used in the main subprograms aren't considered until they're ready to be called.

Stepwise refinement, then, is a term we usually reserve for working on problems, while top-down design is more broadly applied to describe our approach to programming. In the long run, we'll see that top-down design is also concerned with methods of scheduling, debugging, testing, and modifying code.

why use them?

There are several reasons why stepwise refinement and top-down design are important programming methods. Most obvious is the combined strategy's divide and conquer aspect. A formidable programming problem may turn out to be a combination of easily solved subproblems—in like a lion, and out like four or five lambs. Even if a crucial procedure is beyond our abilities at present, we can still work on the program because we've made independent subdivisions in the problem. As a result, the final program is modular. It's composed of separate pieces that can be written and tested by themselves, and then eventually merged together.

finding the seams

In real-life programming projects, the ability to find the seams of a problem or program is the earmark of a good programming manager. If several people are to work on a single program effectively, each must have a clearly delineated task. Each individual has to know exactly how her piece of the program interacts with the whole. Stepwise refinement and top-down design slice a problem up in a natural, intuitive manner.

thinking in English

Stepwise refinement and top-down design also let a programmer plan most of a program without actually writing in Pascal. It's easier to think in English than in any sort of computerese, and tackling a problem from the top puts off the nitty-gritty of encoding for as long as possible. Outlining a program in terms of its procedures (and procedures and functions *within* procedures) provides a transitional phase between words and code.

Here are two outlines: one demonstrates stepwise refinement as an approach to programming problems, and the other shows how procedures are part of top-down program design. Notice how smoothly they merge together—the plan for breaking down a problem goes hand-in-hand with the guide for building a program.

Stepwise Refinement of a Problem

1. State the problem simply, decomposing it into its logical subproblems.
2. If you can immediately figure out how to encode all of the subproblems, you're done. These will be the major procedures of your program. If the subproblems are too complex . . .
3. Refine the subproblems into smaller, more basic subproblems. Their solutions are written as procedures or functions within procedures.

Top-Down Design and Procedures

1. Write the statement part of the main program first. In a program of any size, this will mainly consist of procedure calls. Each procedure should solve one part of the original problem.
2. The main program's statement part should be simple enough for a non-programmer to read and understand, yet detailed enough to give a programmer an idea of how the program works.
3. If a procedure is particularly complicated, or does more than one job, it should probably be broken down into sub-procedures.

length of subprograms

> Remember that a procedure isn't a rug for sweeping code under! One page (or screenful) of code is enough for any human to try to read and understand. If the procedure is longer, *try to break it down.*

As programmers get more experienced, the individual procedures they write tend to become more complex. This is because one's bag of programming tricks becomes more sophisticated—a program segment the novice perceived of as requiring several procedures suddenly seems easy. However, a procedure should never become a *deus ex machina*, or miraculous black box within a program.*

public library project

Let's look at an example of our methods. Suppose that a public library wishes to computerize its operations—a fairly ambitious programming project. The first step in cutting it down to size is a basic problem decomposition. However, we might just as well call this a top-down description of the program's main procedures:

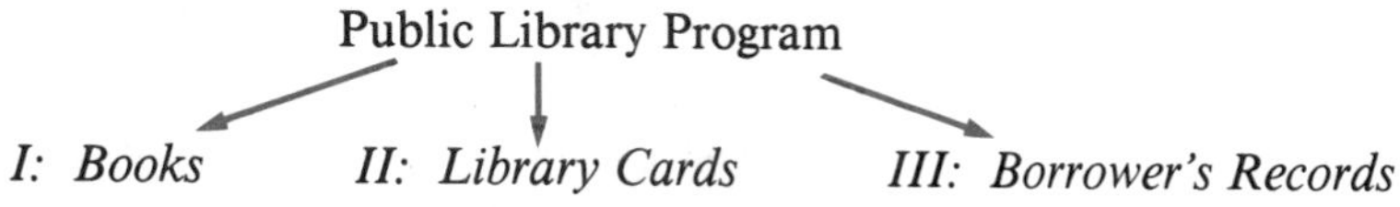

If we've left anything out, we can always backtrack to this step of the refinement. Let's go a stage further, and restate each of the first level's entries:

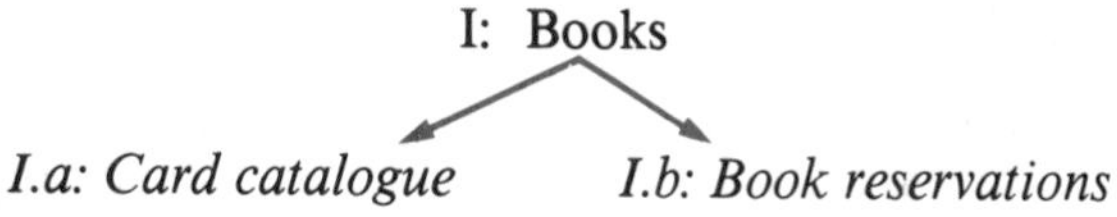

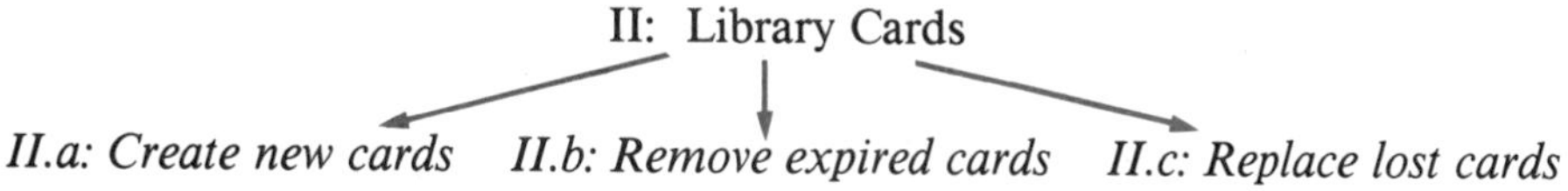

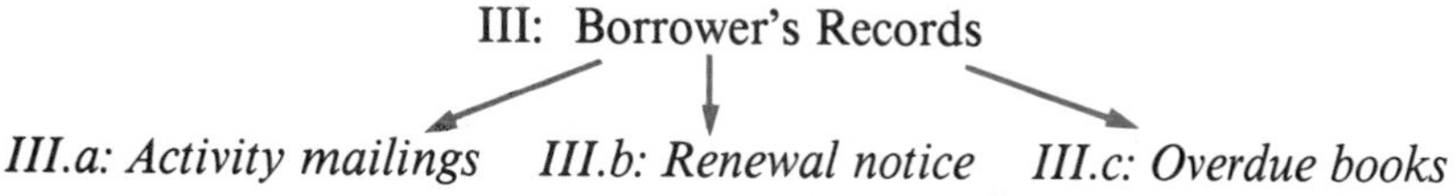

Are there still parts of the problem we don't understand? Is our design still too abstract for a programmer to encode? Let's add more detail:

* The *deus ex machina* ending was a popular dramatic device in early Greek theater. The plots were usually so hopelessly entangled by the final act that the playwright would lower a minor deity onto the stage for the express purpose of resolving the sticky points and winding up the play. *Deus ex machina* has come to symbolize a suspiciously providential, not quite fair, intervention.

I.*a*: Card Catalogue →	*I.a.i: Add books to catalogue* *I.a.ii: Delete books from catalogue* *I.a.iii: Search for books*
I.*b*: Book Reservations →	*I.b.i: Search for books* *I.b.ii: Inform current borrower* *I.b.iii: Print hold message*
II.*a*: Create New Cards →	*II.a.i: Print card form* *II.a.ii: Get new card information*
II.*b*: Remove Expired Cards →	*II.b.i: Remove card from permanent file* *II.b.ii: Check for outstanding books* *II.b.iii: Inform borrower*
II.*c*: Replace Lost Cards →	*II.c.i: Find old card information* *II.c.ii: Print card form*
III.*a*: Activity Mailings →	*III.a.i: Get activity information* *III.a.ii: Inform borrower*
III.*b*: Renewal Notice →	*III.b.i: Get old card information* *III.b.ii: Inform borrower*
III.*c*: Overdue Books →	*III.c.i: Check for overdue books* *III.c.ii: Calculate fine* *III.c.iii: Inform borrower*

Our refinement pays off as we get down to problems easy enough to solve directly—*print card form*. We can also recognize that some of the technical details—*calculate fine*—aren't important to the overall structure of the program and can be delayed. In fact, the program's procedures are largely laid out for us by name already. Our biggest problem will be to decide which parameters each procedure should expect. As an extra bonus, we find that some of our program segments (like the *inform borrower* segments) are similar enough to be written once, then shared.

Antibugging and Debugging 3-5

OF ALL THE PASCAL WE'VE PRESENTED SO FAR, only subprograms might help prevent more trouble than they cause. Their syntax—what reserved words go where?—follows the syntax of main programs closely, so you'll usually have plenty of reference models at hand. Bugs associated with parameters often result from confusing value parameters and variable parameters.

> If a subprogram only *uses* a value, declare a value parameter.
> If a subprogram *changes* or *returns* a value, use a variable parameter.

Error messages like the ones shown below will be common when you begin to declare parameters. Don't forget that the wording and extent of error messages may vary from system to system.

```
NUMBER OF ARGUMENTS DOES NOT AGREE
WITH PARAMETER LIST DECLARATION
```

order of arguments

This message means that a subprogram call contained more (or fewer) arguments than the subprogram expected to receive. There has to be a one-to-one correspondence between parameters and arguments, and they have to be correctly ordered. A misordered procedure call might produce:

```
EXPRESSION GIVEN (VARIABLE REQUIRED)
FOR VARIABLE PARAMETER
```

The value of a defined constant can't be changed within a program. Thus, making it the argument of a variable parameter has to be illegal.

```
CONSTANT ILLEGALLY PASSED TO A VARIABLE PARAMETER
-- VARIABLE EXPECTED
```

type of arguments

Value and variable parameters, like any Pascal variables, belong to some particular type. Their arguments must be of appropriate types for a procedure or function call to be valid. If they're not...

```
ARGUMENT TYPE NOT IDENTICAL TO TYPE OF VARIABLE PARAMETER
EXPRESSION TYPE CLASHES WITH TYPE OF VALUE PARAMETER
```

function bugs

Most of the errors that occur in function declaration are just the result of oversight. There are two main rules to remember when writing functions. First, specify the function's type at the end of the function heading. It can have any simple type, either ordinal or *real*.

Second, don't forget to assign the function its value. An omitted assignment might not be spotted by the compiler, since the assignment isn't specified as a syntax rule. Unfortunately, the missing assignment is sometimes equally hard for the programmer to find—it's such an obvious bug that we tend to overlook it.

accidental recursion

A serious problem is the accidental creation of a recursive function or procedure call—a subprogram that calls itself. The appearance of a subprogram's name serves as a call or invocation of that subprogram. Function *Double*, below, inadvertently invokes itself during its own execution.

```
function Double (Argument: integer): integer;
   {Incorrect example that contains a recursive call.}
   begin
      Double := Double (Argument) * 2
   end; {Double}
```

Double contains a recursive call to itself in the assignment statement. What is the value of *Double*(*Argument*) on the right hand side? The computer will try to call the function to find out. That call leads to another, and another, and another. Where does it all end? Find out when we discuss recursion in Chapter 7.

A similar example is only spotted through an error message that complains about a shortage of arguments to the function:

```
function Increment (Argument: integer): integer;
   {Incorrect example that contains a recursive call.}

   begin
      ...
      Increment := Increment + 1;    etc.
```

The error message is:

```
Increment := Increment + 1;
               ↑  NOT ENOUGH ARGUMENTS TO "INCREMENT"
```

order problems

A final error in subprogram declarations comes when subprograms are inadvertently declared in the wrong order. It may be a rude shock to get an error message like:

```
Increase (NewValue, OffSet);
↑ "INCREASE" -- IDENTIFIER UNKNOWN.
  UNDECLARED PROCEDURE.
```

when you know perfectly well that you *have* declared procedure *Increase*. However, you can't call *Increase* in a subprogram that is defined earlier than *Increase* is. If you do, you'll get an error message.

Let's leave syntax problems, and turn our attention to a more programming-oriented aspect of using subprograms. The most common error in procedure usage is quite serious, even though the program it's found in may execute perfectly well. Can you spot it?

```
begin {main program}
   RunProgram        {procedure call}
end. {main program}
```

The error is using a procedure at all! Does it make the program any easier to read? No, because it doesn't break down the program's action. Does it make the program any easier to write? Again, no, because we're just substituting a long, complicated procedure for a long, complicated program. The example above is merely a sham subprogram that doesn't take advantage of the procedure's benefits.

Pascal Summary

• block: the body of a program, procedure, or function—its definitions, declarations, and statements.

• procedure: a subprogram that represents a sequence of program statements:

```
procedure TheProcedureName (parameter declarations);
   local constants;
   local variables;
   local subprograms;
   begin
      statement;
        ...
      statement
   end;
```

• function: a subprogram that represents a value. Unlike a procedure, a function is given a type (in its heading), and assigned a value (in its statement part):

```
function TheFunctionName (parameter declarations): ItsType;
   local constants;
   local variables;
   local subprograms;
   begin
      statement;
        ...
      TheFunctionName := a value
   end;
```

• call: the invocation of a procedure or function.

• argument: the value or variable, in parentheses, that accompanies a procedure or function call. Multiple arguments are separated by commas.

• value parameter: a local variable whose starting value is supplied, as an argument, during a subprogram call. Changing the value parameter has no effect on the argument. A typical heading that uses them is:

```
function ItsName (ValueParameter: AType;
                  ValP1, ValP2, ValP3: integer): ItsType;
```

• variable parameter: a local identifier, known in the subprogram, that is an alternative name for a variable supplied as an argument in the subprogram call. Changing the variable parameter also changes the argument variable. A typical heading that uses them is:

```
procedure ItsName (var VariableParameter: ItsType;
                   var VarP1, VarP2, VarP3: real);
```

Important Facts

- No procedure or function should be more than a page or 'screenful' long.
- A local identifier is created within a subprogram. A global identifier is created in the main program. However, we may think of identifiers as being relatively local or global.
- The scope of an identifier is the area of a program in which it's recognized. Identifiers are recognized in enclosed procedures and functions.
- Constants should be capitalized so that they can be easily recognized if they are used within an enclosed subprogram. However, variables should never be used this way, because that would create side effects—use value or variable parameters instead.
- If a local and global identifier have the same name, the local identifier's definition takes precedence.
- If a subprogram uses a value *from* the main program, pass it to a value parameter. If a subprogram computes or changes a value *for* the main program, pass it to a variable parameter.
- The argument of a value parameter can be any value with the same type. A variable parameter's argument has to be a variable, though. There must always be an argument for every parameter.
- Stepwise refinement is a problem-solving strategy that involves repeatedly restating a problem in terms of smaller, simpler, subproblems.
- Top-down design is a programming strategy that encourages the use of modular subprograms.
- The Golden Rule of Functions: If a subprogram is supposed to calculate more than one value for the main program, write it as a procedure.

Self-test Exercises

3-1 What kind of definitions or declarations that appear in ordinary program can't show up in procedures and functions?

3-2 Suppose that a local and global variable have the same identifier. How does the computer tell them apart in your program?

3-3 Suppose that *First, Second, Third*, and *Fourth* are *char* variables in ascending order. Write a procedure that reverses their order.

3-4 How could you reverse the digits of a three-digit number?

3-5 How can you tell the difference between constant, procedure, and variable identifiers?

3-6 What's a good guideline for the length of a procedure or function?

3-7 Suppose that you've written procedure *PrintNumbers*, below. What series of calls (followed by a *writeln*) will print this sequence: 1, 1, 2, 3, 5, 8, 13, 21, 34? Don't worry about printing the commas, of course.

```
procedure PrintNumbers (First, Second: integer);
   begin
      write (First, Second, First+Second)
   end; {PrintNumbers}
```

3-8 What's the difference between a parameter and an argument?

3-9 What is a *side effect*? How can it cause trouble?

3-10 A program produces the following compile-time error message:

```
var Time:   integer;
    ↑ "Time" is already defined in procedure "Clock"
```

However, *Time* is the very first entry in the variable declaration part of procedure *Clock*. What could have caused the error message?

3-11 What is the output of program *Quiz*?

```
program Quiz (output);
var A, B, C: integer;
procedure Subprogram (D: integer; var E: integer; C: integer);
   var A: integer;
   begin
      A := C + 1;
      E := D + C - 1;
      C := (C * 2)
   end; {Subprogram}
begin {Quiz}
   A := 2;
   B := 4;
   C := 6;
   Subprogram (B, C, A);
   writeln (A, B, C)
end. {Quiz}
```

3-12 Write a procedure that is passed a *real* value, and returns separately its whole part, and the first four digits of its fractional part.

3-13 It's very unlikely that the situation below will ever appear in a real program, but it is real Pascal. What is the program's output?

```
program HardToBelieve (output);
var Number: integer;
procedure DoubleAndAdd (var First, Second: integer);
   begin
      First := 2*First;
      Second := 1+Second
   end; {DoubleAndAdd}
procedure AddAndDouble (var First, Second: integer);
   begin
      First := 1+First;
      Second := 2*Second
   end; {AddAndDouble}
begin
   Number := 3;
   DoubleAndAdd (Number, Number);
   writeln (Number);
   Number := 3;
   AddAndDouble (Number, Number);
   writeln (Number);
end. {HardToBelieve}
```

3-14 What Pascal types can a function represent values of?

3-15 When can a function identifier appear on the left-hand side of an assignment statement?

3-16 Can the type of a function depend on the type of its argument? In other words, could we write a function that returns a *real* value if its argument is *real*, and represents an *integer* if its argument is *integer*?

3-17 What's the difference between top-down and bottom-up testing and debugging? Is one better than the other?

3-18 What's wrong with this function definition?

```
function SluggingPercentage (AtBats, Singles, Doubles, Triples, Homers: integer): real;
  {This function computes the average number of bases attained per hit.}
  begin
    SluggingPercentage := Singles+(2*Doubles)+(3*Triples)+(4*Homers);
    SluggingPercentage := SluggingPercentage / AtBats
  end; {SluggingPercentage}
```

More Exercises

3-18 Product expiration dates are often encoded to discourage consumers from complaining. A common technique is to use letters instead of numbers in dates. Suppose that the White Bread Mfg. Co. Inc. encodes the months as the letters 'A' through 'L', each digit of the day's date as the letters 'Q' through 'Z' and the year as the letters 'Z' through 'A' plus 1970, where 'Z' represents 1, and 'A' is 26. Days that would otherwise have only one digit are preceded by a zero. Write a program that decodes an expiration date.

3-19 Nadine Riverdale is going to get a job selling hot tubs. She can choose between three payment arrangements: *a*) a straight salary of $325 per week; *b*) a salary of $3.50 per hour for a 40-hour week, plus a 15% commission on sales, or, *c*) no salary at all, with a 20% commission, plus $1.00 for each item sold.

Write a program that Nadine can use to decide which plan is best for her, once she gets an idea of how many hot tubs she can expect to sell each week.

3-20 The Klutz Brothers were famous traveling thermometer-makers of the last century. Unfortunately, they had a rather pixyish sense of humor, and a poor understanding of physics. Joachim Klutz would often set the freezing point of his thermometers at, say, 50 degrees, and give a boiling point of 99, or 275. His brother Fred followed the same whimsical pattern.

Write a program that uses procedures to convert the temperature on one of Joachim's thermometers to an equivalent temperature in Fred's notation. Obtain the freezing and boiling points of each thermometer from the program user.

3-21 Write a program that adds and subtracts time. Its starting input should be a time of day, entered with a colon between the hours and minutes (e.g. 12:37). The program user should be able to have the program add or subtract (indicated by entering a plus or minus sign) any number of hours and minutes from this time.

3-22 One difficulty people have with stepwise refinement is deciding exactly how much of a refinement to make at each level. Suppose that you have the problem of giving directions between two places in your town. Write directions for *a*) a life-long resident; *b*) a newcomer to town; *c*) a foreigner; *d*) a small but intelligent child; *e*) your pet snail.

3-23 Monica Marin is going to go on the television game show Tic Tac Dough. Unfortunately, Monica isn't too familiar with even the rules of ordinary Tic Tac Toe. To help her, we'll write a program that prints completed games. Write a program that outputs a Tic Tac Toe board, asking for the contents of each square as it goes along.

3-24 Write procedures to produce block letters. Naturally, you'll have to do some analysis of the letter characters before you begin. To help out, we've divided the capital letters into the four groups below. Does this help you with your problem? How?

A M T U V W Y   B C D E K   H I O X   F G J L N P Q R S Z

3-25 In the game of Hangman, a player tries to guess letters in a secret word. With each wrong guess, the stick figure of a hanging man is partially drawn. When six wrong guesses have been made, the figure is complete, and the player loses the game.

Write procedures to draw the hanging man as he looks after each guess. In other words, you should draw six pictures, with each picture incorporating the previous one. (Hint: Start with a *DrawHat* procedure, then let the *DrawHead* procedure call it, etc. Each procedure should call the procedure defined before it.)

3-26 Ask a user to enter a three digit number whose first digit is greater than its last. Now reverse the number, and subtract the reversal from the original number. Reverse this number, and add it to its unreversed form. What's the answer? Is it ever different? (There are two general exceptions, but you may have to find them by thinking, rather than by computer.)

3-27 If people can read minds, why can't computers? Our first trick lets the computer read a number from our minds. Here's how a human magician would perform the feat: Present a spectator with a large number, and have her circle any digit but 0. Have her read out the remaining digits, one at a time, in any order. When she's done, the magician names the circled digit.

How does the magician do it? She performs the operation *Number* **mod** 9, and subtracts the answer from 9. This is the value of the circled digit. Why does it work? Well, all depends on the original large number. When the calculation *OriginalNumber* **mod** 9 is performed, the result must be 0. We say that such a number has a *digital root* of 9. We can guarantee that a number's digital root is 9 by a variety of means:

a) Start with a number, rearrange its digits in any order, then subtract the smaller from the larger.

b) Start with a number, add its digits together, then subtract this sum from the original number.

c) Multiply any number by 9.

d) Start with any number, find the sum of its digits, multiply by 8, and add the result to the original number.

e) Start with a number, add two rearranged versions of the same number to it, then square the answer.

All of these operations result in a number whose digital root is 9. Thus, the spectator (or program user) can start with *any* number, and by following the magician's apparently meaningless directions turn it into a suitably magical number.

Revise this problem for the computer. Remember that half of any successful magic trick lies in patter, so be sure to write a talkative program.

3-28 Draft a syntax for declaring procedures in your new high-level language. How can you explain where procedure declarations should be made? Should an extra **end** (or whatever *you* call it) mark the end of the procedure declaration?

3-29 Do you think that your private programming language needs parameters? Can you include them in a way that simplifies their declaration? How about requiring parameters by banning global identifiers from subprograms? Come up with an alternative syntax for a procedure heading.

3-30 Naturally your new programming language will have to include functions. What do you think about extending the idea of functions to encompass definable operators? In other words, how about letting the programmer define the effect of an operator on its operands (for instance, the effect of adding *char* values)? Can you write a reasonable set of rules for defining new operators? What might they be?

'Our final example is a program that finds Fibonacci . . .'

4

Taking Control of Execution: the **for** Statement

In their original definition and explanation of Pascal, Kathleen Jensen and Niklaus Wirth pointed out that...

> 'Essential to a computer program is action...a program must do something with its data—even if that action is the choice of doing nothing!'*

The most interesting of Pascal's actions are its *control statements*—statements that control other statements. In Pascal, as in almost every programming language, there are two types of control statements—those that *loop*, and those that *choose*. Looping statements repeat actions; actions are performed again and again until the correct count, or an appropriate condition, is reached. Choice statements decide actions. They determine whether or not an action is taken at all.

The **for** statement will serve as our introduction to control statements. It's Pascal's most straightforward loop—it repeats an action a given number of times. As we start to use the **for** statement we'll learn about some Pascal details that are often confusing to beginning programmers—*compound* and *empty* statements. These statements play supporting roles to the control statements by helping to specify or limit actions.

Section 4-2 is optional. It provides an early introduction to *arrays* and *strings*. Arrays are variables that can store more than one value; an array might store 10 *integers*, or 1,000 *chars*. Strings are a special variety of arrays that usually store words. The **for** statement is particularly convenient for dealing with array variables, so some instructors like this early introduction. You can skip this section without worry—the formal introduction to arrays doesn't come until Chapter 11.

As usual, section 4-3 covers debugging and antibugging. In addition to giving **for** advice, it talks about *defensive* programming and modularity, and goes over the annoying bugs associated with compound and empty statements. Read it!

* Kathleen Jensen and Niklaus Wirth, *Pascal User Manual and Report*, Springer-Verlag 1974.

for Statements and Program Actions 4-1

for demonstration program

LET'S START WITH AN EXAMPLE. PROGRAM *ShowFor*, below, demonstrates the repetitive nature of the **for** statement.

```
program ShowFor (output);
   {Demonstrates the for loop.}
var LoopCount: integer;
begin
   writeln ('This program shows what a for loop does.');
   for LoopCount := 1 to 5 do
      writeln ('This is loop number ', LoopCount:1);
   writeln ('All done.')
end.
```

```
This program shows what a for loop does.
This is loop number 1
This is loop number 2
This is loop number 3
This is loop number 4
This is loop number 5
All done.
```

The **for** statement's action is shaded. The Pascal phrase:

for *LoopCount* := 1 **to** 5 **do**

for outline

instructs the computer to repeat an action (in this instance, an output statement) five times. The general form of a **for** statement is:

for *counter variable* := *initial value* **to** *final value* **do**
  action;

The reserved word **downto**, in place of **to**, reverses the counting process. For backward counting to work, the initial value must be greater than the final value. In chart form, we can show the **for** statement as:

for statement

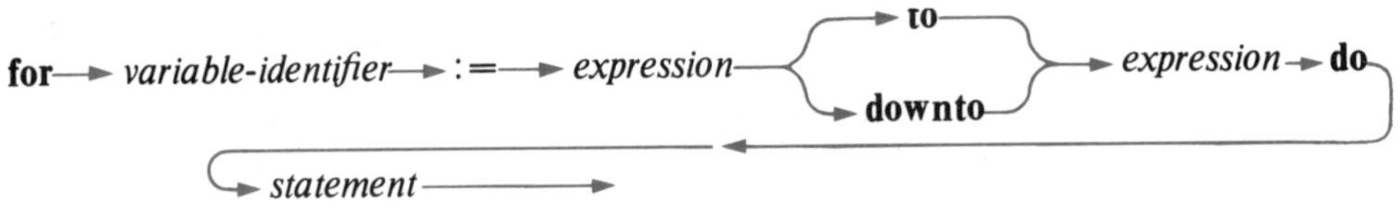

Pascal uses a rather clever mechanism to keep track of the number of times the action *loops*, or repeats. Instead of giving the exact number of times we want the action to occur, we state expressions that give the initial and final values of a locally declared program variable.

> The variable used to control a **for** statement is called the *counter variable*. It can belong to any ordinal type.

the counter variable

When a **for** statement is entered, its counter variable is assigned the initial value. The counter variable is *incremented*, or increased to the next higher value, each time the **for** statement's action is carried out. When the counter variable represents the final value, the loop iterates one last time, and the program moves on to the next statement. In any event, no action is taken if the difference between the initial and final values is less than zero.

Why use such a round-about method to say how many times the loop should repeat? We do it out of necessity, since the counter variable can belong to any of Pascal's ordinal (counting) types. In *ShowFor*, the counter variable was an *integer*, and its value increased by 1 on each circuit of the **for** loop. The initial value is 1, the final value is 5, and the action is repeated

(*final value* – *initial value*) + 1

times—in other words, five times.

But suppose we wanted to 'count' by characters? Program *AlphabetSoup*, below, shows that we can use *char* values as easily as *integers*.

counting by characters program

```
program AlphabetSoup (output);
   {Uses for loops to print the alphabet forward and backward.}
var CounterCharacter: char;
begin
   for CounterCharacter := 'A' to 'Z' do
      write (CounterCharacter);
   writeln;
   for CounterCharacter := 'z' downto 'a' do
      write (CounterCharacter);
   writeln
end.
```

```
ABCDEFGHIJKLMNOPQRSTUVWXYZ
zyxwvutsrqponmlkjihgfedcba
```

Five rules govern possible values of the counter variable. They are revisited, with examples, in the antibugging section.

real counters are forbidden

1. The counter variable, initial value, and final value must all belong to the same ordinal type.

They may not be of type *real*, because it makes no sense to talk of incrementing a *real* value—there is no next *real*. This statement:

for *Counter* := 1.0 **to** 5.0 **do** *action*;

is illegal, because *Counter* may not be a *real*-valued variable.

local counter

2. The counter variable must be locally declared.

This means that a global variable can't be used as a counter variable within a subprogram. The counter variable must be declared in the procedure or function it's used in.

evaluating the bounds

3. The expressions that give the counter variable's initial and final values are evaluated when the statement is first entered.

Consequently, the number of times the loop iterates cannot be modified from within the loop's action. Making assignments to variables that represent the initial and final values will not affect the counter variable or its limits.

assigning the counter

4. It's an error to make an assignment to the counter variable from within the loop's action.

The counter variable, like any other variable, represents a value within the action of the **for** statement. But although it may be *used* within the **for** loop's action, it may not be *changed* there. Trying to change the value through an assignment or input statement will be an error.

Together, rules 3 and 4 are intended to keep programmers (and programs) honest. The documentation implicit in the control statement's first line—that it will repeat for a certain number of times—cannot be undermined or invalidated by changing values from *within* the loop.

counter is undefined

5. The value of the counter variable is undefined on exit from the **for** statement.

In effect, the variable is in the pristine condition it held when it was first declared. It should be reinitialized before being used in an expression.

Self-Check Questions

Q. The first lines of some **for** statements are shown below. How many times do each of these statements call for an action to take place? Assume that these assignments have been made: *LastLetter*:= 'F', *LowerBound* := –5, and *UpperBound* := 3.

a) **for** *Index* := 0 **to** 5 **do** *some action*;
b) **for** *LetterID* := *LastLetter* **downto** 'B' **do** *some action*;
c) **for** *Pointer* := –5 **to** 3 **do** *some action*;
d) **for** *Count* := *abs*(*LowerBound*) **downto** *trunc*(4.92) **do** *some action*;
e) **for** *Index* := 5 **to** 5 **do** *some action*;
f) **for** *BadCount* := *UpperBound* **to** *LowerBound* **do** *some action*;
g) **for** *AnotherBadCount* := 3 **downto** 6 **do** *some action*;

A. The actions of examples *f* and *g* will not take place at all. A 'repetition,' by the way, is a single instance of an action.

a) 6 repetitions.
b) 5 repetitions.
c) 9 repetitions.
d) 2 repetitions.
e) 1 repetition.
f) 0 repetitions—*UpperBound* is greater than *LowerBound.*
g) 0 repetitions—3 is less than 6.

A Pascal Program's Actions

The **for** loops we've seen so far have been somewhat pathetic examples because their actions have all been single *writeln* statements. In this section we'll see that control statements can regulate a variety of actions:

assignment statements
procedure calls
compound statements
control statements
empty statements

Assignment statements and procedure calls are actions we're already familiar with. Use of a procedure call is one way we can get a **for** statement to make a sequence of statements—the procedure's contents—repeat. In the example below, procedure *PrintSquareAndCube* might invoke one statement, or 1,000. What's important is that, to the **for** statement, a single action is being controlled.

```
for Counter := 1 to 20 do
  PrintSquareAndCube (Counter);
```

We won't always have a procedure handy, though, when we want a sequence of statements to be treated as a single action. The compound statement comes to the rescue.

> We can group several statements into a single action by putting them between a **begin** and an **end**. This forms a *compound statement*.

In chart form, we have:

compound statement

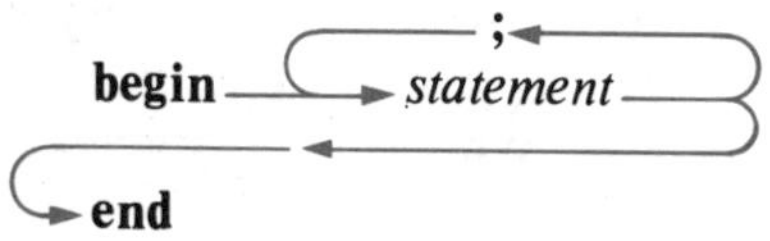

The **begin** and **end** play the role of statement parentheses by marking the boundaries of an action. For example, procedure *AddNumbers*, below, requires that two actions be repeated. First, a number has to be read, then it must be added to a running sum. Note the use of parameters: *Several* is a value parameter that comes from the calling program; its value is used within *AddNumbers*. *Sum*, in contrast, is a variable parameter; it is modified within the procedure for the benefit of the calling program.

compound statements

```
procedure AddNumbers (Several: integer; var Sum: integer);
   {Read and add a sequence of Several numbers.}
   var Count, Current: integer;
   begin
      Sum := 0;
      for Count := 1 to Several do begin
         readln (Current);
         Sum := Sum + Current
      end {for}
   end; {AddNumbers}
```

No semicolon immediately precedes the **end** of a compound statement. Actually, you should just remember that there *never* need be a semicolon right before any **end**, no matter where it appears.

nested statements

A compound statement can include control statements as well. The internal statement is said to be *nested* inside the outer statement, and is treated as a single statement. For example:

```
for Outer := 1 to 3 do begin
   for Inner := 1 to 2 do
      write ('Hip, ');
   writeln ('Hooray!')
end; {for}
```

↓ ↓ ↓ ↓ ↓

```
Hip, Hip, Hooray!
Hip, Hip, Hooray!
Hip, Hip, Hooray!
```

The last kind of statement available to Pascal programmers is not what we'd usually think of as comprising an action.

A semicolon can indicate an *empty* or null statement.

empty statements

The semicolon itself isn't the empty statement—you should recall that it's Pascal's statement separator. However, the compiler (running rings around itself logically), assumes that every semicolon was preceded by a statement. In effect, a semicolon creates an empty statement that is sometimes needed to fulfill syntax requirements. It acts like a bandage on the Invisible Man by letting us (and the compiler) see a statement that isn't really there.

Self-Check Questions

Q. What is the output of this segment of code?

```
for Descendant := 9 downto 0 do
    writeln ((2*Descendent) + 1);
```

A. It prints the odd numbers from 19 through 1.

Q. What about this segment? Is it legal?

```
for Ascendant := 1 to 10 do begin
    ; ; ;
end
```

A. The statement doesn't do anything, but it's perfectly legal Pascal. The **for** statement's action is a compound statement that contains four empty statements (since there are three statement separators).

Focus On Programming: **for** Example . . .

problem: drawing bars

Let's warm up by getting some more practice with procedures and parameters. Program *Bars*, below, uses two value parameters. Its procedure *DrawBar* is a 'utility' procedure that draws a line of characters with a **for** statement. (It might later be used in a bar-graphing program.) The length of the bar, and the character used to draw it, are arguments to each call of *DrawBar*. They provide starting values for the value parameters *Length* and *BarCharacter*.

bar-drawing program

```
program Bars (output);
    {Draws three rows of characters using the for statement.}
const DOLLARSIGN = '$';
var Income: integer;
    Symbol: char;
procedure DrawBar (Length: integer; BarCharacter: char);
    {Prints BarCharacter exactly Length times.}
    var Counter: integer;
    begin
        for Counter := 1 to Length do
            write (BarCharacter);
        writeln
    end; {DrawBar}
begin
    Income := 20;
    Symbol := '#';
    DrawBar (12, 'X');
    DrawBar (3*5, Symbol);
    DrawBar (Income, DOLLARSIGN)
end. {Bars}
```

↓ ↓ ↓ ↓ ↓

```
XXXXXXXXXXXX
##############
$$$$$$$$$$$$$$$$$$$$$
```

When *DrawBar* is called, it's given two arguments—the values of *Length* and *BarCharacter*. Since they go to value parameters, they can be expressions of any sort, as long as each has the correct type. Incidentally, the declaration of *Counter* within *DrawBar* isn't just good programming practice. It's required by the regulation that **for** loop counter variables be locally declared.

problem: averaging numbers

Program *FindAverage*, below, uses a variable parameter to help average a sequence of numbers. Here the **for** statement is outside the procedure—*GetValues* is called 50 times to read in a number, and update the variable parameter *Sum*. Since *Sum* is a variable parameter, its argument (the global variable *Total*) is updated at the same time. *FindAverage* neither prompts for nor echoes input values, so it's strictly oriented toward use with a data file that contains 50 numbers.

averaging program

```
program FindAverage (input, output);
   {Averages NUMBEROFVALUES input values.}
const NUMBEROFVALUES = 50; {Amount of input expected.}
var Counter: integer;
    Total, Average: real;
procedure GetValues (var Sum: real);
   var Number: real;
   begin
      read (Number);
      Sum := Sum+Number
   end; {GetValues}
begin
   Total := 0;
   for Counter := 1 to NUMBEROFVALUES do
      GetValues (Total);
   Average := Total /NUMBEROFVALUES;
   writeln ('The average of ', NUMBEROFVALUES:1, ' values is', Average)
end. {FindAverage}
```

↓ ↓ ↓ ↓ ↓

```
23 1e+02 -29.4 836 7.72 740 19 3 0.85 782 8.3 5 893
4 2 89 8.47 923.1 8934 -78.4 93 612 9.23 -9 0.07823 3
83 -21.9 4 1213 63 089 34.7 937 72.09 659 72 95.23
63 9 8.723 -943 912 30 6.75 832 8.312 3 754.3 -8
The average of 50 values is 3.79103064600000e+02
```

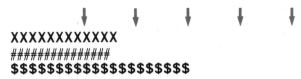

Pseudocode

A few pages back we saw that control statements could be nested within other control statements. Let's consider a simple case of one of the more diabolical forms of nesting—nested **for** loops. At the same time we'll introduce a problem-solving approach that helps us deal with these situations. Here's the problem:

problem: printing patterns

> Write a program that prints a rectangular pattern of stars of any given width (or number of columns) and depth (or number of lines). For example, the pattern below is six columns wide, and four lines deep.

```
* * * * * *
* * * * * *
* * * * * *
* * * * * *
```

This kind of task cries out for a **for** statement. Let's try to solve it using stepwise refinement. As we go, we'll write our algorithm in *pseudocode*. Pseudocode is an intermediate language between English and Pascal. Proportions of each are prescribed by the programmer, but the closer to completion the solution is, the more Pascal appears.

Pseudocode lets us describe an algorithm in Pascal-like terms, but without being restricted by the syntax rules of Pascal programs. It's far more natural and convenient than the flowcharts programmers once employed for drafting programs.

> Should you floss all your teeth? No—just the ones you want to keep. Should you pseudocode all your programs? No—just the programs you hope will run!

Let's get back to our problem. The first step of a refinement is to recognize that the pattern is really a single line that's repeated several times. In pseudocode we can write:

first refinement

for *the correct number of lines*
  print a single line;

Each line, in turn, is generated by repeating one action—printing a star—as many times as there are columns.

second refinement

for *the correct number of columns*
  print a single star;

Joining these partial solutions leads to a nested **for** loop.

pseudocode refinement

for *the correct number of lines*
  for *the correct number of columns*
    print a single star;

Converting the pseudocode into Pascal is a routine matter. Already, you can see the outlines of Pascal code; in fact, we'll use the exact same indenting when we actually write our **for** statements. First we have the code for a single line, spacing between each star:

```
for StarCount := 1 to ColumnNumber do
   write ('*  ');
```

Each line of stars must be followed by a *writeln* that forces output, and puts the printer in position for the beginning of the next line.

```
for LineCount := 1 to NumberOfLines do begin
   for StarCount := 1 to ColumnNumber do
      write ('*  ');      {This prints only a }
   writeln                {single line of stars.}
end;
```

The completed program is shown below.

pattern program

```
program PrintPattern (input, output);
   {Prints a grid of stars using nested for loops.}
var LineCount, StarCount,        {The for loop counter variables.}
    NumberOfLines, ColumnNumber: integer;
begin
   writeln ('This program will print a grid of stars.');
   writeln ('You supply the dimensions.  How wide is it?');
   readln (ColumnNumber);
   writeln ('How deep should it be?');
   readln (NumberOfLines);
   for LineCount := 1 to NumberOfLines do begin
      for StarCount := 1 to ColumnNumber do
         write ('*  '); {This is the entire inner loop}
      writeln
   end {outer loop}
end. {PrintPattern}
```

```
This program will print a grid of stars.
You supply the dimensions.  How wide is it?
10
How deep should it be?
3
*  *  *  *  *  *  *  *  *  *
*  *  *  *  *  *  *  *  *  *
*  *  *  *  *  *  *  *  *  *
```

avoiding nesting

If the concept of nested loops is hard for you right now, you can keep it at arm's length by using procedures. An outer loop can just call a procedure that implements the inner loop. For example, this procedure declaration:

```
procedure PrintOneLine (ColumnNumber: integer);
  {Prints ColumnNumber stars.}
  var StarCount: integer;
  begin
    for StarCount := 1 to ColumnNumber do
      write ('*  ');
    writeln
  end; {PrintOneLine}
```

gives us a procedure that could have been used like this in program *PrintPattern*:

```
for LineCount := 1 to NumberOfLines do
  PrintOneLine (ColumnNumber);        etc.
```

Self-Check Questions

Q. The two program segments below might have been written in place of the pattern-printing code of *PrintPattern*. Unfortunately, each one contains a subtle error that causes incorrect output. What will each segment print?

```
for LineCount := 1 to NumberOfLines do        {first segment}
  for StarCount := 1 to ColumnNumber do
    write ('*  ');
writeln;
```

```
for LineCount := 1 to NumberOfLines do        {second segment}
  for StarCount := 1 to ColumnNumber do begin
    write ('*  ');
    writeln
  end; {inner loop}
```

A. Both segments suffer from improper nesting. The first segment prints the first row of stars correctly. However, the *writeln* is in the wrong position, and forces *every* row of stars to be printed on a single line of output. In other words, the *writeln* does not get executed until all the stars have already been printed out. Thus, the output will be one line of stars, (*NumberOfLines* * *ColumnNumber*) long.

The second segment has the reverse ailment. The *writeln* takes effect after each individual star. This causes the output to be a tall stack of stars, one star wide, and (*NumberOfLines* * *ColumnNumber*) stars high.

Pseudocode with Stepwise Refinement

problem: finding Fibonaccis

Our final example is a program that finds Fibonacci numbers. This series begins 0, 1, then each subsequent number is the sum of the previous two. We'll state the problem like this:

> Imagine that the values in the Fibonacci sequence are numbered. Write a program that lets a user request the *m*th through *n*th Fibonacci numbers.

We'll use the techniques of stepwise refinement and pseudocoding to work toward a solution. A first refinement of the problem is just:

first refinement

> *skip the first m−1 Fibonacci numbers*;
> *print the mth through nth Fibonacci numbers*;

It doesn't take much to turn this into a Pascal-like pseudocode in a second refinement step:

second refinement

> **for** *the first m−1 Fibonacci numbers*
>   *get the next Fibonacci number*;
> **for** *the mth through nth Fibonacci numbers*
>   *get the next Fibonacci number*;
>   *print it*;

It looks like *get the next Fibonacci number* will require yet another refinement step. What is the current Fibonacci number? It's the sum of the previous two. This means that if we remember the *last* Fibonacci, and know the current one, we can always generate the next number. We'll propose the pseudocode algorithm shown below. It's a lot like our old friend procedure *Switch*; it gives two variables new values, but has to use their present values in the process.

> *let a temporary variable get the sum of Last and Current*;
> *Last gets the present value of Current*;
> *Current gets the present value of Temporary*;

procedure or function?

Should this pseudocode for finding a Fibonacci be implemented as a procedure, or as a function? Well, if all we wanted was the next Fibonacci number, a function would be appropriate. After all, a function should be used when we want a subprogram to calculate and return a single value.

In this case, though, we want to maintain the ability to figure out subsequent Fibonacci numbers as well. This means that we have to return two values—the last Fibonacci, as well as the newest. Since the subprogram will change two values, a procedure with two variable parameters is right for our purposes.

One more detail will require our attention before we can translate our pseudocode into Pascal. Will our algorithm find the first Fibonacci in the series? No. Since it has to start with 0, 1, the first Fibonacci our procedure computes will be the third. We'll have to remember this when we write the **for** loop that skips the first $m-1$ Fibonacci numbers.

Fibonacci program

```
program PrintFibonaccis (input, output);
    {Prints the mth through nth Fibonacci numbers.}
var Counter, FirstFib, LastFib, {will represent m and n}
    CurrentFibonacci, NextFibonacci: integer;
procedure GetNextFibonacci (var Last, Current: integer);
    {Generates the next Fibonacci number.}
    var Temporary: integer;
    begin
        Temporary := Last + Current;
        Last := Current;
        Current := Temporary
    end; {GetNextFibonacci}
begin
    writeln ('This program finds the mth through nth Fibonacci');
    writeln ('numbers. Enter m and n. Be sure m is at least 3.');
    readln (FirstFib, LastFib);
    writeln ('Fibonaccis ', FirstFib:1, ' through ', LastFib:1, ' are:');
    CurrentFibonacci := 0; {Initialize the sequence.}
    NextFibonacci := 1;
    for Counter := 3 to FirstFib-1 do
        GetNextFibonacci (CurrentFibonacci, NextFibonacci);
    for Counter := FirstFib to LastFib do begin
        GetNextFibonacci (CurrentFibonacci, NextFibonacci);
        write (NextFibonacci)
    end; {for}
    writeln
end. {PrintFibonaccis}
```

```
This program finds the mth through nth Fibonacci
numbers.  Enter m and n.  Be sure m is at least 3.
10  14
Fibonaccis 10 through 14 are:
      34          55          89         144         233
```

Self-Check Questions

Q. What will happen if you give program *PrintFibonaccis* a value of *n* that's less than *m*? A value smaller than 3 for *m*?

A. Neither input will cause a program error, although we might not get useful output. If a **for** statement's initial value is greater than its final value, the loop simply won't take any action. As a result, an *n* smaller than *m* won't print any Fibonacci numbers. An *m* less than 3 will simply give us incorrect output, since the smallest Fibonacci the program can print (under any circumstances) is the third in the series.

One-Dimensional Arrays* 4-2

IN CHAPTER 1 WE LEARNED HOW TO declare simple variables—variables that were used to store single values of Pascal's standard simple types. In this optional section, we'll take an advance look at a *structured* variable—the **array**—that some instructors like to introduce along with the **for** statement. This section can be skipped without harm, because its contents won't be referred to again until Chapter 11.

The simple variables we have used so far have shared a characteristic so obvious that it's hardly borne mentioning: each variable has referred to a single value only. We can, however, declare variables that store more than one value. These are known as *structured*, rather than simple, variables. *Array* variables are the most commonly used form of structured variables. For example:

array demonstration program

```
program ArrayUser (input, output);
   {Reads in 10 values, then prints them in reverse order.}
type TenValues = array [1..10] of integer;
var i: integer;        {the for loop's counter variable.}
   Hold: TenValues;
begin
   writeln ('This program will read ten integers, then print');
   writeln ('them in reverse. Please enter ten numbers.');
   for i := 1 to 10 do          {Get the values.}
      read (Hold [i]);
   for i := 10 downto 1 do          {Now print them in reverse order.}
      write (Hold [i]:3);
   writeln
end. {ArrayUser}
```

```
This program will read ten integers, then print
them in reverse.  Please enter ten numbers.
8 17 22 5 93 66 18 41 59 74
 74 59 41 18 66 93  5 22 17  8
```

In program *ArrayUser*, above, *Hold* is an array variable that can hold ten different values. According to the shaded code, we use *Hold* as a temporary storage place for holding our input values before they're printed out again. Notice in particular the line of code that begins with the word **type**. This line customizes our array variable (*Hold*, of type *TenValues*) by limiting it to holding ten values, all of type *integer*.

```
type TenValues = array [1..10] of integer;
var Hold: TenValues;
```

More formally, an array is said to have *elements*, which are its stored values. In Pascal, an array can have almost any number of elements, but

* This section is optional.

array elements

they must all be of the same Pascal type. For instance, we might have an array that holds *integer* or *char* values. However, we can't create an array that sometimes holds one type, and sometimes another. *Hold*, above, is an array of *integers*.

The *size* of the array is the number of elements that it contains. An array's size is given in an interesting way that recalls the method used to state the number of times a **for** statement is intended to loop. Instead of explicitly stating the size of the array, we give the *bounds* of the *subscript* that we'll use to refer to individual array elements. In effect, each element is numbered with a subscript (much like a mathematical subscript). The bounds give the starting and ending values of this 'numbering,' which might be 1 through 10 (as above), but could just as easily run from 'A' through 'J.' *Hold*, above, is subscripted by the integers 1 through 10, and has a size of ten.

subscripting

Now, when we've declared ordinary variables thus far, a **var** declaration has been sufficient. This is because the standard simple types *integer, real, char*, and *boolean* are predefined in every Pascal system. Arrays are different, though. Before an array's type identifier can be used in a variable declaration, it must be defined in a *type definition*.

> First *define* the array type. Then *declare* the array variable.

The *type definition part* of a program or subprogram comes just before the variable declaration part. It begins with the reserved word **type**, and fits into our general block outline like this:

type definition part

heading
definition part
  constant definitions
  type definitions
declaration part
  variable declarations
  procedure and function declarations
statement part

program outline

The definition of an array type contains three necessary pieces of information:

1. What is the identifier, or name, of the type?
2. What are the bounds that determine the array's size? Actual values *must* be given when the array is defined—the bounds can't be supplied as variables whose values are found when the program is run.
3. What is the type of the elements the array variable will store?

array type definition

In outline form, the definition of an array type is:

type *identifier* = **array** [*bounds*] **of** *element type* ;

As the examples below show, two periods (..) go between the starting and ending values that state an array's bounds. All three arrays below have five elements, but each stores a different type of value:

FiveIntegers = **array** [1..5] **of** *integer*;
FiveChars = **array** [−2..2] **of** *char*;
CharBounds = **array** ['A'..'E'] **of** *real*;

Note that the bounds need not begin with 1; indeed, they don't even have to be *integer* values. Furthermore, the bounds can have a different type than the stored elements.

type-name bounds

In some circumstances, bounds can be given with a type name instead of with explicit bound values. We'll employ this technique when we want to define an array type whose bounds are the first and last values of type *char*. For example:

LetterCount = **array** [*char*] **of** *integer*;

An array type defined like this will be legal on any Pascal system. Had we used particular bound values for the first and last characters, we might find ourselves in trouble on Pascal systems with different character sets.

Self-Check Questions

Q. How many elements does each of the array types defined below have?

a) **type** *Store* = **array** [0..7] **of** *integer*;
b) **type** *Points* = **array** [-50..50] **of** *real*;
c) **type** *SmallLetters* = **array** ['d'..'h'] **of** *char*;
d) **type** *Equivalents* = **array** ['1'..'9'] **of** *integer*;
e) **type** *Code* = **array** [*char*] **of** *char*;

A. Don't forget to declare variables as well as defining their types.

a) 8 elements of type *integer*.
b) 101 elements (don't forget the '0'th) of type *real*.
c) 5 elements of type *char*.
d) 9 elements of type *integer*.
e) As many *char* elements as there are values in type *char*.

Accessing Array Elements

Suppose we make these type definitions and variable declarations:

type *Hourly* = **array** [1..24] **of** *real*;
Alphabet = **array** ['A'..'Z'] **of** *integer*;
Grades = **array** [1..100] **of** *char*;
Month = **array** [1..12] **of** *integer*;
Units = **array** [1..60] **of** *real*;

```
var Barometer: Hourly;
    Envelopes: Alphabet;
    English: Grades;
    DayCount: Month;
    Minutes, Seconds: Units;
    Initial, Days, Current: integer;
```

Since an array variable represents a collection of values, rather than a single value, we must use a special method to refer to its individual elements.

using subscripts

> To assign or inspect one value of an array variable, follow the variable's name with the subscript of a particular element. The subscript goes between square brackets.

Here are some examples of accesses of array elements:

```
Barometer [1] := 29.27;
writeln (Barometer [1]);
English [10] := 'A';
English [11] := English [10];
read (Envelopes ['T']);
Envelopes ['R'] := Envelopes [succ('S')];
```

> An array subscript may take any form, as long as it is a legal Pascal expression. However, the subscript's value must fall within the bounds given in the array's definition.

form of subscripts

We can use any representation of a value—a constant, function call, or even an array value—as a subscript. For example:

```
for Initial := 1 to 24 do Barometer [Initial] := 0.0;
for Days := 1 to 12 do read (DayCount [Days]);
English [sqr(5)] := English [10 div 3];
DayCount [1] := 2;
Barometer [ DayCount[1] ] := 0.0;
```

Obviously, though, the subscript value has to be legal—within the bounds established by the array type definition. If the subscript is too large or small the program will immediately crash.

> Two array variables may be assigned to each other if they have the exact same type.

assigning to arrays

This is the assignment rule that holds for every variable. Assigning one array to another has the same effect as assigning their elements one at a time. For example (assuming that *Seconds* has been initialized), the assignment:

```
Minutes := Seconds;
```

is the exact equivalent of:

```
for Current :=1 to 60 do
    Minutes [Current] := Seconds [Current];
```

Some Array Examples

The array type lets the programmer declare a large number of variables without having to go to a lot of work. Our first example, program *ArrayUser*, showed one typical application—saving input values. Program *Reverse*, below, accomplishes a similar task. Input values (in this case, characters) are saved, then printed out in reverse order.

array reversal program

```
program Reverse (input, output);
    {Reverses thirty characters' worth of input.}
type ShortLine = array [1..30] of char;
var i: integer;
    Letters: ShortLine;
begin
    writeln ('Please enter 30 characters'' worth of input.');
    for i := 1 to 30 do
        read (Letters [(30 -i) + 1]);
    for i := 1 to 30 do
        write (Letters [i]);
    writeln
end. {Reverse}
```

```
Please enter 30 characters' worth of input.
Rock and roll is here to stay.
.yats ot ereh si llor dna kcoR
```

Note, though, that the algorithm of program *Reverse* is slightly different from that of *ArrayUser*. The shaded statement holds the difference. By cleverly computing a subscript, we are storing the values in reverse order as we read them in. We might have also made the simpler modification:

```
for i := 30 downto 1 do
    read (Letters [i]);
```

problem: counting digits

Array variables are also prized for their assistance in helping us count values. For instance, suppose that we have, as input, a long sequence of numbers. We want to count the number of times each digit character occurs. We'll end up knowing how many 0's, 1's, 2's, etc. there were. How can an array help?

Well, in previous examples we've used array elements to hold input values. But we could just as easily use each element of an array to hold a running count. Since an array element can hold an *integer*, and since we can easily add 1 to a stored value, it doesn't seem that keeping count will pose a problem. We initialize the element to 0, then occasionally add one to its value as necessary.

But can we associate one array element with each digit character? If we're going to have counts for all the digits, we'll need a '0's element,' a '1's element,' and so on. Stop and think for a moment before you read on.

The solution is to define an array whose elements hold *integers*, but are subscripted by the digit characters:

> **type** *Totals* = **array** ['0'..'9'] **of** *integer*;
> **var** *Digits*: *Totals*;

Then we take a clever step. As we read in digit characters, we use each input value as an array subscript, rather than as a new value to be stored in an element.

> *read* (*CurrentDigit*);
> *Digits* [*CurrentDigit*] := *Digits* [*CurrentDigit*] + 1;

The pseudocode for a digit counting program might be:

refinement

> *initialize the counter array*;
> *find out how many digits there are*;
> **for** *that many digits*
>   *read a digit*;
>   *increment its count*;
> *print the results*;

where *initialize the counter array* is:

> **for** *every element in the array*
>   *initialize it to zero*;

As we might imagine, *print the results*, which also requires that we go to every array element, will be quite similar. The completed program is shown below.

digit counting program

```
program ArrayDigitCounter (input, output);
  {Counts the number of times each digit appears in a sequence of numbers.}
type Totals = array ['0'..'9'] of integer;
var Digits: Totals;
    CurrentDigit: char;
    Count, Limit: integer;
begin
  for CurrentDigit := '0' to '9' do          {initialize the array.}
    Digits [CurrentDigit] := 0;
  writeln ('How many digits long is your input value?');
  readln (Limit);
  writeln ('All right, enter the value.');
  for Count := 1 to Limit do begin          {actually count the digits}
    read (CurrentDigit);
    Digits [CurrentDigit] := Digits [CurrentDigit] + 1
  end;
  writeln ('The number of times each digit occurred is:');
  for CurrentDigit := '0' to '4' do
    write (CurrentDigit,':', Digits [CurrentDigit]:2, '      ');
  writeln;
  for CurrentDigit := '5' to '9' do
    write (CurrentDigit, ':', Digits [CurrentDigit]:2, '      ');
  writeln
end. {ArrayDigitCounter}
```

↓ ↓ ↓ ↓ ↓

```
How many digits long is your input value?
25
All right, enter the value.
9373654849568291274393603
The number of times each digit occurred is:
0: 1    1: 1    2: 2    3: 5    4: 3
5: 2    6: 3    7: 2    8: 2    9: 4
```

Self-Check Questions

Q. Suppose that the input of program *ArrayDigitCounter*, above, were known to contain spaces and letters as well as digit characters. Where would the program crash? What modifications would we have to make to avoid this problem?

A. The program would crash when we attempted to increment an element subscripted by a non-digit character—because our type definition doesn't create such elements. If *Count* were redefined in this manner:

```
type Count = array [char] of integer;
```

the problem could be avoided. Note that it would still be necessary to initialize extra sections of the array to 0 so that an error would not occur when their counts are incremented. Assume that *Current* is a variable of type *char*:

```
Digits [' '] := 0;
for Current := 'a' to 'z' do Digits [Current] := 0;
for Current := 'A' to 'Z' do Digits [Current] := 0;
```

More Array Programming

Our examples so far have used arrays as relatively passive recipients of values. Let's consider some examples in which arrays, and array subscripts, are used more actively in dealing with values. We'll use the definition and declarations given below.

```
type Vector = array [1..10] of integer;
var First, Second, Third: Vector;
```

problem: copy arrays

Assume that array *First* has been initialized. Write a code segment that assigns to each element in *Second* the corresponding value from *First*.

This problem could hardly be simpler. We know how to use a **for** statement to step through *First*. The same counter variable can find our place in *Second*:

```
for i := 1 to 10 do
   Second [i] := First [i];
```

problem: sum arrays

Assume that *Second* and *Third* have been initialized. Write a procedure that stores their sum, element-by-element, in *First*.

Once again we want to step through more than one array at a time, so we'll use the same technique. Notice, in procedure *SumElements*, the use of arrays as value and variable parameters.

array summing procedure

```
procedure SumElements (Full1, Full2: Vector; var Sum: Vector);
   {Add Full1 and Full2 into Sum, element-by-element.}
   var i: integer;
   begin
      for i := 1 to 10 do
         Sum [i] := Full1 [i] + Full2 [i]
   end;
```

A call of *SumElements* might be:

```
SumElements (Second, Third, First);
```

problem: sum subarrays

Assume that *First* has been initialized. Store values in *Second* according to the following rule: The *i*th value of *Second* should equal the sum of the first through *i*th value of *First*.

This problem is a bit more complicated. First of all, can we sum the values in a single array? Our pseudocode will be something like:

```
for every element of the array
   add its value to a running total;
```

The code is well within our means:

```
TempSum := 0;
for Current := 1 to 10 do
   TempSum := TempSum + First [Current];
writeln ('The total sum is', TempSum);
```

Solving our problem, though, requires a series of sums—the sum of the first through first values, the first through second values, first through third, etc. In pseudocode, we want:

first refinement

```
for sub-arrays of length 1 through 10
   sum the values of the sub-array;
   assign this sum to our results array;
```

As you might expect, we can immediately expand this pseudocode by developing the shaded section:

second refinement

```
for sub-arrays of length 1 through 10
   initialize a sum variable;
   for every element of the array
      add its value to the running sum;
   assign this sum to our results array;
```

Procedure *SubSums* (part of program *SumSubArrays*, below), implements our pseudocode in Pascal. Notice once again the use of array-typed value and variable parameters.

subarray summing program

```
program SumSubArrays (output);
   {Stores the sums of array subsequences.}
type Vector = array [1..10] of integer;
var First, Second: Vector;
   i: integer;
procedure SubSums (Data: Vector; var Results: Vector);
   {Stores partial sums of Data into Results}
   var SubLength, Current, TempSum: integer;
   begin
      for SubLength := 1 to 10 do begin
         TempSum := 0;
         for Current := 1 to SubLength do
            TempSum := TempSum + Data [Current];
         Results [SubLength] := TempSum
      end {for}
   end; {SubSums}
begin
   for i := 1 to 10 do First [i] := i; {Initialize First to 1, 2, 3, etc.}
   SubSums (First, Second);
   for i := 1 to 10 do write (First [i]); {Print the stored values.}
   writeln;
   for i := 1 to 10 do write (Second [i]); {Print the stored sums.}
   writeln
end. {SumSubArrays}
```

1	2	3	4	5	6	7	8	9	10
1	3	6	10	15	21	28	36	45	55

Self-Check Questions

Q. The code segment below is purported to reverse the contents of the array *Statement*. Does it? Assume that *Statement* is a ten-element array of *char* values whose initial value is 'Bruce!Boss'.

```
for Current := 1 to 10 do
   Statement [Current] := Statement [(10-Current) + 1];
```

A. The code segment contains one of the oldest bugs in the book—it inadvertently destroys one of the two values it tries to exchange. After execution, the contents of *Statement* would be 'ssoB!!Boss'.

A correct exchange uses a temporary variable to effect the exchange of values. Note that we don't travel through the entire array—every value in the first half (the values of *Current*) is switched with its corresponding value in the second half.

```
for Current: = 1 to 5 do begin
    Temp: = Statement [Current];
    Statement [Current]: = Statement [10 – Current + 1];
    Statement [10 – Current + 1]: = Temp
end;
```

String Types

In general computer science terminology, the term *string* refers to any sequence of characters—usually a word or line. Nowadays, dealing with strings is such a common computer application that many languages treat strings as basic data types, much like *real* or *integer*. Pascal doesn't include the string type as a built-in type, and it has been criticized for this omission. We find that string-handling mechanisms are a common extension to Pascal (as in UCSD Pascal).

Nevertheless, even Standard Pascal lets us declare arrays that allow some conveniences for dealing with strings. A *string-type* array definition is superficially like any other array definition, but must obey these three rules:

string rules

1. The array's elements must be of type *char*.
2. The word **array** must be preceded by the word **packed**.*
3. The lower array bound must be 1.

In the example below, *Short* and *Long*, below, are string-type arrays. *Verb, Noun*, and *Phrase* are known as string variables:

```
type Short = packed array [1..4] of char;
     Long = packed array [1..20] of char;
var Verb, Noun: Short;
    Phrase: Long;
```

String variables have all the properties of any other one-dimensional array variables, *plus*:

string properties

1. A string variable can have a string constant (a sequence of characters between single quote marks) assigned to it all at once—not just one element at a time. The constant must have the same length as the variable, of course.
2. String variables can be output in their entirety—again, not just one element at a time.
3. String variables and constants can be compared (generally to determine alphabetical order) by employing the relational operators described in 6-1.

* This is a special instruction to the compiler, and is discussed further in Chapter 11.

string assignments

Rule 1 makes the assignments below legal. Note that when the string constant has fewer characters than the variable has elements, blanks have to be added to the string constant to make the two lengths equal.

```
Verb := 'Sing';   {assignment of string constant}
Noun := Verb;   {assignment of identical array}
Phrase := 'Rather short          ';  {note 8 added blanks}
```

Rule 2 makes these output statements legal:

```
writeln (Verb, Noun);
writeln (Phrase);
```

↓ ↓

```
SingSing
Rather short
```

Strings can also be inspected one element at a time, just like all arrays. This is the method that *must* be used for string input—neither a *read* nor *readln* statement can read in an entire array at once.

string reading program

```
program StringInput (input, output);
   {Demonstrates character-by-character string input.}
type String = packed array [1..10] of char;
var Word: String;
   i: integer;
begin
   writeln ('Please enter a ten-letter word.');
   for i := 1 to 10 do
      read (Word[i]);
   writeln ('You entered: ', Word)
end. {StringInput}
```

↓ ↓ ↓ ↓ ↓

```
Please enter a ten-letter word.
oh my gosh
You entered: oh my gosh
```

Note that in program *StringInput*, replacing the shaded **for** loop with a single input statement (like *readln* (*Word*)) would be illegal.

arrays of strings

String variables are seldom used by themselves. To declare large numbers of array variables, programmers use a clever technique—they define arrays whose elements are strings. For example:

```
type Word = packed array [1..10] of char;
     WordList = array [1..100] of Word;
var OneWord: Word;
    WholeList: WordList;
```

The variable *OneWord*, of type *Word*, is a string array of the sort we've just been experimenting with. Variable *WholeList*, of type *WordList*, is also an array (technically, it's a two-dimensional array, which we'll discuss at length in Chapter 11). The elements of *WholeList*, though, are structured themselves. They are string arrays, and not the simple-type values we've used so far in this section.

Using arrays of strings is surprisingly easy. Let's develop a program that uses the array techniques we've learned so far:

problem: string storage

> Write a program that reads in up to 100 ten-letter names. Let the user ask for a printout of a sublist of names (e.g. the twentieth through fifty-ninth).

A pseudocode restatement of the problem gives us:

refinement

```
find out how many names there will be;
for that many names
  load one name;
find out which names should be output;
for the correct starting through finishing name
  print the name;
```

Our solution is implemented as program *StoreNames*, below. Note the use of parameters with array types. As usual, the choice of value or variable parameters depends on application. An array whose value is modified (as in procedure *LoadOneName*) must be passed to a variable parameter.

string storage program

```
program StoreNames (input, output);
   {Maintains an array of strings.}

type Name = packed array [1..10] of char;
     NameList = array [1..100] of Name;

var OneName: Name;          {each name as it's read in}
    WholeList: NameList;    {the entire list of names}
    Number,                 {the total number of names}
    Start, Finish,          {the bounds for name output}
    i: integer;             {a loop counter variable}

procedure LoadOneName (var Current: Name);
   {Reads in the characters of one string.}
   var i: integer;
   begin
      for i := 1 to 10 do
         read (Current [i])
   end; {LoadOneName}
```

```
begin
   writeln ('How many 10-letter names will you enter?');
   readln (Number);
   writeln ('Enter your names, one per line.');
   for i := 1 to Number do begin
      LoadOneName (OneName);
      WholeList [i] := OneName;
      readln {go to the next line.}
   end; {we've read in the list of names.}
   writeln ('Enter the first and last numbers of the names you want.');
   readln (Start, Finish);
   for i := Start to Finish do
      writeln (WholeList[i])
end. {StoreNames}
```

Self-Check Questions

Q. Suppose that program *StoreNames* contained this procedure declaration:

```
procedure Initialize (var Entire: NameList; Specific: Name);
   var i: integer;
   begin
      for i := 1 to 100 do
         Entire [i] := Specific
   end; {Initialize}
```

Are any of these legal calls of *Initialize*? Why or why not?

a) *Initialize (WholeList, OneName)*;
b) *Initialize (OneName, WholeList)*;
c) *Initialize (WholeList* 'BLANKBLANK');
d) *Initialize (WholeList* 'XYZ');
e) *Initialize (WholeList, WholeList*[10]);

A. For a call of *Initialize* to be legal, the variable parameter *Entire* must have as an argument a variable of type *NameList*. The value parameter *Specific* has a weaker requirement—its argument need only be a value that could be assigned to *Specific*. Calls *a, c*, and *e* are legal (assuming that *OneName* and *WholeList*[10] have been initialized themselves). Call *b* is illegal because its arguments are reversed. Call *d* is illegal because the argument 'XYZ' has only three letters, rather than the required ten.

Antibugging and Debugging 4-3

THE VARIETY OF STATEMENTS INTRODUCED in Chapter 4 will, inevitably, be accompanied by a host of potential syntactic and semantic bugs. Let's begin by reviewing some of the rules associated with **for** statements.

As we pointed out in 4–1, it is an error to try to change the value of a **for** loop's counter variable from within the loop. This goes both for assignments, and for the use of *read* or *readln* with the counter variable as an argument. In effect, the counter variable is *read-only*; it may be inspected, but not modified.

counter variable bugs

For example, the **for** loop below attempts to print only odd numbers by 'secretly' incrementing *Counter* within the loop. The assignment is an error, though, because the counter variable can only be changed before or after the **for** statement.

```
for Counter := LowOdd to HighOdd do begin
   writeln (Counter);
   Counter := Counter + 1          {Invalid assignment}
end; {for}
```

Another sort of attempt at modifying **for** loops is simply ineffective. Since the expressions that are used to form the initial and final values of the **for** loop's counter variable are evaluated before the loop is entered, changes to variables that might form these expressions have no effect on the loop. For example, this segment:

```
Lower := 1;
Upper := 3;
for Counter := Lower to Upper do begin
   Lower := 0;
   Upper := 1000; {Has no effect on the counter variable.}
   writeln ('Hello.')
end; {for}
```

prints 'Hello' only three times, instead of one thousand and one times. The assignments made in the shaded segments are valid, but the initial and final values of the loop's counter variable have already been calculated and stored away. Consequently, the shaded statements serve no useful purpose.

compound bugs

Compound statements can cause problems for a while. Suppose you've written a program that refuses to compile. Although you're sure the program ends with an **end**, you keep getting a compile-time error message like:

```
"END" EXPECTED -- END OF PROGRAM NOT FOUND
```

> Make sure that every **begin** is matched with an **end**.

It's easy to inadvertently leave out an **end**, and cause an error that's hard for the compiler to pinpoint. As far as the compiler is concerned, the last **end** in the program is merely the closing bracket of some compound statement or subprogram written *within* the program.

comment **ends**

Most programmers use two methods to keep track of **ends**. First, *comment them*:

```
for Counter := 1 to Limit do begin
    ...
end; {Limit for}
```

The second technique is to indent, and make **ends** line up under the control statements they close. Of course, this trick only works as well as you let it. If 70 or 80 lines of program come between a **begin** and an **end**, lining up matching pairs is more of a job for a surveyor than a programmer.

length of subprograms

> A procedure, control statement, or compound statement that extends over more than a single screenful of code, or page of program listing, should be broken down into procedures.

Don't forget that the format used in typing a program has absolutely no effect on semantics. The general style of indenting we've used should be adhered to, because it simplifies the job of checking code. The two samples shown below are deliberately misleading. Their appearance says one thing, but their output tells a different story.

compound statement bugs

```
program ThreeCheers (input, output);

const HOWMANY = 3;

var Cheers: integer;

begin
   for Cheers := 1 to HOWMANY do
      writeln ('Hip hip, hooray!');         {This looks like a compound}
      writeln ('Congratulations.')          {statement, but it isn't.}
end. {ThreeCheers}
```

```
Hip hip, hooray!
Hip hip, hooray!
Hip hip, hooray!
Congratulations.
```

```
program Congratulations (input, output);
const HOWMANY = 3;
var Cheers: integer;
begin
   for Cheers := 1 to HOWMANY do begin
      writeln ('Hip hip, hooray!');         {This doesn't look like a}
   writeln ('Congratulations.')             {compound statement, but it is.}
   end
end. {Congratulations}
```

```
Hip, hip, hooray!
Congratulations.
Hip, hip, hooray!
Congratulations.
Hip, hip, hooray!
Congratulations.
```

Moral: Code is hard enough to read even *with* indenting. Don't make it unnecessarily difficult.

The purpose of a compound statement is to make two or more statements (including procedure calls) appear to be a single statement. Is this a legal compound statement?

```
begin
   begin
      begin
         writeln ('Hi.')
      end
   end
end;
```

Yes, even though it's nested. It's no more or less improper than the expression (((5)))+3 is. Even *this* is a legal compound statement, equivalent to the one above:

```
begin write ('H'); begin begin write ('i.') end; begin end; writeln end end;
```

empty statements

We can also try to clarify empty statements by taking them to excess.

```
begin
   begin ; ;
      begin ; ;
         writeln ('Hi again.') ; ;
      end ; ;
   end ; ;
end;
```

This is a perfectly legal compound statement, even though it's fairly bizarre. Since the semicolon has a syntactic meaning in Pascal, though, accidentally misplacing it within a **for** statement can cause a calamity. What's the matter with this **for** loop?

```
for Counter := 1 to 5 do ;
   DoSomething;
```

The statement is supposed to call procedure *DoSomething* five times. Unfortunately, the semicolon right after the **do** forms an empty statement. This empty statement happens (for lack of a better word) five times, and the procedure is only called once.

Defensive Programming

The procedures and functions we've started to employ can be used as antibugging tools in a variety of ways. To make programs easier to read and understand, subprograms should be commented extensively. Mark the start of each procedure or function declaration with a box that explains its purpose, as shown below.

```
(*  *   *   *   *   *   *   *   *   *   *   *   *   *
*                 PROCEDURE REALIGN                 *
*  REALIGN IMPLEMENTS THE HOSPITAL RULE             *
*  LIMIT REALIGNMENT ALGORITHM.  PARAMETERS         *
*  AFFECTED ARE:                                    *
*       DELTA, EPSILON:  INITIALIZED;               *
*       PERMEABILITY:  UPDATED;                     *
*  FUNCTION AUDIT (SEE ABOVE) IS ALSO CALLED.       *
*   *   *   *   *   *   *   *   *   *   *   *   *  *)
```

Professionally produced code is usually commented like this. In addition to clarifying the action of each subprogram, comment boxes make individual procedures or functions easy to locate in a long program listing. In fact, you'll probably find that merely putting a few blank lines between each subprogram makes your code more understandable.

precommenting

When a program is long and has many procedures it's a good idea to *precomment* them at the beginning of the program. Describe the program's action in terms of its procedure calls.

```
(*  *   *   *   *   *   *   *   *   *   *   *   *   *
*                 PROGRAM SCRAMBLER                 *
*  THIS PROGRAM CAN BE USED TO ENCODE OR            *
*  DECODE DOCUMENTS OR COMMUNICATIONS.  IT          *
*  CALLS PROCEDURES:                                *
*       INSTRUCTIONS                                *
*       CHOOSEOPTION                                *
*       ENTERCODEKEY                                *
*       ENCODE, DECODE  (ONE OPTION)                *
*       PRINTRESULTS                                *
*  ALL PROCEDURES ARE DESCRIBED BELOW.              *
*   *   *   *   *   *   *   *   *   *   *   *   *  *)
```

program history

In larger programs, the first page of comments may be as far as the reader gets. An outline like the one below contains all relevant information about the program and its history.

```
(*  *   *   *   *   *   *   *   *   *   *   *   *
*            PROGRAM NAME                          *
*            AUTHOR(S)                             *
*            DATES OF MODIFICATIONS                *
*            PURPOSE OF PROGRAM                    *
*            DESCRIPTION OF ALGORITHM              *
*            LIST OF PROCEDURES                    *
*            IMPLEMENTATION NOTES                  *
*   *   *   *   *   *   *   *   *   *   *   *   *)
```

Procedures are useful when it comes to debugging. A particularly handy application is a *snapshot* procedure that prints the current value of all program variables. Why would anybody want such a procedure?

> The Golden Rule of Debugging
>
> When you're sure that everything you're doing is right, and your program *still* doesn't work, one of the things you're sure of is wrong.

snapshot procedures

Frequently, a variable whose value you're certain of actually represents another value entirely. This holds true for experienced programmers as well as novices. Snapshot procedures should be used at the first sign of trouble; experienced programmers often build them into programs as a matter of course. Calls for snapshots can be spread liberally around a program during testing, and then turned into comments or edited out when the program is operational. For example, this sequence of procedure calls:

```
GetInputValues (A, B, C, D, E);
PrintAllValues (A, B, C, D, E);
ProcessData (B, C, E);
PrintAllValues (A, B, C, D, E);
PrepareOutput (A, B, D);
PrintAllValues (A, B, C, D, E);
```

is quickly modified when the program works:

```
GetInputValues (A, B, C, D, E);
{ PrintAllValues (A, B, C, D, E); }
ProcessData (B, C, E);
{ PrintAllValues (A, B, C, D, E); }
PrepareOutput (A, B, D);
{ PrintAllValues (A, B, C, D, E); }
```

> Programming in a manner that helps prevent errors is called *defensive programming*.

Some of Pascal's best features are partly intended to help us program defensively. Procedures and functions are useful in this regard because they let us write modular programs.

> A program is modular if it can be divided into components that are relatively independent of each other, and of the main program.

It's not hard to see that a procedure or function, with inputs and outputs specified in its parameter list, fits the implied definition of a program module.

program modularity

Modularity is an important asset when it comes to antibugging and debugging. Programs that can be dealt with one module at a time are easier to read, write, and understand than programs that consist of one long statement part. For the small effort of writing a test program driver, a procedure or function module can be written and tested by itself. When the subprogram works, it can be plugged into the main program.

As you might imagine, modular programs are also a lot simpler to fix, since a faulty module can be replaced without a lot of program rewriting. In fact, a module from an entirely different program can be inserted if its 'connections' to the calling program—its list of parameters—match up.

A final point about subprogram modularity is that it is spoiled by referring to a global variable from within a procedure or function. A side-effect, or direct assignment to a global variable from a subprogram, is as incongruous and unsettling as a nail protruding from the bottom of an iron might be, so *don't do it*. If a global variable's value is to be changed, declare and use a variable parameter.

Pascal Summary

- **for** statement: a loop that repeats an action a predetermined number of times:

  for *counter variable* := *initial value* **to** (*or* **downto**) *final value* **do**
  action;

- compound statement: a sequence of statements, between a **begin** and **end**, that are treated as a single action:

```
begin
   statement;
      ...
   statement
end;
```

- empty statement: a non-action, shown with a semicolon.

Important Facts

• A **for** loop's counter variable, initial value, and final value must all have the same Pascal type.

• The counter variable must be locally declared.

• The expressions that give the counter variable's initial and final values are evaluated when the loop is first entered. Changing them won't change the number of times the loop iterates.

• It's an error to try to make an assignment to the counter variable within the loop.

• The counter variable is undefined when the loop is exited.

• Pseudocode is a Pascal-like English, used for outlining and refining programs. Programs should always be planned and designed in pseudocode before being coded in Pascal.

• A modular subprogram accomplishes one specific program task, and communicates with the main program through parameters.

• Procedures and functions should be commented clearly. These comment boxes are the parts of your program most likely to be read.

• A snapshot procedure prints the values of program variables, and can be 'commented out' after debugging. It's one form of defensive program.

• The Golden Rule of Debugging: When you're sure that everything you're doing is right, and your program *still* doesn't work, one of the things you're sure of is wrong.

Self-test Exercises

4-1 How many statements will a loop that goes from 1 **to** 1 execute? A loop that goes from 1 **to** 0?

4-2 What's the output of this code?

```
Limit := 10;
for Counter := 1 to Limit do begin
    write (Counter+Limit:3);
    Limit := 5
end;
writeln;
```

4-3 Write a **for** statement that prints the even numbers between 1 and 25.

4-4 What Pascal type can't the counter variable of a **for** statement be?

4-5 What is the value of *Count* after this code is executed?

```
for Count := 10 downto 2 do
    writeln (Count);
```

4-6 Write code that prints the first letter of the first line of input, the second letter of the second line, etc. Stop on the *Last* character of line *Last*.

4-7 How many 'Hubba's do each of these print?

```
for Rub := 1 to 3 do
    for Dub := 1 to 3 do
        for Tub := 1 to 3 do
            writeln ('Hubba');
```

```
for Sub := 1 to 3 do
    for Pub := 1 to 3 do
        for Lub := Sub to Pub do
            writeln ('Hubba');
```

4-8 Write a procedure that reads ten numbers, and prints the difference between successive pairs. Thus, only nine numbers are printed.

4-9 Write a procedure that averages a series of numbers. The length of the series should be passed as a value parameter, and the average value should be returned as a variable parameter.

4-10 What is a snapshot procedure? What is its purpose?

More Exercises

4-10 Write a program to print every even number from 0 to 100. Every other letter from 'A' to 'Z'. Every fifth number from 0 to 100. Every sixth number from 2 to 110. Every third letter, starting with 'C'. Every fourth character in your computer's character set (better find out how many characters there are).

4-11 The cost of operating a small Beverly Hills bumper gold-plating company can be given by this formula:

$$Cost = Units^3 - 7\ Units^2 + \$432$$

where *Units* stands for the number of bumpers that are gold-plated each day. How many bumpers should be produced each day to minimize operating costs? The number is smaller than twenty.

4-12 Write a program to print a temperature conversion table. Calculate and print the Fahrenheit equivalents of all Celsius temperatures *at 10 degree intervals* from 0° to 250°. The conversion formula is:

$$C = 5/9\ (F-32)$$

4-13 List the integers from 1 to 20, their squares, square roots, cubes, and fourth roots, all in a five column table. There are a number of ways to write this program; implement one, and describe another.

4-14 Write a program to produce a table of factorials. Prompt the user for the upper limit of the table, i.e. how many numbers it should contain. Can you write the program to *a*) work from 1 factorial up, *b*) compute and print from the upper limit down, *c*) do only one additional multiplication for each additional factorial figured?

Write another program to produce a table of factorials. This time, however, ask the user for the upper *and* lower limits of the table. Only print the factorials of numbers within (and including) these limits.

4-15 The square of the sum of any series of numbers starting with 1 is equal to the sum of the cubes of each individual number. Prove that this is true for the sums of the series 1 ... 10 through 1 ... 20.

4-16 Here's the mechanism of a number-guessing game. Write it as a program. Begin by giving the computer a number between 2 and 9, and a number that contains that many digits. The longer number, however, may not contain any zeros, nor may any two of its digits be the same (e.g. 3, 927, and 7, 4729135 are valid pairs).

Now the fun begins. Take the leftmost digit of the large number, double it, add 1, and multiply by 5. Add the result to the next number to the right. Double this sum, add 1, and again multiply by 5. Continue this process until you reach the rightmost digit. From this final number subtract a number with the following properties: it is as many digits long as the original large number, and it consists only of fives. Divide the result by 10. Does it look familiar? Why does the process do what it does?

4-17 A series is called *geometric* if each value in it (called a *term*) is the product of a particular number (called the *common ratio*) and the preceding term. For example, the sequence: ¼, 1, 4 is geometric, with a common ratio of 4. The next number in the series will be 16—the last term times the common ratio. Naturally, the common ratio can be found by dividing any term by the term before it.

Write a program that will find the *n*th term of a geometric series. The program user should have the options of entering *a*) the first two terms; *b*) the first term and the common ratio; *c*) any two consecutive terms and one either term's position; *d*) any single term, its position, and the common ratio. Naturally, the user must also enter a value for *n*. (Bonus: let the user ask for a term whose position is *less* than that of the given term or terms.)

4-18 It's time to compute final grades. Write a program that reads in 10 sets of 6 grades and computes *weighted* averages as follows: The first and second grades count for 10% each, the midterm for 25%, the next assignment for 20%, the next for only 5%, and the final exam for 30%. Print each grade, the weighted average for each student, and the average for the entire class.

4-19 A Fibonacci series can actually begin with *any* two numbers—the important rule is that each subsequent number must be the sum of the two prior numbers. Thus 10, 11, 21, 32, 53 is the beginning of a perfectly valid sequence.

Write a program that computes the first ten members of any Fibonacci series. Use it to verify the following conjecture: The sum of the first ten members of a Fibonacci series is 11 times the value of the seventh element of the sequence. Can you turn this into a magical feat of lightning mental calculation?

4-20 Many computer systems, particularly interactive ones, operate on a *timesharing* basis. The computer distributes its time among many users, allotting each one a fraction of a second to use the entire computer. Because most computer jobs are completed very quickly, a user on a lightly loaded system has the illusion of having the computer all to herself. However, when the computer is given long jobs the distribution system begins to break down. The computer can only finish part of a job in its apportioned time, and must return (possibly many times) to complete it entirely. This, unfortunately, creates the illusion of *many* users on the computer.

Ricki Gould is a not very bright systems programmer who has come up with a plan to discourage submission of long programming jobs. She penalizes long jobs by progressively reducing the amount of time the computer spend working on them. The reduction is 10% per 'return;' thus, if the first time allotment is one second, the second will be only .9 seconds, and the third only .81 seconds.

Write a program that computes and graphs the amount of time the computer will spend on a program that takes from 1 to 500 'visits' to run. Assume that the first visit is one second. What is the problem with Ricki's plan?

4-21 Write a procedure that computes *a* to the *b* power (using a **for** loop), and *b* to the $1/a$ power (by formula). A call of this procedure should look like this:

FigurePowers (*Inside, Outside, InsideToTheOutside, OutsideInverseInside*);

Inside, Outside, and *InsideToTheOutside* are all of type *integer*, while *OutsideInverseInside* is *real*.

4-22 Another way of finding the *n*th term of a geometric sequence like a_1, $a_2 \ldots a_n$ (as discussed in an earlier problem) involves using the formula:

$$a_n = a_1 \text{ times } (Common\ Ratio)^{n-1}$$

In words, we've said that the *n*th term equals the first term times the common ratio raised to the $n-1$ power.

Write a procedure that finds the *n*th term of a geometric sequence. It should be passed the values of the first term and the common ratio, and return the value of the *n*th term.

4-23 Monica Marin makes $10,000 per year at her part-time job. Her boss, who has a sadistic mind, offers Monica one of the following raises: either a ten percent increase every year, with a thousand-dollar bonus right away, or an increase of one-twelfth of ten percent each month and no bonus.

Monica decides that the offer she should take depends on how long she plans on continuing at her job. Write a program that shows how much she can expect from each offer for each of the next twenty years.

4-24 The charm below was formed from an ancient magic word. Write a program that contains a procedure to draw a symbol from a word (of up to fifteen letters) provided by the user, and another procedure that computes the number of paths the magic word can be read by, starting from the top of the charm.

```
          A
         B B
        R R R
       A A A A
      C C C C C
     A A A A A A
    D D D D D D D
   A A A A A A A A
  B B B B B B B B B
 R R R R R R R R R R
A A A A A A A A A A A
```

4-25 Add a statement that allows iteration to your personal computer language. Try requiring your equivalent of a **for** to have a matching **end** at the end of the statement. What bugs will this help prevent?

'brute force implies that we repeat an unsophisticated solution step many, many times…'

5

Making Choices: the **case** Statement

Have you ever used an automatic bank teller machine? After inserting your bank card and punching in a secret code, you have a choice of transactions—deposit, withdraw, check balances, transfer funds, etc. When you hit the appropriate button, the machine asks for more details, and moves along with the transaction. If you're withdrawing money, it eventually counts out the correct number of bills.

If you've ever gone through this sequence you've run an interactive computer program. The bank card and code number let you 'log on' to the bank's computer, and the buttons you push belong to a highly specialized keyboard. And no matter what language the bank's computer is programmed in, it uses control statements similar to Pascal's.

Pascal's **case** statement is the topic of section 5-1. It gives a program the power to choose between alternatives. An automatic teller program would use a **case** statement to decide which procedures—deposit, withdraw, balance, or transfer—to call. The **case** statement lets a single program do a variety of different jobs.

In section 5-2 we'll shift gears considerably, and take a break from details of Pascal coding. We'll begin to consider comparisons—but not of Pascal programs. Instead, we'll learn some measures of the algorithms that programs are based on. First, we'll learn how to estimate the *running time* of programs through an analysis of their algorithms. Run-time analysis gives us an idea of the relative *efficiency* of a particular approach. Then, we'll see why a problem-solving strategy called *brute force* can be desirable even though it may lead to algorithms that are not efficient at all.

The anti- and debugging section, 5-3, contains some advice about using top-down design to help avoid bugs. The techniques we suggest—structured walkthroughs and stub programs—will be increasingly useful as your programs get longer and more involved.

The **case** Statement 5-1

WHY BREAK A TRADITION? PROGRAM *ElectionDetection*, below, uses a **case** statement to take an action that depends on the value of *Year*. Although the program contains four potential output statements (shaded), only one is executed.

case demonstration program

```
program ElectionDetection (input, output);
   {Determines how close an election year is.}
var Year: integer;
begin
   writeln ('What year is this?');
   readln (Year);
   case (Year mod 4) of
      0: writeln ('This is an election year.');
      1: writeln ('Last year was an election year.');
      2: writeln ('The election was two years ago.');
      3: writeln ('The election will be next year.')
   end {the case statement}
end. {ElectionDetection}
```

```
What year is this?
1987
The election will be next year.
```

The first line of the **case** statement contains an ordinal-valued *case expression*.* Then comes a list of the **case** expression's potential values (called the *case constant list*), and the proper action to take for each one. The reserved word **end** completes the statement. It isn't preceded by a semicolon.

Its syntax chart looks like this:

case statement

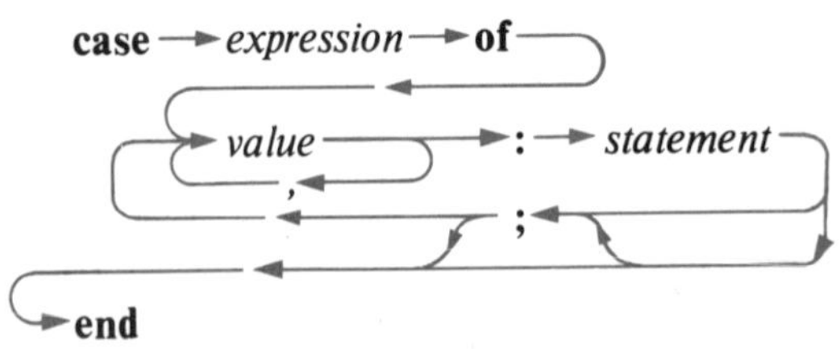

* To refresh your memory, an ordinal value is a value of any simple type except *real*.

case expression

The **case** expression is frequently just a variable identifier. In *ElectionDetection*, though, *Year* **mod** 4 is the **case** expression. The values given in the constant list must be of the same Pascal type as the **case** expression. Incidentally, in this context the word *constant* means that actual values (like 4 or 'D') must be given. Expressions that represent values can't appear in the **case** constant list.

case constants

Sometimes, the same action may be initiated by two or more possible values of the **case** expression. In this situation, the constants are separated with commas:

```
case Score of
    10: writeln ('Exceptionally Good');
    8, 9: writeln ('Good');
    5, 6, 7: writeln ('Barely Passing');
    3, 4: writeln ('Flunking');
    0, 1, 2: writeln ('Exceptionally Flunking')
end;
```

As long as no constant calls for two different actions (that would be illegal), the order in which values are specified is irrelevant. This **case** statement is semantically identical to the one above—it has the exact same effect:

```
case Score of
    7, 6: writeln ('Barely Passing');
    3, 4: writeln ('Flunking');
    10: writeln ('Exceptionally Good');
    2, 0, 1: writeln ('Exceptionally Flunking');
    8, 9: writeln ('Good');
    5: writeln ('Barely Passing')
end;
```

give all values

The Golden Rule of case Constant Lists

Every potential value of the **case** expression must be specified in the **case** constant list. It's an error for the **case** expression to represent a value that is not given.

Consequently, it's important to be very precise when prompting for a value that serves as a **case** expression. (You may want to check the quick discussion of sets in 6-2 to find ways of avoiding this error. It's easy to follow.)

empty statements

When some value of the **case** expression doesn't really require an action, the empty statement comes to the rescue. For example, procedure *ConsiderReadings*, below, delivers a message for most, but not all, of the possible values of *Reading*. If *Reading* has a value of 4, 5, 6, or 7, an empty statement is executed—nothing happens.

using an empty statement

```
procedure ConsiderReadings (Reading: integer);
   {Demonstrates use of the empty statement.}
   begin
      case Reading of
         0: writeln ('Instrument test cancelled.');
         1, 2, 3: writeln ('Check controls--reading too low.');
         4, 5, 6, 7: ;
         8, 9, 10: writeln ('Check gauge--reading too high.')
      end {case}
   end; {ConsiderReadings}
```

Naturally, the actions associated with the **case** constant list can be any of Pascal's statements. Here's a model case statement that includes one of everything we know about so far.

model **case** statement

```
case expression of
   const1: Late := Early; {assignment statement}
   const2: DoItToIt; {procedure call}
   const3, const4, const5:  ; {empty statement}
   const6: begin
              statement; {compound statement}
              statement
           end;
   const7: for Count := Lo to Hi  do begin
              statement; {control statement}
              statement
           end {for}
end; {of the case statement}
```

We feel compelled to apologize for the stilted reserved words Wirth used for the **case** statement. A more natural effect might have been achieved with, say:

```
when expression equals        {This isn't legal Pascal.}
   value1 do action;
   value2 do action;    etc.
```

Wirth used the reserved words **case** and **of** because they're traditional in programming languages. When you become *PFC*'s (Programmers First Class), and design your *own* programming languages....

Self-Check Questions

Q. Which of these values could be used in a **case** statement's constant list?

a) *Time*	*b*) *Year* **div** 4	*c*) 5+2
d) *ord*('H')	*e*) 'B'	*f*) *B*
g) 9	*h*) −4	*i*) *true*

A. The *integer* values 9 and −4 are valid, as is the *char* value 'B'. Answer *i*, *true*, is a *boolean* value, and may also be used. The remaining values—*Time, B, ord*('H'), *Year* **div** 4, and 5+2—are identifiers or expressions, and may not be used.

Focus on Programming: Nested **case** Statements

The **case** statement is used whenever several alternative actions are possible. But what if one choice depends on another? Let's write a program that scores the children's game of *Scissors, Rock, Paper*. Two *char* inputs will represent the two players. There are only three rules—Scissors cut Paper, Rock crushes Scissors, and Paper covers Rock. Our pseudocode shows why we have to make choices in sequence:

refinement

get the input;
depending on what the first player has
   decide if the second player wins or loses;

First we have to check the first player's value to see which rule to follow. Then, we can issue a ruling depending on the second player's choice.

Program *Scissors*, below, implements our pseudocode. The actions associated with the three possible *FirstPlayer* values 'S', 'R', and 'P' are intentionally written in three different ways, to show different styles of using compound statements and nested control statements.

scissors game program

```
program Scissors (input, output);
   {Demonstrates nested case statements.}
var FirstPlayer, SecondPlayer: char;
begin
   writeln ('Enter plays for two players--S, R, or P.');
   readln (FirstPlayer, SecondPlayer);
   case FirstPlayer of
      'S': case SecondPlayer of
              'S': writeln ('Scissors tie scissors.');
              'R': writeln ('Scissors are crushed by rock.');
              'P': writeln ('Scissors cut paper.')
           end; {inner case}
      'R': begin
              writeln ('Rock ties rock. ');
              case SecondPlayer of
                 'S': writeln ('But rock crushes scissors.');
                 'R': writeln ;
                 'P': writeln ('But rock is wrapped by paper.')
              end {inner case}
           end; {compound statement}
      'P': begin
              write ('Paper ');
              case SecondPlayer of
                 'S': write ('is cut by scissors.');
                 'R': write ('wraps the rock.');
                 'P': write ('ties paper.')
              end; {inner case}
              writeln
           end {compound statement}
   end {outer case}
end. {Scissors}
```

↓ ↓ ↓ ↓ ↓

```
Enter plays for two players--S, R, or P.
PR
Paper wraps the rock.
```

Self-Check Questions

Q. What outputs will this data produce from *Scissors*?

a) **SS** *b*) **RR** *c*) **RS** *d*) **R P**

A. *a*) Scissors tie scissors.
b) Rock ties rock.
{blank line}
c) Rock ties rock.
But rock crushes scissors.
d) Note the space between **R** and **P**. Since the space is read as a *char* value, a run-time error occurs. The program has no output.

Sophisticated **case** Programming

A considerable amount of effort is expended on writing programs that analyze input in one form or another. Let's develop an interesting example that relies on the **case** statement:

problem: odd/even counting

> Write a program that will determine how many odd, even, and zero digits there are in a sequence of input numbers. Don't bother to count spaces or commas. There are 50 characters in all.

Clearly this will require a loop—we have to look at characters again and again. In pseudocode, we have:

first refinement

```
for the correct number of times
    get an input value;
    count it properly;
print the results;
```

To *count it properly*, we'll pseudocode a **case** statement:

second refinement

```
case Current of
    a zero:  add to the zero count;
    an odd number:  add to the odd count;
    an even number:  add to the even count;
    a space or comma:  ignore it;
```

Program *CountDigits*, below, solves our problem. It's designed for data file use. Note the use of value and variable parameters in the declaration of procedure *StoreCount*—you should review Chapter 3 if they cause you any trouble.

```
program CountDigits (input, output);
    {Count odd, even, and zero digits in input.}
const NUMBERINLIST = 50;
var ListCounter, Evens, Odds, Zeros: integer;
    Current: char;
procedure StoreCount (ThisChar: char;
                      var Ecount, Ocount, Zcount: integer);
    {Increments the proper total.}
    begin
        case ThisChar of
            ',', ' ': ;            {ignore these}
            '2', '4', '6', '8': Ecount := Ecount+1;
            '1', '3', '5', '7', '9': Ocount := Ocount+1;
            '0': Zcount := Zcount+1
        end {case}
    end; {StoreCount}
begin
    Evens := 0;
    Odds := 0;          {Initialize the 'total' variables}
    Zeros := 0;
    for ListCounter := 1 to NUMBERINLIST do begin
        read (Current);
        StoreCount (Current, Evens, Odds, Zeros)
    end; {for}
    write ('There are ', Zeros:1, ' zeros, ', Odds:1, ' odd ');
    writeln ('numbers, and ', Evens:1, ' even numbers.')
end. {CountDigits}
```

odd/even counting program

2,597 18 528 637 9,083,002 6 47,100 319 10 590,093

```
There are 8 zeros, 19 odd numbers, and 9 even numbers.
```

We will see the same technique reappear in our next problem—writing a program that counts internally generated numbers:

problem: testing 'random' functions

Write a random number generator. Test its operation with a driver program.

Where do random numbers come from? Before computers were widely available, the most common sources were large tables. The ultimate version was probably a book published by the Rand Corporation that contained one million randomly distributed digits. (In a random distribution, there is an equal likelihood that any given integer will be 0, 1, 2 . . . 9.)

Nowadays, programming a computer to produce random numbers is elementary. Indeed, many Pascal implementations will have predefined

er
ɔn

random functions (but you should copy ours if you want your programs to be Standard Pascal). One common algorithm is to pick a starting number (called the *seed*), then subject it to this sequence of mathematical operations:

Seed := ((*MULTIPLIER* * *Seed*)+*INCREMENT*) **mod** *MODULUS*;

the seed

(All the identifiers on the right-hand side of the assignment, besides *Seed*, are *integer* constants, given below.) The assignment gives *Seed* a value that satisfies the relation:

$0 \leqslant Seed < MODULUS$

If we divide by *MODULUS* (using the *real* division operator), we'll have a value such that:

$0 \leqslant Seed < 1$

pseudo-random sequences

Repeating the assignment and extra division produces a *pseudo-random* sequence of numbers. Although the numbers are randomly distributed, it is possible to predict what the series will be. Furthermore, the sequence will eventually repeat itself.

```
function Random (var Seed: integer): real;
   {Generates a pseudo-random number such that 0<=Random<1.}
   const MODULUS = 65536;         {These are 'magic' numbers}
         MULTIPLIER = 25173;      {that produce a pseudo-random}
         INCREMENT = 13849;       {sequence of numbers.}
   begin
      Seed := ((MULTIPLIER*Seed)+INCREMENT) mod MODULUS;
            {Pick an integer from 0 through MODULUS-1}
      Random := Seed/MODULUS
            {Adjust it to fall between (or including) 0, and 1.}
   end; {Random}
```

We wrote *Random* as a function because it's usually called as part of an expression, rather than as a statement. However, *Random* is one of the rare functions that requires a variable parameter. To use *Random* in a program, declare a global *integer* variable *Seed*, and initialize it before the first call of *Random*. Because *Seed* is changed by each call of *Random*, it must be passed as a variable parameter.

Now, any initial value of *Seed* generates a particular sequence of numbers. As a result, if *Seed* is initialized to the same number every time a program that contains *Random* is run, the program will always work with the same random series. This is a lifesaver during debugging, because you know what numbers to expect. However, a game program isn't much fun if its random elements are the same each time you play.

Programmers usually solve this problem by using a nonstandard function that returns a constantly changing *integer* (or a *real* value that can be rounded or truncated). For example, most Pascal implementations have a function that represents the current time of day. Although the inclusion of such a function makes a program nonstandard (because it isn't Standard Pascal), it's sometimes the only solution.

initializing the seed

Can we test *Random* as easily as we tested function *tan*, back in Chapter 3? No. Although we might write a driver that prints the first ten or twenty numbers in the pseudo-random sequence it produces, such a small sample won't do us too much good. It's also easy enough to call the function a few thousand times:

```
for Count := 1 to 10000 do
    writeln (Random(Seed));
```

problems with testing

But how useful would this segment's output be? Nobody can inspect a list of ten thousand twenty-two digit *real* numbers and declare that they're randomly distributed.

Why don't we modify the function call to produce a number in some reasonable *integer* range, say 1 through 10? Since *Random's* output currently falls between 0.000... and 0.999... we can multiply by 10 and truncate (to get a number in the range 0 through 9), then add 1 to the result. We can use a **case** statement and ordinary variables to keep track of the loop's output.*

TestRandom's well-labeled output assures us that our function, as well as our method for generating a number within a particular range, both work reasonably well. Had we managed to generate a number outside the range 1 through 10, the **case** statement would have caused a run-time error and crash. The completed program is shown below.

random function testing program

```
program TestRandom (input, output);
    {Checks the distribution of the Random function's output.}

const NUMBEROFTRIALS = 10000;

var One, Two, Three, Four, Five, Six, Seven, Eight, Nine, Ten,
                    Counter, Seed: integer;

function Random (var Seed: integer): real;
    {Generates a pseudo-random number such that 0<=Random<1.}

    const MODULUS = 65536;
          MULTIPLIER = 25173;
          INCREMENT = 13849;

    begin
        Seed := ((MULTIPLIER*Seed)+INCREMENT) mod MODULUS;
        Random := Seed/MODULUS
    end; {Random}
```

* In Chapter 11 we'll see that using **array** type variables would be even more suitable.

```
begin
   One := 0;  Two := 0;  Three := 0;
   Four := 0;  Five := 0;  Six := 0;
   Seven := 0;  Eight := 0;  Nine := 0;
   Ten := 0;
   writeln ('Please enter a seed.');
   readln (Seed);
   writeln ('Distribution of ', NUMBEROFTRIALS:1,' trials of Random:');
   for Counter := 1 to NUMBEROFTRIALS do begin
      case (1+trunc(10*Random(Seed))) of
         1: One:=One+1;  2: Two:=Two+1;  3: Three:=Three+1;
         4: Four:=Four+1;  5: Five:=Five+1;  6: Six:=Six+1;
         7: Seven:=Seven+1;  8: Eight:=Eight+1;  9: Nine:=Nine+1;
         10: Ten:=Ten+1
      end {case}
   end; {for}
   writeln ('1''s':5, '2''s':5, '3''s':5, '4''s':5, '5''s':5,
            '6''s':5, '7''s':5, '8''s':5, '9''s':5, '10''s':5);
   writeln (One:5, Two:5, Three:5, Four:5, Five:5,
            Six:5, Seven:5, Eight:5, Nine:5, Ten:5)
end. {TestRandom}
```

```
Please enter a seed.
471
Distribution of 10000 trials of Random:
  1's  2's  3's  4's  5's  6's  7's  8's  9's 10's
 1022 1057 1018 1015  991 1014  978 1007  917  981
```

Self-Check Questions

Q. Can you find a bug in this program segment? Assume we're using the *Random* function defined above.

```
WildCard := Random(Seed);
writeln ('The number we picked was', Random(Seed));
```

A. A programmer who expects this segment to print the value of *WildCard* will be disappointed. The second call of *Random*(*Seed*) represents an entirely different number. The segment should have been written as:

```
WildCard := Random(Seed);
writeln ('The number we picked was', WildCard);
```

Harder Combinations

Let's continue with the development of programs that involve nested statements. Our problem will be:

problem: graphing data

Write a program that makes a bar graph of this data:

	England	*France*	*Japan*
1985	26	41	33
1986	34	44	26
1987	44	49	20
1988	48	49	17
1989	51	51	5

Frisbee Production
(*in ten thousand frisbee lots*)

Using computers to present information in a more understandable or dramatic manner is a very common application. Now, a program's output gives no indication of the work that went into producing it. As far as many program users are concerned, the output *is* the program.

label output

> Label program output, and present it in a clear, readable manner. Don't force a program user to read a program's code to understand its results.

A first refinement of the problem doesn't cause any trouble. We're just massaging it into a more Pascal-like form.

```
for each year from 1985 to 1989
    draw three bars of the correct length, using different symbols;
```

The outline of a program falls into our lap.

first refinement

```
for each year from 1985 to 1989
    draw the three bars;
    label the year;
```

And what does 'draw the three bars' turn out to be? We take another step, and change only that sentence.

second refinement

```
for each year from 1985 to 1989
    for each of the three countries
        draw a single bar of the correct length, using the correct symbol;
    label the output;
```

Another refinement gives us the rough outline of a program.

third refinement

```
for Year := 1985 to 1989
    for each country's symbol
        DrawBar (Production, Symbol);
    writeln (Year);
```

The *for each country's symbol* part of the last refinement is going to cause some problems. We'll have to perform some sleight of hand to make the **for** loop count by symbols. The program segment below shows a common programming trick that gets us out of our bind.

```
for SymbolCounter := 1 to 3 do begin
   read (Production);
   case SymbolCounter of
      1: DrawBar (Production, '#');
      2: DrawBar (Production, '$');
      3: DrawBar (Production, '%')
   end {case}
end; {for}
```

Since we couldn't count by symbols, we counted by numbers, and made it have the proper effect. Such a trick is called a *kludge* (klooj). A kludge is the programming equivalent of jury-rigging. It's a quick and dirty solution that often works cleverly and well.

kludges

It's interesting, incidentally, to think about why our kludge is clever. It combines the *counting* of a **for** statement, and the *selection* of a **case** to form a 'new' control statement. The merger of disparate abilities can be powerful, but is often difficult to invent because we tend to see certain tools in their most ordinary roles. A quick mental exercise demonstrates the way people tend to automatically classify knowledge along familiar lines.

> Think about animals for a bit. Can you name five small animals? Five furry ones? Five ferocious ones? What other categories might you come up with?
>
> Now think about cities. Can you list five hot cities? Five large cities? Five cities with sea-harbors? Again, try to think of some other categories.
>
> Now comes the test. *Name five cities whose names are the names of animals.* This one isn't so easy—there doesn't seem to be a city/animal intersection in the mind.

The moral, applied to programming, is this:

> Although it's useful to understand and categorize statements by *application*, or specific examples of their use, thinking about them in terms of *attribute*—the abstract features that distinguish one statement from the next—can lead to new and unexpected combinations.

The completed program, along with its output, is shown below. Note our use of constants to make the kludge a little cleaner.

bar graphing program

```
program GraphMaker (input, output);
   {Prints a bar graph.  Data file oriented.}
const ENGLAND = 1;
      FRANCE = 2;
      JAPAN = 3;
var Year, SymbolCounter, Production: integer;
procedure DrawBar (Length: integer; BarCharacter: char);
   {Draws a Length-long sequence of BarCharacter.}
   var Counter: integer;
   begin
      for Counter := 1 to Length do
         write (BarCharacter);
      writeln
   end; {DrawBar}
begin
   for Year := 1985 to 1989 do begin
      for SymbolCounter := ENGLAND to JAPAN do begin
         read (Production);
         case SymbolCounter of
            ENGLAND: DrawBar (Production, '#');
            FRANCE: DrawBar (Production, '$');
            JAPAN: DrawBar (Production, '%')
         end {case}
      end; {SymbolCounter for}
      writeln (Year)
   end; {Year for}
   writeln;
   writeln ('Key to symbols:  #=England  $=France  %=Japan')
end. {GraphMaker}
```

↓ ↓ ↓ ↓ ↓

```
26 41 33
34 44 26
44 49 20
48 49 17
51 51 5
```

```
##########################
$$$$$$$$$$$$$$$$$$$$$$$$$$$$$$$$$$$$$$$$$
%%%%%%%%%%%%%%%%%%%%%%%%%%%%%%%%%
        1985
##################################
$$$$$$$$$$$$$$$$$$$$$$$$$$$$$$$$$$$$$$$$$$$$
%%%%%%%%%%%%%%%%%%%%%%%%%%
        1986
```

```
############################################
$$$$$$$$$$$$$$$$$$$$$$$$$$$$$$$$$$$$$$$$$$$$$$$$$
%%%%%%%%%%%%%%%%%%%%
       1987
################################################
$$$$$$$$$$$$$$$$$$$$$$$$$$$$$$$$$$$$$$$$$$$$$$$$$
%%%%%%%%%%%%%%%%%
       1988
###################################################
$$$$$$$$$$$$$$$$$$$$$$$$$$$$$$$$$$$$$$$$$$$$$$$$$$$
%%%%%
       1989

Key to symbols:  #=England  $=France  %=Japan
```

Let's continue using the techniques of pseudocoding and stepwise refinement to solve our final, and most difficult, problem.

problem: finding embedded words

The word *therein* is interesting because at least eleven words can be 'cut' from it, without rearranging any letters. Find them.

A little bit of massage is in order here. Suppose that we start with the first letter and print it, then print the first two, then the first three, etc. We can easily pick out the real words—*the, there*, and *therein.*

t th the ther there therei therein

Unfortunately, this is only a partial solution. We have to print the words that start with the second letter, *h*, as well.

h he her here herei herein

More words—*he, her*, etc.—spring to view. Obviously, if we repeat the process and print all the words that begin with the third letter, then the fourth letter, and so on, we'll have printed every possible word. But can we do this by computer? Using pseudocode, we can describe our algorithm as:

first refinement

for *each letter in 'therein'*
    print the subwords that begin with that letter;

So far, so good—but we need plenty of additional refinement to turn our pseudocode into Pascal. The repeated action of our pseudocode must be broken into two stages—generate a subword, then print it.

second refinement

for *each letter in 'therein'*
    for *every subword that begins with that letter*
        print that word;

A programmable algorithm is beginning to take shape. Adding a refinement of *print that word* helps even more.

third refinement

for *each letter in 'therein'*
    for *every subword that begins with that letter*
        for *the subword's first through last letters*
            print that letter;

The innermost step is practically written in Pascal. Let's imagine that the letters of *therein* are numbered 1 through 7. A **case** statement (used in a manner reminiscent of the kludge from program *GraphMaker*) will serve to print the letter that corresponds to a particular number.

trying a kludge

```
procedure Print (LetterNumber: integer);
   begin
      case LetterNumber of
         1: write ('t');
         2: write ('h');
         3, 5: write ('e');
         4: write ('r');
         6: write ('i');
         7: write ('n')
      end
   end; {Print}
```

We can imagine a paper demonstration of *Print* with *First* equal to 1, and *Last* set to 7:

testing it

```
for LetterNumber := First to Last do
   Print (LetterNumber);
writeln;
```

```
therein
```

Now that we can print a word, we have to figure out a method of generating subwords. Let's look at the subwords of *therein*, and label each word's last letter:

1	2	3	4	5	6	7
t	*th*	*the*	*ther*	*there*	*therei*	*therein*

Instead of fixing *Last* at 7 (as we did in our paper demonstration) we should let it range from the word's first letter through its seventh. Trace through this code by hand to make sure it works.

a more elaborate test

```
{Print the subwords of therein.}
for Last := First to 7 do begin
   for LetterNumber := First to Last do
      Print (LetterNumber);
   write ('   ') {Space between words.}
end;
writeln;
```

```
t   th   the   ther   there   therei   therein
```

All that's left is to figure out a way of supplying this secondary loop with every 'first' letter in *therein*. But wait! We already know how to solve this problem with a **for** loop. Just let *First* represent the current first letter of *therein*.

final refinement

```
for First := 1 to 7
    for every subword that begins with the first letter
        for the subword's first through last letters
            print that letter;
```

We've already tested our Pascal version of the shaded pseudocode. If you want, you should reread the code of the inner loops, and trace its output for different starting values of *First*. The completed program is shown below.

embedded word finding program

```
program SearchWord (output);
   {Prints all possible subwords of 'therein'.}
var First, Last, LetterNumber: integer;
procedure Print (LetterNumber: integer);
   begin
      case LetterNumber of
         1: write ('t');
         2: write ('h');
         3, 5: write ('e');
         4: write ('r');
         6: write ('i');
         7: write ('n')
      end
   end; {Print}
begin {SearchWord}
   for First := 1 to 7 do begin
      for Last := First to 7 do begin
         for LetterNumber := First to Last do
            Print (LetterNumber);
         write ('   ') {Space between words.}
      end; {Last loop}
      writeln
   end {First loop}
end. {SearchWord}
```

```
            ↓      ↓      ↓       ↓        ↓
t    th    the    ther    there    therei    therein
h    he    her    here    herei    herein
e    er    ere    erei    erein
r    re    rei    rein
e    ei    ein
i    in
n
```

The words we were able to find are:

the there he her here herein ere re rein I in

Do you think that we could have written program *SearchWord* without using stepwise refinement, or relying on pseudocode? Frankly, a triply-nested **for** loop is enough to frighten the most experienced programmer.

the moral

> The way we approached the solution—develop an algorithm, then encode it in an organized way—protected us from having to make massive leaps of faith in our code.

Analysing Algorithms 5-2

LET'S STOP WORRYING ABOUT THE DETAILS of Pascal code for a while, and consider algorithms and programs in a more abstract way. To begin with, what's the difference between the two?

> An algorithm is a general method for solving some kind of problem. A program is an implementation of an algorithm; a particular algorithm put into practice.

Now, in our discussions so far we've generally talked about the 'goodness' of algorithms and programs in subjective phrases. A good program has been described in terms of certain characteristics—it does the job, or its output is well-labeled, or the program has good comments and is easy to understand.

However, we can form an entirely different basis of comparison between programs or algorithms by considering their relative *efficiency*.

efficiency

> In broad terms, efficiency is the measure of an algorithm's (or program's) impact on a computer. An algorithm or program is efficient if it accomplishes our goals with a minimal usage of computer resources.

Computers have only two basic resources at their disposal—*space* and *time*. This means that we can describe the impact of a program on a computer in two practical ways:

How much computer memory will the program require?

How long will the program take to execute?

computer resources

Space is not of much concern to us right now. The programs we've developed thus far have had modest space requirements, and will continue so for a long time. Still, the notion that space can be a limiting factor is hardly foreign nowadays—almost every software ad (for spreadsheets, databases, etc.) states the minimum memory needed to run the program.

Time is a more relevant consideration. By using a computer's built-in clock we can determine to the nearest milli- or microsecond how long it takes a program to execute. However, actual *running time* is a poor means for comparison between algorithms because it isn't universal. It will vary considerably depending on such unrelated factors as:

how well the algorithm was implemented in a computer language;

the speed of the computer the program is run on;

the compiler used to translate the program into executable form;

the computer's operating system;

other computer system loads.

As a result, actual running time measurements usually say more about the computer than about the algorithm. True running time measurements are generally employed for comparisons between computers, or between compilers for a particular language, or between different methods of coding a given algorithm.

How, then, do we compare algorithms? By getting an idea of the number of steps a program based on the algorithm will take.

proportional measures

> The running time of an algorithm is *proportional* to the number of steps it takes to carry the algorithm out.

This is a pretty reasonable notion. It says that, regardless of particular implementations, compilers, or computers, an algorithm that takes N steps to carry out will have a running time about twice that of an algorithm that only requires $N/2$ steps.

As you might imagine, it isn't necessary to figure out exactly how many steps an algorithm will require in order to get an idea of what its proportional running time will be. In fact, computers run so fast that a rough approximation is sufficient to characterize an algorithm. This approximation will usually be related to the amount of input the program expects, or the amount of output it will produce, or the 'size' of a value the algorithm's computations will be based on.

Let's compare two different algorithms for summing a sequence of numbers. In pseudocode, our algorithms are:

two test algorithms

{A *summing* algorithm}
find out how long the sequence is;
initialize the running total to zero;
for *1 to the last number in the sequence*
  add the current number to a running total;
print the answer;

{*Gauss'* algorithm from Chapter 2}
find out how long the sequence is;
sum the series with Gauss' formula;
print the answer;

Now we'll actually implement the algorithms:

```
program AddSeries (input, output);
   {Add a sequence with a summing algorithm.}
var N, Sum, Counter: integer;
begin
   writeln ('This program will add the first N numbers.  Enter N.');
   readln (N);
   Sum := 0;
   for Counter := 1 to N do
      Sum := Sum + Counter;
   writeln ('The grand total is ', Sum:1)
end. {AddSeries}
```

It's easy to count the statements that will be executed in *AddSeries*. There are two *writelns*, a single *readln* and initializing assignment, and a loop that will execute *N* assignments. The total is *N*+4, or about *N*. For all practical purposes, if *N* doubles, then the running time of the program will double as well. We're in a position to say something about the summing algorithm itself.

linear running time

Since the running time of a program based on the summing algorithm will change by about the same amount that *N* changes, the algorithm is said to be *linear*, or directly proportional to *N*.

Just how 'good' is the summing algorithm? Consider a program based on Gauss' algorithm:

```
program Gauss (input, output);
   {Implements Gauss' algorithm for summing a sequence.}
var N, Sum, Counter: integer;
begin
   writeln ('This program will add the first N numbers. Enter N.');
   readln (N);
   Sum: = round ((1 + N) * (N / 2));
   writeln ('The grand total is', Sum :1)
end. {Gauss}
```

Program *Gauss* has only 4 statements. A more practical way of stating this fact, though, is to say that Gauss' algorithm requires a constant number of statements *regardless* of the value of *N*.

constant running time

An algorithm like Gauss' algorithm is said to have *constant* running time, since it doesn't vary with the value of *N*.

For any large value of *N* a constant algorithm (like Gauss) is clearly preferable to a linear algorithm (like the summing algorithm). Just how much better the algorithm is in practical terms will depend on the actual value of N. It's important to realize that comparing the statement counts of the programs themselves is quite misleading. It means almost nothing to say that program *Gauss* runs 104/4, or 26, times faster than *AddSeries* since this number will change with implementation, computer, and N itself. Describing the algorithm in terms of N is the only realistic basis of comparison.

N^2 running time

Just for fun, let's look at an algorithm that's much slower—an N^2 algorithm. Program *SumSubSeries*, below, implements a summing algorithm for adding subseries of numbers. Given a number N, it tells us the sums of the subsequences 1..1, 1..2, 1..3,... 1..N.

subseries summing program

```
program SumSubSeries (input, output);
   {Sums all subsequences of a series of integers.}
var i, j, N, Sum, Total: integer;
begin
   writeln ('Enter the limit.');
   readln (N);
   Total := 0;
   for i := 1 to N do begin
      Sum := 0;
      for j := 1 to i do
         Sum := Sum + j;
      Total := Total + Sum
   end;
   writeln ('The sum of the subtotals is ', Total:1)
end. {SumSubSeries}
```

```
Enter the limit.
12
The sum of the subtotals is 364
```

analyzing the algorithm

This algorithm is a little harder to analyze exactly. A quick inspection gives us the algorithm's main feature—it requires a loop within a loop. The outer loop will iterate N times. However, the outer loop includes more than one statement—there are two assignments, as well as an inner loop. The overall 'cost' of the outer loop, then, will be:

$N * (2 +$ the cost of statements in the inner loop)

What about the inner loop? The first time it's entered only one statement will be executed. The second entry will execute two statements, then three, and so on. On the last run through the inner loop N statements will be executed. On average, about $N / 2$ statements will be executed. The running time of our algorithm will be proportional to $(2 * N) + (N * N / 2)$, or N^2.

Big O Notation

As we noted earlier, we'll generally find a particular factor N—the number of characters that have to be inspected, the size of a file that must be sorted, etc.—that has primary influence over an algorithm's running time.

> *Big* O, or 'order of,' notation is used to express the running time of an algorithm in terms of N. For the purpose of big O notation, constant factors (constant multiples of, or additions to, N), or smaller terms involving N, are ignored.

Saying that an algorithm is $O(N)$ means that it takes on the order of N steps. Similarly, an $O(N^2)$ algorithm will require about N^2 statements. We say 'about' and 'on the order of' because the number of steps may be multiplied by a constant, or have a factor added. Some typical big O values are:

typical Big O algorithms

$O(1)$ *Constant* time. The running time of the algorithm won't be affected by data, as in Gauss' algorithm. *Example*: Any algorithm that works by evaluating a formula.

$O(log_2 N)$ *Logarithmic* time. Running time increases very slowly with N, since $\log_2 N$ only doubles when N is squared. For instance, $\log_2 1{,}000$ is 10, while $\log_2 1{,}000{,}000$ is just 20. *Example*: Binary search—the 'split the remainder' algorithm you follow when you look up a number in a telephone book N names long.

$O(N)$ *Linear* time. Running time is dependent on N; if N doubles, then running time doubles as well. *Example*: Searching through a list of length N, starting at one end.

$O(N\ log_2 N)$ No special name. Usually implies that a linear algorithm invokes a $log_2 N$ algorithm. Doesn't increase much faster than N alone. *Example*: Storing N numbers in a phone book in the first place.

$O(N^2)$ *Quadratic* time. Running time increases with the square of N; when N triples, its running time goes up nine times. *Example*: Sorting a list of N elements by multiple passes, pulling out the largest one each time.

$O(N^3)$ *Cubic* time. When N is 1,000, N^3 is one billion. This time increases by eight whenever N doubles. *Example*: Matrix multiplication.

$O(2^n)$ *Exponential* time. If N is 10, running time is about 1,000; but doubling N (to 20) increases its running time to 1,000,000! Algorithms with exponential times are considered to be impractical. *Example*: Most brute-force code-breaking methods require exponential time algorithms.

Brute Force and Efficiency

Now that we have an idea of how to measure it, there is a strong temptation to worry about the efficiency of our programs. However, this tendency is largely misplaced. In terms of program *coding*, concern about the effect of minor variations in statement usage has all but disappeared. Believe it or not, programmers used to worry about such questions as which of these expressions:

$$a * (b + c) \qquad vs. \qquad (a * b) + (a * c)$$

would compile and execute more quickly. The answer varies from machine to machine, of course, and is practically irrelevant in any case. The few milliseconds that would be saved by knowing the correct answer are insignificant.

A more realistic approach to efficiency lies in recognizing that algorithm, not code, is the proper area of concern. An improved algorithm will pay off regardless of implementation, and the study of different algorithms is usually the content of the second or third computer science course.

Surprising as it may seem, though, we won't even always want to seek out the most efficient algorithm. Instead, we'll devise algorithms that use a time-honored method of problem solving know as *brute force*.

Solving a problem by brute force is not exactly what it sounds like—we don't write the problem on a piece of paper, then stomp on it until an answer crawls out. Instead, brute force implies that we repeat an unsophisticated solution step many, many times. The classic brute force solution was the Count of Monte Cristo's plot for his escape from the dungeons of the Chateau d'If.* Did he have a carefully planned route, split-second timing, and a diversion set up to distract the guards? No. Instead, he had a spoon, and fourteen years to spend in digging himself out. *That's* brute force.

brute force

Now, brute force tends to sound like a nasty method of solution, to be eschewed in favor of clever, elegant algorithms whenever possible. Although this is true in an abstract sort of way, real-life considerations make brute force methods a natural part of everybody's problem-solving repertoire. Suppose, for example, that you have to find out the number of distinct two-letter combinations that can be made with the letters *a, b, c, d*, and *e* (e.g. *ab, ac, ad*, etc.). Stop for a moment and figure out the answer.

Of course there's a formula for figuring it out (there's always a formula), but what is it? 5 factorial divided by 2 factorial? 5 factorial over (5−2) factorial? 5 factorial minus 2 factorial? (Or does that have something to do with the formula for permutations?) In the time it takes to figure out the correct formula, we could write out every combination, count them up, and move on to bigger and better things.

Consider the problem Gauss faced in adding his series of numbers. Although he solved it in a rather elegant manner (not surprisingly, since his only tools were his head and his chalkboard), he might have come up with this familiar brute force solution had he access to a computer.

* As related in *The Count of Monte Cristo* by Alexandre Dumas.

```
program AddSeries (input, output);
var Sum, Counter: integer;
begin
   Sum := 0;
   for Counter := 1 to 100 do
      Sum := Sum + Counter;
   writeln ('The grand total is ', Sum:1)
end.
```

```
The grand total is 5050
```

AddSeries performs the computer equivalent of 'writing down all the combinations.' Its linear running time algorithm is clearly less efficient than Gauss' formula even now, and it gets worse as the length of the sequence gets longer. Why, then, should we bother fooling around with inefficient, brute-force algorithms? We see three reasons.

advantages of brute force

> Reason 1: Exploring a brute-force algorithm can lead to a better understanding of the problem.

There's a saying to the effect that you don't really understand a subject until you teach it. Why? Because teaching forces you to make a thorough, step-by-step analysis of the subject matter.

as thinking strategy

Brute force is a thinking strategy, like any of the strategies we listed in the Introduction. It's used to *expand* a problem, to *separate* it into its constituent parts, to *simulate* the process a machine might use in solving it, to *exaggerate* the amount of repetition that may go into an algorithm, to *focus* attention on details of the problem or solution that might otherwise go unnoticed . . . the list could go on and on. Sometimes the best way to a clever solution lies in formulating a deliberately unclever answer, and then looking at it, and improving it.

> Reason 2: The real costs of a programming project are not always what they seem. Efficiency is a relative term.

ease of implementation

The cost of computer time is only one factor in the price of a programming effort. Human costs—the time, effort, and wages of programmers—are usually greater than machine costs, and the gap is widening. This doesn't mean that grossly inefficient algorithms or quick and dirty programming methods should be tolerated. However, the savings that a more efficient method provides may be illusory. A brute-force algorithm is often the clearest and simplest way to do all or part of a job. A more efficient algorithm may exist, but it may not be cost-beneficial to discover it. Furthermore, an 'improved' algorithm might make the final program more complicated and difficult to understand.

> Reason 3: Brute-force algorithms tend to be adaptable. They are often easier to modify than more elegant, but more specialized, algorithms.

Consider Gauss' algorithm. The formula:

$$\textit{sum of numbers from first to last} = (\textit{first} + \textit{last}) * \textit{last}/2$$

adaptability

is certainly efficient, but it's useless for solving other sum of the series problems. What about finding the sum of the squares of every number from 1 to 100? Or their cubes? Or their square roots? Our brute-force solution is a snap to adapt to solving these problems. Gauss' method is hopelessly narrow.

the moral

The real bottom-line of algorithms and programs, whether brute-force or elegant, is simple—*does it work*? In *The Psychology of Computer Programming*, Gerald Weinberg tells a story about a rescue programmer who was brought in to design a program to schedule the production of automobiles. The original programmer on the job was highly indignant over the rejection of his program, and complained that the new program was less than half as efficient as his discarded version. "However," retorted his relief, "my program works, and yours doesn't. If the program doesn't have to work, I can come up with an algorithm that runs twice as fast as yours!" Yes indeed!

Antibugging and Debugging 5-3

WE'VE PROBABLY NEVER EXPLAINED THE difference between debugging and testing carefully enough.

> *Debugging* is what *you* do before you consider a program completed. *Testing* is what a program user does as she makes your program crash.

The programmer, faced with a particularly recalcitrant program, tends to think only of getting it to compile—if it works for a particular set of data, so much the better. This is debugging. But someone who must actually use (or grade the quality of) your program applies stiffer criteria. It doesn't matter much that the program compiles, since that's the bare minimum expectation. Nor is the user concerned with its operation under ideal conditions. Instead, she tries to find your program's limitations: to make it produce wrong results, or to crash. *That's* testing.

Thus, debugging tries to get rid of known bugs, while testing is an attempt to show that more bugs still exist. It's an unfortunate fact that both methods have severe limitations. The effectiveness of debugging depends largely on the diligence and experience of the programmer.

the moral

> The Golden Rule of Testing
>
> Although program testing may show the *presence* of bugs, it can't guarantee their *absence*.

Stub Programming

We have to conclude that as programs get more complicated, testing and debugging alone may not be enough to produce reliable code. Instead, we have to write programs in a manner that will help insure that errors are caught or avoided. *Stub* programming is a method that allows for error and improvement.

> A *stub* program is a stripped-down, skeleton version of a final program. It doesn't implement details of the algorithm or fulfill all the job requirements. However, it does contain rough versions of all subprograms and their parameter lists. Furthermore, it can be compiled and run.

A stub program helps demonstrate that a program's structure is plausible. Its procedures and functions are primitive, unsophisticated versions of their final forms, but they allow limited use of the *entire* program. For example, if we were writing a payroll program, we might begin by developing a stub program that handles a fixed group of workers who each put in 50 hours per week, receive the same rate of pay, and declare the same number of dependents.

dummy subprograms

The stub program approach is especially useful for beginning programmers, who are often forced to start working before they know enough Pascal to write the entire program. 'Dummy' procedures let novices get a head start on the program, without requiring implementation of the hard parts.

In developing a stub program, we start by writing a program's main modules. In the illustration below, *A, B,* and *C* demonstrate the major workings of a program, but they call dummy subprograms.

the stub approach

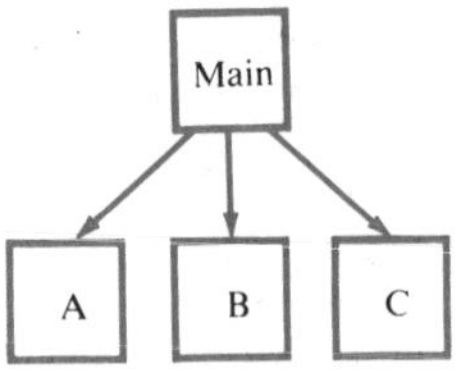

Next, the dummy procedures and functions—*M, N, O, P*—are expanded and debugged, but the program's smallest details still aren't implemented.

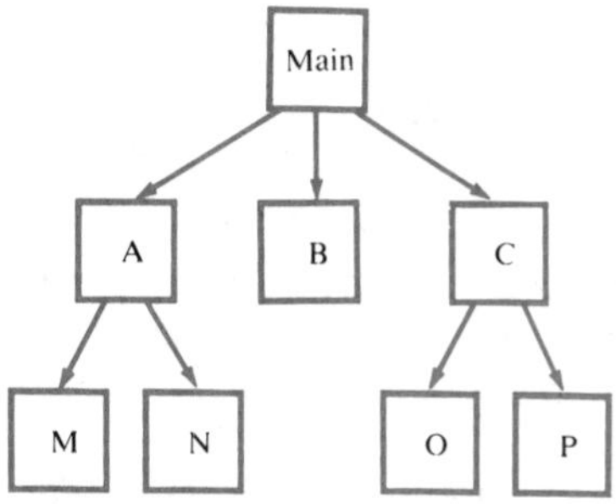

Eventually, the remaining subprograms—*X, Y, Z*—can be completed, and tested as they are added to the main program.

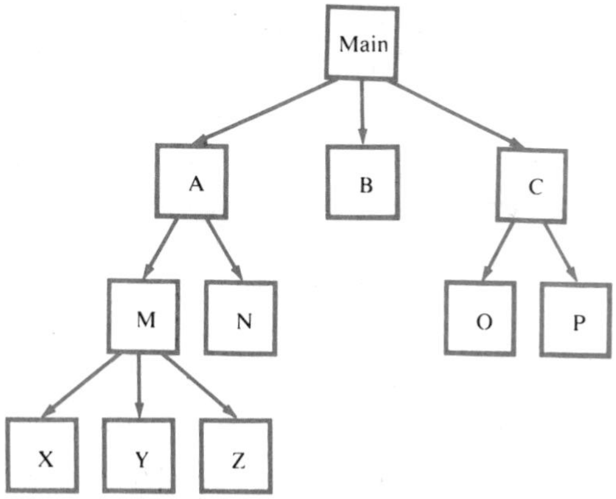

top-down debugging

It's easy to appreciate that stub programming complements stepwise refinement. In fact, stub programs allow for something unexpected—*top-down debugging*.

Stub programs let a large system be debugged and tested *as it is built*.

How can a program be tested or debugged before it's in operating shape? The dummy modules of stub programs can support rough runs on the computer. The proposed program can also be subjected to the intense scrutiny of your programming team—usually yourself and anybody else you can collar for ten minutes.

structured walkthroughs

A *structured walkthrough* is a guided tour of a partially completed program. It's an explanation *and defense* of the program's algorithm and implementation.

Working on a program tends to develop a mind set in the programmer that renders obvious mistakes invisible. Merely explaining a program aloud can give you a totally new view of it.

Top-down debugging of Pascal code has advantages too. To begin with, major program connections are tested first, which means that major bugs and shortcomings are detected early in the game. Furthermore, testing and debugging are distributed throughout the entire writing process. You're not forced to do all your program fixing just before the program is scheduled to be completed (which is invariably when the computer is least available). Finally, even if a program isn't completely finished by the due date it's a preliminary *working* version—and not just a useless mess of code.

The bottom-up approach follows the opposite tack. We start out by writing and debugging a program's smallest and least important subprograms:

Then, the separate procedures and functions are incorporated into a subsystem of the main program:

bottom-up module building

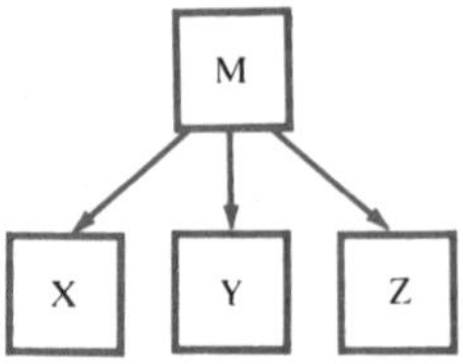

Finally, we put subsystems together to complete the program. This is the first time that they can be tested as a unit.

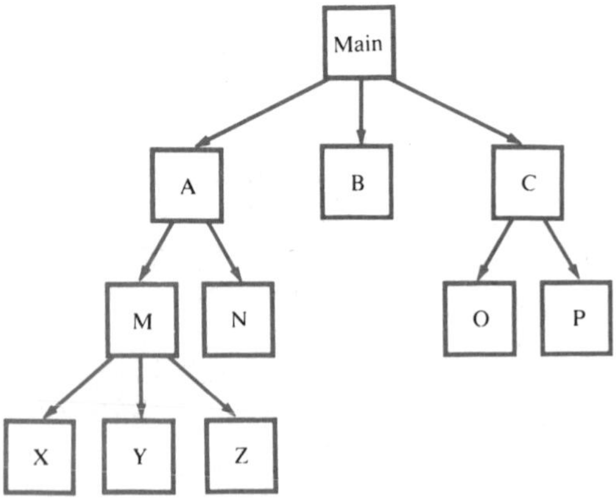

In practice, the first version of a stub program will contain many procedures that look like this:

stub procedures

```
procedure TranslateCharacters (Old, New: char; Distance: integer);
  {This procedure will take care of character translation—stub version.}
  begin
    writeln ('In procedure TranslateCharacters. Arguments are');
    writeln ('Old: ', Old, ', New: ', New, ', Distance: ', Distance)
  end;
```

The procedure does almost nothing for the action of the final program. However, it makes a considerable contribution to the final program's design.

commenting-out code

Another technique for incorporating top-down design into programs involves the judicious use of comment brackets. We'd like to be able to have our high-level procedures ready to call lower-level code, even if the more detailed subprograms haven't even been written in the abbreviated form suggested above. 'Commenting out' segments of a **case** statement does the trick:

```
ReadCommand (Command);
case Command of
  'A': Add;
  'D': Delete;
{ 'F': Find;
  'S': Skip;
  'T': Translate;
  'V': Verify }
end;
```

The comment brackets can be moved, call-by-call, as the underlying procedures are actually written. In this segment, 'F', 'S', 'T', and 'V' will be written later.

case Bugs

Once again, suppose that you've written a program that just won't seem to compile. Even though every **begin** has a matching **end**, the same compile-time error message keeps showing up:

```
"END" EXPECTED -- END OF PROGRAM NOT FOUND
```

> Make sure your **case** statement ends with an **end**.

This error is common because the syntax of the **case** statement is different from the other Pascal control statements. Only the **case** statement has to end with an **end.** Although this turns out to be an inconvenience in Pascal, most recently developed languages follow the **case** format—every statement has the equivalent of a closing **end.** This system is called *full bracketing*. If you think about it for a bit, you'll see that its intention, and effect, is to put the compound statement out of business.

Accidentally misplacing a semicolon within a **case** statement can cause a calamity. We've used a semicolon instead of a colon on the third line below.

> **case** *Selector* **of**
> 1: *DoFirstThing*;
> 2; *DoSecondThing*;
> 3: *DoThirdThing*; etc.

Can you predict the error messages the program segment might generate? They're rather subtle:

```
1 :  DOFIRSTTHING;
2 ;  DOSECONDTHING;
     MISSING "BEGIN"
↑UNDECLARED PROCEDURE "2"
↑"2" MAY NOT BE AN IDENTIFIER
```

Since '2' is preceded and followed by semicolons—statement separators—the compiler assumes that it is some kind of statement. However, 2 hasn't been defined as a procedure, and is an illegal identifier in any case.

missing **case** constants

The **case** statement can also be the cause of a run-time error. The message below appears when the **case** expression takes on a value that wasn't included, along with an appropriate action, in the constant list.

```
ABNORMAL TERMINATION --
VALUE OF CASE EXPRESSION NOT IN CONSTANT LIST
```

Although this is an error in Standard Pascal, some implementations of Pascal don't deal so harshly with an unanticipated **case** expression value. In these versions of Pascal, the **case** expression 'falls through.' No value was specified, and no action is taken.

Why is a Pascal control statement implemented in different ways? Well, when he designed Pascal, Wirth felt that the constant list was part of the **case** statement's documentation. Letting a program continue operation when the **case** expression had a value *not* specified might be misleading to a program reader. Thus, an unanticipated value was supposed to generate a run-time error; a note that something unexpected was happening.

case extensions

However, some Pascal implementors took a different view. They thought it was perfectly reasonable to expect the unexpected, and to provide a means of dealing with it less disastrous than a run-time crash. A simple approach was to ignore the offending **case** expression, as described above. Another innovation was the exception clause—a specific 'else' or 'otherwise' action to be taken if the value of the **case** variable could not be found on the value list. These are nonstandard *extensions*, or additions, to Pascal.

Check your own Pascal system, and see which philosophy its implementors adhered to. You should note any extensions inside the front cover. Naturally, even if your system is nonstandard, you can usually write programs according to Standard Pascal. You will find that you must make a subjective decision: Is it better to write an absolutely standard program, sure to run on every system (even though it is very inflexible and prone to crashes), or to write your programs for a friendlier (although nonstandard) environment? Questions like this must usually be answered in every individual case—there are no hard and fast rules to apply.

One final point deals with certain functions, like *Random*, that represent different values on subsequent calls. This can lead to hard-to-find bugs. For instance, assume that function *Random* computes and represents a random number. A dumb, but nonetheless common, mistake is to try to inspect *Random's* value twice in a row—perhaps first to print it, and then as part of an assignment. If you expect to find the same random number twice you'll be very unhappy. Using an auxiliary variable to hold the function's value stops this problem.

Pascal Summary

• **case** statement: used when a choice is made between two or more alternatives. The decision is based on the value of the **case** expression; this value—and an associated action—is given in a **case** constant list. The action may be any Pascal statement:

```
case expression of
   const1: Late := Early; {assignment statement}
   const2: DoItToIt; {procedure call}
   const3, const4, const5:  ; {empty statement}
   const6: begin
              statement; {compound statement}
              statement
           end;
   const7: for Count := Lo to Hi  do begin
              statement; {control statement}
              statement
           end {for}
end; {of the case statement}
```

Important Facts

• The **case** expression and values in the **case** constant list must all have the same Pascal type.

• The constant list must contain an action for every possible value of the **case** expression.

• An empty statement is used to specify an inaction if no action is required.

• Some implementations may allow a value that isn't in the **case** constant list to 'fall through' without ill effect, but this is a nonstandard extension.

- Big *O* notation describes an algorithm's relative efficiency. It relates an algorithm's running time to the amount of data it will process.
- Although we can time a program, and make small changes in its code to try to make it run faster, we'll generally try to improve an algorithm when we want to improve efficiency.
- Brute-force algorithms are usually inefficient, but we'll use them 1) because they can help us understand a problem better, 2) because programmer time may be more valuable than computer time, and 3) because brute-force algorithms are often more adaptable than elegant algorithms that are highly specialized.
- A structured walkthrough is a guided tour of a program. It's intended to give other experienced programmers an opportunity to spot errors and make suggestions before your program is finally coded.
- A stub program relies on dummy modules—partially implemented subprograms—to help develop and demonstrate a large program.
- A kludge is a programming trick that may be necessary on occasion. However, the use of kludges isn't overly encouraged.
- The Golden Rule of **case** Constant Lists: Every potential value of the **case** expression must be specified in the **case** constant list.
- The Golden Rule of Testing: Although program testing may show the presence of bugs, it can't guarantee their absence.

Self-test Exercises

5-1 What's the minimum number of reserved words that appear in a **case** statement?

5-2 Suppose that the code below is the beginning of a **case** statement. What values should appear in the statement's constant list?

```
case -((ord(CapitalLetter)-ord('A')) mod 5) of   etc.
```

5-3 What is the purpose of this **case** statement?

```
write(n);
case n of
    1: writeln('st');
    2: writeln('nd');
    3: writeln('rd');
    4, 5, 6, 7, 8, 9: writeln('th')
end;
```

5-4 Simplify this **case** statement as much as you can.

```
case ItemNumber of
    0: writeln('Hats');
    1: writeln('Bats and Cats');
    2: writeln('Slats');
    3: writeln('Hats');
    4: writeln('Bats and Cats');
    5: writeln('Hats')
end;
```

5-5 An angle is given as a positive *real* number of degrees. Angles from 0° to (but not including) 90° fall in the first quadrant, 90° to 180° are in the second, 180° to 270° are in the third, and 270° to 360° are in the fourth quadrant. The series of quadrants starts all over again at 360°. Write a procedure that reads the value of an angle, and prints out the angle, and the quadrant it falls in.

5-6 What's wrong with this **case** statement?

```
case Grade of
  'A'..'D': writeln ('Passing');
  'F': writeln ('Failing')
end;
```

5-7 What are the possible outputs of this program segment? Assume that *First* and *Second* are *char* variables, and that the only possible inputs are **AB**, **BA**, **AA**, and **BB**.

```
readln (First, Second);
case First of
  'A': case Second of
         'A': write ('It');
         'B': write ('is')
       end;
  'B': begin
         write ('an');
         case Second of
           'A': write ('Ancient');
           'B': write ('Mariner')
         end
       end
end;
writeln;
```

5-8 Why is the Ancient Mariner a lousy ballplayer?

5-9 Write a procedure that counts the number of times the digits 4, 8, and 9 appear in forty characters worth of input.

5-10 What's the output of this procedure?

```
procedure Quiz;
   var Counter: integer;
   begin
      for Counter := 1 to 9 do
         case Counter mod 5 of
            0: write ('often ');
            1: write ('What ');
            2,4: write ('is ');
            3: write ('not ')
         end; {case}
      writeln
   end; {Quiz}
```

5-11 Write a procedure that counts the number of times the digits 2, 3, and 6 appear in *x* many digit-characters worth of input. If a **case** statement is used to winnow the input, does it make sense to pass 2, 3, and 6 as parameters?

5-12 Can good test data prove that a program doesn't have any bugs? What can it show?

More Exercises

5-12 What happens in your Pascal system if the value of the **case** expression is not contained in the **case** structure's constant list? Is any kind of **else** or **otherwise** clause allowed?

5-13 Write a markup/sale program. It should give the user the option of specifying a percentage markup or reduction, then compute a sales price.

5-14 Write a program that takes the values of a two-card blackjack hand as input, and prints out the point total of the hand. Note that input values may include the *char* values 'A', 'K', 'Q', and 'J', and that an ace's value is either 1 or 11. (Hint: an ace will always be 11 unless you have two aces. You may want to require that values be input in descending order.)

5-15 A simple conversion of letter grades to their equivalent grade points is easy. However, allowing the letter grade to be modified by a plus or minus complicates the matter. Write a program that shows the grade-point ranges of letter grades (including plus and minus grades). Use whatever conversion table applies at your school.

5-16 Before Great Britain went decimal, foreigners arriving at London's Heathrow Airport were usually rather confused about money. A traveller might know the exchange rate for one particular unit of English currency of money, as shown below, but have no idea about other sorts of conversion. Write a program which, after establishing the current exchange rate for *any* of the denominations shown, will convert any amount of U.S. currency into appropriate English amounts.

12 pence = 1 shilling
5 shillings = 1 crown
4 crowns = 1 pound
21 shillings = 1 guinea

5-17 Relative gravities of most planets in the solar system, the Sun, and the Moon, are shown below. They let us find what a given weight on Earth would weigh on each body.

Sun	27.94	Mercury	.37	Venus	.88
Moon	.17	Mars	.38	Jupiter	2.64
Saturn	1.15	Uranus	1.17	Neptune	1.18

Write a program that lets a user find her weight on any of these. It should ask her to enter the first letter of the planet or body she wants, and then, if there's an ambiguous situation (as we find for *S* or *M*) it should prompt her for the second letter. In other words, a nested **case** structure is required.

5-18 Write a program that, when given a television channel, will print out its call letters. (Why wouldn't this work with radio station frequencies?) Be sure the program works for any channel from 2 through 13, even if you have to print a message pointing out that a particular channel isn't assigned.

5-19 Write a program that extends felicitations on auspicious occasions like birthdays and anniversaries, as well as general greetings on holidays and special occasions. Have the user enter a single-letter code to specify the message required, along with any numerical information (age, which anniversary) required. Limit the numerical data to the range 1..10, and print the word (e.g. 'First', or '3rd') instead of the number.

5-20 Write a program that accepts as input a four-digit *integer*, then prints out the number in English. In a simple version, assume that the third digit is not 1. For example, the input **4713** is illegal. A harder program will allow all four-digit input.

5-21 Local necromancers have come up with the following method of finding a day. Begin by expressing the year, month, and date you're interested in as numbers.

Add 10 to the month, and subtract 1 from the year. Let a variable C equal the year **div** 100, and another variable, named A, equal the year **mod** 100. Set a third variable called B equal to 13 times the number of the month, then subtract 1 and **div** by 5, then add A **div** 4, and C **div** 4. The number of the day of the week (where Sunday is 0) equals $B + A$ plus the number of the day of the month minus twice C, all **mod** 7.

Incidentally (because of a shortage of eye of newt), this algorithm won't work when the day of the month sought is the first or second. Write a program that prints out the day of the week Halloween falls on (or fell on) in 1066, 1492, 1776, and 2001.

5-22 Although telephone numbers currently consist only of digits, they used to begin with two letters followed by five digits. For example, what we now refer to as 548-0276 was once known as KI8-0276. The prefix 'KI' stood for 'Kingsbridge', and was the name of the local exchange.

A number of exchange names are shown below. Write a program that reads in a telephone number written in the form 'KI8-0276' (i.e. with the initials of one of the exchanges), then prints it with the exchange name fully spelled out, as in 'Kingsbridge 8-0276'. Be sure to provide test data.

Purdue	*Maltby*	*Rhinelander*
Roseland	*Elgin*	*Excelsior*
Cambridge	*Paradise*	*Central*

5-23 Write a program that, when given the call letters shown below, will print the broadcast frequency assigned to them. (Hint: first check the first letter—it may be unique. Then check the second letter, and if these match, the third.) Be sure to declare each procedure *before* you use it, even if it's used in another procedure.

ABC 94.4	NBC 102.4	CBS 102.9
CAB 88.9	NBA 93.4	NTR 104.4
BBC 97.4	AAA 101	TVA 106.9

5-24 Write a bank account program that keeps track of current balances, service charges, and interest. The program user should begin by telling the program the number of transactions that have to be recorded. Interest, at an annual rate of 6%, should be paid on the average balance in excess of $1,000, and a service charge of fifty cents should be levied on each withdrawal.

5-25 How many one, two, three, four, and five letter combinations can you make from five different letters? Come up with a formula or a program that computes the answer.

5-26 Compound interest rates can be significantly greater than simple rates, because interest is paid on interest already accrued. Write a program that compares the benefit of simple interest with interest compounded monthly, weekly, daily, and hourly. Let the program user enter an interest rate, amount of original principal, and time period.

5-27 Write a checkbook/savings passbook balancing program. Have the user enter the number of transactions she wants to make and her current balances, then let her make deposits, withdrawals, and balance checks. Finally, post new balances (including interest) and summarize account activity (how much was deposited, withdrawn, and the number of transactions made) for the month.

5-28 The executives of a large oil company are in a quandary. Although they can sell all the No. 1 oil available, supplies are limited. An ambitious vice president suggests the following plan: As the delivery truck goes along its route, the driver should replace the delivered No. 1 oil with oil of an inferior grade. The replacement isn't 1:1 (if it were, the truck would come back full!). Instead, it goes according to this schedule:

No. 2 oil—replace 75%   *No. 3 oil—replace* 50%   *No. 4 oil—replace* 25%

Only one kind of replacement oil is used on any given day.

Write a program that will help customers sue the oil company by telling them how much No. 1 oil they actually received on any particular delivery day. Variables in each day's run include the starting contents of the delivery truck, the number of customers served, and the amount of oil in each delivery. Since nobody is sure what grade of oil was used for replacement each day, show figures for each of the three possible adulterants. Make sure that your output will look good in court.

5-29 Procedures that help draw graphs are an essential part of many programs. Write a loop that could graph the function $f(x)=x$ over the range 1 to 10. In other words, plot a graph whose first value is 1, second is 2, etc. Don't worry about printing the x or y axis. Note that although this particular graph is easy to plot either vertically or horizontally, it's usually less trouble to print graphs vertically—in effect, on their sides.

5-30 Try drawing an x axis on the graph. Write a loop that graphs the same function for all *integer* values of x from -10 to 10. Print a vertical line (signifying 0—the x axis) down the center of the page.

5-31 Drawing plane figures from dots or stars is not too intellectually stimulating, but counting the number of dots required to draw a figure can be. Not unreasonably, these numbers are known as *figurate* numbers, and come in all varieties—triangular numbers, square numbers, pentagonal numbers, etc. Three of these figures are shown below.

In 1665, Blaise Pascal wrote a *Treatise On Figurate Numbers*, in which he came up with a general equation for finding figurate numbers. The number of dots required to draw a figure with a given number of dots per side (*DotsPerSide*) is:

Triangle=$(DotsPerSide^2+DotsPerSide)/2$;
Square=$DotsPerSide^2$;
Pentagon=$(3*DotsPerSide^2-DotsPerSide)/2$;
Hexagon=$2*DotsPerSide^2-DotsPerSide$.

Write a figurate number program. It should be able to compute figurate numbers for the shapes shown above, and print a table of the first 10 figurate numbers for each shape. Moreover, the program should *draw* any of the figures on demand. (Bonus: find the general equation that relates number of sides, number of dots per side, and figurate number.)

5-32 How would you use the random number generator we developed in this chapter to choose a number, evenly divisible by 3, between (and including) 69 and 123?

5-33 How would you use the random number generator we developed in the text to pick a *real* number in the range 3 through 33 by *fourths*? (e.g. 3.25, or 29.75.)

5-34 In the text, our random number generator produced a *real* that was greater than or equal to 0, but less than one. We could use it to choose a random *integer* greater than or equal to A, and less than or equal to B, by using the formula:

$$Random\ Integer = A + trunc\ ((B-A+1)*Random\ (Seed)$$

How would you change this formula if *Random* (*Seed*) represented a number greater than 0, and less than or equal to 1?

5-35 Add a statement that lets a program make alternative choices to your personal computer language. Can you make any improvements on Pascal's syntax? What will you do if the **case** expression's value isn't found in the list of **case** constants? Can you specify a general alternative action?

'boolean expressions can also be tricky (but always, as Mr. Spock would say, perfectly logical).'

6

Programming Decisions: the **if** Statement

What's the use of *boolean* values? There aren't many of them—just *false and true*—and apparently it's possible to read deep into a Pascal textbook without using either one. Yet, *boolean* values are going to turn out to be the most useful values of all, because they let programs make *decisions*.

This chapter introduces *boolean* values along with the **if** statement. Section 6-1 begins with a discussion of *boolean* values and the *relational* operators. We'll show how the **if** statement requires *boolean* expressions, and write some example programs.

Section 6-2 describes how the *boolean* operators **and**, **or**, and **not** construct more complex *boolean* expressions. A final relational operator, called **in**, gives us a quick and easy way of error-checking a program's entry to a **case** statement, and can often be used to simplify *boolean* expressions.

Finally, in 6-3, we'll learn about a problem-solving approach called *exhaustive search*. We'll also consider ways of making a search less exhausting by limiting a problem's *solution space*, and look at our first long program. 6-4 points out potential bugs, and suggests that debugging code be *embedded* into all programs for convenience.

Understanding *boolean* values through and through is a key part of learning to program. Now, some people are a little wary of *booleans* because they seem too logical—after all, they're named after George Boole, the creator of logical calculus. It turns out, to the contrary, that *booleans* are nice because they make programs *less* formal, and more natural. 'Common sense' values is a better description of them than logical values. If a *boolean* expression seems to be unfathomable, relax. You're probably trying too hard.

boolean Expressions and **if** Statements 6-1

LIKE ALL EXPRESSIONS, *BOOLEAN* EXPRESSIONS represent values. The simplest examples are the constants of the ordinal type *boolean*:

false *true*

The *odd*(*x*) function also represents a *boolean* value—*false* if its *integer* argument *x* is even, and *true* if it's odd. We can state longer *boolean* expressions by using the *relational* operators.*

relational operators

Math	*Pascal*	*English*
$=$	=	*equal to*
$<$	<	*less than*
$\leqslant$	<=	*less than or equal to*
$>$	>	*greater than*
$\geqslant$	>=	*greater than or equal to*
$\neq$	<>	*not equal to*

Some relational operators require two symbols because the keyboards of most terminals are too restricted to show characters like ≠.

In high school math, the relational operators were used to build equalities and inequalities. We've usually seen them restricting the value of an expression in a context like this:

if $b^2 - 4ac > 0$ *the expression has two real, unequal roots*
if $b^2 - 4ac = 0$ *the expression has two real, equal roots*
if $b^2 - 4ac < 0$ *the expression has two imaginary, unequal roots*

booleans are assertions

> Pascal uses the fact that equalities and inequalities always make an assertion (claim) that has to be either true or false. This makes them *boolean*-valued expressions.

For example, this expression is either *true* or *false*:

LowerLimit>5

It asserts that a variable or constant named *LowerLimit* has an *integer* or *real* value greater than 5. The expression:

ApplicantsAge<=65

claims that the value of *ApplicantsAge* is less than or equal to 65. There's no need to restrict comparisons to *integer* or *real* values, because these expressions:

Finished='Y' 'X'<>*chr* (63)

form *boolean* expressions just as plausible as their numerical counterparts. Since character sets are ordered, even this expression makes sense:

SecondLetter>=*FirstLetter*

* One other relational operator, **in**, is discussed in section 6-2.

It confirms or denies the alphabetical ordering of two *char* variables.

relational operands

The operands of the relational operators (the values that are being compared) must generally be of the same ordinal type. *reals* may be compared to each other, and to *integers*, but the vagaries of *real* arithmetic make these comparisons unreliable. (For example, the *real* value 3.0*(10.0/3.0) frequently equals 9.99999999... instead of 10.0.)

At any rate, a relational operator clearly can't have operands of totally unrelated types. Is *true* $<$ 16? Is 'A' <> 5? These expressions are existential rather than *boolean*. They contain type clashes that would cause compile-time error messages.

It's also important to recognize that the relational operators can't be used in a manner that's very common in mathematics—to show multiple inequalities. The mathematical phrase $5 < X < 10$ has no meaning in a Pascal program. We'll see how to express such relations in 6-2; this particular example is correctly written as ($5 < X$) **and** ($X < 10$).

boolean constants

Constants and variables can also be used to represent *boolean* values. The value of a user-defined constant can't be computed in its definition, so the topic of defining *boolean* constants is disposed of in short order. Note that these definitions are not *boolean* expressions, even though '=' is a relational operator under other circumstances.

```
const THISPROGRAMWORKS = false;
      TESTING = true;
```

boolean variables are declared in the variable declaration part, along with *integer, real*, and *char* variables. As usual, the order of these declarations is irrelevant, because no type is more important than any of the others.

```
var Balance: real;
    Heir, Broke: boolean;
    TattooOnRightShoulder: char;
    Temperature: integer;
    NotDivisibleBy2: boolean;
```

> Assignments to *boolean* variables are like all other assignment statements. An expression is evaluated, and its result value is given to the variable.

The constants of type *boolean* (*false* and *true*), user-defined *boolean* constants (like *TESTING*, above), and *boolean* variables may all appear on the right-hand side of assignment statements.

assignment to *booleans*

```
Heir := true;
ActivateDebuggingProcedures := TESTING;
Broke := Balance<=0;
NotDivisibleBy2 := odd(Temperature);
Broke := Heir;
```

Self-Check Questions

Q. Assume that we've made assignments as shown. Evaluate each expression.

Grade := 'C'; *RealValue* := 3.97; *IntegerValue* := 5;

a) *RealValue* <= 5E+00	*b*) *IntegerValue* <> *Grade*
c) *IntegerValue* < *RealValue*	*d*) *round*(*RealValue*+1) = *IntegerValue*
e) (*ord*('D')−1) <= 34	*f*) *Grade* <> *chr*(*trunc*(*RealValue*) +6∗*IntegerValue*)

A. In evaluating expressions *e* and *f*, we've assumed the ordering of the ASCII character set.

a) *true*	*b*) This is a type clash.
c) *false*	*d*) *true*
e) *false*	*f*) *false*

Q. Suppose that *Willy* and *Nilly* are *boolean* variables. What will the value of *Willy* be after assignment 1 if *Nilly* is *true*? *false*? Is there anything wrong with assignment 2 syntactically? From the viewpoint of conciseness or clarity?

```
Willy := Nilly = false;   {Assignment 1}
Willy := Nilly = true;    {Assignment 2}
```

A. The first assignment statement gives *Willy* the opposite value of *Nilly.* If *Nilly* equals *true, Willy* becomes *false,* and if *Nilly* represents *false, Willy* takes on the value *true.** The second assignment statement has correct Pascal syntax, but is redundant. It should have been written as:

```
Willy := Nilly;
```

because the expression *Nilly=true* is identical to the value of *Nilly.*

* Soon, we'll use the **not** operator to make the same assignment as: *Willy* := **not** *Nilly*.

The **if** Statement

Now that we've grasped the basics of *boolean* expressions, let's use a control statement that requires them.

> The **if** statement lets a program choose between taking two alternative actions.

Its general form is:

if *boolean expression*
  then *action*
  else *alternative action*

The statement's syntax chart shows an option (omitting the **else**) that we won't get to for a few pages.

if statement

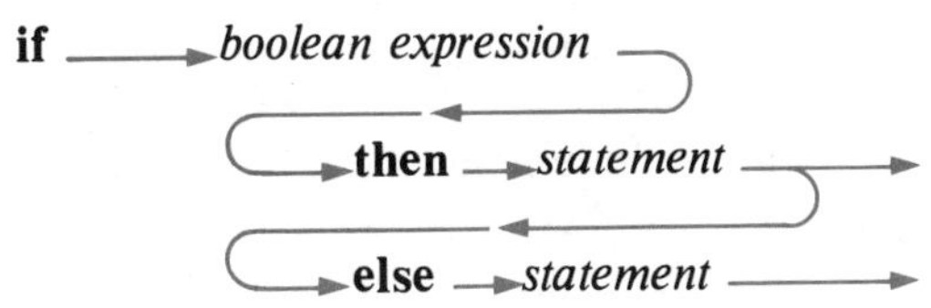

how it works

When an **if** statement is entered, its *boolean* expression is evaluated. If it's *true*, the **then** action is carried out, and the alternative **else** action is skipped. If the *boolean* expression represents the value *false*, the **then** action is jumped over, and the **else** action is executed instead. In either case, only one of the two actions is taken. For example:

if demonstration program

```
program SquareRoot (input, output);
   {Computes square roots. Error-checks input using if.}
var RootExists: boolean;
    Argument, Answer: real;
begin
   writeln ('Please enter a number.');
   readln (Argument);
   RootExists := Argument >= 0;
   write ('The square root of ', Argument:2:2);
   if RootExists then begin
      Answer := sqrt(Argument);
      writeln (' is', Answer:2:2)
   end {then}
   else writeln (' is imaginary. Sorry!');
   writeln ('Thanks for using this program.')
end. {SquareRoot}
```

```
Please enter a number.
-24.6
The square root of -24.60 is imaginary.  Sorry!
Thanks for using this program.
```

Although the auxiliary (not strictly necessary) variable *RootExists* provided the *boolean* expression in *SquareRoot*, we could have correctly said:

if *Argument* >=0 **then** etc.

Program *SquareRoot* used an **if** statement (shaded) to *error-check* its input. Without this check, the program would crash when given negative input.

robustness

> Error-checking input helps make programs *robust*—less sensitive to user errors or misuse. They end gracefully instead of crashing.

When **if** statements are used, they should be formatted in a way that highlights their alternative actions. However...

> The Golden Rule of Coding
>
> *Syntax determines semantics.* Spacing and indentation is for the benefit of human program readers. The computer only obeys **begin**, **end**, semicolons, and the like.

Although syntax, and not appearance, controls the semantics (effect) of Pascal code, programs should still be easy for humans to read. This program layout clearly distinguishes between the **if** statement's actions and the rest of the program:

if statement layout

```
   ...
statement;
if boolean expression then begin
   statement;
      ...
   statement
end {then}
else begin
   statement;
      ...
   statement
end; {else}
statement;          etc.
```

When an **if** statement's alternative actions are just single statements (like assignments or procedure calls) the **begin** and **end** of compound statements can be omitted.

```
program EasyOrder (input, output);
   {Prints two input letters in alphabetical order.}
var First, Second: char;
begin
   writeln ('Please enter two letters.');
   readln (First, Second);
   write ('In alphabetical order, ', First, ' and ', Second, ' are ');
   if First>Second
      then writeln (Second, ' ', First)
      else writeln (First, ' ', Second)
end. {EasyOrder}
```

```
Please enter two letters.
XM
In alphabetical order, X and M are M, X
```

an **else** rule

The two formatting styles can also be combined, as they were in program *SquareRoot*. However, a picayune syntax rule is extremely important: the reserved word **else** is *never* preceded by a semicolon. We'll examine this small, but crucial, detail in the Antibugging section.

Self-Check Questions

Q. Rewrite this assignment as an **if . . . then . . . else** statement.

Finished := *Response* = ´Q´;

A.

if *Response* = ´Q´
  then *Finished* := *true*
  else *Finished* := *false*;

Programming with the **if** Statement

We'll frequently want a program to decide whether or not to execute a single action, rather than choose between two alternative actions. Pascal provides a convenient variation.

> The **else** portion of an **if** statement can be omitted entirely.

Such a statement is like an ordinary **if** statement whose **else** action is an empty statement. Check back to the syntax chart and trace the no-**else** option.

Program *PostageMeter*, below, demonstrates the simplified **if** statement. As before, we've tried to make the program robust by anticipating user errors. Several checks are phrased as *boolean* expressions—Was the weight accidentally entered as a negative number? Is it less than the minimum? Is the letter to go special delivery? If any expression is *true*, an appropriate response is evoked.

no-**else** demonstration program

```
program PostageMeter (input, output);
   {Computes charges for first class and special delivery mail.}
const BASICCHARGE = 0.18;          {The one-ounce rate.}
      OUNCECHARGE = 0.17;          {Each additional ounce.}
      SPECIALCHARGE = 2.00;        {Special delivery surcharge.}
var Weight, Postage: real;
    Response: char;
    SpecialDelivery: boolean;
begin
   writeln ('How heavy is your letter, in ounces?');
   readln (Weight);
   if Weight < 0.0 then Weight := abs(Weight);
   if Weight < 1.0 then begin
      writeln ('Minimum weight charge is one ounce.');
      Weight := 1.0
   end;
   Postage := BASICCHARGE+((Weight-1.0)*OUNCECHARGE);
   writeln ('Do you want special delivery?  Answer ''Y'' or ''N''.');
   readln (Response);
   SpecialDelivery := Response = 'Y';
   if SpecialDelivery then Postage := Postage+SPECIALCHARGE;
   writeln ('The ', Weight:1, '-ounce postage charge is', Postage:5:2)
end. {PostageMeter}
```

```
How heavy is your letter, in ounces?
0.5
Minimum weight charge is one ounce.
Do you want special delivery?  Answer 'Y' or 'N'.
Y
The 1.0E+00-ounce postage charge is 2.18
```

the dangling **else** problem

An abbreviated **if** statement that nests an **if** complete with its **else** clause can appear ambiguous at first sight. An unindented example shows the problem. Which **if** statement is the **else** action, *statement2*, associated with?

```
if B1
then if B2
then statement1
else statement2
statement3
```

> The Golden Rule of **if** Statements
>
> In Pascal, an **else** is always the alternative action of the *nearest* prior **then** action.

Thus, *statement2* is executed if *B1* is *true*, and *B2* is *false*.

nested **if** statements

```
if B1 then
   if B2
      then statement1
      else statement2;
statement3;          etc.
```

As always, we hasten to point out that altering the code's physical appearance has no effect on the program. Procedure *TwoDwarves*, below, shows the effect of the nesting rule.

```
procedure TwoDwarves (Sleepy, Grumpy: boolean);

   begin
      if Sleepy then
         if Grumpy
            then writeln ('I''m grumpy and sleepy.')
            else writeln ('I may be sleepy, but I''m not grumpy.');
      writeln ('I hope you''re satisfied.')
   end;
```

This association can be changed by hiding the inner **then** within a compound statement.

changing **else** association

```
procedure TwoMoreDwarves (Sneezy, Dopey: boolean);

   begin
      if Sneezy then begin
         if Dopey then writeln ('I''m sneezy and dopey.')
      end
      else writeln ('I''m not sneezy, but I might be dopey.');
      writeln ('Bother me again and I''ll bite your leg.')
   end;
```

Let's get back to writing programs that solve problems. Our next example requires a sequence of **if** statements.

problem: making change

> Write a change-making program that accepts as input a price and amount of money tendered, then prints the minimum number and type of coins required for change.

> When writing a program that simulates a real-life process, it's a good idea to try imagining the steps you'd go through yourself.

Who hasn't made change? First, you count out the dollars, then the half-dollars, and so on through the pennies. Frankly, the change-making algorithm of program *ChangeMaker* isn't going to be a great advance in computer science:

first refinement

count out the dollars;
count out the half-dollars;
count out the quarters;
count out the dimes;
count out the nickels;
count out the pennies;

On the other hand, it's still a challenge to write a program that imitates the fine steps a human change-maker takes almost automatically. A real-life clerk would inform the customer if she were shortchanged, and so should our program. A person doesn't think about pluralizing words, but we'll have to teach the computer to add an 's' to plural coin names. A human wouldn't bother announcing the coins that she *wasn't* returning as change, and neither should *ChangeMaker*. We'll have to modify our pseudocode outline to make it clear that useless or misleading work will be avoided:

second refinement

find out the price and amount tendered;
decide if there's enough money;
if *there's no change*
    then *say thanks*
    else
        if *there are dollars in the change, return them*;
        if *there are half-dollars in the change, return them*;
            . . .
        if *there are pennies in the change, return them*;

A second imperative is to make *ChangeMaker* as well-written as possible. Its output should be clear. It should be robust, and able to deal with the 'unexpected' situations we just mentioned. It should be self-documenting where possible, but comments should be added to clarify less-than-obvious features. Finally, it should take advantage of procedures to minimize the length and complexity of its code. The completed program is shown below.

change making program

```
program ChangeMaker (input, output);
   {Computes minimum coinage for making change.  Data file oriented.}
const DOLLAR=100;
      HALFDOLLAR=50;
      QUARTER=25;
      DIME=10;
      NICKEL=5;
      PENNY=1;
var Price, Tendered: real;  {Amounts are input as real dollar amounts...}
    Change: integer;         {...but are dealt with as pennies in the program.}
    MoneyIsDue: boolean;
procedure ComputeChange (Unit: integer; var Change: integer);
   {Prints number of coins.  Reduces Change by that many Units.}
   var Pieces: integer;
   begin
      Pieces := Change div Unit;
      Change := Change mod (Pieces * Unit);
      write (Pieces:1);
      case Unit of
         100: write (' dollar');
         50: write (' fifty-cent piece');
         25: write (' quarter');
         10: write (' dime');
         5: write (' nickel');
         1: write (' cent')
      end; {case}
      if Pieces>1  {Take care of multiple coins.}
         then writeln ('s')
         else writeln
   end; {ComputeChange}
begin {ChangeMaker}
   readln (Price, Tendered);
   MoneyIsDue := Price>Tendered;
      {Express the potential change in pennies.}
   Change := abs(trunc(100*(Price-Tendered)));
   if Price = Tendered
      then writeln ('Thanks!')
      else begin
         if MoneyIsDue
            then writeln ('Too little!  You''re short by')
            else writeln ('Your change is exactly');
         if Change>=100 then ComputeChange (DOLLAR,Change);
         if Change>=50 then ComputeChange (HALFDOLLAR,Change);
         if Change>=25 then ComputeChange (QUARTER,Change);
         if Change>=10 then ComputeChange (DIME,Change);
         if Change>=5 then ComputeChange (NICKEL,Change);
         if Change>=1 then ComputeChange (PENNY,Change)
      end {else}
end. {ChangeMaker}
```

```
11.95 8.21
Too little!  You're short by
3 dollars
1 fifty-cent piece
2 dimes
4 cents
```

Self-Check Questions

Q. What's wrong with the *boolean* expression in this statement?

if *Finished=true* **then** etc.

A. As a *boolean* variable, *Finished* represents either the value *true* or *false*. *Finished=true* represents the exact same value. Thus, the redundant way the expression is written forces the computer to go through the unenlightening exercise of determining that (*true=true*) is *true*, or that (*false=true*) is *false*.

Short Circuiting **if** Statements

The **if** statements in program *ChangeMaker* were basically independent of each other. Since the statements were in sequence, each statement's *boolean* expression was evaluated regardless of the previous statement's effect. However, by nesting **if** statements we can arrange them in a manner that short-circuits the process. If a *boolean* test is ever failed, the remaining tests will be skipped.

We'll usually want to take advantage of this technique when we're examining a lot of data. Problems that are sure to require it typically begin 'Find a number such that...,' and then list the characteristics of the answer. The Stolen Gold Shipment Mystery is a typical example.

problem: stolen gold

> Three desperadoes robbed a shipment of gold bars late one night. They escaped to their hideout, and resolved to divide their booty in the morning. However, as soon as one of the bandits heard the others snoring, he divided the stolen gold into three equal piles, finding one bar left over. He buried one of the three piles under a tree, along with the extra bar. Then he went to sleep, sure that he had protected his interest in the treasure. Naturally, the other two outlaws were no more honest than the first. Each in turn crept to the cache of gold, divided it three ways, and found one bar left over, which he kept along with 'his' third.
>
> Soon came morning and the final three-way division. Oddly enough, this division also left one odd bar remaining. The highwaymen fought over this bar, and in an unprecedented three-way draw, shot each other dead.

The problem we pose is this: Each of the four three-way divisions left exactly one bar. How many bars could have been in the entire shipment? Assume that the shipment contained no more than 500 bars.

We can solve the gold shipment mystery by mimicking the action of the bandits (the same approach we used for making change). We'll test each number between 1 and 500 to see if it, after the repeated divisions and subtractions, still leaves a remainder of 1. In pseudocode we have:

refinement

```
for every number from 1 through 500
   if the first bandit's division leaves a remainder of 1 then
      if the second bandit's division leaves a remainder of 1 then
         if the third bandit's division leaves a remainder of 1 then
            if the final division leaves a remainder of 1 then
               we've got a possible answer
```

Picture what will happen when a program based on this pseudocode runs. Suppose our trial number passes the first division. If it fails the second division, the third and final trials are not made. Nesting the statements abbreviates the loop. Only numbers that pass each test will be considered in subsequent tests, and only numbers that pass every **if** test will be printed as solutions.

stolen gold program

```
program StolenGold (output);
   {Demonstrates nested if statements.}
var TrialNumber, DividedNumber: integer;
begin
   for TrialNumber := 1 to 500 do
      if (TrialNumber mod 3) = 1 then begin {First bandit.}
         DividedNumber := 2*(TrialNumber div 3);
         if (DividedNumber mod 3) = 1 then begin {Second bandit.}
            DividedNumber := 2*(DividedNumber div 3);
            if (DividedNumber mod 3) = 1 then begin {Third bandit.}
               DividedNumber := 2*(DividedNumber div 3);
               if (DividedNumber mod 3) = 1 then
                  writeln (TrialNumber:3, ' is a solution.')
            end
         end
      end
end. {StolenGold}
```

```
 79 is a solution.
160 is a solution.
241 is a solution.
322 is a solution.
403 is a solution.
484 is a solution.
```

Sophisticated *boolean* Tests 6-2

THREE 'WORD-SYMBOLS'—**and**, **or**, and **not**—are the *boolean* operators. Just as the word-symbol **div** takes *integer* operands to form an *integer*-valued expression, the *boolean* operators use *boolean* operands to create *boolean*-valued expressions.

boolean operators can combine several tests that would otherwise require a series of **if** statements. The first, **and**, joins two conditions into a single expression.

the **and** operator

> If we have two *boolean* values (call them *Condition* and *Decision*), the expression:
>
> *Condition* **and** *Decision*
>
> is evaluated as *true* if both *Condition* and *Decision* are *true*. If either or both of them are *false*, the entire expression is *false*.

We can use **and** in any *boolean* expression. It can help set the condition of an **if** statement:

```
if (Value>5) and (Value<10) then
   writeln ('The value is within limits.');
```

or appear on the right-hand side of an assignment:

```
Capital := (Letter>='A') and (Letter<='Z');
```

For example, program *Palindrome*, below, reads in a five-letter word, and decides whether or not it's spelled the same forward and backward.

palindrome program

```
program Palindrome (input, output);
   {Recognizes five-letter palindromes.}
var c1, c2, c3, c4, c5: char;
begin
   writeln ('Please enter a five-letter word.');
   readln (c1, c2, c3, c4, c5);
   write (c5, c4, c3, c2, c1);
   if (c1=c5) and (c2=c4) then write (' is')
                          else write (' is not');
   writeln (' a palindrome.')
end. {Palindrome}
```

```
Please enter a five-letter word.
opera
arepo is not a palindrome.
```

The second operator, **or**, yields a result of *true* if one or the other (or both) of its operands has the value *true*. This idea isn't nearly as strange as it sounds—the English sentence:

If I do well on the midterm, or ace the final, then I'll pass.

is a perfect example of '**or**ing' two values:

> **if** (*I do well on the midterm*) **or** (*I ace the final*) **then**
> *I'll pass*

the **or** operator

> The *boolean* operator **or** is less restrictive than **and** is. The expression:
>
> *Condition* **or** *Decision*
>
> is *true* if either *Condition* or *Decision*, or both of them, are *true*. It's only *false* if *Condition* and *Decision* are both *false*.

For example, this program segment:

```
if (PurchasePrice<=BankBalance) or CreditIsGood then begin
    writeln ('Who should I make the check out to?');          etc.
```

lets a check be written if there's enough money in the bank to cover the purchase (*PurchasePrice<=BankBalance*), or if the value of the *boolean* variable *CreditIsGood* is *true*. Naturally, it's all right for both conditions to be *true*, too.

The third *boolean* operator, **not**, is analogous to the minus sign in math. It reverses a *boolean* condition.

the **not** operator

> The **not** operator's result is the opposite of its operand. The expression:
>
> **not** *Condition*
>
> represents *true* if *Condition is false*, and *false* otherwise.

not negates the very first (and *only* the first) *boolean* value to follow it.

```
if not odd(InputValue) then
    writeln (InputValue, 'couldn''t possibly be prime.');
```

using parentheses

As you might expect, we can use parentheses within *boolean* expressions. In arithmetic expressions, parentheses play two roles. First, they circumvent the operator hierarchy, so that:

$$2 * 2 + 2 = 6 \qquad (2 * 2) + 2 = 6 \qquad \textit{but} \qquad 2 * (2 + 2) = 8$$

Second, the presence of parentheses usually makes the effect of complex expressions less ambiguous to program readers. *boolean* expressions use parentheses for the same reasons.

> The Golden Rule of *boolean* Operators
>
> Equalities and inequalities must be parenthesized when **not, and** or **or** appear in an expression.

Parentheses *must* be used in these expressions.

> **not** (*Key*='T')
> (*Voltage*=110) **and** (*Amperage*<10)
> (*Limit*<5) **or** (*Limit*>=10)
> (*Temperature*>80) **and** *Sunny*

Operator precedence is the reason. All of the *boolean* operators have higher precedence than the relational operators, so this expression:

> *A*>*B* **or** *C*>*D*

is misinterpreted by the computer as:

> *A*> (*B* **or** *C*) >*D*

which is meaningless (unless *A, B, C*, and *D* are *boolean* expressions—in Pascal, *false* is 'less than' *true*).

Parentheses may also be required to put together expressions that include two or more different *boolean* operators.

boolean precedence

> The order of precedence in the *boolean* operator hierarchy is: **not, and, or. not** has the most precedence, while **or** has least.

Suppose we want an action to take place if *Condition* and *Decision* are both *false*. This statement:

> **if not** *Condition* **and not** *Decision* **then** etc.

does the job. These expressions:

> **not** *Condition* **and** *Decision*
> **not** *Condition* **or** *Decision*

might sound good in English, but their effect in Pascal is unexpected—only *Condition* is being **not**ed. In fact, we'll give the strange advice that you forget about the relative *boolean* operator precedences entirely, since...

always use parentheses

> When **not, and,** or **or** appear in *boolean* expressions, it's good programming practice to use parentheses as internal documentation, even if they don't affect the expressions' value.

This expression uses the smallest legal number of parentheses—zero:

> **if not** *Hot* **and** *Humid* **or** *Raining* **then** etc.

But this version is self-documenting and unambiguous:

> **if** ((**not** *Hot*) **and** *Humid*) **or** *Raining* **then** etc.

If *boolean* operator precedence makes an expression long enough to be unwieldy or confusing, it can usually be rewritten by following the *distri-*

butive laws, as shown below. Assume that *p*, *q*, and *r* are *boolean*-valued expressions or variables:*

distributive laws

(*p* **or** *r*) **and** (*q* **or** *r*) = (*p* **and** *q*) **or** *r*
(*p* **and** *r*) **or** (*q* **and** *r*) = (*p* **or** *q*) **and** *r*

A similar set of relations is known as *De Morgan's* laws:

De Morgan's laws

(**not** *p*) **and** (**not** *q*) = **not** (*p* **or** *q*)
(**not** *p*) **or** (**not** *q*) = **not** (*p* **and** *q*)

boolean expressions may seem hard to evaluate at first, but looking at them one term at a time helps bring them into perspective. The effect of the *boolean* operators can be summarized in this *truth table*:

truth tables

not *true* is *false*
not *false* is *true*

true **and** *true* is *true*
true **and** *false* is *false*
false **and** *false* is *false*

true **or** *true* is *true*
true **or** *false* is *true*
false **or** *false* is *false*

Sometimes we'll know that an expression will be *false* even before each subexpression is evaluated, as in this program segment:

```
if (Denominator<>0) and ((Numerator/Denominator)>Fraction) then
    writeln ('We have a lucky winner!');
```

An output statement is executed if *Denominator* doesn't equal zero, and if the quotient of *Numerator* and *Denominator* exceeds *Fraction*. Now, if *Denominator* does equal zero, the entire expression will be *false*, because both operands of **and** must be *true* for the expression to be *true*. Unfortunately, the computer doesn't think ahead—it usually tries to evaluate the expression by carrying out the division.

full evaluation

In Pascal, we must assume that *boolean* expressions are always completely evaluated.

Since division by zero is an affront to all thinking women, men, and computers, a run-time error occurs and the program crashes. The segment should be rewritten to make the two evaluations explicitly consecutive, and not inadvertently simultaneous.

avoiding division by zero

```
if (Denominator<>0) then
    if (Numerator/Denominator)>Fraction then
        writeln ('We have a lucky winner!');
```

* Why *p*, *q*, and *r*? It's traditional, and tradition builds character.

Self-Check Questions

Q. Write each of these relations or conditions as a *boolean* expression.

a) *ConditionMet* is *true*
b) $50 \leq Time \leq 100$
c) *Letter* is 'V' or *Goals* is less than 4
d) $A < 27$, $B > 6$, $C \neq 13$, and *Char* isn't 'T'
e) $A < 27$, $B > 6$, $C \neq 13$, and *Char* isn't 'T', or, on the other hand, $50 \leq Time \leq 100$
f) *State* is neither *High* nor *Low*.

A. Note the necessary use of parentheses around relational expressions.

a) *ConditionMet*
b) (*Time*>=50) **and** (*Time*<=100)
c) (*Letter*='V') **or** (*Goals*<4)
d) (*A*<27) **and** (*B*>6) **and** (*C*<>13) **and** (*Char*<>'T')
e) ((*A*<27) **and** (*B*>6) **and** (*C*<>13) **and** (*Char*<>'T'))
or ((*Time*>=50) **and** (*Time*<=100))
f) (*State*<>*High*) **and** (*State*<>*Low*)

Q. One limitation of the **or** operator is that it's unable to differentiate between a single *true* operand and two *true* operands. Suppose that we want an action to be carried out if *A* is *true*, or *B* is *true*, but absolutely *not* if both of them are *true.* Write a *boolean* expression that accurately states our condition.

A. The expression we have to create is known as an *exclusive or.*

(*A* **and not** *B*) **or** (*B* **and not** *A*)

Some languages, but not Pascal, include a special operator, **XOR**, to state this condition.

Q. Express the meaning of these *boolean* expressions in English.

not (*A* **or** *B*) **or** (*A* **and** *B*) {Condition 1}
(*A* **and** *B*) **or** (**not** *A* **and not** *B*) {Condition 2}

A. The conditions stated are known as *equivalence.* The expressions are *true* if *A* and *B* are both *true* or if both are *false.* Thus, equivalence is the exact opposite of the exclusive **or**.

A Little Ado About Sets and **in**

Our final dealings in *boolean* matters involve a neat relational operator called **in**. It indicates whether or not a value is included in a larger group, or *set*, whose members can be defined as we wish.*

* A number of other operations can be performed with sets, but we're not going to encounter them formally until Chapter 14.

the **in** operator

> The relational operator **in** forms the following *boolean* expression:
>
> *value* **in** [*a listed set of ordinal values*]
>
> This expression represents *true* if *value* belongs to the specified set, and *false* if *value* isn't mentioned.

case error checking

A typical application of set expressions is to error-check entry to a **case** statement. Recall that it's a run-time error if the value of the **case** expression doesn't appear in the constant list. It doesn't take much conceptual rewording to see that the constant list contains the *set* of values the **case** expression may safely assume. The expression *could* be checked in advance like this:

```
if ((Score>=0) and (Score<=10)) or (Score=15) then
  case Score of
    10: writeln ('Exceptionally Good');
    8, 9: writeln ('Good');
    5, 6, 7: writeln ('Barely Passing');
    3, 4: writeln ('Flunking');
    0, 1, 2: writeln ('Exceptionally Flunking');
    15: writeln ('Something tells me you cheated.')
  end; {case}
```

But this is a clumsy way to protect our **case** statement. A better method involves using the sets and the **in** operator.

defining sets

> A set can be defined by listing its members, separated by commas, between *square brackets* ([ ]). All the members of a set must be of one ordinal type.

For example, the set of integers from 0 to 9 is:

[0, 1, 2, 3, 4, 5, 6, 7, 8, 9]

whereas the set of *char* values that represent the digits is:

['0', '1', '2', '3', '4', '5', '6', '7', '8', '9']

Note that each *char* constant is put in single quotes, as usual.

set shorthand

> If the members of a set are sequential ordinal values—*integers* in numerical order, or *char* values in the order of their collating sequence—we can simplify things a bit by using two periods between the first and last members, much as we would use an ellipsis in English.

[0 .. 9]   ['A' .. 'Z']   ['0' .. '9']

Two or more ordered sequences, like the set of upper- and lower-case letters, can be shown in a single expression like this:

Letter **in** [´a´ .. ´z´, ´A´ .. ´Z´]

The *Score* example is rewritten as:

```
if (Score in [ 0 .. 10, 15 ]) then
   case Score of
      10: writeln (´Exceptionally Good´);
      8, 9: writeln (´Good´);
      5, 6, 7: writeln (´Barely Passing´);
      3, 4: writeln (´Flunking´);
      0, 1, 2: writeln (´Exceptionally Flunking´);
      15: writeln (´Something tells me you cheated.´)
   end; {case}
```

two final points

Two final points end our discussion of sets. First, any representation of a value can be used in the set definition—it doesn't have to be one of the constants of the type.

```
if (Value in [ (ErrorRange–Correction) .. HighBound ] ) then begin
   etc. {Expressions can appear in the set definition.}
```

The second point is that in a set *non*-membership test, the entire *boolean* set expression is put in parentheses and preceded by the **not** operator.

```
if not (NextCharacter in [ ´0´ .. ´9´ ] ) then
   writeln (´You must enter a digit´);
```

Self-Check Questions

Q. Is it possible for this to be a valid expression?

InputValue **in** [−15 .. 25, ´f´ .. ´w´]

A. It couldn't possibly be a good *boolean* expression, because we've tried to define a set that contains two different types of values—*integer*, and *char*. The members of a set, and the value whose membership we're checking, must all belong to the same ordinal type.

Focus On Programming: Exhaustive Search, Reading Programs 6-3

IN CHAPTER 5, WE SAID THAT BRUTE-FORCE solutions, while not necessarily efficient or elegant, are often the easiest kind to implement quickly and correctly. They may waste the computer's time, but they save ours. A specialized form of brute force is called *exhaustive search*. Instead of designing an algorithm to produce a final answer directly, we examine the problem's *solution space*—all of its potential answers—to find one or more that are correct.

solution spaces

A famous problem that's often solved through exhaustive search is the Traveling Salesman problem. A salesman must visit seven different cities on his sales route. He can start anywhere, and visit them in any order. Is there some technique he can use to minimize the distance he has to travel? A solution that seems too obvious to work turns out to work well—write a program that figures out how long every possible route is, and take the shortest one.

Computers are good at solving problems by exhaustive search because they can go through large solution spaces quickly. Unfortunately, the pioneers of programming learned that the computer is a Sorcerer's Apprentice. Although a computer increases the speed at which one can perform calculations, it also vastly accelerates the rate at which one can make mistakes and produce nonsense. Worse yet, even correct programs can produce output in such quantity as to be virtually useless. Let's look at a problem that might lead us into such a trap.

problem: embedded word

> The letters 'ergro' appear in the middle of an ordinary word. They are preceded by three letters, and are followed by the same three letters in the same order. The first letter is a vowel, and the other two are different consonants. What is the word?

Program *AllPossibilities*, below, implements a simple exhaustive search algorithm. It prints every possible word formed by prefixing and following 'ergro' with the same three letters. We've shown the first few lines of its output.

an exhaustive search program

```
program AllPossibilities (output);
  {Prints all possible outputs of the form XXXERGROXXX.}

var Ch1, Ch2, Ch3: char;

begin
  for Ch1 := 'A' to 'Z' do
    for Ch2 := 'A' to 'Z' do
      for Ch3 := 'A' to 'Z' do
        writeln (Ch1, Ch2, Ch3, 'ERGRO', Ch1, Ch2, Ch3)
end. {AllPossibilities}
```

```
↓     ↓     ↓     ↓     ↓
AAAERGROAAA
AABERGROAAB
AACERGROAAC          etc.
```

All we have to do now is scan the output and find an ordinary word. But how much output *is* there? *Ch3* will change 26 times for each increment of *Ch2*. *Ch2*, in turn, changes 26 times for every advance of *Ch1*. The *writeln* in *AllPossibilities*, then, is executed 26*26*26 times.

The number of lines of output produced by *AllPossibilities* equals the solution space it searches—17,576. The sheer size of this output makes it worthless. Even if we modified the program to print eight columns of twenty-five lines each, more than eighty-five pages would be generated. If we want to solve this problem realistically, we have to figure out a method of limiting the solution space that is searched.

How can we go about improving our algorithm? Well, if you recall program *StolenGold*, you'll remember that we used nested **if** statements to short-circuit the loop when a potential answer was known to be invalid. As a result, *StolenGold* automatically winnowed out the incorrect answers. *AllPossibilities*, on the other hand, relies on the program *user* to do the dirty work.

limiting the solution space

We can begin to reduce the solution space by using all the information in the problem statement. The first letter is a vowel, and the other two are different consonants. *FewerPossibilities* incorporates these checks into our basic algorithm.

a less exhausting search

```
program FewerPossibilities (output);
  {Reduces the amount of output.}

var Ch1, Ch2, Ch3:  char;

begin
  for Ch1 := 'A' to 'U' do
    if Ch1 in ['A','E','I','O','U'] then
      for Ch2 := 'B' to 'Z' do
        if not (Ch2 in ['E','I','O','U']) then
          for Ch3 := 'B' to 'Z' do
            if not (Ch3 in [Ch2, 'E','I','O','U']) then
              writeln (Ch1, Ch2, Ch3, 'ERGRO', Ch1, Ch2, Ch3)
end. {FewerPossibilities}
```

```
↓     ↓     ↓     ↓     ↓
ABCERGROABC
ABDERGROABD
ABFERGROABF          etc.
```

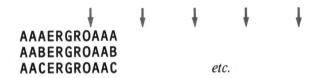

When we multiply **for** loops to find the number of words *FewerPossibilities* prints, we should discount iterations that don't result in output because one of the **if** statements isn't passed. The first loop goes all the way 5 times (for A, E, I, O, and U). The next loop passes 21 times—once for each consonant—and the final loop succeeds only 20 times. Thus, *FewerPossibilities* churns out 5*21*20, or 2100, words to check.

Is *FewerPossibilities* more efficient than *AllPossibilities*? Certainly, even though the code is longer and now involves *boolean* checks. The improvement in our basic algorithm has reduced the solution space the user must pore over by a factor of eight.

FewerPossibilities can be improved by using our knowledge of English to limit the solution space even further. For example, 'Q' couldn't be one of the consonants because it can't be followed by a 'U'. If we add it to the sets of disallowed characters, our output is reduced to 5*20*19, or 1900, words. Taking out 'X' and 'Z' brings us down to 1530 possibilities. Beyond this the advantages of limiting the solution space must be weighed against the potential of letting the correct answer slip by.*

Reading Programs

In *The Psychology of Computer Programming*, Gerald Weinberg warns that program reading is a dying art. 'Just as television has turned the heads of the young from the old-fashioned joys of book reading,' he says, 'so have terminals and generally improved turnaround made the reading of programs the mark of a hopelessly old-fashioned programmer.' He goes on to admit that working face-to-face with a giant computer is probably more exciting than contemplating other people's programs. However, he concludes that there's something to be gained even by laughing at other programmer's bad examples.

Our final example for this chapter is a long program for you to read. The problem it solves is very different from *AllPossibilities*:

problem: bowling scores

> Write a program that keeps a running total of bowling scores for one player. Program input will be the number of pins knocked down with each bowled ball, and its output should be the player's score up to that point.*

Clearly, we're not going to worry about solution spaces here! Our problem, once more, is imitation. We want to copy the actions a human scorekeeper takes to score a frame. Let's not cheat you out of your money's worth of stepwise refinement:

* So what's the word? *Underground*.

first refinement

get one ball's score;
get another ball's score if necessary;
wrap up a previous spare if necessary;
wrap up a previous strike if necessary;
finish scoring this frame if possible;
start all over again;
if the tenth is a spare or strike, do special handling;

To refresh your memory of the rules, a spare frame's score is increased by the next ball, while a strike frame's score is increased by the sum of the next two balls. If a spare or strike is scored in the tenth and final frame, the bowler gets to bowl one or two extra balls. We can refine our rough pseudocode by imagining a scorekeeper's actions in more procedural terms.

second refinement

initialize all program variables;
for *each of 10 frames*
  get the first ball's score;
  get the next ball's score, if the first wasn't a strike;
  if *we've had two strikes, score the frame two frames back*;
  if *we're riding on one strike, score the last frame*;
  if *we're working on a spare, score the last frame*;
  if *the current frame has scored less than ten, score the current frame*;
  update the game condition variables;
if *there was a strike or spare on the tenth frame*
  process the extra frame;

What does a human scorekeeper have to know as she goes along? Naturally, she has to keep track of the number of pins knocked down by each ball. She also has to know what happened in the last frame, and sometimes, in the frame before that. A human scorekeeper has a scoresheet to keep all these notes on. As Pascal programmers, we have program variables:

outline of variables

Score
Frame
FirstBall — *integer variables*
SecondBall
NumberOfPins

LastTwoWereStrikes
LastWasStrike — *boolean variables*
LastWasSpare

What about the jobs a scorekeeper does? We turn to procedures:

outline of procedures

GetTheNextBall
HandleFrame
TwoMoreBalls
OneMoreBall

At this point, we could return to our last refinement and restate it in far more precise terms. Instead, we'll jump right to the end. Program *BowlingScore*, which appears over the next few pages, is the final result of our refinements. We'd like you to read *BowlingScore*, and see what you can learn from it.

state variables

How can you go about reading a program as long as *BowlingScore*? A good way to begin is by skimming. Read over the main program and try to get a feel for the different *states* that prevail during execution. What frame are we on? Are we working on a strike or spare? Exactly when do we make the transition from one frame to the next? From one state to the next?

reading programs

Next, read through the procedures. Are their names self-explanatory? Perhaps a note in the margin will help you remember a detail of a procedure's operation. What is the program state on entry to the procedure, and on exit? What values does each procedure change? Note that most of our comments are intended to help delineate the structure of the program rather than to explain its algorithm. Does this help or hinder your understanding of the program?

Go back to the main program and see how it uses its procedures. Go to the beginning of the main **for** loop and pose a state—say, there was a spare on the previous frame, or a strike, or perhaps the first bowled ball is a strike. What happens? Mentally run some sample input through the program to see what it does.

Read the program to see how we used procedures and control statements to divide execution into well-defined actions. Why did we use a **case** statement for two-way choice in procedure *HandleFrame*? Could the **if** statements be further nested? Is there unnecessary repetition in our coding? Are all the variables we declared really needed? Could the *boolean* conditions be restated in a better way?

Finally, appraise the program. What are its shortcomings? Does it always work? How well does it error check input? How robust is it? Can its output be made more attractive? How could it be modified for an interactive programming environment?

the moral

> Reading another person's program can be a difficult job. However, it can give an insight into programming that can't be taught in a class.

Learn to criticize your own programs by practicing on ours.

bowling program

```
program BowlingScore (input, output);
   {Keeps bowling score for one player. Error checks for valid input.}
var Score, Frame: integer;
    LastTwoWereStrikes, LastWasStrike, LastWasSpare: boolean;
procedure GetTheNextBall (var NumberOfPins: integer; Max: integer);
   {Reads a ball value and makes sure it's between 0 and Max.}
   begin
      read (NumberOfPins);
      if NumberOfPins < 0 then begin {Assume 0 for a negative entry.}
         writeln ('Negative ball value; assuming 0.');
         NumberOfPins := 0
      end
      else if NumberOfPins > Max then begin {Assume spare for too-large value.}
         writeln ('Ball value too large; assuming ', Max:1);
         NumberOfPins := Max
      end
   end; {GetTheNextBall}
procedure HandleFrame (Frame: integer; var Score: integer;
      var LastTwoWereStrikes, LastWasStrike, LastWasSpare: boolean);
   {Score one frame, update the strike and spare state variables.}
   var FirstBall, SecondBall: integer;
   begin
      GetTheNextBall (FirstBall, 10);
      case FirstBall = 10 of {Was it a strike?}
         true: SecondBall := 0;
         false: GetTheNextBall (SecondBall, 10-FirstBall)
      end; {case}
         {Complete the scoring of earlier frames if necessary.}
      if LastTwoWereStrikes then begin
         Score := Score + FirstBall + 20;
         writeln ('Frame ', Frame-2:1, ' Score ', Score:1)
      end;
      if LastWasStrike and (FirstBall < 10) then begin
         Score := Score + FirstBall + SecondBall + 10;
         writeln ('Frame ', Frame-1:1, ' Score ', Score:1)
      end;
      if LastWasSpare then begin
         Score := Score + FirstBall + 10;
         writeln ('Frame ', Frame-1:1, ' Score ', Score:1)
      end;
      if (FirstBall + SecondBall) < 10 then begin
         Score := Score + FirstBall + SecondBall;
         writeln ('Frame ', Frame:1, ' Score ', Score:1)
      end;
```

```
        {Update the game state variables—what are we working on?}
      LastTwoWereStrikes := LastWasStrike and (FirstBall = 10);
      LastWasStrike := FirstBall = 10;
      LastWasSpare := (FirstBall < 10) and ((FirstBall + SecondBall) = 10)
    end; {HandleFrame}
procedure TwoMoreBalls (var Score: integer; LastTwoWereStrikes: boolean);
    {A special case—get two more balls for a strike in the tenth frame.}
    var FirstBall, SecondBall: integer;
    begin
      GetTheNextBall (FirstBall, 10);
      case FirstBall = 10 of {Was it a strike?}
        true: GetTheNextBall (SecondBall, 10);
        false: GetTheNextBall (SecondBall, 10-FirstBall)
      end ; {case}
        {Complete the scoring of the ninth frame, if necessary.}
      if LastTwoWereStrikes then begin
        Score := Score + FirstBall + 20;
        writeln ('Frame 9 Score ', Score:1)
      end;
        {Finish by scoring the tenth frame.}
      Score := Score + FirstBall + SecondBall + 10;
      writeln ('Frame 10 Score ', Score:1)
    end; {TwoMoreBalls}
procedure OneMoreBall (var Score: integer);
    {Another special case—get one more ball for a tenth frame spare.}
    var FirstBall: integer;
    begin
      GetTheNextBall (FirstBall, 10);
      Score := Score + FirstBall + 10;
      writeln ('Frame 10 Score ', Score:1)
    end; {OneMoreBall}
begin {BowlingScore}
    {Initialize the game's state variables.}
    Score := 0;
    LastTwoWereStrikes := false;
    LastWasStrike := false;
    LastWasSpare := false;
      {Process the score for each frame.}
    for Frame := 1 to 10 do
      HandleFrame (Frame, Score, LastTwoWereStrikes,
                                      LastWasStrike, LastWasSpare);
      {Take care of special cases in the tenth frame.}
    if LastWasStrike
      then TwoMoreBalls (Score, LastTwoWereStrikes)
      else if LastWasSpare then OneMoreBall (Score)
end. {BowlingScore}
```

```
              ↓       ↓       ↓       ↓       ↓
9 1   0 10   10   10   6 2   7 3   8 2   10   9 0   9 1   10
Frame 1 Score 10
Frame 2 Score 30
Frame 3 Score 56
Frame 4 Score 74
Frame 5 Score 82
Frame 6 Score 100
Frame 7 Score 120
Frame 8 Score 139
Frame 9 Score 148
Frame 10 Score 168
```

Antibugging and Debugging 6-4

MOST AUTOMOBILE ACCIDENTS HAPPEN close to home, because that's where people do most of their driving. By the same token, the **if** statement probably tends to generate more than its fair share of bugs, because it appears in just about every program.

One small bug that's extremely hard to find is caused by a misplaced semicolon. For example, in the segment below, *GetMoreData* is called whether *ReadingData* is *true* or *false*. Can you see why?

```
if ReadingData then;
    GetMoreData;
NextStatement;    etc.
```

empty statement bugs

Reformatting the segment makes the bug stand out. The compiler thinks that the **if** statement controls an empty statement:

```
if ReadingData then
    ;        {This empty statement is the statement's action.}
GetMoreData;
NextStatement;    etc.
```

The same error occurs when an **else** is followed by a semicolon. Note that these are *semantic* errors. They are syntactically correct, so the programs they appear in will compile. However, their effect is unintended. Preceding an **else** with a semicolon, in contrast, is strictly a syntax error. The semicolon's effect is to dissociate an **if** statement's **else** and **then** parts. The compiler will complain about the sudden appearance of the reserved word **else**.

An extremely common mistake is to neglect to express an **if** statement's action as a compound statement. As we've said before, program format has no effect on program semantics. This segment doesn't do what it appears to:

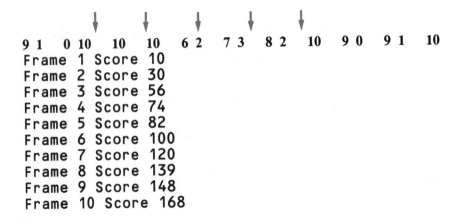

compound statement bugs

```
if Searching then
   PrintCurrentValues (HobNob, Goblin, Munchkin);
   UpdateInput (ChangeData);
   writeln ('I hope everything works!')
else
   GetRawInput (NewData);
   writeln ('Moving on to computations.');
FigureThingsOut;     etc.
```

If we format it the way the computer reads it, we can see why the compiler will complain about a meaningless **else**.

```
if Searching then PrintCurrentValues (HobNob, Goblin, Munchkin);
UpdateInput (ChangeData);
writeln ('I hope everything works!')
else          {What is this word doing here?}
GetRawInput (NewData);
writeln ('Moving on to computations.');
FigureThingsOut;     etc.
```

Now, errors like this are usually due to carelessness. The action (or alternative action) of a statement may have originally been just one statement or procedure call. If the program is modified, and additional actions are added, it's easy to overlook the need for a **begin** and **end**. Defensive programming helps obviate the problem.

> Many programmers write *every* action as a compound statement. Reading an unnecessary **begin**, **end** pair doesn't cost the computer anything, and it may save lots of trouble later on.

boolean bugs

boolean expressions cause a whole raft of semantic and syntactic bugs. A common error occurs if you forget that **and** and **or** don't literally mean 'and' and 'or.' Suppose that the proper response to some question is either 'A' or 'B.' This assignment is meaningless in Pascal:

```
RightAnswer := Response = ('A' or 'B');
```

because **or** is a *boolean* operator, and is only used to compare *boolean* values. The statement is rewritten correctly as:

```
RightAnswer := (Response = 'A') or (Response = 'B');
```

Errors also occur in translation from English to Pascal. For example, the English phrase:

neither *A* nor *B*

translates into Pascal as:

not *A* **and not** *B*

rather than:

not *A* **or not** *B*

keep *booleans* simple

Using **not** in complex *boolean* expressions can also be tricky (but always, as Mr. Spock would say, perfectly logical). It's an interesting fact that negative expressions—those containing a **not**—are often harder to understand than positive ones—especially when they start to stretch out, like this:*

not not not not not not not ($X > Y$)

It's particularly important to keep track of parentheses. These two expressions are not identical in meaning:

not (*Hot* **and** *Tired*)   (**not** *Hot*) **and** (**not** *Tired*)

although they appear to be rather similar. This expression:

not (*Hot*) **or not** (*Tired*)

states the same as the left-hand expression above. You can prove that we're right by constructing a truth table, as we did in 6-2. Show the result of each expression for all possible values of *Hot* and *Tired*.

What do you think precipitated this error message?

```
IF NOT NEXTCHARACTER IN ['a'..'z'] THEN
       ↑OPERAND OF "NOT" MUST BE OF TYPE BOOLEAN
```

An error caused by the high precedence of the **not** operator—greater than the other relational and *boolean* operators—shows up in 'negative' set expressions:

if not *NextCharacter* **in** ['a'..'z'] **then**   etc.

The precedence of **not** (which exceeds that of the relational operators, including **in**), makes the compiler think we're trying to **not** the value of *NextCharacter*, which would be meaningless. The expression must be rewritten with parentheses:

if not (*NextCharacter* **in** ['a'..'z']) **then**   etc.

The precedence hierarchy of *boolean* and relational operators, from greatest to least, is:

* Miller, Lance A., *Programming For Non-programmers*. Intl. Journal of Man-Machine Studies, 1974, vol. 6, pp.237-260.

operator precedence

not	*most*
and	
or	
= <> < <= > >= **in**	*least*

You can appreciate that there are often a variety of ways to express identical conditions, some considerably more obscure than others. Any expression that's difficult to decipher should be rewritten by using parentheses, the Distributive laws, or De Morgan's laws.

A final common bug is to mistakenly assume that two **if** statements with opposite conditions are always the same as an **if** statement with an **else** alternative. Can you name the circumstances that would make this program segment:

```
if BitCount<0 then Twiddle(BitCount);
if BitCount>=0 then Twaddle(BitCount);
```

order matters

differ in effect from this one:

```
if BitCount<0
   then Twiddle(BitCount)
   else Twaddle(BitCount);
```

Suppose that *Twiddle* modifies the value of its argument *BitCount*, and makes it equal to or greater than zero. In the first program segment, both *Twiddle* and *Twaddle* might be called then. In the second segment, only one procedure is—never both—no matter what *Twiddle* does to *BitCount*.

Embedding Debugging Tools

Samuel Johnson may or may not have been accurate in his observation that remarriage is the triumph of hope over experience. Programming without planning for bugs, though, certainly demonstrates a failure to have learned from the past.

> Building debugging *writelns* and snapshot procedures into your programs is called *embedding* debugging code.

An obvious technique to follow in building-in debugging code is to use **if** statements and constants to switch parts of the program on and off:

```
const DEBUGGING = true;
         ...
if DEBUGGING then begin
   writeln ('Debugging point 7.');
   Print (X,Y,Z);    etc.
```

In long programs, however, the use of **if** statements may not allow a fine enough control of diagnostic output. We may want to have a switch with intermediate positions, and not just the *boolean* equivalent of 'ON' and 'OFF.' A constant can be defined with a wider range of values, and used to control a **case** statement when convenient.

debugging levels

```
const DEBUGLEVEL = 3;
    {Available debugging levels:
        0: all diagnostics off.
        1: entry to procedures announced.
        2: entry and exit of all subprograms announced.
        3: parameters printed on entry to subprograms.
        4: conditions printed at control statements.
        5: special instructions followed.        }
                ...

case DEBUGLEVEL of
    1: writeln ('Welcome to procedure CheckInput');
    3: writeln ('CheckInput:  Parameter Data: ', Data);
    5:    etc.
```

Another approach is to make debugging levels additive, so that every level implies all the actions of the lower levels as well. A sequence of nested **if** statements does the trick here:

additive debugging levels

```
if DEBUGLEVEL >= 1 then begin
    writeln ('Welcome to procedure CheckInput');
    if DEBUGLEVEL >= 2 then begin
        writeln ('CheckInput:  Parameter Data: ', Data);
        if DEBUGLEVEL >= 3 then begin
            {additional debugging levels}
                ...
        end {Level 3 debugging}
    end {Level 2 debugging}
end; {Level 1 debugging}
```

Pascal Summary

- **if** statement: allows a decision on whether or not to take an action, or which of two actions to take. A *boolean* expression is evaluated; if it's *true* the **if** statement's action is taken. If it's *false*, the action is skipped, or an alternative **else** action (if there is one) is taken instead.

if *boolean expression* **then** *action*;
{or}
if *boolean expression*
then *action*
else *action*;

- relational operators: used to compare two values of the same simple type:

Math	*Pascal*	*English*
$=$	=	*equal to*
$<$	<	*less than*
$\leqslant$	<=	*less than or equal to*
$>$	>	*greater than*
$\geqslant$	>=	*greater than or equal to*
$\neq$	<>	*not equal to*

- *boolean* operators: used to build *boolean*-valued expressions:

not *A*	the opposite of its operand
A **and** *B*	*true* if both operands are *true*
A **or** *B*	*true* if either operand is *true*

- set expression: the **in** operator creates a *boolean* expression that is *true* if an ordinal expression is found within a set of values:

Number **in** [*Test, Result, In, Out*] *Letter* **in** ['A'..'M']

- precedence: The precedence of operators found in *boolean* expressions is:

not	*most precedence*
and	
or	
<, >, <=, >=, =, <>, **in**	*least precedence*

Important Facts

- The constants of type *boolean* are *false, true*. *boolean* expressions are always fully evaluated in Pascal.
- De Morgan's laws, the distributive laws, and truth tables can be used to simplify or help you understand *boolean* expressions.
- The Golden Rule of *boolean* Operators: equalities and inequalities must be parenthesized when **not**, **and**, and **or** appear in an expression (because of the low precedence of the relational operators).
- When **if** statements follow each other, each one's *boolean* expression is evaluated—the statements are independent. In contrast, if the **if** statements

are nested, the evaluation may be short circuited. Statements nested more deeply will be skipped once a test is failed.

- The Golden Rule of **if** Statements: an **else** is always the alternative action of the nearest prior **then** action. Put an **else** action in a **begin** ... **end** to get around this association.
- The Golden Rule of Coding: syntax determines semantics. Spacing and indentation is for the benefit of human program readers.
- We can never assume that program input will be correct, but using **if** statements to check values helps make programs robust.
- Exhaustive search algorithms, a brute-force programming method, inspect a problem's entire potential solution space. We'll often try to refine such algorithms to partially limit the solution space that must be searched.
- Diagnostic error-checking code, which can be switched on and off by setting constants, is often built into programs. Such embedded debugging tools let the programmer obtain diagnostic program output during debugging, and need not be removed once the program is operational.

Self-test Exercises

6-1 If a *boolean* expression contains both relational operators (like =, <, and >) and *boolean* operators (like **and** and **or**), why will some of its terms (subexpressions) need to be put in parentheses?

6-2 Which of these *boolean* expressions are logically equivalent?

a) (*Finished* **and not** *Bankrupt*) **or** (*Bankrupt* **and not** *Finished*)
b) (*Finished* **or** *Bankrupt*) **or not** (*Bankrupt* **and** *Finished*)
c) *Finished*<>*Bankrupt*

6-3 Under what circumstances will the output statement be executed? Assume that *StillSearching* and *Found* are *boolean* variables.

```
if StillSearching = Found then
    writeln ('Value located.');
```

6-4 Is this legal Pascal? Assume that *Entry* and *Standard* are *integer* values.

```
case Entry<Standard of
    true: writeln ('Entry is less than Standard.');
    false: writeln ('Standard is greater than or equal to Entry.')
end;
```

6-5 The negation operator (an ordinary minus sign) changes the sign of its operand. Write a function *ReturnNegative* that returns its *real* operand as a negative number.

6-6 Write a *boolean* function *IsADigit* that reflects whether or not its *char* argument is a digit character.

6-7 Suppose that you want to pick a number from 4 through 7 under the following conditions: there is a 35% chance of picking 4, a 15% chance of picking 5, a 19% chance of picking 6, and a 31% percent chance of picking 7. How could you use the random number generator we developed in the text to make the pick?

6-8 Write a *boolean* function *Divisible* that returns *true* if its first argument is evenly divisible by its second argument, and *false* otherwise.

6-9 Rewrite the following statement using two **if...then** statements.

```
if (2*X) > Y
    then begin Y := 2*Y; X := X/2 end
    else writeln ('Able was I ere I saw Elba.');
```

6-10 What is the output of this program segment?

```
writeln (1=2, 2=2, (2+3)=7);
```

6-11 Compare these two program segments:

```
if (a<=b) and (a<=c)
  then Smallest := a
  else if (b<=c) and (b<=a)
    then Smallest := b
    else Smallest := c;
```

```
Smallest := a;
if b<Smallest then
  Smallest := b;
if c<Smallest then
  Smallest := c;
```

Is there any difference between them? Explain.

6-12 What's the difference between these two program segments? Which is better, and why?

```
readln (Amount);
if Amount>500
  then OverRun (Amount);
if (Amount>300) and Amount<=500)
  then UnderRun (Amount);
if (Amount>150) and Amount<=300)
  then WriteCheckFor (Amount);
if (Amount<=150)
  then ReCompute (Amount);     etc.
```

```
readln (Amount);
if Amount>500
  then OverRun (Amount)
  else if Amount>300
    then UnderRun (Amount)
    else if Amount>150
      then WriteCheckFor (Amount)
      else ReCompute (Amount);     etc.
```

6-13 Write a procedure that determines if one *integer* is evenly divisible by another. Both numbers should be passed as parameters.

6-14 Write a loop that reads in 100 positive *integers* in the range 1 through 500, and determines the largest even and smallest odd.

6-15 Suppose that the two statements below appear, as shown, in a program. What single **if** statement could you replace them with?

```
if n>=2 then n := 3*n+1;
if n>=7 then n := n-7;
```

6-16 Write a set definition that defines, for upper-case letters, *a*) the vowels, *b*) the consonants.

6-17 Write a loop that reads in 250 characters, and prints out the number of digits and punctuation marks.

6-18 The four program segments below all purport to add the even numbers between 1 and 5. What are the advantages and disadvantages of each?

```
{Example 1}
Sum := 0;
for Counter := 1 to 5 do
    if not odd(Counter) then
        Sum := Sum + Counter

{Example 3}
Sum := 6
```

```
{Example 2}
Sum := 0;
for Counter := 2 to 4 do
    if not odd(Counter) then
        Sum := Sum + Counter

{Example 4}
Sum := 5
```

More Exercises

6-18 Write a program that finds the 'middlemost' of five numbers.

6-19 An *Armstrong number* is a number of n digits that is equal to sum of each digit raised to the nth power. For example, 153 (which has three digits) equals $1^3 + 5^3 + 3^3$. Find the other three Armstrong numbers below 999.

6-20 Take a four-digit number. Add the first two digits to the last two digits. Now, square the sum. Surprise! you've got the original number again. Find the three numbers that have this special property.

6-21 The following instruction appears on a computer science final exam: "Make a statement. If the statement is true, you'll flunk the exam. If the statement is false, you'll flunk the entire course." What's the correct answer to avoid flunking?

6-22 One of the bugs associated with *boolean* expressions is the appearance of an unexpected alternative, not ruled out by the statement of the expression. Here are some everyday examples of this phenomenon.

Two people played seven games of chess, yet each won the same number of games. How could this be? Some months have 31 days, and some months have only 30. How many months have 28 days? I have two coins in my pocket that total fifty-five cents. One of the coins is not a nickel. What are the two coins?

6-23 Write a loop that sums the squares of the first 333 odd integers.

6-24 Write a procedure that takes two *integers* as parameters, and prints them in ascending order. Do the same with three *reals*. Four *char* values (in alphabetical order, of course).

6-25 Write a program to produce a table of factorials for odd or even numbers only. Prompt the user for the upper limit of the table. If the user asks for odd factorials, and gives an even upper limit, what should happen? Modify the program to give reasonable output for a negative limit input.

6-26 An peculiar property of the Fibonacci series is that if any given number is squared, it equals the product of the preceding and subsequent numbers, sometimes plus 1, and sometimes minus 1. Write a program that computes the correction for the first hundred Fibonacci numbers—should one be added or subtracted? Is any pattern apparent?

6-27 A perfect square is a number whose square root is an *integer*. Now, it's easy to make a table of the first n perfect squares—it just takes a **for** loop that prints the square of its counter variable. Finding all perfect squares between any two numbers takes a bit more doing, because the standard *sqrt* function has a *real* result that may be a tiny bit off. For example, *sqrt*(16) might equal 4.00000000001E+00, or 3.9999998888E+00. However, we can test for perfect squares like this: Given any *integer*, find its *real* square root, round this number, and then square it. If the result equals the original number, the original number is a perfect square.

Write a program that prints all perfect squares between any two numbers a and b.

6-28 A college bookstore wants to estimate its business for the next year. Experience has shown the clerks that sales depend greatly on whether a book is required or merely recommended, and whether or not it has been used before. A new, required book will sell to 90% of prospective enrollment, but if it's been used before, only 65% will buy. Similarly, 40% of the prospective enrollment will buy a newly recommended book, but just half that many buy a book that was recommended in the past.

Write a program that accepts as input a book code, the book's single-copy cost, the current number of volumes on hand, the prospective class enrollment, and data that indicates whether the book is required, recommended, and has or hasn't been used in the past. Each book is identified by a one-letter subject code, followed by an integer book code. As output, show all the input information, together with the number of books that must be ordered (if any), the total cost of all book orders, and the expected profit if the store pays 80% of list price.

6-29 Improve the above program to take more sophisticated considerations into account. Suppose that the store's cost drops to 75% of list on all orders of 10 to 50 books, and 70% on all orders of more than 50. However, also assume that the sales projections may be overstated by as much as 10%. Have your program compute the purchase sizes that will maximize potential profits.

6-30 The terms of a revolving credit account are as follows:

Unpaid Balance	*Interest Rate/Month*
\$0—\$500	1½%
\$500.01—\$1000	1¼%
over \$1000	1%

Balance	*Minimum Payment*
\$0—\$10	Balance
\$10.01—\$250	\$10
over \$250	10% of Balance

Write a program that given an unpaid balance, adds on the interest due, and prints out the minimum payment. Accept a payment, and then print a record of the transaction, including the next month's balance and minimum payment.

6-31 Here's another in our series of computer-magician programs. Write the following algorithm as a program: Ask somebody to pick a three digit number, and to think of the number as being *ABC* (where *A, B*, and *C* are the three digits of the number). Now, find out the remainders when the numbers formed by *ABC, BCA*, and *CAB* are divided by 11. Have the computer call these remainders *X, Y*, and *Z*, and add them three up as $X+Y$, $Y+Z$, and $Z+X$. If any of the sums is odd, increase or decrease it by 11—whichever operation results in a positive number less than 20. Finally, divide each of the sums in half. The resulting digits are *A, B*, and *C*.

It's a nice touch to include a 'calculator' as part of this program. Don't forget to have all output be as spellbinding as possible.

6-32 What goes on within the computer is hidden from a program user, and for this problem it's just as well. Pick a number between 1 and 100, cube it, and give it to the computer. Call this *UsersCube*. Here's how the computer can figure out the cube root—the original number. Begin with a table of cubes for the numbers 0 through 9:

$0^3=0$ $1^3=1$ $2^3=8$ $3^3=27$ $4^3=64$
$5^3=125$ $6^3=216$ $7^3=343$ $8^3=512$ $9^3=729$

Note that each cube ends with a different digit.

The computer finds the cube root of *UsersCube* in two steps. The second digit of the root equals the cube root of the number in the table whose cube ends with the same digit as *UsersCube*. The first digit of the desired cube root is found by discarding the final three digits of *UsersCube*, and comparing the remaining figures to the cubes in the table. The first digit of our cube root is the cube root of the number that is less than, or equal to, these remaining figures. For example, the second digit of the cube root of 117649 is 9 (by comparing last numbers), and the first digit is 4 (the cube root of 64, the figure nearest but not greater than 117). Write a program that carries out this weird computation.

6-33 Although one likes to think of computers as representing the ultimate in mathematical calculation, the interior of a computer is really a sort of Never-never Land, where the axioms of ordinary arithmetic are occasionally suspended. In other words, although $A+B$ may equal C, it is not necessarily true that B is equal to $C-A$. This can be very disconcerting.

Write a program that computes the following sum:

$$1 - 1/2 + 1/3 - 1/4 + \ldots - 1/1000$$

Try figuring it in several ways: working from right to left (and left to right), subtracting the sum of *all* the negative terms from the sum of the positive terms (again going right to left and left to right), summing the two series, etc. Why do you think there are differences in your results? By the way, the actual sum (to 25 decimal places) is:

0.6930971830599452969172323

6-34 A target used for throwing darts allows these scores: 7, 15, 19, 23, 29, and 37. Suppose that the purpose of a game is to throw six darts and score exactly 100 points. What are the five ways such a score can be achieved?

6-35 Sam Loyd tells of a roulette system, named after a Lord Rosslyn, that enabled a lucky player to win 777,777 francs at Monte Carlo. In the Rosslyn system, a player makes only even-money bets (we'll ignore the house percentage) in the following manner: first, make 7 consecutive one-franc bets, then 7 forty-nine-franc (7^2) bets, then 7 bets of 7^3 francs, 7 bets of 7^4, 7^5, 7^6, and 7^7 francs. Thus, forty-nine bets are made in a row, win or lose.

The problem we pose is this: How many bets, at what stakes, were won to produce winnings of exactly 777,777 francs? Don't forget to deduct losing bets from the winnings.

6-36 Write a function *Ceiling* that takes a *real* argument, and returns as an *integer* result the closest whole number above (for positive arguments) or below (for negative arguments).

6-37 A large North American country (whose name we can't cite for copyright reasons) levies taxes at the following rates: 2% on the first $4,000 of income, 3% on the next $2,000, 4% on the next $2,000, 5% on the next $2,000, and so on, to a maximum of 15% on all income in excess of $28,000. No special breaks are given to couples that file jointly.

Write a program in two parts. The first part should compute the average tax rate on any amount of income. The second part should determine the effective penalty for filing a joint return.

6-38 Write a function *IsAnInteger* which determines whether or not its argument is an *integer* value. Then, find three cases where the function doesn't work.

6-39 Extend your new programming language to allow *boolean* choice. Define the two forms of **if** statements as two entirely different statements. Can their syntax be simplified, or written in a way that helps prevent errors?

'Recursive programs are self-referencing, which will probably seem a little weird…'

7

Making Actions Continue: the Conditional Loops

Most conversations about the capabilities of computers are dominated by the subject of their incredible speed. Computers are so fast that the speed of light (or of electricity, really) sometimes becomes a limiting factor in their design.

The looping statement is the bridle programmers use to harness computer speed. Want to slow down a machine? Find the first few hundred prime numbers, or use addition and subtraction to perform multiplication and division! A single looping statement lets us state a condition that might not be satisfied for thousands, or millions, of repeated program steps.

We've already seen one of Pascal's loops—the **for** statement. The **for** is limited, though. While we might use it to see if the numbers between *a* and *b* have some property, we can't use a **for** to find the first *n* numbers with the same property—we don't know how many numbers we'll have to inspect.

The *conditional loops* **repeat** and **while** come to the rescue. In both cases, a *boolean* condition (such as *NumbersFound*=*n*) must be met to make looping stop. As a result, the **repeat** or **while** loop's action helps to determine when the loop is finished. We'll begin section 7-1 with a look at the **repeat** statement, and then move on to the **while** loop. They are very similar; their difference is that the **repeat** loop's action takes place at least once, while a **while** loop might be skipped entirely. Section 7-2 explores a variety of loop applications.

Section 7-3 describes an approach to programming known as *recursion*. Recursive programs are self-referencing—they call themselves—which will probably seem a little weird at first. Recursion can be used for repetition without loops, and it is *de rigueur* in more advanced programming courses. However, it's optional reading for most students using this text. This section also describes **forward** subprogram declarations.

Section 7-4, which contains our usual antibugging and debugging hints, is particularly important reading for this chapter. It goes over a variety of the semantic errors that occur with loops.

Note: The next chapter, 8, is devoted to a particular set of loop applications—those that involve working with characters (often known as *text processing*). Since Chapter 8 won't involve any new statements, you may want to look at its material for some extra loop programming practice.

The **repeat** and **while** Statements 7-1

LIKE MOST CONTROL STATEMENTS, the **repeat** uses a *boolean* expression to control the execution of an action.

> The **repeat** statement's action takes place, then its *exit condition* (a *boolean* expression) is evaluated. The loop's action is repeated until the exit condition is met.

looping and terminating

If the expression that represents the exit condition is *false*, the exit condition is *not* met, and the loop's action is iterated (repeated). If the expression is *true*, the exit condition *is* met. The loop is terminated and the program moves on to the next statement. In outline form, the **repeat** statement looks like this:

repeat
    action
until *boolean expression*; {the exit condition}

The statement's syntax chart is:

repeat statement

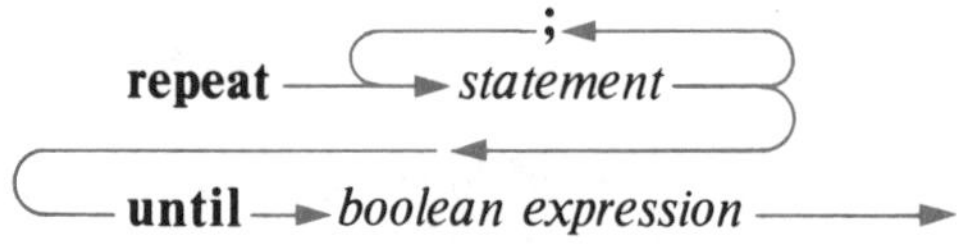

exit only at the loop end

What happens if the **repeat** loop's exit condition suddenly becomes *true* while we're in the midst of executing the loop's action? Are we snatched out of the loop and plunked down at the end of the entire statement? No, because the action of a loop is an unbreakable unit. We will never exit from the middle of a loop. The exit condition is evaluated only after the loop action has been completely carried out.

A **repeat** statement can control any of Pascal's actions. However, compound statements are unnecessary.

> Since the reserved words **repeat** and **until** show the extent of the loop, and mark its first and last statements, the **begin** and **end** of a compound statement are unnecessary.

These two statements are absolutely identical in effect:

compound statements unnecessary

repeat
    statement;
    statement
until *ExitCondition*;

repeat
    begin
        statement;
        statement
    end
until *ExitCondition*;

Program *NumberLength*, below, shows a **repeat** statement at work. The program counts the digits in an *integer* by repeatedly removing the 'ones' column, until the number equals zero.

count the digits program

```
program NumberLength (input, output);
    {Counts digits by repeated division.}
var InputNumber, NumberOfDigits: integer;
begin
    NumberOfDigits := 0;
    writeln ('Please enter an integer.');
    readln (InputNumber);
    write (InputNumber:1);
    repeat
        InputNumber := InputNumber div 10;
        NumberOfDigits := NumberOfDigits+1
    until InputNumber=0;
    writeln (' has ', NumberOfDigits:1,' digits.')
end. {NumberLength}
```

```
Please enter an integer.
-3829
-3829 has 4 digits.
```

while statement

The **while** statement is also a conditional loop, but its condition is checked prior to entering the loop, instead of on exit. The loop's action is not executed at all if the entry condition is not met.

In the first part of the **while** statement, a condition is stated as a *boolean* expression. It determines whether or not the loop will be entered (because it's an *entry condition*), and when the loop will terminate (because it implies an exit condition—the opposite of the entry condition—as well).

entry, exit conditions

In a sense, the entry condition serves as an **if** statement—a *boolean* expression must be *true* for the statement to be entered. But since the **while** is a loop statement, the expression is evaluated again after the action is completed. If it's still *true*, the action gets repeated. If the entry condition has become *false*, the action is skipped entirely, and the program moves on to the next statement.

```
while boolean expression do {the entry condition}
    action;
```

In chart form, the **while** statement is:

while statement

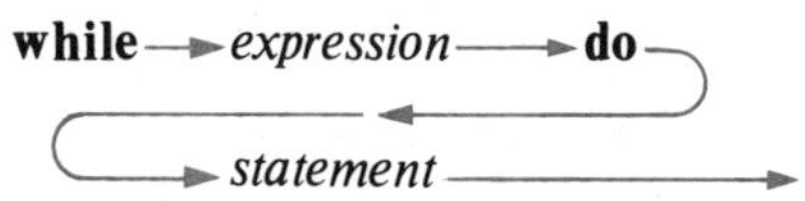

Program *LongDivision*, below, uses a **while** statement to simulate the effect of the **div** and **mod** operators. It employs a simple brute-force algorithm—repeated subtraction. However, since the dividend may be smaller than the divisor, it's possible that no subtractions will be required. Thus, a **while** loop (whose action may be skipped) is superior to a **repeat** loop (whose action always occurs at least once) in this application.

long division program

```
program LongDivision (input, output);
   {Simulates div and mod for data file input.}
var Dividend, Divisor, Wholes, Remainder: integer;
begin
   Wholes := 0;
   readln (Dividend, Divisor);
   writeln ('The integer quotient of ', Dividend:1, ' and ', Divisor:1, ' is');
   Remainder := Dividend;
   while (Remainder-Divisor)>=0 do begin
      Remainder := Remainder-Divisor;
      Wholes := Wholes+1
   end; {while}
   writeln (Wholes:1, ', with remainder ', Remainder:1)
end. {LongDivision}
```

```
22 5
The integer quotient of 22 and 5 is
4, with remainder 2
```

No matter what the action of a **repeat** or **while** loop is, the Golden Rule of loops must be observed.

the condition must change

The Golden Rule of Loops

If a loop is entered, it must end eventually. Therefore, the entry or exit condition has to contain a variable whose value is changed by the loop's action.

Without this update, one repetition is just like the next, and the loop repeats an infinite number of times. For example, this program segment's exit condition will never be met, because the *boolean* expression (*Counter* = 100) will always be *false*.

```
Counter := 0;
repeat
    writeln (Counter)
until Counter=100;
```

Although endless, infinite loops are programming errors, they won't hurt the computer. Systems usually have a built-in limit on the number of statements a single program may execute (or on the amount of computer time a program may devour) to protect users from inadvertent infinite loops. An endlessly iterating loop will eventually crash, with an epitaph like 'Statement Limit (or 'Time Limit') Exceeded.'

infinite loops

It's not hard to appreciate how similar the **while** statement is to the **repeat**. Their main difference is simply stated.

repeat vs. **while**

> The action of a **repeat** statement will take place at least once; the **while** loop's action may not be executed at all. The **repeat** statement's exit condition, when met, causes looping to stop. The **while**'s entry condition, when met, causes looping to continue.

Since in many cases either loop would work equally well, when should one use a **repeat** statement, and when a **while**? Unfortunately, this is an essay question—it doesn't have a single correct answer. On one hand, the ordinary English meanings of the reserved words help clarify a programmer's intentions. 'Repeat' implies that an action will take place at least once, and the **repeat** statement supports this contention. By the same logic, 'while' lets an element of doubt creep in—maybe the action won't take place at all—that accurately reflects the **while** statement's usage.

On the other hand, programmers often use a **while** statement even when they're sure the loop's action will take place at least once. Why? Because placing the loop's condition in the first line might make the program a little easier to read. This is especially true when a **repeat** statement involves negated conditions. This statement:

```
repeat
    action
until not A or not B;
```

is error-prone and hard to read. Using a **while** lets us restate the conditions more clearly:

```
while A and B do
    action;
```

the moral

> Common sense and clarity, more than any abstract rule of correct usage, should be the programmer's guide.

Pascal has been criticized for including two control statements that are so similar, on grounds that they make the language more complicated, but no more powerful. What do *you* think?

Self-Check Questions

Q. What's wrong with these exit conditions? Why are they probably in error?

```
      repeat
          SomeActions
   a. until true
   b. until false
   c. until abs(Counter) < 0
   d. until (Value>10) and (Value<=5)
   e. until (Value<=10) or (Value>=11)
```

A. All these exit conditions are either always *true* (*a, e*), or invariably *false* (*b, c, d*). There is no way any of them can be modified. Thus, the '*true*' loops will only take place once, and the '*false*' loops will repeat forever.

Conditional Loop Basics

Let's look at some of the basics of using conditional loops. Increasing program robustness is a common looping job. For instance, we might use a loop to give the program user a chance to correct improperly entered data. Procedure *CheckInput*, below asks the user to enter a value from *Lower* through *Upper*. The request is repeated until a legitimate value is entered.

input error check program

```
procedure CheckInput (var Value: integer; Upper, Lower: integer);
   {Gets and returns a Value between Lower and Upper.}
   begin
      repeat
         writeln ('Enter an integer from ', Lower:1, ' to ', Upper:1);
         readln (Value);
         if Value<Lower then
            writeln (Value:1,'was too small.  Try again.')
            else if Value>Upper then
               writeln (Value:1,' was too large.  Try again.')
      until Value in [Lower .. Upper]
   end; {CheckInput}
```

improving robustness

Interactive programs should include error-checking and mistake-correcting loops whenever possible. Nothing is more infuriating than a computer program that won't let a user change input she knows is wrong.

Conditional loops are essential when an unknown amount of data is to be read and processed. Program *DataAverage*, below, computes the average value in a sequence of positive numbers. Since it couldn't possibly be part of the program's data, a negative number is used to mark the end of input. The program's main loop iterates until this end marker is read. If the data list is empty, *DataAverage* prints an explicit message.

average until sentinel program

```
program DataAverage (input, output);
    {Averages a series of numbers.  -1 marks the end of data.}
const SENTINEL = -1;
var Value, Total, Average: real;
    Counter: integer;
begin
    Total := 0;
    Counter := 0;          {Initialization}
    Average := 0;
    read (Value);
    while Value<>SENTINEL do begin          {Process the data.}
        Total := Total+Value;
        Counter := Counter+1;
        read (Value)
    end; {while}
    if Counter=0
        then writeln ('No data entered.')
        else begin
            Average := Total/Counter;
            writeln ('The average of ', Counter:1, ' values is', Average)
        end {else}
end. {DataAverage}
```

```
23.9   85.68   227E02   0.00863   75
93.44   71   14.7E-03   66   -1
The average of 9 values is 2.56833814777778e+03
```

Program *DataAverage* is interesting because it exercises three basic loop concepts.

sentinel, counter, accumulator

> A *sentinel* is a character or value used to mark the end of relevant input data. A *counter* variable keeps track of the number of values we've read. An *accumulator* keeps a running sum of values we've seen.

Sentinels, counters, and accumulators will turn up in applications other than averaging sequences of numbers. However, averaging is interesting because it demonstrates the interdependence of these three. The antibugging section presents a sequence of buggy program segments that attempt to find averages, but err slightly in spotting a sentinel, or in maintaining the values of counters and accumulators. Read it!

A potential error we will deal with now, though, must be consciously avoided in many basic loop applications. It occurs when a loop can be exited for more than one reason. If the *boolean* expression that states a loop's exit condition involves multiple conditions, we might find ourselves leaving a loop without knowing exactly why. The problem develops in a situation like this:

problem: find the letter 't'

Assume that you have as input to a program a sequence of 35 characters. Find the position of the first 't'—if there is one.

Our pseudocode is brief and to the point:

refinement

```
repeat
    read a letter;
    count it
until we read a 't' or read 35 characters;
print the position of the 't';
```

The shaded section is easily implemented as:

```
PositionCounter := 0;
repeat
    read (Letter);
    PositionCounter := PositionCounter + 1
until (Letter = 't') or (PositionCounter = 35);
```

But what do we do next? Although we have left the loop, we're not sure why. We can't just claim that the 't' was found at position *PositionCounter*, because there might not have been a 't' at all. However, checking the value of *PositionCounter* and printing 'No t found' if it equals 35 might be wrong too—the 't' could be in the last position.

> Don't jump to a conclusion about why you left a multi-condition loop. Find out why the loop terminated before you act.

We complete the code above by checking the value of *Letter*. Our sample input comes from the most famous 't' party of all.*

t-finding program

```
program FindT (input, output);
    {Looks for a 't' in input.}
const LIMIT = 35;
var PositionCounter: integer;
    Letter: char;
begin
        PositionCounter := 0;
        repeat
            read (Letter);
            PositionCounter := PositionCounter + 1
        until (Letter = 't') or (PositionCounter = LIMIT);
        if (Letter = 't')
            then writeln ('t is in position ', PositionCounter:1)
            else writeln ('No t found.')
end. {FindT}
```

Why is a raven like a writing desk?
t is in position 26

* The answer, of course, is that Edgar Allan Poe wrote on both.

boolean Functions

Our final discussion point on basic loop operations touches on the use of *boolean* functions. When they're used to state loop entry or exit conditions, *boolean* functions let programmers write code that is concise, yet still explicit in purpose. For instance, consider this code segment:

```
{Loop until Number is within a valid range of responses.}
repeat
   readln (Number)
until ((Number>=20) and (Number<=30)) or (Number=35)
```

Proclaiming the condition as a function does the same job in an unobtrusive, self-explanatory manner.

```
repeat
   readln (Number)
until Valid(Number)
```

Valid, declared below, takes the details of the *boolean* expression and puts them in a function declaration where they belong.

```
function Valid (Number: integer): boolean;
{Valid is true if its argument is 35, or between 20 and 30, inclusive.}
begin
   Valid := ((Number>=20) and (Number<=30)) or (Number=35)
end; {Valid}
```

We can find ourselves developing a funny relationship with program comments. On one hand, we insist on their importance as a part of the documentation of every program, but on the other, we continuously try to write code that needs no commenting. But as the programs we write become large and complex, *boolean* functions become a necessity in stating conditions.

why use them?

boolean functions help clarify the flow of a program, and let Pascal code retain some of the informality of pseudocode. Although *boolean* function declarations may clutter up a short program, they're invaluable in larger programs, or wherever complex *boolean* conditions must be stated.

There are several *boolean* functions whose names frequently pop up in Pascal programs. Like *Valid*, they establish a condition:

```
function No (Value: real): boolean;
   begin
      No := Value=0
   end; {No}
```

in an English-like, easy to comprehend manner.

```
repeat
    PlayTheGame
until No(TurnsLeft);
while No(ValueEntered) do
    PromptForValue;
if No(ErrorConditions)
    then ProcessTransactions
    else RepeatLastTransaction;
```

Focus on Programming: Loops and Testing 7-2

problem: number guessing

WITH CONDITIONAL LOOPS AT OUR DISPOSAL the variety of programs we can write is hugely increased. Let's warm up with a game that uses the random number function we wrote a few chapters back:

> Write a program that picks a number in the range 1 through 100, and challenges a program user to guess it. Allow seven tries, and tell the user if she's too high or low.

Clearly a **for** loop would never do for this sort of problem—seven is the maximum number of tries, not the required number. Instead, we want to repeat a sequence of actions—allow a guess, then check it—until the game is either won or over. In a first pseudocode refinement, we have:

first refinement

```
get a seed for the Random function;
pick a random number;
repeat
    let the user guess;
    respond to the guess
until the guess is right or all the guesses are used up;
report on the game winner;
```

Note that when we leave the loop, we won't be sure of why we left. The user might have guessed correctly, or run out of guesses, or both.* We'll have to check before giving our congratulations or condolences.

What kind of interaction will the program user require? Well, her guess will either be too high, too low, or exactly right. Since these three possibilities are mutually exclusive, we can use nested **if** statements to choose an appropriate response:

second refinement

```
get a seed;
pick a random number;
repeat
    let the user guess;
    if guess is high then give high error message
        else if guess is low then give low error message
            else if guess is right then record it
until the guess is right or all the guesses are used up;
if the guess was right, offer congratulations;
```

* The authors must confess that in the first edition of *Oh! Pascal!* we forgot the last possibility ourselves—we failed everybody who didn't guess the number until the seventh try. Oops!

The completed version of program *NumberGuess* is shown below. Notice our unsubtle method of initializing *Seed*—we just ask the user to enter a number without mentioning why we want it. As you read *NumberGuess* try to figure out why seven guesses should be enough to find the computer's number.

number guess program

```
program NumberGuess (input, output);
   {Challenges a user to guess a number within 7 tries.}

const GUESSLIMIT = 7;

var Number, Guess, Count, Seed: integer;
    Solved: boolean;

function Random (var Seed: integer): real;
   {Generates a pseudo-random number such that 0<=Random<1.}
   const MODULUS = 65536;
         MULTIPLIER = 25173;
         INCREMENT = 13849;
   begin
      Seed := ((MULTIPLIER*Seed)+INCREMENT) mod MODULUS;
      Random := Seed /MODULUS
   end; {Random}

begin
   writeln ('Play a guessing game.  Enter a number between 1 and 100.');
   readln (Seed);
   Number := 1 + trunc(100*(Random(Seed)));
   writeln ('Thanks.  Now, I''m thinking of a number from 1 through 100.');
   write ('You have ', GUESSLIMIT:1, ' tries to guess it.   ');
   Count := 0;
   Solved := false;
   repeat
      Count := Count+1;
      writeln ('Take a guess.');
      read (Guess);
      if Guess <Number
         then write ('Uh oh ... that number was too small.   ')
         else if Guess >Number
            then write ('Sorry, but that number was too big.   ')
            else Solved := true
   until Solved or (Count=GUESSLIMIT);
   if not Solved
      then writeln ('You lose!  The right number was ', Number:1)
      else writeln ('Congratulations!   ', Guess:1, ' was exactly right.')
end. {NumberGuess}
```

```
Play a guessing game.  Enter a number between 1 and 100.
91
Thanks.  Now, I'm thinking of a number from 1 through 100.
You have 7 tries to guess it.  Take a guess.
50
Sorry, but that number was too big.  Take a guess.
25
Sorry, but that number was too big.  Take a guess.
13
Uh oh ... that number was too small.  Take a guess.
19
Sorry, but that number was too big.  Take a guess.
16
Uh oh ... that number was too small.  Take a guess.
18
Sorry, but that number was too big.  Take a guess.
17
Congratulations!  17 was exactly right.
```

Generating Test Data with Loops

Our next example involves implementing, rather than devising, an algorithm. Although it requires a conditional loop, the example is primarily interesting because of the variety of techniques it employs. The program implements Sir Isaac Newton's method of finding a number's square root.* His algorithm is:

> Take a guess at the number's square root. The assignment:
>
> *Guess* := ((*Number* / *Guess*)+*Guess*) / 2;
>
> gives a number that is closer to being correct, no matter how wild the original guess was (as long as it wasn't 0).

We can make the value of *Guess* more and more accurate by repeatedly carrying out the assignment. However, we'll eventually tax the computer's precision, and continued guessing won't make our answer any more correct. Thus, we want to write a program that repeats the assignment shown above until the difference between successive guesses is very small—say, 10E–09. (Incidentally, this method won't work well for numbers with very large square roots.) In pseudocode, the loop we desire looks like this:

* Don't forget that he, like Gauss, didn't have a computer (or even a calculator).

first refinement

give NewGuess an initial value;
repeat
OldGuess gets the value of NewGuess;
compute the new value of NewGuess
until *NoSignificantChange*(*OldGuess, NewGuess*);

Note our pseudocode *boolean* function call, complete with arguments. Not only is it perfectly clear as pseudocode, but we won't anticipate too much change when we actually code it in Pascal.

problem: test Newton's method

Now, writing a program that implements Newton's algorithm isn't too challenging for us, so we'll try to enliven the job. Let's write a program that *tests* Newton's method by using it to find the square roots of various numbers. We'll use a random number function to generate test numbers, as well as wild first guesses at their square roots. At the same time, we'll count how many iterations Newton's method takes to arrive at the root, and compare its result to that of the standard function *sqrt*. Our pseudocode of a *SquareRoot* function expands to:

second refinement

pick a number to solve for;
print the number;
assign a wild first guess of its square root to NewGuess;
print the guess;
repeat
OldGuess gets the value of NewGuess;
compute the new value of NewGuess;
update the guess counter
until *NoSignificantChange*(*OldGuess, NewGuess*);

We won't bother writing up a further refinement of a *TestNewton* program, since we've already worked on most of its components. Instead, let's try a program outline:

program outline

program *TestNewton*;
const *the starting seed, the number of trials we want, and the upper limit on numbers and guesses*;
var *the number we're examining, the seed, and a counter for trials*;
function *RandomInteger--gets Seed and UpperLimit, returns an integer*;
function *SquareRoot--gets Number, returns its square root*;
function *NoSignificantChange--gets the two most recent guesses, and returns true if they're very close*;
begin
initialize the seed;
label the program output;
for *some number of trials*
pick a Number
print Number
print SquareRoot (*Number*), *sqrt* (*Number*)
end.

The completed program is shown below. Notice that *RandomInteger* is a slightly modified version of our old function *Random*. It differs by returning an *integer* between 1 and an upper limit, rather than a *real* between 0 and 1.

Newton testing program

```
program TestNewton (input, output);
  {Tests Newton's method of finding square roots.}

const STARTINGSEED = 187;
      NUMBEROFTRIALS = 10;
      UPPERLIMIT = 10000;

var Number, Seed, Counter: integer;

function RandomInteger (var Seed: integer; UPPERLIMIT: integer): integer;
  {Generates a pseudo-random integer from 1 through UPPERLIMIT.}
  const MODULUS = 65536;
        MULTIPLIER = 25173;
        INCREMENT = 13849;
  begin
    Seed := ((MULTIPLIER*Seed)+INCREMENT) mod MODULUS;
    RandomInteger := 1+trunc(UPPERLIMIT*(Seed/MODULUS))
  end; {RandomInteger}

function SquareRoot (Number: real): real;
  var OldGuess, NewGuess: real;
  GuessNumber: integer;
  function NoSignificantChange (Old, New: real): boolean;
    const EPSILON = 10E-09;
    begin
      NoSignificantChange := abs(Old-New)<EPSILON
    end; {NoSignificantChange}
  begin {SquareRoot}
    NewGuess := RandomInteger(Seed, UPPERLIMIT);
      {Take a wild first guess.}
    write (trunc(NewGuess):15);
    GuessNumber := 0;
    repeat
      GuessNumber := GuessNumber+1;
      OldGuess := NewGuess;
      NewGuess := ((Number/OldGuess)+OldGuess)/2
    until NoSignificantChange(OldGuess, NewGuess);
    write (GuessNumber:8);
    SquareRoot := NewGuess
  end; {SquareRoot}
```

```
begin {TestNewton}
   Seed := STARTINGSEED;
   writeln ('Number':6, 'First Guess':15, 'Tries':8, 'Newton':12, 'sqrt':12);
   for Counter := 1 to NUMBEROFTRIALS do begin
      Number := RandomInteger(Seed, UPPERLIMIT);
      write (Number:6);
      writeln (SquareRoot(Number):12:5, sqrt(Number):12:5)
   end
end. {TestNewton}
```

Number	First Guess	Tries	Newton	sqrt
398	9689	14	19.94994	19.94994
121	6579	14	11.00000	11.00000
5559	5521	11	74.55870	74.55870
6771	1498	9	82.28609	82.28609
7096	8394	12	84.23776	84.23776
6907	7754	12	83.10836	83.10836
7355	7527	12	85.76130	85.76130
4123	818	9	64.21059	64.21059
1177	4638	12	34.30743	34.30743
4513	8656	12	67.17887	67.17887

Using All the Loops

Our final program will call on all the programming techniques we've learned so far (top-down design, stepwise refinement, pseudocoding, etc.), as well as all the Pascal, from subprograms (procedures and functions) to loops (**repeat**, **while**, and **for**). The problem we pose involves implementing a brief numerical algorithm for producing *numerical palindromes*—numbers that are the same forward and backward.

problem: palindromic numbers

> Write a program that produces palindromic numbers by following this algorithm: Start by taking a number. If it isn't a palindrome, reverse the number, and sum the number and its reversal. If the new number isn't palindromic, reverse the new number, then add it to the reversal. Eventually, the number will become a palindrome.

For example, the number 101 is a palindrome. 561, however, isn't. To follow the algorithm given above we reverse 561, then add: 561+165=726. Since 726 isn't palindromic either, we repeat the process: 726+627=1,353. As 1,353 still isn't a solution, we must invoke our algorithm once more: 1,353+3,531=4,884. It has taken us three reversals to produce a palindrome.

A first refinement of our algorithm produces this pseudocode:

first refinement

get the number;
while *it's not a palindrome*
    reverse the number;
    add the number and its reversal;
print the answer;

checking palindromes

How can we tell if a number is a palindrome? A one-digit number is easy—it's always a palindrome. A two-digit number is a palindrome if its digits are the same. Three-digit numbers are palindromic if the first digit equals the last. It doesn't take a college degree to realize that a number is a palindrome if the first digit is the same as the last, the second equals the next-to-last, etc.

We'll assume that, if we can pull out individual digits, we can spot a palindrome. Now, an *integer's* last digit is the remainder of a division by 10:

the last digit = *the number* **mod** 10

Its first digit is the whole portion of a division:

the first digit = *the number* **div** (10 *to the* (*number of digits* − 1) *power*)

It seems that if we want to find a number's first digit, we have to know the number of digits in the entire number. Fortunately, we've already written a program that does the job—program *NumberLength*, in section 7-1. Since we can always find the first and last digits, (and, thus, can compare them), we can assume that determining whether or not a number is a palindrome is within our power.

reversing the number

What about reversing a number? Any programmer who can count a number's digits should find this trivial. We initialize a 'running total' variable to zero, then just repeat the following algorithm:

determine the last digit of the number;
add it to ten times the 'running total' variable;
remove the last digit from the original number with **div**;

until the original number has been reduced to zero.

A much subtler problem is going to cause more trouble. Suppose that a number requires many reversals before it becomes a palindrome. For example, 89 must be reversed 24 times before becoming the palindrome 8,813,200,023,188. Stop reading for a moment, and try to figure out why this is a cause for concern. Program *Oops*, below, should give you a hint. Although *MAXINT* is implementation-defined, the figure we show is typical.

```
program Oops (output);
   {Prints the value of MAXINT.}
begin
   writeln (MAXINT)
end.
```

```
    ↓     ↓     ↓
2147483647
```

integer overflow

> Attempting to assign an *integer* variable a value greater than *MAXINT* causes an *integer overflow*, (and usually a crash).

Even though *MAXINT* is a large number, most non-palindromes will exceed it after ten or eleven reversals and additions. If we want our program to be robust, we have to find a method of anticipating overflow situations. A clever technique is to use ratios—if a tenth of some number exceeds a tenth of *MAXINT*, then the actual number is greater than *MAXINT*. A function *InDangerOfOverFlow* can use this strategy to report on our current situation.

We're now in a better position to refine our pseudocode in more procedural (and 'functional') terms.

second refinement

while *the user wants to keep running the program*
  get the starting number;
  count its digits;
  while not *Palindrome* **and not** *InDangerOfOverFlow*
    reverse the number;
    add it to the original;
  print the results for that starting number;

graceful degradation

What results should the program have? If the number can be turned into a palindrome, we should print the palindrome and the number of steps required. If it requires too many steps for the computer to handle, the program should *degrade gracefully* by printing an error message—not halt abruptly with a crash, or print incorrect results.

A more interesting question involves determining whether to print the palindrome, or the error message. Once more, it seems, we've devised a loop whose multiple exit conditions leave us unsure of why we left. Fortunately, we can use existing *boolean* functions—an additional call of either *Palindrome* or *InDangerOfOverFlow* will let us know why the loop terminated.

why use particular loops?

The text of program *ProducePalindromes* appears over the next few pages. As you read it, try to recognize why we've used each particular loop statement as we have, even when another loop statement could have worked. For example, finding a number's first digit involves computing a divisor that equals 10 to the *NumberOfDigits*−1 power. Our code (in function *Palindrome*) uses a **for** statement:

for *Counter* := 1 **to** *NumberOfDigits*−1 **do**
  Divisor := *Divisor* * 10;

even though a **while** or **repeat** might have achieved the same effect. Why? How come we used a **repeat** loop in procedure *CountTheDigits*? Could a **while** have worked? Finally, why does the entire program repeat **until**, instead of continuing **while**?

palindrome program

```
program ProducePalindromes (input, output);
   {Produces palindromic numbers. Watches for integer overflow.}

var Original, Reversed, Reversals: integer;

procedure ReverseTheNumber (Original: integer; var Reversed: integer);
   {Reverses and returns a copy of its first parameter.}

   begin
      Reversed := 0;
      while (Original<>0) do begin
         Reversed := (Reversed*10) + (Original mod 10);
         Original := Original div 10
      end
   end; {ReverseTheNumber}

function InDangerOfOverFlow (Original: integer): boolean;
   {Determines if Original will cause integer overflow when reversed
    and added. Procedure ReverseTheNumber, above, is called.}

   var Reversed: integer;

   begin
      Original := (Original div 10);
      ReverseTheNumber (Original, Reversed);
      InDangerOfOverFlow := (Original+Reversed) > (MAXINT div 10)
   end; {InDangerOfOverFlow}

function Palindrome (Original: integer): boolean;
   {Determines if Original is palindromic.
    Procedure CountTheDigits is declared within this procedure.}

   var Divisor, Counter, NumberOfDigits, FirstDigit, LastDigit: integer;

   procedure CountTheDigits (Original: integer; var NumberOfDigits: integer);
      {Counts the number of digits in Original.}

      begin
         NumberOfDigits := 0;
         repeat
            Original := Original div 10;
            NumberOfDigits := NumberOfDigits+1
         until Original=0
      end; {CountTheDigits}
```

```
    begin {Palindrome}
        Palindrome := true; {Initialize Palindrome.}
        CountTheDigits (Original, NumberOfDigits);
        Divisor := 1;
            {Compute 10 to the NumberOfDigits-1 power.}
        for Counter := 1 to NumberOfDigits-1 do
            Divisor := Divisor*10;
        for Counter := 1 to NumberOfDigits div 2 do begin
                {Compute and compare the first and last digits.}
            FirstDigit := Original div Divisor;
            LastDigit := Original mod 10;
            if FirstDigit<>LastDigit then Palindrome := false;
                {Get rid of the first and last digits of Original.}
            Original := (Original mod Divisor) div 10;
            Divisor := Divisor div 100
        end {for}
    end; {Palindrome}
begin {ProducePalindromes}
    writeln ('Please enter a positive integer.');
    readln (Original);
    repeat
        write (Original:1, ' took ');
        Reversals := 0;
        while not Palindrome (Original) and
                not InDangerOfOverFlow (Original) do begin
            ReverseTheNumber (Original, Reversed);
            Reversals := Reversals+1;
            Original := Original+Reversed
        end; {while}
        if InDangerOfOverFlow (Original)
            then writeln ('too many reversals to convert.')
            else writeln (Reversals:1, ' reversals to become ', Original:1);
        writeln ('Play again?  A negative entry ends the program.');
        readln (Original)
    until Original<0
end. {ProducePalindromes}
```

```
Please enter a positive integer.
86
86 took 3 reversals to become 1111
Play again?  A negative entry ends the program.
563
563 took 11 reversals to become 88555588
Play again?  A negative entry ends the program.
89
89 took too many reversals to convert.
Play again?  A negative entry ends the program.
-1
```

Recursive Programming Methods* 7-3

recursive sentence-reverse program

CONSIDER THIS program:

```
program Reverse (input, output);
   {Recursively reads a sentence of input, and echoes it in reverse.}
procedure StackTheCharacters;
   var TheCharacter: char;
   begin
      read (TheCharacter);
      if (TheCharacter<>'.') then
         StackTheCharacters;          {A recursive call.}
      write (TheCharacter)
   end; {StackTheCharacters}
begin
   writeln ('Please enter a sentence.');
   StackTheCharacters;
   writeln
end. {Reverse}
```

```
Please enter a sentence.
This is not a palindrome.
.emordnilap a ton si sihT
```

Program *Reverse* takes an ordinary sentence of text as input, and prints it out in reverse. It accomplishes this with a *recursive* procedure, *StackTheCharacters.*

recursion defined

> A procedure or function that calls itself is said to be *recursive*.

When *StackTheCharacters* is first invoked, a character is read as input to the local variable *TheCharacter*. Then (unless the first character was a period) *StackTheCharacters* is called again. Note that the final statement of the first call—*write* (*TheCharacter*)—is still pending. However, leaving uncompleted statements behind is nothing new; we do it almost every time we call a procedure or function. Sooner or later we'll get back to this output statement, and print the value of the first character.

recursive calls

Now let's look at the second call of *StackTheCharacters*. Once again, a new local variable (*TheCharacter*) is created, a new letter is read to give *TheCharacter* its value, and (assuming it wasn't a period), *StackTheCharacters* is called once more. Eventually, when the pending *write* (*TheCharacter*) is executed, the second character's value will be printed.

Since it's hard to visualize what happens in a series of identical procedure calls, computer scientists use a metaphor to help explain recursion.

* This section is optional, and can be returned to at any time.

the stack

> The variables and pending statements of a partially executed program or subprogram are said to go on a *stack* within the computer.

When we jump out of a subprogram (by calling another procedure or function) all currently active variables, along with any pending statements, are added to the stack. The number of times this can occur—the height of the stack—is only limited by the memory resources of the computer.

If we only look at the input statements executed during program *Reverse*, we'll see something like the series shown below. Although we keep creating local variables named *TheCharacter*, Pascal's scope rule (that the most local variable takes precedence) gives the current input value to the most recently created variable.

building the stack

```
read (TheCharacter);          {Reading in 'T'.}
   read (TheCharacter);          {Reading in 'h'.}
      read (TheCharacter);          {Reading in 'i'.}
         ...          {Intermediate calls...}
            read (TheCharacter);          {Reading in 'm'.}
               read (TheCharacter);          {Reading in 'e'.}
                  read (TheCharacter);          {Reading in '.', the last call.}
```

The chain of calls to *StackTheCharacters* continues until we read the period that ends the sentence. At last we'll get past the **if** statement. We can finally complete the last invocation of *StackTheCharacters* by printing the character most recently read—the period. Since this particular invocation of *StackTheCharacters* is finished, the program 'returns' to where it was when the procedure call was made—to the calling procedure, and eventually to the main program. In effect, the computer executes this series of statements:

undoing the stack

```
                  write (TheCharacter);          {Printing out '.'.}
               write (TheCharacter);          {Printing out 'e'.}
            write (TheCharacter);          {Printing out 'm'.}
         ...          {Intermediate calls...}
      write (TheCharacter);          {Printing out 'i'.}
   write (TheCharacter);          {Printing out 'h'.}
write (TheCharacter);          {Printing out 'T'.}
writeln          {This is the last statement in the main program.}
```

Now, a stack is actually created in any series of procedure or function calls—the sequence need not be recursive. The stack can, and usually does, grow and shrink during the course of a program. However, it will always be empty when a program ends normally.*

* This simplified explanation of stacks helps explain how the computer keeps track of scope within a program. *All* identifiers defined in a subprogram are put on the stack when the subprogram is invoked. Then, when an identifier is used, the computer looks down the stack for the identifier's most recent definition or declaration. Although the stack may contain several different usages of a single name, the most recent definition is the first one found.

Procedure *StackTheCharacters* is a good introduction to recursion because it lets you see how the stack is used in an obvious way. In *StackTheCharacters*, each time the recursive procedure was invoked, useful local variables and uncompleted statements were left on the stack. But now, let's look at an example that is recursive, but which makes minimal usage of the stack.

Program *IntegerReverse*, below, leaves the minimum amount of business undone. All that each call of procedure *ReverseDigits* leaves behind is its final **end**. When the very last call is made (when (*TheNumber* **div** 10) equals zero), the entire stack of procedure calls can end without further ado.

recursive *integer-reverse* program

```
program IntegerReverse (input, output);
  {Recursively reverses the digits of an integer.}
var Number: integer;
procedure ReverseDigits (TheNumber: integer);
  begin
    write (TheNumber mod 10:1);
      {Output the rightmost digit in a one-space field.}
    if (TheNumber div 10) <> 0 then ReverseDigits (TheNumber div 10)
      {If there are more digits, strip off the rightmost one and pass the result.}
  end; {ReverseDigits}
begin
  writeln ('Please enter a positive integer.');
  readln (Number);
  ReverseDigits (Number);
  writeln
end. {IntegerReverse}
```

```
Please enter a positive integer.
789254
452987
```

end recursion

> This kind of recursion is called *end* or *tail* recursion. When the procedure makes its recursive call, no unfinished statements are left on the stack.

A procedure that uses end recursion is usually easy to write iteratively (using a looping statement). For example:

iterative reversing procedure

```
procedure IterativeReverse (TheNumber: integer);
  begin
    repeat
      write (TheNumber mod 10:1);
      TheNumber := TheNumber div 10
    until (TheNumber = 0)
  end;
```

Self-Check Questions

Q. Is the procedure in *Print* recursive? Should it be? What does it do?

```
program Print (input, output);
procedure Echo;
   var TheCharacter: char;
   begin
      read (TheCharacter);
      write (TheCharacter);
      if TheCharacter <> '.' then Echo
   end; {Echo}
begin
   writeln ('Please enter a sentence.');
   Echo;
   writeln
end. {Print}
```

A. Procedure *Echo* offers another demonstration of end recursion. Although a stack is created, it doesn't contain any statements to be executed. The series of *TheCharacter* local variables is saved, but gets thrown away when the recursive calls end. The stack is created, but not used. A **while** loop would do the job perfectly well, because the program just echoes a line of input.

```
Please enter a sentence.
This is not a palindrome.
This is not a palindrome.
```

More Complicated Recursion

Our first two examples kept recursion simple by minimizing the numbers of statements and variables involved. Our next recursive procedure will be the most complicated, even though it's just intended to help us play a game:

> The *Towers of Hanoi* game is played with three pegs, and a pile of disks of different sizes. We start with all the disks stacked on one peg, as shown:

problem: towers of hanoi

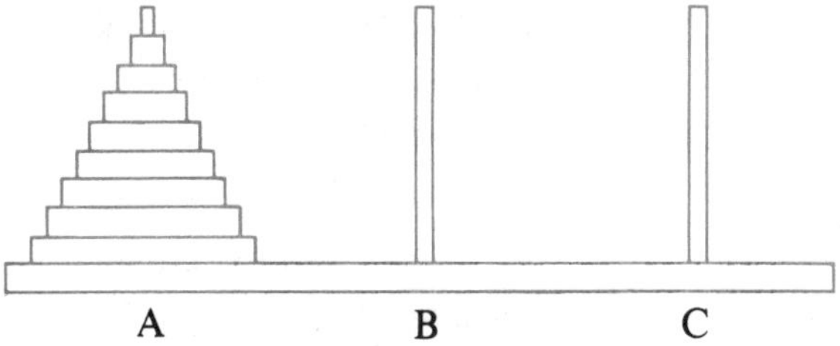

The object of the game is to move the entire stack from peg A to peg C, while obeying two rules:

the rules

1. Only one disk can be moved at a time.
2. A larger disk can never go on top of a smaller one.

Write a program that gives step-by-step instructions for moving a stack of height n from peg A to C.

The original version of this game was supposedly played as a religious rite with a set of three diamond needles and sixty-four golden disks. The end of the game was supposed to mark the end of the world.

the 1 or 2-disk problem

Let's try to get a handle on how the moves are made for stacks of various heights. Clearly a height of 1 is trivial—we move the disk directly from A to C. What about a height of 2? We put the top disk out of the way—to B. Then the bottom disk goes to C, and the smaller disk from B to C.

the 3-disk problem

With a stack of height 3 it gets interesting. Let's suppose, though, that we restate the problem (as we're liable to do when we're up to something). Instead of moving 3 disks from A to C, let's move 2 disks from A to B—we already know how to move two disks from one peg to another. Next, move the third disk directly to C. Finally, make another two-disk move, from B to C. We've switched all three disks.

the 4-disk problem

How about starting with 4 disks? Once more, let's begin by restating the problem. Can we move 3 disks from A to B? Sure—it's essentially the same as moving them from A to C. Then we switch the fourth disk directly from A to C, and, finally, transfer 3 disks from B to C.

developing a recursive statement

As you can probably gather, we've insisted on restating the problem in a particular way each time so that we can develop a special insight. We begin to solve the Towers of Hanoi problem for a stack of height n by trying to solve it for a stack of height $n-1$. This solution must wait until we solve for $(n-1)-1$, and so on. Eventually we get to the trivial case of n equaling 1, and can begin to work our way back up.

induction

Almost without realizing it, we've used a high-priced method of thinking called *induction*. We start by solving a simple case of the Towers of Hanoi problem—a tower of height one or two. Then, we show that even if we start with a larger number, we can always work our way down to a problem that we know how to solve. This is the heart of what will become our recursive solution to the problem.

Now we're ready to make a recursive statement of our solution. To move n disks from peg A to peg C:

the recursive Hanoi algorithm

1. Move $n-1$ disks from A to B.
2. Move 1 disk from A to C.
3. Move $n-1$ disks from B to C.

In steps 1 and 3, of course, we will use the remaining peg as an auxiliary 'holding' peg.

In understanding program *Hanoi*, below, it may help to imagine that the three pegs are arranged in a circle rather than in a line. The actual pegs that *FromPeg, ToPeg*, and *UsingPeg* represent will change (they'll actually seem to rotate). However, we'll always eventually find ourselves fulfilling the second step of our algorithm, and announcing a particular move.

Towers of Hanoi program

```
program Hanoi (input, output);
  {Recursively solves the Towers of Hanoi problem. Moves disks from A to C.}
var Height: integer;
procedure Move (Height: integer; FromPeg, ToPeg, UsingPeg: char);
  {Recursive procedure for determining moves.}
  begin
    if Height = 1
      then writeln ('Move a disk from ', FromPeg, ' to ', ToPeg)
      else begin
        Move (Height-1, FromPeg, UsingPeg, ToPeg);
        writeln ('Move a disk from ', FromPeg, ' to ', ToPeg);
        Move (Height-1, UsingPeg, ToPeg, FromPeg)
      end {else}
  end; {Move}
begin
  writeln ('How many disks are you going to start with?');
  readln (Height);
  Move (Height, 'A', 'C', 'B')
end. {Hanoi}
```

```
How many disks are you going to start with?
4
Move a disk from A to B
Move a disk from A to C
Move a disk from B to C
Move a disk from A to B
Move a disk from C to A
Move a disk from C to B
Move a disk from A to B
Move a disk from A to C
Move a disk from B to C
Move a disk from B to A
Move a disk from C to A
Move a disk from B to C
Move a disk from A to B
Move a disk from A to C
Move a disk from B to C
```

Recursive Functions

Functions can be written recursively, just like procedures. Function *Sum*, below, uses a series of recursive calls to add a series of numbers from 1 to its argument *Limit*.

recursive summing function

```
function Sum (Limit: integer): integer;
   {Recursively sums the series 1 through Limit.}
   begin
      if Limit<=1
         then Sum := Limit
         else Sum := Limit + Sum(Limit-1)
   end; {Sum}
```

A comparable iterative function would be:

iterative summing function

```
function IterativeSum (Limit: integer): integer;
   {Iteratively sums the series 1 through Limit.}
   var TemporarySum: integer;
   begin
      TemporarySum := Limit;
      while Limit>1 do begin
         Limit := Limit-1;
         TemporarySum := Limit+TemporarySum
      end;
      IterativeSum := TemporarySum
   end; {IterativeSum}
```

However, both functions, if called in the same program, will produce the same results.

```
writeln (Sum(5), IterativeSum(5));
writeln (Sum(100), IterativeSum(100));
```

```
   15       15
 5050     5050
```

The stack produced by *Sum* is a bit peculiar because it contains a series of partially completed assignment statements.

stacking recursive function calls

> The general outline of *Sum* is typical of recursive functions—the recursive call occurs in the middle of an assignment statement. Thus, the stack serves to delay the evaluation of an expression.

Let's assume that *Sum* is called with 5 as its first *Limit* argument, as above. Remember that the **if** statement in function *Sum* looks like this:

```
if Limit<=1
   then Sum := Limit
   else Sum := Limit + Sum(Limit-1)
```

Here's the stack of partial assignments that's made in the sequence of calls:

```
Sum := 5 + Sum (5-1); {first}
  Sum := 4 + Sum (4-1); {second}
    Sum := 3 + Sum (3-1); {third}
      Sum := 2 + Sum (2-1); {fourth}
        Sum := 1; {fifth}
```

None of the stacked assignments can be completed until *Sum* gets a non-recursive value—the fifth assignment, which doesn't depend on calling *Sum* again. Let's follow the sequence of assignments as they're completed.

```
        Sum := 1; {fifth}
      Sum := 2 + 1; {fourth}
    Sum := 3 + 3; {third}
  Sum := 4 + 6; {second}
Sum := 5 + 10; {first}
```

the limit call

> The last of a series of recursive calls is the *limit* call. The circumstances that give rise to the limit call form the exit condition of the recursion.

infinite recursion

By our definition of the function, *Sum's* limit call occurs when its argument is 1. An *infinite* recursion occurs if the exit condition can't be met, and the limit call is never made.

Once we understand how *Sum* is implemented recursively in Pascal, it's instructive to look at a recursive statement of its algorithm in English.

If *Limit* is 1 or less, the sum of 1 to *Limit* is *Limit*.

recursive addition

If *Limit* exceeds 1, the sum of 1 to *Limit* is *Limit*—plus the sum of 1 to *Limit*−1.

As you can see, this definition—like all recursive definitions—is essentially circular, since it's defined in terms of itself. If you're having trouble understanding recursion, take a deep breath and start again—it's well worth the effort.

Another definition that's easy to state recursively in English is that of the *n*th Fibonacci number:

If *n* is 1 or 2, the *n*th Fibonacci number is 1.

recursive Fibonaccis

If *n* is 3 or more, the *n*th Fibonacci number is the sum of the previous two.

To nobody's surprise, this algorithm works perfectly well when transliterated into Pascal.

recursive Fibonacci program

```
program TestFibonacci (input, output);
   {Tests a function that recursively generates Fibonacci numbers.}
var Test1, Test2, Test3, Test4: integer;
function Fibonacci (Which: integer): integer;
   begin
      if (Which=1) or (Which=2)
         then Fibonacci := 1
         else Fibonacci := Fibonacci(Which-1) + Fibonacci(Which-2)
   end; {Fibonacci}
begin
   writeln ('Reading four test entries.');
   readln (Test1, Test2, Test3, Test4);
   writeln ('Fibonacci numbers', Test1:4, Test2:4, Test3:4, Test4:4, ' are:');
   write (Fibonacci(Test1), Fibonacci(Test2));
   writeln (Fibonacci(Test3), Fibonacci(Test4))
end. {TestFibonacci}
```

```
Reading four test entries.
1 7 15 25
Fibonacci numbers   1   7  15  25 are:
        1        13        610      75025
```

problem: exponentiation

Let's go on to our third and final recursive function example. Our first two functions each used a single value parameter. This time, we'll work with two value parameters; one will remain constant, while the other declines on each recursive call. Our problem is to raise some number X to the nth power, where n is and *integer*.

Defining a *Power* function in English is easy—'multiply X by itself n times.' However, this sounds like an invitation to a **for** loop. Before you read on, try to state a recursive algorithm.

Our recursive solution uses the same sort of thinking as our solution to the Towers of Hanoi problem—we give it in terms of a restatement:

the recursive statement

If n equals 1, X to the n equals X.
If n is greater than 1, X to the n equals X times X to the $n-1$.

In reading the code of function *Power*, below, note the necessity of two value parameters. Each possible step of our recursive algorithm requires that we know the values of both X and n. However, as you can easily see in the algorithm, X remains constant while n declines steadily.

recursive power function

```
function Power (X: real; n: integer): real;
   {Recursively calculates X^n. Assume n>0.}
   begin
      if n = 1
         then Power := X
         else Power := X * Power (X, n-1)
   end; {Power}
```

Although we won't show it here, *Power* (like *Fibonacci*) can easily be implemented as an iterative function. In fact, every recursive procedure or function can be written in a non-recursive manner. Since recursion isn't absolutely necessary, why should it be used at all? The answer takes several tacks. In a few instances (such as reversing a string of characters of unknown length) recursion is the best way to solve the problem. Our main alternative is the impractical one of declaring enough variables to deal with every possible character sequence.

why use recursion ?

Another reason is that the implementation of recursive algorithms or definitions can be nearly trivial. We'll encounter some other recursively defined functions in the Exercises, and look at a variety of recursive algorithms in Chapters 11 and 16. A more sophisticated reason for recursion will arise when we encounter *recursive data structures* in Chapter 15. Although we won't get into such data structures now, they also pose problems that are stated and solved recursively.

Finally, recursive solutions can be more elegant than their iterative counterparts. We'd hate to say that shortness is a virtue in itself, but recursive subprograms can often be written more briefly and clearly than iterative ones. When you become comfortable with recursion, and start to recognize 'standard' recursive algorithms, you'll appreciate the ease with which such algorithms can be put into programs.

Self-Check Questions

Q. What is the intention and effect of function *RawPower*, below? What restriction of *Power* does it remove?

```
function RawPower (X: real; n: integer): real;
   {Recursively calculates X^n. Assume ?}
   begin
      if n = 0
         then RawPower := 1
         else if n > 0
            then RawPower := X * RawPower (X, n-1)
            else RawPower := 1 / RawPower (X, -n)
   end; {RawPower}
```

A. *RawPower* is considerably more robust than *Power*. It is still a recursive procedure whose algorithm is nearly identical to *Power's*. However, it can raise *X* to a power smaller than 1. In other words, *n* can be any *integer*, positive, negative, or zero.

Q. What is the largest number of times the innermost **else** will be entered, above?

A. At most, the call *Power* (*X*, $-n$) will occur once.

forward References

In Chapter 3 we learned that once a procedure or function has been declared, its name has meaning in other parts of the program, including 1) the main program's statement part, 2) the statement part of the subprogram itself, and 3) the statement parts of subprograms declared after the procedure or function we're concerned with.

procedures calling procedures

We're quite familiar with calls of the first sort, and we've just been looking at calls of the second kind. The third case calls for an example. Suppose that we make the following declarations:

```
program Main (input, output);
global declarations;
procedure Early (parameter list);
   local declarations
   begin
      statements
   end;
procedure Late (parameter list);
   local declarations;
   begin
      statements
   end;
begin {Main}
   ...         etc.
```

Procedure *Early* can be called in procedure *Late*, or in the main program. Procedure *Late* can't be called in *Early*, though, because it hadn't been declared when *Early* was written.

mutual recursion

Occasionally, the 'declare before you call' rule will seem to paint the programmer into a corner. Suppose that a procedure must call another procedure that hasn't been declared yet, but which will be declared by the end of the subprogram declarations. This can happen when procedure *A* calls procedure *B*, which, in turn, calls procedure *A* (sometimes called *mutual recursion*). We're in a fix—which declaration should come first?* The *forward declaration* comes to the rescue.

forward declarations

> A *forward declaration* tells the compiler that a subprogram identifier is valid, and may be used in a program before the actual subprogram declaration takes place.

how identifiers are validated

When a program is first compiled, the compiler scans (reads) the code from start to finish. As it goes along, it reads constant, variable, and subprogram declarations and creates an internal table of known identifiers. If the compiler encounters an identifier that hasn't been declared, it assumes that an error has been made. It jumps to the conclusion that the identifier won't *ever* be declared, and prints an error message.

* This brings to mind the old Rhode Island law: 'When two trains meet on a track, neither train shall move until the other one has passed.'

The **forward** declaration puts the subprogram's name into the table of valid procedure and function identifiers. This doesn't mean that the subprogram need not be declared at all, or that the declaration can occur outside of the subprogram declaration part. A **forward** declaration is merely used to vary the order of declarations.

forward syntax

The complete subprogram heading, complete with parameter list, is followed by the word **forward**. Then, when the subprogram is actually declared, the parameter list is not repeated. **forward** is a statement, and should be preceded and followed by a semicolon.

using **forward**

```
procedure Second (var M,N: integer; P: char); forward;
procedure First (A,B: integer; var X: real);
  local declarations
  begin
    statements;
    Second (argument list)        {Call procedure Second.}
      . . .
  end; {First}
procedure Second;       {The parameter list is omitted.}
  local declarations
  begin
    statement part
  end; {Second}
```

Because a forward declaration may come well before the actual procedure or function declaration, it's usually a good idea to repeat the parameter list as a comment when the subprogram is finally declared.

```
procedure Second; {var M,N: integer; P: char}
  local declarations          etc.
```

This is an excellent programming practice that adds documentation with almost no effort.

Functions may be **forward**-declared too. The normal function heading, complete with parameter list and function type, is followed by the word **forward**. When the actual declaration of the function takes place, the parameter list and function type are omitted. For example:

```
function DeclaredLater (Parameter: integer): char; forward;
procedure CallManyFunctions (parameter list);
  begin
    rest of the procedure declaration
    includes a call of DeclaredLater
  end;
function DeclaredLater;
    {The parameter list and function type are omitted}
  begin
    rest of the function declaration
  end;
```

As usual, it's a good idea to include the parameter list and function type as a comment of the real function declaration.

```
function DeclaredLater {(Parameter: integer): char;}
  etc.
```

why **forward**?

Why use **forward** declarations? As noted, we sometimes have to. However, even if they're not absolutely required (as with the procedures above, whose declarations could have simply been reversed), **forward** declarations can help make a program more readable. Sometimes it seems like a good idea to put the shortest, most easily understood procedures at the beginning, and **forward** declare a long, complicated routine they all call and use. It's equally plausible that we might want to do exactly the opposite, and start out with the hardest, least familiar procedure instead of burying it deep within the procedure declarations. Some programmers (and we don't advise this) **forward** declare *every* subprogram, to help keep track of the parameters each one expects to receive.

Antibugging and Debugging 7-4

MOST OF THE BUGS ASSOCIATED WITH conditional loops are semantic. The programs they're found in will compile, but won't work properly. Naturally, these are the worst kind of bugs, because they can only be found by program testing, or by visual inspection of the code itself. We can only say that a program is *correct* if we can show that it will work for all possible input data.

Reliance on testing is often ill-advised, because it can lead programmers into an unnecessarily fatalistic state of mind. A computer scientist named Graham once observed that "We build programs like the Wright brothers built planes. Build the whole thing, push it off a cliff, let it crash, and start all over again." However, we've already pointed out that a program test is only as reliable as the test data it's provided with.

Proving that entire programs are correct (sometimes called *program verification*) is a task that requires a considerable amount of fasting and prayer. We'll discuss the issue at length in section 9-2. Still, it's fairly easy to become confident that a single loop statement will *usually* work. Three potential situations must be considered.

boundary conditions

1. The loop won't be entered when it should be.
2. The loop won't ever be exited.
3. The loop will terminate after the wrong number of iterations.

We can generally assure ourselves of a loop's correctness by closely examining its *boundary conditions*—the exact circumstances of its first and last iterations.

Entry: Can the entry condition be met? Have all its variables been initialized? Do we want a **repeat** loop or a **while** loop? Does the loop have to be conditional at all—might a **for** loop work?

Exit: Can the exit condition be met? Is the entire loop action being repeated, or just its first statement? Are **and**s and **or**s being used correctly in the exit condition? Does some statement in the loop's action make it certain that the exit condition eventually *will* be met?

Off-by-one: Trace execution of the loop action through its first and final few iterations, step-by-step. Will all variables have their expected values when the loop is terminated? Is it possible that the loop takes place one time too often? Once too few?

This is by no means a formal proof of a loop statement's correctness. However, even a casual check like this should be performed while the code is still on paper, before it's even run. A little bit of effort now can prevent a lot of trouble in the long run.

execution profiles

Many programmers will develop *execution profiles* of their programs for help in debugging and antibugging.

> An *execution profile* is a count of the number of times each statement is executed, or the number of times every subprogram is called.

auxiliary counters

This sort of information is useful for improving the efficiency of programs, as well as for spotting runaway loops. An auxiliary counter variable can be inserted into a loop, and instructed to print during debugging runs (perhaps if a constant named *DEBUGGING* is *true*, as suggested in our discussion of embedded debugging code). For instance:

```
Iterations := 0;
while Looping do begin        {Loop 7}
   ...        {the loop's action}
   Iterations := Iterations+1
end;
if DEBUGGING then writeln ('Loop 7:', Iterations);
```

Similar variables can be used to count procedure or function calls. Some Pascal systems will have profilers built into their compilers, and can be told to spit out a profile after running a program.

Accumulator, Counter, and Sentinel Bugs

Focusing on standard loop components—sentinels, accumulators, and counters—can help draw attention to some bugs. (Recall from 7-1 that a sentinel marks the end of valid input, an accumulator sums values, and a counter keeps track of the number of values seen thus far.) These components appear in loops in varying guises, but the problem of summing and averaging a sequence of input numbers displays them most clearly. Let's state the problem:

problem: find the average

Write a code segment that finds the average value in a sequence of non-negative numbers. The sequence ends with a negative number.

Here's our first stab at encoding a solution. Can you spot the bug?

'adds sentinel' bug

```
{incorrect segment—adds the sentinel}
Sum := 0;
Count := 0;
repeat
   read (Number);
   Sum := Sum + Number;
   Count := Count + 1
until Number < 0;
if Count <>0 then Average := Sum / Count;
```

As the comment indicates, we add the sentinel by accident. The counter is 'correct,' but the accumulator stores an extra value.

Let's try again. This time, though, we'll try to be smarter—we'll read the first number before we enter the loop and add it to the accumulator. Can we avoid mistakenly adding the sentinel like this?

'empty list' bug

```
{incorrect segment—won't detect an empty list}
read (Number);
Sum := 0;
Count := 0;
repeat
   Sum := Sum + Number;
   Count := Count + 1
   read (Number)
until Number < 0;
if Count <>0 then Average := Sum / Count;
```

Well, we're getting a bit closer—but only if there are values to average. Suppose that the very first value entered is the sentinel? Not only will both the counter and the accumulator show incorrect values, but the sentinel won't even be seen in the right place. By the time we check for a negative value we'll have read the second input.

Let's go back to the drawing board. Our most obvious mistake was using a **repeat** loop, since entry to the loop wasn't even checked. We'll start from the beginning, using a **while** loop.

'initialization' bug

```
{incorrect segment—entry condition not initialized}
Sum := 0;
Count := 0;
while Number >= 0 do begin
   read (Number);
   Sum := Sum + Number;
   Count := Count + 1
end;
if Count <>0 then Average := Sum / Count;
```

We're still in hot water. Our quest for simplicity neglected to initialize *Number* before trying to enter the loop. A fix is easy, though:

'skipped value' bug

```
{incorrect segment—first value skipped, sentinel counted}
read (Number);
Sum := 0;
Count := 0;
while Number >= 0 do begin
   read (Number);
   Sum := Sum + Number;
   Count := Count + 1
end;
if Count <>0 then Average := Sum / Count;
```

It seems that we've really gone from the frying pan to the fire. Again, both the accumulator and counter will be off by one value—the first input will be skipped if the loop is non-empty. However, if the list isn't empty, the sentinel will be added and counted incorrectly. We need a fifth try:

correct at last!

```
{correct segment}
read (Number);
Sum := 0;
Count := 0;
while Number >= 0 do begin
   Sum := Sum + Number;
   Count := Count + 1;
   read (Number)
end;
if Count <>0 then Average := Sum / Count;
```

> Look before you loop. Don't make *any* assumptions about input, and always put the check before the action.

Here's a final example that contains one of the bugs shown in the incorrect examples above. Can you spot it?

another off-by-one bug

```
program BuggyConversion (input, output);
   {Tries to read an integer one digit at time.}
var Digit: char;
    Number: integer;
begin
   Number := 0;
   writeln ('Enter an integer followed by a letter.');
   repeat
      read (Digit);
      Number := ord(Digit) - ord('0') + (10*Number)
   until not (Digit in ['0'..'9']);
   writeln ('The number is ', Number:1)
end. {BuggyConversion}
```

```
Enter an integer followed by a letter.
25A
The number is 267
```

BuggyConversion's error is of the off-by-one variety. It expects a sentinel to mark the end of valid input, but inadvertently includes the sentinel's value in its calculations. Although *BuggyConversion* manages to exit the loop perfectly well, it adds the ordinal value of 'A' to the accumulator *Number* before printing its results.

In general terms, successful models of loops that read and process input check it for validity before processing. In contrast, unsuccessful, incorrect versions process new items before making sure they're valid. The models to follow are:

loop processing models

```
get a data item; {while version}
while the data is valid
   process the data;
   get more data;
```

The **repeat** loop version only works if we're sure that there really is input available:

```
get a valid data item; {repeat version}
repeat
   process the data;
   get more data
until the data isn't valid;
```

Naturally, off-by-one errors are not limited to programs that read input. Such mistakes can be extremely serious because they don't always produce obviously incorrect output. Consider the following program segment. It's supposed to add the numbers from 1 through 100.

```
Sum := 0;
NextNumber := 1;
repeat
   Sum := Sum+NextNumber;
   NextNumber := NextNumber+1
until NextNumber>=100;
```

checking boundary conditions

Mentally check the loop's boundary conditions. Does it begin properly? Yes, *Sum* gets 1, 3, 6 etc. as it adds 1, 2, 3 and so on. What about the upper boundary? After *Sum* is increased by 99, *NextNumber* is incremented to 100. But wait...this means that the exit condition is met. The loop is exited, and the final value of *Sum* is off by 100. The exit condition should have been *NextNumber*>100.

A final set of basic loop bugs are caused by misplacing semicolons, or neglecting to create compound statements. For example, this program segment is intended to compute 5 factorial (5*4*3*2*1). Although it won't find any factorials, it won't generate any error messages either.

empty statement bugs

```
Product := 1;
Counter := 2;
while Counter<=5 do;
   Product := Product * Counter;
   Counter := Counter + 1;
writeln (Product);
```

There are two flaws in this code. As written, it will have no output at all, because it never gets past the line that says '**do**;'.

> Don't ever forget that a semicolon—an empty statement—is a form of action.

Thus, the only action taken by the loop is a non-action. Naturally, *Counter* never increases beyond its starting value of 2, and the empty statement is repeated again and again, until the computer's time or statement limit is exceeded.

compound statement bugs

Even if we get rid of the semicolon, we've still got a problem. The computer cares no more about our neat indenting than we care about the computer's machine language. It sees this code:

```
while Counter<=5 do
   Product := Product * Counter;
Counter := Counter + 1;
writeln (Product);
```

As far as the computer is concerned, the assignment to *Product* is the loop's sole purpose. To correctly encode our intentions, both statements should be put together into a compound statement.

```
while Counter<=5 do begin
   Product := Product * Counter;
   Counter := Counter + 1;
end;
writeln (Product);
```

Pascal Summary

- **repeat** statement: repeats an action until a *boolean* condition is satisfied:

```
repeat
   statement;
      ...
   statement
until boolean condition
```

- **while** statement: repeats an action for as long as a *boolean* condition is *true*:

  while *boolean condition* **do**
  action;

- Basic models for loop processing:

  get a data item; {**while** version}
  while *the data is valid*
  process the data;
  get more data;

Only use the **repeat** version if you're sure there's input:

  get a valid data item; {**repeat** version}
  repeat
  process the data;
  get more data
  until *the data isn't valid*;

Important Facts

- A **while** loop has an explicitly stated entry condition that must be met if the statement's action is to take place. A **repeat** loop has no entry condition. Therefore, a **repeat** statement's action will always take place at least once, but a **while** loop's action may not occur at all.
- Both loops have an exit condition that must be met for the loop to end—the **repeat** condition is stated explicitly, but the **while** exit condition must be inferred from the loop's entry condition.
- A sentinel value is sometimes used to mark the end of input data relevant to a loop. A counter counts the number of values seen so far, while an accumulator sums them.
- When a loop can be left for more than one reason, don't jump to any conclusions. Add an **if** test to clarify the situation before acting.
- Loops should be used to improve program robustness by giving the user a chance to check, and correct, her input.
- When possible, programs should degrade gracefully. They should give some idea of why the program fails, instead of simply failing abruptly, or producing incorrect results.
- Off-by-one errors are the most common looping bug. Try to avoid them by mentally checking the boundary conditions under which a loop will be entered or exited.
- An execution profile of a program's activity can be created by installing counter variables in loops and subprograms, and printing their values periodically.
- The Golden Rule of Loops: If a loop is entered, it must end eventually. Therefore, the entry or exit condition has to contain a variable whose value is changed by the loop's action.

Self-test Exercises

7-1 Which of these statements apply only to **while** statements? Only to **repeat** statements? To neither or both?

a) A *boolean* is evaluated before entering the loop.

b) This statement's action never need be a compound statement.

c) A *boolean* is evaluated after entering the loop.

d) Its action takes place at least once.

e) Can become an infinite loop.

f) The exact number of times the loop will iterate can always be determined from the entry or exit condition.

g) Must have a counter variable.

7-2 List three things you can do to help improve a program's robustness.

7-3 This loop is intended to add the first ten numbers. Will it? Why not?

```
Count := 1;
Sum := 0;
while Count < 10 do begin
    Count := Count + 1;
    Sum := Sum + Count
end;
```

7-4 This program segment is intended to read and count characters until a blank is found. What's wrong with it?

```
Count := 0;
read (ch);
if (ch = ' ') then
    repeat
        read (ch);
        Count := Count + 1
    until (ch = ' ');
```

7-5 This bit of code is supposed to read pairs of values, and print them in reverse. Any negative number should end the sequence. Will it work?

```
read (N1, N2);
while (N1 >= 0) and (N2 >= 0) do begin
    read (N1, N2);
    writeln (N2, N1)
end;
```

7-6 Rewrite this program segment as a single **repeat** statement.

```
read (First, Last);
while (First = Start) and (Finish <> Last) do
    read (First, Last)
```

7-7 Rewrite this program segment so that it uses a **while** statement, and does not use a **repeat** statement.

```
Count := -1;
repeat
    read (Number);
    Count := Count + 1
until Number < 0;
```

7-8 Let's try one last rewrite. Redo this program segment as a single **for** statement. It should control a single *writeln* statement—no assignments or other statements will be necessary.

```
i := 25;
repeat
    i := (i div 5) - 1;
    i := i * 5;
    writeln (i)
until i <= 0;
```

7-9 Write a loop that shows the first power of 2 greater than or equal to some input number.

7-10 The number of fish in Lake Lackluster is currently about ten million. Write a loop that determines how long it will take the population to drop to a tenth of this level if the number declines by 2.3% each year.

7-11 Some quick questions. *a*) Punctuate the following sentence so that it makes sense: *Sue while Patti had had had had had had had had had had had a better effect on the teacher.*

b) Although we usually worry about the boundary conditions of a sequence, here's one problem whose secret is locked in the middle. What is the product of the sequence:

$$(X-A)(X-B)(X-C)\ldots(X-Z)$$

c) Suppose that you want to put up a fence in your front yard, which is 100 feet long. How many fenceposts are required to have a post every 10 feet?

7-12 The *greatest common divisor* of two integers is the largest number to divide them both without leaving a remainder. Write a function that determines the greatest common divisor of two *integer* arguments.

More Exercises

7-12 Write a function that sums a geometric series, the absolute value of whose common ratio is less than 1. (For example, the common ratio of 1, 0.5, 0.25... is .5—each term is half of the prior term.) You should use the following formula:

Sum of the series = First term / 1−Common ratio

Thus, the function must be given the first term and the common ratio as arguments. Now, write a program that sums a geometric series *iteratively*, i.e. using brute force. How long does it take for this method to be roughly as accurate (say, within 10E-09) as the 'formula' answer? Use at least five different first term and common ratio values (positive and negative), and chart your results.

7-13 Here's a peculiar form of multiplication. To multiply any two numbers, start halving the larger, and doubling the smaller. Whenever the first number (the one that was originally larger) is odd, remember the second number. Continue until the first number has been reduced to 1. Disregard any fractional remainder of any of the halvings. The product is equal to the sum of the remembered second numbers. For example, 53 times 26 is:

53	26	13	6	3	1
26	52	104	208	416	832

26+104+416+832=53*26=1378

Write a program that carries out this form of multiplication.

7-14 Write a program that finds the first 20 numbers which, when divided by 2, 3, 4, 5, or 6 leave a remainder of 1, and when divided by 7 have no remainder.

7-15 The integer 36 has a peculiar property—it is a perfect square, and is also the sum of the integers from 1 through 8. The next such number is 1225, which is 35^2 as well as the sum of 1 through 49. Find the next number that is a perfect square, and is also the sum of the series 1..*n*.

7-16 In the Battle of Hastings, Harold's Saxons arranged themselves in a number of solid squares, each of the same size. This was unfortunate for the attacking Normans, who were unable to pierce Harold's defenses from any side.

Late in the day, Harold decided to enter the fray himself. However, Harold's men (who by this time were in thirteen squares) were unable to make an opening for him without spoiling one of their squares. An armour bearer who fortuitously happened to be standing by noted that, with the addition of Harold, the soldiers would be able to form one very large square. How many men were in each of the small squares, and how many were in the large one? (Hint: you'll find the method of checking for perfect squares we gave in the exercises for Chapter 6 helpful.)

7-17 In the last chapter's exercises we presented a dartboard problem. Six possible scores could be obtained—7, 15, 19, 23, 29, and 37. We asked you to find the five ways of obtaining 100 points with six darts.

Repeat the exercise. This time, however, you should minimize the problem's solution space as much as possible. Improve your basic algorithm so that your program executes as few statements as possible.

7-18 A miser once inherited a sum of money in cash and coin—equal numbers of dollar bills, half dollars, and quarters. She divided the money between eight hiding places, putting the same number of dollar bills and each kind of coin in each place.

The very next day, however, the miser became afraid that one of the hiding places would be uncovered. She redistributed the money, as equally as before, among only seven places. Then, the very next day she felt compelled to cache her money in only six locations. This she was able to do. Unfortunately this was the limit of her ingenuity. The next day she tried to assort her money evenly among only five hiding places. When she was unable to do this, she burst a blood vessel and died, leaving the money to *her* miserly heirs, and starting the whole process over again.

The question we pose is this: How much money did the miser start with, and how many of each coin and bill were there? ($294, 168)

7-19 Write a simple-minded inventory program. Allow for five different products, and have the program user enter the starting inventories of each. Implement the following commands: 'A' is add inventory, 'O' is order and remove from inventory, 'P' is print inventory, and 'Q' is quit. Each input line should consist of one of these commands and, if necessary, a product code and amount.

Try to make this program as idiot-proof as possible. Besides error-checking input (and discarding lines that are mistaken), the program should warn of inventory shortages and print the totals of orders that could not be completely filled.

7-20 In many industries set-up costs are so high that manufacturers will produce much larger quantities of an item than they can reasonably hope to sell quickly. However, warehousing costs can limit the practical size of a production run.

Nadine Riverdale (thanks to the great success of her hot tub sales) is currently in the bulldozer manufacturing business. Experience has shown her that profit on the nth dozer equals $\$500+100(ln(n))$. However, the cost of building parking lots to store them on continually rises, and the kth parking lot she builds will cost $\$100(2k-1)$. In practice, she builds a new parking lot after finishing the manufacture of every ten machines.

The question we pose is this: How many bulldozers should Nadine build if she wants the difference between her total profit, and the cost of storing the machines, to be as large as possible?

7-21 Pick-up-stones is an easy game of position. Twenty-one stones are put in a pile, and players take turns removing 1, 2, or 3 stones from the pile. The last player to go wins.

Write a program that uses the best possible strategy to play Pick-up-stones. Then modify it to accept these variations: X stones go into the original pile, Y stones may be picked up each turn, and the last player loses.

7-22 Pick a number between 1 and 100. Now, write a program that will guess the number within seven turns. To help the program, tell it if its guesses are too high or too low.

7-23 Here's a magical card trick. Let's see how you can turn it into a program. The trick works like this: Nine cards of a single suit (with values from Ace to Nine) are dealt out, face down. Several people each pick a different card. The first person must double the number on her card, add 1, multiply by 5, and give the result to the second player. She adds this number to the value of her own card, then also multiplies by 2, adds 1, multiplies by 5, and passes on the final value. Each person in turn adds the value given her to the value of her card, then carries out the prescribed operations.

When everybody has completed their multiplications and additions we can begin the magic. Make a number that contains as many fives (and only fives) as there are card-choosers. Subtract this from the number calculated by the very last person. Now, divide by 10. The result is a number whose digits are the chosen cards in correct order. Don't forget to have your program say *Abracadabra.*

7-24 It's time for the circus to pay its annual bird and animal tax. The circus owner, however, is a little short on cash, and can't quite afford the bill, which is figured at a rate of $5.50 per bird, and $7.29 per animal. To stall the tax collector, the owner has a clown tell city hall that the circus own 36 heads, and 100 feet altogether, and isn't sure how much tax to pay. Write a program that figures out how many animals and birds are in the circus, and what the tax bill should be.

7-25 Business assets can be depreciated (for tax purposes) in three different ways. In *straight-line* depreciation, the asset's value decreases by the same amount each year over its entire useful life. A second accepted practice of computing depreciation uses the *double-declining balance* method. An asset's 'book value' (its original value less depreciation) is diminished each year by $2/n$, where n is the asset's life. Thus, the depreciation allowed each year is the book value times $2/n$. This accounting method allows quicker depreciation in the first few years.

The *sum-of-the-digits* method is a bit more complicated. Suppose that an asset's useful life is n years. Add the digits from 1 through n (we'll call this the *YearTotal*). The depreciation allowed in the ith year is $(n-i)+1$ divided by *YearTotal*.

Write functions that compute the depreciation allowed each year using each of the methods described above. Use them in a program that prints a depreciation schedule over n years for an asset that originally cost *Price* dollars.

7-26 The Internal Revenue Service lets taxpayers switch from the double-declining balance method to straight-line depreciation whenever they want. Why would a taxpayer want to do this? Write a program that determines the most beneficial time to make the accounting switch.

7-27 Recall that function *SquareRoot* was designed to make successive approximations of a square root, until the difference between one guess and the next was very small. Our definition of 'very small' was that the difference between the old guess and the new guess be less than 10E−09.

Copy function *SquareRoot*, possibly rewriting it as a program or procedure. See if it works for very large and very little inputs, by comparing its output with the answer computed by the standard function *sqrt*. (Hint: it won't.) Redefine function *NoSignificantChange* to produce more accurate results. Two possible variations are:

NoSignificantChange:= abs(Number−sqr(New)) < Epsilon;
NoSignificantChange:= abs(Number−sqr(New)−1) < Epsilon;

Analyze these (either on paper, or with a test program). Are either or both of them reasonable? Come up with two more plausible ways of describing a 'very small' difference that work for a wide range of inputs.

7-28 Implement the *integer* operators **div** and **mod** as functions.

7-29 Here are a few problems for certain of the numbers between 1,000 and 9,999.

a) Find a number that meets the following conditions: it is a perfect square between 1,000 and 9,999, its first two digits are the same, and its last two digits are the same.

b) Find two numbers, between 1,000 and 9,999, which are equal to the sum of the cubes of their digits.

c) Find three numbers that are members of the following select group: they are four digit perfect squares, and each is equal to the square of the sum of its first two and last two digits.

d) Four numbers, when squared, consist of only even numbers and are greater than 1,000 and less than 9,999. What are they?

One of these problems doesn't quite fit in. Which one? How does realizing this affect your program?

7-30 When the Greeks discovered that π was an irrational number (and couldn't be expressed as a fraction), they were rather upset. It didn't seem right that the perfect simplicity of mathematics be challenged by such a figure, so they suppressed the knowledge of pi's existence, and resorted to more complex methods of circle measurement.

One of their problems was to determine the area of a circle. They were able to get an approximate answer by inscribing a regular polyhedron (i.e. a many-sided figure) within the circle, and then computing the polyhedron's area with elementary trigonometry. Write a program that determines the accuracy of this method. Show your results graphically. How many sides will the polyhedron have when it challenges the accuracy of your computer?

7-31 Bidding gets fast and furious at auctions, and it's possible to spend a lot of money very quickly. A friend of ours went to an auction, and in just ten minutes managed to spend half of her money. Oddly enough, she now had as many pennies as she had previously had dollars, but only half as many dollars as she had previously had pennies. How much did she start with, and how much did she spend?

7-32 The largest common factor *LCF* of two positive integers *a* and *b* (where $a>=b$) can be defined as *a* if *b* is zero, and the largest common factor of *b* and *a* **mod** *b* otherwise. Implement this function both recursively and non-recursively.

7-33 Write a recursive procedure that computes and represents any requested Fibonacci number. Do you have to place any limits on input?

7-34 Implement this recursive function. What operation does it carry out?

MysteryFunction (X, Y) is X if Y=1.

MysteryFunction (X, Y) is X + *MysteryFunction* $(X, Y-1)$ otherwise.

7-35 Devise a statement for conditional iteration. Do you think that equivalents of both **while** and **repeat** are necessary? Can you think of a syntax that would allow you to exit from the middle of a loop? When might this be desirable?

'These days, the average computer is far more likely to be found crunching words...'

8

Character-Oriented Computing: Text Processing

When the authors were boys, computing meant numbers, plain and simple. 'Number crunching' was what computing was called, and it was hard to imagine using computers for anything else. But as even our most youthful (or ancient) readers are aware, there has been a gradual change in computer applications. These days, the average computer is far more likely to be found crunching words than numbers.

Word crunching is usually known as *text processing*, since a sequence of characters is called text. Solving text processing problems is quite a bit of fun. They give us the opportunity to wrestle with hard programming problems, but, since they hardly involve any math at all, don't give us cause to regret having flunked (or not taken) calculus.

Section 8-1 introduces programming for processing text. Two standard *boolean* functions, *eof* and *eoln*, are the only new Pascal features in this section. These functions help us deal with text in its most familiar form—as a sequence of lines, each composed of characters. We'll see some of the standard text processing loops, then deal with some considerably more complicated text-oriented problems.

Section 8-2 is optional reading. It describes methods of creating input and output *files* that serve as alternatives to the standard *input* and *output* mechanisms. We also introduce the *file window*, which can be used to take a peek ahead at the value we're about to read. Instructors who rely heavily on text-oriented programming, or who make extensive use of files other than *input* and *output*, may require this material now. However, it won't be assumed at all until files are formally introduced in Chapter 13.

As usual, the final section, 8-3, deals with debugging and antibugging techniques, and describes some of the bugs that are typical of text processing loops.

Text Processing 8-1

WORK WITH CHARACTERS (AS OPPOSED to numbers) is called *text processing*—any sequence of characters forms text. Procedure *EchoOneLine*, below, gives us an idea of what text processing involves. The procedure reads in a line of text (that contains an unknown number of characters) one character at a time, and echoes each character as it goes along.

```
procedure EchoOneLine;
   {Read and echo a single line of text.}
   var CurrentCharacter: char;
   begin
      while not eoln do begin        {While not at the end of line...}
         read (CurrentCharacter);          {...read and echo characters.}
         write (CurrentCharacter)
      end;
      writeln;        {Print a carriage return.}
      readln          {Dump the end-of-line character.}
   end; {EchoOneLine}
```

EchoOneLine calls the standard (predefined) function *eoln*. The unpronounceable *end-of-line* function (people usually just spell out *eoln* when referring to it) is used to watch for the end of an input line.

review of *read* and *readln*

Let's begin our discussion of text processing by reviewing the operation of *readln* and *read*. *readln* finds the value of its parameter (or parameters), and then throws the rest of the line away. For example, suppose we have the following text in a data file (or ready to type into an interactive keyboard):

When I am grown to Man's estate
I shall be very proud and great.
And tell the other girls and boys
Not to meddle with my toys.

When this input is given to program *EchoFirstLetter*, below, only the first value is read from each line. The rest of the input line is skipped.

readln demonstration program

```
program EchoFirstLetter (input, output);
   {Demonstrates the effect of readln.}
var Character: char;
begin
   readln (Character);      write (Character);
   readln (Character);      write (Character);
   readln (Character);      write (Character);
   readln (Character);      write (Character);
   writeln
end. {EchoFirstLetter}
```

↓ ↓ ↓ ↓ ↓

```
WIAN
```

discarding the line

> Calling *readln* without any argument discards any values left on the current line of input. The next character read will be the first character of the next line.

The standard procedure *read* doesn't discard anything. When we use *read* to input *char* values, no character—not even a blank space—is ever thrown away. Assume that the input of *ReadEachCharacter* is the text sample we showed above.

read demonstration program

```
program ReadEachCharacter (input, output);
   {Demonstrates the effect of read.}
var Character: char;
begin
   read (Character);        write (Character);
   read (Character);        write (Character);
   read (Character);        write (Character);
   read (Character);        write (Character);
   writeln
end. {ReadEachCharacter}
```

```
When
```

All the output of *ReadEachCharacter* came from the first line of input. We'd have to do quite a few more *reads* before getting to the beginning of the second line. Don't forget that when *real* or *integer* values are obtained with either *read* or *readln*, blanks and line-ends serve only to separate values, and are otherwise ignored.

the end-of-line

Now, for the convenience of both people and machines, text input in Pascal is divided into lines, just as in the example above. A special non-printing *control character*, which varies from system to system, usually marks the end of each line.* Thus, every punched card represents a line of input in batch systems, and an end-of-line marker is generated whenever a card is read. In interactive systems, hitting the carriage return or new-line key sends the end-of-line character to the computer. When data files are stored in the computer, the end-of-line marker is usually hidden, and doesn't show up in a count of the number of characters the data file holds. But in any case...

the *eoln* function

> A call of the *boolean* function *eoln* represents *true* if the character we're about to read is the end-of-line character (whether we can see it or not). Otherwise, *eoln* represents *false*.

Calling *eoln* causes the computer to examine the next character without disturbing it in any way. If it's the end-of-line character, *eoln* is

* For the purpose of our discussion, we can assume that it's always done this way.

true, because we're at the end of a line. If the next character is a digit, punctuation mark, letter, etc. we're obviously *not* at the end of a line of input yet, and *eoln* represents the value *false*.

what is the end-of-line?

> Although the end-of-line character has a special meaning to the computer, this cachet is lost once we read it as part of a Pascal program. Instead of printing as a carriage return, the end-of-line character is read and printed out as a blank space.

The end-of-line character is rather like an enchanted jewel. As long as we're content to merely look at it, it retains its special significance. However, once we touch it, the spell is broken (and it turns into a toad). If we read and echo the end-of-line character we'll just print a blank.

the next line

The character immediately following the end-of-line character is, for all practical purposes, the first character of the next line of input. However, we still have to read (or otherwise dispose of) the end-of-line character on our way to the next line. Procedure *ReadOneLine*, below, uses a **while** loop to read input, character by character, until the end of the current line is reached. Then, it reads the end-of-line character—the last character on the current line. A call of *ReadOneLine* is equivalent to a call of the standard procedure *readln*, because it leaves us at the beginning of the next line of input.

imitating *readln*

```
procedure ReadOneLine;
   {Imitates the effect of readln.}
   var Character: char;
   begin
      while not eoln do read (Character);
      read (Character)
   end; {ReadOneLine}
```

> The only way to generate (print) an end-of-line character from within a program is to use the standard procedure *writeln*.

creating an end-of-line

Were we to input the end-of-line character from a data file or interactive terminal keyboard, and immediately echo it to the lineprinter or screen, it would not cause a carriage return. Subsequent output will appear on the same line, until we call procedure *writeln*.

problem: echo a line of text

Let's use this information to write a procedure that reads and echoes a full line of text—complete with carriage return (the end-of-line marker). In words, our algorithm is:

refinement

```
while it's not the end of the line
   read a character (using read);
   ready the character for printing (using write);
force printing of all output (by using writeln);
get ready for another line of input (by using readln);
```

To nobody's surprise, we find ourselves writing our starting example—procedure *EchoOneLine*.

```
procedure EchoOneLine;
  {Read and echo a single line of text.}
  var CurrentCharacter: char;
  begin
    while not eoln do begin          {While not at the end of line...}
      read (CurrentCharacter);              {...read and echo characters.}
      write (CurrentCharacter)
    end;
    writeln;          {Print a carriage return.}
    readln            {Dump the end-of-line.}
  end; {EchoOneLine}
```

Self-Check Questions

Q. What would happen if we wrote *EchoOneLine* with a **repeat** statement instead of a **while** statement, like this?

```
procedure EchoWithRepeat;
  {A faulty procedure for echoing a line of text.}
  var Character: char;
  begin
    repeat
      read (Character);
      write (Character)
    until eoln;
    writeln;
    readln
  end; {EchoWithRepeat}
```

A. We've made a faulty assumption—one of the most serious in text-processing programs—by assuming that the line definitely contains something to read. But what if it doesn't? Suppose that the first line of input is empty, and contains only the end-of-line character. Then:

1. We read the end-of-line character.
2. We ready it (really a space) for printing.
3. Is *eoln true* yet? Not necessarily, because the character we're about to read is the first character of the second line. Thus, *eoln* will only be *true* if this line is blank as well.

Never assume that there will be input. Always allow for the possibility that a line may be blank.

The Idea of a File

So much for a single line of text. What about a series of lines, though? For all practical purposes, a *series* of lines is just as organized—complete with beginning and end—as the characters that form a *single* line. Computer scientists have developed a pleasant fiction to describe this line-by-line sequence of characters.

> As far as a Pascal program is concerned, its input comes from an imaginary entity called a *file*.

Programmers who use data files already employ files for input. The idea of a file of input probably won't upset users of punched cards too much either, since a stack of cards might as well be called a file as anything else. Video terminal programmers, on the other hand, must submit to a more willing suspension of disbelief, because an interactive terminal keyboard isn't any more full of information than is a ball point pen. Still, a Pascal program acts as though all its input is coming from a file that consists of zero or more lines of data.

Now, just as the end of each input line is marked by an end-of-line character, the end of the entire file is flagged with an end-of-file character.* It's used by the *end of file* function, *eof*.

the *eof* function

> A call of *eof* causes the computer to inspect the very next input character, without otherwise disturbing it. If it's the end-of-file character, *eof* is *true* because we're at the end of the input file. If it's any other character, there must still be data in the file and *eof* is *false*.

The *eof* function is necessary when we don't know how much input a program is going to receive, and when no explicit sentinel character marks the end of input. A general outline of programs that use *eof* to process *char* input is:

```
while not eof do begin
    get the data;
    process the data
end;    etc.
```

The internal processing of an *eof* loop need not be complicated. Perhaps the simplest example counts the number of lines in input:

counting lines

```
LineCount := 0;
while not eof do begin
    LineCount := LineCount + 1;
    readln          {Discard the current line.}
end;
```

* As with the end-of-line character, this may not be literally true. The end-of-file character may not actually be there as part of the file.

Another easy code segment counts the number of characters in input:

counting characters

```
CharCount := 0;
while not eof do begin
   CharCount := CharCount + 1;
   read (Ch)          {Discard the current character.}
end;
```

However, we must realize that we're including any end-of-line characters in our count.

Although we'll develop more specialized examples in the next section, widespread applications of *eof* require it to be used in conjunction with *eoln*. Program *EchoText*, below, illustrates one of the most common models of text processing programs. It reads and echoes an entire input file one line at a time. In doing so, it maintains the line structure of its input—whenever *eoln* is *true*, a *writeln* prints a new carriage return.

EchoText is a very important and widely-used model. You should identify and understand:

1. the outer loop that processes lines, while keeping an eye out for the end of the input file.
2. the inner loop that processes characters, while watching for the end of the current line.

Note that the shaded portion is equivalent to procedure *EchoOneLine*.

the basic text-processing program

```
program EchoText (input, output);
   {Uses nested while loops to echo a file of text.}
var CurrentCharacter: char;
begin
   while not eof do begin
      while not eoln do begin
         read (CurrentCharacter);
         write (CurrentCharacter)
      end; {eoln while}
      writeln;
      readln
   end {eof while}
end. {EchoText}
```

Two special rules apply to the end-of-file character.

The Golden Rules Of *eof*

A program cannot read the end-of-file character. Furthermore, when *eof* is *true*, *eoln* is undefined.

reading past *eof*

The end-of-file character can be heard, but not seen. Trying to read the end-of-file character (or even worse, trying to read *past* it), causes one of the quickest crashes in Pascal.

ATTEMPT TO READ PAST EOF

Thus, (**not** *eof*) is usually used as the *entry* condition of a **while** loop, and not as the *exit* condition of a **repeat** loop.

Self-Check Questions

Q. Procedure *EchoText*, above, contains two pairs of input and output statements:

```
read (CurrentCharacter);        {first pair}
write (CurrentCharacter);
  ...
writeln;                        {second pair}
readln;
```

Can the order of calls in either the first or second pair be reversed?

A. The first pair is a *read, process* sequence. The calls couldn't be switched, because without input, there is nothing to process.
The second pair is different. The *writeln* makes sure that all the pending *writes* are printed, along with issuing an end-of-line. The *readln* arranges for a new line of input (if there is one). Since these tasks are entirely separate, the calls could be switched without doing any damage.

Concentrating on Numbers

Many programs that are not intended to process text still require the tools of text processing. Improving program robustness is a common motivation. For example, a program that expects numerical input is exceptionally sensitive to its environment. An inadvertent nonblank or non-digit character can cause a type clash, and program crash.

A basic form of run-time error checking helps prevent the problem. Since all input may be read as a sequence of *char* values, we can read a number's digits one at a time, then convert them into the number they represent (e.g. turn the sequence '1', '3', '7', into 137). Any non-digit characters that are encountered can be skipped. We'll make creating an error-proof input procedure our first problem:

problem: reading *integers*

Write a procedure that reads an *integer* as a sequence of characters. Error check all input, and ignore any leading non-digits.

What are the basic steps of our *integer* reading procedure? First, we have to get rid of any spaces or other characters that precede the number. Then, we must employ the *ord* function to represent the digit characters as numbers. An assignment from Chapter 2 shows us the way:

ConvertedToInteger := *ord* (*InputCharacter*) − *ord* ('0');

Finally, we should continue to read in digits of the number until we reach a non-digit. We'll simplify the task slightly by only allowing positive *integer* input.

first refinement

find a digit;
convert it into an integer;
add it to ten times the value of the digits read so far;
keep reading and converting until we get to a non-digit;

As usual, we'll need a second refinement to express our algorithm in more procedural form.

second refinement

```
initialize a variable Number to 0;
repeat
    read a character
until we read a digit;
repeat
    convert the digit into an integer;
    add the digit to 10*Number;
    read in the next character
until we read a non-digit;
```

The completed procedure, shown below, implements the algorithm. It's worth studying the special techniques it employs (especially the use of sets, and the *ord* function), because the same methods will show up in many text processing programs and procedures.

integer-reading program

```
procedure ReadANumber (var Number: integer);
    {Reads positive integer input as a sequence of characters.}
    var Character: char;
    begin
        Number := 0;
        repeat          {remove extraneous non-digits.}
            read (Character)
        until Character in ['0'..'9'];
        repeat          {convert the digit characters to the integer}
            Number := (10*Number)+(ord(Character) - ord('0'));
            read (Character)
        until not (Character in ['0'..'9'])
    end; {ReadANumber}
```

A considerable portion of *ReadANumber* is devoted to error checking. It's worth the trouble—suppose we have a program segment with input as shown:

```
writeln ('Please enter a positive integer.');
ReadANumber (Number);
writeln ('The number is ', Number:1);
```

↓ ↓ ↓ ↓ ↓

```
Please enter a positive integer.
bkjw(*#n;,)(_hg$^&71439H!Am
The number is 71439
```

Self-Check Questions

Q. Suppose that we wanted to make *ReadANumber*, above, even more bulletproof. How can we avoid reading a number that's greater than *MAXINT*?

A. We'll use the same trick we employed in our numerical palindrome program from section 7–2. A simple addition to the second **repeat** statement's exit condition (shaded) ensures that we remain a comfortable distance away from *MAXINT*:

```
repeat
   ...
until not (Character in ['0'..'9'])) or (Number > (MAXINT /10)
```

Continuing with Numbers

A problem that's somewhat related involves converting numbers from one base to another. When we work with a base greater than 10, ordinary characters *must* appear within numbers. For example, the hexadecimal (base 16) system's digits are '0', '1', '2', '3', '4', '5', '6', '7', '8', '9', 'A', 'B', 'C', 'D', 'E', and 'F'. Our problem is:

problem: hex conversion

> Write a program that reads and converts hexadecimal numbers to base 10 notation.

Hex values (like those of binary and octal—base 8—notation) often come up when we're dealing with computers at the machine level. For example, the hex value B equals 11 in decimal (base 10) notation; F is 15, B1 is 111, and AB is 115.

We can start to develop an algorithm for converting hexadecimal numbers into ordinary decimals by looking at an assignment from *ReadANumber*:

```
Number := (10*Number)+(ord(Character) - ord('0'));
```

a conversion algorithm

Number represents the numerical value of the digits already read in, while *Character* is the digit that currently belongs in *Number's* 'ones' column. Since *Number* is base 10, we have to multiply it by 10 before adding *Character* on. The same principle converts numbers of any base *B* to base 10. Before the decimal value of a new digit is added to the digits converted so far, they must be multiplied by *B*.

Program *ConvertHex*, below, computes the decimal equivalents of its hexadecimal input. As you can see, it conforms to the outline (proposed earlier) for processing *char* input:

```
while not eof do begin
   get the data;
   process the data
end;
```

It's worth making a special effort to recognize that *ConvertHex* treats its input as a long sequence of *char* values. The line structure of its input is ignored. Why can't there be more than one space (or carriage return) between each input value?

hex conversion program

```
program ConvertHex (input, output);
    {Converts hexadecimal numbers to base 10.}
const BASE = 16;
var Character: char;
    Number, Decimal: integer;
procedure GetDecimalEquivalent (Character: char; var Decimal: integer);
    {Gives Decimal the base 10 equivalent of Character.}
    begin
        case Character of
            '0','1','2','3','4','5','6','7','8','9':
                            Decimal := ord(Character)-ord('0');
            'A','B','C','D','E','F':
                            Decimal := (ord(Character)-ord('A'))+10
        end
    end; {GetDecimalEquivalent}
begin {ConvertHex}
    while not eof do begin
        Number := 0;
        read (Character);
        write ('The decimal equivalent of hex ');
        repeat
            write (Character);
            GetDecimalEquivalent (Character, Decimal);
            Number := (BASE * Number)+Decimal;
            read (Character)
        until not (Character in ['0'..'9', 'A'..'F']);
        writeln (' is ', Number:1)
    end {while}
end. {ConvertHex}
```

```
A 10 1A
F00 ABCDEF
The decimal equivalent of hex A is 10
The decimal equivalent of hex 10 is 16
The decimal equivalent of hex 1A is 26
The decimal equivalent of hex F00 is 3840
The decimal equivalent of hex ABCDEF is 11259375
```

echoing *integer* input

ConvertHex ignored the line structure of its input, and treated the end-of-line character as an ordinary space. However, similarly constructed programs that read *integer* and *real* data require us to use *readln* to move from line to line. Suppose that we want to read and echo *integer* input. Since blanks and end-of-lines are ignored except as value separators, this data-file-oriented program segment would seem to do the job:

```
{incorrect program segment}
while not eof do begin
    read (IntegerValue);
    writeln (IntegerValue)
end;
```

Unfortunately, as we'll see below, the program this segment appears in will crash as it tries to read past end of file! When we rewrite the segment (on the next page) we'll see that we still have to keep the line structure of input in mind. The reason has to do with the way that *read* works.

> If *read* is given an *integer* or *real* variable as a parameter, it skips characters until it comes to a nonblank.

problems with reading numbers

In other words, when the statement:

read (*IntegerValue*);

is executed, the program jumps over spaces or end-of-lines, and reads the first nonblank value it finds (which, we hope, is an *integer*).

If we try to read another *integer* value, the process is repeated. The space or spaces that come before the next *integer* are skipped, and the *integer* is read in. Thus, after reading a numerical value, the computer is always about to read (and possibly ignore) a space, or an end-of-line character.

Let's jump ahead to the end of the program's input data.

the last end-of-line

> By default, there is always an end-of-line character at the end of an input 'file' in Pascal.

Suppose we've just read what we (but not the computer) know is the program's last input number. The loop above asks itself:

Is this the end of the program's input?

Then it answers:

No. There is at least one blank space left—the last end-of-line character. Perhaps there is more data.

Since the program doesn't think that it's reached the end of the file, procedure *read* starts to repeat the **while** loop's action. It begins to skip spaces, looking for another *integer*. In the process, the program tries to read the end-of-file character, and it crashes.

> To avoid the problem of reading past end of file, *integer* and *real* data must be read on a line-by-line basis.

Although this may be conceptually distasteful, it isn't difficult. *If there are no extra blanks at the end of each line*, we can rewrite the incorrect program segment from the last page as:

correct model for number processing

```
{General-purpose outline for programs that read integer or real data.}
while not eof do begin
    while not eoln do begin
        read (IntegerValue);
        Process (IntegerValue)
    end; {We've reached the end of a line.}
    readln {Discard the rest of the line.}
end;
```

Understanding this technique is essential for writing correct programs. This is true whether input comes from a data file or from the keyboard.

Self-Check Questions

Q. Suppose that blank spaces follow a program's last *integer* or *real* input value. Will the program segment shown above work?

A. No. After the last numerical value is read in, *eoln* isn't *true* yet. The *readln* won't be executed, and the program will crash. A method of solving this problem (by using Pascal's *file window*) is discussed in the optional section 8-2, and again in Chapter 13.

Bottom-Up Module Testing: A Long, Hard Program

Our final example is a rather long program that will give us a considerable amount of practice in the areas of writing and testing program modules. Like many text-processing problems, it involves looking at text as a sequence of characters, and then recognizing (and possibly modifying) patterns in that sequence. The problem is:

problem: gerund conversion

> Write a program that finds infinitive verb forms in ordinary English text, and changes them to gerunds.

The infinitive of a verb is its 'to be' form: to see, to run, to dance, to sing.* A gerund is a verb with an 'ing' ending: seeing, running, dancing, etc. To simplify the problem, we'll assume that whenever 'to' appears in a sentence, the next word is a verb.

This problem isn't easy to solve—a glance ahead to the code of its solution will make this obvious. Nor do the program's procedures fall into the neat pieces that make top-down programming methods (like stepwise refinement) so attractive.

a bottom-up strategy

However, converting infinitives to gerunds *does* provide a realistic set of motivations for exploring alternative programming strategies; in particular, a *bottom-up* approach to solving our problem. Although we'll keep using stepwise refinement to help break the problem down, we'll encode trial versions of our modules. This means that we'll be making some low-level decisions about algorithm and implementation *before* thoroughly decomposing the problem.

The bottom-up approach lets us make some necessary tests of our ideas and methods as we go along. Although the problems given in textbooks can usually be solved by a methodical programmer on the first try, we'll find that making mistakes is a necessary part of learning how to convert infinitives to gerunds.

A first breakdown of the problem is obvious, even though it may prove to be a bit simplistic:

first refinement

while *there are characters to read*
  look for infinitives;
  change them to gerunds;

How can we recognize an infinitive verb? Well, the definition above is clearcut—the word 'to' is always the start of an infinitive. What are the characteristics of a 'to' that comes before another word?

what is a 'to'?

1. It is always preceded by a blank.
2. It contains the letters 't' and 'o'.
3. It is always followed by a blank.

Thus, recognizing the word 'to' requires that we keep track of four letters. If we encounter a blank that is followed by 't', an 'o', and another blank, we've found a 'to'. If the required series of matches breaks down at any point, we know that we don't have a 'to', and can print the letters that have already been read. In the pseudocode below, a pound sign '#' is used to represent the character that didn't match:

* Most people's contact with infinitives is due to the ancestral prohibition against splitting them, e.g. to barely see, to quickly run.

finding a 'to'

```
while there are still letters to read
  read a letter. Is it a ' '? If so...
    then read a letter. Is it a 't'? If so...
      then read a letter. Is it a 'o'? If so...
        then read a letter. Is it a ' '? If so...
          then we have a 'to'
        else print what we have so far—' ','t','o','#'
      else print what we have so far—' ','t','#'
    else print what we have so far—' ','#'
  else print what we have so far—'#'
```

How come the pseudocode is nested so deeply? Well, sometimes we'll echo the characters we read in, and sometimes we won't. We have to store the characters first, then make a decision about whether or not we want to print them. The solution to a different problem—spotting the end of a 'to'—wouldn't require such deep nesting, but it wouldn't be appropriate for our gerund conversions. We've made a trial implementation of the pseudocode in program *FindTo*, below, and supplied some test data to check our method.

'to'-finding test program

```
program FindTo (input, output);
  {Trial program for recognizing the word 'to' in text.
   Prints an asterisk after every 'to'.}
const BLANK = ' ';
      ASTERISK = '*';
var ch0, ch1, ch2, ch3: char;
begin
  while not eof do begin
    read (ch0);
    if (ch0=BLANK) and not eof then begin
      read (ch1);
      if (ch1='t') and not eof then begin
        read (ch2);
        if (ch2='o') and not eof then begin
          read (ch3);
          if ch3=BLANK then
            write (ch0, ch1, ch2, ASTERISK, ch3)
          else write (ch0, ch1, ch2, ch3) {ch3 wasn't BLANK}
        end else write (ch0, ch1, ch2) {ch2 wasn't 'o'}
      end else write (ch0, ch1) {ch1 wasn't 't'}
    end else write (ch0) {ch0 wasn't BLANK}
  end; {while}
  writeln;
end. {FindTo}
```

To begin with to, to end into too. To wit, to do. to be.

```
To begin with to, to* end into too.  To wit, to* do.  to be.
```

Although our trial sentence isn't too grammatical, it tests *FindTo* in likely 'to'-finding situations. Notice that the output is incorrect—the 'To' that begins the test sentence is ignored because it isn't preceded by a blank, and because it starts with a capital 'T'. The program also fails when a 'to' has two blanks before it. We'll have to improve the 'to'-finding algorithm later.

how good is testing?

FindTo is useful because it tests our *algorithm* as well as its *implementation*. However, before we rely on it, we have to remember one of our Golden Rules:

> Testing can show the presence of bugs, but never their absence. A program test is only as realistic as the test data.

What about turning infinitives into gerunds? We'll expand our initial pseudocode:

second refinement

while *there are characters to read*
    read and echo characters until we find a 'To' *or* 'to';
    if *we find one*
        read and echo characters until the end of the next word;
        add an 'ing' *to it*;

Unfortunately, a few mental test cases will find flaws in the second part of our conversion method. Adding 'ing' just won't suffice. Consider these verbs:

rules for gerunds

Infinitive	*Gerund*	*Rule*
see	*seeing*	*add 'ing'*
fall	*falling*	*add 'ing'*
send	*sending*	*add 'ing'*
like	*liking*	*drop final e; add 'ing'*
run	*running*	*double last letter; add 'ing'*

If we examine the last few letters of the verb we can make some provisional rules for creating gerunds:

Characteristic	*Example*	*Action*
Last two letters the same	*see, sell*	*Add 'ing'*
Last two letters consonants	*sing, send*	*Add 'ing'*
Last letter 'e'	*like, bake*	*Drop the 'e', add 'ing'*
Next-to-last letter a vowel	*run, stir*	*Double last letter, add 'ing'*

Our experience with *FindTo* should also make us wary of the *until the end of the next word* part of our pseudocode. Although the 'to's we looked for were always followed by blanks, almost any punctuation mark will signify the end of a verb. As before, we need a program that tests our algorithm—the set of rules for recognizing and modifying verbs—and gives us practice in implementing it.

a moving window

Program *TestConversion*, below, uses an interesting technique to find the end of a word. Taken together, variables *Ch1, Ch2*, and *Ch3* represent the three most recently read characters. In effect, they form a moving 'window,' three characters wide, into our input text. The four shaded statements print the oldest character from the window, remove it, and then bring the next character into our field of view. Contrast the window technique to the method (deep nesting) used in program *FindTo*. Could that method be used here? Would it be appropriate?

gerund conversion test program

```
program TestConversion (input, output);
   {Test program for printing every input word as a gerund.}
const BLANK = ' ';
var ch1, ch2, ch3: char;
      {Used to form a moving window of the current 3 input characters.}
begin {TestConversion}
   while not eof do begin
      read (ch1, ch2, ch3); {Every verb has at least 2 letters.}
      while not (ch3 in [BLANK, ',', ';', '!', '?', '.']) do begin
         write (ch1); {Advance the window until we}
         ch1 := ch2;  {reach the end of the word.}
         ch2 := ch3;
         read (ch3)
      end; {while}
      {Now that ch1 and ch2 represent the last 2 letters,
       we can convert the verb into a gerund.}
   if (ch1=ch2) or (not (ch1 in ['a','e','i','o','u'])
                    and not (ch2 in ['a','e','i','o','u']))
      then write (ch1, ch2, 'ing', ch3) {RULE: see, fall, or send}
      else if ch2='e'
         then write (ch1, 'ing', ch3) {RULE: like}
         else write (ch1, ch2, ch2, 'ing', ch3) {RULE: run}
   end; {while not eof}
   writeln
end. {TestConversion}
```

↓ ↓ ↓ ↓ ↓

see be sing sway know fall come go eat quit

```
seeing bing singing swayying knowwing
falling coming gooing eatting quitting
```

(We, and not the program, are responsible for splitting the output over two lines.) As before, a well-chosen set of test data has exposed some flaws in our algorithm. However, the **if** statements that implement our rules for making gerunds can easily be extended. Perhaps by the time we return to the *TestConversion* algorithm we'll have a more precise set of guides.

What else do we have to worry about? Well, when an infinitive appears at the beginning of a sentence, we'll have to capitalize the verb. This gives us two problems—knowing when we're at the beginning of a new sentence, and capitalizing a letter. We'll deal with the new sentence problem first.

state variables

How do we represent the knowledge that we are, or are not, at the beginning of a sentence? If you recall the bowling program *BowlingScore*, you'll recognize that we require a *boolean* 'state' variable. Initially, it will be *true*. It becomes *false* once we process the first letter of the first word, then *true* again when we reach one of the ordinary English sentence terminators '.', '!', or '?'.

finding the end of a sentence

Procedure *SpotEndOfSentence*, below, updates the state variable *NewSentence* by checking the value of the most recently read character *LastCh*. It contains one additional refinement to the algorithm outlined above—it is smart enough to recognize that *NewSentence* remains *true* as we read the blank letters that follow the end of a sentence. In our final program, *SpotEndOfSentence* will have to be called frequently, since we're potentially at the end of a sentence whenever we reject a potential 'to', or convert a known verb.

```
procedure SpotEndOfSentence (LastCh: char; var NewSentence: boolean);
  {Sets the state variable NewSentence.}
  begin
    NewSentence := (LastCh in ['.', '!', '?'])
                    or (NewSentence and (LastCh=Blank))
  end; {SpotEndOfSentence}
```

Capitalizing a lower-case letter is our next problem. Let's write this as a function that is given a lower-case letter as its argument, and returns a capital letter. Program *ConvertToCapital*, below, tests the function.

capitalization test program

```
program ConvertToCapital (input, output);
  {Trial program that converts lower-case letters to capitals.}
var ch: char;
function Capitalized (ch: char): char;
  {Represents its argument as a capital letter.}
  begin
    Capitalized := chr((ord(ch)-ord('a'))+ord('A'))
  end; {Capitalized}
begin
  while not eof do begin
    read (ch);
    write (Capitalized(ch))
  end; {while}
  writeln
end. {ConvertToCapital}
```

↓ ↓ ↓ ↓

abcxyz
ABCXYZ

At last we've come up with a trial program that seems to work!

review of the modules

Now that we've written rough versions of the basic modules of a verb-conversion program, let's review the mistakes we found. Go back and look at our test run of program *FindTo*. You'll see that *FindTo* failed to recognize the word 'to' when the 't' was capitalized. Spotting a capital 'T' as well as a lower-case one is easily fixed with a set definition:

if (*ch1* **in** ['t', 'T']) **and not** *eof* **then** etc.

FindTo also didn't spot a 'to' when it was the first word of the first sentence of input. Fortunately, we've just solved this problem: We can begin processing with the state variable *NewSentence* initialized to *true*. If *NewSentence* is *true*, we won't require that a potential 'to' be preceded by a blank space.

A more serious problem came with *TestConversion's* poor rule table. Most errors came from unnecessarily doubling the verb's last letter. Inspecting the test output leads to more accurate rules. Note that there's an implicit **else** between each rule change below. Thus, 'sway' and 'quit' don't follow the 'next-to-last letter a vowel' rule.

final gerund-conversion rules

Characteristic	*Example*	*Action*
The word is 'be'	*be*	*Add 'ing'*
Last letter is 'w', 'y', or 'o'	*sway, know, go*	*Add 'ing'*
Last two letters the same	*see, sell*	*Add 'ing'*
Last two letters consonants	*sing, send*	*Add 'ing'*
Two vowels before last letter	*quit, eat*	*Add 'ing'*
Last letter 'e'	*like, bake*	*Drop the 'e', add 'ing'*
Next-to-last letter a vowel	*run, stir*	*Double last letter, add 'ing'*

The completed version of program *Gerunds*, along with test data, is shown over the next few pages. Its procedures are rewritten versions of our test programs, and their functions should be readily apparent. The only assumption we've made about input is that it follows ordinary English sentence structure—a 'to' that doesn't begin a sentence is only preceded by a single blank.

the moral

> The bottom-up method of programming should be used to gain experience with the parts of a program. However, it should never be a justification for starting to code without first developing an algorithm, and pseudocode draft of your program.

gerund conversion program

```
program Gerunds (input, output);
  {Converts infinitive verbs to gerunds.}
const BLANK = ' '; {Used in all subprograms.}
var NewSentence, ToFound: boolean;
procedure SpotEndOfSentence (LastCh: char; var NewSentence: boolean);
  {Sets the state variable NewSentence.}
  begin
    NewSentence := (LastCh in ['.', '!', '?'])
                    or (NewSentence and (LastCh=BLANK))
  end; {SpotEndOfSentence}
procedure FindTo (var NewSentence, ToFound: boolean);
  {Searches for the words 'to' and 'To'. '#' represents an unknown character.}
  var ch0, ch1, ch2, ch3: char;
  begin
    ToFound := false;
    while not eof and not ToFound do begin
      read (ch0);
      if ((ch0=BLANK) or NewSentence) and not eof then begin
        if NewSentence and (ch0='T') then ch1 := ch0 else read (ch1);
          {This corrects the special case of a 'T' at the start of input.}
        if (ch1 in ['t', 'T']) and not eof then begin {We have a 't' or 'T'}
          read (ch2);
          if (ch2='o') and not eof then begin {We have a 'to' or 'To'}
            read (ch3);
            if (ch3=BLANK) and not eof then begin {We have a 'to ' or 'To '}
              ToFound := true; {Mark it, and space between words if necessary.}
              if not NewSentence then write (ch0)
            end else begin {ch3 wasn't BLANK}
              write (ch0, ch1, ch2, ch3);
              SpotEndOfSentence (ch3, NewSentence)
            end {We've printed ' to#' or ' To#'}
          end else begin {ch2 wasn't 'o'}
            write (ch0, ch1, ch2);
            SpotEndOfSentence (ch2, NewSentence)
          end {We've printed ' t#' or ' T#'}
        end else begin {ch1 wasn't 't' or 'T'}
          write (ch0, ch1);
          SpotEndOfSentence (ch1, NewSentence)
        end {We've printed ' #'}
      end else begin {ch0 wasn't BLANK}
        write (ch0);
        SpotEndOfSentence (ch0, NewSentence)
      end; {We've printed '#'}
      if eoln then begin writeln; readln end
    end {while}
  end; {FindTo}
```

```
procedure ConvertToGerund (var NewSentence: boolean);
  {Prints the current input word as a gerund.}
  var ch0, ch1, ch2, ch3: char;
  begin
    ch0 := BLANK; {If we're here, the last letter was a blank.}
    read (ch1, ch2, ch3);        {Every verb has at least 2 letters.}
    if NewSentence then ch1 := chr((ord(ch1)-ord('a'))+ord('A'));
    while not (ch3 in [BLANK, ',', ';', '!', '?', '.']) do begin
      write (ch1); {Create a moving window that finds}
      ch0 := ch1; {the last 2 letters in the verb.}
      ch1 := ch2;
      ch2 := ch3;
      read (ch3)
    end;
      {ch1 and ch2 represent the last 2 letters, so convert the verb into a gerund.}
    if (((ch0=BLANK) or NewSentence) and ((ch1='b') or (ch1='B')
                                         and (ch2='e')) {be}
      or (ch2 in ['o', 'w', 'y']) {go, know}
      or (ch1=ch2) {tell}
      or (not (ch1 in ['a','e','i','o','u'])
              and not (ch2 in ['a','e','i','o','u'])) {sing}
      or ((ch0 in ['a','e','i','o','u']) and (ch1 in ['a','e','i','o','u']))) {quit}
      then write (ch1, ch2, 'ing', ch3)
      else if ch2='e'
        then write (ch1, 'ing', ch3) {like}
        else write (ch1, ch2, ch2, 'ing', ch3); {run}
    if eoln then begin writeln; readln end;
    SpotEndOfSentence (ch3, NewSentence)
  end; {ConvertToGerund}
begin {Gerunds}
  NewSentence := true;
  while not eof do begin
    FindTo (NewSentence, ToFound);
    if ToFound then ConvertToGerund (NewSentence);
  end
end. {Gerunds}
```

↓ ↓ ↓ ↓ ↓

To see is to deceive, but to eat is to believe.
Mary liked to lift weights, but John went to surf.
It is better to give than to receive. To get there
is half the fun. To err is human; to forgive divine.
I like to do something; I like to seek. To be is nothingness.
To go is to live; to do is to be. To see is to believe.
Some like to sled; some to eat; and some to sit.
Others like to play, but not to stew.

```
Seeing is deceiving, but eating is believing.
Mary liked lifting weights, but John went surfing.
It is better giving than receiving.  Getting there
is half the fun.  Erring is human; forgiving divine.
I like doing something; I like seeking.  Being is nothingness.
Going is living; doing is being.  Seeing is believing.
Some like sledding; some eating; and some sitting.
Others like playing, but not stewing.
```

The File Window and External Files* 8-2

NO MATTER HOW CAREFULLY WE CODE, THERE seem to be some text processing tasks that are well-nigh impossible. For instance, suppose that a line of input contains a series of non-digit characters, and then a number. Is there any way to skip the non-digits so that we're about to read the number? Or, if this problem is too mathematical, suppose that a line of input contains a series of blanks, and then a word. Is there any way to skip the blanks so that we're about to read the word?

We've just seen instances of both these tasks in our programs for reading numbers, and for changing infinitives to gerunds. It may seem unreasonable, but given the tools we know about so far, the job can't be done—we'll always end up going one character too far. Fortunately, Pascal comes to the rescue with a 'lookahead' mechanism for inspecting the upcoming character.

the file window

> The *file window* represents the first character that would be obtained in the next call of *read* or *readln*. The file window is denoted by the file's name followed by an up-arrow (↑) or circumflex (∧).

(We'll always use the up-arrow in this text.) For our purposes, the file window is a read-only buffer variable. It can be inspected (i.e. compared or written out), but not changed by being assigned to. Other file window features are discussed in Chapter 13.

The character that is about to be read from ordinary *input* is called *input*↑. In a few pages we'll see that other files have windows as well. The file window comes in handy when we want to know what character is coming next, but don't wish to disturb it in any way.

The number-reading example gives us the key to most file window applications. Use of the file window is appropriate when we want to stop *before* actually reading something. Being able to stop at the right place is often a key component in writing modular code. For instance, suppose we know that a line of input contains a number hidden amongst a variety of non-digit characters. We want to skip characters up to, but not including, the start of the number. In pseudocode we have:

* This brief introduction to the use of the file window and the declaration of external textfiles is optional. Its material is covered in Chapter 13.

```
while we're not about to read a digit
   read the next character;
```

Our Pascal code uses the *input* file window. Assume the *char* variable *Ch*:

skipping leading non-digits

```
{Correct method of skipping leading non-digits.}
while not (input↑ in ['0' .. '9']) do
   read (Ch);
```

Why won't the alternative code segment shown below work?

```
{Incorrect method of skipping leading non-digits.}
read (Ch);
while not Ch in ['0' .. '9']) do
   read (Ch);
```

It won't work because it goes too far. By the time we stop reading, we'll have already given *Ch* the first digit of the number.

Let's solve an expanded version of the problem we opened with:

problem: compress blanks

> Write a program that reads and echoes input, while making the following modification: any sequence of blanks should be printed as a single space.

Since there might be blanks at the beginning of our input, we'll make a check for blanks our first order of business. In addition, since skipping blanks might bring us to the end of the file, we'll check for end-of-file before we read and echo a word.

first refinement

```
while there are still characters to consider
   if we're about to read a blank
      print a blank;
      repeat {Skip blanks}
         read and ignore blanks
      until we're about to read a nonblank
   if not eof
      repeat {Echo a word}
         read and echo characters
      until we're about to read a blank
```

Note how use of the file window keeps our code conceptually neat—we can write *SkipBlanks* and *EchoAWord* procedures that are called on time, rather than one character late.

Will we encounter any difficulties in skipping blanks? Unfortunately, the answer is yes. Why won't this code work for skipping blanks?

skipping blanks

```
{incorrect way to skip blanks}
while input↑ <> ' ' do read (Ch);
```

the file window can't represent *eof*

Imagine an empty file. If we skip characters until the file window doesn't contain a blank, we'll eventually find that we try to skip past the end of the file. Will adding a check for *eof* help? No.

Inspecting the file window when *eof* is *true* is an error in Standard Pascal.

The correct code for skipping blanks is shown below. It requires an auxiliary *boolean* variable *Finished*. Don't be put off if you find this procedure hard to write and understand—so do most computer science faculty!

correctly skipping blanks

```
{Skip blanks to a nonblank or eof.}
Finished := false;
repeat
   if eof then Finished := true
         else if input↑=' ' then read (Ch)
                           else Finished := true
until Finished;
```

The completed version of our space-compressing program is:

blank compressing program

```
program CompressBlanks (input, output);
   {Demonstrates the file window in compressing blanks.}
procedure SkipBlanks;
   {Skips input blanks until eof or a nonblank.}
   var Finished: boolean;
      Ch: char;
   begin
      Finished := false;
      repeat
         if eof then Finished := true
               else if input↑=' ' then read (Ch)
                                 else Finished := true
      until Finished
   end; {SkipBlanks}
procedure EchoAWord;
   {Echoes characters until it reaches a blank.}
   var Ch: char;
   begin
      repeat
         read (Ch);
         write (Ch)
      until input↑=' '
   end; {EchoAWord}
begin {CompressBlanks}
   while not eof do begin
      if input↑=' ' then begin
         write (' ');
         SkipBlanks
      end; {if}
      if not eof then EchoAWord
   end; {while}
   writeln
end. {CompressBlanks}
```

Here is text that
contains blank spaces, and

empty lines.

`Here is text that contains blank spaces and empty lines.`

Self-Check Questions

Q. What is the last procedure that program *CompressBlanks* calls—*SkipBlanks* or *EchoAWord*?

A. It might not seem that we can answer this question without knowing exactly what the input of *CompressBlanks* looks like. We can, though, because of an important fact about text input: There is always an end-of-line at the end of the last line. As a consequence, *SkipBlanks* will always be the last procedure called.

External Files

Consider a program that gets input, and produces output, yet has nothing to do with a terminal keyboard or screen:

file copy program

```
program Duplicate (Old, New);
   {Demonstrates copying of external textfiles, from Old to New.}
var Old, New: text;   {The external files' type.}
    Current: char;
begin
   reset (Old);     {Prepare to read Old.}
   rewrite (New);   {Prepare to write New.}
   while not eof (Old) do begin
      while not eoln (Old) do begin
         read (Old, Current);
         write (New, Current)
      end; {eoln loop}
      readln (Old);
      writeln (New)
   end {eof loop}
end. {Duplicate}
```

textfiles

Program *Duplicate*, above, copies the contents of file *Old* into file *New*. These files are known as *textfiles*, because they store text, or sequences of *char* values. (Readers who have used what we've called 'data-file oriented' programs may already be familiar with such files.)

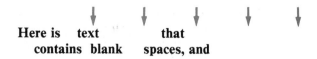

> A textfile variable is declared with the predefined type *text*. An assignment may not be made between two file variables, even though they have the same type.

Textfiles are interesting for several reasons.

textfile properties

1. Textfiles can be made permanent. Unlike other program variables, which only exist for the life of a program, textfiles keep their contents after a program is finished.
2. The length of a textfile isn't limited, except by the computer's memory. For all practical purposes, we can add additional characters and lines to a textfile indefinitely.
3. The standard procedures and functions that are normally applied to *input* and *output* can be used with any textfile. This applies to the file window as well.

program parameters

> To use a permanent textfile, name it as a *program parameter* in the program heading. Textfiles can go in place of, or in addition to, the normal program parameters *input* and *output*. Then, declare it as a variable of type *text*.

You can see that we carried out these two steps with the external files *Old* and *New* in program *Duplicate*.

```
program Duplicate (Old, New);
   ...
var Old, New: text;
```

Before we use a textfile, we have to prepare it for use. This is an unusual step that isn't applied to any other sort of Pascal variable.

reset and *rewrite*

> Procedure *reset* prepares a file to be inspected or read. Procedure *rewrite* readies a file to be generated or written. Applying *rewrite* to a file removes any contents it may currently have.

The call is accompanied by the particular file's name in parentheses. From program *Duplicate* we have:

```
reset (Old);    {Prepare to read Old.}
rewrite (New);  {Prepare to write New.}
```

files must be variable parameters

A special restriction applies to textfile variables used as arguments to subprograms written by the programmer. They must be passed to variable parameters; a file-type variable may not be defined as a value parameter.

Actually using a textfile variable is very much like using ordinary *input* and *output*. When we're getting input from a textfile we'll want to be able to read values, to check for the file's end, to discard lines, or to check for the end of a line. Similarly, when we're sending output to a textfile we'll want to be able to print values and lines.

> Any of the procedures or functions used for ordinary input and output may be given a textfile identifier as a first argument. The subprogram then acts on that textfile.

textfile I/O

Naturally, we can only use the input-oriented subprograms with a textfile that has been *reset*, and the output-oriented procedures with a file that has been readied for output through a call of *rewrite*. For example:

while not *eof* (*Old*) **do** ... etc.
while not *eoln* (*Old*) **do** ... etc.
read (*Old, Current*);
write (*New, Current*);
readln (*Old*);
writeln (*New*);

default I/O

The only reason that we haven't had to provide *input* and *output* as arguments to these subprograms is that *input* and *output* are the default textfiles. In other words:

eof	really means	*eof* (*input*)
read (*Ch*)	really means	*read* (*input, Ch*)
write (*Ch*)	really means	*write* (*output, Ch*)
writeln	really means	*writeln* (*output*)

As mentioned, we can take advantage of the file window in working with textfiles. If we had a textfile called *Old*, and prepared it for reading with a call of *reset*(*Old*), then *Old*↑ would represent the very first character in *Old*. If *Current* were a *char*-type variable, we could read this first character with the call *read* (*Old, Current*).

We'll wrap up with a short program designed to exercise our file handling abilities. We won't even try to dignify program *FileExercise* by claiming that it solves some sort of problem! Try to figure out what it does before you read its belated pseudocode.

textfile demonstration program

```
program FileExercise (input, output, Data, Results);
    {Performs a few textfile manipulations.}
var Ch1, Ch2: char;
    Data, Results: text;
begin
   reset (Data);
   while input↑ = Data↑ do begin
      read (Ch1);
      read (Data, Ch2)
   end;
   rewrite (Results);
   while not eof do begin
      read (Ch1);
      write (Results, Ch1)
   end;
   while not eof(Data) do begin
      read (Data, Ch2);
      write (Ch2)
   end;
   writeln
end. {FileExercise}
```

Program *FileExercise* is clearly just an excuse to use external files and the file window. First, it compares the contents of file *Data* with characters entered by the program user. As soon as a mismatch occurs, it sends the rest of the user's input to file *Results*. Finally, it prints the remainder of *Data* on the screen. In pseudocode, the program is outlined as:

Ignore all input that matches file Data;
Save the rest of the user's input in file Results;
Print the rest of Data;

Self-Check Questions

Q. In program *FileExercise* we read input relatively continuously. First we read it but ignored it, then we echoed input into file *Results*. Only after there wasn't any input left did we print the remaining contents of file *Data*. Our question is: Could we have taken these last steps in reverse? In other words, could we have printed *Data* before taking sending the rest of the user's input to *Results*?

A. Yes. Data available as input remains available even if we temporarily stop reading it, perhaps to deal with other files, or to produce any sort of output.

Antibugging and Debugging 8-3

PROBLEMS WITH THE PREDEFINED FUNCTIONS *eof* and *eoln* are endemic to text-processing programs. They work fine in the 'standard' processing models, but if your program does something out of the ordinary—watch out! Gripes about the operation of *eof* and *eoln* are among the most frequently heard complaints about Pascal.

> *eof* and *eoln* are *true* when we are *about* to reach the end of the file or line, and neither before nor after.

when are they true?

eoln causes problems in this regard when we read the end-of-line character itself. *eoln* is *false* at this point, because we're about to read the first character of the *next* line—even if there isn't any next line.

eof's problem is the opposite. If *eoln* is *true*, *eof* is *false*. Why? Because when *eoln* is *true*, we're about to read the end-of-line character—not the end-of-file character. There has to be a final *readln*—to get rid of this last end-of-line character—at the end of most text processing loops.

Unexpected encounters of the end-of-file kind tend to be unhappy experiences for the programmer. Consider the program segment below. It's intended to print every other line of a file—the first, third, fifth lines, etc.

```
{incorrect attempt to print every other line}
while not eof do begin
   while not eoln do begin
      read (Ch);
      write (Ch)
   end; {eoln}
   readln;          {get rid of the end-of-line}
   writeln;         {print the current line}
   readln           {skip the next line}
end; {eof}
```

```
Although I work, and seldom cease,
At Dumas pere and Dumas fils.
Alas, I cannot make me care
For Dumas fils and Dumas pere.
```

```
Although I work, and seldom cease,
Alas, I cannot make me care
```

Works fine—until we change the input:

```
The forehead of Shelley was cluttered with curls,
And Keats never was a descendant of earls,
And Byron walked out with a number of girls.
```

```
The forehead of Shelley was cluttered with curls,
And Byron walked out with a number of girls.
ABNORMAL TERMINATION --
ATTEMPT TO READ PAST END-OF-FILE.
```

Input of an odd number of lines causes the crash. *eof* is *true* after our *readln* at the end of the third line, but we try to skip the next line (with another *readln*) anyway. The bug is fixed with an extra check:

correct line-skipping code

```
{correct way to print every other line}
while not eof do begin
   while not eoln do begin
      read (Ch);
      write (Ch)
   end; {eoln}
   readln; {get rid of the end-of-line}
   writeln; {print the current line}
   if not eof then
      readln {skip the next line}
end; {eof}
```

always check for *eof*

> Don't undermine the checks that are posted at the start of the loop. Check for *eof* or *eoln* whenever you read extra lines or characters inside the loop.

synchronization bugs

A common class of text processing bugs are called *synchronization* errors. At some point, an off-by-one error enters the text processing loop and won't go away. A typical synchronization bug requires the user to enter an extra carriage return every now and then. This kind of bug is often found in highly interactive programs that obey many user commands.

What happens is this: Some commands are just one character or one line long. After reading the command, the programmer calls procedure *readln* to get rid of the end-of-line, so that the next command can be read eventually.

find the extra *readln*

Sometimes, though, a single command will require several characters or lines of input. The programmer may call a procedure that specializes in reading these multi-line commands—and which, for some reason, includes a *readln* of its own. This isn't at all unusual, since the more complicated procedure may have been written and tested in a driver program that required the *readln*.

Whatever the reason, we end up with two *readlns*—one in the procedure, and another back in the main program. Each one is just intended to flush the remnants of the current command line. The extra *readln* is usually not apparent until we expect a prompt for an additional command. The prompt doesn't appear until we impatiently hit the return key.

This kind of bug is hard to find because it seems to be somewhere that it isn't. The problem appears to lie with the current command since, after all, the previous command had worked perfectly well. Hopefully, an awareness of the problem will help you avoid it.

Pascal Summary

• *eoln*: a *boolean* function that is *true* if the character about to be read is the carriage return or end-of-line character:

```
{read and echo one line of text}
while not eoln do begin
   read (Character);
   write (Character)
end;
writeln;
```

• *eof*: a *boolean* function that is *true* if the character about to be read follows the end of the last line of input:

```
{count the number of input lines}
LineCount := 0;
while not eof do begin
   LineCount := LineCount + 1;
   readln
end;
```

• text processing models: programs that do line-by-line character processing usually consist of two nested loops. The inner loop processes the characters found on a single line, and watches for the end of the line. The outer loop watches for the end of input, and does line-oriented operations. For example:

```
while not eof do begin
   while not eoln do begin
      read characters;
      process them
   end; {inner loop}
   execute readlns or writelns
end; {outer loop}
```

Important Facts

• A sequence of character input is called *text*. Text is almost invariably divided into lines, each of which ends with a carriage return or end-of-line character. The entire sequence of lines is thought of as forming a *file*.

• The carriage return or end-of-line character itself is read and echoed as a space. Its effect can only be obtained with *writeln*.

• Procedure *readln* discards the remainder of the current line, through and including its end-of-line character.

• Synchronization bugs can occur when an off-by-one error enters a text processing loop, and the computer's notion of the current line differs from the user's. Beware of unnecessary *readlns*.

• There is always an end-of-line character at the end of the last line of text input.

• The Golden Rules of *eof*: A program cannot read the end-of-file character. Furthermore, when *eof* is *true*, *eoln* is undefined.

• Bottom-up programming techniques are useful for gaining experience with individual program modules. Procedures or functions are written and tested independently (in driver programs) before being refined and incorporated into the main program.

Self-test Exercises

8-1 Can you read the end-of-line character? What does it look like? What happens when you echo it?

8-2 Suppose that we're reading text. Write code that will show if we're at the end of the file or at the end of the current line (both can't be true at once). If neither of these is true, show whether or not the next character is an ordinary space.

8-3 When *eoln* is *true* we're at the end of a line of text. A call of the input procedure *readln* will put us at the beginning of the next line of text, ready to read its first value. What is the effect of a call of *readln* if there *is* no next line? Is it an error? What about a call of *readln* when *eof* is *true*?

8-4 What is the effect of this code? Assume that *eof* isn't *true*.

```
while not eoln do begin
    while not eoln do begin
        read (Character);
        write (Character);
    end
    readln;
    writeln;
end;
```

8-5 Write a procedure *GetNextLetter* that 'filters' text. It should read characters until it finds a letter (disregarding spaces, numerals, and punctuation), then return the letter as a variable parameter. If you reach the end-of-file before finding a letter, print an error message.

8-6 How can we read and store the end-of-line character?

8-7 What happens to input that isn't read during the course of a program?

8-8 Write a procedure that finds the 'smallest' and 'largest' lower-case letters (alphabetically speaking) in a series of characters. Return these letters to a calling program as variable parameters.

8-9 Read our solution to the problem above, and name the circumstance under which the expression *Largest=Smallest* is *true*.

8-10 Write a general-purpose procedure to read and echo a series of characters. Input will terminate either with a sentinel character, or at the end-of-file. The possible sentinel will be passed as a parameter of the procedure, along with a *boolean* value that indicates whether we should look for the sentinel, or for the end of the file. For example, the call:

ReadAndEcho ('\', *true*);

indicates that the backslash character acts as a sentinel, whereas:

ReadAndEcho (' ', *false*);

means that echoing should cease at end-of-file. Be sure *to* check for an empty file in either case, and *not* to print the sentinel character.

More Exercises

8-10 Write a program that:

a) Counts and prints the number of values in a series of numbers;

b) Finds the average value;

c) Finds the largest and smallest value in the series;

d) Prints the positions of the high and low numbers.

The series of numbers *should* end with −999. However, it's quite possible that the end-marker will fall off on the way to your computer. Make sure that the program doesn't try to read past the end-of-file. Naturally, you should allow for peculiar cases, such as a series one number long.

8-11 Write a program that converts an octal (base 8) number into hexadecimal (base 16) notation. Print the hexadecimal digits 10, 11, 12, 13, 14, and 15 as the letters 'A', 'B', 'C', 'D', 'E', and 'F'. What limits must you set on allowable input?

8-12 Write a procedure *Count* that is passed two parameters of type *char*, and counts the number of times they appear in a text file. Modify it to count the number of times the integers '3' and '8' appear.

8-13 A series of blank lines are sometimes used to separate different parts of input data. Write a program that will read and echo characters, line by line, until two blank lines in a row are input.

8-14 Write a simple program to count the number of words and sentences in a sample of input text. Assume that every blank marks the end of a word, and that a period marks the end of a sentence. Assume that the end of input is marked by *a*) a backslash (\), *b*) *eof*.

8-15 Write a program to count the number of words and sentences in a sample of input text. Assume that input ends when *eof* is *true*. Make sure the program can handle real-life ambiguities—for example, this . . . is not three sentences; nor are the two blank spaces after a colon or period both word-enders. Modify your program to count the number of input lines, and to issue an announcement when there's an obvious punctuation error—no space, or the wrong number of spaces, after (or before) a punctuation mark, word, or sentence. The announcement should say what number line the error occurs on.

8-16 Write a program to find the average number of characters per word, and words per sentence, in a sample of input text. You may revise either of the programs above to handle the job.

8-17 Write a simple text processing program that reads input text (that may be split over many lines) and echoes it in such a way that each line has ten words. Then, modify the program so that the fortieth character of each line is in the last word printed. Don't forget to make a rule for what happens if the fortieth character is a space. In any case, ignore spaces that appear at the beginning of a line.

8-18 Write a program that translates its input into Pig Latin. Be sure to think of special circumstances—punctuation at the end of words, words that start with vowels, words beginning with capital letters, etc.

8-19 Write a program that reads through a sample of text and prints out all *integer* values it encounters, as well as their sum. Digits that occur within words should be ignored. For example, the input 'If I were 21, instead of 53, I'd probably punch you in the nose a 2nd time' should produce as output the numbers 21 and 53, along with their sum, 74. A function *ConvertToInteger* will probably prove quite useful.

8-20 Write a function that reads a real number written using the 'E' notation as a sequence of characters, and returns the *real* value it represents.

8-21 Write a program that reads text, and prints out every letter that occurs twice in a row. (Bonus: write the program, possibly using recursion, so that it prints out the actual word instead.) Have it analyze the following input: "Miss Metteer, a bookkeeper of all excess cottonseed bills, looked at a corrupt terra cotta Cossack."

8-22 Write a program that reads text, and spots words that contain three or more consecutive letters in alphabetical order. Have your first sample input be: "A stupid, laughing, crabcake, displaying calmness, deftly hijacked the first canopy."

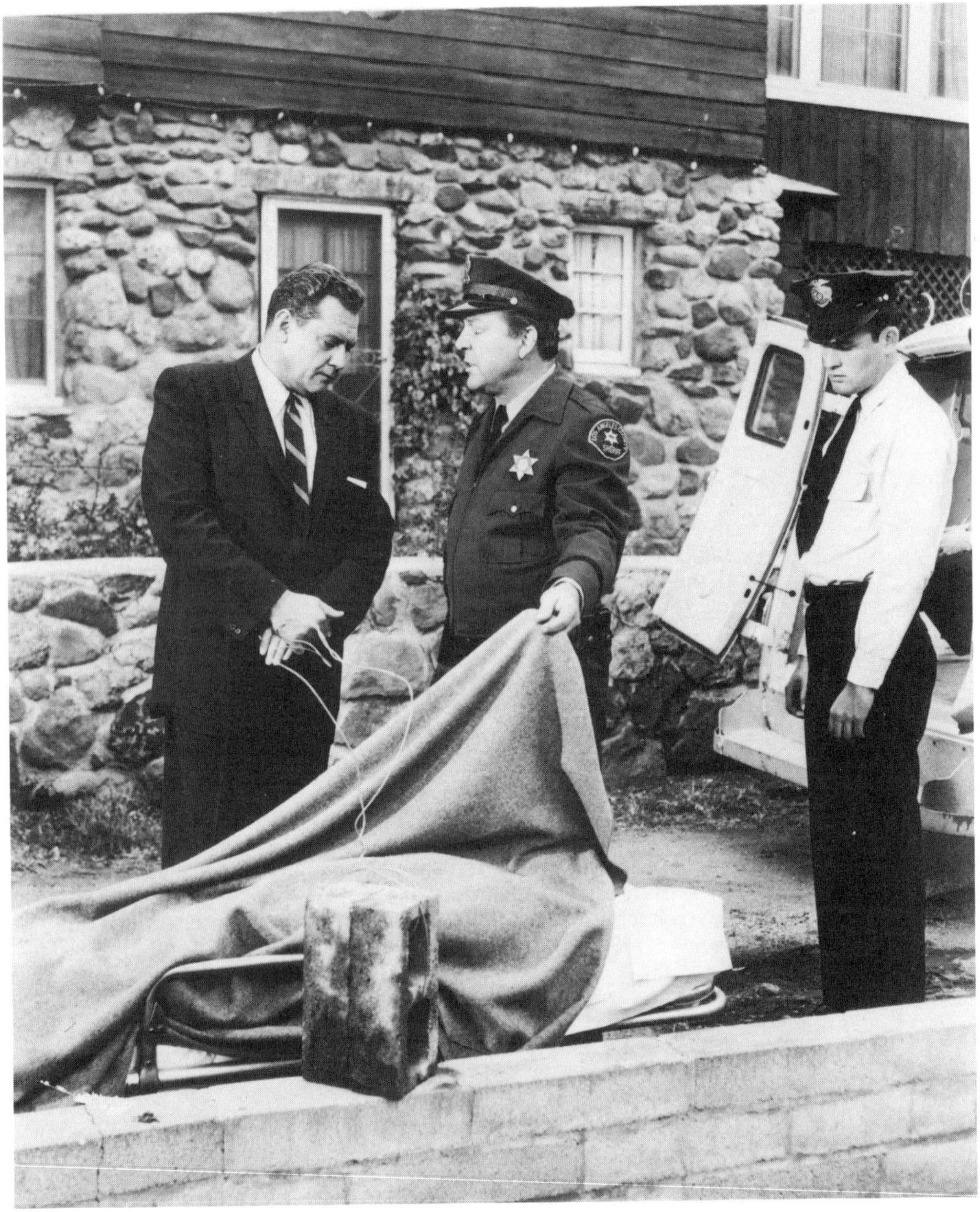

'Like Perry Mason, we can cause a proof to collapse simply by demonstrating a reasonable doubt...'

9

Extending the Ordinal Types

When the first computer languages were developed, everything—commands, identifiers, values, etc.—had to be expressed in ones and zeros. One of the first language improvements let programmers use octal (base 8) numbers instead of binary. Then, letters were introduced, which meant that variables and commands could be given names instead of numbers. However, the same basic units of measure (usually just *reals, integers*, and *char*) had to be used to describe every value imaginable.

The world, though, is filled with plenty of values that have perfectly good names of their own. This month might be January or July. Today's weather could be sunny, cloudy, raining, or breezy. A playing card can be a heart, spade, club, or diamond. There are many such groups of values, and in Pascal, unlike most other languages, any group of named values can be the basis of an *enumerated ordinal type* that's defined by the user.

The types we'll learn to define in 9-1 can be used like the standard ordinal types—their values can be stored in variables, passed as parameters, defined as constants, etc. In effect, Pascal is extended to include new types and values as part of its vocabulary.

Groups of values can be restricted as well as extended. By defining *subrange* types, we can limit variables to represent a particular segment (a subrange) of any ordinal type. We'll learn how to declare subranges of both standard and enumerated ordinal types.

Section 9-2 raises a concern that becomes more important as our programs become larger. The study of ways of establishing *program correctness* is a very active area of research in Computer Science. We'll describe some of the methods used to help develop some assurance that programs will actually do what they're designed for. We'll focus on one formal method, called *program proving* or *verification*, and see some of the difficulties it entails.

The anti- and debugging section, 9-3, includes some details about enumerated types and subranges, and should be read along with the regular text.

Enumerated Ordinal Types 9-1

THE FIRST FEW LINES OF THE PASCAL program below introduce *enumerated ordinal types*. Two new ordinal types (*Fruit* and *Vegetable*) are defined in the shaded *type definition part* of *Menu.*

```
program Menu (input, output);
   {Demonstrates an enumerated type definition.}
type Fruit = (banana, apple, orange, pear);
      Vegetable = (cabbage, leeks, beets, okra);
var Appetizer, Dessert: Fruit;
      Entree: Vegetable;
begin        etc.
```

Fruit and *Vegetable* are enumerated ordinal types. Like the standard ordinal types, they consist of an ordered group of simple values. The standard ordinal types, which are predefined in every Pascal implementation, are:

standard ordinal types

integer: The whole numbers from −*maxint* to *maxint*.

char: The character set, in a particular collating sequence.

boolean: The values *false, true.*

Don't let the word 'ordinal' confuse you. It just means that the values of any given type are ordered and countable, and can be compared to each other. The letter 'A' is less than 'C', and *true* is 'greater' than—and certainly not equal to—*false.* The ordinal types, in conjunction with type *real*, are Pascal's simple types.

> An *enumerated* ordinal type is a group of values named and ordered by the programmer. Variables can be declared to be of such a type, and may be assigned any value of that type.

For example, given the definitions and declarations from *Menu*:

defining enumerations

```
type Fruit = (banana, apple, orange, pear);
      Vegetable = (cabbage, leeks, beets, okra);
var Appetizer, Dessert: Fruit;
      Entree: Vegetable;
```

we can make assignments like:

```
Appetizer := apple;        {Appetizer gets the value apple.}
Dessert := Appetizer;      {Dessert is apple too.}
Entree := leeks;           {Entree is leeks.}
Entree := cabbage;         {Change Entree to cabbage.}
```

We couldn't give variables *Appetizer* or *Dessert* values of type *Vegetable*, since that would cause a type clash. We can, however, compare values or variables that have the same type:

```
if Appetizer = apple then
   writeln ('An apple a day keeps the doctor away.');
if Appetizer = Dessert then
   writeln ('Too much of a good thing is no good at all.');
```

type definition part

The *type definition part* is an optional portion of every Pascal program and subprogram. We can describe a program in terms of its parts as:

program heading
definition part
    constant definitions
    type definitions
declaration part
    variable declarations
    procedure and function declarations
statement part

Or, we can use reserved words to outline a potential program:

program *heading*;
const *definitions*;
type *definitions*;
var *declarations*;
procedure or **function** *declarations*;
begin
    statements;
end.

enumerated type syntax

The reserved word **type** introduces the type definition part. The *type identifier* is followed by an equals sign, and the type's value identifiers, or *constants*, within parentheses and separated by commas. Naturally, both type identifier and constants must be named in accordance with Pascal's identifier syntax. We can chart an enumerated type definition as:

enumerated type definition

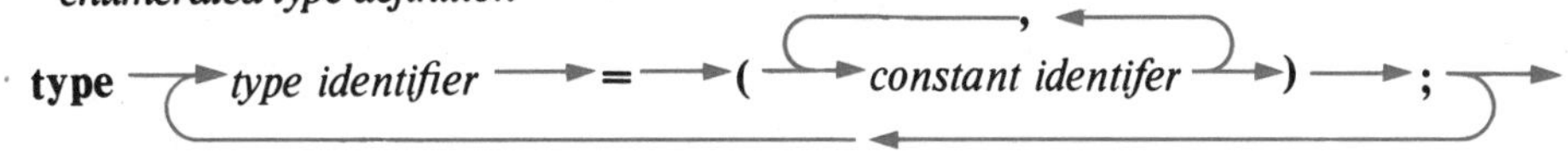

pred, succ, ord

> The predecessor function *pred*(*x*), successor function *succ*(*x*), and ordinal function *ord*(*x*) may all be given arguments of any ordinal type, including standard types and types enumerated by the programmer.

```
type RouletteResult = (red, black, green);
   PokerHand = (OnePair, TwoPair, Triples, Straight, Flush, StraightFlush);
   WeekDay = (Monday, Tuesday, Wednesday, Thursday, Friday);
   WeekEnd = (Saturday, Sunday);
```

Don't forget that the first ordinal number is 0, not 1. For the types defined above, we find that:

ambiguous type membership

> *ord*(*black*) is 1 {the second value of type *RouletteResult*}
> *pred*(*TwoPair*) is *OnePair*
> *succ*(*Tuesday*) is *Wednesday*

An important restriction on the enumeration of ordinal types is that no value can belong to more than one type. This rule makes type membership unambiguous. We could *not* make the following definition:

```
type WeekDay = (Monday, Tuesday, Wednesday, Thursday, Friday);
     WeekEnd = (Friday, Saturday, Sunday); {Illegal definition.}
```

The ordinal position of *Friday*, as well as its type, is unclear. Is it the last value of type *WeekDay*, or the first value of *WeekEnd*?

> We can define constants of *any* ordinal type.

ordinal constants

However, such definitions will invariably occur within an enclosed subprogram. Why? The ordinal type must be defined before its constants can be used—but the constant definition part comes before the type definition part in the current block. Note that the constants of ordinal types aren't put in quotes, because that would make them text constants.

```
const FAVORITE = apple;        {A constant of type Fruit.}
      HOUSECOLOR = green;      {A constant of type RouletteResult.}
      DAYOFF = Wednesday;      {A constant of type WeekDay.}
      BIRTHDAY = 'Monday';     {This is text—not a
                                member of type WeekDay.}
```

Self-Check Questions

Q. Is this the beginning of a valid control statement? Assume the definitions of program *Menu*.

```
if Appetizer <> Entree then      etc.
```

A. No, because comparing values of different types causes a type clash. We can no more compare *apple* and *leek* (even for inequality) than we could compare 'S' and *true*.

Q. Is this a valid type declaration? Why or why not?

```
type Letters = ('A', 'B', 'C', 'D', 'E', 'F');
```

A. It's illegal. 'A', 'B', etc. are not identifiers—they're constant values of type *char*. The definition doesn't conform to Pascal syntax. We *could* use *A, B, C*, etc., as identifiers, but only if we omitted the single quote marks.

Focus on Programming: Enumerated Types

Enumerated ordinal types enjoy all the rights and privileges of the standard ordinal types, with one major limitation.

> The constants of enumerated ordinal types *cannot* be read with *read* or *readln*, nor printed using *write* or *writeln*. They have no *external character representation*.

no enumerated I/O

Unlike values of the standard types, enumerated type values can't be input from a keyboard or data file, nor output to a screen or lineprinter.* (In section 11-2 we'll see how to fake input and output of user-defined ordinal values. When we discuss files, we'll learn a bit more about internal and external representations of values.) Aside from this exception, enumerated ordinals are used just like the standard ordinal values.

> Enumerated values can be used to set the limits of a **for** statement, or in the constant list of a **case** statement.

We can demonstrate both these features with our next example:

problem: employee payroll

> Write a program that computes an employee's weekly pay. Assume that we're paying time-and-a-half for Saturday, and double-time for Sunday work.

We'll read in the hours day by day, and make adjustments for overtime as we go along. In pseudocode our algorithm is:

first refinement

for *each day of the week*
  read in the number of hours worked
  make a weekend overtime bonus adjustment if necessary

A variable *Workday*, that take on values corresponding to the days of the week, lets us refine the pseudocode:

second refinement

for *Workday* := *Monday* **to** *Sunday*
  read in the number of hours worked
  make a weekend overtime bonus adjustment if necessary

How can we arrange for the Saturday and Sunday overtime rate? Why not use a **case** statement?

case *Workday* **of**
  Saturday: *arrange for time-and-a-half*
  Sunday: *arrange for double-time*
  Monday, Tuesday, Wednesday, Thursday, Friday: *pay single-time*
end;

* Why not? Although there is a justification for restricting enumerated ordinal types to internal program use, its explanation is beyond the scope of this book. Ask around on the street, or write Dr. Wirth at ETH in Switzerland and query him directly. Be sure to enclose a self-addressed, stamped envelope.

All that really remains is the definition of a new ordinal type:

data type definition

```
type Day = (Monday, Tuesday, Wednesday,
                        Thursday, Friday, Saturday, Sunday);
```

The addition of input, output, and a few calculations turn our pseudocode into program *Payroll*. Notice that *Payroll* is quite limited; it's practically a stub program. It only handles one worker, at a single hourly wage and benefit rate. It only accepts full (i.e. *integer*) hours of work. It doesn't error-check input. Nonetheless, *Payroll* works, and can be upgraded later.

employee payroll program

```
program Payroll (input, output);
   {Computes one employee's weekly payroll using enumerated types.}
const BENEFITRATE = 2.73;          {Benefits add $2.73/hour.}
   {Benefits are only paid on actual hours worked, not overtime.}
type Day = (Monday, Tuesday, Wednesday,
                        Thursday, Friday, Saturday, Sunday);
var Workday: Day;
    HourlyRate, TotalWages, HoursCredited, Benefits: real;
    HoursWorked: integer;
begin
   writeln ('Please enter the hourly wage rate.');
   readln (HourlyRate);
   TotalWages := 0.0;
   Benefits := 0.0;
   writeln ('Enter hours worked daily from Monday through Sunday.');
   for Workday := Monday to Sunday do begin
      read (HoursWorked);
      case Workday of
         Saturday: HoursCredited := 1.5*HoursWorked;
         Sunday: HoursCredited := 2.0*HoursWorked;
         Monday, Tuesday, Wednesday, Thursday, Friday:
                              HoursCredited := HoursWorked
      end; {case}
      Benefits := Benefits + (HoursWorked *BENEFITRATE);
      TotalWages := TotalWages +(HoursCredited *HourlyRate)
   end; {for}
   TotalWages := TotalWages+Benefits;
   writeln ('Total wages for the week are $', TotalWages:2:2)
end. {Payroll}
```

```
Please enter the hourly wage rate.
9.37
Enter hours worked daily from Monday through Sunday.
8 8 6 9 10 0 4
Total wages for the week are $581.98
```

enumerated ordinals as parameters

Value parameters and variable parameters can belong to enumerated ordinal types. The result of a function may also be an enumerated value.

We'll get used to seeing—and placing—new and unusual type identifiers in the headings of procedures and functions. For example, here's a quick way to print the value of a parameter of type *Day*:

kludge for printing enumerations

```
procedure PrintDay (Word: Day);
   {Prints the name of a Day-type value.}
   begin
      case Word of
         Monday: writeln ('Monday');
         Tuesday: writeln ('Tuesday');
         Wednesday: writeln ('Wednesday');
         Thursday: writeln ('Thursday');
         Friday: writeln ('Friday');
         Saturday: writeln ('Saturday');
         Sunday: writeln ('Sunday')
      end
   end; {PrintDay}
```

NextWorkingDay, shown below, is a function that returns a value of type *Day*. Given an argument of type *Day*, it finds and represents the next working day. Constants *FirstDay* and *LastDay* mark the beginning and end of the work week.

```
function NextWorkingDay (Today: Day): Day;
   {Represents the next (sometimes first) value of Day.}
   const FIRSTDAY = Monday;
         LASTDAY = Friday;
   begin
      if (Today>=FIRSTDAY) and (Today<LASTDAY)
         then NextWorkingDay := succ(Today)
         else NextWorkingDay := FIRSTDAY
   end; {NextWorkingDay}
```

scope of ordinals

Once a type has been defined, its name, and the names of its constants, are known in all subprograms—unless they are locally redefined.

The same scope rules apply to type and constant identifiers as to variable and subprogram identifiers. However, the identifiers of types (and their constants) are usually preserved globally. Since they are often used for communication between different parts of a program, they're seldom redefined.

As you might imagine, it's not really necessary to define enumerated ordinal types to make a program work. They're desirable because they let us program in understandable terms—*Monday* is obviously the day Monday, whereas an *integer* variable named *Day*, with value 1, might reasonably refer either to Sunday *or* Monday. The enumerated type feature lets programmers work with abstractions—ideas or values that have meaning to people, but not to machines. How the computer deals with these values is not our concern—we're programmers, not mechanics. In the next few chapters we'll see more of the ways that Pascal adapts to real-world conceptions and representations of data.

why enumerate ordinal types?

Self-Check Questions

Q. Suppose we make the assignment *Alpha* := *Beta*. Is there any way to tell if *Beta* is a variable? A constant of an ordinal type? A function call?

A. No. An identifier (like *Beta*) is just the representation of a value. We can't determine what sort of value *Beta* is from its context.

Q. Though we've seen that values of enumerated ordinal types can be used with any control statement, there are a few pitfalls to beware of. What's wrong with these program segments?

```
WorkDay := Monday;
while WorkDay<=Sunday do begin
    read (Hours);
    Total := Total+Hours;
    WorkDay := succ(WorkDay)
end;
```

```
WorkDay := Monday;
repeat
    read (Hours);
    Total := Total+Hours;
    WorkDay := succ(WorkDay)
until WorkDay=Sunday;
```

A. The left-hand program segment tries to use a **while** loop to cycle through the days of the week. Unfortunately, its exit condition is that *WorkDay* be greater than *Sunday*. As far as our program is concerned, there is no day greater than *Sunday*—the program crashes when it tries to give *WorkDay* the successor to *Sunday*.

The second segment bends over too far backwards in an attempt to avoid making the same error. Its exit condition is that *WorkDay* equal *Sunday*; consequently, the number of hours worked on Sunday is never read in.

Focus on Programming: Subrange Types

The ordinal types we've just learned to define represent entire ranges of values. We can restrict variables to representing *part* of the range of an ordinal type by defining another kind of ordinal type—an *ordinal subrange*.

```
type Day = (Monday, Tuesday, Wednesday,
                    Thursday, Friday, Saturday, Sunday);
     Weekday = Monday..Friday;        {Subrange of Day.}
     Weekend = Saturday..Sunday;      {Subrange of Day.}
     HoursInADay = 0..24;             {Subrange of integer.}
     CapitalLetters = 'A'..'Z';       {Subrange of char.}
```

```
var CardNight, SickDay: Weekday;
    SailingDay, GameDay: Weekend;
    HoursWorked: HoursInADay;
    FirstInitial, MiddleInitial: CapitalLetters;
```

> A *subrange* definition gives a type identifier (name) to a particular segment of any standard or enumerated ordinal type.

limits of subranges

Although a variable of type *Day* may represent any of the days, *CardNight* (a variable of the *Weekday* subrange) can only represent one of the values *Monday* through *Friday*. Similarly, *HoursWorked* can only represent an *integer* value from 0 through 24—the values included in the ordinal subrange *HoursInADay*. Trying to assign it a value from outside this restricted range (say, −4 or 29) will cause a type clash and program crash. As far as the computer is concerned, we're trying to assign it a value of a different type entirely. In chart form, the definition of an ordinal subrange is:

ordinal subrange

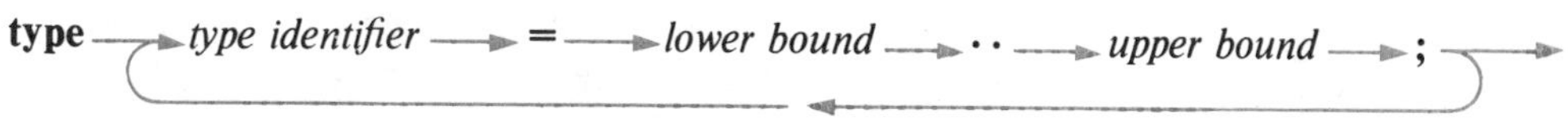

Notice that two dots (..) are used to mean 'through and including'. We used the same symbol earlier when we discussed a method of set declaration. There is also a shorthand way to define subranges.

> The range of values a variable can represent may be specified when a variable is declared—but not when a parameter is declared.

shorthand subrange declarations

```
type Day = (Monday, Tuesday, Wednesday,
                    Thursday, Friday, Saturday, Sunday);
var CardNight, SickDay: Monday..Friday;
    SailingDay, GameDay: Saturday..Sunday;
    HoursWorked: 0..24;
    FirstInitial, MiddleInitial: 'A'..'Z';
```

The variables declared with this shorthand are just like the variables in our last declaration, and represent the same limited range of values. User-defined constants can also be used to set the limits of a subrange, although variables, function calls, or other expressions may not be. The effect of this restriction is to prohibit any attempt to determine the bounds of a subrange during program execution.

> Variables should be declared as subrange types whenever practical, *particularly in large programs*.

why use subranges?

Since this calls for some changes in your programming habits, we'll try to justify our new dictum. Ordinal subranges are desirable for three reasons—self-documentation, program efficiency, and antibugging. We'll consider them in turn.

documentation

1. Self-documentation. Knowing the range of values that a variable is going to represent, and saying so at the time of variable declaration, helps demonstrate that you have a firm grasp of what your program does.

   It also helps another person who may be working on your program *get* an idea of appropriate values within a program. The declaration:

```
KilnTemperature: integer;
```

says nothing, whereas:

```
KilnTemperature: 400..1200;   {or, better yet...}
KilnTemperature: 400..MaximumTemperature;
```

is informative. Note that the decision to use the long or shorthand method of creating ordinal subranges is generally optional (except as noted in the next section).

efficiency

2. Program efficiency. A variable declared to represent only a limited range of values can be dealt with (by the compiler) in a more economical manner than a variable that can represent *any* value of its type.

   This is really the least important reason. Under certain circumstances, though, a program may require so many variables that limiting the storage they require is a valid programming consideration.

antibugging

3. Antibugging. Pascal's requirement that variables be of some particular type is a form of antibugging. Restricting the values that a variable may represent to a range of values we know it *should* have extends the protection. We help assure ourselves (and the computer) that any operations we'll try to carry out will make sense.

   Real life often places limits on the values that a variable can reasonably represent. A payroll program may 'work', but allow 37 deductions, or −2. A checker-playing program might devote a considerable amount of time looking for the ninth row of a checkerboard. A computer croupier could spin a computer roulette wheel, and decide the ball has landed on number 39—which doesn't exist.

   These are all obviously bugs that should, and could, be spotted or prevented by the programmer. The most annoying aspect of bugs, though, is that you don't see them until it's too late. When a program announces that the sum of two and two is five, the programmer knows that something has gone wrong, and takes another look at her code. The results of a more complex program, however, are more likely to be taken for granted—even if some input datum or partial result hidden within the program is totally absurd.

the moral

> Subrange types provide a constant check on variables and assure us that they have values appropriate to their application. They help prevent a very dangerous kind of program—one which appears to be reliable, but is not.

Using subranges doesn't absolve the programmer of responsibility for error checking and keeping track of data within a program. The subrange philosophy is rather nihilistic—if a variable takes on an inappropriate value, the program stops! Relying on run-time crashes to do error checking is like using telephone poles (instead of brakes) to stop your car. Still, strong type checking makes Pascal sympathetic to a programmer's woes—data inevitably gets screwed up for reasons beyond the control of programmer, program user, or computer. Subrange types won't make programs work, but they will make it easier to debug programs and to keep them running.

Program Correctness* 9-2

HOW DO WE SHOW THAT A PROGRAM works? A few weeks ago we might have given the obvious reply—*run it*. By now, though, we've probably learned to be a bit more cautious. We understand that, at best, running a program (and checking its results) shows that it works for a particular set of data. Making up a broader range of test data gives us a stronger feeling that the program will always work, but even testing is usually limited to ferreting out bugs whose symptoms we can imagine in advance.

In this section we'll look at some of the methods used to gain assurance about the correctness, or reliability, of programs. Now, it's tempting to think that we can simply prove that any program will always work, just as we might prove that a mathematical theorem is correct. However, we'll find that confidence in the correctness of programs is much like confidence in the correctness of engineering methods, rather than the more abstract notions of correctness in mathematics.

what is confidence?

What do we mean when we talk about developing confidence? Well, confidence lets us ride in airplanes, or cross bridges. We can't prove that a bridge won't ever fall down once it's in place, but we can feel certain enough about it to trust the bridge with our lives. A combination of tests join to give us this confidence. The bridge may follow the same design as other structures. We can build models for aerodynamic testing in a wind tunnel, and employ mathematical formulas for the design of structural members. We may even go so far as to stress randomly selected beams, cables, and the like to the point of destruction, in order to establish minimum strength levels.

* This section is optional.

Program tests are merged in the same manner to give us confidence in code. Some features are trusted because they've worked in similar programs, while others are allowed because the programmer and her peers believe that they will work. Parts of a program may have to undergo exhaustive testing by being run on carefully gathered real data, while for others, artificially manufactured data is good enough. Finally, some portions of the code may be so crucial that we have to try to prove, on paper, that they will always work.

Let's consider some of the less formal methods before we see what a program proof looks like. The first sort of testing most programs undergo can be called *bench testing*. The programmer explains her work to another programmer, or small group of programmers, in a structured walkthrough of the code. This kind of examination is useful for two reasons. First, programmers less intimately involved with actual coding may spot conceptual errors that have escaped previous notice. Second, the discussion can lead to useful suggestions for tests that can be made at later stages of production.

bench testing

Static analysis of the program is a step that's usually reserved for very large systems. Static analyzers are programs that examine the source code (e.g. the Pascal version) of a program without actually running it. They're able to spot certain kinds of errors that aren't always found by the compiler. One kind of error is the use of uninitialized variables in assignments, or as arguments to value parameters. A more interesting error that can be found through static analysis is the existence of unreachable code segments that won't ever be run, no matter what program input is.

static analysis

Trace tools give us a window into program execution as the program runs. A simple kind of trace will print a message every time a subprogram is entered; arranging for a count and display of totals is barely more difficult. A trace tool might also keep track of changes in the value of a particular variable, or group of variables. In the hands of an expert, a trace is an invaluable tool for spotting potential errors in program design. As terminals with graphics capability become more widely available, we can expect to see trace tools become more widely available and exploited.

trace tools

Finally, "data testing" is a method we should be quite familiar with. Builders of large systems often create "data generators"; programs that can automatically produce data that has a set of characteristics specified by the programmer. The output of a data generator might be sophisticated data intended to make a program follow every possible execution path, or it might simply be a long sequence of five-letter words. With huge amounts of test input available, it's no surprise to find programmers also creating automated tools for checking raw program output as well.

The methods we've mentioned here give only a rough overview of the kinds of tests that can be performed. To give you an idea of what a fertile field program testing is, consider a totally unexpected variation called *mutation testing*. In this approach, as exhaustive a set of test data as possible, with known results, is prepared. Next, programs are systematically

mutation testing

mutated by having small errors introduced: a plus sign might be changed to a minus sign, or a constant might be increased by 1. The mutated program is then run on the original test data. If it works (i.e. it has the same results as the original program), we can conclude either that there is something very wrong with our original program, or that our test data is too weak to be useful. What an idea!

It's easy to imagine that a large program might require *all* of the different testing approaches described here to give us confidence that the program will really work. Even then, though, our faith in the program depends largely on its prospective application. We have greater faith in less important programs because we don't pay a high price for their failure. An interrupted video game may be annoying, but the manufacturer's desire to bring it to market will probably outweigh concern about some minor residual bugs. It's easy enough to refund the user's quarter if she's unlucky enough to find the bug the hard way.

limits on confidence

A program that controls a weapons system, on the other hand, is a different matter entirely. The recognition that no one test method is sufficient to guarantee that a program is correct and error-free is a cause for alarm, particularly when there is no way to undo a mistake. Indeed, there may not be *any* way to test such systems adequately.

Program Proofs

In recognition of the limits of program testing, computer scientists have tried to develop other methods of gaining confidence in programs.

> A *program proof* is a 'paper' analysis of a program that attempts to formally verify that the program will always produce a correct result.

In one sense, a program proof *is* like a mathematical proof. A mathematical proof tries to justify the correctness of a mathematical statement—a theorem. A program proof tries to give us the same sort of assurance about a sequence of code statements—a program.

However, there is also an important difference between the two kinds of proofs. A mathematical proof tries to show that following a certain sequence of steps will result in an irrefutable conclusion. A program proof, in contrast, tries to show that the conclusion reached by following a series of steps will always be correct. The mathematical sort of proof works well when we want to show that, in principle, an algorithm will work. However, proving an actual implementation—a completed program—requires a different sort of tack.

assertions

> The proof of a program is based on a series of *assertions* about the values of program variables and data.

An assertion is a statement that we expect to be true. Typically, we'll use *boolean*-valued expressions (like $a<>b$) to make assertions.

In general, we'll find that assertions come in pairs—there's an assertion right before a program action, then one immediately following it. We can think of the opening assertions as giving *preconditions*, while the closing assertions state *postconditions*. If you note that one statement's postcondition can be the next statement's precondition, you can begin to picture how program proofs are established. First, we make assertions about the effect of each statement:

preconditions, postconditions

{*assertion1*} *Statement1*; {*assertion2*}
{*assertion2*} *Statement2*; {*assertion3*}
{*assertion3*} *Statement3*; {*assertion4*}

verifying sequences

Then, by applying simple rules of logic, we can remove intermediate assertions:

{*precondition*} *Statement1*;
Statement2;
Statement3; {*postcondition*}

In practice, we usually work in the opposite manner, by starting with the outlying assertions, and attempting to develop assertions for parts of the program, then parts of those parts, etc.

Now, it's pretty easy to see how to make some kinds of assertions. Suppose that we want to divide A by B and save the result in C. The closing assertion is a check on the operation—our assertion that the answer is correct is $A = B * C$. However, if we want to be assured that we will survive the division we need an opening assertion as well—that B isn't 0. The sequence of assertions (in comment brackets) is:

```
{B<>0}
C := A/B;
{A=B*C}
```

verifying loops

Looping statements are more interesting because assertions before and after the loop aren't sufficient to make a proof. Why not? Well, if the assertions are to actually prove anything, they must also establish that we arrive at the loop's end—that the loop isn't infinite!

variant and invariant assertions

A loop's *invariant* assertion is a statement about the loop that is true both before and after each iteration of the loop. Its companion is a *variant* assertion whose truth will change between the loop's initial and final iterations. This is sometimes called the loop's *bound function*.

These two assertions serve complementary purposes in a loop proof. The invariant assertion makes a statement about the correctness of the loop's action, which is why it must always be true. The truth of the variant assertion, in contrast, is changed by the loop's action. It helps assure us that the loop will eventually be terminated, which is why it's also known as a bound function. The invariant assertion helps make sure that the loop doesn't do the *wrong* thing, while the variant assertion ensures that it does do the *right* thing.

For instance, suppose that we want to do *integer* division by repeated subtraction. The code segment below implements an algorithm we probably all learned in second or third grade:

problem: proving division by subtraction

```
Remainder := Dividend;
Quotient := 0;
while Remainder >= Divisor do begin
   Remainder := Remainder - Divisor;
   Quotient := Quotient + 1
end;
```

developing the invariant

If this loop is correct, we should arrive at proper values for *Quotient* and *Remainder*. First, what's our invariant assertion? Well, both before and after each loop iteration there should be a special relationship between the dividend, divisor, quotient, and remainder:

{*Dividend* = (*Divisor*∗*Quotient*)+*Remainder*}

Since *Dividend* isn't changed within the loop, we don't have to worry about monkey business that would require us to save *Dividend's* original value, and make our invariant more complicated. As long as the invariant relation is true, we can be confident that our loop is, at the very least, not doing the wrong thing.

need for a bound

However, the invariant relation isn't enough. Suppose that the loop's action made no assignments to either *Quotient* or *Remainder*. Although the invariant assertion would still stay true, it wouldn't assure us that the loop would ever end. We need to state some sort of bound that is approached by the loop's action, but which can act as a threshold beyond which the loop won't venture.

The variant assertion:

{*Remainder* >= *Divisor*, and *Remainder* declines}

does the trick. Its truth is potentially changed on each iteration of the loop—each time we change the value of *Remainder*. Eventually it becomes false; we pass the bound or threshold, and the loop is terminated. It is no accident that it forms the entry condition of the loop. The entire loop, complete with assertions, is:

```
Remainder := Dividend;
Quotient := 0;
{Dividend = (Divisor*Quotient)+Remainder}
while Remainder >= Divisor do begin
   Remainder := Remainder - Divisor;
   {Remainder >= Divisor, and Remainder declines}
   Quotient := Quotient + 1
   {Dividend = (Divisor*Quotient)+Remainder}
end;
```

As usual, we've made everything look easy by coming up with the correct answer on our first try. Let's consider a false proof, though. Suppose that we had chosen as our variant assertion the relation *Quotient* <= *Dividend*. We would still make progress toward loop termination, since we increment *Quotient* on each pass through the loop. Since it provides an upper bound on the loop, it's reasonable to think that the assertion is a good bound function.

a false proof

Unfortunately, it's the *wrong* bound function. Before we reach the limit it sets, we'll have allowed the invariant assertion to become incorrect. Our attempted proof would fail, even though we set a threshold and approached it.

Difficulties In Proving Programs

The idea that we can prove that a program is correct is intensely appealing, since it would greatly increase our confidence in programs. True, verification seems complicated at first; but then again, so do mathematical proofs. Unfortunately, the promise of program proving has not been realized in as full a manner as was originally hoped. Let's investigate the reasons.

Two conditions have to be satisfied if we want a program proof to work. First, the action of a program statement can't undermine our assertions about what the statement will do. Although this notion seems obvious (we clearly wouldn't have a statement that directly contradicts an assertion), there are subtle difficulties that are easy to overlook. For instance, mathematical proofs don't have to worry about whether or not the axioms of mathematics will apply, but program proofs do. The machine code that takes care of computer arithmetic may never have been formally proven—and it may not always obey the rules!

correctness

Second, the assertions we make have to define the entire 'universe' of the program. Any necessary assertions that are left out cause gaping holes in the program proof that may not be detected until the program fails. For instance, suppose that a routine should sort three variables into increasing order. It's not enough to prove that the variables are in order when the routine ends. We can't ignore the possibility that the routine might have accidentally given all the variables the *same* value.

completeness

> The need to satisfy these two conditions—correctness and completeness—make program proofs very difficult to develop.

In mathematical proofs, small errors will not necessarily have a negative impact on the proof as a whole. It may be that an individual step is incorrect or misstated. However, this sort of error won't always invalidate the overall goal of the proof—a fact can be true even if our explanation of it is faulty. Mathematical proofs usually fail because of larger conceptual errors.

For programs, though, the smallest step is vitally important to the conclusion of the program proof. The tiniest untested assumption about a data value in a program can suffice to undo an elaborate program proof.

limits of proofs

More importantly, though, the knowledge that such errors can occur in proofs without being detected by expert computer scientists tends to undermine our confidence in the absolute reliability of program proofs at all.

Like Perry Mason, we can cause a proof to collapse simply by demonstrating a reasonable doubt about its correctness. As a result, programs are actually proved only in a limited set of cases; and then only for relatively small program segments that are written with eventual proof in mind.

automated verification

Incidentally, you may be tempted to suggest that, since keeping track of small details is so important, program proving would be a perfect job for a computer. Why not write a program that could automatically check the correctness of a proof?

It's a good idea until you imagine what such a program's first job would be. Obviously we'd want to run it on itself. But what will we make of the answer? Suppose that the program announces that its own code is correct. Can we trust it? Worse yet (in a much more likely outcome) suppose that the automated verifier announces that its own code is *wrong*. Oh no! Back to the drawing board...

benefits of program proving

Even though few programs are formally verified, the techniques used to prove programs are widely applied as an aid to program development. In one aspect, the assertions that we might use to prove a program will turn up as detailed comments about the state of variables before and after a procedure or function call, or on the successful completion of a loop. Proof methods are also employed during the development of especially confusing program segments. In particular, ideas of loop invariants and bounding conditions are used to help assure ourselves that algorithms are correctly stated in the first place.

Another application of proof techniques is manifested by features built into programming languages. The availability of subrange types is a good example. A variable declared to have a subrange type is essentially a variable accompanied by an assertion—that is constantly checked—about the range of the variable's values. *Exception handling*—the specification of special notification procedures to be followed when errors are encountered—is another feature of recently developed programming languages.

Finally, programs can be written in a 'rough proof' form. You see, for many kinds of programs it almost seems easier to write the proof first, then tailor the code to fit the verification. In practice, when programs must be proved the development of proof and code usually go hand in hand. Even when the code is not intended to be exhaustively proved, writing code as though it will be verified can lead to less error-prone programs.

Antibugging and Debugging 9-3

ON OCCASION, WE MAY DEFINE SUBRANGES that are overlapping, similar, or even (apparently) the same. Understanding the differences between these subrange types is a confusing problem even for experienced programmers. For example:

```
type CapitalLetter = 'A'..'Z';
var FirstInitial, MiddleInitial: CapitalLetter;
    LastInitial: 'A'..'Z';
```

Are *FirstInitial* and *LastInitial* variables of the same type? A reasonable person, seeing that the subrange definitions are equivalent, would say yes. Unfortunately, Pascal requires us to be more precise.

identical vs. compatible types

> In Pascal, a distinction is drawn between variables whose types are exactly *identical*, and those that are merely *compatible*. Only variables declared with the same type identifier are identical.

In the case above, the types of *FirstInitial* and *MiddleInitial* are identical to each other, but not to *LastInitial*. We can still make an assignment between *FirstInitial* and *LastInitial* because they are compatible.

underlying types

> Two variables are compatible if they represent values of the same *underlying* type, even though they may be restricted to representing subranges of that type.

```
type LowRange = 1..5;
     MidRange = 1..10;
     HighRange = 6..20;
var LowValue: LowRange;
    MidValue: MidRange;
    HighValue: HighRange;
    AnyValue: integer;
```

LowValue, MidValue, HighValue, and *AnyValue* are clearly not of identical types, because they're all declared with different type identifiers. However, their underlying ordinal type (in this case, *integer*), determines type compatibility. Thus, the assignments:

```
MidValue := LowValue;
AnyValue := LowValue;
```

will always be legal, because *MidValue, LowValue*, and *AnyValue* all represent *integers*, and the subrange of *LowValue* falls within the subrange of *MidValue* (and is compatible with the *integer* range of *AnyValue*). However, this won't always be the case. These assignments:

```
LowValue := MidValue;
MidValue := HighValue;
HighValue := AnyValue;
```

may or may not be valid, depending on the values of *LowValue, MidValue, HighValue*, and *AnyValue* when the assignment actually takes place. If values are in the wrong subrange, a type clash will occur. Incidentally, checks on the plausibility of such assignments often aren't made until the program is run.

Is there any reason to define an ordinal subrange as a distinctly named type? Yes,—we may want to use it to make declarations.

subrange parameters

When a value parameter, variable parameter, or function is created, its type must have a name. The shorthand method of specifying ordinal subranges can't be used.

Moreover, procedure and function headings are type-checked very strictly. A variable parameter's type *must* be identical to its argument. Of all the variables declared above, only *LowValue* can be passed as an argument to procedure *DoesSomething*, below.

procedure *DoesSomething* (**var** *SmallNumber*: *LowRange*);

It's the only variable whose type is identical to the variable parameter *SmallNumber*.

Since value parameters treat their arguments as values, they need not have identical types. As long as parameter and argument are type-compatible, a run-time error occurs only for an 'out-of-range' argument.

Self-Check Questions

Q. Could this be a valid function heading?

function *ConvertToSmall* (*BigNumber*: 6..20):1..5;

A. No. Only type identifiers can appear in a subprogram heading—the shorthand method won't work. Written properly, the heading would be:

function *ConvertToSmall* (*BigNumber*: *HighRange*): *LowRange*;

Pascal Summary

- type definition: the reserved word **type** followed by the names and definitions of one or more types. A type definition follows constant definitions, and precedes variable declarations. It creates a new class of values:

  program *heading*;
  const *definitions*;
  type *definitions*;
  var *declarations*;
  procedure *or* **function** *declarations*;
  statements.

• enumerated type: a set of values named and ordered by the programmer. It's defined with a type identifier followed by the identifiers of the constant values of the type:

type *Motown* = (*Temptations, Smokey, MarvinGaye, Supremes*);
    Eighties = (*BruceSpringsteen, Prince, RickyLee, ElvisCostello*);

• subrange type: the name given to one particular range of any ordinal type. Defined with a type identifier followed by the first and last values in the subrange. The subrange values must be in the same order as their underlying type:

type *Subrange* = *First..Last*;
    Smalls = 1..10;

Important Facts

• The constants of an enumerated ordinal type must be distinct. No enumerated type can share the same values.

• Enumerated type constants are considered to belong in the order they're defined in. This is reflected in use of the *pred, succ*, and *ord* functions. The numbering of enumerated ordinal values starts with zero.

• Enumerated ordinal type constants can't be input or output because they have no external character representations.

• Subrange types are useful because they help make programs self-documenting, and incorporate automatic run-time checks on variable values into programs. They may also contribute to efficiency.

• Two variables have the same, identical, type only if they're declared with the same type identifier. A variable parameter and its argument must have identical types. Assignments between two variables of the same, identical type will always be valid.

• Variables or values are compatible, as distinct from identical, if they have the same underlying type. The argument of a value parameter must have a compatible type. Assignments between compatible variables might not be valid, since they might represent (or be allowed to represent) different subranges of the underlying type.

• A correct program produces correct results for all possible inputs. Since it is very difficult to prove that programs are correct, a variety of test methods are used to build confidence in programs.

• An assertion is a formal statement about the current state of a program that is either true or false. A loop's invariant assertion is supposed to be true at all times. Its variant assertion sets the loop's bound—its truth will eventually change.

Self-test Exercises

9-1 What distinguishes an ordinal type from the *real* type?

9-2 What's wrong with this definition and declaration?

```
type Hue = (Red, Blue, Green, Yellow, Violet);
var Green, Yellow: Hue;
```

9-3 Which of these are legal type definitions?

```
type Positive = 1..MAXINT;
     GradePoints = 0.0..4.0;
     Numbers = integer;
     Scientific = real;
     Alphabet = 'Z'..'A';
```

9-4 Name one circumstance that would make this an illegal definition.

```
type Hand = (Straight, Flush, StraightFlush);
```

9-5 Suppose that you can't be sure of the range of values a variable should represent until you actually run your program. Is it a good idea to declare the variable like this:

```
var Lower, Upper: integer;
    TheVariable: Lower..Upper;
```

and then input the values of *Lower* and *Upper* at runtime?

9-6 Suppose that we've made these definitions and declarations:

```
type Rainbow = (Infrared, Red, Orange, Yellow, Green, Blue, Violet, Ultraviolet);
     Spectrum = Infrared..Blue;
var HotColors: Infrared..Green;
    Colors: Rainbow;
    CoolColors: Yellow..Ultraviolet;
```

a) Which variables could be arguments to value parameters of type *Rainbow*?
b) Which variables could be arguments to value parameters of type *Spectrum*?
c) Which variables could be arguments to variable parameters of type *Spectrum*?
d) Which variables could be arguments to this value parameter:

```
procedure AnyProcedure (Hue: Infrared..Ultraviolet);
```

9-7 Can a program print the value of a variable whose type has been defined by the programmer?

9-8 The standard function *ord* will give us the ordinal position of a value of any ordinal type. Suppose that we've made this type definition:

```
type Weather = (Hail, Sleet, Snow, Rain, Pestilence, Plague);
```

What is the value of *chr*(*ord*(*Pestilence*) + 1);

9-9 Suppose that we've defined a type *Day* whose constants are the days *Monday* through *Sunday*, and then declared a variable *Today* of that type. What bugs can you find in this program segment?

```
for Today := Sunday to Monday do begin
    writeln (Today);
    Today := succ (Today)
end;
```

9-10 How can we find out the type of a constant value?

9-11 Suppose that you have a variable that represents some value of an enumerated ordinal type. How can you make it represent the very *first* value of that type?

'Large-scale programming over the past decade has been such a tar pit . . .'

10

Software Engineering

By now you've surely noticed that the music always plays just before the shark attacks. This is dramatic foreshadowing; it sets the audience's mood for what's about to happen.

To a certain extent, the same technique is used in textbooks. Introductions, like this one, give you an idea of what's contained in the chapter ahead. Right now we'll carry the approach further, and give you an idea of what's involved in programming on a larger scale than we've done so far.

Software engineering is our first topic. The programs we write in class are usually thrown away after they're graded, but real-life *software systems* stick around for years. Software has a long lifetime that begins when problems are first being considered for computer solution, and doesn't end until the software is discarded or completely replaced. The different stages of the software *life cycle* are the subject of section 10-1.

The second section, 10-2, contains a rough overview of the *structured types—arrays, records, files*, and *sets*—that will be discussed in the next four chapters. Variables with structured types let us describe data in our terms, rather than the machine's. A quick look at all the structured types before studying them in detail will help you better understand their applications. You'll also get a good idea of how different types are used together, and how they can be combined into more complex structures.

Since this chapter simply surveys material, there aren't any exercises found at the end. Enjoy!

Software Engineering* 10-1

SOFTWARE ENGINEERING IS THE SCIENCE of the development of *software systems*—programs, large and small, that will be used to solve real problems. Like more traditional engineering endeavors, the study of software engineering is largely motivated by a desire to avoid repeating mistakes—mistakes that were only belatedly recognized as involving engineering at all. The opening paragraphs of a seminal text on software engineering (written barely a decade ago) describe the situation:

> 'No scene from prehistory is quite so vivid as that of the mortal struggles of great beasts in the tar pits. In the mind's eye one sees dinosaurs, mammoths, and sabertoothed tigers struggling against the grip of the tar. The fiercer the struggle, the more entangling the tar, and no beast is so strong or so skillful but that he ultimately sinks.

the tar pit

> 'Large-system programming has over the past decade been such a tar pit, and many great and powerful beasts have thrashed violently in it. Most have emerged with running systems—few have met goals, schedules, budgets. Large and small, massive or wiry, team after team has become entangled in the tar. No one thing seems to cause the difficulty—any particular paw can be pulled away. But the accumulation of simultaneous and interacting factors brings slower and slower motion. Everyone seems to have been surprised by the stickiness of the problem, and it is hard to discern the nature of it. But we must try to understand it if we are to solve it.'**

Airline reservations systems (like the one described later in this chapter) are just one category of the dozens of software systems that have fallen into the tar pit Brooks describes. Sometimes the development effort is entirely unsuccessful; a satisfactory system isn't constructed. Other systems may be accepted by the end user, but be late, over budget, poorly suited to the intended application, or hamstrung by inefficient use of system resources. In either case, the programmer and user are equally dissatisfied with the end result.

software life cycle

The study of software engineering starts with the recognition that the development of software is a long-term process. It begins well before any program coding is done, and continues long after a program is thought to be finished. This continuing development process is known as the *software life cycle*. It can be divided into these distinct phases:

1. *Analysis* of the problem.
2. *Specification* of the software's abilities.
3. *Design* of the software.
4. *Implementation* or coding.

* This section is optional, but it is strongly recommended.

** *The Mythical Man-Month*, by Frederick P. Brooks, Jr. Addison-Wesley Publishing Co., 1975. pg. 4.

5. *Testing* of the completed system.
6. *Maintenance* and evolution of the system.

Although our studies have focused mainly on coding, it is just one step in the process. As programs become larger and more complex, the earlier and later steps become increasingly important.

Analysis

Analysis of the problem is the first, and probably most difficult, step in the software life cycle. The real life problems faced by potential computer users are a far remove from the neatly prepared exercises presented in computer science textbooks. This is not because real life problems are any more difficult; indeed, the reverse is quite often the case. Instead, it is because customers and programmers often speak very different languages. As a result, simple problems can be misunderstood, or difficult ones understated.

The analysis phase tries to answer the question 'What should the software do?' in a manner that will be meaningful to the software designer. Simply saying that the software should 'keep our books,' or 'monitor our test equipment,' or 'give sample Pascal examinations' doesn't give much direction. Instead, the analyst must work with the end user to answer many questions about the system. The system is pictured both as it is now, and as it may come to be:

questions for analysis

- what will the system's input be? what output should the system produce?
- will these requirements change? how seriously? how often?
- what sort of people will use the system? can they be specially trained?
- will there be errors in input? in stored data? how should errors be fixed?
- what kind of equipment is available? what can be obtained?
- how fast should the system work? how reliable does it have to be?
- will the system grow? in what directions?

software prototypes

One current area of computer science research that's intended to help with the problems of analysis is *rapid software prototyping*. The idea of building prototypes, or test models, is common to many engineering disciplines. A prototype is a scaled-down model that can be examined and tested before any commitment is made to a final design. Prototyping is especially appropriate for software systems, since it helps facilitate communication between user and designer in the problem-analysis phase of program design.

Software prototyping relies on the idea that many software components—routines for input, output, data sorting—are more or less independent of the systems they're found in. These building blocks can be joined, with a minimum of new code, to rough out a prototype of the end-user's system. This working model can be used to help give the user an idea of a computer's capabilities, as well as to give the software analyst a feel for the users' needs. The user interface, or method the user employs to communicate with the program, is an area that's particularly suited for evaluation through prototyping.

Requirements Specification

The specification of a software system's requirements is a formal statement of its capabilities, capacities, and constraints. Whereas the analysis phase was intended to determine in general terms what the proposed system was supposed to do, the requirements specification states in detail what the finished system *will* do.

A requirements specification will be referred to throughout the entire software development process. It can act as the contract between programmer and end user, and is often the only point of contact between the two groups. If a feature or requirement isn't specified in the requirement, it's not liable to show up in the final product. The requirements specification will also generally be the standard against which the final system is tested.

Specification of software requirements is a more difficult task than it might appear to be at first glance. Consider the variety of areas that a specification has to define:

details of the specification

- It must state the specific abilities of the system—the commands that will be available to the user. These are the system's *functional requirements*.
- It has to specify the assumptions that will be made about the systems' input, users, response time, data—its operating environment.
- It must define the system's limitations—how many users will there be, how much data need be handled, etc.
- It has to describe any special hardware requirements, or any restrictions imposed by hardware limitations.
- It must specify possible modifications to the system that have to be allowed for in the system's design.
- It should describe the nature and extent of documentation that are supposed to accompany the system. A preliminary users' manual may be required as well.

The functional specification is the most visible part of a requirements document. In small systems, stating functional requirements is a pretty straightforward task. A list of allowed commands may be all that is needed. In more complex systems, though, a list of commands may not be enough—we'll need a better mechanism for describing the big picture.

A variety of schemes have been developed to help in stating specifications. Most of them are elaborate charting systems; terms like *actigram, data-flow diagram*, and *Warnier diagram* abound. However, most specifications systems are built around a common theme: they describe a program in terms of its data—how it is stored and transferred, and what can be done with it in the process.

Once we begin to talk about data, programs can't be far away. Before we begin to code, though, we have to go through the design phase.

Design

The first two steps of the software life cycle determine *what* should be done. The design phase specifies *how* is should be done. The end result of the design phase is a *software blueprint* that can be implemented with a minimum of difficulty.

software blueprint

The importance of the design phase is probably the most underrated aspect of the software life cycle. Although it is inconceivable that one would embark on the construction of, say, a building without a detailed plan of action in hand, software projects are routinely undertaken with the barest minimum of advance planning.

structured design

How do we go about designing software, and how is a software design shown? *Structured design* has become a generic term for programming with an emphasis on modular design. Many of the design techniques we take for granted now were first formalized in a series of structured design texts and seminars put together by Larry Constantine and Ed Yourdon.* In particular, the emphasis on designing relatively independent program modules, whose interconnections are specified in parameter lists, is characteristic of structured design. Many of the top-down programming techniques we've mentioned in past chapters, including stub programming, evolved naturally out of the desire to keep programs modular.

flowcharts

Flowcharting is the method originally used to make precise descriptions of a program's activity. A flowchart is a sequence of boxes, connected by arrows, that shows a program's flow of control. There is actually a government standard for the shapes of boxes—a diamond indicates a decision, a parallelogram is input or output, and so on. Flowcharting is very popular in languages, like FORTRAN, in which programs can make sudden jumps to unexpected places.

pseudocode

Pseudocoding is quite familiar to us by now, and it seems like a self-evident idea. However, in the early 1970's, pseudocode was just an experimental alternative to flowcharting. A number of formalized pseudocoding systems were defined as *program design languages*, or PDL's. It's interesting to note that Pascal (which wasn't widely available at the time) and other recently designed languages incorporate many of the techniques they suggested.

* Such as *How to Manage Structured Programming*, by Ed Yourdon, YOURDON Inc. 1976 (and dedicated 'to my first, third, and fourth wives . . .').

other formal systems

Hierarchy and Input-Process-Output, or HIPO, charts are part of a typical formal system for software design and specification (in this case, one developed by IBM). Although they were intended to be used as system documentation, these charts have also been found to be useful in system design. Hierarchy charts give a modular presentation of the work a program does, while input-process-output diagrams are more detailed pictures of the action of individual modules.

Regardless of the system used to design and specify code, the design phase has two goals. First, any ambiguities located in the requirements specification should be found and clarified. Second, there should be a detailed guide prepared for the next step—coding.

Coding

For most of the history of computing, coding the main program has been thought of as the programmer's main activity. Surprisingly, surveys consistently show that program coding occupies only about 20% of the time and effort involved in producing software systems. Nevertheless, carefully made specifications and designs are all for naught if they are not well-implemented.

The software engineer looks at the coding phase of programming in several different ways. First, there's the code itself. What language, or languages, should be used? How long should subprograms be? What rules should be followed for defining identifiers? How should the code be laid out? How efficient must it be? How detailed should comments be? Are any kinds of programming tricks forbidden?

Next, there's the programming staff. How can work be divided? What are the responsibilities of individual coders? How closely should programmers be supervised? How should proposals for coding be reviewed? How much communication should there be between programmers, and how can it be arranged? How can we estimate the difficulty of specific program segments?

Finally, there are the methods used to produce the code. What electronic tools are there for coding support? How are different versions of programs maintained? How should debugging or testing code be built into the software? Will different hardware—terminals, printers, interactive equipment—have any effect on programmer productivity?

Of all the phases of software development, coding is probably the least formalized. One reason is that the management of coding efforts has turned out to differ from other kinds of management in unexpected ways. A particularly instructive example comes from attempts to apply general notions of manpower to coding. Now, in most sorts of organized activity—drafting, or claims processing, or chopping wood—the volume of work accomplished grows in rough proportion to the amount of effort expended. As a consequence, doubling effort doubles results—or halves completion time, more or less.

The unanticipated results of applying this rule to programming gave Brooks the title of his book: *The Mythical Man-Month*. He found that most project managers treated software production just like other sorts of production. When a project fell behind schedule, they would add additional programmers. To their astonishment, they often found that adding help made matters worse! Extra programmers only made the project fall further behind schedule. Brooks characterized this experience rather cynically in Brooks' Law: *Adding manpower to a late software project makes it later*.

the mythical man-month

On close inspection we can recognize the two characteristics of software production that give the law its grain of truth. First, new staff must be trained. Even if they are expert programmers, the current project must be explained; they have to be brought up to speed in the project's goals, rules, coding strategies, etc. Second, they must communicate as they work, since a program's modules can never be made entirely independent of each other. A group of n people can meet in $n(n-1)/1$ different pairs; which means that doubling a group from three programmers to six increases the number of meetings they can hold by a factor of *five*.

A variety of solutions have helped improve the situation. Insistence on modular software design reduces the amount of communication needed between groups, and helps reduce the impact of delays in software production. A very effective approach suggested by Brooks and others is the creation of *programming teams*, in which outstanding 'superprogrammers' are given sufficient staff support to avoid unnecessary distractions. Such teams include a 'copilot' who helps the superprogrammer with design, a 'language lawyer' who specializes in knowing the ins and outs of a particular language or programming system, an 'editor' in charge of documentation, a 'program clerk' who can handle secretarial details that require technical expertise, etc.

programming teams

Testing

The test phase of the software life cycle can involve as much time and effort as the coding phase. No matter how carefully a program is planned and coded, it will still contain bugs and imperfections. In addition, large software systems may not even be fully assembled until the test phase begins. A ship's maiden voyage is traditionally a shakedown cruise; a program's first run marks the start of the test period.

The test phase has several goals. Most obviously, we want to find bugs introduced during the coding process. The attempt to find this sort of bug relies on methodical testing of individual program modules. This is usually known as *module testing*. Many of the program testing techniques we've discussed elsewhere are employed in this phase.

module testing

Next, modules are put together to form systems or subsystems. This is sometimes called *integration testing*, since we are integrating the activity of different modules. The bugs found during integration testing are generally due to design errors. These will typically involve the interface

integration testing

between separate modules. Code may have been implemented correctly, but programmers may have labored under false impressions of the input their particular modules could expect, or the output they were supposed to produce. If problems found in integration testing involve basic data storage methods they can be very serious, and involve a considerable amount of code rewriting.

acceptance testing

In the final testing step, the completed system is presented to its end users for *acceptance testing*. Well-managed software systems will usually work their way into this phase slowly by *alpha* and *beta* site testing. The system is distributed to a limited number of sites for feedback and refinement before it is presented for final validation and acceptance. Unfortunately, problems that come up in acceptance testing sometimes date back to the original analysis and specifications phases. The program does what is called for in the design, but the design itself may be incomplete or incorrect from the end user's point of view.

The testing scheme described here is, of course, a bottom-up approach. Since bottom-up approaches tend to hide early errors until late in the game, top-down approaches to system testing, like the stub programming methods described in section 5-3, are becoming more popular. Some techniques mentioned earlier—particularly rapid software prototyping—will also help the situation.

Maintenance and Evolution

Software may outlive its usefulness, but it never wears out. Once an individual or organization has put effort into learning (or adapting to) a particular software system, there is a great tendency to prefer modification of existing software over the acquisition of new software. Even armed with this understanding, it will probably come as a great surprise to find that maintenance and modification of a program can cost two to four times as much as its original coding—or up to 80% of the costs contained in the entire software life cycle.

correction

There are a number of motivations for modifying software once it is presumed to be complete. A first category involves *correction*. Although the rate at which bugs are found declines drastically, they usually appear throughout a software system's entire lifetime. Occasionally they will fall into the 'bug or feature?' column, especially when a user employs a poorly-documented or unintended command.

perfection

A second motivation for modification is the desire to improve the system's usefulness—*perfective* changes. Surprisingly, a successful system may require the most modifications, since it may be widely adopted in environments other than it was originally intended for. The addition of new features, or fine-tuning and improvement (perhaps by using new algorithms) of existing features are typical of this kind of modification and evolution.

adaptation

A third category of modifications are sometimes called *adaptive* changes. These are mandated by changes in the system's operating environment. They may be caused by improvements in the hardware system, or by changes in external software the system relies on; for instance, a change in the computer's operating system.

The understanding that maintenance accounts for such a large portion of software costs has been one of the prime motivating factors in the development of software engineering. Well-understood systems—say, automobiles—are designed with maintenance in mind. As a result, their construction is fairly modular, and points that need to be checked regularly are easily accessible.* Software is only recently developing this kind of self-awareness. The embedded debugging tools mentioned in section 6-4 are a perfect example of built-in aids for program maintenance.

toolbox software

One approach intended to improve the maintainability of systems involves the creation of *toolbox software*. A system is conceived of as being a collection of relatively independent tools, each with a specific task. The UNIX** operating system is typical of the toolbox approach. For instance, it doesn't contain a word-processing program, per se. Rather, it has separate programs (editors, formatters, printers, etc.) that a user can tie together to provide the function of a word-processor. Boxes of tools may produce larger systems, but they make it easier to improve specific tools as technology or understanding improves, or as needs change.

integrated software

When adapted to the consumer market, toolbox systems generally appear as *integrated software* systems. In these systems, a single program is capable of a variety of functions. *Framework* and *Symphony* are two commercially available products that are typical of integrated systems. They each combine brand-name editors, spreadsheets, databases, etc. into a single program. However, integrated systems have been criticized for going too far—in attempting to create a single, easily-marketed product, the maintainability of the component parts is lost. At this point, only time will tell how well the integrated systems will fare in the marketplace.

Meet The Types 10-2

ONE OF THE MAIN ADVANTAGES OF PROGRAMMING in Pascal is that we can design variables with different structures. A simple variable can only store a single value, but when a variable belongs to a *structured type*, it generally stores several, and can be used in a variety of new ways. We'll introduce Pascal's structured types by seeing how a large program might employ them.

Our example for this chapter will be an airline reservation program. Now, the data such a program uses tends to organize itself into certain kinds of packages. For example:

* There are notable exceptions. Consider, for example, the Chevy Monza, which required that the engine be partly removed in order to change the spark plugs!
** UNIX is a registered footnote of Bell Laboratories.

An airline might fly 4 or 5 different types of airplane. Each plane has a different number of rows and aisles of seats.

Every flight has a number, flight schedule, departure and arrival gates, fares, plane type, etc.

data storage requirements

Every airline has files of information—new fare schedules awaiting approval, flight plans that may be modified, rules and regulations that are being revised—that are permanently stored. They may require revision before being given to the reservation computer, or may only be read or printed out on rare occasions.

Every city on an airline's route has a set of connections to other cities which can be flown to nonstop. Every flight has a set of discounts and special fares associated with it.

If we were actually writing a reservation program we'd want to be able to declare each of these packages as a single variable:

A 'plane' variable that stores data on an organized arrangement of seats. In Pascal, we'd use an *array* variable.

Pascal data types

A 'flight' variable that holds several different types of information. In Pascal, this requires a *record* type.

An 'information' variable, that can be used for permanent storage of data. The *file* type is Pascal's answer.

A 'connections' variable that stores one or all of a group of values simultaneously. Pascal's *set* type is called for.

Let's look at the structured types—array, record, file, and set—named above. Bear in mind that this is only an overview, and that each type will be discussed in detail in subsequent chapters. As you read, make a mental note of two important facts associated with each structured type. First is its method of *creation*; the process we have to go through in order to declare a variable with a given internal structure. Second, get an idea of the means of *access* to each variable. When a single variable has more than one piece of data associated with it, we must follow rules to get information.

The **array** Type (Chapter 11)

What does an airline ticket agent do when she reserves your seat on a flight? First, she probably prompts the computer to print a picture of the seats that are available. Then, by naming one seat in particular (say, '14D'), she updates the stored chart, and reserves a seat for you.

What does a computer programmer do when she has to represent the seating plan of an airplane within a program? Well, a plane's seating plan is more or less a grid, in which each seat can be referred to by a row number and aisle letter. Different plans are distinguished by different numbers of rows and aisles. In English, we might describe the seating plan of a plane like this:

Seating plan—grid, rows 1 through 30, aisles A through J—of taken or not.

In Pascal, a programmer defines a new type:

type *SeatingPlan* = **array** [1..30, 'A'..'J'] **of** *boolean*;

As you can see, the method of creation of the actual Pascal code is very similar to our English version.

Seating plan becomes the identifier *SeatingPlan*
grid becomes the reserved word **array**
rows 1 through 30, aisles A through J becomes [1..30, 'A'..'J']
of becomes the reserved word **of**
taken or not taken becomes *true* or *false*—the type *boolean*

The *array* type is used in many computer languages. According to the dictionary, an array is an orderly arrangement of things, and Pascal takes this idea to its logical limit. Although a grid is usually a two-dimensional assortment (like the squares in a piece of graph paper), a Pascal array type can have *any* number of dimensions. We might define an array type with one dimension:

type *Aisle* = **array** ['A'..'J'] **of** *boolean*;

Or, we could define a type with three dimensions, like a three-dimensional Tic-Tac-Toe board.

type *BoxStatus* = (*Empty, X, O*);
    TTTBoard = **array** [1..3, 1..3, 1..3] **of** *BoxStatus*;

Note that our first two examples created types that contained *boolean* values, while the third type contained 27 (for there are 27 squares on a 3 by 3 by 3 Tic-Tac-Toe board) values of type *BoxStatus*, which are defined as *Empty, X*, and *O*.

The type definition was the major part of our job. Declaring variables of new types is easy.

var *DC10SeatTaken, L1011SeatTaken, B747SeatTaken*: *SeatingPlan*;

DC10SeatTaken is an variable of type *SeatingPlan*. *SeatingPlan*, in turn, is an array, with two dimensions, of *boolean* values.

The method of access to values in array-typed variables is unusual, but not unreasonable. The variable identifier is accompanied by the coordinates of the particular value we want to access:

TTTBoard[2,2,2] := *X*; {Put an 'X' in the central box}
DC10SeatTaken[14, 'H'] := *true*; {We've just reserved seat 14H}
if not *L1011SeatTaken*[21, 'B'] **then**
    writeln ('That seat is free. Do you wish to reserve it?');

In Pascal, square brackets serve double-duty—they're used with both set and array types.

We can also create arrays that represent different structures—in effect, structures of structures. One of the most common variations is an array of records—our next topic.

The **record** Type (Chapter 12)

Arrays store many values, but they must all have the same type. Suppose, though, that we want a single variable to store a number of data items that are related, but have *different* types. For instance, let's look at some of the data that might be connected with an airplane flight to Phoenix.

Phoenix— *Flight number* (*integer*)
Departure and Arrival Time (*real*)
Terminal (*char*)
Gate Number (*integer*)
On Time, Cancelled, Sold Out (*true or false*)

Many flights, to many cities, will have the exact same categories of information associated with them. What we require is a new *type* of variable that's capable of storing all this data—in effect, a record. In Pascal, the record is an official type:

```
type FlightData = record
                     FlightNumber: integer;
                     DepartureTime, ArrivalTime: real;
                     Terminal: char;
                     GateNumber: integer;
                     OnTime, Cancelled, SoldOut: boolean
                  end;
var Phoenix, StLouis, Denver, Miami, Buffalo: FlightData;
```

In the example above, we've used a number of city names (*Phoenix*, *StLouis*, etc.) as variable identifiers. These variables are of the record type *FlightData*. What exactly is the structure of *FlightData*? It's composed of several 'internal' variables, called *fields*. Can the fields be broken down further? Not in this example—they're all of the standard simple types.

What about getting at the values stored in a record variable's fields? There are several methods of access, but we'll just look at the most common. If a variable has a record type, we can follow its name with a period (.) and the name of the field (or internal variable) we wish to access. This lets us make assignments:

```
Phoenix.FlightNumber := 27;
Phoenix.Terminal := 'E';
Denver.DepartureTime := Buffalo.ArrivalTime+ 0.5;
StLouis.SoldOut := true;
```

We can also access record-typed variables for output:

```
writeln ('Flight to Miami leaving at gate ', Miami.GateNumber);
```

Why do records use this syntax for access? It's really totally arbitrary—Wirth could just as easily have used the possessive ' 's ' of English:

Patti's phone number ~ *Patti.PhoneNumber*
Buffalo flight's terminal ~ *Buffalo.Terminal*

Pascal records, like real-life records, are hardly ever used singly, and programmers often create data types that contain many records. For example, suppose that an airline numbers its flights 1 through 100. Clearly, this calls for 100 copies of a *FlightData* record to be stored in an array:

```
type FlightData = record
                    DepartureTime, ArrivalTime: real;
                    Terminal: char;
                    GateNumber: integer;
                    OnTime, Cancelled, SoldOut: boolean
                  end;
     OutboundFlights = array [1..100] of FlightData;
var PanAm, United, American, TWA: OutboundFlights;
```

Try to figure out what the statement below does. It's just a matter of combining methods of access.

```
writeln (United[48].DepartureTime);
```

With a little inspection, the answer should reveal itself—the statement prints the departure time of United Airlines flight 48.

The **file** Type (Chapter 13)

In Chapter 8 we explained that a Pascal program thinks its output comes (and output goes to) a file of data. So far, the files we've used have actually been devices—*input* is generally a keyboard or card reader, while *output* is almost always a lineprinter or terminal screen. However, programs often use real files—data that's been stored within the computer for a program to interpret, or program results that are saved instead of being printed out immediately.

In Pascal, we can create new file types for storing data. We begin by defining a file type—what type of data does the file contain?—then declare variables of that type. In practice, many of the files we'll be using are of type *char*. A predefined identifier, *text*, is used to indicate a file of *char*. It's as though every Pascal program contained the definition:

```
type text = file of char;
var Data, RateProposal: text;
```

Sometimes file variables are only used during the course of a program (as though they were computer scratchpads). These are called *internal* files. Other files are stored permanently, and are called *external* files. Because external files are, in a sense, parameters of a program, they're named in the program's heading.

```
program ComputeSomething (output, Data, RateProposal);
```

This program heading allows program *ComputeSomething* to receive input from two sources—the files *Data* and *RateProposal*. *ComputeSomething's* output can go to the standard output, or it might be put into one of the external files.

The method of access to files is both familiar and unexpected. We already know a method of access to textfiles. To read a value from textfile *Original*, and echo it to textfile *Copy*, we'd say:

read (*Original, Value*);
write (*Copy, Value*);

As you can see, we've given each of the standard procedures *read* and *write* an extra argument—the name of the file we're reading or writing. Without this extra argument, the computer would assume we want to read from the standard input, and write to the standard output.

In comparison to other types of variables, access to files is restricted in a peculiar manner. Before a file can be read from, it must be *reset*. This puts us at the beginning of the file. As we read values, we move toward the file's end. By resetting the file we can start from the beginning again whenever we like. However, there's no way to get anywhere else in the file besides reading it again, line by line.

Files are written in the same manner. By calling a procedure named *rewrite*, we begin with a blank file to which we can add data. However, we can only add values to the end of the file, because calling *rewrite* again erases the file.

Because of these limitations on access to their stored values, files are often called *sequential access* types—each value must be stored or retrieved in sequence. In contrast, a type like the array is called *random access*. Its values can be assigned or retrieved in any order.

The **set** Type (Chapter 14)

Suppose that we've made the enumerated type definition below. It's nothing new—it just creates a range of values that can be used within a program.

type *City* = (*Memphis, Houston, Detroit, Eugene, Flagstaff, Raleigh*);

The *set* type is used to create variables that can represent any, none, or all of the members of an ordinal type. The *all* must be qualified, because Pascal implementations can limit the number of members a set can have. Usually, though, a set can contain as many members as the computer has characters. The creation of set-typed variables follows this pattern:

type *City* = (*Memphis, Houston, Detroit, Eugene, Flagstaff, Raleigh*);
    Connections = **set of** *City*;
var *FromMemphis, FromHouston, FromDetroit, FromEugene,*
        FromFlagstaff, FromRaleigh: *Connections*;

The various *From...* variables are all of type *Connections*. What is the type of *Connections*? Potentially, it can contain the entire set of *City* values.

Accessing set-type variables involves two separate ideas. First is the method of making assignments. A set variable's values are given between square brackets. As in the shorthand method of set declaration, two dots (..) can be used to indicate contiguous values:

> *FromMemphis* := [ ]; {An empty set}
> *FromHouston* := [*Detroit, Flagstaff*];
> *FromDetroit* := [*Eugene..Raleigh*];
> *FromMemphis* := *FromDetroit*;
> *FromRaleigh* := *FromHouston*+*FromMemphis*;
>   {This is called 'set union'}
> *FromEugene* := *FromRaleigh* * *FromDetroit*;
>   {This is called 'set intersection'}
> *FromFlagstaff* := *FromMemphis*–*FromHouston*;
>   {This is called 'set difference'}

There are three new operations that can be applied to set variables—*union, intersection*, and *difference*. The union of two sets is the combination of their elements; thus, *FromRaleigh* gets all the values included in *FromHouston* and *FromMemphis*. The intersection of two sets contains the values that are members of both sets. In the example above, *FromEugene* winds up representing *Eugene, Flagstaff*, and *Raleigh*—all cities connected to both Houston and Memphis. Finally, the difference of two sets (e.g. *A*–*B*) are the elements left after the members of *B* are taken from *A*. In the assignment above, *FromFlagstaff* is being given the values *Eugene* and *Raleigh*.

The second idea of set values involves their use in *boolean* expressions. When we first used the operator **in** we had to list the members of a set between square brackets. Now, we can just use the name of the set:

> **if** *Detroit* **in** *FromMemphis* **then**
>   *writeln* ('You can fly directly from Memphis to Detroit');

We can also test for set *equality, inequality*, and *inclusion*. We'll briefly review these ideas when we begin to discuss Pascal sets.

Important Facts

• Software engineering studies the development of software systems. The software life cycle can be divided into six stages:

- Analysis of the problem.
- Specification of the software's abilities.
- Design of the software.
- Implementation or coding of the software.
- Testing of the completed system.
- Maintenance and future evolution of the software system.

• A software prototype is a scaled-down, test model of a system. A software blueprint gives a detailed description of final code.

'Almost any group of values that can be organized in a regular manner…'

11

Arrays for Random Access

They say that a topologist is a person who finds a doughnut and a coffee cup identical because they both have the shape of a torus. We can just as reasonably describe a computer scientist as the sort of person who doesn't distinguish between a checkerboard and a topographical map—after all, they can each be described with an array.

The array is the most common computer structure, and is included in practically every programming system from machine language on up. Do you have a list of data values? A table? A grid? A coordinate system? Almost any group of values that can be organized in a regular manner can be stored in an array, because array values are accessed by *location* rather than by *name*.

Section 11-1 describes the syntax of array-typed variables. We'll pay special attention to the two important ideas behind structured variables—the method we use to create them, and the means we use to access their stored values. We'll also learn about *string* variables, which can be used to store words.

In section 11-2 we'll look at some applications of arrays. In addition to developing algorithms that use arrays, and coding them into Pascal, we'll work on designing data structures for their own sake. We'll explore the close relationship between a program's data *types*, its data *structures*, and its algorithm. We'll take a special look at the use of arrays in text processing.

Section 11-3 deals with some specialized applications of *recursion*, and is optional. We describe the idea of *backtracking* algorithms, and see how to implement them recursively. In particular, we'll learn how to apply computer techniques to problems as diverse as maze-searching, and chessboard positioning. Finally, 11-4 covers potential bugs.

Creating Array Types 11-1

STRUCTURED VARIABLE TYPES CAN STORE and represent one or more simple (ordinal or *real*) values. The *array* is one of Pascal's basic structured types. Array variables, like all structured variables, are created in a systematic way.

> The Golden Rule of Types
>
> *Define*, then *declare*. First, define a structured type, then declare variables of that type. New types must always be declared before they can be used in subsequent definitions.

Structured types are defined along with ordinal types in a program's (or subprogram's) type definition part. Some portions of the type definition are the same for every type. The reserved word **type** always opens the type definition part, each type has a unique identifier, and an equals sign always precedes the type's specific details.

The definition of an array-structured type tells the compiler three things:

elements, bounds, dimensions

1. What is the type of the array's *elements*—its stored values?
2. What is the array's *size*—how many elements will the array hold?
3. What are the array's exact *dimensions*—in what order will the elements be stored, and how will we refer to individual elements?

Specifying the type of the elements is easy—the values of any single ordinal, structured, or *real* type may be stored in a given array. The *number* of elements is given by the lower and upper *bounds* of each array dimension. Finally, these bounds also indicate how values will be stored, and what names should be used to access individual elements.

Once an array type is defined, we can declare variables of that type. In outline form the definition and declaration look like this:

array syntax

type *array-type identifier* = **array** [*dimensions*] **of** *element-type identifier*;

var *ArrayVariable identifier*: *array-type identifier*;

The syntax chart of an array type definition contains some options we haven't mentioned yet, but it'll be useful for reference.

array type

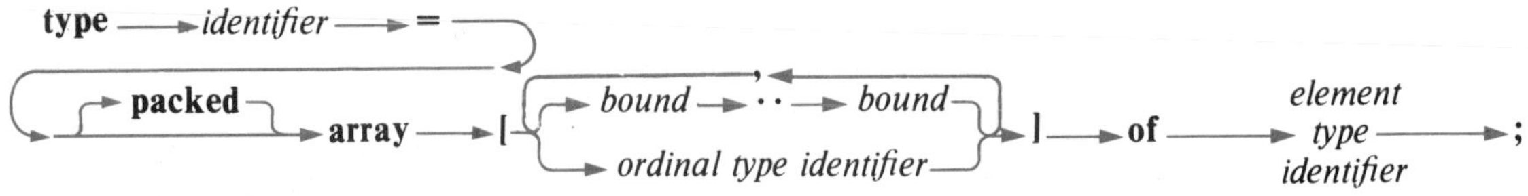

array bounds

An array dimension is specified by its limit values—the *array bounds*—which must belong to an ordinal type. The bounds are separated by two dots (..) that have their usual Pascal meaning of 'through and including.' If an array has more than one dimension, the pairs of array bounds are separated by commas.

An array that has only one pair of bounds is called *one dimensional*. However, arrays of two, three, or more dimensions can be created by giving additional pairs of array bounds. The entire dimension specification goes between the square brackets.

```
type CapitalLetters = array ['A'..'Z'] of element type;          {1 dimension}
     DailyReadings = array [1..24] of element type;              {1 dimension}
     SeatingPlan = array ['A'..'M', 1..44] of element type;      {2 dimensions}
     GameBoard = array [1..3, 1..3, 1..3] of element type;       {3 dimensions}
```

Array bounds can also be values of enumerated ordinal types. However, the bounds must be given with the constants of each type, or with user-defined constants. Variable identifiers, or other expressions, may *not* be used as array bound values. For example:

sample array bounds

```
const LASTROW = 'Z';
      MAXIMUM = 20;
type Days = (Monday, Tuesday, Wednesday, Thursday,
                                   Friday, Saturday, Sunday);
    Desserts = (Tart, Torte, Cake, Pie, IceCream, Mousse);
    SeatingPlan = array ['A'..LASTROW, 1..MAXIMUM] of element type;
    NumberOfHelpings = array [Tart..Mousse] of element type;
    WorkSchedule = array [Monday..Friday] of element type;
    DailyHelpings = array [Monday..Sunday, Tart..Cake] of element type;
    ServingsBySeat = array ['A'..LASTROW, 1..MAXIMUM, Tart..Cake]
                           of element type;
```

An ordinal or subrange type identifier (except *integer*) can take the place of specific array bounds. The dimension thus stated has bounds equal to the first and last members of the type.

type identifier as bound

This shortcut makes these two definitions equivalent:

```
type NumberOfHelpings = array [Tart..Mousse] of element type;
     NumberOfHelpings = array [Desserts] of element type;
```

The second method can be used to define an array whose bounds are the first and last characters, even when you don't know what the first and last *char* values are. Note that an array defined by its dimension type (like *char*) is portable. A *char*-dimensioned array will run on every computer, regardless of its character set.

type *CharacterCount* = **array** [*char*] **of** *element type*;

The definition of an array type is completed by naming the type of its elements.

array elements

> An array's elements may belong to any ordinal, *real*, subrange, or structured type.

Some arrays whose elements are ordinal values are:

type *SquareStatus* = (*Black, White, Empty*);
CheckerBoard = **array** [1..8, 1..8] **of** *SquareStatus*;
Word = **array** [1..15] **of** *char*;
Vegetables = (*Leeks, Yams, Spuds, Okra, Artichokes*);
GroceryOrder = **array** [*Leeks..Artichokes*] **of** *integer*;

Naturally, we can combine these in any way imaginable. To play checkers with vegetables, we add the definition:

CheckerBoard = **array** [1..8, 1..8] **of** *Vegetables*;

Self-Check Questions

Q. What is the size of each of these arrays—how many elements can be stored in a variable of each array type?

a) **type** *Storage* = **array** [1..5, 1..10] **of** *char*;
b) **type** *Measurements* = **array** [−5..10] **of** *real*;
c) **type** *Seats* = **array** [−5..5, 'A'..'G'] **of** *integer*;
d) **type** *TruthTable* = **array** [*boolean*] **of** *integer*;
e) **type** *Crate* = **array** [1..50, 1..10, 1..25] **of** *real*;
f) **type** *Graph* = **array** [1.0..100.0] **of** *char*;

A. Notice that the number of stored values can become quite large when an array has more than one dimension.

a) 50 (5∗10).
b) 16 (Don't forget the '0'th value).
c) 77 (11∗7 letters).
d) 2 (We've used the shorthand method of saying *false..true*).
e) 12,500 (50∗10∗25).
f) Illegal—bounds can't be *real*.

Accessing Array Elements, String Types

Individual elements are stored in and retrieved from array-type variables according to their *location* within the array. The location is given by a *subscript*; a name that comes from the arrays used in physics and mathematics. Now, in noncomputer applications an array subscript is written in small letters just below the normal line of text, like $Matrix_{i,j}$ (hence the name *sub*script). In Pascal, an array variable's subscript is given between square brackets.

array subscripts

> To access a single array element, follow the array variable's name by the element's subscript between square brackets. If more than one subscript is required (for multi-dimensional arrays), separate the subscripts with commas. Subscripts can also be *computed*, since any subscript can be a variable or expression.

random access

(The subscript is usually read as 'sub *whatever*.' *ChessBoard*[1,1] would be spoken as 'ChessBoard sub 1 *pause* 1.') According to the box above, the array is a *random access* type, because we can immediately access any of its elements. Given proper declarations, these are all valid assignments:

```
Initials['S'] := Initials['S'] + 1; {Add 1 to the value of Initials['S']}
Dinner[Leeks] := 5; {Assignment to a GroceryOrder variable.}
readln (Dinner[Yams]); {Read a value into Dinner[Yams]}
Boeing747['E', 4] := Taken; {Occupy seat E4—2 subscripts required.}
GameBoard[Upper, Center, Left] := X; {Move—three subscripts are needed.}
```

Any representation of a value can be an array subscript. All the subscripts in the following examples are computed.

computed subscripts

```
Scores[5+2] := NewValue;
Scores[Counter] := NewValue;
Scores[Counter+3] := NewValue;
Scores[trunc(7.62)] := NewValue;
Scores[Scores[OldScore]] := NewValue;
```

Naturally, the subscript must refer to a location within the array bounds. In the antibugging section we'll see how an 'out-of-range' subscript causes an immediate program crash.

We will find that, when the type of variables becomes more complicated, accessing values stored in an array element may require some patience. However, working methodically and breathing slowly will get us through the most complicated definitions.

> Assignments may be made between variables with *identical* array types.

assignment between arrays

Such 'complete array' assignments are sometimes used to initialize arrays. 'Identical' is printed in italics, above, to reinforce a subtle point we made in our discussion of subrange types. In Pascal, two variables have identical types only if they're declared with the same type identifier. Two array-type variables that are exactly alike in every detail *except type name* are not identical. (More formally, there is no structural equivalence of types in Pascal. If this sentence doesn't make sense to you, don't read it.)

We'll take this opportunity to introduce an option of array definitions called *packing*.

packing

When it appears in an array type declaration, the reserved word **packed** instructs the compiler to conserve space when storing the array (to 'pack' it), and to allow certain operations on the array.

For most practical purposes, a packed array is just like a non-packed one. The space conservation feature is seldom important to us because a good compiler will minimize storage space by itself. Some people even feel that forcing the programmer to decide when to pack an array runs counter to a basic principle of Pascal—that the programmer shouldn't have to worry about details of machine operation. We'll look at the exact operation of packed variables in Appendix A.

string types

One particular type of packed array in Pascal is unlike all the others. A packed array of *char*, like the one defined below, is usually called a *string*, and is used for storing text.

type *String* = **packed array** [1..15] **of** *char*;

string requirements

For an array type to be a string, three conditions must be met. First, it has to be packed, as we've just said. Second, it can only store *char* values. Third, its lower bound has to start with 1. Naturally, it can only have one dimension.

Thus, strings have three extra requirements. However, they also have three special advantages over ordinary arrays:

string advantages

1. We can use the relational operators to compare the alphabetical ordering of two strings.
2. We can output the entire string at once, instead of one *char* element at a time.
3. We can give a text value to the entire string with an assignment statement (but *not* with an input statement).

Don't forget that these features apply only to packed arrays of *char*, and not any other type. We'll look at a number of string applications in section 11-2.

Arrays and **for** Loops

Before we start to use array types in data structures, let's explore some of the nitty-gritty of array manipulation. The archetypical problem involves visiting every element of the array to modify it, print its value, or just to inspect it in the hope of finding something interesting. The **for** statement is custom-made for travelling through arrays because its counter variable can be used as an array subscript. Regardless of the ordinal type of an array dimension, we can create a **for** loop counter variable with the same type.

For example, procedure *LoadArray*, below, reads initializing values for the array *CompleteArray*. If *LowValue* and *HighValue* are legitimate bound values for the array, they're also good for setting the initial and final values of a **for** loop intended to traverse the array:

array-initializing procedure

```
procedure LoadArray (var CompleteArray: ArrayType;
                     LowValue, HighValue: TheirType);
   {Reads data into an array of type ArrayType.}
   var CurrentIndex: TheirType;
   begin
      for CurrentIndex := LowValue to HighValue do
         read (CompleteArray[CurrentIndex])
   end; {LoadArray}
```

The same method can be applied to a two-dimensional array. Suppose we have the following definition and declaration. We're deliberately giving *Grid* a peculiar set of array bounds—there's no reason for them to start at 1.

```
type Grid = array [-5..5, 3..14] of integer;
var Table: Grid;
```

problem: finding the largest element

Assume that all the elements of *Table* have already been initialized. How can we find the largest value stored? The natural inclination is to search through the array column by column and row by row. A single row might be inspected with:

```
for every column in the row
   keep track of the largest value found;
```

Because we have many rows, we'd look at each in turn:

refinement

```
for each row
   for every column in the row
      keep track of the largest value found;
```

We'll rewrite the pseudocode with nested **for** statements. Notice that we cleverly initialize *Largest* to the least possible *integer* value, *−MAXINT*, since no legal value can be smaller.

largest-element procedure

```
procedure FindLargest (var Table: Grid);
   {Finds the largest element in a Grid-type array.}
   var Largest, Row, Column: integer;
   begin
      Largest := -MAXINT;
      for Row := -5 to 5 do
         for Column := 3 to 14 do
            if (Table[Row, Column] > Largest) then
               Largest := Table[Row, Column];
      writeln ('The largest value in Table is ', Largest:1)
   end; {FindLargest}
```

What happens if an array has three or more dimensions? Suppose that we want to study the way that space has been appropriated in a campus office building over the last decade or so. A ten-story building that has twenty offices available on each floor can be described with a two-dimensional array. For our purposes, though, a third dimension is required—time.

problem: initializing multi-dimensional arrays

```
const NUMBEROFOFFICES = 20;
      NUMBEROFFLOORS = 10;
      CURRENTYEAR = 1986;

type Departments = (Unassigned, Botany, Embroidery, Reeling, Writhing);
     Building = array [1..NUMBEROFOFFICES, 1..NUMBEROFFLOORS,
                       1970..CURRENTYEAR] of Departments;
```

In a preliminary survey of the building we'll mark each office *Unassigned*. This means that:

refinement

```
for each office
    for each floor
        for each year
            mark the office Unassigned;
```

Aside from the extra **for** loop, procedure *Empty* is much like procedure *FindLargest*.

multi-dimensional initializing procedure

```
procedure Empty (var TheBuilding: Building);
   {Assigns Unassigned to each element of TheBuilding.}
   var Office: 1..NUMBEROFOFFICES;
       Floor: 1..NUMBEROFFLOORS;
       Year: 1..CURRENTYEAR;
   begin
      for Office := 1 to NUMBEROFOFFICES do
         for Floor := 1 to NUMBEROFFLOORS do
            for Year := 1970 to CURRENTYEAR do
               TheBuilding[Office, Floor, Year] := Unassigned;
      writeln ('Building now ready for occupancy.')
   end; {Empty}
```

For manipulating arrays, a bottom-up approach can be just as valid as top-down. Recall that we discussed bottom-up programming earlier, in reference to using drivers to test modules of large programs. When it's used to deal with small programs, though, the bottom-up method can be described as: *Find the rule, then devise the algorithm*.

inductive leap

> The bottom-up approach often leads to an *inductive leap* to the solution of a problem.

This is just a fancy way of saying that if you look at a problem and its solution long enough, the exact chain of steps that turns a problem into a solution may suddenly jump into your mind. It's often called the 'aha!' method of problem solving.

problem: storing ordered values

For example, how can we initialize a two-dimensional array to this table of values?

```
 1  2  3  4
 5  6  7  8
 9 10 11 12
13 14 15 16
```

Let's make a definition and declaration:

type definition

```
type Matrix = array [1..4, 1..4] of integer;
var Board: Matrix;
```

Now, stare at the table above and examine the relationship between the coordinates of each array element, and the value it contains. Eventually, you'll say 'Aha! The value stored at row *i* and column *j* equals (4*(*i*−1))+*j*.' This formula is our rule. The assignment:

```
Board[i, j] := 4*(i-1) + j;
```

will be the centerpiece of any algorithm that initializes *Board*.

Initializing *Board* means that the assignment above must be made for every *i, j* combination within the array. Fortunately, this is a skill we already possess—we visited every element of a two-dimensional array in *FindLargest*. We'll modify it to perform the initialization.

ordered value storing procedure

```
procedure InitializeBoard (var Board: Matrix);
    {Initializes Board to a particular table of values.}
    var i, j: integer;
    begin
        for i := 1 to 4 do
            for j := 1 to 4 do
                Board[i, j] := 4*(i-1) + j;
    end; {InitializeBoard}
```

Programmers often use single-letter identifiers (traditionally starting with *i*) as array subscripts or **for** loop counter variables. Why? Well, orientation often changes unexpectedly in array manipulations—what once were rows are now columns, and vice versa. In such cases identifiers that are clearly abstract (like *i, j, k*), are superior to identifiers whose meaning is subject to misinterpretation by the program reader (say, *Height, Width, Depth*).

problem: array transposition

Let's copy the *Board* array to another *Matrix*-type variable. Instead of making a direct copy, though, we'll transfer values as shown below. (This is called *transposing* the array.)

Board				*Copy*			
1	2	3	4	1	5	9	13
5	6	7	8	2	6	10	14
9	10	11	12	3	7	11	15
13	14	15	16	4	8	12	16

Apply the bottom-up approach again. If you pencil in *i, j* coordinates you'll find that the rule is *reversal*. Each value stored in element *i, j* of *Board* moves to element *j, i* of *Copy*. Once again, we modify the nested **for** loops of *FindLargest*.

transposition procedure

```
procedure ReverseBoard (Board: Matrix; var Copy: Matrix);
   {Copy becomes a reversal of Board.}
   var i, j: integer;
   begin
      for i := 1 to 4 do
         for j := 1 to 4 do
            Copy[i, j] := Board[j, i]
   end; {ReverseBoard}
```

problem: array reflection

Our final rearrangement of *Board* will be to effect the transformation shown below.

Board now				*Board transformed*			
1	2	3	4	4	3	2	1
5	6	7	8	8	7	6	5
9	10	11	12	12	11	10	9
13	14	15	16	16	15	14	13

The transformed pattern above is a mirror-image or *reflection* of the original. But suppose that we want to rearrange *Board* itself, instead of copying it somewhere else. Try to come up with a rule, and its implementation. Then, compare your result to procedure *Reflect*, below.

reflection procedure

```
procedure Reflect (var Board: Matrix);
   {Reflects Board onto itself.}
   var i, j, Temporary: integer;
   begin
      for i := 1 to 4 do {For each horizontal row...}
         for j := 1 to 2 do begin {...for the first half of the row...}
            Temporary := Board[i, j]; {...switch the 1st and 4th,}
            Board[i, j] := Board[i, 4-j+1]; {and 2nd and 3rd, values.}
            Board[i, 4-j+1] := Temporary
         end          {The current row i has been reversed.}
   end; {Reflect}
```

Self-Check Questions

Q. In procedure *Reflect* , *j* only goes from 1 to 2—just half the row. Why don't we let *j* go all the way to 4? What will happen if we do?

A. Try tracing execution of *Reflect*. On any row, we first switch the first and last values, then the second and third values. So far, all is well. However, if we continue to switch values (third for second, and fourth for first) we'll simply put the row in its original order. Thus, we only switch values for half the row. If we let *j* go to 4, *Reflect* would have no effect.

Focus On Programming: Arrays 11-2

A BASIC EQUATION OF PROGRAMMING PROVIDES the title of one of Niklaus Wirth's textbooks: *Algorithms + Data Structures = Programs.* Now, an algorithm is the sequence of steps a program takes, but what is a data structure?

> A *data structure* is a set of rules for storing and manipulating data.

Just as a program's algorithm relies on the *statements* a programming language allows, its data structures are founded on the *data types* built into the language.

So far, we've taken a lopsided view of Wirth's equation by concentrating on algorithms. From now on, though, we'll devote more time to thinking about data type definitions, and their implications for data structures. We have three main reasons:

1. Many of the problems we'll encounter don't really need to be solved, in the sense of finding unknown answers. Their difficulty lies in *implementation*—defining appropriate data types, and using them with comparatively simple arithmetic or input and output routines.

importance of data structures

2. As the equation given above implies, there can be a trade-off between the complexity of an algorithm, and the data structures it uses. A sophisticated type definition can minimize the length and difficulty of a final program.
3. The character of an entire program can be changed by slight modifications of a data structure. Thus, data type definitions are more important than their size in a program listing implies.

An algorithm that compensates for a too-simple data structure can become unnecessarily complex and detailed. This is one basis of objections to languages like BASIC and FORTRAN. Although their control statements are comparable to Pascal's, their general lack of abstract data types (they only have arrays) forces programmers to waste time explaining data in terms the language can handle. It's no accident that computer journals and advanced programming texts usually show algorithms in some form of Pascal.

In this section we're going to look at several categories of problems whose solutions use data structures based on array types. In some cases we won't even go beyond the definition of a data type. These examples should indicate that there is no single array-type problem. As you read, notice how algorithms and data structure designs take advantage of different array features—random access, the ability to store different types of values, the ease with which all array elements can be visited, the option of calling for any number of dimensions, different applications of subscripts, etc. As you go along, it's also a good idea to mentally propose alternate types that accomplish the same ends as the ones we demonstrate.

Inventory

A classic application of arrays is inventory. In its simplest expression, we are told of a store that contains a row of bins or cubbyholes, numbered 1 through 10, each filled with some amount of stock.

```
type Inventory = array [1..10] of integer;
var Stock: Inventory;
```

As sales or stock figures come in we can update the inventory:

```
Stock[3] := Stock[3]-5;
```

Here, five units of product 3 have been sold. Is this a satisfactory system? Well, it might be if we were programming in 1956. To begin with, products have names—no manufacturer numbers her products 1 through 10. Fortunately, the abstract notion of an enumerated ordinal type comes to our rescue—we can name inventoried products. For the rest of this example we'll assume we're in the garment industry.

type definition

```
type Style = (Flares, StraightLeg, BellBottom, BootCut, Leisure, Chinos);
    Inventory = array [Flares..Chinos] of integer;
var Stock: Inventory;
```

This improvement moves us rapidly into the '60s. Although our data type lets us name styles of pants, it still doesn't reflect the real world. For instance, pants come in different waist sizes as well as styles. We should add a second dimension to the array:

expanded definition

```
type Style = (Flares, StraightLeg, BellBottom, BootCut, Leisure, Chinos);
    WaistSize = 25..48;
    Inventory = array [Flares..Chinos, 25..48] of integer;
var Stock: Inventory;
```

The data type now has a position for each style of pants in 24 different sizes. It stores a total of 144 values—six styles times 24 sizes.

How many pairs of pants do we have in stock—i.e. what is the sum of the stored values? Assuming *WaistSize* variable *CurrentSize*, *integer* variable *TotalCount*, and *Style*-type variable *CurrentStyle*, we can travel through the array and count.

summing array elements

```
{Count all waist sizes in each style.}
TotalCount := 0;
for CurrentStyle := Flares to Chinos do
   for CurrentSize := 25 to 48 do
      TotalCount := TotalCount+Stock[CurrentStyle, CurrentSize];
writeln ('Total stock is ', TotalCount:1, ' pairs of pants.');
```

Here is where we start to notice that our data type has become a data structure—the data type definition meshes with Pascal's basic algorithmic actions. We might just as easily, and correctly, go through it in sideways order:

alternative summing code

```
{Count all styles in each waist size.}
TotalCount := 0;
for CurrentSize := 25 to 48 do
   for CurrentStyle := Flares to Chinos do
      TotalCount := TotalCount+Stock[CurrentStyle, CurrentSize];
writeln ('Total stock is ', TotalCount:1, ' pairs of pants.');
```

Can the data structure be brought up to the 80's? Yes. In the old days, computer users (who had no knowledge of programming) frequently found themselves at the mercy of programmers who didn't understand business, and didn't care to learn. This resulted in programs more attuned to the programmer (or computer) than to the end user. Nowadays it's generally accepted that programs should be written to meet applications—requirements shouldn't have to be tailored to meet a programmer's whim. In fact, one reason for books like this is to teach people what they can expect from computers.

What does this have to do with pants? Our next step is to realize that pants come in different lengths, and are manufactured from a variety of materials. We'll declare new types *Length* and *Material*, and add another two dimensions to the array.

further expansion of the definition

```
type Style = (Flares, StraightLeg, BellBottom, BootCut, Leisure, Chinos);
     WaistSize = 25..48;
     Length = (Short, Medium, Long);
     Material = (Denim, Corduroy, Polyester, Cotton);
     Inventory = array [Flares..Chinos, 25..48,
                        Short..Long, Denim..Cotton] of integer;
var Stock: Inventory;
```

abstracting information

Now, declaring third and fourth dimensions for the *Stock* variable was an important conceptual step. We stored information about pants in the way we *perceived* it, instead of trying to mimic the appearance of pants on a shelf. We reached, and went beyond, the limit of an array as a literal picture of reality.

Although a one-dimensional array is close to our original row of bins or cubbyholes, a four-dimensional array only relates to the way we *think* about inventory. A four-dimensional show room cannot be constructed on a sales floor, but a type definition creates one within the computer. Finding the stock of boot-cut pants, size 34 medium, made of denim, requires a single statement:

```
writeln (Stock[BootCut, 34, Medium, Denim]);
```

We can quickly devise a function that counts and represents the number of pairs of pants of any given style and material. We go through the array as before, but keep two of the subscripts constant.

another element summer

```
function CountStyles (TheStyle: Style; TheMaterial: Material;
                      Stock: Inventory): integer;
  {Sums array elements.}
  var CurrentLength: Length;
      TotalCount: integer;
      CurrentSize: WaistSize;
  begin
    TotalCount := 0;
    for CurrentLength := Short to Long do
      for CurrentSize := 25 to 48 do
        TotalCount := TotalCount +
          Stock[TheStyle, CurrentSize, CurrentLength, TheMaterial];
    CountStyles := TotalCount
  end; {CountStyles}
```

A program might include the statement:

```
if CountStyles(BootCut, Denim, Stock)<(OriginalOrder–ExpectedSales) then
  writeln ('Sales of boot cut Denim pants are above expectations.');
```

We've discussed an inventory problem for several pages without ever mentioning an algorithm. Nonetheless, the problem is substantially solved because of our choice of data type. Any operation we're liable to want a program to perform—adding or diminishing stock, analyzing merchandise on hand, projecting sales or supplies—is easy to accomplish because of the manner in which we've structured our data.

Self-Check Questions

Q. Suppose we make this definition. How many elements does *Stock* have?

```
type Style = (Flares, StraightLeg, BellBottom, BootCut, Leisure, Chinos);
     WaistSize = 25..48;
     Length = (Short, Medium, Long);
     Material = (Denim, Corduroy, Polyester, Cotton);
     Inventory = array [Style, WaistSize, Length, Material] of integer;
var Stock: Inventory;
```

A. We've used the shorthand method to define *Inventory*. It stores 6 times 24 times 3 times 4 values, or a grand total of 1,728 *integers*.

Counting

Another popular array example (that varies with the season) is to impart organization to a collection of data values. In fall, we write programs that make predictions, hold elections, tabulate votes, and look for voter fraud. Come winter, we take examination scores, rank them, and decide who passes and who fails. In spring, baseball standings get figured out. Summer tends to be slow, devoted to searching for license plates, library books, and telephone numbers.

In any case, the notion of searching and sorting collections of values is widespread. We'll begin with a counting problem:

problem: count characters

> Count the number of characters in a text sample. Print a table of the frequency of the lower-case letters.

An analysis like this is usually the first step in code-breaking programs. This particular problem is intriguing because of the role array subscripts play. A starting pseudocode might be:

refinement

initialize counts;
while *there are characters to count*
    count each character;
    keep a running total;
for *every lower-case letter*
    print its relative frequency (*count/total*);

How can we use arrays to our advantage here? The last part of the pseudocode gives us a hint. Suppose that we had an array that stored *integers*, but used characters as its index values. We could initialize the array to zeros, then store the number of times ´a´ appeared in *CountArray*[´a´], the number of times ´b´ showed up in *CountArray*[´b´], etc. Each time we read a *Character*, we increment *CountArray*[*Character*] by one. Printing the count is just a matter of indexing through the ´a´..´z´ segment of the array.

Here's a type definition that lets us implement our pseudocode cleanly and easily:

type definition

type *CharacterArray* = **array** [*char*] **of** *integer*;

This creates an array type whose bounds are the first and last *char* values, whose elements are *integers*, and whose subscripts are the individual characters. With it, we can use the array element subscripted by a character to store the number of times that character appears as input. In program *CountTheCharacters*, below, we've assumed we're using the ASCII set of 128 characters.

character counting program

```
program CountTheCharacters (input, output);
    {Count input characters, print relative frequency of lower-case letters.}
const NUMBEROFCHARACTERS = 128;
type CharacterArray = array [char] of integer;
var CountArray: CharacterArray;
    Character: char;
    Letters,                {Letters counts lower-case letters.}
    Lines: integer;         {Lines counts lines for producing neat output.}
begin
    for Character := chr(0) to chr(NUMBEROFCHARACTERS-1) do
        CountArray[Character] := 0;  {Initialize the array.}
    Letters := 0;
    while not eof do begin  {Count all the character frequencies.}
        read (Character);
        if Character in ['a'..'z'] then Letters := Letters+1;
        CountArray[Character] := CountArray[Character]+1
    end; {while}
    Lines := 1;
    for Character := 'a' to 'z' do begin  {Print the output table.}
        write (Character, ' =');
        write ((CountArray[Character] / Letters)*100:6:2, '%   ');
        if (Lines mod 5) = 0 then writeln;
        Lines := Lines+1  {New-line every fifth write.}
    end; {for}
    writeln
end. {CountTheCharacters}
```

We had *CountTheCharacters* analyze its own listing, and got these results:

```
a =  9.90% b =  0.96% c =  5.11% d =  1.60% e = 13.90%
f =  2.24% g =  1.12% h =  4.95% i =  5.27% j =  0.00%
k =  0.00% l =  2.08% m =  0.64% n =  6.87% o =  5.11%
p =  1.44% q =  0.32% r = 14.22% s =  4.31% t = 12.14%
u =  3.83% v =  0.48% w =  1.28% x =  0.00% y =  1.76%
z =  0.48%
```

Searching

If counting things is a major theme of programming, then searching for them is certainly one of the primary minor chords. Let's consider some of the techniques we'll use in searching through arrays. For all our examples, we'll assume the following array type definitions:

basic definitions

```
type NumberArray = array [1..20] of integer;
     LetterArray = array [1..20] of char;
var Numbers: NumberArray;
    Letters: LetterArray;
```

In our first searches, we'll assume that we're dealing with arrays that are *unordered*. Later, we'll see a variety of methods that can be used if we know that an array's values are in numerical or alphabetical order.

problem: find the first 7

Find the position of the first 7 stored in *Numbers*.

Once we've found the 7 we can stop searching. Our code, then, would seem to have a simple exit condition—we search *Current* elements, one by one, until *Numbers[Current]* equals 7. But what if no 7 is found? Our *boolean* exit condition has to be a bit more complicated, as we see below:

```
Found := false;
Current := 0;
while (Current < 20) and not Found do begin
   Current := Current + 1;
   Found := Numbers[Current] = 7
end;
if Found then
   writeln ('The 7 was in position', Current);
```

When stated in this manner, our code avoids several potential search problems. We won't be thrown if there isn't any 7, or if the 7 is in the last position. We're not going to belabor this particular problem now, since the Antibugging section discusses the pitfalls associated with the simplest of searches.

Let's change the problem slightly:

problem: find the last 7

Find the position of the last 7 stored in *Numbers*.

This change will require a different strategy—and a different loop. Our first problem didn't necessarily require that we search the entire array, so we used a conditional loop. Now, though, we'll be looking at every value, so a **for** loop does the trick:

```
Position := 0;
for Current := 1 to 20 do
   if Numbers[Current] = 7 then
      Position := Current;
if Position <> 0 then
   writeln ('The last 7 was in position', Position);
```

Now, a clever reader might point out that we waste a great deal of effort following this approach, since we have to search the entire array. 'Why not just start from the end, and find the first value?,' she might reasonably ask. We'll use this approach to solve our next problem.

problem: non-blank length

Suppose that we have a series of words stored in array *Letters*. Find the length of the series—how many letters are stored?

It's tempting to think that we can start searching *Letters* from the beginning, with finding a blank space providing an exit condition. However, the problem statement mentions *words*—a series of letters interspersed with blanks. How do we know when we've reached the blank that marks the end?

The solution, of course, is to turn the problem around. Instead of starting with the first element and looking for a blank, we'll start with the very last element, and try to find a non-blank. The code is implemented as function *UsefulLength*. Note that, in this case, returning a length of 0 is a valid response.

non-blank length function

```
function UsefulLength (Letters: LetterArray): integer;
   {Finds the 'useful' (non-blank) length of Letters.}
   var Position: integer;
   begin
      Position := 20; {the length of Letters}
      while (Letters[Position]=' ') and (Position>1) do
         Position := Position - 1
      if Letters[Position]<>' '
         then UsefulLength := Position
         else UsefulLength := 0
   end; {UsefulLength}
```

When a list is unordered, a simple *linear search*, from one end to the other, is the only appropriate strategy. However, when a list is ordered, there are many more effective approaches.

problem: is the value present?

Suppose that *Numbers* is an ordered array of *integer* values. Is there an 8 stored in the array?

We'll write three different solutions to this simply stated problem. First, we'll encode a *linear search* that is quite similar to our search for the 7. In pseudocode, we have:

refinement

```
while we haven't seen a larger value
   move on to the next larger element;
```

When you read the code below, decide what the value of *Location* is if the value *isn't* found.

```
Location := 1;
Located := false;
while (Location < 20) and not Located do
   if Numbers[Location] >= 8
      then Located := true
      else Location := Location + 1;
Located := Numbers[Location] = 8;
```

Note that this search can be simplified considerably if we're sure that the number we're looking for is actually present. A common solution is to store the sought number in the last element of the array; in effect, as a sentinel. If you plan on using this method, define the original array with one extra element from the beginning. Then, we can dispense with the auxiliary *boolean* variable, and simply search until we find the sentinel value.

using a sentinel

Now, the linear search we just used worked its way toward the sought value one element at a time. It's not hard to imagine that we could find the value a bit faster if we could take larger jumps. This is the basis of the *quadratic search* algorithm:

quadratic search

refinement

```
pick a good jump size;
while the next jump won't take us too far
    take the next jump;
while single steps don't take us too far
    implement an ordinary linear search;
save the position if we've found the value;
```

The square root of the total length of the array turns out to be a convenient size for the big jumps (hence the name of the search—quadratic means square). In the code below, we will assume that the number we seek is *Value*, and that the length of the array is *MAX*.

quadratic search procedure

```
procedure Quadratic (Value: integer; Numbers: NumberArray;
                                          var Position: integer);
  {Quadratic search for Value. Position will be 0 if it's not found.}
  var Jump: integer;
      TooFar, Found: boolean;
  begin
    Jump := round (sqrt (MAX+1));
    Position := 1;
    TooFar := false;
    {Jump until we get close.}
    while not TooFar and ((Jump + Position) <= MAX) do
      if Numbers[Jump + Position] > Value
        then TooFar := true
        else Position := Position + Jump;
    {Now, single step to the value.}
    Found := false;
    while (Position < MAX) and not Found do
      if Numbers[Position] >= Value
        then Found := true
        else Position := Position + 1;
    {Finally, store a zero if we didn't find Value.}
    Found := Numbers[Position] = Value;
    if not Found then Position := 0
  end; {Quadratic}
```

Our final search method will not be given the analysis it deserves here, since we return to it in Chapter 16. It is the *binary search* algorithm, and is the fastest of the methods we've seen. While the quadratic search took jumps equal to the square root of the array's size, the binary search takes jumps up to half the size of the array.

binary search

Assuming, as we have been, that the array is ordered, we start by looking at the middle element. If it's too high, we look at the middle of the bottom half of the array, while if our guess is too low, we look at the middle of the top half. We repeat this step—'split the remainder'—until we find the value we want, or decide that it doesn't exist.

Binary search is the basic *divide and conquer* algorithm. You may wish to look at the number guess program we wrote in Chapter 7 for another example. It used binary search to find which number (in the range 1 through 100) we were thinking of. A typical series of guesses might be 50, 25, 37, 43, 40, 41, 42, which would imply guesses that are too high, low, low, high, low, low, and correct. In pseudocode, a first refinement of the binary search algorithm is:

divide and conquer

first refinement

repeat
    compute a guess
until *we find the value* **or** *decide to stop looking*;

How do we *compute a guess*? Well, we start by knowing the lower and upper bounds of the array, so adding them, then dividing by two, gives us a good starting 'middle.' The insight we need for computing successive middles is that, after each wrong guess, the old middle becomes the new lower or upper bound. In actual practice, we'll add or subtract 1 each time, since we've already checked the old middle. A second refinement is:

second refinement

get the lower and upper bounds;
repeat
    compute a middle;
    if *it's low*
        then *make it (plus 1) be the new lower bound*
        else *make it (minus 1) be the new upper bound*
until *we find the number* **or** *decide to stop looking*;
decide why we left the loop;

We've implemented the actual code as a function, below. Once more, we'll return the array position 0 if we can't find the value we're looking for. Note the clever method we use to decide when we've looked long enough—our lower and upper bounds will cross. Be sure you believe that this will actually happen before you leave the example behind.

the bounds may cross

binary search function

```
procedure Binary (Value: integer; Numbers: NumberArray;
                                var Position: integer);
  {Binary search for Value. Position will be 0 if it's not found.}
  var Midpoint, Left, Right: integer;
  begin
     Left := 1;
     Right := MAX;
     repeat
        Midpoint := (Left + Right) div 2;
        if Value < Numbers[Midpoint]
           then Right := Midpoint - 1
           else Left := Midpoint + 1
     until (Value = Numbers[Midpoint) or (Left > Right);
     if Value = Numbers[Midpoint]
        then Position := Midpoint
        else Position := 0
  end; {Binary}
```

Self-Check Questions

Q. In the best case, how many elements will have to be inspected to find a value hidden in an array using the methods described above?

A. Just one—the value could always be in the first place we look no matter which of the methods we use.

Q. In the worst case, how long will each search method (linear, quadratic, and binary) take? How many elements will have to be inspected to find the most hidden value, or a value that isn't there?

A. Since the linear search works one element at a time, its worst case time will be N for an N-element array. The quadratic search, at worst, will take square-root-of-N, less 1, big jumps, plus the same number of single steps. The worst case, then, is roughly twice the square root of N. The binary search algorithm has the best performance—only $log_2 N$ inspections in the worst case.

Strings

The word *string* is commonly used to describe a **packed array** of *char* elements used to hold text values. As noted earlier, string types have three advantages over ordinary array types:

string advantages

1. Strings can be compared alphabetically with the relational operators.
2. Strings can be output in their entirety, instead of one element at a time.
3. Strings can be assigned text constants all at once, rather than one element at a time.

string rules

Some simple rules apply to the definition of string types. First, they have to be **packed**. Second, their single subscript has to start with 1. Third and finally, they must store *char* values.

Strings aren't particularly difficult to work with, and their applications are so diverse that we're going to demonstrate some procedures for string operations—your time is better spent programming with strings than in trying to figure out *how* to. Program *OrderWords*, below, demonstrates the three main string operations—input, output, and comparison.

string demonstration program

```
program OrderWords (input, output);
   {Demonstrates input, output, and comparison of strings.}

const BLANK = '               '; {WORDLENGTH blank spaces}
      WORDLENGTH = 15;

type String = packed array [1..WORDLENGTH] of char;

var First, Second: String;

procedure ReadString (var Word: String);
   {Reads the first WORDLENGTH nonblank characters.}

   var Counter: integer;
       Character: char;

   begin
      Word := BLANK;
      Counter := 0;
      read (Character);
      while (Character<>' ') and (Counter<WORDLENGTH) do begin
         Counter := Counter+1
         Word[Counter] := Character;
         read (Character)
      end;
   end; {ReadString}

procedure WriteString (var Word: String);
   {Prints nonblank elements of Word.}

   var Counter: integer;

   begin
      Counter := 0;
      repeat
         Counter := Counter+1;
         if (Word[Counter]<>' ') then write (Word[Counter]);
      until (Word[Counter]=' ') or (Counter=WORDLENGTH)
      write (' ') {Put a blank after each string.}
   end; {WriteString}
```

```
begin {OrderWords}
   writeln ('Enter two words.');
   ReadString(First);
   ReadString(Second);
   writeln ('The words are ', First, ' and ', Second);
   writeln ('In alphabetical order the words are...');
   if First<Second
      then writeln (First, Second)
      else begin
         WriteString(Second);
         WriteString(First);
         writeln
      end
end. {OrderWords}
```

```
Enter two words.
Hello Goodbye
The words are Hello          and Goodbye
In alphabetical order the words are...
Goodbye Hello
```

string input

How do we program a computer to read a word? According to procedure *ReadString*, very carefully. We read one character at a time until we reach the end of the word (indicated by a blank character), or until the array of *WORDLENGTH* characters is filled. Since we initialized the string to all blanks at the beginning of the procedure, we need not change any remaining characters from a previous word to blanks. Furthermore, no matter how short the input word is, each value stored in the string array will be defined.

Reading characters one at a time, however tedious it may be, is the only way that text can be input to a string variable. Neither *read* nor *readln* can be used to read more than one character at a time.

string output

What about output of strings? There are really two methods. The first, implemented in procedure *WriteString*, roughly parallels *ReadString*. Characters are printed, one at a time, until we've printed all *WORDLENGTH* characters, or run out of nonblank characters to print.

A second method of string output is especially useful for making columns of words. It relies on a special rule of Pascal.

An array type that has been defined as a packed array of *char* values (as a string) may be output in its entirety using *write* or *writeln*.

Naturally, when strings are printed like this, any padding blanks that fill the remainder of the array are printed as well. As defined, variables *First* and *Second*, of type *String*, hold fifteen characters each. If *First* and *Second* store the strings 'Hello' and 'Goodbye' the blanks that follow the words will show up in output.

write (*Second*);
writeln (*First*);
writeln (*First, Second*);

```
   ↓     ↓     ↓     ↓     ↓
Goodbye        Hello
Hello          Goodbye
```

string assignment

Program *OrderWords* demonstrates only one of two methods for making assignments to string variables. We've already pointed out that a complete array assignment can be made between any arrays of *identical* types. The assignment:

First := *Second*;

is valid because *First* and *Second* are both of type *String*.

However, string types are unique in allowing text constants *of the proper length* to be honorary strings.

> A text constant with *n* characters may be assigned to a packed *char* array variable with *n* elements.

These two assignments have the exact same effect:

First := *BLANK*;
Second := '   ';

because a) *BLANK* and the fifteen blank spaces both represent sequences of fifteen *char* values, and b) for purposes of assignment, they are both compatible with values of type *String*.

string comparison

Program *OrderWords* makes one final point—string-type values can be compared with the relational operators (<, >, =, <=, >=, <>). The result of such a comparison depends on alphabetical order, according to the computer's collating sequence. When both upper and lower-case letters are involved, this can have unexpected consequences. For example, these words are in alphabetical ordering according to three different systems:

English ....Ant, art, ball, Bat
ASCII ....Ant, Bat, art, ball
EBCDIC.................art, ball, Ant, Bat

Many programs require the ordering of strings. A typical data type definition is:

```
type String = packed array [1..15] of char;
     WordList = array [1..100] of String;
var Word: String;
    Vocabulary: WordList;
```

We've just seen how to assign values to, and access the values of, variables like *Word*. The same rules of assignment and access hold when string values are the elements of an array.

```
Vocabulary[32] := Word;
for Counter := 1 to 100 do
   writeln (Vocabulary[Counter]); {Print the entire vocabulary list}
```

elements of two-dimensional arrays

How about making a direct assignment to one of the elements of one of the strings stored in *Vocabulary*? Suppose we want to store ´B´ as the fifth character of the twelfth word. There are two methods:

```
Vocabulary[12] [5] := ´B´;
Vocabulary[12, 5] := ´B´;
```

As you can see, the first method is a logical application of the array method of access—we patiently access each array in turn. The second method is another of Pascal's shorthands; it recognizes that the definition of *Vocabulary* is tantamount to that of a two-dimensional array. Both are equally correct.

enumerated ordinal output

In Chapter 9 we mentioned that strings can be used to fake the output of enumerated ordinal values (which cannot be written directly). For example, *Monday, Tuesday, Wednesday*, etc. might be constants of an enumerated ordinal type, but 'Monday', 'Tuesday', 'Wednesday', etc. are the English words we use to describe them. We can print the names of each constant with a cute technique—the string table—thought up by the first Pascal programmer.

To Build A String Table...

First, define an enumerated ordinal type and a string type. Then, create an array that is subscripted by the enumerated ordinal type, but whose elements belong to the string type.

Each enumerated ordinal value will be the subscript of a string—the English word we associate with the ordinal value. For example, suppose that we make the following definitions and declarations:

```
type DayWords = (Monday, Tuesday, Wednesday, Thursday,
                                   Friday, Saturday, Sunday);
     String = packed array [1..9] of char;
     StringArray = array [DayWords] of String;
var Today: DayWords;
    WordTable: StringArray;
```

By suitably initializing the *WordTable* array, we can use it to print the English representation of the *DayWords* type variable *Today*. This is a fairly common application, and you should understand it.

string tables

```
   {Initialize the array.}
WordTable[Monday] := 'Monday   ';
WordTable[Tuesday] := 'Tuesday  ';
WordTable[Wednesday] := 'Wednesday';
WordTable[Thursday] := 'Thursday ';
WordTable[Friday] := 'Friday   ';
WordTable[Saturday] := 'Saturday ';
WordTable[Sunday] := 'Sunday   ';
   {Demonstrate how it works.}
for Today := Monday to Sunday do
   writeln ('Today is ', WordTable[Today]);
```

↓ ↓ ↓ ↓ ↓

Today is Monday
Today is Tuesday
Today is Wednesday
Today is Thursday
Today is Friday
Today is Saturday
Today is Sunday

The same method also simulates the input of enumerated ordinal values. Begin by reading in the string, then search through the string table for an equal (i.e. identical) string. The index of that stored string is the ordinal constant equivalent to the input string. In Chapter 13 we'll see how to use files as an easier way to initialize the array.

Arrays and Text Processing

The text processing programs we dealt with in Chapter 8 were limited in a very fundamental way. They treated text as a stream of characters that could be modified in passing, but could not be saved for later perusal. As a result, we could exchange the values of two characters, but changing the order of two lines was beyond our power.

Using arrays for text processing will change all that. We'll find that we're able to do text *editing*, and can manipulate words or lines as easily as characters or numbers. We'll state our problem like this:

problem: text editing

> Define a data type suitable for a text editing program. Create commands that would be useful for basic editing or formatting functions—centering, deleting text, moving or copying, etc.

A plain top-down approach to this problem seems reasonable. However, instead of dividing the editor into modules—separate commands—

and designing and implementing each one individually, let's try a different technique: writing *primitives*.

> A *primitive* procedure is a low-level, special-purpose subcommand that can be used by different program modules.

primitives

We'll use the primitives to implement the subtasks that our modules will ultimately require. If we design primitives carefully, we'll find that each module is just a series of calls to primitive procedures. In contrast, we might find that too rigid an adherence to stepwise refinement could lead us to considerable duplicated effort.

Looking for, and writing, primitives is a useful approach in programs (like text editors) that have many similar commands. Instead of developing a series of nearly identical modules, we try to break each module down into underlying subcommands that may never be explicitly requested in the problem statement. An awareness of the potential of primitives is important as an alternative to strictly modular program development.

Our first programming consideration, though, is a data type definition. Suppose that we limit our editor to files *MAXLINES* lines long, with *MAXCHARS* characters allowed on each line. We'll keep the actual values low for now, so that we can print all our stored data on a single 'screen' during debugging.

data type limits

```
const MAXLINES = 20;
      MAXCHARS = 50;
```

It's pretty obvious that we'll want to represent our data as a two-dimensional array. However, we have two choices of how to do it. We can define a straightforward array:

```
type Sheet = array [1..MAXCHARS, 1..MAXLINES] of char;
var Whole: Sheet;
```

Or we can make the definition in a more roundabout way:

```
type Line = packed array [1..MAXCHARS] of char;
     Page = array [1..MAXLINES] of Line;
var Work: Page;
```

array of *char* vs. **array of** *Line*

What's the difference between these data types? They both define two-dimensional arrays, and each stores the same number of characters. We can use the same doubly nested **for** loop to travel through either, and, by changing the values of our constants, we can change the size of each array just as easily. Superficially, the two types are the same; at first glance, variable *Whole* and *Work* seem interchangable.

advantages of *Page*

As a data structure, though, the *Page* type definition, used to define *Work*, will turn out to be considerably more convenient. Defining our type as a one-dimensional array of lines, instead of as a two-dimensional array of characters, lets us take advantage of Pascal string capabilities. We'll be thinking about our data in a line-oriented way (for printing, moving, copying, deleting, etc.). When each line is a string, we can print, move, copy, or delete the line in its entirety in a single stroke. If we have to work on a single line of the array, it can be passed as an argument to a procedure, without dragging the rest of the array along.

Let's turn to primitives. Suppose that we have a two-dimensional array *Work* of type *Page*, above. Imagine some of the things we'd want to do to a single line:

delete part of the line;
delete its contents entirely;
center the line;
shift the line to obtain a ragged right or left margin;
number the line;

Now comes the hard part. Can we boil this group of possibilities down to a handful of primitive? Well, the basic piece of information we need to know is the length of the text portion on each line. We wrote an appropriate function (*UsefulLength*) a while back. Let's redo it as a procedure:

length-finding primitive

```
procedure FindLength (ThisLine: Line; var Length: integer);
  {Finds the 'useful' (non-blank) length of ThisLine.}
  var Position: integer;
  begin
    Position := MAXCHARS; {the length of ThisLine}
    while (ThisLine[Position]=' ') and (Position>1) do
      Position := Position - 1
    if ThisLine[Position]<>' '
      then Length := Position
      else Length := 0
  end; {FindLength}
```

We'll also need to be able to delete individual characters on the line:

blanking primitive

```
procedure Blank (var ThisLine: Line; Start, Finish: integer);
  {Replace elements Start through Finish with blanks.}
  var Current: integer;
  begin
    for Current := Start to Finish do
      ThisLine[Current] := ' '
  end; {Blank}
```

Finally, we'll need to be able to shift a sequence of characters within the line. This wouldn't seem to be to hard, but a problem may arise if we're not careful. We have to be sure that we don't move a character into an element that we haven't yet moved, but nevertheless intend to move soon. For instance, imagine shifting 'ABC ' one element to the right. We have to shift 'C', then 'B', then 'A'. If we move 'A' first, we'll screw up the rest of the move.

Procedure *ShiftRight*, below, takes care of our moving problem—but only if we want to move characters to the right. As you read, try to figure out how we might have written a procedure that shifts equally well both ways.

```
procedure ShiftRight (var ThisLine: Line; Start, Finish, Distance: integer);
   {Shift elements Start through Finish right by Distance.}
   var Current: integer;
   begin
      for Current := Finish downto Start do
         ThisLine[Current+Distance] := ThisLine[Current]
   end; {ShiftRight}
```

shifting primitive

Now that we have three primitives at our disposal, it's not hard to implement the other commands we imagined. Assume that we're dealing with the *Current* line of the *Work* array. Deleting a line is taken care of with:

the delete command

```
Blank (Work[Current], 1, MAXCHAR);
```

Shifting a line to the right takes a series of calls.

the right-adjust command

```
FindLength (Work[Current], Length);
ShiftRight (Work[Current], 1, Length, MAXCHARS-Length);
Blank (Work[Current], 1, MAXCHARS-Length);
```

Centering involves exactly the same sequence of primitives—only the arguments change:

the centering command

```
FindLength (Work[Current], Length);
ShiftRight (Work[Current], 1, Length, (MAXCHARS-Length) div 2);
Blank (Work[Current], 1, (MAXCHARS-Length) div 2);
```

Numbering a line will also involve calls of our primitives. We make sure that a number (say, two digits long, plus a blank) will fit, then make room for it. The code below stops at the point of adding the number to the beginning of the line.

the numbering command

```
FindLength (Work[Current], Length);
if (MAXCHARS-Length) >= 3 then begin
   ShiftRight (Work[Current], 1, Length, 3);
   Blank (Work[Current], 1, 3);
   {actually insert the number}
      ...
end;
```

The same approach—thinking about the primitives that underly commands—pays off with two-dimensional problems. Assume that our array is filled with text from line 1 through 20, but that we want to remove lines 6 through 15 (a total of 10 lines). Stop for a moment, and try to describe the command *delete 6, 15* as a sequence of primitives.

Obviously we'll want to fill lines 6 through 15 with blank characters. But that's not enough for a text editor—we have to move lines 16 through 20 down into the breach. This move will actually take two steps. First, we'll copy line 16 to 6, 17 to 7, and so on. Then, we'll have to fill 16 through 20 with blanks. If we don't take the last step, we'll have two copies of the last 5 lines of the array—lines 6 through 10 will be identical to 16 through 20.

deleting lines

How many primitives have we discovered? Two—a line blanking primitive, and one for shifting lines down. As a sequence of primitives, the delete command is:

the delete command

LineBlank (6, 15);
ShiftDown lines 16 to 20 by 10 lines;
LineBlank (16, 20);

Draw a picture in the margin if you can't follow this sequence.

Why bother with the first *LineBlank*? Well, even though it's not really necessary (we could just *ShiftDown* over the lines we want to delete) it's useful as an antibugging technique. If we wanted to, we could print the contents of the data array after each step to make sure we were doing the right thing. If we were to imagine a call of a *Delete* procedure, complete with arguments, it might be:

Delete (*Start, Finish, TotalLength*);

What about copying text? After the deletions above, we have information on lines 1 through 10. Suppose that we want to make an extra copy of lines 1 through 5 on the lines following line 7. We'll need to make room for the new lines (by shifting lines 8 through 10 up, out of harm's way), and then make the copies line by line. In primitive terms, we have:

the copy command

ShiftUp lines 8 through 10 by 5 lines;
LineBlank (8, 12);
Duplicate 1 through 5 into 8 through 12;

The *ShiftUp* primitive is similar to our earlier *ShiftDown*, while *Duplicate* is really a brand new primitive. Were we to imagine a call of a *Copy* procedure, complete with arguments, it would look like this:

Copy (*Start, Finish, AfterLine, TotalLength*);

How about moving lines? Let's move lines 4 through 7 to a new home following line 10. Assume that (after our previous set of moves) we have a total of 15 lines. We make room for lines 4 through 7, then copy them to their new home. Once the copy is completed, we delete the original lines 4 through 7. Finally, lines 7 on are moved down to fill the space vacated by the original 4 through 7. In terms of primitives, we have:

the move command

ShiftUp lines 11 though 15 by 4 lines;
LineBlank (11, 14);
Duplicate 4 through 7 into 11 through 14;
LineBlank (4, 7);
ShiftDown lines 8 through 19 by 4 lines;
LineBlank (16, 19);

Are you still with us? Again, some scribbling in the margin might help. Note that a move doesn't require any additional primitives. In fact, it's really the combination of two earlier commands:

Copy (4, 7, 10, *TotalLength*);
Delete (4, 7, *TotalLength*);

Since the number of lines of text stored in the array changes from call to call, we find that a *TotalLength* variable is passed each time. Were we to write the *Move* command as a procedure call, we'd have:

Move (*Start, Finish, AfterLine, TotalLength*);

text input to arrays

Now that we have the hang of developing primitives, let's take a brief look at some code. In particular, we'll see about getting data in the first place. Our problem is to read in text while preserving its line structure. It's tempting to use the standard text processing model:

```
while not eof do begin
   while not eoln do begin     etc.
```

But suppose that we have more than *MAXCHAR* characters on one input line, or more than *MAXLINE* lines in all? Our program would crash at an attempted illegal array access. We have to incorporate checks for these statutory limits into our code. First we have a procedure for reading a single line:

single line input procedure

```
procedure LoadLine (var ThisLine: Line);
   {Read a line of text into ThisLine.}
   var Count: integer;
   begin
      ThisLine := BLANK;
      Count := 0;
      while not eoln and (Count <MAXCHARS) do begin
         Count := Count + 1;
         read (ThisLine[Count])
      end
   end; {LoadLine}
```

Procedure *LoadEditor*, below, uses *LoadLine*. Note that in addition to loading our main array, it also returns the count of how many lines were read in—the useful length of our data structure.

multiple line input procedure

```
procedure LoadEditor (var Data: Page; var TotalLength: integer);
   {Initialize the main data structure. Also returns the number of lines read.}
   begin
      TotalLength := 0;
      while not eof and (Length < MAXLINES) do begin
         TotalLength := TotalLength + 1;
         LoadLine (Data[TotalLength]);
         readln
      end
   end; {LoadEditor}
```

Recursive Array Programming 11-3

A LARGE NUMBER OF INTERESTING PROGRAMMING problems involve recursive array manipulation. The array is useful because it stores large amounts of data, while recursion is handy because it lets our manipulation of the data be described easily. In this section we'll look at problems that involve using recursion to inspect or modify the contents of an array.

The recursion we'll be using here differs from the examples presented in Chapter 7 in an interesting way. Back then, we used recursion to solve problems that were stated 'one dimensionally,' so to speak. We would recursively progress along one particular path until we found the end of the sentence (or evaluated an expression, or reached the beginning or end of a series). Then, we'd tumble all the way back to the start of the sequence of recursive calls, and the program would be finished.

Now, though, we'll use recursion to allow algorithms that require movement in several 'dimensions,' some of which may be false starts, and others of which might help lead in the right direction.

backtracking algorithms

> *Backtracking* algorithms involve a series of trial and error solutions. We travel toward a solution until we know we're heading in the wrong direction, then backtrack to where we think we took the incorrect turn. Then, we try again.

The children's game of 'Hot and Cold' uses a classic backtracking algorithm. One player takes guesses as to what the second player is thinking of. The second player tells the first if a guess is hot (close) or cold (far from the truth). Since in-between degrees of warmth are allowed (warmer, cooler, 'now you're practically boiling to death!' etc.), the first player is continually guessing and backtracking.

Backtracking algorithms are particularly suited to recursive programming methods. Each recursive call creates a context, or environment, associated with one step toward a solution. The sequence of steps that got us there is preserved in the series of recursive calls. Were we to look at the

* This section is optional, of course.

'stack' of recursive calls, we'd generally find it growing and shrinking repeatedly as we search further toward—or back away from—potential solutions.

Maze Searching

Searching through a maze is an ideal problem for recursive solution. We'll state the problem like this:

problem: maze searching

> Imagine that you are trapped in the center of a maze. Find all paths to the outside world.

We'll assume that the maze is given to us as a pattern of asterisks (marking walls) and blanks (marking potential paths). We'll always start in position 6,6. For example, this is a 12 by 12 maze, with our starting position (at 6,6) marked with a '!':

```
*** ********        *** ********
***    *****        ***!!!!*****
*** **  ****        ***!**!!****
***   *  ***        ***!!!*!!***
***** ** ***        *****!**!***
*****!** ***        *****!**!***
***** ******        ***** ******
*****   ****        *****   ****
****  * ****        ****  * ****
*   **  ****        *   **  ****
* *    *****        * *    *****
* **********        * **********
```

The maze — *A false path*

First, let's agree on our representation of the maze. We can store the maze as a two-dimensional array of *char* that goes from 1 to *MAXCOL* horizontally, and from 1 to *MAXROW* vertically. When we initially read in our data, we'll put a * in each 'wall' location, and leave potential paths blank. As we search the maze, we'll mark each step with a '!'. We'll know that we're at an exit if we find ourselves on row 1 or *MAXROW*, or at column 1 or *MAXCOL*. Our Pascal type definition is:

data type definition

> **type** *ArrayType* = **array** [1..*MAXROW*, 1..*MAXCOL*] **of** *char*;
> **var** *Maze*: *ArrayType*;

Now, how does one get out of a maze? Well, if you're Theseus, you trail a string behind you on the way in, then trace it back out again. Even if you don't have any string, a simple rule—stick to one wall, and always turn right—will eventually get you out of the maze.

Working with a computer, though, imposes certain limitations. Perhaps there's no Minotaur chasing us, but there's no string, either. Moreover, the path may be too narrow for a 'stick to a wall' rule. We may not be able to turn right, and if we reach a dead end, we'll have to back out (as shown in the right-hand illustration, above). We're more in the position of the monster than of Theseus!

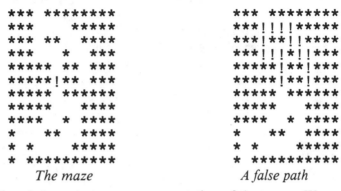

Fortunately, the phrase 'back out' gives us a hint. Recall that one effect of recursive procedure calls is to create a stack of partially executed subprograms. Each one can have variables and pending statements associated with it. If each step down a path involves a recursive procedure call—building the stack—we can also imagine that exiting the sequence of procedure calls will back us out along our original path.

using the recursive stack

How can we state a maze searching method recursively? Let's try some inductive thinking as a warmup exercise. Suppose that we're one step away from an exit. Can we get to the door? Sure—just take one step in any direction. It may take several tries (once in each direction) but we'll certainly find the way out.

using induction

Suppose that we're two steps away. Can we get to the spot that's only one step away? For sure again, even though it may take us a few tries. Now comes the clever step—our inductive leap. What if we're N steps away? Can we get to be one step away? Of course. No matter what N starts at, we can always get to $N-1$. Since N keeps going down, it will eventually reach 2, and we'll be home free. No matter how many steps away we are, we can always get to a position we're sure we know how to solve.

Being clever was easy compared to our next task—stating our algorithm recursively:

first refinement

To search a maze (from the current spot)...
mark the current spot as part of the way out;
if *we're at the exit, print the maze*
  else *search a maze (from a new starting position)*;

We've added a new step to the mental warmup we worked on. Each time we call the *search a maze* procedure we mark our present position. The maze itself is passed as a value parameter to each call of the procedure. Note that the path of positions we've marked grows one step longer on each call. You can think of it as a snapshot of our current state—where we are, and how we got there.

The key to the algorithm is finding the new starting position. If we can—if there's no wall there—we'll *search a maze* starting one step to the left. Then, if we can, we'll *search a maze* starting one step up. Then we'll search to the right, and finally down, each time making sure that we're not running into a wall. The shaded section below corresponds to the **else** part shaded above:

second refinement

To search a maze (from the current spot)...
mark the current spot as part of the way out;
if *we're at the exit, print the maze*
  else if *we can, search a maze (starting one step left)*;
    if *we can, search a maze (starting one step up)*;
    if *we can, search a maze (starting one step right)*;
    if *we can, search a maze (starting one step down)*;

Once more, the maze, with our current position marked on the pathway out, is passed as a value parameter to the *search a maze* procedure. In effect, we are always searching a maze that has already been partially searched. The computer maintains a stack of copies of the maze—one for each of the partially completed procedure calls. Each copy shows the path that led to that particular location. If we're at the exit, the current copy of the maze shows the way out.

If we don't get to an exit, nothing happens at all. Suppose we take a left turn into a dead end. Since we can't go left, forward, or right, that particular invocation of the procedure ends, and its copy of the maze (with an incorrect path out) is removed. The completed program is shown below.

maze searching program

```
program ThreadTheMaze (input, output);
  {Recursively find and print all exit paths from a maze.}
const MAXROW = 12;
      MAXCOL = 12;
      POSSIBLEPATH = ' ';
      THEWAYOUT = '!';
type ArrayType = array [1..MAXROW, 1..MAXCOL] of char;
var Maze: ArrayType;
procedure StoreTheMaze (var Maze: ArrayType);
  {Reads in the maze.}
  var i,j: integer;
  begin
    for i := 1 to MAXROW do begin
      for j := 1 to MAXCOL do read (Maze[i, j]);
      readln
    end
  end; {StoreTheMaze}
procedure PrintTheMaze (Maze: ArrayType);
  {Print the maze contents, showing the exit path.}
  var i,j: integer;
  begin
    for i := 1 to MAXROW do begin
      for j := 1 to MAXCOL do write (Maze[i, j]);
      writeln
    end;
    writeln {Space between solutions.}
  end; {PrintTheMaze}
function AtAnExit (row, col: integer): boolean;
  {Tells whether or not we are on the border of the maze.}
  begin
    AtAnExit := (row in [1, MAXROW]) or (col in [1, MAXCOL])
  end; {AtAnExit}
```

procedure *ExploreTheMaze* (*Maze*: *ArrayType*; *Row*, *Col*: *integer*);
  {Recursive procedure for searching the maze.}
  begin
    Maze [*Row*, *Col*] := *THEWAYOUT*;
    if *AtAnExit* (*Row*, *Col*)
      then *PrintTheMaze* (*Maze*)
      else begin
        if *Maze* [*Row*−1, *Col*] = *POSSIBLEPATH* **then**
          ExploreTheMaze (*Maze*, *Row*−1, *Col*);
        if *Maze* [*Row*, *Col*+1] = *POSSIBLEPATH* **then**
          ExploreTheMaze (*Maze*, *Row*, *Col*+1);
        if *Maze* [*Row*+1, *Col*] = *POSSIBLEPATH)* **then**
          ExploreTheMaze (*Maze*, *Row*+1, *Col*);
        if *Maze* [*Row*, *Col*−1] = *POSSIBLEPATH)* **then**
          ExploreTheMaze (*Maze*, *Row*, *Col*−1)
      end {**else**}
  end; {*ExploreTheMaze*}

begin
  StoreTheMaze (*Maze*);
  ExploreTheMaze (*Maze*, 6, 6) {We start in the center of the maze.}
end. {*ThreadTheMaze*}

```
*** ********
***    *****
*** **  ****
***   *  ***
***** ** ***
***** ** ***
***** ******
*****   ****
****  * ****
*   **  ****
* *    *****
* **********
```

the input maze

```
***!********
***!    *****
***!**  ****
***!!!*  ***
*****!** ***
*****!** ***
***** ******
*****   ****
****  * ****
*   **  ****
* *    *****
* **********
```

```
*** ********
***    *****
*** **  ****
***   *  ***
***** ** ***
*****!** ***
*****!******
*****!!!****
****  *!****
*!!!**!!****
*!*!!!!*****
*!**********
```

The Eight Queens Problem

One of the best known examples of backtracking in programming is the *Eight Queens* problem. It's simply stated:

problem: eight queens

> A queen can move in any direction—vertically, horizontally, or diagonally—on a chessboard. Is it possible to place eight queens on a board so that no queen endangers another? How?

It turns out that the problem has many solutions. Our busy friend Gauss attacked the problem in 1850 (when he was 73), but he wasn't able to find all of them (so at last we'll be able to surpass him!). How can we go about approaching it?

working by hand

Let's imagine that we're trying to solve the eight queens problem by hand. We get a chessboard, and eight pieces to use as queens. Almost immediately we can realize that the board should be divided into eight columns. Since we can't have more than one queen in any column (because that would endanger her), we try placing one queen in each.

the solution space

How many different ways can eight queens be put in eight columns? Since each queen can go to eight 'row' positions, the total number of different boards is 16,777,216 (8^8). An exhaustive search of this huge solution space might be a little too tedious even for a computer. Fortunately, it's not hard to see how to avoid checking most of them: As soon as we find a single bad row position, we'll stop looking at possible boards that incorporate that position. Let's look at an example.

limiting the solution space

Positioning the first queen is easy—she goes to the top of the first column. The second queen is a bit harder. The top row of the second column is out (that would put two queens on the same row), as is the second row (that would put two queens on the same diagonal). Our third try works, though, and we have two safely positioned queens. Note that, by not bothering to check any of the boards that start out with two queens in the top row or on the first diagonal, we avoid checking 524,288 ($2*8^6$) illegal positions. We've begun to limit our solution space very successfully.

Putting a queen in the third row isn't much harder. Again, the top position is out, since the first queen guards the top row. The third row is out because we've just put the second queen there. The second and fourth positions aren't any good either—diagonal problems with the second queen. We end up putting the third queen five rows down.

Let's jump ahead. The board on the left, below, shows the positions of the first five queens. Where will the sixth queen go? Stop for a second and try to figure out what to do next.

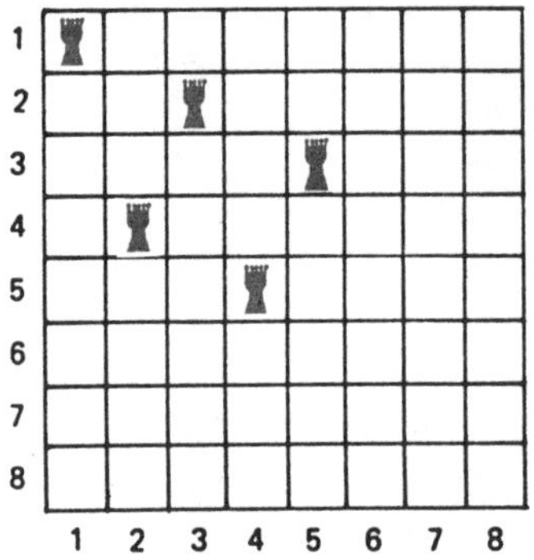

We're stuck

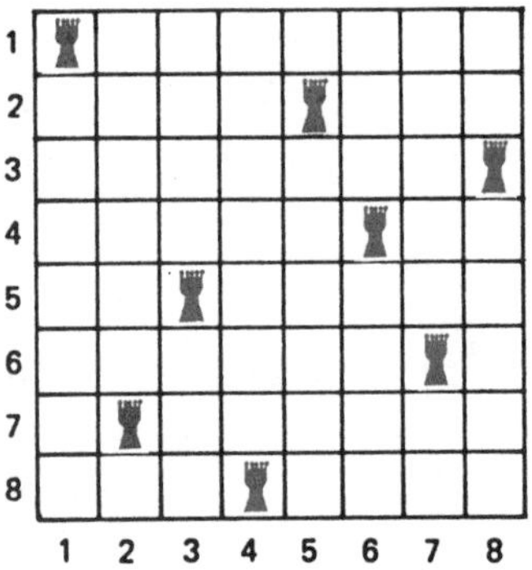

A solution

backtracking

Inspection will show that the sixth queen can't go anywhere without being taken by another queen. What do we do now? It's time for a second clever step—backtracking. We backtrack one step (by putting the fifth queen down a row), and try again.

An actual solution to the problem is shown, above, at the right. If you compare the solution to our starting position, you'll see that we've had to back up many times. The fifth queen isn't the only one that's been repositioned. In fact, only the very first queen is still in its original starting place.

Now, our mental exercise has given us two clues to a computer solution. First, we limit our solution space by ending one line of search whenever we reach a bad board. Second, we backtrack to a previous position whenever we get stuck at a dead end.

How far will we have to backtrack? Sometimes simply repositioning the queen in the previous column will suffice. We won't always be able to reposition, though, since a queen may eventually reach the eighth position in its column. If this happens we'll have to backtrack two or more columns, until we get to a queen that can be moved.

why use recursion?

As we've found earlier, the need for backtracking leads us toward a solution that uses a recursive stack. Although we may work on a single board (a global *Board* variable that's passed as a variable parameter) we stack our individual moves through a series of recursive calls. Each call represents one queen placement; but before the call ends, we'll pick the queen up, and return to a previous board layout.

Let's move on to the hard part of solving the Eight Queens problem—a recursive statement of our queen-positioning algorithm.

first refinement

```
to put a queen in column (N)...
  repeat
    try to put a queen in the current row;
    if it worked, put a queen in column (N+1);
    remove the last queen we set down;
    advance to the next row in this column
  until we get to the eighth row;
```

The shaded portion is our recursive call. Each call is temporarily suspended whenever we're able to legally place a queen. As a result, a long series of 'remove the queen and advance to the next row' statements remains stacked.

Let's look at a second refinement. This time, we'll deal with more of the bookkeeping details—when do we stop advancing? when do we have a solution? etc.

second refinement

```
to put a queen in column (N)...
  repeat
    if the current row is safe then
      place the queen;
      if we're not in the eighth column yet
        then put a queen in column (N+1)
        else print the board—we have a solution;
      remove the queen;
    advance to the next row in this column
  until we get to the eighth row
```

determining safe positions

Let's consider the shaded section of our second refinement. How do we know when a position is safe? It's easy enough to do this by eye—we just look down the row or diagonal for another queen—but how can we store the same information in a program? It's time once more for an Aha! solution. Obviously we won't want to search the entire row or diagonal every time, so try to think of a simple means of putting an entire row or column off limits.

Well, let's suppose that we number the rows 1 through 8. It's not hard to imagine a *Safe* array of eight *boolean* values—each one representing an entire row—that's initially *true*, but can be set to *false* whenever we put a queen in the appropriate row.

Diagonals are a little bit tougher until we have a crucial insight. Imagine that each row, column position is an i, j coordinate. It turns out that every position in a given left-leaning diagonal has the same $i+j$ sum, while each position in a particular right-leaning diagonal has the same $i-j$ difference. How lucky for us! We can check any position's safety by looking at single elements from three arrays—one for the row, and one for each diagonal. (We assume that we'll never even try to put two queens in the same vertical column.)

The completed program is shown below. As you read it, try to imagine a sequence of recursive calls. It helps to start out in a deliberately bad position—stuck at the end of a column, say—that will require a sequence of backtrack steps. It is also an excellent exercise to try to state the program nonrecursively. The problem has 92 possible solutions, but we've only shown the first 3.

eight queens program

```
program EightQueens (input, output);
  {Recursive solution to the Eight Queens problem.}

type Play = array [1..8, 1..8] of boolean;
     RowCheck = array [1..8] of boolean;
     LeftDiagonalCheck = array [2..16] of boolean;
     RightDiagonalCheck = array [-7..7] of boolean;

var Board: Play;
    SafeRow: RowCheck;
    SafeLeftDiag: LeftDiagonalCheck;
    SafeRightDiag: RightDiagonalCheck;
    Row, Column, i: integer;

function Safe (Row, Col: integer; SafeRow: RowCheck;
                    SafeLeftDiag: LeftDiagonalCheck;
                         SafeRightDiag: RightDiagonalCheck): boolean;
  {true if a queen can be safely placed in the current position.}
  begin
    Safe := SafeRow[Row] and SafeLeftDiag[Row+Col]
                              and SafeRightDiag[Row-Col]
  end; {Safe}

procedure Print (Board: Play);
  {Print the current board layout.}
  var i,j: integer;
  begin
    for i := 1 to 8 do begin
      for j := 1 to 8 do
        if Board[i,j] then write ('Q') else write ('*');
      writeln
    end; {outer for}
    writeln {Space between solutions.}
  end; {Print}
```

```
procedure TryColumn (Column: integer; var Board: Play);
   {Recursive procedure for attempting queen placement.}

   var Row: integer;

   begin
      Row := 1;
      repeat
         if Safe (Row, Column, SafeRow, SafeLeftDiag, SafeRightDiag) then begin
            SafeRow[Row] := false; {set the queen}
            SafeLeftDiag[Row+Column] := false;
            SafeRightDiag[Row-Column] := false;
            Board[Row, Column] := true;
            if Column < 8
               then TryColumn (Column+1, Board)
               else Print (Board);
            SafeRow[Row] := true; {remove the queen}
            SafeLeftDiag[Row+Column] := true;
            SafeRightDiag[Row-Column] := true;
            Board[Row, Column] := false
         end; {the row was safe}
         Row := Row + 1;
      until Row > 8
   end; {TryColumn}

begin
   for Row := 1 to 8 do SafeRow[Row] := true; {initialize}
   for i := 2 to 16 do SafeLeftDiag[i] := true;
   for i := -7 to 7 do SafeRightDiag[i] := true;
   for Row := 1 to 8 do
      for Column := 1 to 8 do
         Board [Row,Column] := false;
   TryColumn (1, Board) {make the first recursive call}
end. {EightQueens}
```

```
Q*******
******Q*
****Q***
*******Q
*Q******
***Q****
*****Q**
**Q*****
```

```
Q*******
******Q*
***Q****
*****Q**
*******Q
*Q******
****Q***
**Q*****

Q*******
*****Q**
*******Q
**Q*****
******Q*
***Q****
*Q******
****Q***
```

Antibugging and Debugging 11-4

WHEN IT COMES TO BUGS, THE ARRAY TYPE can be relied on to separate the engineers from the poets. Although dealing with single array elements is usually mastered in short order, the systematic processing that most arrays require involves thinking on a different wavelength entirely. In other words, don't be too alarmed if you feel that you just weren't cut out to understand arrays. You may not have been.

array searching bugs

Certain bugs inevitably turn up during array processing. A classic problem that's been the subject of many articles involves searching an array for a value that might not be present. For example, suppose we define a variable *TheArray* as an **array** [1..20] **of** *integer*. The following program segment is intended to find the subscript of the stored value 0 (zero).

```
{incorrect segment}
Counter := 1;
while TheArray[Counter]<>0 do
    Counter := Counter+1;
writeln ('A zero is stored at subscript ', Counter:1);
```

This code works perfectly if 0 is actually stored somewhere in *TheArray*. If it isn't, though, we'll eventually try to see if *TheArray*[21] equals 0. Since there is no such location—*TheArray* only has 20 elements—the program crashes with a message like this:

```
ABNORMAL TERMINATION -- SUBSCRIPT OUT OF RANGE
```

The message indicates that a run-time error occurred because the array subscript is out of its valid range 1..20. A correct program segment would include a check to ensure that *Counter* never exceeds 20. What do you think of this version?

```
{incorrect segment}
Counter := 1;
while (Counter<20) and (TheArray[Counter]<>0) do
    Counter := Counter+1;
writeln ('A zero is stored at subscript ', Counter:1);
```

Suppose that *TheArray* still doesn't contain a zero, or holds a zero in element 20. In either case, the segment's output will be:

```
A zero is stored at subscript 20
```

As you can see, we've escaped the frying pan only to find ourselves in the fire. Another test has to be added to the end of the segment to make sure that we've really found the zero.

check after the loop

```
{correct segment}
Counter := 1;
while (Counter<20) and (TheArray[Counter]<>0) do
    Counter := Counter+1;
if TheArray[Counter]=0
    then writeln ('A zero is stored at subscript ', Counter:1)
    else writeln ('No zeros.');
```

Leaning over too far backwards can lead to a bump on the back of your head. Make sure that you don't search past the end of an array, and be wary of finding something that you weren't looking for.

Ordinal subranges can cause a special kind of problem if the programmer isn't careful. The following definition sets the stage for the bug:

```
type Letters = 'A'..'Z';
     CountArray = array [Letters] of integer;
var LetterCount: CountArray;
    CurrentPosition: Letters;     etc.
```

subrange bugs

Suppose we want to travel through the array and inspect each element (with procedure *Inspect*) until a variable or function named *SomethingHappens* is *true*, or until we reach the end of the array. Will this program segment work?

```
{incorrect segment}
CurrentPosition := 'A';
repeat
    Inspect (LetterCount[CurrentPosition]);
    CurrentPosition := succ(CurrentPosition)
until SomethingHappens or (CurrentPosition>'Z');
```

Not if we try to assign *CurrentPosition* the successor of 'Z'. Any assignment that causes *CurrentPosition* to exceed its subrange crashes the program with a message like:

```
ABNORMAL TERMINATION --
OUT-OF-RANGE ASSIGNMENT TO VARIABLE "CURRENTPOSITION"
```

Will this change make the program work?

```
{incorrect segment}
CurrentPosition := pred('A');
repeat
    CurrentPosition := succ(CurrentPosition)
    Inspect (LetterCount[CurrentPosition]);
until SomethingHappens or (CurrentPosition='Z');
```

No. The value that *pred*('A') represents falls outside the *Letters* subrange as well. As before, we need an extra **if** test to make the loop work.

```
{correct segment}
CurrentPosition := 'A'
Inspect (LetterCount[CurrentPosition]);
if not SomethingHappens then
    repeat
        CurrentPosition := succ(CurrentPosition);
        Inspect (LetterCount[CurrentPosition])
    until SomethingHappens or (CurrentPosition='Z');
```

Potential bugs shouldn't discourage you from using ordinal subranges (or arrays). However, subranges and arrays both tend to generate off-by-one errors that could easily be avoided by checking entry and exit conditions.

two-dimensional bugs

Arrays of two or more dimensions are sometimes confusing. One common problem comes from using too many nested loops to inspect an array. Suppose, for example, that we have a two-dimensional array and want to examine the values stored along one of its diagonals—*TheArray*[1,1], *TheArray*[2,2], etc. An intuitive, but incorrect, solution uses two **for** loops. Assume that we have an array whose dimensions are 1..*Last* and 1..*Last*.

```
{incorrect segment}
for Row := 1 to Last do
    for Column := 1 to Last do
        Examine (TheArray[Row, Column]);     etc.
```

This program calls *Examine* for *every* value stored in *TheArray*. A correct version requires only a single loop, regardless of the diagonal being searched. The 1,1, 2,2 3,3... diagonal is searched with:

searching diagonals

```
{correct segment}
for Mark := 1 to Last do
    Examine (TheArray[Mark, Mark]);     etc.
```

Just for comparison, see how the opposite diagonal is searched:

```
{another correct segment}
for Mark := 1 to Last do
    Examine (TheArray[Mark, (Last-Mark)+1]);     etc.
```

Frequently we'll want to compare an array element to its neighbors. If we're at element *i,j*, we'll be looking at *i*–1,*j*–1; *i*–1,*j*; *i*–1,*j*+1; *i,j*–1; *i,j*+1; *i*+1,*j*–1; *i*+1,*j*; and *i*+1,*j*+1. There's nothing particularly difficult about cycling through an array to make the check for every *i, j* pair. However, not every element *has* a neighbor on every side! Trying to check the neighbors of an element on any side row or column will cause a subscript error.

checking boundary conditions

> Think about the boundary conditions of searches, especially when you're dealing with border locations.

A piece of debugging folk wisdom we passed along some time ago has a special application when dealing with arrays. We said that 'when you're sure everything is right and the program still doesn't work, then one of the things you're sure of is wrong.' This is particularly true when array subscripts are being computed. Now, an incorrect subscript won't always cause a program crash—it might just cause incorrect results. If a program performs strangely for inexplicable reasons, it's a good idea to use a snapshot statement or procedure to look at subscript values during execution.

subscript snapshots

```
{This output statement was added for debugging.}
writeln ('Subscripts before the call of DoSomething are: ',
            Computed(i), Margin/Border-1, Row*Column);
DoSomething (TheArray [Computed(i), Margin/Border-1, Row*Column]);
```

It's amazing how often an inspection like this solves the mystery.

One point about passing large variables (like arrays) as parameters is worth mentioning, even though it seldom has an effect on your programming practice. It has to do with the storage space required by value and variable parameters.

arrays as parameters

> A value parameter is a *copy* of its argument. Any variable, regardless of its structure, is duplicated in its entirety.

As you might imagine, this can cause problems when very large data structures (like big arrays) are passed as value parameters. Although computers can hold a great deal of data, storage space is finite. With this in mind, programmers sometimes pass large data structures as variable parameters, even if they have no intention of changing the variable's contents within the procedure.

> A variable parameter is a *renaming*, or aliasing, of its argument. It requires a minimal amount of storage space, and doesn't really depend on the size of its argument variable.

Unfortunately, using this trick subverts the protection provided by value parameters. A programmer too concerned about conserving storage space may find herself making unexpected changes in global variables.

> The Golden Rule of Space
>
> A program that works and uses a lot of space is better than one that very efficiently doesn't work at all.

Pascal Summary

• array: a structured type that lets a variable hold many values—the array's elements—of one type.

```
type AnArray = array ['A'..'Z'] of real;
       Triples = array [1..10, 1..10, 1..10] of char;
var Test: AnArray;
     Lottery: Triples;
```

• string type: a **packed array** of *char* values. It can only have one dimension, which must start at 1:

```
type TypicalString = packed array [1..20] of char;
var Word: TypicalString;
```

• subscript: the value used to denote one particular array element. The subscript can be computed during program execution:

```
Word [1] := 'A';
Test ['A'] := Test ['B'];
Lottery [1, 2, 3] := Lottery [Alpha, Beta, Coopa];
```

If a sequence of subscripts is correct (e.g. [1], ['A']) for accessing an array element, the subscripts can be merged into a single pair of brackets (e.g. [1, 'A']). This situation can occur when we define arrays of array-type elements.

Important Facts

• The Golden Rule of Types: Define, then declare. First, define a structured type, then declare variables of that type.

• An array is known as a random access type because array elements can stored or inspected in any order.

- The size of an array (the number of elements it can hold) is determined by its dimensions. The bounds that set the dimensions can have any ordinal type. There's no limit on the number of dimensions an array can have, although the computer may restrict an array's total size.
- The bounds that set array dimensions must be given with actual values, known when the program is compiled (with the exception given below). They can't be variables or expressions that aren't computed until the program is finally run.
- The name of an ordinal type can be used instead of actual values in giving an array dimension. It's as though the first and last values of the type were given instead.
- An array's elements can have any type, but all of an array's elements must have the same type. A 'complete array' assignment can be made between two array variables with the exact same type.
- Value parameters and variable parameters with structured types must be declared with type names. Their types can't be described 'on the spot.'
- String type array variables can be compared, and assigned to or printed all at once (rather than on element at a time). Values must still be read in element-by-element, though.
- The most common array bugs involve subscripts that are out of the range of the array's definition. Printing 'subscript snapshots' is a good debugging technique.
- Array-searching loops usually have multiple exit conditions, since the sought value may not be found. Be sure to check the reason for loop termination before assuming that you've found what you were looking for.
- The Golden Rule of Space: A program that works and uses a lot of space is better than one that very efficiently doesn't work at all.

Self-test Exercises

11-1 How can the dimensions of an array be defined?

11-2 Can the values stored in an array be arrays? Give two different examples.

11-3 Suppose that we define an array type like this:

```
type StoredArray = array [1..10] of integer;
     StoringArray = array [1..10] of StoredArray;
```

Assume that a variable of type *StoringArray* is called *DataBank*. Which of these assignments to *DataBank* is correct?

```
DataBank [3] [4] := 200;
DataBank [3, 4] := 200;
```

11-4 Which of the problems listed below require arrays for an elegant solution?

a) Find the (alphabetically) least word in a series of words.

b) Compute the sum of a series of numbers.

c) Find the second largest number in a sequence of input numbers.

d) Read in exactly two hundred numbers, and sort them in decreasing order.

e) Read in as many as two hundred numbers, and print all the numbers that fall within a certain range.

11-5 What kind of arrays can be compared for equality? Must the arrays be of identical types?

11-6 A word-processing program requires you to store up to one hundred words. The longest word is eight characters long. Define a suitable data type.

11-7 Suppose that you are using a selection sort to put an array of *integer* values into ascending order. Which of the starting sequences shown below will require the most updates? The fewest? How many will they require?

a)	10	9	8	7	6	5	4	3	2	1
b)	10	1	9	2	8	3	7	4	6	5
c)	2	3	4	5	6	7	8	9	10	1
d)	1	10	2	9	3	8	4	7	5	6
e)	5	4	3	2	1	10	9	8	7	6

11-8 Suppose that you have an array as defined and declared below. Initialize the odd-subscripted elements (*List* [1], *List* [3], etc.) to 'O', and the even-subscripted elements to 'E'. Use a single **for** loop, and no **if** statements.

```
type Storage = array [1..50] of char;
var List: Storage;
```

11-9 Suppose that a checkerboard is represented with an 8 by 8 array of *boolean*, and that every occupied position is marked *true*. At present, position *Board* [*Row, Column*] is occupied. The code below is intended to find if any other squares in the same row or column are also occupied. What bug does the segment contain?

```
AlsoOccupied := false;
for Counter := 1 to 8 do
    if Board [Row, Counter] then AlsoOccupied := true;
for Counter := 1 to 8 do
    if Board [Counter, Column] then AlsoOccupied := true;
```

11-10 A magic square is an n by n array of the *integer* values 1 through n^2. The values of each row and column, and the main diagonals, have the same sum. Write a function that inspects an n by n magic square, and verifies that it contains the proper numbers for potential magic squaredom. (However, you need not add up each row, column, or diagonal.) Assume that the maximum value of n is passed as an argument to your function, and is no more than ten.

More Exercises

11-10 Charting sales, prices, investments, etc. is a common business computing application. However, careful thought must go into the chart's design if it's going to be readable, and fit on a page or screen. An appropriate scale must be determined, symbols and labels must be decided on, and, above all, the chart had better not come out sideways.

Write a general-purpose set of graphing routines. Assume that some rule for generating data points will be provided further down the line. Within reason, your routines should be able to compute an appropriate number of data points and scale them. The user should also be able to specify the orientation of the horizontal and vertical axes.

11-11 Most charts are used to compare several sets of data points, rather than show one group by itself. For instance, business programmers are often called on to produce a single chart that compares product sales, profits, or stock prices. Write a program that plots more than one set of data points on a single graph, possibly rotated as above. Use a different symbol for each quantity, and some neutral symbol when two or more data points are identical.

11-12 Although Pascal is supposed to be an international programming language, all its reserved words and pre-defined identifiers are in English. This feature has not been welcomed in certain countries. To help foreign sales of *Oh! Pascal!*, write a program that takes a Pascal program as input, and substitutes non-English equivalents for all its reserved words and predefined identifiers. Be sure to ignore words that appear as text output or constants, or within comments.

11-13 Sam Loyd tells a story about the Russian army at the time of the Russo-Japanese war. It seems that 20 regiments were in a continuous process of formation. The first had 1,000 men, the second had 950, the next 900, and so on down to the twentieth regiment, which garrisoned only 50. During each week, 100 men were added to each regiment, and at week's end, the largest regiment was sent to the front.

Apparently, the commander of the fifth regiment was a wonderful chess player. To delay his eventual trip to the front, the general of the army (who happened to be his chess partner) sent him only 30 new recruits each week. Write a program that tells which regiment is sent to the front each week, shows the status of the remaining regiments, and determines exactly how long it takes for the chess-playing commander to go to the front.

11-14 When writing card-game programs, it's often convenient to imagine that the cards are numbered 1 through 52, and have an array of this length serve as a deck. A formula can be used to decide exactly what number and suit each card represents. How can such a programmed deck of cards be shuffled?

Two solutions immediately present themselves. The first is to travel along the array, and exchange the current card with the card at a random subscript between 1 and 52. The second idea is similar to the first, except that we don't choose cards from the already-shuffled portion of the deck. Thus, we exchange the first card for one between 1 and 52, the second for a card between 2 and 52, and so on.

If you're mathematically inclined, you'll see that the first shuffling method produces 52 to the 52nd power different hands, while the second results in 52 factorial hands. Do both methods produce fair shuffles? Write a program that simulates the shuffling of a very small deck of cards, and test or prove your theory.

11-15 Suppose that we have a four-by-four checkerboard. How can ten checkers be arranged on the board (disregarding the rules of checkers) so that the largest number of horizontal, vertical, or diagonal rows contain an even number of checkers? How many such rows are there? (16)

11-16 Here's a problem in array searching. Represent the illustration below as a two-dimensional array. Now, starting at any 'R', how many paths can be followed to spell out 'RADAR'? Don't forget the 'R's on the diagonals, and in the center.

```
R A D A R
A D A R A
D A R A D
A R A D A
R A D A R
```

(Hint: To avoid falling off the edge of the array, store blanks all around the edges of a 7 by 7 array.)

11-17 In *transposition ciphers*, a message is encrypted by having its letters rearranged in a regular manner. For example, if we write Ambrose Bierce's remark that 'patience is a minor form of despair disguised as a virtue' like this:

```
Patience
isaminor
formofde
spairdis
guisedas
avirtue.
```

we can read the vertical columns as through they were words in a sentence:

Pifsga asopuv taraii immisr eiorst nnfddu codiae eress.

Write a program that will encode and decode plain text in this fashion. Try to make the coding algorithm more sophisticated—perhaps by reading diagonal columns, or by having a secret key that controls the order that columns are read in. Be sure that your code is very well documented!

11-18 In *The Cloven Viscount*, Italo Calvino tells how the Viscount Medardo of Terralba suffered the misfortune of being split in half by a cannonball. The two halves (one good, and the other bad) survived, but underwent many trials before being reunited.

Some years later Medardo found himself in charge of guarding a field that looked very much like a checkerboard. Medardo put two soldiers in two of the four 'squares' closest to the center, and arrayed fourteen others in different squares around the field. However, he arranged all the soldiers in such a way that, if a cannonball happened to fly horizontally, vertically, or diagonally across the field, no more than two soldiers would be hit. (You see, he wanted to minimize the odds that any of them would suffer the same fate he had.) How were the sixteen soldiers posted?

11-19 An old-time flat of eggs held 64 eggs, arranged in a square. Suppose that an otherwise empty flat already holds two eggs in corners diagonally opposite each other. How many more eggs can be put into the flat without having more than two eggs in any horizontal, vertical, or diagonal row?

11-20 Write procedures or functions to perform these string handling tasks.

a) Determine if the non-blank portions of two strings are longer than the maximum length of the string.

b) Concatenate two strings to form a third.

c) Extract a string from within a string. Pass as parameters the original string, the starting position in it, the length of the portion to be extracted, and the new string.

d) Insert a string within a string. Pass the original string, the replacement string, and a starting position within the original. Be sure to preserve the remainder of the original string.

e) Do an insertion like the one above, but dispose of the remainder of the original string.

f) See if a string is a sub-string of another string.

11-21 The game *Life* was developed by a mathematician named John Conway. It's intended to provide a model of life, death, and survival among simple organisms that inhabit an n by m board. The current population of the board is considered to comprise one generation. There are only three rules, as follows: 1) every empty cell with three living neighbors will come to life in the next generation; 2) any cell with one or zero neighbors will die of loneliness, while any cell with four or more neighbors will die from overcrowding; 3) any cell with two or three neighbors will live into the next generation. All births and deaths occur simultaneously.

Why is *Life* a game? Well, it turns out that although some starting populations die out quickly, others form interesting patterns that repeat, grow, or move across the board as they go from generation to generation. Write a program that plays *Life*. Let the program user specify the locations of the starting population, as well as the number of generations that should be shown as output.

11-22 In a gambling game called *Treize* a deck of cards is shuffled, then laid face up one at a time. As the cards are dealt, the dealer counts 'One, two, three...' etc., up through Jack, Queen, and King. The count is repeated four times. Bets can be placed on whether or not a dealt card's value will coincide with the value spoken by the dealer.

Write a program that calculates the chances of making a match. 'Chances' can be described as the number of shuffles that allow at least one match, divided by the complete number of potential shuffles. However, it's not necessary to work with a complete deck of 52 cards. Start with a deck of two cards, and increase the deck size one card at a time until the difference between two deck-sizes is less than .001.

11-23 The game of Nim and its many variations should be familiar to you. The players start with several rows of markers, and take turns removing some number of markers from any row. The player who goes last either wins or loses.

Write a program that plays a perfect game of Nim. Starting positions, the maximum number of markers that can be removed in a turn, who goes first, and which turn wins should be optionally supplied by the player.

11-24 Bring the array into your new language. Is an equivalent to the reserved word **of** really necessary? How might it help or hinder the programmer? Can you think of any operations that are frequently performed on arrays (like matrix multiplication) that might be predefined in your language?

'Programs that involve games can bring out the best in a programmer...'

12

E Pluribus Unum: Records

Ever since the Cro-Magnons introduced interior decoration to the Pleistocene epoch, information has been stored in many different ways. Usually, we tend to think only of storage *media*, beginning with paintings on stone walls, and advancing past clay tablets and papyrus to microfilm and magnetic tape. But looking at storage *organization* makes just as much sense. A filing cabinet, a three-ring binder, and a packet of 3 by 5 index cards all represent approaches to the basic problem of keeping data in a way that's secure, yet easy to find.

The **array** was one approach to the data-storage problem. The **record** type is the second of Pascal's structured types. Now, the actual physical storage the compiler uses is irrelevant to us. We don't know or care if the computer puts its data on magnetic tape, disk, or even tissue paper with a crayon. As far as we're concerned, types differ only in terms of organization—how information is stored in them, and then how it's located and gotten out again.

In section 12-1 we'll see how values of different types can be stored as *fields* within a single record. We'll pay special attention to two aspects of every structured type—its method of creation, and its methods of access. We'll also see how a new control statement, called the **with** statement, is sometimes used to aid in accessing records.

Our focus on programming in 12-2 will use records in conjunction with arrays for developing powerful new data structures. This combination is perhaps the most ubiquitous in programming; we combine the array's random access and ease of travel with the record's ability to hold values of different types.

Section 12-3 is optional reading at this time. It describes a more sophisticated use of records called *record variants*. Although we include this section here for completeness, it's seldom necessary to use record variants in ordinary programming applications. Finally, 12-4 covers potential bugs, and takes a last look at record variants.

Defining Record Types 12-1

THE DECLARATION OF A RECORD-TYPE variable begins with a definition of the record variable's type.

field list

> The details of a record type are its *field list*, given between the reserved words **record** and **end**. A record's fields can be of any type—standard or user-defined, simple or structured.

We can draw a simplified chart of a record types's definition as shown below. It will be expanded after the discussion of record variants in 12-3.

record type

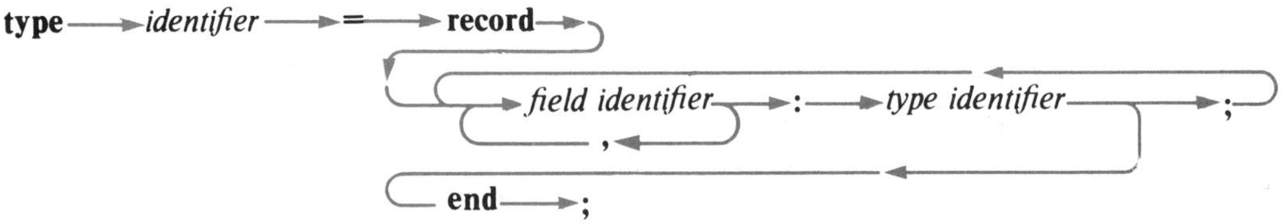

A boilerplate record definition is helpful:

model record-type definition

```
type (type identifier) = record
                    field identifier, field identifier: real; {or...}
                    field identifier: ordinal type identifier; {or...}
      {Field list}  field identifier: structured type identifier; {or...}
                    field identifier: subrange identifier; {or...}
                    field identifier: subrange bounds {No semicolon}
                 end;
```

The definition and declaration below show that specifying a record's fields is a lot like declaring a series of variables.

```
type Study = record
               Units, HoursPerWeek: integer;
               Grade: char;          {The record's fields.}
               Passed: boolean
             end; {Study type definition.}
var WeavingClass: Study;
```

For all practical purposes, the record's fields (*Units, HoursPerWeek, Grade*, and *Passed*) are ordinary variables—we can make assignments to them, use them in input and output statements, etc. In a few paragraphs we'll learn exactly how to access fields.

scope of fields

A special feature of field identifiers is their limited scope. The field identifiers of a given record have their own *name list* in the computer, and don't conflict with identifiers used in other records, or elsewhere within the program.

The *Study* record type was easy to define because all its fields belong to standard types. Our next definition, of record type called *Class*, requires several ordinal and structured types that describe a class more realistically. Notice that ordinal types and subranges are defined before they're used to provide the types of fields. Records, in turn, are defined before being used in other structured types themselves.

```
type GradeLetters = 'A'..'F';
     Quarter = (Fall, Winter, Spring);
     CourseStatus = (Passed, Failed, Incomplete, WithDrawn);
     WhenTaken = record
                       Term: Quarter;
                       Year: 1980..1985
                    end; {WhenTaken}
     Class = record
                   Hours, Units: 1..5;
                   Grade: GradeLetters;
                   Results: CourseStatus;
                   Taken: WhenTaken          {A record within a record}
                end; {Class}
var Weaving, Wefting, Warping: Class;
```

WhenTaken, a record type, can provide the type of one of *Class's* fields because *WhenTaken* was defined first. The reverse wouldn't be allowed. Nesting of record definitions can go more than two levels deep, as long as each type is defined in the proper sequence.

problem: chessboard data definition

An array of structured elements is just as easy to create. As an example, let's design a structure to represent a chessboard. The board itself can be a two-dimensional array. What will each square of the board store?

1. Whether or not the square is occupied.
2. The value of the piece (if any) on each square.
3. The owner of the piece.

An individual square clearly calls for a record type. In the type definitions below, we first define ordinal types, then the record type that uses them, and finally the array whose elements the records are.

chessboard type definition

```
type OwnerColor = (None, Black, White);
     PieceValues = (Empty, Pawn, Knight, Bishop, Rook, Queen, King);
     Squares = record
                     Occupied: boolean;
                     Piece: PieceValues;
                     Owner: OwnerColor
                  end; {Squares definition}
     ChessBoard = array [1..8, 1..8] of Squares;
var Board: ChessBoard;
```

Methods of Access To Records

There are three different ways to access the values stored in a record-typed variable.

1. Individual fields can be accessed with the 'period' notation we showed in Chapter 10.
2. The **with** statement lets us access fields without having to employ the period notation.
3. The complete record can be accessed in a single assignment statement—*all* the fields of one record variable can be assigned to the corresponding fields of another.

When Wirth designed Pascal, he realized that people often access several of a record's fields at one point in a program (perhaps to initialize or update them). The 'period' notation for accessing individual fields can become quite tedious, especially if the record has a long name. Wirth made Pascal programming a bit easier by providing two shortcuts for record assignments.

Let's define a record type to experiment with:

```
type CurrentConditions = (Clear, Cloudy, Raining);
     Weather = record
                 Temperature: -25..125;
                 Barometer: real;
                 Present, Outlook: CurrentConditions
               end;
var Morning, Noon, Evening: Weather;
```

Here's a series of assignments to *Morning* that use the 'period' notation. The record variable's identifier is followed by a period, and the name of a field.

period notation

```
Morning.Temperature := 73;
Morning.Barometer := 30.16;
Morning.Present := Cloudy;
Morning.Outlook := Raining;
```

If weather conditions are identical at midday, we can take a shortcut and assign all the *Weather* fields in one fell swoop, like this:

complete record assignment

```
Noon := Morning;
```

This single assignment is equivalent to the series of assignments below. Every field of *Noon* gets the value of its counterpart in *Morning*.

```
Noon.Temperature := 73;
Noon.Barometer := 30.16;
Noon.Present := Cloudy;
Noon.Outlook := Raining;
```

> Complete record assignments can only be made between records of an *identical* type.

We might call this the 'complete record' assignment method. As with complete array assignments, both record variables must be declared with the *same* type identifier, or else the computer considers them to belong to different types. This kind of assignment is often used to initialize records stored in an array.

The third method of access to record-typed variables uses the **with** statement. Its sole purpose is convenience.

the **with** statement

> When a record variable's identifier is given in the **with** statement (**with** *RecordName* **do**), its fields can be accessed directly during the statement's action. The period notation is not required.

According to the syntax chart below, more than one record-type variable identifier can be specified. (We'll explain this further in a page or two.)

with statement

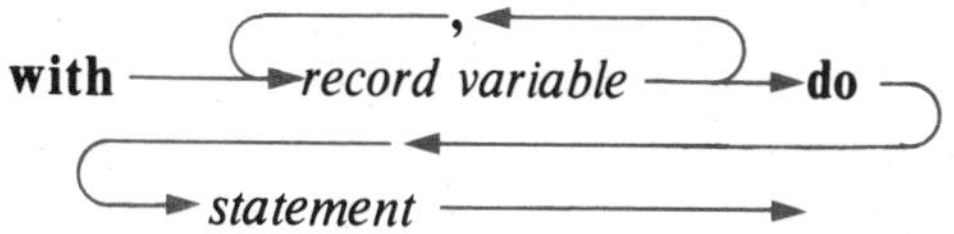

The **with** statement's action is almost invariably a compound statement (so that two or more fields can be accessed during the course of one action). The series of assignments below is clearly equivalent to either of the last two examples.

using **with**

```
with Noon do begin
   Temperature := 73;
   Barometer := 30.16;
   Present := Cloudy;
   Outlook := Raining
end;
```

Either the period notation or the **with** statement can be used for any inspection or alteration of a record's fields—for assignment (as above), or for input and output. Consequently:

```
writeln (Morning.Temperature);
readln (Morning.Barometer);
```

is the same as:

```
with Morning do begin
   writeln (Temperature);
   readln (Barometer)
end;
```

How can we access a record that is a field of another record? Consider these definitions and declarations.

fields of fields

```
type PressureRecord = record
                          Systolic, Diastolic: 50..200
                        end; {PressureRecord}
     PatientRecord = record
                         Temperature: real;
                         BloodPressure: PressureRecord
                       end; {PatientRecord}

var Low, Normal, High: PressureRecord;
    TodaysPatient: PatientRecord;
```

A top-down approach is the key to taking apart structured variables. *TodaysPatient* is a variable of type *PatientRecord*. A *PatientRecord* structure contains two fields. The first, *Temperature*, stores a value of type *real*. The second field, *BloodPressure*, is itself a record. What's *it* composed of? As defined, it's a record structure named *PressureRecord*, containing two fields—*Systolic* and *Diastolic*. Each of these fields can represent values in the subrange 50..200.

> To analyze the structure of *TodaysPatient* we asked the same question—What is the structure of *this*?—over and over again. To access the fields contained in *TodaysPatient*, apply the same principle. First, access the record, then, access any records contained in the record.

```
TodaysPatient.Temperature := 98.6;
TodaysPatient.BloodPressure.Systolic := 120;
TodaysPatient.BloodPressure.Diastolic := 90;
```

The **with** statement can be used to make dealing with nested records (like *TodaysPatient*) easier.

arguments to **with**

> The **with** statement can be given any number of record-structured variable identifiers as 'arguments.' This construct is equivalent to a series of nested **with** statements.

In other words, this **with** statement:

```
with Record1, Record2 do begin   etc.
```

is the exact semantic equivalent of:

```
with Record1 do
   with Record2 do begin    etc.
```

Similarly, both program segments below have the same effect. However, segment 2 uses **with** in a more sophisticated way by giving it two arguments.

```
with TodaysPatient do begin                      {Segment 1}
   Temperature := 98.6;
   BloodPressure.Systolic := 120;
   BloodPressure.Diastolic := 90
end;

with TodaysPatient, BloodPressure do begin       {Segment 2}
   Temperature := 98.6;
   Systolic := 120;
   Diastolic := 90
end;
```

In some potential applications of the **with** statement, the scope of field identifiers must be taken into account. Suppose that a statement begins:

scope of **with**

```
with Low, Normal do begin   etc. {Two PressureRecord variables.}
```

Within this **with** statement, is a mention of the identifier *Systolic* equivalent to *Low.Systolic*, or to *Normal.Systolic*?

> The scope of nested records is similar to normal scope. The innermost record variable's field identifiers take precedence.

Thus, the last mentioned record variable's fields are accessed—*Systolic* really means *Normal.Systolic*. You can gather that, under certain circumstances, using a **with** statement may be inappropriate.

Once the idea of field access is firmly rooted in your mind, you'll appreciate that it doesn't really matter how deep a variable's structure is. Inspection and alteration of fields may become more tedious:

This.That.TheOther.SomeMore.StillGoing := *Here.We.Go.Again.Value*

but certainly no more complicated. Let's consider an example. Suppose that we've made these definitions and declarations:

arrays of records

```
type OwnerColor = (None, Black, White);
     PieceValues = (Empty, Pawn, Knight, Bishop, Rook, Queen, King);
     Squares = record
                  Occupied: boolean;
                  Piece: PieceValues;
                  Owner: OwnerColor
               end; {Squares definition}
     ChessBoard = array [1..8, 1..8] of Squares;
var LastMove, CurrentMove: Squares;
    Board: ChessBoard;
```

Assume that a white pawn is stored in element 5,2 (its starting position). The statements below put a white pawn two rows up, on 5,4. Since *Board*[5,4] refers to an element that's an entire record, we must use record-access methods to get at a single field. Any of the examples shown below will do the job.

identical alternatives

```
Board[5,4] := Board[5,2];                    {1}

Board[5,4].Occupied := true;
Board[5,4].Piece := Pawn;                    {2}
Board[5,4].Owner := White;

CurrentMove.Occupied := true;
CurrentMove.Piece := Pawn;
CurrentMove.Owner := White;                  {3}
Board[5,4] := CurrentMove;

with Board[5,4] do begin
   Occupied := true;                         {4}
   Piece := Pawn;
   Owner := White
end;
```

You may note that we haven't emptied the square where the pawn used to be—right now it's in two places at once.

Combining methods of access (as in the *Board* example) can be carried to any length. Suppose that a record-typed variable contains an array-typed field. We might find ourselves making an assignment like:

```
Schedule.Monday[3, PM] := Busy;
```

Schedule.Monday refers not to a single value, but to an array of values. We have to give the subscript of the exact element ([3, *PM*]) we wish to change. An array of records of arrays is equally plausible:

```
Room[273].Monday[9, AM] := Busy;
```

In this example, we begin with a one-dimensional array called *Room*, whose elements are records. Each record contains a two-dimensional array field called *Monday*. By reading the assignment one step at a time (and breathing very slowly), we can conclude that Room 273 will be busy on Monday at 9 A.M.

Self-Check Questions

Q. What do you think about this assignment? Is it legal?

```
TodaysPatient.BloodPressure := Normal;
     {Assume we've assigned values to the fields of Normal.}
```

A. Yes. A few pages ago, we saw that assignments may be made between any two records of identical types. The field *BloodPressure* and the variable *Normal* are both of type *PressureRecord*.

Data Structuring: Arrays of Records 12-2

RECORDS ARE RARELY USED BY THEMSELVES. WE will almost invariably find them being employed in conjunction with other data types; in particular, with arrays. In this section we'll focus on the definition of more complicated data types.

As we go along, we'll continue to recognize the distinction between Pascal definitions of data *types*, and algorithmic definitions of data *structures*.

> A data *type* describes a particular kind of data. A data *structure* describes the way the data is stored.

data types, data structures

As a data type, an array stores a sequence of values of one particular type. As a data structure, an array carries additional information related to the program's algorithm. For instance, the stored values may be in alphabetical or numerical order. They may bear some special relation to the array's subscripts. The array may just be used to keep track of when the values arrived.

In this section we'll pay special attention to data type definitions, and see how the structures they allow affect program algorithms. For our first set of examples, we won't even bother to write programs, since type definitions, and the structures they imply, will accomplish most of the programming job.

Boards and Games

An interesting class of data structuring problems can be broadly categorized as board or game-type problems. They generally call for arrays of records—arrays whose elements are structured themselves. For example:

A baseball game consists of nine innings.
A football game has four quarters.
A bowling match contains ten (sometimes eleven) frames.
A chessboard has 64 squares whose color and contents vary.
A Monopoly board has squares that represent properties, and usually include schedules of rents and buildings.
Computer games like Adventure, Hunt the Wumpus, and Zork contain many rooms filled with unknown objects, and connected in various ways.

Programming the games described above pose problems of keeping score, remembering positions, locating players, and the like. Do they require real algorithms? Well, although winning play might need some sort of algorithm, the programmer basically manages data by tracking scores and board positions.

> Data structures, rather than algorithms, are often the key to solving data-based problems. We can simplify a potential program with a data structure that makes it easy to do the arithmetic of scorekeeping, or the graphics of board positioning.

lateral thinking

Because the design of data types and structures is largely a mental exercise, a problem solving technique called *lateral thinking* can be put to good use. Lateral thinking is a name Edward DeBono invented to describe the process of repeatedly exploring and reconsidering possible solutions before committing ourselves to one particular method. For example, a lateral approach to digging for buried treasure would entail digging many shallow holes, instead of one hole that is very deep.

alternative data types

A lateral programmer might propose several potential data types before writing a program that relies on one of the alternatives. Experienced programmers can do this in their heads, but novices should sketch out some proposals on paper. For example, consider these two possible data type definitions for a program that scores a baseball game.

```
type Team = (Pirates, Mets, Astros, Giants, Yankees, Angels);
     Inning = (Top, Bottom);
     AtBats = record
                  TeamUp: Team;
                  Runs, Hits, Errors: integer
              end;
     Game = array [1..9, Top..Bottom] of AtBats;
```

```
type TeamName = packed array[1..15] of char;
     Inning = (Top, Bottom);
     Statistics = array [1..9] of integer;
     TeamStatistics = record
                          Name: TeamName;
                          Runs, Hits, Errors: Statistics
                      end;
     Game = array [Top..Bottom] of TeamStatistics;
```

These data type definitions create two different ways of viewing and storing the exact same information. Choosing one over the other as the basis of our final data structure will depend on our ultimate application.

Programs that involve games (especially imaginary ones) can bring out the best in a programmer when it comes to design problems. Some game boards have an obvious representation—for instance, checkerboard games almost always call for a data type that is an **array** [1..8,1..8] of some record type. A board game like Monopoly, on the other hand, which appears to require a two-dimensional array, can be described as a single, long line of boxes—a one-dimensional array. Declaring a two-dimensional

Monopoly board is unnecessary and slightly misleading because, aside from an occasional trip to Jail, the game moves in a straight line.

A game in which *nothing* moves in a straight line also calls for a one-dimensional array of records. *Hunt the Wumpus* is often found on interactive computer systems. Here's a description of a simple version.

problem: Hunt the Wumpus

> You are in the cave of the Wumpus. The Wumpus likes you very much—especially for breakfast. To avoid being eaten, you must locate the Wumpus, and shoot it with your bow and arrow.
>
> The Wumpus cave has 20 rooms, connected by narrow passageways. You can travel in any direction—North, South, East, or West—from one room to another. You also know the number of the room each passageway leads to. However, there are hazards to beware of. Some rooms contain bottomless pits, and others contain bats that will pick you up, and carry you to another room. One room contains the Wumpus. Entering a room that holds a pit or the Wumpus causes instant death. Fortunately, when you are one room away you can feel the breeze from a pit, hear the bats, or smell the Wumpus,
>
> To win the game, you must shoot the Wumpus. When you shoot an arrow, it travels through three rooms—you can tell the arrow which tunnel to take as it passes through each room. Don't forget, though, that the tunnels often turn unexpectedly. You may end up shooting yourself. You have 5 arrows. Good luck.

A single refinement step is enough to state the rules of Hunt the Wumpus in an approximation of a Pascal program:

refinement

```
initialize the cave;
put the player in her first room;
if adjoining rooms have hazards, give warning;
repeat
   get the action—Move or Shoot?;
   case Action of
      Move: begin
               find out the direction;
               move;
               if adjoining rooms have hazards, give warning
            end;
      Shoot: begin
               find out the arrow directions;
               shoot;
               update arrow count;
               is Player or Wumpus killed?
            end
   end {case}
until (Player is dead) or (Wumpus is dead);
```

Stop and think for a moment. Does this pseudocode really help us write the final program? No. Our *real* problem is designing a data structure suitable for representing the Wumpus Cave.

A good first step in this situation is to illustrate our data. The picture below has room numbers, contents (**B**at, **P**it, or **W**umpus), and connections between a number of the rooms.

the Wumpus cave

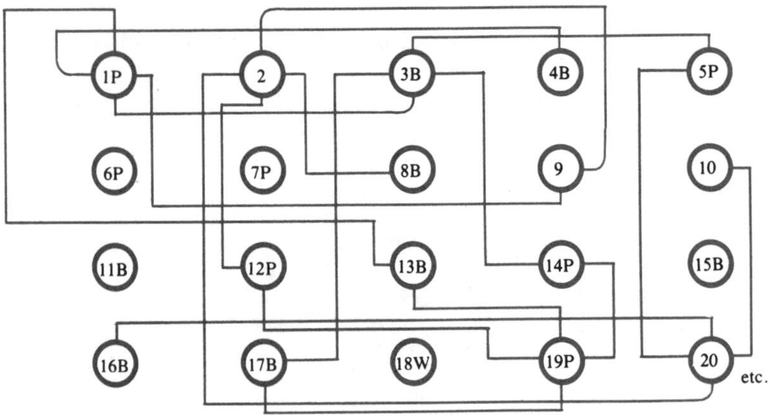

Now we have to turn a data picture into a data type. How will the rooms be connected? As you can see, it's practically impossible to draw the cave *picture* in only two dimensions. At least three dimensions, and probably four, are needed to make rooms that seem to be right next to each other actually adjoin. But is a multi-dimensional array *type* needed to hold the cave of the Wumpus? Before you read on, stop for a moment and think how you'd represent the entire group of rooms.

The answer lies in considering the way we will use the stored data. Our main concern in playing is to know the contents of the current room, and the numbers of adjoining rooms. Suppose that we define *Rooms* as a record that holds just this information. We can draw a new and quite different picture of a room as a record with two fields. The *Contents* field represents any of the *Hazard* values. The second field is an array, subscripted by *Directions*, that contains *RoomNumbers* values.

a single room

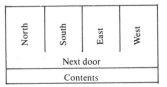

On the left, above, we've drawn a *Rooms* record in terms of its field and subscript names. The right-hand picture shows the values a typical *Rooms* record contains.

the entire cave

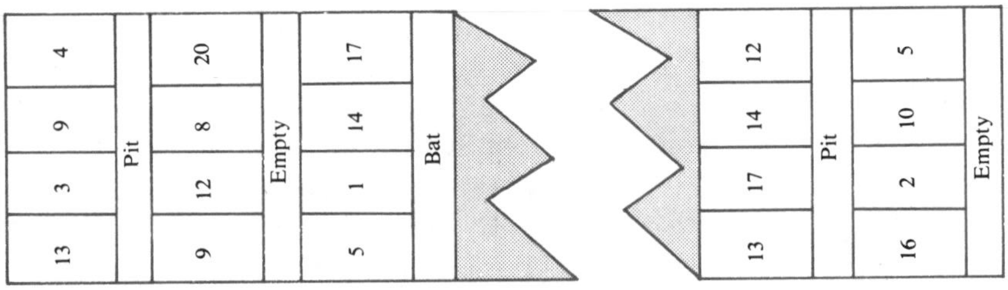

What about drawing the entire cave as a line of rooms? The map above contains the same information as our original picture. At this stage we can turn the drawing into a Pascal type definition.

Wumpus type definition

```
const MAXIMUMNUMBEROFROOMS = 20;

type Hazard = (Pit, Bat, Wumpus, Empty);
    RoomNumbers = 1..MAXIMUMNUMBEROFROOMS;
    Directions = (North, South, East, West);
    PassageWays = array [North..West] of RoomNumbers;
    Rooms = record
                Contents: Hazard;
                NextDoor: PassageWays
            end;
    Cave = array [1..MAXIMUMNUMBEROFROOMS] of Rooms;
      {We could have said array [RoomNumbers] of Rooms.}

var WumpusCave: Cave;
    CurrentRoomNumber: RoomNumbers;
```

Let's fill rooms 1 and 2 with data according to the map. For purposes of illustration, we'll use two different methods of access.

initializing the rooms

```
WumpusCave[1].Contents := Pit; {Initialize Room 1.}
WumpusCave[1].NextDoor[North] := 13;
WumpusCave[1].NextDoor[South] := 3;
WumpusCave[1].NextDoor[East] := 9;
WumpusCave[1].NextDoor[West] := 4;


with WumpusCave[2] do begin {Initialize Room 2.}
    Contents := Empty;
    NextDoor[North] := 9;
    NextDoor[South] := 12;
    NextDoor[East] := 8;
    NextDoor[West] := 20
end;
```

> One characteristic of a good data structure is to minimize the effort a programmer must expend to examine data.

For example, at one stage of the game we must check neighboring rooms to see if they contain hazards. Procedure *CheckForHazards*, below, does the job quickly and neatly. Notice how the expression *NextDoor[Neighbor]* is used as an array subscript.

inspecting a room

```
procedure CheckForHazards (CurrentRoomNumber: RoomNumbers;
                           WumpusCave: Cave);
  {Check out the neighbors of a Wumpus cave room.}
  var Neighbor: Direction;
  begin
    with WumpusCave[CurrentRoomNumber] do
      for Neighbor := North to West do
        case WumpusCave[NextDoor[Neighbor]].Contents of
          Empty: ;
          Bat: writeln ('I hear bats!');
          Pit: writeln ('I feel a breeze!');
          Wumpus: writeln ('I smell a Wumpus!')
        end {case}
  end; {CheckForHazards}
```

Is *CheckForHazards* perfect? Not really. One programmer might object that it allows duplicated warnings, and that a clever player could figure out which room contains what hazard. Another programmer might object to our data structure, since the expression:

WumpusCave[NextDoor[Neighbor]].Contents

is unappealing on aesthetic grounds—it takes a concerted effort to understand it. We tried to head off this objection by using a **with** statement and well-named variables.

One of the less visible features of *CheckForHazards* is its use of the subrange *RoomNumbers* as the type of *CurrentRoomNumber*. This is a built-in safety check on the value passed to *CurrentRoomNumber*, assuring us that the room we're examining exists. It is precisely for such applications that ordinal subranges were created.

We'll leave Hunt the Wumpus now. Although a program to play the game is fairly long, it is well within our abilities as programmers—given a suitable data structure.

Ordering

In Chapter 11 we wrote a program (*CountTheCharacters*) that determined the frequency with which lower-case letters appeared in a text sample. Our program printed its frequency chart in alphabetical order. It's not unreasonable, though, to want the output printed in order of frequency, from the most used letter to the least. To get such a chart we'll have to order our collected data.

Sorting data is one of the most thoroughly analyzed topics in computer science; people can write entire books about it (and they have). We, too, will return to the subject in section 16-1. For now, though, we won't be intimidated, because some basic methods can work very well. A very obvious sorting routine known as a *selection sort* works like this:

Suppose that we have an array of *integer* values.

18	35	22	97	84	55	61	10	47

selection sort

Search through the array, find the largest value, and exchange it with the value stored in the first array location.

97	35	22	18	84	55	61	10	47

Next, find the second largest value in the array, and exchange it with the value stored in the second array location. This is identical to the first trip through the array, except that we don't look at the first value—we already know it's the largest. We've shaded the portion we're not inspecting.

97	84	22	18	35	55	61	10	47

Now, repeat the 'select and exchange' process, each time beginning the search one value further along the array. As we go along, we'll be building an ordered array of values (shaded). Eventually, we'll get all the way to the end of the array—which has to be the smallest stored value—and the array will be ordered.

97	84	61	18	35	55	22	10	47
97	84	61	55	35	18	22	10	47
97	84	61	55	47	18	22	10	35
97	84	61	55	47	35	22	10	18
97	84	61	55	47	35	22	18	10

Another sorting algorithm that's similar is called *bubble sort*. This method usually requires fewer comparisons, but many more exchanges than the selection sort does. It tends to take more time to run than a selection sort. A bubble sort works like this:

Begin with the same array as before:

18	35	22	97	84	55	61	10	47

bubble sort

Compare the first value with the second. If the second is larger, exchange them.

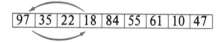

35	18	22	97	84	55	61	10	47

Next, compare the second and third values, exchanging them if the third is larger.

35	22	18	97	84	55	61	10	47

Then compare (and possibly exchange) the third and fourth values, the fourth and fifth, etc. until you reach the end of the array. Note that the smallest stored value ends up stored in the last position (shaded).

35	22	97	84	55	61	18	47	10

Now, go back to the beginning of the array and start all over again. Work your way through the array comparing and exchanging values again. However, since the smallest value is already at the far right, you need not compare the final value.

35	97	84	55	61	22	47	18	10

Repeat the process of comparison and exchange without bothering the final *two* values.

97	84	55	61	35	47	22	18	10

As you can see, an ordered list is forming on the right. Continue the process of comparison and exchange, ignoring the last *three* values this time.

97	84	61	55	47	35	22	18	10

This particular array is already ordered. If it weren't, it *would* be when we got to the point of only comparing the first two values.

In a sense, the smallest values 'bubble' to the right side of the array.

Implementing these sorting algorithms will require a new data structure. Recall that we stored the values produced by *CountTheCharacters* in a one-dimensional array that was subscripted by letters, and stored *integer* values. Although such an array is easy enough to sort, the relationship between stored numbers and subscript characters can't be preserved. We'll wind up with an ordered array of numbers (the number of times each character appeared) but no idea of what characters they refer to.

Instead, we'll have to define an array whose elements store a character, and also the number of times that character has appeared. In other words, we'll need a one-dimensional array of records.

type definition

```
const ARRAYLIMIT = 26;
type CharData = record
                  TheCharacter: char;
                  Count: integer
                end; {CharData}
     RecordArray = array [1..ARRAYLIMIT] of CharData;
var OrderedArray: RecordArray;
```

Actually counting characters with this new data structure means we'll have to modify our counting algorithm. However, we'll save that problem for a rainy day and assume that an array variable named *OrderedArray*, of type *RecordArray*, already stores the number of times each letter appears in a long text sample. For the purposes of our example, we'll assume that *OrderedArray*[1].*TheCharacter* is ´a´, while *OrderedArray*[26].*TheCharacter* is ´z´.

Since both the selection sort and bubble sort algorithms require many array values to be exchanged, procedure *Switch*, below, will come in handy. When called, it will be passed two array elements (of type *CharData*) as parameters.

element-switching procedure

```
procedure Switch (var First, Second: CharData);
  {Exchanges the fields of two CharData values.}
  var Temporary: CharData;
  begin
    Temporary := First;
    First := Second;
    Second := Temporary
  end; {Switch}
```

As you read procedures *SelectionSort* and *BubbleSort*, below, bear in mind that each procedure rearranges records according to their *Count* fields. With slight modifications, they could be used to sort arrays of almost any type. The fact that we defined *ARRAYLIMIT* as a constant will make any conversion easier. As an aid in comparing the effects of each sort, we've kept count of the number of switches and comparisons each method requires. Assume the data of *CountTheCharacters*.

selection sort procedure

```
procedure SelectionSort (var OrderedArray: RecordArray);
  {Uses a selection sort algorithm to order an array of records.}
  var First, Largest, Comparisons, Switches: integer;
      Current: 1..ARRAYLIMIT;
  begin
    Comparisons := 0;
    Switches := 0;
    for First := 1 to ARRAYLIMIT-1 do begin
      Largest := First;
      for Current := First to ARRAYLIMIT do begin
        Comparisons := Comparisons+1;
        if OrderedArray[Current].Count
                > OrderedArray[Largest].Count then
          Largest := Current
      end; {Current for}
      Switches := Switches+1;
      Switch (OrderedArray[Largest], OrderedArray[First])
    end; {First for}
    writeln (Comparisons:2,' comparisons,  ', Switches:2,' switches.')
  end; {SelectionSort}
```

```
350 comparisons, 25 switches.
```

bubble sort procedure

```
procedure BubbleSort (var OrderedArray: RecordArray);
  {Uses the bubble sort algorithm to order an array of records.}
  var Last: 2..ARRAYLIMIT;
      Current: 1..ARRAYLIMIT;
      Comparisons, Switches: integer;
  begin
    Comparisons := 0;
    Switches := 0;
    for Last := ARRAYLIMIT downto 2 do
      for Current := 1 to Last-1 do begin
        Comparisons := Comparisons+1;
        if OrderedArray[Current].Count
                  <OrderedArray[Current+1].Count then begin
          Switches := Switches+1;
          Switch (OrderedArray[Current], OrderedArray[Current+1])
        end {if}
      end; {Current for}
    writeln (Comparisons:2,' comparisons,  ', Switches:2,' switches.')
  end; {BubbleSort}
```

```
325 comparisons, 132 switches.
```

When you read the procedures, you can realize that *SelectionSort* and *BubbleSort* are interesting because of the nearly opposite way they use array subscripts. Look again for a moment.

comparing the algorithms

The difference between *SelectionSort* and *BubbleSort* shows up in the number of comparisons and switches, and, more subtly, in the ordering they produce. Although both procedures correctly order the letters, the exact order of letters with the same frequency differs. This discrepancy doesn't cause any problems, but it exemplifies the sort of detail we always have to be aware of. Were we to print the contents of *OrderedArray* after each sort we'd see:

Ordering of SelectionSort

```
r = 14.22% e = 13.90% t = 12.14% a =  9.90% n =  6.87%
i =  5.27% o =  5.11% c =  5.11% h =  4.95% s =  4.31%
u =  3.83% f =  2.24% l =  2.08% y =  1.76% d =  1.60%
p =  1.44% w =  1.28% g =  1.12% b =  0.96% m =  0.64%
v =  0.48% z =  0.48% q =  0.32% x =  0.00% j =  0.00%
k =  0.00%
```

Ordering of BubbleSort

```
r = 14.22% e = 13.90% t = 12.14% a =  9.90% n =  6.87%
i =  5.27% c =  5.11% o =  5.11% h =  4.95% s =  4.31%
u =  3.83% f =  2.24% l =  2.08% y =  1.76% d =  1.60%
p =  1.44% w =  1.28% g =  1.12% b =  0.96% m =  0.64%
z =  0.48% v =  0.48% q =  0.32% j =  0.00% k =  0.00%
x =  0.00%
```

Focus on Programming: Harder Data Design

Let's carry our next problem all the way to the end, defining a data type, then seeing how our algorithms will help define a data structure. The problem is:

problem: letter-pair frequency

> Write a program that counts the occurrences of all letter pairs in a sample of text. Disregard differences between lower- and upper-case letters. Summarize the program's findings.

For example, the word *draft* contains four letter pairs: *dr, ra, af*, and *ft*. The great number of possible pairs—26∗26, or 676—is the reason we'll have to summarize output in some manner. A first refinement of the problem gives us:

first refinement

> **while not** *eof*
>   *count the pairs;*
> *print the most frequently occurring pairs*;

Counting letter pairs isn't all that different from counting single characters. Previously, we incremented the elements of a one-dimensional array subscripted by *char* values. *CharacterArray*['p'], for example, held the number of times the character 'p' had appeared in input. Why not keep track of letter pairs with a two-dimensional array? Suppose we define a type *PairArray* like this:

type definition

```
type PairArray = array ['a'..'z', 'a'..'z'] of integer;
```

The element subscripted by ['a','a'] will hold the number of times the pair 'aa' has been encountered.

> More important, the data *type*—an array that holds *integers*—will be a data *structure*. The way the data is stored will have as much information as the numbers themselves.

How will we get the two subscript values? Let's use a technique we practiced in program *Gerunds*, back in Chapter 8, in which we kept a moving window, two characters wide, on the input sample. Again, we'll have a data type (a two-character array) that becomes a data structure because of the way we use it as a steadily advancing window. We can refine *count the pairs* to:

second refinement

```
read the first character;
while not eof
   read the second character;
   update element [first character, second character];
   advance the window—first character gets the value of the second character;
```

This pseudocode is still too rough. The problem statement requires us to treat upper- and lower-case characters equally. Have we? Our next refinement will have to allow for character conversion, and include a provision for ignoring non-letter characters as well.

program output

But let's start worrying about output. The array of type *PairArray* will have 676 elements, each representing the number of times one letter pair has appeared. Since we won't want to print them all, it seems reasonable that we print, say, the hundred letter pairs that occur most often. Our job, then, will be to order the data of the *PairArray* array.

Unfortunately, we can't reorganize the 676 elements without losing the information they impart. We'll have the numbers, but we won't know what letter pairs they correspond to. We'll need a new data type and structure. Suppose we define a type that can hold a letter pair:

```
type ShortString = packed array [1..2] of char;
```

and a type that holds a pair and the number of times it appeared:

extending the type definition

```
{type definition continued...}
     PairData = record
                  Pair: ShortString;
                  Number: integer
                end;
```

You can imagine that we might search the two-dimensional *PairArray* for its largest entry, then store the entry's *i, j* coordinates in the *Pair* field, and the entry itself in the *Number* field. This is the most frequently occurring pair.

Finding the largest entry is easy enough, but what about the 100 largest entries? One way to find them involves using an *insertion sort* algorithm. It requires an array of 100 elements, each capable of storing a letter pair, and the number of times it's occurred. We'll store the elements in order from most frequent to least. The algorithm looks like this:

insertion sort

Get a new count and pair;
Starting with the first element in the ordered array
    move to the right until we find an element with a smaller count;
insert the new element in front of it;

Note that, if we actually make an insertion, the 100'th element will get bumped off the list.

In practice, the ordered-elements array is defined to have one extra element—101 rather than 100:

```
{type definition continued...}
        OrderArray = array [1..101] of PairData;
```

The extra element serves as a bumper at the end of the array, and lets us use an ordinary **while** loop to search for a smaller value. If we didn't use this bumper, we'd inevitably find ourselves trying to check the array's 101st element (unless we resorted to fancy coding). We discussed this problem in Chapter 11's antibugging section.

What exactly will we print? The number of times each pair occurred will be meaningless without the total number of pairs. So, let's report on the total number of pairs found, and give the individual pair figures as a percentage of the total. We can refine our pseudocode once more as:

third refinement

```
initialize the pair counting and ordering arrays;
read the first character;
while not eof
   read the second character;
   if it's a capital then convert it to lower case;
   if the first and second characters are both lower case
      update element [first character, second character];
   advance the window—first character gets the value of the second character;
for every element of the PairArray-type variable
   insert it in an ordered array;
for every element of the ordered array
   print the letter pair, and its relative frequency;
print the total number of pairs counted;
```

Program *Doubles* implements this pseudocode. We've given it the contents of this entire section, including programs, as input.

letter-pair frequency program

```
program Doubles (input, output);
   {Computes the frequency of letter pairs in a text sample.
    Prints the hundred most frequent pairs.}
type PairArray = array ['a'..'z', 'a'..'z'] of integer;
     ShortString = packed array [1..2] of char;
     PairData = record
                   Pair: ShortString;
                   Number: integer
                end;
     OrderArray = array [1..101] of PairData;
var ch1, ch2: char;
    Pairs: PairArray;
    Ordered: OrderArray;
    Total, Current: integer;
procedure Initialize (var Pairs: PairArray; var Ordered: OrderArray);
   {Initialize Pairs and Ordered to 0's.}
   var ch1, ch2: char;
       i: integer;
   begin
      for ch1 := 'a' to 'z' do
         for ch2 := 'a' to 'z' do
            Pairs[ch1, ch2] := 0;
      for i := 1 to 101 do
         Ordered[i].Number := 0
   end; {Initialize}
procedure BuildThePairsTable (var Pairs: PairArray; var Total: integer);
   {Counts the occurrences of each character pair.}
   var ch1, ch2: char;
   function DeCapitalized (Capital: char): char;
      {Represents its capital argument as a lower-case letter.}
      begin
         DeCapitalized := chr(ord('a')+(ord(Capital)-ord('A')));
      end; {DeCapitalized}

   function BothValid (ch1, ch2: char): boolean;
      {Represents true if both arguments are lower-case letters.}
      begin
         BothValid := (ch1 in ['a'..'z']) and (ch2 in ['a'..'z'])
      end; {BothValid}
```

```
    begin {BuildThePairsTable}
      ch1 := ' ';
      Total := 0;
      while not eof do begin
        read (ch2);
        if ch2 in ['A'..'Z'] then ch2 := DeCapitalized(ch2);
        if BothValid(ch1, ch2) then begin
            Pairs[ch1, ch2] := Pairs[ch1, ch2]+1;
            Total := Total+1
        end; {if}
        ch1 := ch2
      end {while}
    end; {BuildThePairsTable}

procedure Insert (Current: integer; var Ordered: OrderArray;
                  HowMany: integer; ch1, ch2: char);
    {Insert a new element into position Current in Ordered.}

    var i: integer;

    begin
      for i := 100 downto Current do
          Ordered[i+1] := Ordered[i];
      Ordered[Current].Pair[1] := ch1;
      Ordered[Current].Pair[2] := ch2;
      Ordered[Current].Number := HowMany
    end; {Insert}

procedure PrintTheTable (Ordered: OrderArray; Total: integer);
    {Prints the contents of Ordered.}

    var Counter: integer;
        Subtotal: real;

    begin
      Subtotal := 0.0;
      for Counter := 1 to 100 do begin
        write (Ordered[Counter].Pair, ' ',
               (Ordered[Counter].Number / Total)*100:4:2, '%   ');
        Subtotal := Subtotal+(Ordered[Counter].Number);
        if (Counter mod 6) = 0 then writeln {make the output table neat}
      end;
      writeln;
      writeln ('Output represents:   ',
               (Subtotal / Total)*100:4:2, '% of ', Total:1, ' pairs.')
    end; {PrintTheTable}
```

```
begin {Doubles}
   Initialize (Pairs, Ordered);
   BuildThePairsTable (Pairs, Total);
   for ch1 := 'a' to 'z' do
      for ch2 := 'a' to 'z' do begin
         Current := 1;
         while (Ordered[Current].Number >=Pairs[ch1, ch2])
                                                  and (Current <=100) do
            Current := Current+1;
         if Current <=100 then
            Insert (Current, Ordered, Pairs[ch1, ch2], ch1, ch2);
      end; {for}
   PrintTheTable (Ordered, Total)
end. {Doubles}
```

```
th 2.79%  fi 2.74%  in 2.32%  he 2.10%  re 1.98%  ar 1.94%
er 1.84%  or 1.72%  fr 1.70%  ra 1.37%  nt 1.33%  on 1.31%
en 1.28%  fb 1.20%  es 1.18%  te 1.17%  it 1.14%  al 1.13%
at 1.06%  an 1.04%  ch 1.03%  ha 1.01%  st 0.99%  rr 0.98%
co 0.97%  le 0.97%  ed 0.91%  ti 0.90%  nd 0.90%  be 0.89%
ro 0.88%  ay 0.86%  to 0.86%  of 0.85%  is 0.81%  ou 0.80%
ir 0.78%  rd 0.78%  ri 0.78%  se 0.77%  ta 0.76%  ic 0.75%
ng 0.75%  me 0.74%  de 0.71%  io 0.70%  ur 0.68%  ct 0.67%
ec 0.66%  pa 0.65%  om 0.63%  rs 0.60%  we 0.59%  ea 0.59%
ca 0.58%  pr 0.57%  ve 0.57%  ll 0.57%  mp 0.57%  as 0.56%
da 0.56%  ne 0.55%  oo 0.53%  um 0.53%  el 0.51%  ai 0.49%
em 0.49%  ns 0.49%  wi 0.47%  am 0.46%  us 0.45%  ac 0.44%
fo 0.43%  ot 0.41%  pe 0.41%  rt 0.41%  so 0.41%  ge 0.39%
va 0.39%  et 0.36%  ts 0.36%  bo 0.35%  il 0.35%  un 0.35%
si 0.34%  ex 0.34%  im 0.33%  ow 0.32%  ho 0.32%  li 0.31%
tr 0.31%  ue 0.31%  bl 0.30%  hi 0.30%  do 0.29%  nu 0.29%
oc 0.28%  pu 0.28%  ut 0.28%  di 0.28%
Output represents:  78.47% of 17396 pairs.
```

Records With Variants* 12-3

THE RECORDS WE'VE DEFINED SO FAR HAVE each had a fixed contingent of fields. However, Wirth enhanced Pascal records by allowing the definition of *record variants*. When we use record variants, the effective number and type of fields in a single record may change during the course of a program. This means that two variables can be of an identical record type, yet have different numbers or types of fields.

We'll discuss record variants briefly. First we'll consider a record that has *only* a variant part, then we'll define a record with a fixed part *and* a variant part. Finally, we'll establish the syntax of record variants. Let's begin with a data structuring problem that illustrates the need for record variants in the first place.

Suppose that we're recording measurements that describe several four-sided figures. The table below shows that each shape is defined by a different group of dimensions.

why do we need variants

Shape	*Required Dimensions*
Square	*Side*
Rectangle	*Length, Width*
Rhomboid	*Side, AcuteAngle*
Trapezoid	*Top, Bottom, Height*
Parallelogram	*Top, Side, ObtuseAngle*

Now, if a program required us to store these dimensions we could easily define five different records—one for each shape. Or, it might be more convenient to define a single record that serves to record the dimensions of *any* of the shapes, like this:

```
type Shape = (Square, Rectangle, Rhomboid, Trapezoid, Parallelogram);
     Dimensions = record
                    WhatShape: Shape;
                    Side, Width, Length, Top, Bottom, Height: real;
                    AcuteAngle, ObtuseAngle: 0..360
                  end;
```

shortcomings of records

Each field of type *Dimension* is fixed, and every variable of type *Dimensions* contains the exact same fields. Unfortunately, this causes two problems for the programmer. First of all, it's possible to make useless assignments to a variable of type *Dimensions*, such as recording the angles of a square. Second, every variable will have extra (and unnecessary) fields. If a program contained many hundreds or thousands of such variables, this waste of storage space might be important.

Record variants come to the rescue. If you examine the definition of *Dimensions*, it's obvious that the *WhatShape* field tells us which fields are actually required in the rest of the record. For example, if *WhatShape* is *Square*, all we really need is a *Side* field. All the others are superfluous.

the tag field

> The idea that the value of one field could or should determine the rest of the structure is the basis of record variants. One field is designated to be a *tag* or marker field—a field whose value tags or marks the proper group of *variant* fields.

Dimensions is redefined below as a record with variants. *WhatShape* is the tag field, and the record contains five groups of variant fields.

a record with variants

```
type Shape = (Square, Rectangle, Rhomboid, Trapezoid, Parallelogram);
     Dimensions = record
                    case WhatShape: Shape of     {The tag field}
                      Square: (Side1: real);
                      Rectangle: (Length, Width: real);
                      Rhomboid: (Side2: real; AcuteAngle: 0..360);
                      Trapezoid: (Top1, Bottom, Height: real);
                      Parallelogram: (Top2, Side3: real; ObtuseAngle: 0..360)
                  end; {Dimensions}
var FourSidedObject: Dimensions;
```

> Each variant's fields must be unique. No field identifier can appear in more than one group. The tag field, in contrast, is shared by each of the variant groups.

Until the tag field has a value, the remainder of the record variant's structure is undefined. At this point, we can only make an assignment to the tag field, *WhatShape*.

```
FourSidedObject.WhatShape := Rectangle;
```

activating variants

Once *WhatShape* has been given a value, the fields associated with that value (given in parentheses in *Dimension's* definition above) are created. The assignment above activates a certain group of fields—in this case, *Length* and *Width*. As long as the value of *WhatShape* is *Rectangle*, these are the only fields that *FourSidedObject* will contain. We can make the assignments:

```
FourSidedObject.Length := 4.3;
FourSidedObject.Width := 7.5;
```

but an attempted assignment to a field in one of the other variant groups (say, *Top1* or *ObtuseAngle*) is an error—it does not exist.

What if the value of the tag field changes? If we now say that:

```
FourSidedObject.WhatShape := Parallelogram;
```

we find ourselves able to access three new, but as yet undefined fields—*Top2, Side3* and *ObtuseAngle*. The former variant fields *Length* and *Width* simply don't exist any more—they've been deactivated and replaced.

> Record variants act as an antibugging device, by restricting the assignments that can be made to a record variable.

advantages of variants

A single record variant definition (like *Dimensions*) has other advantages over the five separate definitions we might have made. Suppose that we want to write a function that computes and represents the area of variable *FourSidedObject*. In function *Area*, below, a single variable of type

Dimensions is passed as a parameter, then dissected within the routine. If we were using five different records, we'd have to write five different subprograms. But since *Dimensions* is defined as a record variant, just one declaration suffices.

```
function Area (Object: Dimensions): real;
  {Computes an area that depends on an active variant.}
  begin
    with Object do
      case WhatShape of
        Square: Area := sqr(Side1);
        Rectangle: Area := Length * Width;
        Rhomboid: Area := sqr(Side2)*sin(AcuteAngle);
        Trapezoid: Area := (Top1+Bottom)/2*Height);
        Parallelogram: Area := Top2 *Side3 *sin(ObtuseAngle)
      end {case}
  end; {Area}
```

using the active variant

Notice how the **case** statement in *Area* parallels the construction of *Dimensions* variant part. Using a tag field as the **case** expression is quite common, and is why record variants are similar to **case** statements.

The variant parts of the *Dimensions* record were *disjoint*, which means that they only shared the tag field. However, Pascal lets us define records that share fields, and have variants as well.

fixed and variant parts

> A record definition may include a *fixed part* and a *variant part*. The fixed part *always* comes before the variant part, and only one variant part is allowed (although variants may be nested).

In the example below, the *Year, Fee*, and *ExpirationDate* fields form *Registration's* fixed part. They, along with the tag field *VehicleType*, are shared by every variant.

```
type Model = (Motorcycle, Car, Truck);
     Registration = record
                      Year: 1915..1987;
                      Fee: real;
                      ExpirationDate: 1986..1990;
                      case VehicleType: model of
                        Motorcycle: (EngineSize: 50..1200);
                        Car: (Cylinders: 2..8; SmogRequired: boolean);
                        Truck: (Axles: 2..10; Weight, Tare: integer)
                    end; {Registration}
```

The current value of the tag field *VehicleType* determines which group of variant fields will be accessible.

Other applications that require records with both fixed and variant fields include employment records, library records, medical records, and the like—any time some storage is specialized, and some general.

Syntax of Variants

The syntax of a record with a variant part is, without doubt, the toughest in Pascal, and it requires a great deal of soul-searching to be understood. By using the reserved word **case** in a misplaced moment of economy, Wirth managed to confuse nearly everybody. The reason is that the **case** of a record variant is only superficially similar to the **case** of a **case** statement.

The definition of a record type has three basic sections, as shown below. We'll look at each in turn, and clarify some of the fine points of record-variant definitions.

```
type RecordName = record
{Fixed Fields}         FieldName: FieldType;
                       FieldName, FieldName: FieldType;
{Tag Field}            case TagField: FieldType of
                         TagValue: (FieldName: FieldType);
{Variant Fields}         TagValue, TagValue: (FieldName: FieldType;
                                     FieldName, FieldName: FieldType);
                         TagValue: ( ) {Empty field list.}
                   end;
```

The *fixed* part we're already familiar with:

fixed part

```
type RecordName = record
                      FieldName: FieldType;
                      FieldName, FieldName: FieldType;
                  {end} {...if there's no tag field and variant part.}
```

Any number of fields may be defined—even none, which makes the fixed part optional.

The tag field follows the last field of the fixed part. It consists of the tag field identifier, and its type, between the reserved words **case** and **of.**

tag field

```
case TagField: FieldType of
```

Because the variant part comes after the last fixed field, no extra **end** matches the **case.** The same **end** that ends the record type definition also terminates the variant part.

The variant part is the most complicated section. Each group of variant fields begins with a 'selector' value (one of the possible values of the tag field), followed by a colon, and the variant fields between parentheses.

variant part

```
{Variant Fields}    TagValue: (FieldName: FieldType);
                    TagValue, TagValue: (FieldName: FieldType;
                                FieldName, FieldName: FieldType);
                    TagValue: ( ) {Empty field list.}
                end;
```

If a tag field selector value (or values) doesn't have any variant fields associated with it, an empty field list must be provided—*no* field names are put between the parentheses (as above).

The syntax chart of a record definition is more complicated than any we've encountered so far. A record type can be shown simply as:

record type

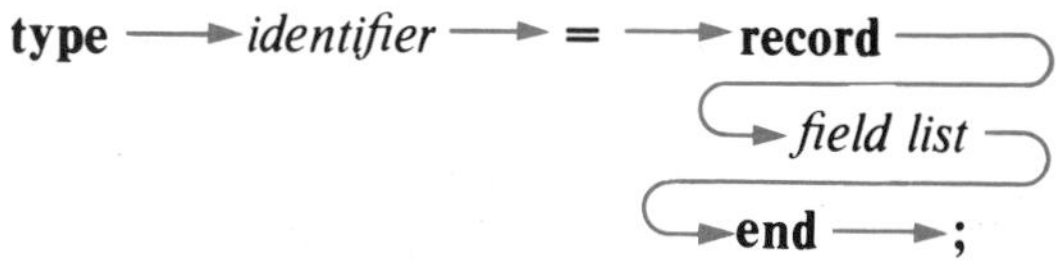

The syntax of a field list is much harder to follow. If you read it carefully, you'll see that the field list is partially defined in terms of itself. This makes it a recursively defined type.

field list

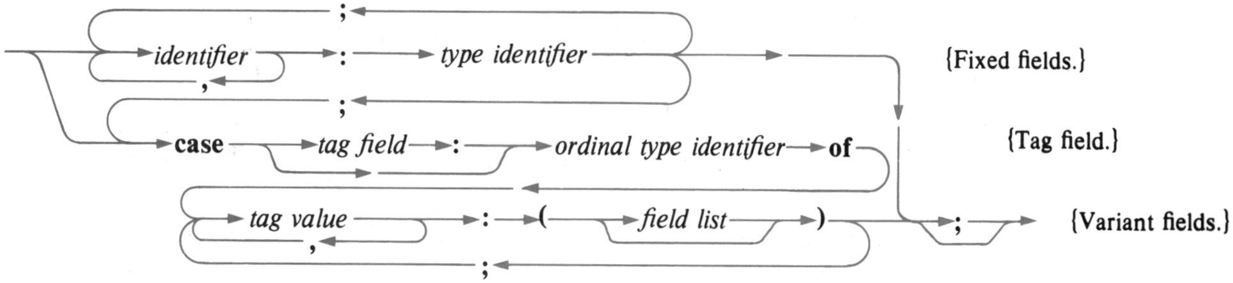

Antibugging and Debugging 12-4

THE MOST COMMON ERROR IN DEFINING record types is to omit the **end** that marks the conclusion of the record definition. Imagine how a compiler might read this program segment:

type *RealEstate* = **record**
Street, Avenue: *integer*;
Price: *real*;
var *Apartment*: *char*;

Since the end of the record definition isn't indicated, the compiler will probably think that **var** is one of *RealEstate's* fields, and print an error message that points out the futility of using reserved words as identifiers, along with a host of other presumed transgressions:

```
type RealEstate = record
                    Street, Avenue: integer;
                    Price: real;
var Apartment: char;
↑RESERVED WORD "VAR" MAY NOT BE FIELD IDENTIFIER
   ↑MISSING COMMA
                  ↑MISPLACED COLON
                    ↑PROBABLE MISUSE OF IDENTIFIER "CHAR"
```

The fact that records and **with** statements have their own form of scope also causes confusion. For example, this is a perfectly legal sequence of definitions and declarations:

```
type InnerRecord = record
                       AnyName: integer
                   end;
     OuterRecord = record
                       AnyName: boolean;
                       Inside: InnerRecord
                   end;
var TestCase: OuterRecord;
    AnyName: char;    etc.
```

scope bugs

In the usual context of a program, the two *AnyName* fields will be distinct from each other, as well as from variable *AnyName*, because a reference to a field is usually prefaced by the name of the record-type variable it belongs to. The assignment below is to the *char* variable *AnyName*.

```
AnyName := 'R';
```

In the next example, the identifier *AnyName* refers to the *boolean* field of *TestCase*. The *integer AnyName* field of *Inside* must be referred to using the period notation, and the global variable *AnyName* cannot be accessed at all.

```
with TestCase do begin
   AnyName := true;
   Inside.AnyName := 5
end;
```

Giving two record names to the **with** statement further restricts the scope of the identifier *AnyName*. The *integer AnyName* field of *Inside* is accessed below. It's the most local because *Inside* is the last record named.

```
with TestCase, Inside do begin
   AnyName := 6
end;
```

with statement bugs

An exceptionally sneaky bug can occur when we use a **with** statement to examine the record-type elements of an array. Suppose that we have an array of 100 elements, and want to examine an element whose *Sum* field is nonzero (we're sure that one exists). Will this code work?

```
{incorrect segment}
Count := 1;
with TheArray[Count] do begin
   while Sum=0 do Count := Count+1;
      ...
   manipulate other fields of TheArray[Count]
end;
```

No, it won't. Instead, if *TheArray*[1].*Sum* equals 0, the **while** loop will become an infinite loop.

> The Golden Rule of **with** Statements
>
> The specific record that a **with** statement has access to cannot be changed during the statement's action. It is determined when the statement is first entered.

The code above must be modified like this:

```
{correct segment}
Count := 1;
while TheArray[Count].Sum=0 do
    Count := Count+1;
with TheArray[Count] do begin
    ...
    manipulate the TheArray[Count] fields
end;
```

A basic source of misunderstanding in dealing with structured variables is the difference between the name of a type, and the name of a variable. The following mistake is quite common. A programmer defines a type...

type definition bugs

```
type Housing = (House, .....Hotel, Vacant);
     Name = packed array [1..20] of char;
     Property = record
                    Address: Name;
                    Rent: real;
                    Buildings: Housing;
                    ...
                end; {Property}
     Board = array [1..24] of Property;
var GameBoard: Board;
```

...and then accidentally refers to the *type* identifier instead of a *variable* identifier in the program:

```
Board[22].Address := 'Boardwalk           ';
    {The variable identifier GameBoard should have been used.}
```

> Type identifiers *never* appear in the statement part. If you see a type identifier in an assignment statement or procedure call, you can be sure it's up to no good.

how variants work

The Pascal headaches caused by record variants extend far beyond their weird syntax. Our discussion was less than candid (we lied) when we said that assigning a value to the tag field activated a particular group of variant fields. In reality, *all* of the record's fields are accessible *all* the time. Understanding why this spells trouble requires a bit of background in how values are stored. Usually, the computer provides a unique portion of its memory for the storage of each field and variable value. As you might imagine, values of different types require different amounts of storage. The illustration below shows how two distinct records might have space allocated for their fields.

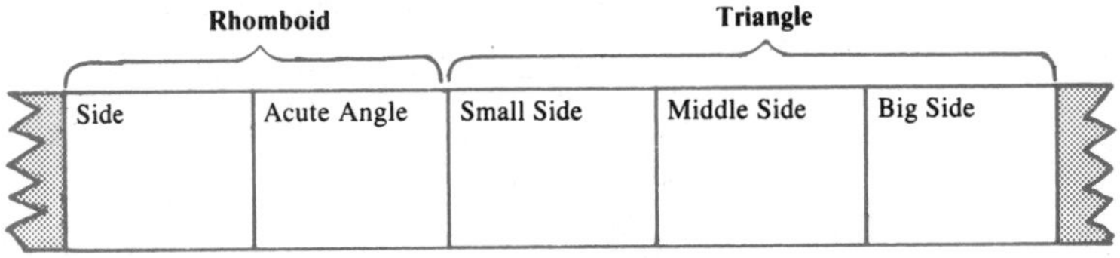

Now, let's imagine that instead of being separate records, the two groups above are variant parts of a single record. The compiler saves space by *overlaying* them—scheduling them for the *same* area in the computer's memory:

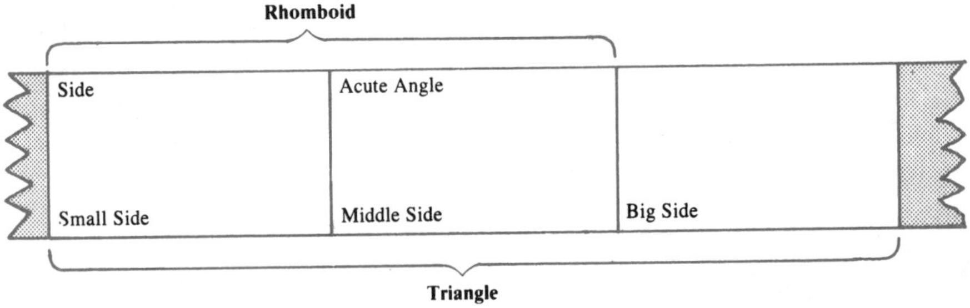

All is well and good as long as we only input and output values of one variant group. Trouble comes when we store values according to one scheme of occupancy, and then mistakenly try to read them according to the other. Although we get a value, it is gibberish. You would think that the compiler would prevent errors of this sort, but it doesn't because of a very specialized option of record variants we didn't shout about.

optional tag fields

A tag field need not be specified for a record variant. However, a type identifier must still be given:

case *TypeIdentifier* **of** etc.

The rest of the variant part's definition proceeds normally.

This feature is error-prone and rarely used. Since the tag field is optional, it can't be checked by the compiler. Thus, *you* should always declare a tag field, and check its value before trying to access fields of a variant part.

Pascal Summary

• **record** type: a structured type that lets a variable store values of different types. The record type definition names the type, and gives the names and types of the record's fields:

```
type Sample = record
                  ANumber: integer;
                  Letter1, Letter2: char
              end;
var RecordVar, RecordSample: Sample;
```

• fields: can be of any type, simple or structured. Fields can be assigned to one at a time:

```
RecordVar. ANumber := 44;
RecordVar.Letter1 := 'W';
```

Or, if two records have identical types, assignment can be made between all fields simultaneously:

```
RecordSample := RecordVar;
```

• **with** statement: used to make assignments to a record's fields, without the necessity of repeatedly referring to the record variable's name:

```
with RecordVar do begin
    ANumber := 26;
   Letter2 := 'X'
end;
```

Important Facts

• A record's fields must have different identifiers. However, different records can share the same identifiers—each record has its own name list. Field identifiers also don't conflict with identifiers defined elsewhere.

• A **with** statement can be given more than one record variable as an argument. This construction is equivalent to a series of nested **with** statements. The last-named (i.e. innermost) variable's fields take precedence.

• Lateral thinking is an approach to problem solving in which alternative strategies are explored before making any commitments.

• The Golden Rule of **with** Statements: The specific record that a **with** statement has access to can't be changed during the statement's action. This rule is mainly of concern when we're looking at record-type elements of array variables.

Self-test Exercises

12-1 True or false: A record must have at least two fields. The fields of a record must have different names. A record must have a different name than any of its fields.

12-2 Is this a legal type definition? Why not?

```
type Unit = record
                Quantity: integer;
                Cut: Style
            end;
     Style = (Mini, Midi, Maxi);
```

12-3 Suppose that the period character were allowed to appear in Pascal identifiers. What problem would this cause? Give an example.

12-4 Which record variables can we make complete record assignments between?

```
type Period = record
                  Months, Days, Years: integer
              end;
     Time = record
                  Months, Days, Years: integer
            end;
var Passage, Interval: Period;
    SnowsOfYesteryear: Time;
```

12-5 Define a record suited for showing the position, and color, of a checker on a checkerboard.

12-6 Latitude and longitude are specified in degrees (°), minutes (´), seconds (˝), and direction (North, South, East, and West). Suppose that a city lies at latitude 22° 17´ 34˝ North, and longitude 53° 41´ 9˝ West. Store this location in variable *City*, as declared below.

```
type CompassPoints = (North, South, East, West);
     Coordinates = record
                       Degrees: 0..180;
                       Minutes, Seconds: 0..60;
                       Direction: CompassPoints
                   end;
     Location = record
                    Latitude, Longitude: Coordinates
                end;
var City: Location;
```

12-7 Why wouldn't the **with** statement below be suitable for making the assignments of the previous question?

```
with City, Latitude, Longitude do begin     etc.
```

12-8 Suppose that we have the definitions and declarations shown below:

```
type PhoneNumber = record
                       AreaCode, Prefix, Number: integer
                   end;
var Home, Office, Car: PhoneNumber;
```

Write code to test if *Home* and *Office* represent the same phone numbers, to check whether *Office* and *Car* are in the same area code, and to set the prefix stored in *Car* equal to the prefix in *Home*.

12-9 A record without a variant part only uses the reserved word **end** once. If a record has a variant part, how many times does the reserved word **end** appear in the record definition?

12-10 What is the purpose of a tag field?

12-11 Assume that *Series* is an array of records, subscripted by a subrange of *integer*. What is the output of the following code? Are we making an assignment to the *Current* or *Current*+1 record inside the **with** statement?

```
Series [Current].Initial := 'A';
with Series [Current] do begin
    Current := Current + 1;
    Initial := 'B'
end;
Current := Current - 1;
writeln (Series [Current].Initial);
```

More Exercises

12-11 Write a program that helps a user plan a menu. Determine the recommended daily allowances of various vitamins and nutritive elements for men, women, and children. Have the program user enter a meal—the data associated with each food item, as well as the number of men, women, and children who will be eating. Print out the proportion of the RDA provided for each diner. Note that you'll have to provide a rule (or random process) for dividing the food.

12-12 Nadine finds a treasure map! It contains the following inscription:

Your good-luck country is a ten-foot square,
And four feet of treasure are buried there.

Nadine takes this to mean that a four-foot treasure chest is buried somewhere under a ten by ten plot of land. Write a program that picks a location for the buried treasure, and lets Nadine take ten guesses of its location. Show what the plot looks like after each hole is dug. Naturally, you shouldn't show the treasure.

12-13 Check reconciliation is the process of comparing a list of checks that have been written against a list of those that have been cashed and returned. The object is to find the number and amount of checks that haven't been cashed (or checks that were cashed for the wrong amount), as well as a current bank balance.

Write a program that reconciles a checking account. Construct a starting 'data base' by taking a beginning balance, and the number and amount of each check written. Then, accept as input the number and amount of each check cashed and returned. Design data types for two situations: *a*) all check numbers are known in advance to fall within a particular range; *b*) check numbers aren't known in advance. However, don't bother sorting input, and write only one program.

12-14 Write an interactive soccer program. This is a program that can be endlessly refined and improved, so set definite goals (ha!) for yourselves. A first version should let two users move two players around a small field, checking for collisions, running into walls, and the like.

A second version can introduce the soccer ball. Improve your graphics output, and allow five 'players' per team. Allow kicking of the ball.

In version three, start to make the game more realistic. Keep track of the strength of players (which should affect their running and kicking ability). Allow scoring and out-of-bounds kicks.

Version four—the sky's the limit. Implement injuries, penalties, etc.

12-15 The tables have turned on Rachel Rustler—a giant chicken from the Pullet Planet is chasing her through midtown Manhattan. As you know, it's easy to get around midtown because the streets are numbered one way, and the avenues the other. Unfortunately, there are horrendous traffic jams all around, and Rachel can only run around the area from 34th to 42nd street, bounded by 1st through 7th avenues. Rachel and the chicken can each can run only one block at a time, but the chicken, because of its size, is able to move diagonally.

Implement an interactive game that has the computer play the role of giant chicken trying to catch Rachel within a given number of turns. A human player, as Rachel, tries to escape. Concentrate on writing the program as a series of refinements and extensions. Begin with a small (5 by 5) board and guide both chicken and Rachel, then increase the size of the board. Develop a strategy for your program to follow in guiding the chicken, and experiment with different starts.

12-16 Suppose that you are about to read in a data value that is either *real*, *integer*, or *char*. Define a record type that is suited for holding any of these values (use record variants if you want, or include a field that indicates which one of the other fields is being used if you don't uses variants). Then, write a procedure to read in the data value and assign it to the appropriate field of the record.

12-17 Define a new syntax, and alternative reserved words, for a record type. Can you make record variants easier to deal with? Do you think that you should change the syntax of a **const** definition to allow the definition of structured constants? What about letting functions represent structured values?

'How can we possibly insert something at the beginning, or in the middle . . . ?'

13

Files and Text Processing

Ask most people to describe what worries them about computers in a single word, and that word is liable to be 'files.' With the aid of computers, it's possible to keep track of enormous amounts of information—or to pull out hidden facts from a mass of raw data. Credit history, police records, tax returns, school records, even the videotapes you rented last week are all on file in various computers.

And how can all that information be used? Can files be put together in ways that weren't originally anticipated? Is it possible to sneak through a file, looking for a single word or name? Can information be surreptitiously inserted into—or removed from—a file?

The creation and use of files is the topic of Chapter 13. The most basic sort of files are used to store characters. These are called *textfiles*, and are discussed in section 13-1. Odds are that the Pascal programs you've been writing all along are stored in textfiles, so they won't be too unfamiliar.

Section 13-2 looks at the notion of a file in general. In it we discuss details of file manipulation, and consider files of ordinal and structured types besides *char*. As usual, we close with an Antibugging section, 13-3, at the end of the chapter.

Making and Using Textfiles 13-1

GARBO SPEAKS! LET'S SAVE HER FIRST SCREEN words for posterity in a file named *Garbo*.

```
program GarboSpeaks (Garbo, output);
    {Creates, and adds to, a textfile named Garbo.}

type text = file of char;

var Garbo: text;

begin
   rewrite (Garbo);
   writeln (Garbo, 'Gimme a viskey, and don'' be stingy.')
end. {GarboSpeaks}
```

file components

> A *file*-type variable stores a sequence of any number of *component* values (except other files).

The syntax chart of a file-type definition is:

file type

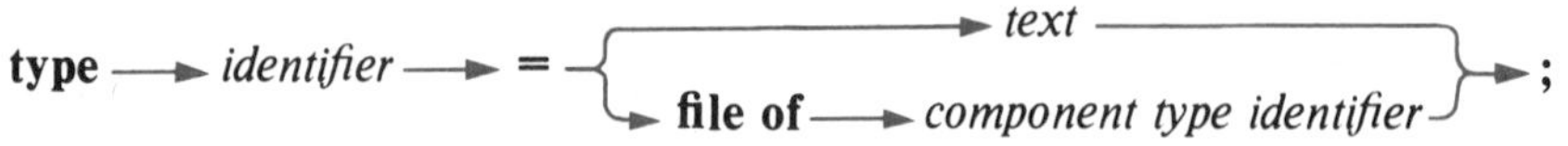

A general notion of files should be familiar to all of us by now, since computer systems rely on the idea of files as storage places. File-type variables can be used to create or gain access to permanently stored files (so-called *external* files), or to create files that only last for the duration of program execution (*internal* files). External and internal files are identical except for the requirement that external files be passed as *file parameters* in a program heading (as *Garbo* is above).

Program *GarboSpeaks* stores *char* components in an external file named *Garbo*. The identifier *Garbo* turns up four times in the program.

file parameters

> 1. Program heading. Permanent, external files must be named in the program heading as *file parameters*. The order of file parameters doesn't matter.

Just as a procedure's parameters connect the procedure to the program it operates in, file parameters set up lines of communication between a program and its environment. That's why most programs have *input* and *output* given as file parameters.

file declaration

2. Variable declaration. Every file variable, whether it is internal and temporary, or external and permanent, must be declared before it can be used in a program. (*Input* and *output* are exempt from this rule.*)

type *text*

In this section we're going to concentrate on files of *char* values, also called *textfiles*. To accommodate special treatment of such files, a structured type *text* is predefined in Pascal. Its definition:

type *text* = **file of** *char*;

is a built-in part of every program (just like the definitions of the ordinal types *boolean* and *char*). As a result, the definition of type *text* in *GarboSpeaks* was redundant and unnecessary—it was already defined.

procedure *rewrite*

3. Procedure *rewrite*. A call of *rewrite* creates an empty file. Any data currently in the file is destroyed.

Since a program may contain several files, the name of the file we want prepared for writing is given as a parameter of *rewrite*:

```
rewrite(Garbo);        {Prepare to write file Garbo.}
rewrite(f);            {Prepare to write file f.}
```

A file's contents can be destroyed at any time with a subsequent call of *rewrite*.

4. Procedures *write* and *writeln*. When a file identifier is given as the first parameter of *write* or *writeln*, program output is sent to that file.

Program output normally goes to the standard file *output*, usually a terminal screen or lineprinter. Output can be directed to a file-type variable instead by naming the file *each time* we call *write* or *writeln*.

```
writeln (f, SomeVariable, Another, 'Que pasa?', AConstant);
writeln (g, V1, V2:3:4);
```

output to files

These calls send output to files *f* and *g*. Note that we can specify the field width of output values, and that textfiles are divided into lines. To put three blank lines into *Garbo*, we'd say:

```
writeln (Garbo);
writeln (Garbo);
writeln (Garbo);
```

The values of any predefined simple type may be written to (stored in) a textfile.

* Other predefined files, that do not have to be declared as variables, are frequently included as extensions to Pascal.

We can also write text values and string (**packed array** [*index*] **of** *char*) values, since they're both sequences of characters. In fact, only values of enumerated ordinal types *can't* be stored in textfiles, since they have no external character representations. In section 13-2 we'll see how to define file variables that can store such values.

Self-Check Questions

Q. What are the final contents of *SampleFile* after *Mistakes* is executed?

```
program Mistakes (SampleFile, output);
var SampleFile: text;
begin
   rewrite (SampleFile);
   write (SampleFile, 'Once, long ago, I thought I made a mistake.');
   rewrite (SampleFile);
   writeln (SampleFile, 'Unfortunately, I found out that I was wrong.')
end. {Mistakes}
```

A. The second call of *rewrite*(*SampleFile*) is an error. It erases the current contents of *SampleFile*, and starts us with a blank file. The final contents of *SampleFile* are 'Unfortunately, I found out that I was wrong.'

Reading From Files

It's time at last to murmur the magical incantation 'Let's have the computer analyze the data.'

```
program Analyze (output, Data);
var Data: text;
    Fact: integer;
      ...  {other variable declarations}
begin
   reset (Data);
   while not eof(Data) do begin
      read (Data, Fact);
      if Fact<25 then      etc.
         ...  {Program continues its analysis.}
end. {Analyze}
```

Like *Garbo, Data* is an external file, named in the program heading. And, like any file, it must be declared as a variable within the program. However, *Data* contains information to be read. It must be handled differently from a file that's being written.

procedure *reset*

The standard procedure *reset* puts us at the beginning of a file, ready to read its first value.

As we said earlier, a program may contain several file variables. The file we want to begin reading must be passed as a parameter to *reset*:

reset(*Data*); {Get ready to read from *Data.*}
reset(*g*); {Get ready to read from *g.*}

Another call of *reset* (with the same parameter) puts us back at the file's beginning. As a result, we can read the file all over again, but must start with its first component. A single file can be read and written (but never at the same time) within a single program. All that are required are appropriately placed calls of *reset* and *rewrite.*

reading from files

When the name of a textfile is given as the first parameter of *read* or *readln*, input is read from that file.

The standard *input* 'file' (keyboard or card reader) usually supplies a program's input. However, we can read data from a different source by naming it each time *read* or *readln* is called. For example:

read (*DataFile, First, Second, Third*);
{Read values of *First, Second*, and *Third* from *DataFile*.}
readln (*g, V1, V2*);

The first input statement reads the values of three variables from *DataFile*. The second statement reads the values of *V1* and *V2* from the file variable *g*, then gets rid of any more values stored on the same line (the typical usage of *readln*).

arguments to *eof* and *eoln*

Functions *eoln* and *eof* can each be given a single file name as an argument. *eoln's* argument must be of type *text*.

while not *eof*(*AnyFileName*) **do** etc.
...
if *eoln*(*AnyTextFile*) **then** etc.

What kinds of values can be read from a textfile? Intuitively it would seem that only *char* input can be read from a file of type *text*. However, we can read data of *any* standard type from a textfile, because it's stored as a sequence of *char* values.

When you sit at a terminal and enter data of any type, you send *char* values to the computer. When the computer expects to read *integer* or *real* values, it automatically converts the characters into values of the proper type. In a similar sense, even though values might differ *within* a program—*integer* is *integer*, *char* is *char*, and never the twain shall meet—they're stored in textfiles as characters. A program can read an *integer* value from a textfile as easily as it can read it from a keyboard or punched card.

There are three Golden Rules of using file-typed variables.

assignments to files are restricted

The Golden Rules of File Variables

Assignments cannot be made between two file-typed variables, even if they're both of the same type (such as *text*).

File variables are either being generated (if *rewrite* was called), or inspected (if *reset* was called)—never both.

File-type variables must always be passed to variable parameters, even if they're not changed within a subprogram.

The first rule's effect is to preclude shortcut methods of making two files identical. A file's contents must be read and written one value at a time. The prohibition against passing files as value parameters is an indirect consequence of this rule.

Self-Check Questions

Q. Suppose that a file named *Storage* contains the following data:

```
10 First Reading
20 Second Reading
30 Third Reading
```

What will the output of program *WillItWork* be?

```
program WillItWork (output, Storage);
var Storage: text;
    Value: integer;
begin
   reset (Storage);
   readln (Storage, Value);          writeln (Value);
   read (Storage, Value);            writeln (Value);
   readln (Storage, Value);          writeln (Value)
end. {WillItWork}
```

A. Its output is unexpected. It is:

```
                ↓    ↓    ↓    ↓    ↓
10
20
ABNORMAL TERMINATION --
ERROR IN TYPE OF INPUT -- INTEGER EXPECTED.
```

What happened? Well, the first input statement (using *readln*) read the value **10**, and discarded the characters remaining on the rest of the line. The second statement (using *read*) read **20** *without* moving on to the next line. When the final input statement tried to read an *integer* value, it mistakenly read the non-*integer* value **Second** into the *integer* variable *Value*, and caused a crash.

Textfile Searches and Insertions

What are some advantages of textfile types over records and arrays? The most important feature is that the size of files is not predetermined. Although the bounds of an array or the fields of a record must be defined in advance, a file can grow almost indefinitely. When a program must store an unknown quantity of data, a file is the data type of choice.

file advantages

Files allow permanent storage of program data. The success of programs that require substantial amounts of input is easily threatened by mistakes in data entry. As a defensive programming measure, data can be placed in a file, and a separate program or procedure written to error-check the file's contents. If the data is correct, the file can be reset and fed to the program proper. If it's incorrect, the program halts so that its data-file can be edited and fixed. You are left with a file of data entries that's known to be error free.

Files also have disadvantages in comparison to other types.

> The information stored in a file cannot be accessed at random.

file disadvantages

Suppose that we want to read the last value stored in a file. Calling the *reset* procedure puts us at the file's beginning. We must read all the way through the file to reach the end—there's no way to jump there automatically. Similarly, how can we easily compare the values on some particular line of two or more files? We have to *reset* and wade through each file (to the proper line) before making a comparison.

We're at a like disadvantage in writing files. The procedure *rewrite* puts us at the beginning of a blank file. Once *rewrite* has been called, we can only add data to the file's *end* (obviously, when a file is empty, its beginning and end are essentially the same). How could we possibly insert something at the beginning, or in the middle, of a file? Calling *rewrite* again erases all we've already written.

Naturally, there are shortcuts we can take to alleviate some of these problems. Since textfiles are divided into lines, we can jump from line to line (via *readln*) without bothering to peruse each line's contents. Let's solve the following problem of file *searching*:*

problem: counting file lines

> Suppose that we have a file of fortunes, one per line. Let the user enter a number (her age, say), then print the fortune found on that number's line.

The pseudocode breakdown of the program will have to include a check, shaded, to make sure that an exceptionally aged user doesn't run past the end of the *Fortunes* file:

* Some problems that involve searching for strings are considered in Chapter 16.

refinement

get the number;
prepare to read Fortunes;
while *we're not at the line we want* **and not** *eof* (*Fortunes*)
get the next line;
count the line;
if *there's a line for the age*
then *print it*
else *print a message*;

Note that, when we leave the loop, we're not sure of why we left. Did we find the correct line number, or did we just run out of file? Did both happen at the same time? Indeed, did we enter the loop at all—perhaps the user is less than a year old! The shaded section of program *FortuneCookie*, below, sees if we're on a proper line before it acts. The program will only print a line from *Fortunes* if we've reached an existing line number *Age*.

line-counting program

```
program FortuneCookie (input, output, Fortunes);
   {Finds and prints one line of textfile Fortunes.}

var Fortunes: text;
    Age, CurrentLine: integer;
    NextCharacter: char;

begin
   writeln ('Feel lucky?  How old are you?');
   readln (Age);
   CurrentLine := 1;
   reset (Fortunes);
   while (CurrentLine<Age) and not eof (Fortunes) do begin
      readln (Fortunes);
      CurrentLine := CurrentLine+1
   end;
   if (CurrentLine<>Age) or eof (Fortunes)
      then write ('You are just plain unlucky.  Don''t tempt fate.')
      else while not eoln (Fortunes) do begin
            read (Fortunes, NextCharacter);
            write (NextCharacter)
      end; {we've printed a line}
   writeln
end. {FortuneCookie}
```

Next, let's solve a problem that involves file *insertions*.

problem: file concatenation

The word *concatenate* means to link together in a series or chain. For example, the concatenation of 'simple' and 'minded' is 'simplem-inded'. Files are concatenated by being joined into a single longer file. Write a program that concatenates two files.

buffer files

Concatenation—putting one file at the head of another—is just a special case of file insertion. We'll find that temporary internal files come in handy for such jobs. They're used as *buffers*, or temporary holding places, while editing permanent external files. Internal files aren't included in the program heading since they, like ordinary program variables, don't exist before or after the program is run.

Suppose that we want to concatenate files *Beginning* and *Ending* into *Beginning*. *Beginning* will end up with its original contents followed by those of *Ending*. There is an almost overwhelming temptation to put the following pseudocode into effect.

{incorrect pseudocode}
prepare to read Beginning;
read it until eof (*Beginning*);
prepare to write Beginning;
prepare to read Ending;
add the contents of Ending to Beginning;

However, we shall resist the temptation—the pseudocode reads to the end correctly, but preparing to write *Beginning* will destroy its contents. To avoid this minor problem, we'll use *Temporary* as a transient, internal buffer file, and take the round-about route the pseudocode below suggests:

refinement

{correct pseudocode}
prepare to write file Temporary;
prepare to read Beginning;
add the contents of Beginning to Temporary;
prepare to read Ending;
add the contents of Ending to Temporary;
prepare to write Beginning;
prepare to read Temporary;
add the contents of Temporary to Beginning;

Notice that the first and third concatenations are really just file copy moves, because we're concatenating an empty file to one that isn't empty. The implemented program is shown below.

file concatenation program

```
program JoinFiles (Beginning, Ending, output);
   {Demonstrates file concatenation.}
var Beginning, Ending, TemporaryFile: text;
procedure Concatenate (var ToFile, FromFile: text);
   {Adds the contents of FromFile to the end of ToFile.}
   var CurrentCharacter: char;
   begin
      reset (FromFile);
      while not eof (FromFile) do begin
         while not eoln (FromFile) do begin
            read (FromFile, CurrentCharacter);
            write (ToFile, CurrentCharacter)
         end;
         readln (FromFile);
         writeln (ToFile)
      end
   end; {Concatenate}
begin
   rewrite (TemporaryFile);
   Concatenate (TemporaryFile, Beginning);
   Concatenate (TemporaryFile, Ending);
   rewrite (Beginning);
   Concatenate (Beginning, TemporaryFile)
end. {JoinFiles}
```

Self-Check Questions

Q. Suppose that the segment below is the statement part of *JoinFiles*, and that all files mentioned have been validly declared. What is its effect?

```
begin
   reset (File2);
   reset (File4);
   reset (File1);
   rewrite (File0);
   reset (File3);
   Concatenate (File0, File1);
   Concatenate (File0, File2);
   Concatenate (File0, File3);
   Concatenate (File0, File4);
   rewrite (File4);
   Concatenate (File4, File0)
end.
```

A. The program concatenates files *File1, File2, File3*, and *File4* into *File4*. *File0* serves as the temporary, internal file.

Textfile Comparisons

We've just seen examples that dealt with file searches and insertions. Let's look at a final problem of file *comparison*.

problem: finding common lines

> We have three textfiles that contain names, one per line, in alphabetical order. We know that there is at least one name in common between the files. Find it.

This problem has historically been characterized as the 'Welfare Cheat' question; we imagine that we're given files that contain the names of welfare recipients in adjoining counties. However, we could just as easily call it the 'Cabinet Felon' problem, and have files that contain the names of Cabinet officers, indicted felons, and major contributors to the party in power.

Our first difficulty will be making the comparisons at all. Now, comparing two lines character by character isn't too hard. This code will compare a line in *File1* to a line in *File2*:

```
{Travel along two lines until a mismatch or eoln.}
Ch1 := ' ';
Ch2 := ' ';
while not eoln(File1) and not eoln(File2) and (Ch1=Ch2) do begin
    read (File1, Ch1);
    read (File2, Ch2)
end;    etc.
```

Trouble starts when we leave the loop without a match. Suppose that we decide that the first line of *File2* is lower, alphabetically, than the first line of *File1*. We should get the second line from *File2*, and compare it to the first line of *File1*.

But what do we make the new comparison between? We'll be at the beginning of the new line from *File2*, but in the middle of the current line of *File1*. They might be equal, but there's no way to back up to the beginning of the line to check. Worse yet, according to our problem, we have *three* files to contend with.

string buffers

Our solution will be to buffer the current line of each file in a particularly convenient manner—as a string. Recall that we can compare strings to each other in their entirety, using the relational operators. If a line of one file is 'low' in relation to the current lines of the other files, we get the next line from that file. In pseudocode:

refinement

```
prepare to read each file;
save the first line of each file as a string;
while all three lines aren't equal
    while the first file's line is lower than any other
        get the next line from the first file;
    while the second file's line is lower than any other
        get the next line from the second file;
    while the third file's line is lower than any other
        get the next line from the third file;
print the common line;
```

Program *FindTheCommonLine*, below, depends on the assumption that *First, Second*, and *Third* really do have a line in common. Increasing its robustness (to make it immune from crashes due to a missing common line) require checks for *eof*, rather than any basic change in our algorithm.

common line-finding program

```
program FindTheCommonLine (First, Second, Third, output);
   {Find and print the common line in textfiles First, Second, and Third.}
const LINELENGTH = 80;
type String = packed array [1..80] of char;
var First, Second, Third: text;
    FirstLine, SecondLine, ThirdLine: String;
procedure GetTheNextLine (var TheFile: text; var TheLine: String);
   {Read a line of text up to LINELENGTH characters long.
    Advance to the next line of TheFile before leaving.}
   const BLANKLINE = '                                                    ';
   var Count: integer;
   begin
      TheLine := BLANKLINE;
      Count := 1;
      while (Count <=LINELENGTH) and not eoln(TheFile) do begin
         read (TheFile, TheLine[Count]);
         Count := Count + 1
      end;
      readln (TheFile)
   end; {GetTheNextLine}
begin
   reset (First);
   reset (Second);
   reset (Third);
   GetTheNextLine (First, FirstLine);
   GetTheNextLine (Second, SecondLine);
   GetTheNextLine (Third, ThirdLine);
   while (FirstLine<>SecondLine) or (FirstLine<>ThirdLine)
                              or (SecondLine<>ThirdLine) do begin
      while (FirstLine<SecondLine) or (FirstLine<ThirdLine) do
         GetTheNextLine (First, FirstLine);
      while (SecondLine<FirstLine) or (SecondLine<ThirdLine) do
         GetTheNextLine (Second, SecondLine);
      while (ThirdLine<FirstLine) or (ThirdLine<SecondLine) do
         GetTheNextLine (Third, ThirdLine)
   end; {outer while}
   writeln (FirstLine)
end. {FindTheCommonLine}
```

Focus On Programming: A Hard Program

Although our next example demonstrates an application of files, it's also important as an exercise in program comprehension. Suppose we are faced with the following problem:

problem: find the missing card

> We are given a deck of playing cards, stored in a file named *PartialDeck*. Were we to read *PartialDeck*, it would begin like this:
>
> **Ten of Spades Four of Hearts Queen of Hearts**
>
> and continue for a total of fifty-one cards. Our job is to write a program that finds the missing card.

This is a task that's easy for a person, but is difficult for a computer. After all, almost any human knows what a deck of cards is, and can design a simple search strategy that yields the missing card. A typical approach would be to pile up all the aces, deuces, etc., and then look for the stack containing only three cards. The missing one can be spotted almost instantly.

A computer, on the other hand, possesses an excellent memory (good enough to remember each card as it is read in), but has no idea of what playing cards are. Our first step in solving the problem might simply be to redefine our givens, using appropriate computer terminology where necessary.

First of all, a deck of cards consists of 52 pairs of values—every possible combination of thirteen number values and four suit values. Second, we have a textfile that contains 51 *triples* of nonblank strings—the number of a card, the word 'of', and the card's suit. This puts us in position for a second step—proposing a program outline.

first refinement

> *Explain to the computer what a deck of cards is by 'giving' it a full deck*;
> *Read in cards from our partial-deck file, and...*
> *Mark them off on the computer's list of a full deck*;
> *Search the computer's list for the card that wasn't found*;

Essentially, we're planning to read in each card and tick it off of a master list of cards. The only card *not* checked off is missing.

designing the data structure

At this point we have to ask a hard question: What is an appropriate data structure for representing a deck of cards? Given the adaptability of Pascal, there are many possible answers. Prime considerations for a very *good* answer are that the deck be easy to create, and that it be easy to use later in the program when we begin reading in card values from the partial-deck file.

When we designed a data structure for Hunt the Wumpus we faced a similar problem. Our response was to use a lateral thinking approach—roughing out a data type and then looking ahead for input, output, or scorekeeping problems that it might cause as a data structure. We did the same thing on our way to proposing the types defined below:

data type definition

```
{Proposed data types for representing a deck of cards.}
type String = packed array [1..8] of char;
     Card = record
              Number, Suit: String;
              Found: boolean
            end;
     Deck = array [1..52] of Card;

var FullDeck: Deck;
```

Some typical assignments to a variable of type Deck would be:

```
FullDeck[13].Number := 'Four    ';
FullDeck[13].Suit := 'Spades  ';
FullDeck[13].Found := false;
```

why use arrays?

Two features of this data structure deserve special attention. The advantages of defining *FullDeck* as an array type should be obvious—we're able to easily traverse the entire deck while loading it, or searching for a particular card. As a result, the quick sequence of statements shown below can eventually be used to find the missing card—the only element of the array whose *Found* field is *false*:

```
Counter := 1;
while FullDeck[Counter].Found do
   Counter := Counter + 1;
   {Increment Counter until the Found field is false.}
```

why use strings?

A more subtle advantage is gained by defining the *Number* and *Suit* fields as strings. As we did in our line-matching program, we're exploiting the fact that our data comes in a textfile, and that string values are easily compared. Suppose we have a *String*-type variable called *NextWord* that holds the first word in the partial-deck file. We can find the first equivalent word stored in *FullDeck* with:

```
Counter := 1;
while FullDeck[Counter].Number <> NextWord do
   Counter := Counter+1;
```

Now that we've defined a basic data structure, we'll take an unusual step. Program *FindTheLostCard* is shown on the next two pages. Instead of developing it from the top down, though, we'll explain it from the bottom up, procedure by procedure. We have two main reasons:

a bottom-up explanation

1. We specified the data structure independently of a full-scale stepwise refinement of the problem. When the working mechanism of a program is intimately tied to its structure(s), making or understanding a refinement can depend on *prior* knowledge of the program's type definitions.

2. Although an algorithm may be clear, details of its implementation can be complex. Knowing the algorithm won't necessarily enable you to follow the program.

We'll learn about *FindTheLostCard* by seeing what it does. As we go along, we'll start to understand how and why it works.

find the missing card program

```
program FindTheLostCard (output, PartialDeck);
   {Finds a missing pattern in a text file.}

type String = packed array [1..8] of char;
     Card = record
               Number, Suit: String;
               Found: boolean
             end;
     Deck = array [1..52] of Card;

var PartialDeck: text;
    FullDeck: Deck;

procedure GetAWord (var TheFile: text; var TheWord: String);
   {String input procedure.}
   const BLANKWORD = '        ';        {8 blank spaces.}
   var Counter : integer;
       CurrentCharacter: char;
   begin
      TheWord := BLANKWORD;        {Initialize TheWord.}
      repeat {Skip leading blanks.}
         read (TheFile, CurrentCharacter)
      until CurrentCharacter<>' ';
      Counter := 1;
      repeat {Read in the word.}
         TheWord[Counter] := CurrentCharacter;
         Counter := Counter+1;
         read (TheFile, CurrentCharacter)
      until (CurrentCharacter=' ') or (Counter>8)
   end; {GetAWord}
```

```
procedure InitializeTheDeck (var FullDeck: Deck);
   {Initializes every field of FullDeck.}

   var Counter: integer;
      NumberFile, SuitFile: text;
      NumberWord, SuitWord: String;

   begin
      rewrite(NumberFile);
      rewrite(SuitFile);
      writeln (NumberFile, 'Ace Deuce Three Four Five Six Seven');
      writeln (NumberFile, 'Eight Nine Ten Jack Queen King');
      writeln (SuitFile, 'Spades Hearts Clubs Diamonds');
      reset(NumberFile);
      reset(SuitFile);
      GetAWord(NumberFile, NumberWord);
      for Counter := 1 to 52 do begin {Load the aces, deuces, etc.}
         GetAWord(SuitFile, SuitWord);
         FullDeck[Counter].Number := NumberWord;
         FullDeck[Counter].Suit := SuitWord;
         FullDeck[Counter].Found := false;
         if ((Counter mod 4)=0) and (Counter<52) then begin
            reset(SuitFile); {After each suit's current number...}
            GetAWord(NumberFile, NumberWord)
         end {...go to the beginning of the Suit file, and get the next card number.}
      end {for}
   end; {InitializeTheDeck}

procedure InspectTheCards (var FullDeck: Deck; var PartialDeck: text);
   {Read PartialDeck and update Found fields in FullDeck.}

   var CardCount, PositionCounter: integer;
      NextWord: String;

   begin
      reset(PartialDeck);
      for CardCount := 1 to 51 do begin
         PositionCounter := 1;          {Start trying to match at the first card.}
         GetAWord(PartialDeck, NextWord);          {Get the 'number' word.}
         while (FullDeck[PositionCounter].Number<>NextWord) do
            PositionCounter := PositionCounter+1; {Match the 'number' word.}
         GetAWord(PartialDeck, NextWord); {Get rid of the 'of'.}
         GetAWord(PartialDeck, NextWord); {Get the 'suit' word.}
         while (FullDeck[PositionCounter].Suit<>NextWord) do
            PositionCounter := PositionCounter+1; {Match the 'suit' word.}
         FullDeck[PositionCounter].Found := true {Mark the card found.}
      end {for}
   end; {InspectTheCards}
```

```
procedure FindTheMissingCard (FullDeck: Deck);
   {Locate the element of FullDeck not marked Found.}
   var Counter: integer;
   begin
      Counter := 1;
      while FullDeck[Counter].Found do
         Counter := Counter+1;
      with FullDeck[Counter] do
         writeln ('The missing card is the ', Number, ' of ', Suit)
   end; {FindTheMissingCard}

begin
   InitializeTheDeck(FullDeck);
   InspectTheCards(FullDeck, PartialDeck);
   FindTheMissingCard(FullDeck)
end. {FindTheLostCard}
```

↓ ↓ ↓ ↓ ↓

Ten of Spades Four of Hearts Queen of Hearts Queen of Clubs Six of Clubs Jack of Hearts Seven of Spades Three of Diamonds Nine of Clubs Nine of Diamonds Ace of Diamonds King of Hearts King of Clubs Five of Spades Eight of Spades Six of Spades Four of Spades Eight of Hearts Seven of Clubs Five of Hearts Jack of Spades Deuce of Clubs Jack of Clubs Five of Diamonds Ace of Spades Queen of Spades Ace of Clubs Seven of Diamonds Three of Clubs Deuce of Hearts Ten of Hearts Queen of Diamonds Eight of Clubs Six of Hearts King of Spades Ten of Clubs Ten of Diamonds Four of Diamonds Deuce of Spades Nine of Spades Nine of Hearts Three of Spades Four of Clubs Three of Hearts Seven of Hearts Deuce of Diamonds Six of Diamonds Five of Clubs Ace of Hearts Eight of Diamonds King of Diamonds

```
The missing card is the Jack    of Diamonds
```

GetAWord

We'll begin our bottom-up analysis with *GetAWord*. It is a basic textfile procedure, designed to read a *String* value (*TheWord*) from any textfile (*TheFile*). Notice that padding with blanks is the first order of business, simplified by the definition of *BLANKWORD*, a constant that consists of eight blank spaces.

GetAWord makes a basic assumption about words—that they do not contain blanks. Thus, the first **repeat** loop skips past any leading blanks, blank lines, or end of line markers that may be in front of the first word. When a nonblank is found, the second **repeat** loop reads characters into *TheWord* until a trailing blank indicates that we've reached the end of the word or line. Note that no check for end-of-file is needed, since an end-of-line (read as a space) always ends a Pascal textfile.

GetAWord makes a safety check on the length of words. Attempting to assign a value to *TheWord*[9] would cause a crash as *TheWord*, by the definition of type *String*, only has index values 1 through 8. However, the procedure simply truncates the input string. The ninth character is lost.

InitializeTheDeck

Procedure *InitializeTheDeck* tells our program what a deck of cards is. It uses internal files to sidestep a lengthy series of assignments in initializing the array variable *FullDeck*. *FullDeck* is loaded in the following pattern: the first stored card, *FullDeck*[1], is the Ace of Spades, then *FullDeck*[2] is the Ace of Hearts, followed by the Aces of Clubs and Diamonds. With the fifth card, *FullDeck*[5], we begin the pattern again, storing the Deuces of Spades, Hearts, Clubs, and Diamonds. As the loading loop progresses, it sets each *Found* field to *false*.

a kludge

How do the internal files fit in? *NumberFile* holds the words that express the number values of files—'Ace', 'Deuce', 'Three', etc. *SuitFile* consists of the suit words 'Spades', 'Hearts', 'Clubs', and 'Diamonds'. The procedure begins by getting the first words of *NumberFile* and *SuitFile*. After pairing these words in *FullDeck*[1], the next suit is obtained, and used to initialize *FullDeck*[2]. Then we get the next suit, and the next. After four cards have been created (when *Counter* **mod** 4 =0), we read the next number word from *NumberFile*, and go back to the beginning of *SuitFile* by resetting it. The process continues until all 52 cards have been initialized.

Note that we could just as easily have initialized *FullDeck* in suit-order, i.e. all the Spades, then Hearts, etc. Why did we decide to go with number-order? We can discover the reason by analyzing *InspectTheCards*. The algorithm it follows is simplicity itself—given an initialized *FullDeck*. First, we find a card's number, then its suit, then we mark it *Found*.

InspectTheCards

InspectTheCards begins by reading the first word of *PartialDeck*. As we know this is a number word (perhaps 'Deuce', or 'Queen') we search through *FullDeck* for an identical *Number* field. Then we call *GetAWord* again, to get rid of the second string in *PartialDeck*—the word 'of'. This accomplished, we read in the third word—the card's suit word—and begin to search *FullDeck*, starting with our current position, for an equal *Suit* field. Given a suit match, we mark the card found. The process is repeated until we've checked in 51 cards.

Are there any potential problems with our implementation of this algorithm? The basic flaw in our procedure is its lack of error-checking—the entire program is not robust. What happens if *PartialFile* contains a word that is neither a number, suit, or 'of'? The program will crash as it attempts to inspect *FullDeck*[53]. A better version of *InspectTheCards* would print out the unmatchable string, along with an error message warning that subsequent program results might be wrong.

FindTheMissingCard

FindTheMissingCard is the simplest procedure in the program. The missing card will be the only card that hasn't been checked in, i.e. for which *FullDeck*[*Counter*].*Found* is *false*. Our decision to represent our data in string form pays off here, because we're able to output the value of the missing card directly.

Files of Simple and Structured Types 13-2

SECTION 13-1 DEALT SOLELY WITH FILES of *char*. However, we can define and declare file variables that store values of *any* structured or simple type, except another file type. For example:

```
type Card = record
              . . . {Definition of Card's fields}
            end;
     CardFile = file of Card;
     Color = (red, blue, green, yellow);
     ColorFile = file of Color;
     NumberFile = file of real;
var Cards: CardFile;
    Numbers: NumberFile;
    Colors: ColorFile;
    OneCard: Card;
    OneNumber: real;
    OneColor: Color;
```

As *text* is the only predefined file type, we have to explicitly define types *CardFile, NumberFile*, and *ColorFile*.

component type

> The values stored in a file are the file's *components*. Their type is the file's *component type*.

The components of file *Cards* are records of type *Card*; the component type of *Colors* is the enumerated type *Color*, etc. File components are stored according to the Pascal compiler's method of internal representation (which we'll explain soon), and usually cannot be read, printed, or created except with a Pascal program.

Access to files is handled by the standard (predefined) procedures *get* and *put*. Using these procedures requires an understanding of the *file window*. It can be thought of as a built-in variable that represents the component stored—or about to be stored—at the current file position.

the file window

> A file is a sequence of component values. The current file position is marked by a *file window*. The file window's identifier is the name of the file, followed by an up-arrow (↑) or circumflex (∧).

(We'll always use the up-arrow.) In effect, the file window contains the file component we're about to read. This helps explain how *eoln* and *eof* work. If the *input* file window *input*↑ holds the end-of-line or end-of-file marker, then function *eoln* or *eof* is *true*. We recommend that you take this opportunity to read or review section 8-2, which contains an optional early introduction to textfiles and the file window.

Every file access (even with *read* and *write*) uses the file window as a buffer, or intermediate storage place, between the computer and the actual file. To read a value from a file, we really 'get' the next value into the file window, and then read the file window. To write a value to a file, we assign the value to the file window, and then 'put' the window into the file.

procedure *get*

> The procedure call *get*(*f*) assigns the next component of file *f* to the file window *f*↑. Any current value of *f*↑ is discarded.

As you might imagine, calling procedure *reset* implicitly involves a call of *get*. The call:

reset(*FileName*);

essentially tells the compiler:

go to the beginning of FileName;
get(*FileName*);

how *read* works

The file window *FileName*↑ now represents the first component of *FileName*. Procedure *read* also uses *get*. The statement *read* (*f*, *X*) is equivalent to:

X := *f*↑;
get (*f*);

The call of *read* gets the value of *X* from a file named *f*. The equivalent pair of statements first assign *X* the current value of the file window, then give the next value in file *f* to *f*↑. Finally, we can describe the effect of *readln*(*f*), where *f* is a textfile, as:

while not *eoln*(*f*) **do** *get*(*f*);
get(*f*);

The current line is discarded, and the file window is left at the beginning of the next line (or at *eof* if there isn't a next line).

Output to file variables uses the other file-access procedure, *put*.

procedure *put*

> The procedure call *put*(*f*) adds the current value of *f*↑ to the end of file *f*.

how *write* works

Thus, *put* is always used after an assignment to the file window, and sometimes after a call of *rewrite*. The standard output procedure *write* also uses *put*. The call *write* (*f*, *X*) is the equivalent of:

f↑ := *X*;
put (*f*);

The call of *write* adds the value of *X* to the file named *f*. The statements above assign the file window the value of *X*, then place this value at the end of file *f*.

limits on I/O

> The standard procedures *write* and *read* can be used with files of any type, but if their file argument is not of type *text*, only one component argument may be given. Procedures *readln* and *writeln* may only be used with textfiles.

The statements *read* (*f, a, b, c*), *readln* (*f*), *write* (*g, a, b, c*), and *writeln* (*g*) are all illegal unless *f* and *g* are files of type *text*.

A final word about the file window will end our discussion. As we said earlier, the file window represents a value of the file's component type (unless it's empty). If the component type is structured, the file window can be used to access stored values. For example, assume the following definitions and declarations:

```
type StoredValues = array [1..100] of real;
     StoreFile = file of StoredValues;
var Storage: StoreFile;
```

structured file components

Storage is a file that can hold many array components. Each array is capable of holding 100 elements. We'll access some elements of the fifth array stored in *Storage*. Naturally, we're assuming that *Storage* has at least five components.

```
reset (Storage); {Does the first get.}
for i := 1 to 4 do
    get(Storage); {Go to the fifth array in Storage.}
Storage↑[10] := 9.39E02;
Storage↑[11] := Storage↑[11]+Storage↑[12];
writeln (Storage↑[23]:4:8); {We can use format controls.}
```

Self-Check Questions

Q. Can *read* and *write* be given file arguments whose type is not *text*?

A. *read* and *write* (but not *readln* or *writeln*) may be given a file argument of any file type.

Focus On Programming: File Merging

Merging two files to form a third is a common programming task. Typically, we'll find ourselves dealing with files whose components are record types. A file might consist of student records, employment records, vehicle records, sales records, etc. All that's really important is that one field of each record stores a name or number that can be used as the alphabetical or numerical basis for file ordering. File merging is similar to file concatenation (as discussed in 13-1), except that now we'll be interleaving individual file components, instead of joining the files end-to-end. We'll state our problem like this:

problem: file merging

> Imagine a record that contains a string-type *Name* field. Suppose that we have two files (call them *Old* and *Current*) whose components are these records. Assume that *Old* and *Current* are each in alphabetical order according to the *Name* fields. Merge them into file *Merged* while preserving this alphabetical order.

What will be involved? Imagine that you're merging two file cabinets by hand into a third (currently empty) cabinet. You open all the cabinets, and get the first record from each of the full ones. The alphabetically 'lower' of the two records goes into the third cabinet, and you pick up another record to replace it. The process of alphabetical comparison, moving, and replacing goes on until one of the original cabinets is empty. Then, since all the records in the remaining cabinet belong at the end of the large cabinet, and are in alphabetical order already, you move them into the large cabinet without making any comparisons.

A Pascal algorithm is much the same. We'll have to prepare *Old* and *Current* for reading, and *Merged* for writing. Then, we should see which file's first record's *Name* field is lower alphabetically. This record gets added to the *Merged* file. Naturally, we have to repeat this process until *Old* or *Current* is exhausted. In pseudocode we have:

refinement

```
prepare to write Merged;
get the first records from Old and Current;
while not the end of either Old or Current
    add the lower record to Merged;
    get the next record from that file;
finally, add the non-empty file's remaining records to Merged;
```

A slight addition to the algorithm will be to have the procedure report on its activities. Without such a message, a merger of two empty files—probably a mistake—would be quite acceptable.

The **while** loop's action is easy to refine into Pascal. Let's assume that *Old's* present record is lowest.

a coding detail

```
OldCount := OldCount+1;
Merged↑ := Old↑;
if not eof(Old) then get(Old)
put (Merged);
```

file merging procedure

The completed procedure is shown below. Note the **case** statement that takes the place of a possibly confusing nested **if** statement. It's perfectly acceptable here, even if it does only control two alternative actions.

```
procedure MergeRecords (var Old, Current, Merged: FileType);
  {Merges Old and Current into Merged while preserving
   the alphabetical ordering of Name fields.}

  var OldCount, CurrentCount: integer;

  begin
    OldCount := 0;
    CurrentCount := 0;
    reset (Old);
    reset (Current);
    rewrite (Merged);

      {Merge files until one of them is empty.}
    while not eof(Old) and not eof(Current) do begin
      case Old↑.Name<Current↑.Name of
        true: begin
                OldCount := OldCount+1;
                Merged↑ := Old↑;
                if not eof(Old) then get(Old)
              end;
        false: begin
                CurrentCount := CurrentCount+1;
                Merged↑ := Current↑;
                if not eof(Current) then get(Current)
              end
      end; {case}
      put(Merged)
    end; {while}

    {Flush the other file into Merged.}
    while not eof(Old) do begin
      Merged↑ := Old↑;
      OldCount := OldCount + 1;
      put(Merged);
      get(Old)
    end;
    while not eof(Current) do begin
      Merged↑ := Current↑;
      CurrentCount := CurrentCount + 1;
      put(Merged);
      get(Current)
    end;
    writeln ('Merger of ', OldCount+CurrentCount:1, ' records complete.');
    writeln (OldCount:1, ' records from file Old.');
    writeln (CurrentCount:1, ' records from file Current.')
  end; {MergeRecords}
```

A Detailed Digression: Numbers in Textfiles

Earlier we said that file components are stored according to the compiler's method of internal representation. We'll explain that now. As you probably know, computer systems store values in a code of zeros and ones that is designed or chosen by the compiler writer. Certain codes (like ASCII and EBCDIC) used for showing characters are standardized, and Pascal compilers are required to translate internal representations into standard *external* representations for output of *char, boolean, real*, and *integer* values. If universal codes weren't available, each computer would need special keyboards, terminals, lineprinters, etc., that could understand the compiler's storage code.*

external character representations

Enumerated ordinal values and types are *not* required by Pascal to have external character representations. A compiler need not decode them into ordinary characters for input and output, or even allow them to be output in any form. Some compilers extend Pascal by giving character representations to ordinal data values—these compilers allow input and output of all ordinal values by automatically encoding and decoding them. Most compilers, though, aren't so generous. If you create a file of an enumerated type *Color* (with values *Red, Blue, Green*, etc.) and manage to inspect it using a text editor, chances are you'll find a meaningless (to us) file of binary or integer values.

real values provide a dramatic illustration. For example, when they're input or output from *text* files (or the standard files *input* and *output*), they are given a character representation. However, when they're stored in a variable whose type is **file of** *real*, the internal, binary representation is used. Thus, while a *text* file of *real* values is readable (to a human), a *real* file of *reals* is not.

use of non-*text* files

Files with component types *real, integer*, and *boolean* are used for three main reasons—speed, size, and accuracy. Because values stored in such files need not be accessed and encoded or decoded individually, input and output of a program's data base can proceed quickly. Secondly, the compiler's coding system can store these types in an extremely compact manner—for example, it might store *false* and *true* as 0 and 1. Finally, stored *real* values tend to degrade slightly (and lose accuracy) after repeated translations from internal to external representation and back. Insofar as possible, their accuracy is maintained by storing them in *real* files.

how *read* works

Let's get back to textfiles. The convenience of automatic conversion between *char* and internal representation of *real* and *integer* values causes a problem with end-of-file checks. Suppose that *f* is a textfile, and that *Data* is an *integer* or *real* variable. The statement *read (f, Data)* is equivalent to:

```
while f↑=' ' do
    get(f);
assign the next value to Data;
```

* In fact, IBM has been accused of devising the EBCDIC code for this very reason.

This means that blank spaces and new-lines are skipped before the numerical value is read. After the value is read, the file window *f*↑ holds the character that immediately follows it.

> However, by default, there is always at least one blank at the end of every textfile.

There's no way to escape from this because the compiler is under strict instructions (from the Pascal Standard) to make sure that every textfile ends with an end-of-line.

What happens, then, if there are trailing blanks at the end of a file when we're trying to read a number—as there are sure to be? *f*↑ is a blank, so *read* skips it, and any blanks that follow. In the process, it tries to *get* the end-of-file character, which causes a program crash. As a result, this convenient scheme for reading and processing data won't work:

problems with *eof*

```
while not eof(f) do begin        {Will crash trying to read past end-of-file.}
   read (f, Data);
   process (Data)
end;
```

Our problem is to write a procedure that skips blanks until a non-blank character is found, or until *eof*(*f*) is *true*. Although it has often been proposed as a solution, the program segment below won't work. Can you figure out why not?

```
while not eof(f) and (f↑=' ') do
   get(f);        {This segment doesn't work either.}
```

> The file window is undefined when *eof* is *true*. It's an error to try to inspect it.

An error occurs when *eof*(*f*) is *true*, because *f*↑ will be inspected when the expression is fully evaluated.

A correct procedure *SkipBlanks* is shown below. It uses nested **if** statements and an auxiliary variable to avoid the error of reading an undefined file window.

blank skipping procedure

```
procedure SkipBlanks (var f: text);
   {Skips blanks until eof(f), or a nonblank is found.}
   var Finished: boolean;
   begin
      Finished := false;
      repeat
         if eof(f)
            then Finished := true
            else if f↑=' ' then get(f)
                           else Finished := true
      until Finished
   end; {SkipBlanks}
```

SkipBlanks should be included in any program that reads *real* or *integer* values from a textfile. It's called prior to any invocation of procedure *read*:

model of *SkipBlanks* use

```
{Model for reading and processing numerical values from textfiles.}
SkipBlanks (f); {Skip leading blanks in case the file is empty.}
while not eof(f) do begin
    read (f, Data);
    process (Data);
    SkipBlanks (f)
end;
```

Self-Check Questions

Q. The procedure shown below sums all the *integer* values in file *Numbers*. Assume that the definition of *NumberFile* is:

```
type NumberFile = file of integer;
```

Is a procedure like *SkipBlanks* necessary? Why or why not?

```
procedure Sum (var Numbers: NumberFile);
    {Sum the components of Numbers.}
    Current, Total: integer;
    begin
        Total := 0;
        reset (Numbers);
        while not eof (Numbers) do begin
            read (Numbers, Current);
            Total := Total+Current
        end;
        writeln ('The sum of the values is ', Total:1)
    end; {Sum}
```

A. The components of *NumberFile* are *integers*, and are stored according to the compiler's method of internal representation. There are no blanks or end-of-lines in *NumberFile*, because they're *char* values. As a result, the value we're about to read is always the next stored *integer* (until we reach the end of the file). Skipping blanks is totally unnecessary.

Antibugging and Debugging 13-3

WE'VE SEEN AMPLE EVIDENCE THAT EACH type has its own quirks, and tends to provoke certain errors. These mistakes usually occur in proportion to the severity of warnings against them—mild 'Bewares!' are usually heeded, but an absolute prohibition promotes a frenzy of crashes. Three common fatal errors that involve files are:

1. Attempting to inspect or read from a file that has not been *reset*.
2. Trying to generate or write to a file without first calling *rewrite*.
3. Reading past the end of a file.

confusing reset and rewrite

The first two bugs are usually the result of oversight, or of inadvertently confusing *reset* and *rewrite*. Unfortunately, some errors of omission that are obvious to us aren't caught by the compiler, since they're syntactically correct. Although this program lacks a call of *rewrite*(*OutsideFile*), it compiles (and crashes) perfectly well.

```
program DoesntRewrite (OutsideFile, output);
var OutsideFile: text;
begin
   writeln (OutsideFile, 'Hi there!')
end.
```

↓ ↓ ↓ ↓ ↓

```
ABNORMAL TERMINATION --
TEMP100937 NOT SET FOR WRITING
```

In some implementations, the run-time error message that's printed is of little help. In the example above, the computer printed its temporary, internal name for *OutsideFile*.

misplacing reset or rewrite

A related error that's hard to find is a misplaced *reset* or *rewrite*. Remember that *reset* puts us at the beginning of a file so that we can inspect it. *rewrite* presents us with an empty file, ready for writing. What program mistakes do you think caused these complaints?

> 'I'm not sure I'm reading the right file—I keep getting the same piece of input.'
>
> 'My program creates a file all right, but when I print the file it only contains the last piece of data I entered.'

Both bugs are probably the result of putting a *rewrite* or *reset* inside a loop that was supposed to write or read a file. The call should have been made just prior to entering the loop action.

eoln bugs

The end-of-line function has always brought grief to Pascal programmers. What's wrong with the following bit of code? It's supposed to echo the contents of *Source* to *SavedOutput*. We'll tell you that *Source* has no leading blanks on any line.

```
while not eof(Source) do begin
    read (Source, CurrentCharacter);
    write (SavedOutput, CurrentCharacter);
    if eoln(Source) then
        writeln (SavedOutput)
end;
```

```
This little piggie went to market;
 This little piggie stayed home.
 This little piggie had roast beef,     etc.
```

The partial contents of *SavedOutput*, shown above, give a broad hint: the second and third lines are indented by one space.

> The end-of-line character is a space that we're about to read when *eoln* becomes *true*.

Since we forgot to get rid of the space at the end of each input line (with a *readln* (*Source*), or even an extra *read*(*Source, CurrentCharacter*)), it showed up at the beginning of the next output line.

Another *eoln* problem is caused by an outlandish, illegal, and quite common extension of Pascal.

weird implementations

> Some nonstandard Pascal implementations automatically remove trailing blanks from the end of every line of text. Other systems *add* blanks to the end of text lines.

If extra blanks appear at (or disappear from) the end of a text line, make sure that the system isn't responsible. This is one of the opportunities you'll get to blame a bug on the compiler, so enjoy it.

Getting an initial value for *eoln* sometimes causes problems in interactive programs. Suppose that this is the beginning of a program.

```
begin {main program}
    while not eoln do begin
        writeln ('Please give an opinion.');
        ProcessTheInput;
          ... etc.
```

> In many interactive Pascal implementations, *eoln* is undefined before the start of input.

As a result, the segment above hangs (without printing the prompt) until input begins. The prompt should have been output before the check of *eoln* was made. This isn't a problem with data file or batch programs because, in effect, all input is ready and waiting at the start of execution.

(Some interactive Pascal systems that were based on the first definition of Pascal won't even allow this code:

```
begin {main program}
   writeln ('Please enter a number.');
   readln (TheNumber);
     ... etc.
```

This is because there's an implicit call of *reset*(*input*) at the beginning of the program. Now, *reset* is supposed to give the file window the first component value of the input file. However, the old Pascal standard specified that there would be no 'first value' until we entered one. As a result, the program would hang, waiting for us to enter a value—any value—so the reset can be completed. This put the programmer in a *Through the Looking Glass* position of entering the data first, and getting the prompt later.)

empty file bugs

Attempting to read past the end of a file is a more serious mistake. The next program segment is sure to fail, given the proper test input:

```
reset (AnyFile);
repeat
   DoSomethingWith (AnyFile)
until eof(AnyFile);
```

An empty input file delivers the death blow, because *eof*(*AnyFile*) is *true* as soon as an empty file is reset.

> Check for end-of-file *before* working with any file.

synchronization bugs

Some of the most annoying file bugs are manifested by disappearing lines, and (for interactive programs) an inexplicable need to type extra carriage returns—we referred to these earlier as synchronization bugs. The root cause is often confusion about exactly what happens at the end of a line. The code below is supposed to read and partially print an input file, echoing the initial nonblank characters on each line. Try tracing through it by hand.

```
{Print leading nonblanks—contains a bug.}
while not eof do begin
   read (CurrentCharacter);
   while CurrentCharacter <> ' ' do begin
      write (CurrentCharacter);
      read (CurrentCharacter);
   end;
   readln;
   writeln
end;
```

If every line begins with nonblanks, and ends with blanks, everything works fine. Suppose, though, that there *are* no extraneous blanks at the end of a line. When the inner loop is exited the value of *CurrentCharacter* is ' '—it is the end-of-line character. What happens when the *readln* is executed? The next line is thrown away. If the program is being run interactively, the user has to enter an extra carriage return (or else there is no next line to get rid of).

bug-prone special cases

Always make sure that textfile routines can handle these three special cases:

1. Blanks at the beginning of a line.
2. Blanks at the end of a line.
3. Lines that are empty.

Since most line-reading bugs are related to mix-ups of *read* and *readln*, there's a real temptation to debug by trying minor variations. This is most common when good editing facilities and a lightly-loaded computer are available—why think about the right way to do something when you can make mistakes so quickly? Take it from us—it doesn't pay. You'll find yourself trading one bug for another.

Textfile programs also frequently call for application of the programming uncertainty principle:

If you're sure that everything is right, and the program still doesn't work, then one of the facts you're sure of is wrong.

The best antibugging technique is to print the file you're working on *as* you work on it. Make sure that you can explain every blank space or empty line that shows up, as well as every full line that *doesn't* appear.

non-text bugs

Non-text files cause more trouble with syntax than semantics. The file window (the file's name followed by an up-arrow or circumflex) is, in effect, the name of a variable. Unfortunately, the up-arrow makes for unusual-looking identifiers. Suppose that we have a file of records. If each record has an array field, we might see these identifiers in a program:

```
TheFile                {Name of the file.}
TheFile↑               {The file window—the name of one record component.}
TheFile↑.TheArray      {An entire array field.}
TheFile↑.TheArray[10]  {One element of the array.}
```

Naturally, all assignments must involve values of an appropriate type.

```
TheFile {can't be assigned to.}
TheFile↑ {may get a record of TheFile's component type.}
TheFile↑.TheArray {may get an array of TheArray's type.}
TheFile↑.TheArray[10] {may get any value of TheArray's element type.}
```

Furthermore, remember that some actions that are all right with textfiles will not work with files of other component types. *eoln* may not be given a non-textfile argument; nor may *readln* or *writeln*. Also, when procedures *write* and *read* are used in conjunction with non-textfiles, they may only be given one additional argument. As a result, only a single component may be written to, or read from, a non-textfile at any one time.

Pascal Summary

• **file** type: used to store any number of values of one type. Only the file type's name, and the type of its components, are given in a file type definition.

type *Numbers* = **file of** *integer*;

• *text*: a predefined type, assumed to be equivalent to:

type *text* = **file of** *char*;

• file window: used as the name of the currently accessible file component. It's the file variable's name followed by an up-arrow or circumflex:

LetterFile↑ := 'T';
write (*NumberFile*↑);

• program parameters: file names given in a program heading. They refer to external files that the program will inspect or add to. Except for the standard program parameters *input* and *output*, program parameters must be declared within the program as well:

program *FileParameters* (*input, Results, Data*);
...
type *DataFileType* = **file of** ... etc.
...
var *Results*: *text*;
Data: *DataFileType*;

Important Facts

• A file is a sequential access type, because file components must be inspected in sequence, starting at the file's beginning.

• Procedure *rewrite* prepares a file for adding components: *rewrite* (*TheFile*). Any contents presently in the file are lost.

• Procedure *put* appends the value of the file window to the file: *put* (*TheFile*).

- Procedure *reset* prepares a file for inspection: *reset* (*TheFile*). The file window *TheFile* ↑ represents the first stored value.
- Procedure *get* advances the file window, so that it represents the file's next component: *get* (*TheFile*).
- The standard input and output-oriented procedures and functions (*read, readln, write, writeln, eof*, and *eoln*) can all be given a file-type variable as an initial argument. The subprograms then apply to that file, rather than to the default *input* or *output*. Naturally, *readln, writeln*, and *eoln* may only be given textfiles as arguments.
- Buffer files are often used as temporary holding places when we wish to insert values into existing files.
- Always, but always, check for end-of-file before you try to get data from a file.
- The Golden Rules of File Variables: First, assignments can't be made between file variables. Second, file variables are either being generated or inspected—never both at the same time. Third, file variables can only be passed to variable parameters, and never to value parameters.

Self-test Exercises

13-1 What are the standard (or predefined) file parameters?

13-2 Under what circumstances can a file be an argument to a procedure?

13-3 Suppose that you are writing a program that gives a lengthy set of frequently-changed instructions to the user. How can you set up your program so that the instruction set can be modified and changed without making any alterations in the original program?

13-4 A company that is converting its employee records to a computerized system has run into an unexpected problem. Although most employee's telephone numbers are entered as a series of seven digits (e.g. 6424951), a few still have their old exchange letters (e.g. KI85276). Show how a program might screen out the old-style phone numbers.

13-5 What is the effect of this code?

```
Counter := 0;
reset (TheSource);          {TheSource is a textfile.}
while not eof(TheSource) do begin
    if eoln(TheSource) then Counter := Counter+1;
    readln (TheSource)
end;
```

13-6 Suppose that you have a file whose component type is a record or array type. Write code to count the number of components in the file.

13-7 How would you modify a common *EchoText* procedure to number each line of output?

13-8 Restate the procedure calls *read*(*FileName, Value*) and *write*(*FileName, Value*) in terms of the more primitive procedures *get* and *put*.

13-9 In our discussion of the playing card problem we defined a record type *Card* like this:

```
type Card = record
              Number, Suit: String;
              Found: boolean
            end;
```

Suppose that we have a file named *TheDeck* whose component type is *Card*. Write code that will print *TheDeck*'s contents.

13-10 How can an assignment be made between two file variables of the same type?

13-11 Write a procedure that finds and prints line *X* of textfile *F*. Assume that *F* contains at least *X* lines.

13-12 The code below is supposed to sum a textfile of integer values. Will it work? What does it (or won't it) do?

```
Sum := 0;
while not eof(Data) do begin
   read (Data, NextValue);
   Sum := Sum+NextValue
end;
```

13-13 The procedure shown below is supposed to skip blanks until it encounters a non-blank, or the end-of-file. Why won't the code work?

```
procedure SkipBlanks (var TheFile: text);
   begin
      while (TheFile↑ = ' ') and not eof(TheFile) do
         get(TheFile)
   end;
```

More Exercises

13-13 Pascal has been criticized because the file parameters in the program heading are not really parameters. The exact name of an external file must be given in the program heading for it to be 'passed' to the program. Thus, it's hard to write many general purpose file-handling programs in Standard Pascal.

To get around this unreasonable restriction, many implementations have some means by which external file names can be passed to a program at run-time. Does your Pascal have such an extension? How does it work?

13-14 Write a segment of code that will read and echo a text file—with two extra spaces between each line.

13-15 As we mentioned in Chapter 1, not all Pascal systems support both upper and lower-case characters. Write a program that changes all the lower-case characters in a Pascal program file to capital letters.

13-16 A number of text editors currently available have a 'wraparound' feature—the editor automatically enters a carriage return after putting as many words as possible on each line. A typist doesn't have to enter carriage returns at the end of each line because the editor does it automatically.

Write a program that makes an input file appear to have been written using a wraparound editor. It should accept input text, either interactively or from a file, but ignore carriage returns. Instead, your program should reprint the text so that every line contains as many whole words as it can. Allow a maximum line length of 80 characters.

13-17 Write a program that asks the user her name and age, then tells her the name and age of the last person to run the program. Be sure that the program gives sensible output to the first user. Then, modify the program to tell any user how many times *she* has run the program (by checking for her name).

13-18 Preparing personalized junk mail poses an interesting programming problem. A 'letter' file contains most of a letter, but has spaces left for the addressee's name and address, and as many references to her name, family, street, and city as possible. An 'address' file contains a series of names and addresses for personalizing letters.

Write a program that creates personalized junk mail. A simple version will require a user to set up letter and address file (possibly using special codes or formats) for the program to manipulate. A more advanced (and interactive) version will work *with* the user to set up the necessary files, making the codes or formats transparent to her.

13-19 The Midwest Grain and Boring Tool Corporation advertises that its employees are not just numbers. This creates problems for their accounting department. As a first step in setting up a payroll, a file of employee names must be alphabetized. This can be done by repeatedly selecting, deleting, and copying elsewhere, the 'lowest' name remaining in the original file. Write a program that does the job.

13-20 In some computerized management information systems an administrator can request a list of all employees who share some characteristic. They may all have the same pay scale, the same supervisor, work in the same department, etc. Write a two-part program that implements such a system. The first part should create a file that holds all relevant information (department, pay, supervisor, etc.) associated with each employee. The second part should act as an information system, that prints the names of all employees that share some feature.

13-21 A large telephone company (whose name you would probably recognize in an instant) has discovered that some of its employees are on the payrolls of more than one department. In an attempt to catch the double-dippers, alphabetized files that contain the names of all the employees in each department have been prepared.

Write a program that compares the employee lists of just two departments, and prints any names that appear on both payrolls. Then, modify your program to deal with four employee lists. Be sure to print the number of payrolls each caught employee appears on.

13-22 Suppose that we have an enumerated ordinal type called *Day* whose constants are *Monday, Tuesday*, etc. We can arrange to print the string equivalents of these constants by defining an array subscripted by *Day*, and storing the strings 'Monday', 'Tuesday', etc. in it. This technique was demonstrated in section 11-2.

A shortcoming of the method we used then was the large number of assignments required—one assignment for each ordinal type constant. Define an ordinal type whose constants are Pascal's reserved words and use internal files to simplify the initialization of the 'string-equivalent' array. (Hint: employ the method we demonstrated in procedure *InitializeFullDeck* to initialize a series of string variables.

13-23 As we mentioned in the last chapter's exercises, Pascal programs are often written in countries whose native language is not English. However, we can assume that there's a one-to-one correspondence between Pascal's reserved words in English, and those in any other language. Thus, if we have a 'data base' of foreign-language equivalents, we should be able to translate any program.

Write a program that reads an ordinary Pascal program, then echoes it with its reserved words translated into another language. Let the user specify the language. However, if that language's equivalents aren't part of your data base, prompt the program user to enter the translations of words that are required (and only those words). Add them to your data base, too. (Warning: Beware of translating programs into a language you only have a partial set of equivalents for.) As before, ignore reserved words that are text constants or output, or fall within comments.

13-24 The authorship of books can often be determined by doing a statistical analysis of the length of words, and the number of words in each sentence. A number of points can be compared—the average or mean length, the median length (half the words or sentences are longer, half are shorter), the standard deviation (which we won't explain), and the skewness (essentially the proportion *mean:median*).

Write a program that is able to read two text files and compute these points of comparison (you need not figure standard deviation if you don't understand it). Have your program venture a guess about whether or not both files were written by the same person (and give its reasons).

13-25 It seems only reasonable that a computer science course should have its bookkeeping done by computer. Write a program that does the job. It should prepare *and maintain* a file of student names, and each student's score on various tests and homework assignments.

Your program should have the following capabilities: adding new students, dropping students, adding new scores, changing incorrect scores, and printing the scores of the entire class. It should also be able to assign different weights to each score and compute final grades. Don't forget to allow for unusual situations, like missed tests.

For extra credit, include an option for statistical analysis of scores and grades, showing means and medians, as well as a histogram of all scores. Be sure to make it idiot-proof.

13-26 Gassalasca Jape, the well known playwright, has written an entire play (entitled *Home Life*) in which two characters (Mildred and Mordred) are always speaking. In order to give readers unable to attend the live performance a true sense of the drama, he wishes to print the two monologues side-by-side. Unfortunately, Gassalasca's publisher refuses to go to the expense of typesetting the play in such a peculiar fashion.

Write a program to help G.J. out. Assume that Mildred and Mordred's soliloquies are in separate files, and that the maximum length of a line in each file is no more than 40 characters. Merge the two files together by concatenating corresponding lines.

13-27 Surely you're familiar with multiple choice questionnaires that appear in magazines. In the very simplest sort, you're told to score 1 point for all 'A' answers, 2 points for 'B's, 3 for 'C's, etc. Unfortunately, when the answers to each question are arranged in the exact same manner, readers are tempted to give answers that result in the most desirable score, instead of answers that are especially truthful. To combat this, point scores are often intentionally assorted—'C' may be 2 points in one question, but 4 points in the next.

Write a two-part questionnaire program. Part One is invoked if the user enters a secret password. It should let her set up a questionnaire file that includes questions, multiple choice answers, and the 'value' of each individual answer.

Finally, it should contain results or conclusions that relate to different ranges of point values (e.g. 'If your score was 125—150, then... etc.).

Part Two is invoked if the password isn't entered. It asks the questions, lets the user pick from the multiple choices, and records the 'value' of each response (which may change for each question). Finally, it should deliver the appropriate conclusion.

13-28 Computer users—word processors as well as programmers—often find themselves in possession of more than one version of a single file. A program that compares two files is extremely useful. Write such a program, and give it the following options:

> *Length and count*: Print the number of characters, words, and lines in each file.
>
> *Difference*: Assume that file *B* has had extra lines added. Print all lines in *B* that are not in file *A*, along with their line numbers.
>
> *Two-way difference*: Assume that extra lines have been added to each file. Print all lines in *A* that are not in *B*, and vice versa. (Hint: use the *Difference* option first to create files of *A* and *B*'s 'extra' lines.)
>
> *Unify*: Create and print a file that is a merger of *A* and *B*.

13-29 Automatic text formatting is a basic computer application. The central task is *text justification*, which means printing text in such a way that each line is the exact same length. This is accomplished by hyphenating words or by inserting extra space between words. Other formatting jobs include spacing between paragraphs, indenting at appropriate places, deciding how long each page should be, and including page numbers and running headings at the top of each page.

Write a text formatter. The difficulty of this program will depend on your definition of the problem. However, every program should have the ability to justify single lines of text by inserting space between words. Assume that additional commands (to start paragraphs, skip space, specify line and page length, etc.) are included in the file of source text, but are somehow distinguished from the regular text; e.g.:

```
.LL 60c           {Line length is 60 characters.}
.PL 25            {Page length is 25 lines.}
.PP               {Start a paragraph—space and indent.}
The end of the world, when it
came, was no surprise to many
of us...     etc.
```

13-30 Although text editors are often thought of as being interactive programs, a number of editing jobs are equally suited for batch processing. One such job involves deleting or changing every instance of some word (or words) in a source file. Write a program that lets a user specify (in a 'command file') words that are to be removed from or replaced in a source file of text. A sample command file might look like this:

> **replace "concieve" with "conceive"**
> **replace "like I told youse" with "as I told you"**
> **delete "ain't"**

13-31 A *pretty-printer* is a program that formats other programs. It reads a file that contains a program, and prints it in a neat, orderly fashion. A pretty-printer doesn't change the syntax or semantic content of the program. Instead, it just lines up all the **begin**s and **end**s and comments, puts extra spaces between subprograms, etc.

Write a simple pretty-printer that is able to handle indentation. Assume that programs it will have to format are laid out in the style of all the programs in this book except that no lines are indented. You'll have to infer the rules we use for indentation, and write a program that is able to recognize the reserved words that cause us to indent or outdent. To make the job a bit easier, don't worry about indenting type definitions, and assume that every control statement regulates a compound statement.

13-32 Add file types to your private programming language. You might want to treat a file as a means of permanently storing data, rather than strictly as a sequential-access type. Thus, you may wish to predefine additional file-handling procedures that ease the job of file insertion and deletion.

'... a collection of values that share some characteristic.'

14

Collections of Values: The **set** Type

For a short word, *set* certainly packs an awful lot of meaning. The Oxford English Dictionary devotes no less than twenty-two pages to its exposition of *set*, and includes one hundred fifty-four definitions.

Even more remarkable than their number is the fact that not one of the one hundred fifty-four definitions of *set* given by the editors of the O.E.D. mentions Pascal. This is sad because Pascal is one of the only programming languages in the world to include a set type. It deserves some kind of recognition.

A Pascal set, like a real life set, is a collection of values that share some characteristic. In Pascal, that characteristic is their type. Sets are the last of Pascal's structured types, and we discuss them fully in section 14-1. The set type is interesting—it's possible to program for a long time without ever needing sets, but once you've used them they seem indispensable. Since sets seldom cause mysterious errors, we haven't included an Antibugging section in this chapter.

Defining and Programming Set Types 14-1

THE SET TYPE IS USED TO CREATE VARIABLES that can represent more than one value of a given ordinal type. The type definition of a set type contains the set type's identifier, the reserved words **set of**, and the type of the values the set will contain. This 'contents' type is called the set's *base type*. For example:

> **type** *CharacterSet* = **set of** *char*;
> *Vitamins* = (*A, B1, B2, B3, B6, B12, C, D, E*);
> *NutritionType* = **set of** *Vitamins*;
> *LowNumbers* = 1..12;
> *GradesRepresented* = **set of** *LowNumbers*;
> *Hues* = (*Red, Blue, Green, Yellow*);
> *Colors* = **set of** *Hues*;

In chart form we have:

set type

> **type** ⟶ *identifier* ⟶ = ⟶ **set of** ⟶ ***base type identifier*** ⟶ ;

base types

The base type of *CharacterSet* is the predefined type *char*, the base type of *NutritionType* is the enumerated ordinal type *Vitamins*, the base type of *GradesRepresented* is the subrange *LowNumbers*, and the base type of *Colors* is the enumerated ordinal type *Hues*.

Although no ordinal type is specifically prohibited from becoming a set's base type, Pascal places a subtle restriction on allowable base types.

set cardinality

> The maximum *cardinality* of a set type (the maximum number of values in its base type) is implementation defined—determined by the author of a system's Pascal compiler. It typically ranges from 64 to 2040 members.

size limits

Does limiting the size of sets ever cause problems? Well, most enumerated ordinal types have too few members to approach the limit. On the other hand, *integer* will never be the base type of a set type because it has too many member values. Most difficulties occur with medium-sized sets, like an *integer* subrange or the computer's set of characters. We may have to severely limit the size of an ordinal type (as we did with *LowNumbers*, above), to make it a legal base type.

Compiler writers generally allow sets to be at least as large as the cardinality of type *char*. In this text, we'll assume that this definition is always valid:

> **type** *TypeIdentifier* = **set of** *char*;

Once a set has been defined, we can declare set-typed variables.

declaring set variables

```
type CharacterSet = set of char;
     Vitamins = (A, B1, B2, B3, B6, B12, C, D, E);
     NutritionType = set of Vitamins;
     LowNumbers = 1..12;
     GradesRepresented = set of LowNumbers;

var InputCharacters, OutputCharacters: CharacterSet;
    FruitVitamins, VegetableVitamins: NutritionType;
    Responses: GradesRepresented;
```

At this point *InputCharacters, OutputCharacters, FruitVitamins*, and the rest don't actually represent any values. They're uninitialized variables with the *potential* of representing any, or all, or none of the values of their base types. Assignments take the usual form: a set-valued expression is assigned to a set-typed variable.

> In set expressions, individual *members* of a set must be put between square brackets. In contrast, the identifier of a set-typed *variable* isn't.

set assignments

Thus, assignments can be made by listing the assignment values between square brackets, or by supplying the name of a set-typed variable. Don't forget that two dots (..) mean 'through and including':

```
OutputCharacters := ['a'..'z', 'A'..'Z', '0'..'9'];
FruitVitamins := [A..B3, B12, C, E];
VegetableVitamins := FruitVitamins;
InputCharacters := [SomeCharacterValue];
OutputCharacters := [chr(74)];
InputCharacters := OutputCharacters;
Responses := [];
```

the empty set

The final assignment is unusual because it makes *Responses* an *empty set*—a set that contains no values at all.

set representation

Don't let Pascal's variety of methods for representing set members confuse you. If the value of *SomeCharacterValue* is 'B', and we assign it to *InputCharacters*, then the three expressions below are all equivalent ways of referring to a set whose base type is *char*, and whose only member is 'B':

```
['B']        [SomeCharacterValue]        InputCharacters
```

set order

A final point about set values is that they're *unordered*. Thus, these are equivalent representations of the same set:

```
[A..B3, C, E]        [E, A..B3, C]
```

Self-Check Questions

Q. We saw above that the empty set is represented by a pair of square brackets. What's it needed for?

A. Like all other variables, set-typed variables are undefined when they're declared. Initializing a set variable to empty—to '[]'—is roughly equivalent to initializing a *real* or *integer* variable to 0.

We also need a way of showing the empty set to determine if a particular set has any members. The *boolean* expression: (*SomeSet* = []) is *true* if *SomeSet* has no members, and *false* otherwise.

The Set Operators

Set expressions can also be constructed with the *set operators*. There are three basic set operations: union, difference, and intersection. They're all quite straightforward, and may even be familiar from grade-school.

set union

Set *union* is, more or less, the 'addition' of sets. The union of two sets (or of two representations of Pascal sets) is a set that contains *all* the members of both sets. The regular addition sign (+) serves as the set union operator.

In its simplest application, a set union updates or adds to the members of a set-structured variable. For instance, suppose that we want to make a record of the letters that appear in a sample of input text.

set union program

```
program FindIncludedLetters (input, output);
    {Use sets to determine which letters appear in a text sample.}
type CharacterSet = set of char;
var Current: char;
    IncludedLetters: CharacterSet;
begin
    IncludedLetters := [];
    while not eof do begin
        read (Current);
        IncludedLetters := IncludedLetters+[Current]
    end;
    writeln ('Letters included were:');
    for Current := 'a' to 'z' do
        if Current in IncludedLetters then
            write (Current);
    writeln;
    for Current := 'A' to 'Z' do
        if Current in IncludedLetters then
            write (Current);
    writeln
end. {FindIncludedLetters}
```

the quick brown fox jumps over the lazy dog
PACK MY BOX WITH FIVE DOZEN LIQUOR JUGS

```
Letters included were:
abcdefghijklmnopqrstuvwxyz
ABCDEFGHIJKLMNOPQRSTUVWXYZ
```

The program segment begins by initializing *IncludedLetters* (defined as a **set of** *char*) to the empty set. Successive values of *Current* are read in and added to the *IncludedLetters* set. When the loop is finished, *IncludedLetters* represents every character that's been read in. Some other set unions are:

> *IncludedLetters* := *IncludedLetters* + *OutputCharacters*;
> *IncludedLetters* := *IncludedLetters* + *OutputCharacters*+['D'..'T'];

Don't forget that the identifiers of set-type variables need not go between square brackets.

Our next set operator can undo a set union.

set difference

> Set *difference* is akin to the 'subtraction' of sets. The difference of two sets is a set that contains all the members of the first set that are not also members of the second set. The set difference operator is an ordinary minus sign (–).

This mouthful is much more sensible than it sounds. When we subtract set *B* from set *A* (*A*–*B*), we're just taking all of *B*'s members away from *A*. For example, suppose that we've made these definitions and declarations:

> **type** *Options* = (*ErrorRecovery, InputChecks, OutputChecks,*
> *Testing, LongMessages*);
>
> **var** *AllOptions, TestOptions*: **set of** *Options*;

A program might begin by initializing *AllOptions* and *TestOptions*:

> *AllOptions* := [*ErrorRecovery..LongMessages*];
> *TestOptions* := [*InputChecks, Testing*];

At this point, *AllOptions* contains every value of type *Options*. We can reduce its membership by using the set difference operator:

> *AllOptions* := *AllOptions* – *TestOptions*;
> {*AllOptions* now contains [*ErrorRecovery, OutputChecks, LongMessages*]}
> *AllOptions* := *AllOptions*–[*ErrorRecovery..OutputChecks*];
> {*AllOptions* now contains [*LongMessages*]}

difference of empty sets

What happens when we try to remove a value that's not included in a set variable? Nothing. Although the second of the assignments below is obviously fruitless, it's perfectly legal Pascal.

```
TestOptions := [];
TestOptions := TestOptions-[InputChecks];
```

To determine which letters do *not* appear in a sample of text, we could use this variation on our earlier program:

set difference program

```
program FindMissingLetters (input, output);
    {Uses sets to find letters that don't appear in a text sample.}
type CharacterSet = set of char;
var Current: char;
    MissingLetters: CharacterSet;
begin
    MissingLetters := ['a'..'z', 'A'..'Z'];
    while not eof do begin
        read (Current);
        MissingLetters := MissingLetters-[Current]
    end;
    write ('Letters not included were:   ');
    for Current := 'a' to 'z' do
        if Current in MissingLetters then
            write (Current);
    for Current := 'A' to 'Z' do
        if Current in MissingLetters then
            write (Current);
    writeln
end. {FindMissingLetters}
```

↓ ↓ ↓ ↓ ↓

```
the charging rhino tripped over a snoozing fieldmouse
PACK MY BOX WITH TWO CHEESEBURGERS TO GO
Letters not included were:  bjkqwxyDFJLNQVZ
```

set intersection

> The *intersection* of two sets is a set that contains all values that belong to both sets. The Pascal multiplication sign (*) is used as the set intersection operator.

If two sets don't contain any common values their intersection is, of course, the empty set. Assume that we've defined the months as an ordinal type. The value of this set expression:

*[January..June, August]***[May..September]*

is the set *[May, June, August]*. The intersection of *[January..May]* and *[July..November]* is the empty set [ ].

Sets are often used to record characteristics of some sort, and intersection can be used to find features shared by several different sets. For example, suppose that *Options* has been defined as a set of some ordinal type. If we declare some variables of this set-type:

var *Luxury, Deluxe, Standard, Economy*: *Options*;

we can make the following assignment:

Luxury := *Deluxe* * *Standard* * *Economy*;

The set variable *Luxury* holds the values (assuming that there are any) that belong to *all* of the other three sets. If there are no common elements *Luxury* equals [ ], the empty set.

Self-Check Questions

Q. Is this a reasonable and correct application of the set union operator?

InputCharacters := ['D'..'T']+[*CurrentCharacter*]+['9'];

A. Although the assignment is correct, it isn't reasonable. There's no need to use the set union operator, because we're not merging set-typed variables. The assignment below works just as well (note that *CurrentCharacter* may be '9' or in the range 'D'..'T'):

InputCharacters := ['D'..'T', *CurrentCharacter*, '9'];

Focus On Programming: *boolean* Set Expressions

We've just seen how to use the set operators with set-valued operands. However, set values can also be used in other kinds of expressions.

> Set operands can also be used with the ordinary relational operators, and with the set relational operator **in**, to form a variety of *boolean* expressions.

set relations

Sign	*Operation*	*Example*
=	set equality	*InputCharacters*=*OutputCharacters*
<>	set inequality	*Responses*<>[1..4, 6..10]
>=	set 'contains'	*Fruit*>=[*A, B2, C*]
<=	set 'is contained by'	*Luxury*<=*Standard*
in	set membership	'D' **in** *Included*

Such expressions are the basis of most set applications, because sets rarely underly a program's main data structure. Instead, we'll usually find them in supporting roles, simplifying error checking or in-program accounting.

> Set-type variables help create conditions that are easy to use in many parts of a program, but which can be quickly modified in a central place.

problem: character substitution

Suppose that we want to print a textfile, substituting asterisks for a set of forbidden values. Assume that we've defined *CharacterSet* as a **set of** *char*. Write a procedure to do the job.

Procedure *Substitute*, below, does the trick. It's passed a file, and a set of characters to be replaced as the file is being output.

character substitution procedure

```
procedure Substitute (var TheFile: text; BadCharacters: CharacterSet);
   {Substitutes asterisks for BadCharacters set members.}

   var CurrentCharacter: char;

   begin
      reset(TheFile);
      while not eof(TheFile) do begin
         while not eoln(TheFile) do begin
            read (TheFile, CurrentCharacter);
            if not (CurrentCharacter in BadCharacters)
               then write (CurrentCharacter)
               else write ('*')
         end; {eoln while}
         readln (TheFile);
         writeln
      end {eof while}
   end; {Substitute}
```

Typical calls of *Substitute* might be:

```
Substitute (ProposedBudget, ['0'..'9']);
Substitute (Speech, ['!']);
```

The first call prints a file named *ProposedBudget* with asterisks instead of numerals, while the second call makes the same substitution for exclamation marks found in file *Speech*.

The set operators let sets store data that might otherwise be kept in an array. For example, let's reconsider the Hunt the Wumpus problem of Chapter 12. We'll modify the problem slightly, so that instead of having tunnels that lead in each of four directions, each room can have *any* number of exit tunnels. In the solution we proposed then, each room of the cave was defined as a record with a *Contents* field (denoting any hazards in the room), and a *NextDoor* array-field to hold the numbers of neighboring rooms. What do you think about using this proposal instead?

return to the Wumpus Cave

```
type RoomValues = 1..20;
    RoomInformation = set of RoomValues;
    Cave = array [RoomValues] of RoomInformation;
var PitRooms, BatRooms, WumpusRoom: RoomInformation;
    CurrentRoom: RoomValues;
    Neighbors: Cave;
```

We've really changed our way of looking at the cave. In the new example, our central data structure is a set of possible room numbers—the *integer* values 1 through 20. Instead of putting hazards into each room of the cave, as we did before, we store the locations of each hazard in set variables:

```
PitRooms := [1, 5..7, 12, 14, 19];
BatRooms := [3, 4, 8, 11, 13, 15..17];
WumpusRoom := [18];
```

The cave itself has become an array of sets. Each set contains the numbers of the rooms that a given room is connected to.

```
Neighbors[1] := [3, 4, 9, 13];
Neighbors[2] := [8, 9, 12, 20];
Neighbors[3] := [1, 5, 14, 17];
```

You'll probably find out the hard way that Pascal's economy in using square brackets with both arrays and sets causes confusion.

Suppose that we find ourselves in room number *CurrentRoom*. We can easily check for *any* hazard in the room with:

```
if CurrentRoom in (PitRooms+BatRooms+WumpusRoom) then
    writeln ('Sorry, but you''re dead!');
```

Or, we can see if danger lurks in a neighboring room by determining if the *Neighbors* set has a non-empty intersection with one of the sets of hazards. To find bats, for example, use:

```
if (Neighbors[CurrentRoom]*BatRooms)<>[] then
    writeln ('I hear bats!');
```

sets vs. *boolean* arrays

An astute reader will notice a great similarity between a set, and an array of *boolean* values that is subscripted by the set's base type. For example, the base type of *BatRooms* is the subrange 1..20. Suppose we declared the following array:

```
type BatArray = array [1..20] of boolean;
var BatsArePresent: BatArray;
```

Imagine that we initialize *BatsArePresent* to *false*, except for rooms 3, 4, 8, 11, 13, 15, 16, and 17—they all contain bats and are set to *true*. The array-typed variable *BatsArePresent* now holds the exact same data as the set-typed variable *BatRooms*. However, it's much less convenient to work with as a data structure because we can't use the set operators. We have to search all the way through *BatsArePresent* to find out something about its contents.

In certain cases, though, sets and *boolean* arrays share the same problems. For example, there's no automatic way to print either all the elements of an array variable (except for a string-type array), or all the members of a set variable. Suppose that we wanted to print out the numbers of the rooms containing bats. Compare these procedures:

```
procedure PrintArrayRooms (BatsArePresent: BatArray);
   var Counter: RoomValues; {1..20}
   begin
      for Counter := 1 to MAXIMUMNUMBEROFROOMS do
         if BatsArePresent[Counter] then
            writeln (Counter)
   end; {PrintArrayRooms}

procedure PrintSetRooms (BatRooms: BatInformation);
   var Counter: RoomValues; {1..20}
   begin
      for Counter := 1 to MAXIMNUMBEROFROOMS do
         if Counter in BatRooms then
            writeln (Counter)
   end; {PrintSetRooms}
```

As you can see, the procedures are practically identical. We have to step through the set almost as though we were travelling through an array.

Self-Check Questions

Q. Given the procedure declaration above, what will be the effects of these procedure calls:

a) *PrintSetRooms (BatRooms *PitRooms);*
b) *PrintSetRooms (BatRooms+PitRooms);*
c) *PrintSetRooms (BatRooms−PitRooms);*

Assume that we've made the following assignments:

BatRooms := [1..4, 7, 11..12, 19];
PitRooms := [4..8, 10, 14, 19..20];

A. Each of the calls sends a different set to *PrintSetRooms*. Values that will be printed are:

a) 4, 7, 19.
b) 1, 2, 3, 4, 5, 6, 7, 8, 10, 11, 12, 14, 19, 20.
c) 1, 2, 3, 11, 12.

Programming With Sets

Our final set application will compare the efficiency of two typewriter keyboards. The *QWERTY* keyboard is the current standard. Its letter keys are laid out like this:

```
Q  W  E  R  T  Y  U  I  O  P
  A  S  D  F  G  H  J  K  L  ;  :  space
Z  X  C  V  B  N  M  .
```

Unfortunately, few of the most frequently used letters (e, t, a, o, n, r, i, and s) appear on the center 'home' row—the row of keys that a typist's fingers normally rest on. As you might expect, continually jumping from one row to another slows and tires even the best typists.

Many new keyboard designs have been proposed. One of these is the *Maltron* keyboard, shown below. Since the most common characters are in the home row, fewer jumps are required while typing.

```
  Q  P  Y  C  B  V  M  U  Z  L
A  N  I  S  F  E  D  T  H  O  R  ;  :  .  space
  J  G  W  K  X
```

problem: typewriter keyboards

Just how beneficial is the Maltron keyboard? Write a program that compares the number of jumps a text sample would require from QWERTY and Maltron typists.

A first refinement is:

first refinement

as long as there are characters to look at
  get the character;
  see if it's on the QWERTY or Maltron home row;
  see if it requires a jump from the QWERTY or Maltron home row;
print conclusions;

why use sets?

Set-typed variables provide the data structure of choice, because we want to see if a particular value belongs to a group of values of the same type. Suppose that we define *CharacterSet* as a **set of** *char*. We can declare variables that represent the 'home' and 'others' characters of the keyboards above, as well as a *Valid* set-variable to help restrict the characters we consider.

What kind of conclusions should the program arrive at? Naturally we want to count the number of jumps that are made. However, this information isn't particularly helpful unless we know the total count of characters considered. The pseudocode below includes these refinements.

second refinement

```
prepare the data file for reading;
initialize the set variables;
while not the end of the input file
   read the next character;
   if it's in the set of valid characters
      see if it's on the QWERTY or Maltron home row;
      see if it requires a jump from the QWERTY or Maltron home row;
      increment the Total count;
print the number of jumps for each keyboard, and the size of the sample;
```

The completed program is shown below. As input, we gave it the complete text of chapters 11 and 12.

typewriter keyboard program

```
program KeyBoards (DataFile, output);
   {Compares the jumps required by QWERTY and Maltron keyboards.}

type CharacterSet = set of char;

var DataFile: text;
   QWERTYHome, MaltronHome, QWERTYOthers,
                           MaltronOthers, Valid: CharacterSet;
   QWERTYJumps, MaltronJumps, Total: integer;
   Current: char;

begin
   Valid := ['a'..'z', 'A'..'Z', ':', ';', '.', ' '];
   QWERTYHome := ['a','s','d','f','g','h','j','k','l',';','A',
                  'S','D','F','G','H','J','K','L',':',' '];
   MaltronHome := ['a','n','i','s','f','e','.','d','t','h','o','r',';',
                  'A','N','I','S','F','E','D','T','H','O','R',':',' '];
   QWERTYOthers := ['a'..'z', 'A'..'Z'] - QWERTYHome;
   MaltronOthers := ['a'..'z', 'A'..'Z'] - MaltronHome;
   QWERTYJumps := 0;
   MaltronJumps := 0;
   Total := 0;
   reset (DataFile);
```

```
    while not eof(DataFile) do begin
        read (DataFile, Current);
        if Current in Valid then begin
            Total := Total+1;
            if (Current in QWERTYOthers) then
                QWERTYJumps := QWERTYJumps+1;
            if (Current in MaltronOthers) then
                MaltronJumps := MaltronJumps+1
        end {if}
    end; {while}
    writeln ('Total number of input characters was ', Total:1, '.');
    writeln ('QWERTY keyboard required ', QWERTYJumps:1, ' jumps.');
    writeln ('Maltron keyboard required ', MaltronJumps:1, ' jumps.')
end. {KeyBoards}
```

```
Total number of input characters was 181967.
QWERTY keyboard required 97574 jumps.
Maltron keyboard required 35713 jumps.
```

Self-Check Questions

Q. Program *KeyBoards* treats its input as a stream of characters, without regard to its line structure. Does this cause any inaccuracy in *KeyBoards'* output?

A. Yes, because the carriage return at the end of each line is read, and recorded, as a space. Thus, the total of input characters considered is really too high, by the number of lines in the input sample.

Pascal Summary

• **set** type: allows the declaration of a variable that can store more than one value of any single ordinal type:

```
type CharacterSet = set of char;
var Bigs, Littles: CharacterSet;
```

• set representation: members of a set are listed between square brackets. A set-type variable doesn't need brackets:

```
Bigs := ['A'..'D', 'F', 'I'];
Littles := Bigs;
```

- set operators: operators that take set-type operands, and have a set-type result. They are:

+	*set union—sum of the members*
−	*set difference—difference of the members*
*	*set intersection—common members*

- set relations: *boolean*-valued set expressions. They are:

Sign	*Operation*	*Example*
=	set equality	*InputCharacters*=*OutputCharacters*
<>	set inequality	*Responses*<>[1..4, 6..10]
>=	set 'contains'	*Fruit*>=[*A, B2, C*]
<=	set 'is contained by'	*Luxury*<=*Standard*
in	set membership	'D' **in** *Included*

Important Facts

- The cardinality of a set is the number of values in its base type—the maximum number of values a set-type variable can represent. This maximum is set by each computer, but it's usually large enough to allow the set of characters.
- The empty set (shown with an empty set of square brackets: [ ]) belongs to every set type.

Self-test Exercises

14-1 Write definitions for, and initialize, set variables for the set of months with 28 days, the set of months with 30 days, and the set of months with 31 days.

14-2 Suppose that we've made these definitions:

```
type Music = (Rock, Roll, Reggae);
     Tunes = set of Music;
var Hits: Tunes;
```

List all possible values of variable *Hits*.

14-3 Evaluate these *boolean*-valued set expressions.

a) ['L', 'N', 'M'] <> ['L'..'M']
b) ['L'..'M'] = ['L', 'N', 'M']
c) [] <= ['L'..'M']
d) ['L', 'N', 'M'] <= ['K'..'M']
e) ['K'..'M'] >= ['L', 'N', 'M']

14-4 Assume that numbers or characters standing in for a number of people have been divided among the following set variables: *Movers, Groovers, Shakers, Quakers, Lovers*, and *Fighters*. Write set expressions that represent the entire group, the *Lovers* and *Fighters*, the *Movers* who aren't *Groovers*, the *Shakers* who are *Quakers* but not *Lovers*, and the people who are neither *Groovers* or *Quakers*.

14-5 Can elements be removed from an empty set? What is the effect of this assignment:

SomeSet := [] – *SomeSetComponents*;

14-6 Suppose that we've made these definitions:

type *Capitals* = 'A'..'Z';
    CapitalSet = **set of** *Capitals*;

Write a function that represents the number of values in a variable of type *CapitalSet.*

14-7 Assuming the definitions of the previous question, find the (alphabetically) greatest value in a non-empty variable (*LetterGroup*) of type *CapitalSet*.

14-8 The code below is intended to find the (alphabetically) lowest value in a variable of type *CapitalSet*. What bug does it contain?

Letter := 'A';
while not (*Letter* **in** *LetterGroup*) **do**
    Letter := *succ*(*Letter*);

14-9 What does it mean to say that the effect of the symbols +, –, and * are *context dependent*?

14-10 If an enumerated ordinal type has *n* constants, then a variable of that type can have (at most) *n* distinct values. Suppose that a set has *n* elements. How many distinct values can a variable of this set type have?

More Exercises

14-10 What is the maximum cardinality of sets in your Pascal implementation? What problems might this limit cause?

14-11 Write a function that determines if a given character is in the set of capital letters, lower-case letters, punctuation, digits, a blank, or an unknown set.

14-12 The *cardinality* of a set is the number of members it contains. Write functions that, given a set variable of a particular type, compute and represent its cardinality, and the lowest and highest (in the ordering of its base type) members it holds.

14-13 Cryptarithmetic problems were once the rage of the country. An arithmetic problem and its answer are given, except that each digit is replaced by a letter. Our job is to decrypt the arithmetic. The example below can be decrypted by a brute force approach. Although ten nested **for** loops are needed, clever use of sets (and an intelligent algorithm) will drastically reduce the number of iterations required.

```
 SEND
 MORE
-----
MONEY
```

14-14 Suppose that the words below are actually sets of char values. It's easy to find a group of words that forms a set representing the entire alphabet. Unfortunately, the problem we pose is this: how many duplicate letters will there be in the group, and what are they? Can you write a program that tries to form the alphabet set while minimizing duplicates?

the quick brown fox jumped over the lazy dog and packed my box with five dozen liquor jugs

14-15 The word 'spare' has five different letters in it. Write a program that prints all possible permutations of these letters. Then, modify your program to print combinations of only two, three, or four letters as well. Remember not to repeat any letters. Before you begin printing, estimate the number of words that will be printed. Finish by figuring out how many of the words have English meanings.

14-16 At last the problem you've all been waiting for—write a computerized dating service. Although a trivial dating program would just try to match people whose interests match, your program should do a more sophisticated job. Try to divide likes and dislikes into distinct groups, and assign relative weights to each group. Thus, your program might pair two people who have few unimportant things in common, but who have, say, an 80% intersection of important interests.

14-17 The game of Bingo is usually played with a square card that contains a grid of numbers. A caller draws numbers at random, and the first player to obtain a vertical, horizontal, or diagonal row of called numbers is the winner. Unfortunately, people who have severe astigmatism are often unable to see the lines and diagonals. They are forced to play Set Bingo, in which the object is to have *all* your numbers called.

Write a program that simulates a game of Set Bingo. Allow for ten players, and give each player's card fifteen numbers. Show each player's card, and at the end of the game print all the numbers that were called. For a bonus, allow the user to specify the number of players. (Hint: use a file of players.)

14-18 Henry Dudeny tells of an old-fashioned game of bowling called *kayles*. Thirteen pins are lined up in a row, but the second one is always knocked down before the start of the game.

Now, with a little bit of practice, a player can always bowl over any single pin, or any two pins that have adjoined from the start. When taking the last turn is the object of the game, a winning strategy is to divide the remaining pins into an even number of similar groups, then copy whatever your opponent does in a group of the same size.

Interactive users should write a program that plays kayles with a user. Include as options the right of going first, the specification of whether the last player wins or loses, and whether or not the computer should play the best possible strategy. Make game output as lively as possible.

Batch users should write a program that plays with itself. To make it a bit more interesting, give each 'player' only a 65% chance of playing the correct strategy.

14-19 Monica Marin is astonished to learn that plants not only listen to people (she talks to her plants, of course), but talk to each other as well. This puts Monica in a quandary. She has seven plants (aethionema, begonia, camellia, daffodil, endymion, ficus, and zinnia), arrayed in a circle, and wants to rearrange them daily so that each plant has the same neighbors as infrequently as possible.

Now, the begonia whispered to Monica one day that n plants could be put in $(n-1)(n-2)/2$ different circular arrangements. What are they for Monica's plants? What would they be if she had thirteen different plants?

14-20 Andrea and Claire owned a very peculiar set of thirteen wooden blocks. Ten of the blocks were marked with the digits 0 through 9 (with only one digit on each block), two more contained multiplication signs, and the last had an equals sign printed on it.

When they played with their blocks, Andrea and Claire divided them equally, each taking five of the digit blocks and one multiplication sign. One day they happened to arrange their blocks in such a way that, by sharing the equals sign, they produced an equation. What is the largest product that could have been on each side of the equation? How was it produced?

14-21 Write a program that prints all of the consonants in a text sample that are followed by vowels.

14-22 Write a program that lets the user specify one or more vowels (and makes sure they *are* vowels), then reads a text file and echoes all words containing the vowels. Modify the program to produce *n* lists of the words that contain only one of the specified vowels, two of them, etc.—through *n* of them.

14-23 How useful are computers in the diagnosis of disease? Write a program that lets a user enter symptoms, then diagnoses her ailment. The program will require a permanent data base of the symptoms associated with a number of diseases. If the user's symptoms match exactly the stored symptoms of a disease, assume she definitely has it. If the user's symptoms are a subset of any group of stored symptoms, inform her that she might have the disease. Finally, if she has some symptoms of any disease (but other symptoms as well), tell her that she shows signs of the disease. A more advanced program would ask for (and specify) further symptoms if a definite diagnosis can't be made.

14-24 In lieu of asking you to prove the four color theorem, we'll pose an easier map coloring problem. Max the Mapmaker believes in the four color theorem. However, he still needs a program to help him color his maps. What he'd like to do is to color an area (say, a state), then tell the computer what color he used, and what the state's neighbors are. He'd like the computer, in turn, to verify that he's used a color different from any of the neighbors. Write Max's program. Incidentally, an exceptionally good program will let Max backtrack and change the color of a state.

14-25 Can we put Max (above) out of business? Write a program that tries to color each of the fifty states automatically. The program should accept as input a list of the states along with each state's neighbors. Warning—you may find that four colors aren't enough. How many different colors does your program require? How would you have to improve your algorithm to make just four colors sufficient?

14-26 Extend your new programming language to include sets. Should you limit a set's maximum cardinality? Does it make any sense to allow sets of structured types? What additional predefined procedures might make it easier to deal with sets?

'A chain of pointers isn't like a ball of string—if the end gets lost . . .'

15

Abstract Data Structures Via Pointers

In *The Medium is the Massage*, Marshall McLuhan argues that information is changed by the medium that conveys it. The same knowledge, transferred in different form, might be understood—massaged into your consciousness—in a different way. As a result, the medium becomes part of the message.

In computer science, programmed data structures are the media in which data is stored and transferred. A genealogical chart (which we'll soon think of as a *tree* structure) has as much information in its connecting lines as in the names it holds. We couldn't easily store the same data in a Pascal file, because it's the wrong medium for storing non-sequential data. The interdependence of medium and message is a fact of programming.

In Chapter 15 we'll be studying the *linked* structures—*queues, stacks*, and *trees*. These aren't predefined data types, but must be programmed using *pointer types* as building blocks. We'll look at linked structures in terms of the operations that can be performed on each, and see how each structure, by its very design, holds a certain amount of useful information.

Section 15-1 explains the mechanics of pointer-type variables, and introduces some of the operations common in setting up linked structures. 15-2 looks in greater detail at the design and use of linked data structures. Finally, 15-3 is devoted entirely to a large example program, and 15-4 deals with bugs.

This is a hard chapter because a lot of non-intuitive and un-obvious material is presented. You should skim through it quickly to get an idea of where the chapter leads, then reread it slowly for learning. Merely seeing and understanding how something is done with pointers isn't enough. You should also be able to duplicate the solution on your own.

Basic Operations with Pointer Types 15-1

AS UNUSUAL, WE WON'T BEGIN WITH AN example. Instead, the next four pages will be a concentrated introduction to the concept and terminology of pointers. Plan to read it twice. Our bottom-up introduction starts with the notion of a *storage location*.

locations

> An area in the computer memory that stores a value is called a *location*. When a Pascal program is directing computer operation, only the values of one particular type may be stored in a given location.* This is the basis of Pascal's strong type-checking—every location has a type associated with it.

allocation and access

A variable declaration makes the computer *allocate*, or set aside, a small portion of its memory as a storage location. An assignment to a variable changes the value stored in 'its' location. For all practical purposes the variable identifier and its location are the same. Because of this, an assignment to an ordinary variable identifier is called a *direct access* of a location.

Pointer variables work a little differently, because a pointer is a variable that *references,* or points to, a storage location.

indirect access

> The contents of the location can be inspected or changed *through* the pointer (called an *indirect* access) if we use special notation. Without this notation, an assignment to a pointer-type variable changes the particular location the variable references, without affecting the contents of that location.

Let's look at a simple example. This definition:

type *NumberPointer* = ↑*integer*;

defines a pointer type. It is read '*NumberPointer* is a pointer to a location of type *integer*.'

reference types

> A *pointer*-type is defined as referencing (or pointing to) a location of a particular type (its *reference type*). An up-arrow (↑) or circumflex (∧) precedes the name of the reference type.

The syntax chart of a pointer's type definition is:

pointer type

type → *identifier* → = → ↑ → *identifier* → ;

* This is not quite true. The location used to store a record variant can accommodate any of the variant groups—they are *overlaid* in a single location big enough for the largest group. If you don't understand this footnote, forget it.

(In this text we'll always use the up-arrow.) The declaration of a pointer-type variable looks like any other variable declaration.

```
type NumberPointer = ↑integer;
var First, Second, Third: NumberPointer;
```

However, we can't assign specific *integer* values to *First, Second*, or *Third*. Instead, they will store the internal computer names associated with particular storage locations.

Like other variables, pointer variables are undefined when they're first declared. The particular location a pointer variable references must be *dynamically* allocated with the standard procedure *new*. A location can be disposed of (for the computer to reallocate later, if necessary) with the standard procedure *dispose*. For example:

dynamic allocation

```
new (First); {Allocate locations for First and Second to reference.}
new (Second);
```

new, dispose

Space in computer memory can be freed for reallocation like this:

```
dispose (First); {Free the location that First pointed to.}
```

First still exists, but it's undefined and doesn't reference any location. It's in the pristine condition it was in before the original call of *new(First)*.

Pascal has a special provision for defining a pointer variable without giving it a location to reference.

nil pointers

> Any pointer variable can be assigned the value **nil**:
>
> *First* := **nil**;
>
> It is now called a *nil pointer*, and doesn't reference a location.

The advantage of a **nil** pointer over one that is simply undefined is that a pointer variable's **nil**/**not nil** status can be checked with a *boolean* expression.

```
{Determine if First references a storage location.}
if First = nil
   then writeln ('Warning!  Nil pointer.  Cannot be accessed.')
   else writeln ('This pointer accesses a stored value.')
```

The value **nil** is unusual in Pascal because it may be assigned to a pointer of *any* type. That's why **nil** is treated like a reserved word.

Our next step is to assign a value to, or inspect the value of, the location a pointer-type variable references.

assigning to locations

> To assign a value to (or read a value from) the location referenced by a pointer variable, follow the pointer's identifier with an up-arrow or circumflex. The pointer must not be **nil**, because a **nil** pointer doesn't have a location.

(As usual, we'll just use the up-arrow.) For example:

```
First↑ := 5;            {Assign 5 to the location First references.}
Second↑ := First↑;      {Assign 5 (the value First references) to Second↑.}
writeln ('The value First accesses is', First↑:2);
readln (Second↑);       {Input a value to the location Second accesses.}
```

We also have to understand how to give a value to the pointer itself, in order to make it access a different location.

addresses

> The value of a pointer is called an *address*. It is the computer's internal notation for a particular location in memory.

If we think of the computer's memory as being a very, very, long array, then an address is like an array subscript. A pointer's value (and thus, the address of the location the pointer references) can be changed in three ways:

changing addresses

1. With procedure *new*. This gives it a brand new address whose contents are undefined.
2. By assigning it the value **nil**, which gives it a null address.
3. By assigning it the address of another pointer of the same type. Both pointers will then access the same location.

In the example below, we make *Second* and *Third* point to the same location by giving them the same address. Then, *Second* is changed to access the same location as *First*.

```
Third := Second;     {These assignments change the locations that Third}
Second := First;     {and Second access, but not the locations' contents.}
```

Note that the assignments can't be reversed.

```
Second := First;
Third := Second;
```

losing locations

After the second pair of assignments, *First, Second*, and *Third* all reference the same location, but the *integer* formerly referenced by *Second* has been cast adrift—the address of its location is lost. We cannot access it, and its storage area cannot be re-allocated by the computer.

How about printing the value of pointers? An address is an internal notation the computer uses for bookkeeping, and it has no external character representation.

using addresses

> The Golden Rule of Pointers
>
> The value of a pointer can't be printed or inspected. It can only be compared (for equality and inequality) to the value of another pointer-variable of the same type, or to **nil.**

```
if (First<>nil) and (Second<>nil) then
   if First = Second
      then writeln ('First and Second reference the same location.')
      else writeln ('First and Second access different locations.');
      {First↑ and Second↑ might be the same anyway.}
```

pointer to structured types

Although pointers to ordinal values (like *integer*) are easy to understand, most pointers reference structured types. An especially common definition is a pointer to a record type that contains a pointer *of the same type* as one of its fields. For example:

```
type DataPointer = ↑DataLocation;
     DataLocation = record
                       a, b, c: integer;
                       d, e, f: char;
                       Next: DataPointer
                    end;
var CurrentRecord: DataPointer;
```

order of pointer-type definitions

A peculiarity of definitions like this is that the pointer type is defined before the reference type—*DataPointer* is defined before *DataLocation*. Since *DataLocation* appears in the definition of *DataPointer*, we seem to have violated the 'define before you use' rule. However, reversing the definitions wouldn't help matters—if we did, we'd have to use *DataPointer* before *it* was defined. Pascal resolves this paradox by sidestepping it.

> In Pascal, pointer type definitions may precede the definitions of their reference types. However, the reverse is not true—a structure may not contain a field or component of a pointer type that has not yet been defined.

Let's summarize the new information presented so far.

1. A pointer type is defined as pointing to a location of any type, using this format:

```
type PointerType = ↑ItsReferenceType;
var PointerVariable: PointerType;
```

summary of pointer facts

2. The dynamic allocation procedure *new* gives a pointer-type variable a location in memory to reference or point to. Procedure *dispose* deallocates and frees this space.

3. A pointer may be given an address only by using *new*, or by assigning it the address of a pointer of an identical type (which makes them both reference the same location). However, any pointer may be

given the null value **nil**. A pointer's address may not be printed or inspected; only compared to other pointer values for equality or inequality.

4. The location that a pointer variable references can be accessed for assignment or inspection by following the variable's name with an up-arrow (or circumflex), e.g. *ThePointer*↑.

5. A pointer may be defined as referencing a type that has not yet been defined (but which will be defined further along in the type definition).

Self-Check Questions

Q. What's wrong with these statements? Assume that we're using pointers to *integer* storage locations.

> *a*) *First* := 5;
> *b*) *Second*↑ := **nil**;
> *c*) *writeln* (*Third*);
> *d*) *First*↑ := *Second*+*Third*;

A. *a*) This statement tries to assign 5 to *First* instead of assigning it to the location *First* references. It should be:

> *First*↑ := 5;

b) The value **nil** may only be assigned to a pointer—not to the location the pointer accesses (unless it too is a pointer). The assignment should be:

> *Second* := **nil**;

c) This output statement attempts to print the value represented by *Third*—which is just the address of a location within the computer—instead of printing the value stored at that location. It should be:

> *writeln* (*Third*↑);

d) This assignment tries to add two addresses instead of adding the values stored at each address. It should be written as:

> *First*↑ := *Second*↑ + *Third*↑;

Addresses may only be compared for equality, and are *never* used in arithmetic expressions.

The Linked Data Structures

Pointers to records are the most frequently defined pointer types. Such records invariably contain one or more pointer fields themselves, and therein lies their beauty: we can dynamically allocate a series of record locations, and tie them together with pointer fields. These are called *linked* structures because pointers form a chain of records.

The notion of linked structures existed long before Pascal. However, pointer types (a Pascal feature) let us easily and transparently implement many linked data-storage schemes. We'll spend the rest of this section looking at the basic linking operations.

Let's begin with an easy example that assumes the definition of *DataType*—we'll soon see that its particulars are not important.

a basic element

```
type ElementPointer = ↑Element;
     Element = record
                  Data: DataType;
                  Next: ElementPointer
               end;
var FirstElement: ElementPointer;
```

This puts us in position to *new* away to our heart's content:

```
new (FirstElement);
new (FirstElement↑.Next);
new (FirstElement↑.Next↑.Next);
new (FirstElement↑.Next↑.Next↑.Next);
```

linked lists

> This particular linked structure is called a *list*. The individual records of a linked list are its *elements*.

A convenient visual notation is used for presenting linked structures. A box or circle represents a record location whose data fields can be labeled individually, or lumped together as 'data.' Each pointer's address—the location a pointer variable or field refers to—is shown with an arrow.* The series of calls to *new*, above, resulted in this structure:

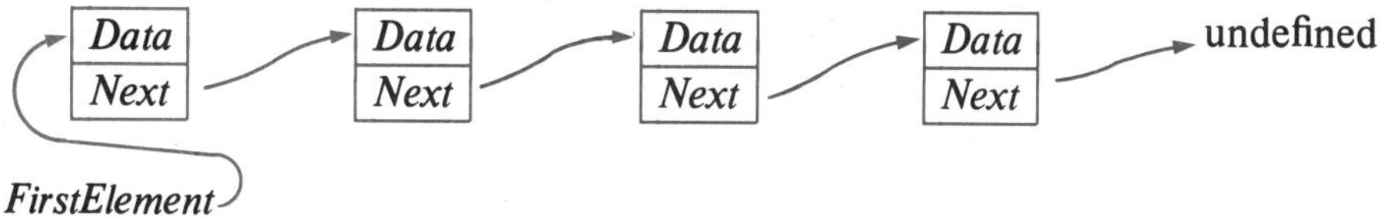

The combination of indirect access and ordinary record notation tends to make expressions long and incomprehensible.

accessing elements

```
FirstElement                {Represents an address}
FirstElement↑               {The record at that address}
FirstElement↑.Data          {One field of that record—a stored value.}
FirstElement↑.Next          {Represents an address}
FirstElement↑.Next↑         {The record at that address}
FirstElement↑.Next↑.Data    {One field of that record—a stored value.}
```

* You can see that we're starting to use visual metaphors.

Now, the illustrated list above shows one of the peculiarities of linked structures. Although the computer has allocated four different locations in memory, only a single identifier—*FirstElement*—is associated with them. This is a source of convenience and confusion. For instance, we can access the entire list through *FirstElement* to make the last record's *Next* field **nil** instead of merely undefined.

FirstElement ↑.*Next* ↑.*Next* ↑.*Next* ↑.*Next* := **nil**;

At the same time, a misstep might cause us to lose contact with part of the list. The assignment below *advances* the pointer variable, so that it references the second record in the list.

FirstElement := *FirstElement* ↑.*Next*;

Unfortunately, this leaves us with no way of accessing the very first list element.

auxiliary pointers

Linked structures usually have several auxiliary pointers associated with them. These pointers act as place markers, maintaining contact with the beginning of a list, its end, our current position, etc.

Suppose that *FirstElement* points to the first link in a list, as in the illustration above. If we had an auxiliary pointer named *CurrentPosition*, and also of type *ElementPointer*, the assignment:

advancing the auxiliary pointer

CurrentPosition := *FirstElement* ↑.*Next* ↑.*Next* ↑.*Next*

would leave the list like this:

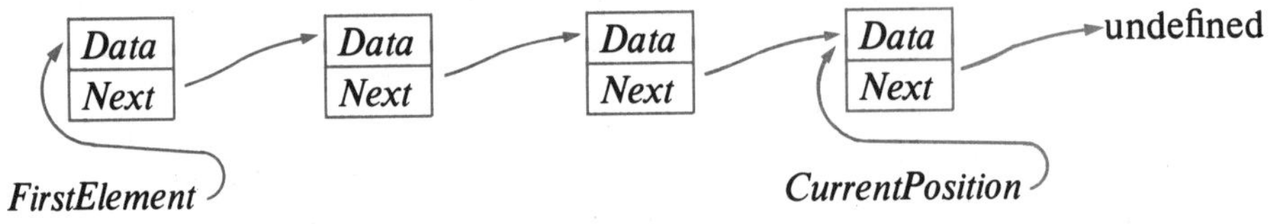

Clearly, the auxiliary pointer makes assignments to the last element of the list much easier to follow:

CurrentPosition ↑.*Data* := *Value*;
CurrentPosition ↑.*Next* := **nil**;

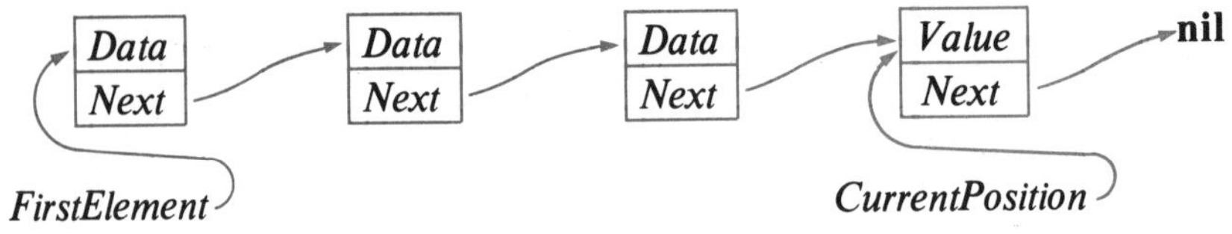

Self-Check Questions

Q. What is the purpose and effect of these statements? Assume the situation of the last paragraph.

new (*CurrentPosition* ↑.*Next*);
CurrentPosition := *CurrentPosition* ↑.*Next*;
CurrentPosition ↑.*Next* := **nil**;

A. These statements extend the chain, but keep *CurrentPosition* pointing to the very last link. The result looks like this:

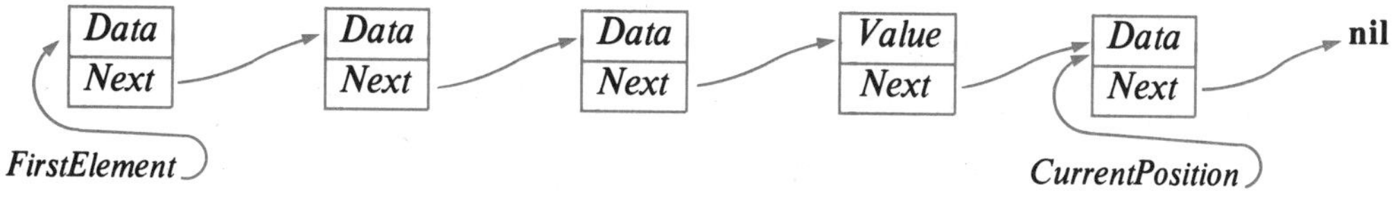

Operations With Links

Like Tinker toys and Lego blocks, the individual elements of a linked structure may be attached to each other in a variety of patterns. However, certain basic operations (like connecting and disconnecting links) are required by most linked structures. In the self-check question above we saw how a linked list could be extended by connecting a new element to its end. The first statement:

new (*CurrentPosition* ↑.*Next*);

allocates a new location. *CurrentPosition* ↑.*Next* now references an undefined record, and the **nil** value is lost. The next statement:

CurrentPosition := *CurrentPosition* ↑.*Next*;

is potentially the most confusing—it advances the current position pointer, moving it to the end of the list. The illustration below shows how the pointer is reconnected.

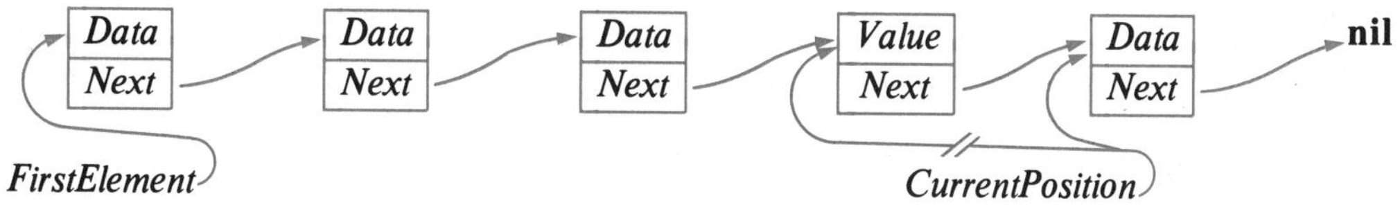

The third and final statement of the list extension makes the new list end **nil.**

CurrentPosition ↑.*Next* := **nil**;

using **nil**

> In general, **nil** should always be used to mark the end of linked structures—a pointer should either have an address or be **nil.**

This makes list searching much easier. If *CurrentPosition* is pointing to a random element of a linked list, we can advance it to the list's end by searching for the **nil**-valued *Next* pointer—the last element.

```
while CurrentPosition↑.Next <> nil do
    CurrentPosition := CurrentPosition↑.Next;
```

Let's write the code for creating a list in the first place. We'll pose the following problem:

problem: make a linked list

> Read and save a sequence of positive numbers. Print the zero or negative number that ends the sequence, then echo the sequence in order.

We'll use an ordinary **while** loop to spot the sentinel, and a linked list to save the numbers. The pseudocode isn't too tough:

refinement

```
initialize the list;
read the first number;
while we're not at the sentinel yet
    add a new element to the list;
    read another number;
print the sentinel;
while we're not at the end of the linked list
    print the current value;
    move to the next element;
```

The Pascal code is shown below. It illustrates some basic linked list methods, and you should be sure to understand it.

linked list program

```
program LinkAndEcho (input, output);
    {Store numbers in a linked list; echo the list.}
type ElementPointer = ↑Element;
     Element = record
                   Number: integer;
                   Next: ElementPointer
               end;
var FirstElement, CurrentElement: ElementPointer;
    TheNumber: integer;
begin
    {Initialize the list and its pointers.}
    new (FirstElement);
    FirstElement↑.Next := nil;
    CurrentElement := FirstElement;
    read (TheNumber);
    while TheNumber > 0 do begin
        {Add each number to the list, then add an element.}
        CurrentElement↑.Number := TheNumber;
        new (CurrentElement↑.Next);
        CurrentElement := CurrentElement↑.Next;
        CurrentElement↑.Next := nil;
        read (TheNumber)
    end ; {while}
    {Note that the current element doesn't store a value.}
    write (TheNumber);
    if CurrentElement<>FirstElement then begin
    {If they both point to the first element, there was no legal input.}
        CurrentElement := FirstElement;
        while CurrentElement↑.Next <>nil do begin
            write (CurrentElement↑.Number);
            CurrentElement := CurrentElement↑.Next
        end {while}
    end; {if}
    writeln
end. {LinkAndEcho}
```

```
12  59  826  959  3  65  -84  444
-84        12        59        826        959        3        65
```

element insertions

Suppose that we wanted to maintain the list in numerical order? We'd read in each new value, search through the list for its proper position, then insert it into the existing list. A single new element, referenced by the pointer *Temporary*, can be appended after the current pointer position with:

```
new (Temporary);
Temporary↑.Next := CurrentPointer↑.Next;
CurrentPointer↑.Next := Temporary;
```

Or, an existing element (referenced by *NewElement*) can be inserted *before* the current pointer position element with:

inserting before the current pointer

```
new (Temporary);
Temporary↑ := CurrentPointer↑;
CurrentPointer↑.Next := Temporary;
CurrentPointer↑.Data := NewElement↑.Data;
dispose (NewElement);
NewElement := CurrentPointer;
CurrentPointer := CurrentPointer↑.Next;
```

As you can see, we engaged in some sleight-of-hand, and didn't really insert the element referenced by *NewElement* into the list. Instead, we created a new, blank element:

```
new (Temporary);
```

gave it the same *Data* and *Next* fields as *CurrentPointer*:

```
Temporary↑ := CurrentPointer↑;
```

inserted it after *CurrentPointer*:

```
CurrentPointer↑.Next := Temporary;
```

stored the new element's data in *CurrentPointer*:

```
CurrentPointer↑.Data := NewElement↑.Data;
```

disposed of the location no longer needed by the new element:

```
dispose (NewElement);
```

arranged for *NewElement* to reference the list element that holds the new *Data* field:

```
NewElement := CurrentPointer;
```

and finally, advanced *CurrentPointer*:

```
CurrentPointer := CurrentPointer↑.Next;
```

If you can follow that sequence, you shouldn't have any trouble with pointers. Here's an outline of the elements involved in the insertion—try filling in the pointers yourself.

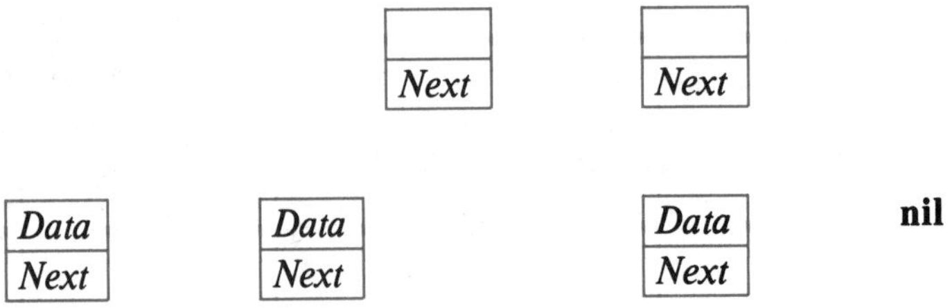

list insertion

Having plenty of auxiliary pointers makes most list manipulations easier. Suppose that we want to insert a new list between two elements of a currently existing list. Two reconnections do the trick, and put the new list between the elements referenced by *CurrentPosition* and *CurrentPosition*↑.*Next*.

NewListEnd↑.*Next* := *CurrentPosition*↑.*Next*;
CurrentPosition↑.*Next* := *NewListStart*;

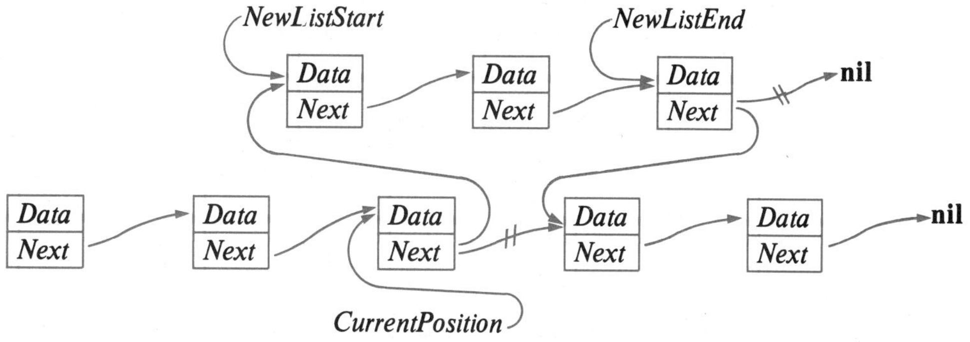

element deletion

Auxiliary pointers are also useful for deleting one or more elements from a list. As long as we don't let part of the list get away (if it does, it's impossible to retrieve), list deletions take only a reconnection or two. Suppose this is the situation.

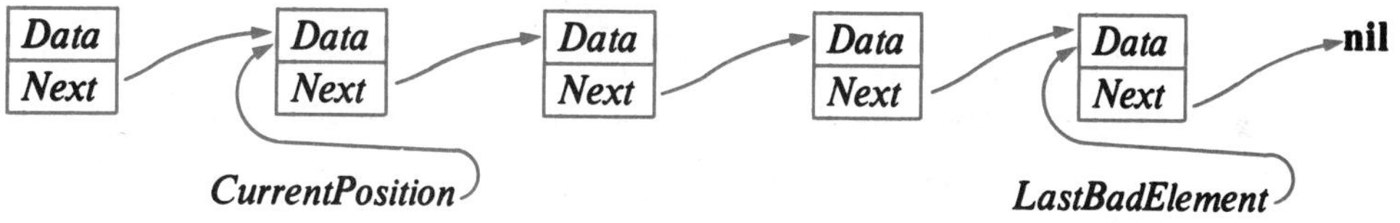

We can delete all elements from (not including) *CurrentPosition*↑ through (and including) *LastBadElement*↑ with:

CurrentPosition↑.*Next* := *LastBadElement*↑.*Next*;

LastBadElement↑ will be retained in the new list if we do:

CurrentPosition↑.*Next* := *LastBadElement*;

Note that we haven't bothered to *dispose* of the elements we cut out.

Let's work out one final problem that will use the techniques we've learned.

problem: adding polynamials

It's a well-known fact that, in any work crew, some people help while others hinder. A *polynamial* is a list of names, in alphabetical order, that gives some idea of the effectiveness of a particular crew. A typical polynamial is:

1 *Bruce* – 5 *Ilana* + 3 *Nadine* + 2 *Patti* –4

Each *term* of the polynamial consists of a name and a number (each person's *inefficient*). Naturally, a person's inefficient may vary (it usually depends on who else is in the crew!). The last term has only a correction factor, and no name.

Our problem is this: Write a procedure that adds two polynamials to form a third.

For example, the sum of these two polynamials is:

(1 *Bruce*) – (5 *Ilana*) + (3 *Naomi*) + (2 *Patti*) –4 plus
(–3 *Alvin*) –3 (*Ilana*) – (1 *Peter*) + 5 equals
(–3 *Alvin*) + (1 *Bruce*) – (8 *Monica*) + (3 *Naomi*) + (2 *Patti*) – (1 *Peter*) +1

We'll work under the assumption that we're given pointers to two existing polynamials. The type definition of a single term must look like this:

type definition

```
type String = packed array [1..5] of char;
    TermPointer = ↑Term;
    Term = record
             Name: String;
             Inefficient: integer;
             Next: TermPointer
           end;
```

The two 'given' pointer variables, then, must be of type *TermPointer*:

```
var First, Second: TermPointer;
```

Our solution will, figuratively, merge two polynamials into a third. Does this kind of problem ring any bells? It should, because we dealt with a similar situation in Chapter 13. Our problem then was to merge two files of records while preserving the alphabetical ordering of the records' *Name* fields. Now we have the additional problem of adding each term's inefficient.

When we merged files we were able to look out for the end of each file. This time we'll watch for the last element in each list—the one with the blank *Name* field. Our pseudocode for creating a new list is:

refinement

```
initialize the new list;
while we haven't gotten to the end of both lists
   if the Name fields are equal, copy it to the new list, adding Inefficients
   else if the First name comes first, copy the whole element to the new list
   else if the Second name comes first, copy the whole element to the new list;
do closing processing on the new list
```

The importance of the last step can't be overemphasized. Files have an end-of-file character added to them automatically, but linked lists must be taken care of by hand.

The coded procedure is shown below. Pay special attention to the *boolean* checks that determine the order of *Name* fields. It's probably a safe assumption that *BLANK* is alphabetically lower than any other *Name* value, but we put in a check just in case it isn't.

polynamial addition procedure

```
procedure AddPolyNamials (First, Second: TermPointer;
                                      var Sum: TermPointer);
  {Create a linked list that adds the terms of two polynamials.}
  const BLANK = '         '; {A Name-sized blank.}
  var SumCurrent: TermPointer; {An auxiliary pointer to the Sum list.}
      Finished: boolean;
  begin
    new (Sum); {We've been passed the pointer, not the list.}
    SumCurrent := Sum; {Sum will stay at the list's head.}
    Finished := (First↑.Name=BLANK) and (Second↑.Name=BLANK);
    while not Finished do begin
      if First↑.Name = Second↑.Name then begin {the names are equal}
        SumCurrent↑.Name := First↑.Name;
        SumCurrent↑.Inefficient := First↑.Inefficient + Second↑.Inefficient;
        First := First↑.Next;
        Second := Second↑.Next
      end {the names were the same}
      else if (First↑.Name<>BLANK) and
              ((First↑.Name < Second↑.Name)
                 or (Second↑.Name=BLANK)) then begin
        SumCurrent↑.Name := First↑.Name;
        SumCurrent↑.Inefficient := First↑.Inefficient;
        First := First↑.Next;
      end {the First list name comes first}
      else begin {First↑.Name was BLANK or > Second↑.Name.}
        SumCurrent↑.Name := Second↑.Name;
        SumCurrent↑.Inefficient := Second↑.Inefficient;
        Second := Second↑.Next;
      end; {the Second list name comes first}
      new (SumCurrent↑.Next);
      SumCurrent := SumCurrent↑.Next;
      Finished := (First↑.Name=BLANK) and (Second↑.Name=BLANK)
    end; {while}
    {Do the closing processing.}
    SumCurrent↑.Name := BLANK;
    SumCurrent↑.Inefficient := First↑.Inefficient + Second↑.Inefficient;
    SumCurrent↑.Next := nil
  end; {AddPolyNamials}
```

Self-Check Questions

Q. Suppose that we have a singly-linked list whose first element is accessed by two pointers—*CurrentPosition* and *PreviousPosition*. Assume that the last element of the list points to **nil**. What is the effect of this code?

```
while PreviousPosition <> nil do begin
    CurrentPosition := PreviousPosition↑.Next;
    dispose (PreviousPosition);
    PreviousPosition := CurrentPosition
end;
```

list disposal

A. The code demonstrates a common *list-disposal* scheme. Each element of the list is disposed of in turn. At the end of the segment, *PreviousPosition* and *CurrentPosition* are both **nil**.

More Link Operations

The basic linked list we've been using all along has an inconvenient shortcoming—it can only be traveled or inspected in one direction. An alteration in the type definition of *Element* solves this problem.

```
type ElementPointer = ↑Element;
     Element = record
                   Data: DataType;
                   Next, Previous: ElementPointer
               end;
```

doubly-linked lists

A list that has backward as well as forward pointers is *doubly-linked*.

Inserting and deleting elements from doubly-linked lists is no more difficult than from singly-linked lists, as long as we remember to reconnect the links in both directions. Procedure *DoubleAppend*, below, puts a new, undefined element after the one accessed by *CurrentPosition*. Note that we have to re-do the links between the new element and *CurrentPosition*↑, and take care of the backward pointer of the element that follows the new one as well. Try to trace the procedure's operation without an illustration.

inserting new elements

```
procedure DoubleAppend (CurrentPosition: ElementPointer);
    var TemporaryPointer: ElementPointer;
    begin
        new (TemporaryPointer);
        TemporaryPointer↑.Next := CurrentPosition↑.Next;
        CurrentPosition ↑.Next := TemporaryPointer;
        TemporaryPointer↑.Previous := CurrentPosition;
        TemporaryPointer↑.Next↑.Previous := TemporaryPointer
    end;
```

The final assignment (to the backward pointer) is most confusing.

TemporaryPointer is a pointer.

TemporaryPointer↑ is the record it references.

TemporaryPointer↑.*Next* is a field of this record. However...

TemporaryPointer↑.*Next* is a pointer too. Therefore...

TemporaryPointer↑.*Next*↑ is a record;

TemporaryPointer↑.*Next*↑.*Previous* is a pointer field, as above.

The overall effect of the assignment is to make the element following the new element point back to the new one, instead of to the element referenced by *CurrentPosition*.

As we have seen, pointers may be passed as parameters. Soon it will seem obvious, but now we'll point out that...

pointers as parameters

> When a pointer is passed as a variable parameter, its address may be changed, as well as the contents of the location at that address. When a pointer is passed as a value parameter, the contents of the location it references can be changed permanently. Changing the address of the value parameter is only a local assignment.

Thus, passing a pointer as a value parameter only partially inhibits our ability to reconfigure the structure it references.

Self-Check Questions

Q. What is the output of this program? What conclusions can you draw about passing pointers as value parameters?

```
program RitesOfPassage (output);
    {Demonstrates some effects of passing a pointer as a value parameter.}
type ElementPointer = ↑Element;
     Element = record
                   Data: char;
                   Next: ElementPointer
               end;
var Current: ElementPointer;
procedure Change (Pointer: ElementPointer);
    begin
      Pointer↑.Data := 'C';              {Which of these}
      Pointer := Pointer↑.Next;          {are local assignments?}
      Pointer↑.Data := 'D'
    end; {Change}
begin
    new (Current);
    Current↑.Data := 'A';
    new (Current↑.Next);
    Current↑.Next↑.Data := 'B';
    writeln (Current↑.Data, Current↑.Next↑.Data);
    Change (Current);
    writeln (Current↑.Data, Current↑.Next↑.Data)
end. {RitesOfPassage}
```

A. *RitesOfPassage* illustrates some of the hazards of passing pointers. The output of the first *writeln* is 'AB', while the second yields 'CD'. During *Change*, alterations to *Pointer* are local, but changes *within* the location it references are global and permanent. The assignment:

Pointer := *Pointer*↑.*Next*;

is negated on return to the main program—*Current* again points to the start of the list. However, assignments to any fields of the record *Pointer*↑, and to other linked records are permanent—the *Data* fields of both records in the list are changed permanently. We could even have globally lengthened the list from within *Change* by adding this statement to the procedure:

new (*Pointer*↑.*Next*)

Data Structures that Use Pointers 15-2

THE STUDY OF STRUCTURES FORMED WITH pointer types is the province of typical second or third computer science courses. We'll jump the gun in this section, and enjoy a brief overview of pointer-based data structures, including *queues, deques, stacks, graphs*, and *trees*. We'll also learn some of the operations and terminology associated with each. We've already encountered linked and doubly-linked lists. The illustration below shows a linked list with auxiliary pointers to its *head* and *tail*.

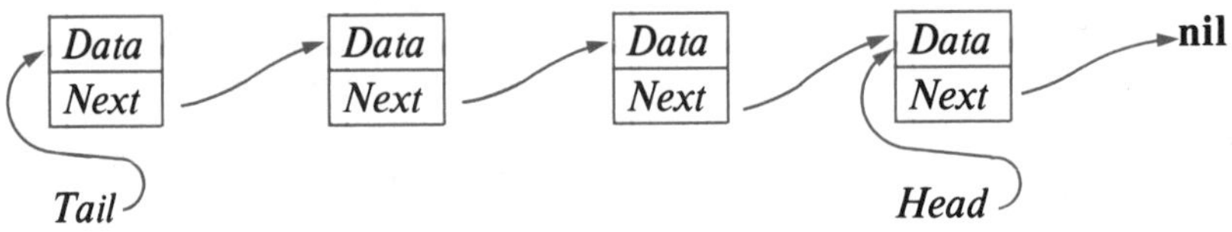

The type definition behind the structure is:

```
type ElementPointer = ↑ListElement;
     ListElement = record
                       Data: DataType;
                       Next: ElementPointer
                   end;
var Head, Tail: ElementPointer;
```

A common application of singly-linked lists is the maintenance of *queues* (kews'). A programming queue is just like a queue that forms inside a bank or outside a movie theater. People (or data) are added to one end and taken from the other—the first in is always the first out. These rules make a queue a queue, and raise it above the level of an ordinary list.

queues

Data structures are characterized by the operations that can be performed on them, as well as by the way they're created.

Although standing in line isn't an especially deep concept, there are some subtleties involved in setting up a queue as a data structure. Suppose that we're working on the basis of the illustration above. An obvious approach would be to add new items to the tail, on the left, and then remove them when they've worked their way up to the head of the queue at the right. Let's see if coding these operations causes any problems. Items are added with:

adding to a queue

```
new (TemporaryPointer);
TemporaryPointer↑.Next := Tail;
Tail := TemporaryPointer;
```

On the other hand, taking an item from the head is pretty difficult, because the head pointer can't be moved backward. Some elaborate code is required.

queue deletion

```
TemporaryPointer := Tail;
        {Start TemporaryPointer at the tail of the list.}
while TemporaryPointer↑.Next <> Head do
    TemporaryPointer := TemporaryPointer↑.Next;
        {This puts TemporaryPointer just before Head.}
Head := TemporaryPointer;
        {Now both pointers reference the next-to-last element.}
TemporaryPointer := TemporaryPointer↑.Next;
        {TemporaryPointer points to the last element, and we can remove it.}
```

A queue doesn't really have to cause this much trouble. We can use a technique called *visual thinking* to get some other (and perhaps better) ideas about how to set one up.

visual thinking

> Visual thinking involves imagining the resolution of a problem in visual, and not algorithmic, terms.

In other words, a visual thinker might try to imagine that she can see a program working (and then try to figure out how or why it works), instead of first trying to come up with its algorithm.

The most famous example of visual thinking is probably that of the chemist Friedrich Kekule, who literally dreamed up the ring-shaped structure of benzene in a vivid reverie in which he saw that a snake biting its own tail could represent a series of linked atoms.* However, the visual approach to problem solving is thoroughly engrained in ordinary thinking. We *look* at problems and *see* their solutions. A bug is due to *oversight*. Wise people are *seers* with great *insight*. We could go on (and McLuhan has).

Visual thinking is particularly applicable to linked structures because the way that elements are connected (and not the type definition of each

* Remember this when we bring up circular lists, below.

element) primarily characterizes a structure. We can radically change a queue representation without altering the basic *ListElement* definition at all. Just imagine a line of people (or list elements) moving from left to right, as above. This time, though, let's have each person point to the person *behind* instead of ahead.

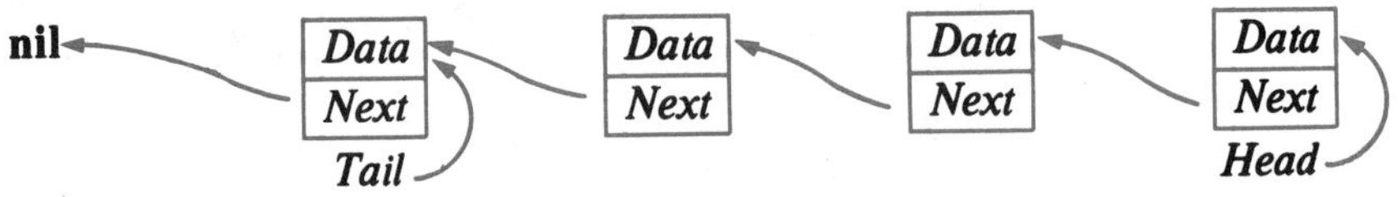

Believe it or not, reversing the pointers will transform our linked list into a convenient representation of a queue. A new element is added with:

```
new (Tail↑.Next);
Tail := Tail↑.Next;
Tail↑.Next := nil;
```

Elements are removed in a similar manner.

```
TemporaryPointer := Head;
if Head↑.Next <> nil then
   Head := Head↑.Next;
```

deques

Now, let's suppose that we want to make a structure similar to a queue, but which relaxes the restrictions on additions and deletions. Although elements will continue to move from the tail to the head, we'll reserve the right to cut into line—even at the head—in order to give some items extra priority. The name *deque* (dek), or double-ended queue, usually describes such a structure. Bearing in mind the difficulty we just had with a single-ended queue, can you propose an approach to implementing a deque?

a better queue

Well, our problem with an ordinary queue was due to the 'directionality' of pointers in a linked list. We can travel and make connections in one direction, but not in the other. Using a doubly-linked list to implement the deque solves the problem. No matter where we are in the deque, we can make insertions or deletions before, after, or at the current element.

```
type TwoElementPointer = ↑StackElement;
     StackElement = record
                       Data: DataType;
                       Next, Last: TwoElementPointer
                    end;
var Head, Tail, ListPointer: TwoElementPointer;
```

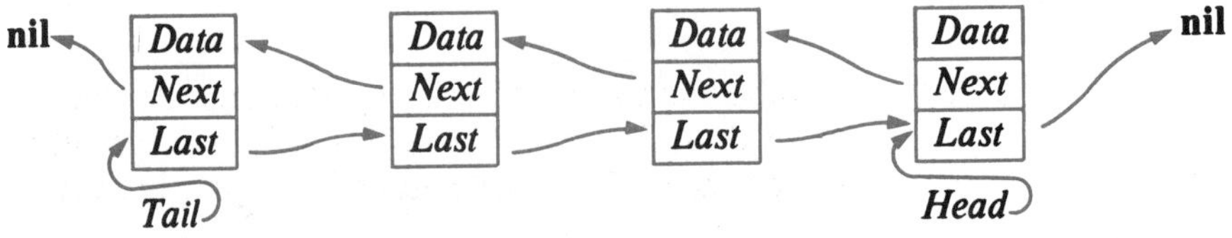

circular lists

How about another variation? Nothing in the definition of *ListElement* says that we have to create lists with heads *or* tails. A *circular* list has no beginning or end—the last element points to the first. A circular list with only one element is interesting, and perfectly legal.

new (*ListPointer*);
ListPointer↑.*Next* := *ListPointer*;

Although some applications specifically require circular data structures, many circular lists are generated because a single 'current position' pointer can act as both a head and tail pointer. For example, this circular list implements a queue:

circular queues

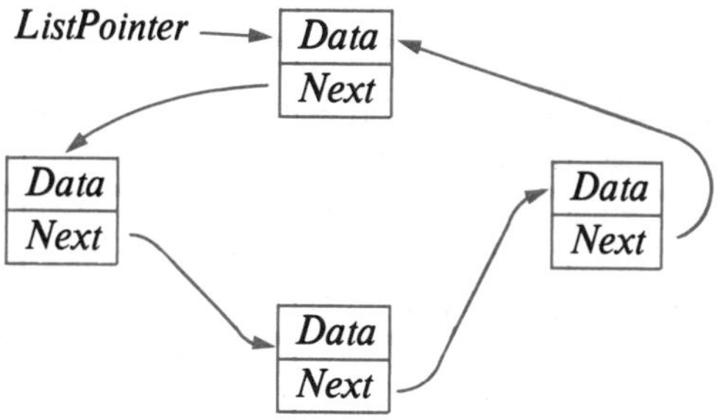

ListPointer points to the end of the queue. A new element is put on the queue with:

new (*TemporaryPointer*);
TemporaryPointer↑.*Next* := *ListPointer*↑.*Next*;
ListPointer↑.*Next* := *TemporaryPointer*;
ListPointer := *ListPointer*↑.*Next*;

The element that's been on the queue the longest is removed with:

TemporaryPointer := *ListPointer*↑.*Next*;
{Point *TemporaryPointer* at the oldest element.}
ListPointer↑.*Next* := *ListPointer*↑.*Next*↑.*Next*;
{Relink the list around it.}

Stacks

Another variation on the usage of lists produces a *stack* structure. Stacks are last in, first out structures—the most recently added element is the first to be taken off. Thus, a stack has a *top*, instead of a head or tail. New elements are *pushed* onto the stack, while old ones are *popped* off. This terminology comes from the most popular image of stacks—the spring-loaded stack of trays in a cafeteria.

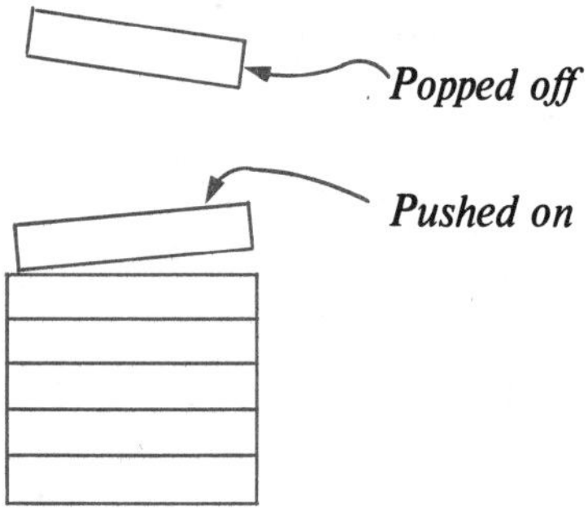

Stack

Implementing stacks requires a simple renaming of the basic linking and unlinking operations, as well as a design decision akin to the choice we made for a queue—should the pointers go up or down the stack? In procedures *Push* and *Pop*, below, we've stayed with our basic, single-pointer, *ListElement* data structure. Each new element points to the current stack, which means that the pointers go down.

Procedure *Push* puts a new element (referenced by *NewElement*) on top of the stack, then advances *Top* there as well. Only *Top* need be passed as a variable parameter.

adding to a stack

```
procedure Push (NewElement: ElementPointer; var Top: ElementPointer);
  {Pushes NewElement on top of a stack.}
  begin
    NewElement↑.Next := Top;
    Top := NewElement
  end; {Push}
```

Pop points *PoppedElement* at the top element of the stack, then moves *Top* down by one element. Because both pointers are permanently changed, they're both passed as variable parameters.

taking from a stack

```
procedure Pop (var PoppedElement, Top: ElementPointer);
  {Pops PoppedElement from a stack.}
  begin
    PoppedElement := Top;
    Top := Top↑.Next;
    PoppedElement↑.Next := nil
  end; {Pop}
```

> A popped element should be isolated from the rest of the stack. Although setting *PoppedElement's* pointer field to **nil** isn't essential, doing so helps prevent inadvertent errors in another part of the program.

If we didn't set its *Next* field to **nil**, *PoppedElement* could still be used to access and change the entire stack.

> Don't forget that an abstract data structure (like a queue or stack) is a set of rules for storing and retrieving data. A programming data type (like a list element) is the means we use to represent the structure in Pascal.

What are stacks and queues used for? Queues are essential when, by accident or design, data can't be relied on to arrive in an orderly fashion. For example, programs that run timeshared computers (which are used simultaneously by several users) use queues to keep track of each user's input. In effect, the computer executes commands at one end of the queue while adding new commands to the other end as they come in. A deque can be used to give commands varying priority by inserting them *within* the queue.

queue applications

Queues are also useful for simulating real-life processes. Suppose that we run a ticket counter, and want to decide if each window should have its own line, or if a single line should feed all the windows. The nature of the problem—customers arriving at irregular intervals, and being served after varying waits—calls for a queue representation.

Stacks tend to have more specialized, computer-oriented applications, and are less representative of real-life phenomena. For example, many kinds of *reversals* use stacks—you may recall our recursive use of the computer's stack in reversing a sentence of input (section 7-3). Arithmetic expressions often take advantage of stacks as well—the order of operators and operands on a stack does away with the need for parentheses.

stack applications

For example, here is the pseudocode of a stack-oriented expression evaluator:

while *we're still reading the expression*
  read a term;
  if *it's an operand, push it on the stack*;
  else if *it's an operator*
    pop the two most recent terms from the stack;
    operate on them;
    push the result on the stack;
pop the top term from the stack;
print it;

For a bit of mental challenge, you might want to think about implementing this algorithm with an explicit stack constructed from pointers and elements. Then, try to figure out how you'd implement it using the computer's stack (through a series of recursive procedure or function calls) instead.

Graphs

A more liberal application of pointers between individual elements leads to a more complicated pointer structure called a *graph*.

> We'll broadly define a *graph* as a pointer structure whose elements are not required to be in linear order.

The picture of the Cave of the Wumpus was a graph, as is this diagram of distances between cities.

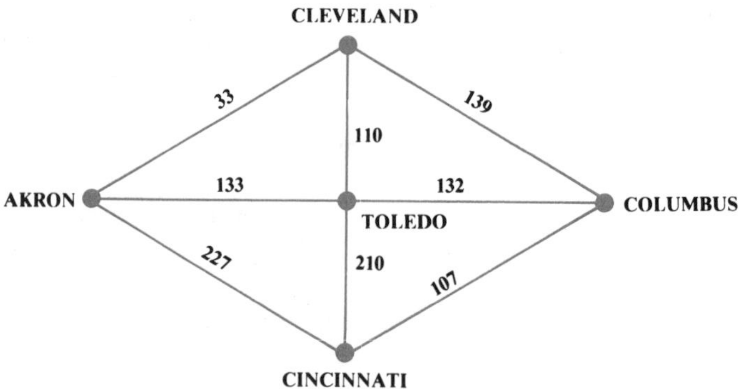

sparse matrix

A much simpler graph can be used to represent a *sparse matrix*. Now, since *matrix* is a rough synonym for a two-dimensional array, a sparse matrix is an array whose component values are almost all identical. As a result, only the non-identical elements are interesting and worth storing. For example, suppose that we want to hold some of the data connected with running a university. *Oh! Pascal! U.* has 100 courses and 10,000 students. How can we keep track of what classes each student is taking, and of which students are in each class?

A reasonable first proposal would be to use a two-dimensional array, with course numbers providing one subscript, and student identification numbers the other. An element is filled in with:

Enrollment [*Course, Student*] := *Taken*;

However, even though such an array would be quite large—one million elements—most of its stored values would be the same—**not** *Taken.* If each student were taking four classes, the array would only be 4% filled. *Enrollment* is clearly a sparse matrix.

Representing the enrollment data with pointers is a much better approach. We want an interlaced network of two sorts of lists—lists of the courses each student is taking, and lists of the students enrolled in each course. The illustration below shows how it's done, and demonstrates some new techniques. To begin with, enrollment data is stored in a record with the following structure:

the underlying data type

```
type String = packed array [1..20] of char;
    CoursePointer = ↑EnrollmentData;
    EnrollmentData = record
                         Course, Student: String;
                         NextCourse, NextStudent: CoursePointer
                     end;
```

A single record is simultaneously a 'students in this course' and 'courses of this student' element. The structure is like that of a doubly-linked list, except that the links are rotated 90° (instead of 180°) to each other.

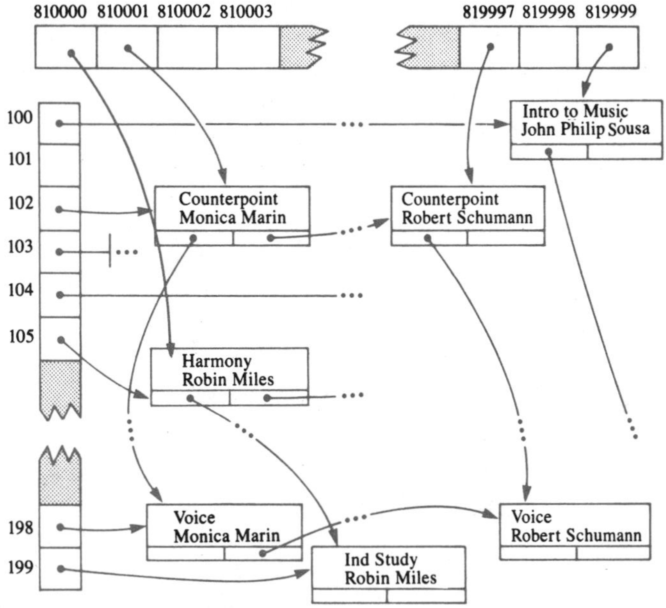

The start of each list is set up in a clever manner. Although we could easily have linked lists of course and student numbers, defining two arrays of type *CoursePointer* takes advantage of the random-access feature of arrays. This lets us find a particular student or course list quickly. The type definition moves along with:

```
{type definition continued}
    CourseNumbers = 100..199;
    StudentNumbers = 810000..819999;        {Class of '81.}
    CourseArray = array [CourseNumbers] of CoursePointer;
    StudentArray = array [StudentNumbers] of CoursePointer;
```

Suppose we want to print the names of all students taking course *TooCrowded*. No sooner said than done.

using the sparse matrix

```
procedure PrintStudentNames (TooCrowded: CourseNumbers;
                             Enrollment: CourseArray);
   {Prints the names of all students in course TooCrowded.}
   var Temporary: CoursePointer;
   begin
      writeln ('Students enrolled in course ', TooCrowded:1, ' are:');
      Temporary := Enrollment [TooCrowded]; {Go to the head of the list.}
      while Temporary <> nil do begin {While there are records to inspect,}
         writeln (Temporary↑.Student); {print the name stored in the record,}
         Temporary := Temporary↑.NextStudent {and advance the pointer.}
      end
   end; {PrintStudentNames}
```

Letting students change their schedules is just a matter of making list insertions or deletions.

Self-Check Questions

Q. Would this code be equivalent to the shaded program segment above? Why or why not?

```
TemporaryPointer := Enrollment [TooCrowded];
repeat
   writeln (Temporary↑.Student);
   Temporary := Temporary↑.NextStudent
until Temporary = nil;
```

A. The code is fine—if any students are taking the class. If nobody has enrolled in course *TooCrowded*, the program crashes attempting to output the *Student* field of a **nil** pointer.

Binary Trees

Of all the data structures that can be represented with pointers, *trees* are probably the niftiest. A *node* at the top of the tree points the way to zero or more different nodes. Each of these, in turn, points to another group of distinct nodes. We can draw a general tree as:

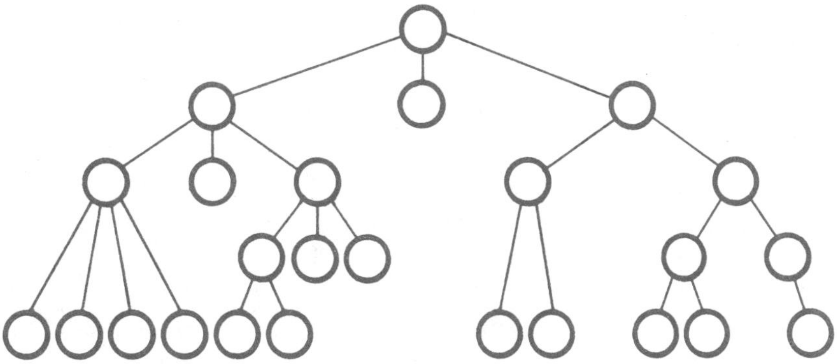

If you look carefully a whole forest is visible—each labeled node points to one or more sub-trees. Now, it's essential that each sub-tree consist of *distinct* nodes—no two sub-trees can share a node. This restriction makes trees *recursively defined* pointer structures. Any tree can be defined as being an element that's linked to one or more trees, or to nothing.

a general tree

tree terminology

The *root* of a tree is its first (topmost) node. The nodes that each element points to are its *children*; it is the *parent*. Finally, a node that has no children is called a *leaf*.

binary trees

Limiting each node to a maximum of two children (i.e. to two potential sub-trees) creates a *binary* (two-part) tree, which is a structure we'll explore in detail. The definition of a binary-node type is much like that of a doubly-linked list element. Only the identifiers have been changed to protect the confused.

a binary tree element

```
type NodePointer = ↑Node;
     Node = record
              Data: DataType;
              LeftChild, RightChild: NodePointer
            end;
```

Since trees are recursively defined, recursive subprograms are convenient for tree structure operations. These usually involve searching trees, or adding additional nodes. We can describe the recursive steps of one tree-searching algorithm in English. (Assume that *CurrentNode* starts by referencing the root.)

To Search a Tree...

recursive tree searching algorithm

1. If *CurrentNode's* left child isn't **nil**, point *CurrentNode* at the left child and search the tree.
2. If *CurrentNode's* right child isn't **nil**, point *CurrentNode* at the right child and search the tree.
3. Print the value stored in the current node.

In practice, each time we return to action 1 (the equivalent of making a recursive procedure call) the values associated with the current node will be saved, along with any pending actions.

> Using recursion allows backtracking without backward pointers.

You may recall using recursion for backtracking in some of our recursive array-manipulation programs in Chapter 11. The tree-searching algorithm is implemented in the recursive procedure *InspectTree*.

binary tree inspection procedure

```
procedure InspectTree (CurrentNode: NodePointer);
  {Visit every node of a binary tree.}
  begin
    if CurrentNode↑.LeftChild <> nil then
      InspectTree (CurrentNode↑.LeftChild);
    if CurrentNode↑.RightChild <> nil then
      InspectTree (CurrentNode↑.RightChild);
    writeln (CurrentNode↑.Data)
  end; {InspectTree}
```

The effect of *InspectTree* can be described as:

> Go down the tree as far as possible, trying to go left, but going right if necessary. Print this node's value. Back up one node, then go down the tree again, following the same strategy—left if possible, right if necessary—until you come to a dead end, or a node you've already visited. Inspect this node, then repeat the search process. When there are no more nodes to search—each child has been visited already—the root has been found, and the entire tree has been inspected.

If you have difficulty imagining the operation of a recursive procedure, stepping through an example on a small tree may help. Looking at the boundary cases of a large tree is also useful.

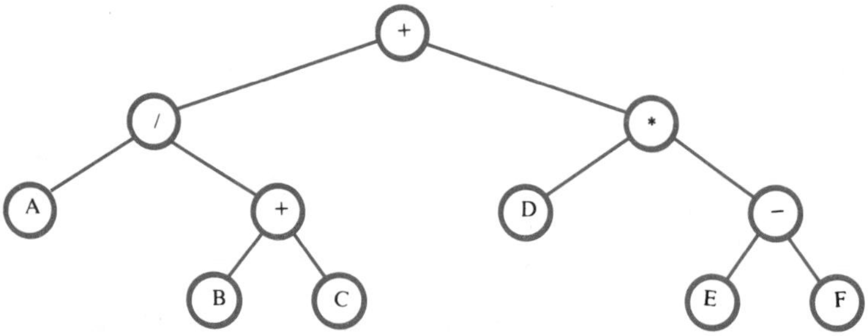

postorder (RPN) search

Suppose we use *InspectTree* to search the binary tree above. Its nodes will be searched in the following order, called *postorder*. *Postfix* and *Reverse Polish* (or *RPN*) are other names for this particular notation.

*A B C + / D E F – * +*

If you own a stack-type calculator you'll recognize this as an arithmetic expression.* In postorder search, a node's sub-trees are inspected before the node itself is. As a result, the root is looked at last.

Self-Check Questions

Q. Suppose that we reorder the three statements of *InspectTree* as shown below. Will the procedure still work? What effect do the changes have?

```
{First variation.}
writeln (CurrentNode↑.Data);
if CurrentNode↑.LeftChild <> nil then InspectTree (CurrentNode↑.LeftChild);
if CurrentNode↑.RightChild <> nil then InspectTree (CurrentNode↑.RightChild)

{Second variation.}
if CurrentNode↑.LeftChild <> nil then InspectTree (CurrentNode↑.LeftChild);
writeln (CurrentNode↑.Data);
if CurrentNode↑.RightChild <> nil then InspectTree (CurrentNode↑.RightChild)
```

preorder search

A. The variations do work, but they change the order in which nodes are visited. The first variation is called a *preorder* search—first a node is inspected, and then its sub-trees. Applied to our earlier tree, we have:

$$+ \ / \ A + B \ C * D - E \ F$$

postorder search

The second modification produces an *inorder* search. The left sub-tree is searched, then the node, and finally the right sub-tree. The path followed is:

$$A \ / \ B + C + D * E - F$$

Programming Binary Trees

The applications of binary trees are unexpectedly diverse. Consider the tree below. Can you guess what it represents?

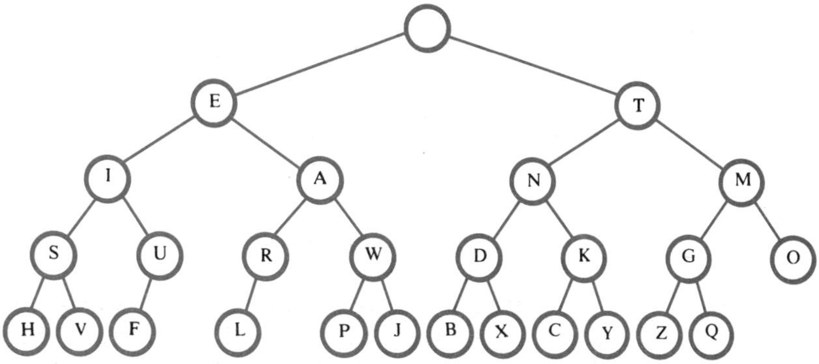

* It's equivalent to $A/(B+C)+D*(E-F)$.

Perhaps the type definition of each node will help.

```
type NextCodeNode = ↑CodeNode;
     CodeNode = record
                    Letter: char;
                    Dot, Dash: NextCodeNode
                end;
var Root: NextCodeNode;
```

As you can probably gather, the tree represents the Morse code. Procedure *Decode*, below, uses the code tree to translate a file of Morse into the letters it stands for. Its parameters are *RootPointer*, which points to the root of the stored code-tree, and *DataFile*, a *text* file of dots, dashes, and spaces. Since we never backtrack (and don't need a stack) *Decode* isn't written recursively. However, we do have to maintain a pointer to the root of the code tree, to start all over again for each new letter.

morse code decoding procedure

```
procedure Decode (RootPointer: NextCodeNode; var DataFile: text);
  {Decodes Morse Code input. Each complete letter must be followed by a blank.}
  var CurrentPointer: NextCodeNode;
      InputCharacter: char;
  begin
    reset (DataFile);
    CurrentPointer := RootPointer;
    while not eof (DataFile) do begin
      read (DataFile, InputCharacter);
      case InputCharacter of
        '.' : CurrentPointer := CurrentPointer↑.Dot;
        '-' : CurrentPointer := CurrentPointer↑.Dash;
        ' ' : begin
                write (CurrentPointer↑.Letter);
                CurrentPointer := RootPointer
              end
      end {case}
    end; {while}
    writeln (CurrentPointer↑.Letter)
  end; {Decode}
```

PACK MY BOX WITH FIVE DOZEN LIQUOR JUGS

binary tree applications

Morse can be stored in a binary tree because the dot/dash code is essentially a series of yes/no questions. Surprisingly, most data can be stored and retrieved using binary trees. An interactive computer game called *Animal* is a good example. The computer plays by trying to guess the name of an animal the player imagines. Although an animal may have many characteristics, considering only one at a time—Is the animal furry? Does it have horns?—reduces its description to a string of binary (two-way) choices. Some sample output from an *Animal* run will help you picture its operation.

```
Think of an animal.
Does it have fur?  Answer yes or no.
no
Does it have tusks?
yes
Does it have big ears?
no
Is it a rhino?                    etc.
```

The *Animal* program relies on two kinds of stored data—characteristics, and (ultimately) the names of animals. The most crucial set of facts—the relationship between characteristic and name—is contained in the binary tree that *holds* the information. The program begins at the tree's root and asks the question stored as a string in that node. Whether the left or right node is visited next visited depends on the answer—sometimes a further question is required (and the process starts again), and sometimes we reach a leaf or final node (and with it, the name of an animal).

Incidentally, the *Animal* program learns as it plays. If it reaches a leaf and guesses wrong, the following transaction takes place.

```
I guessed wrong.  What animal were you thinking of?
a wild boar
Type in an additional question I should have asked.
Does it have bad breath?
Is the correct answer yes or no?
yes                    etc.
```

Internally, a new node is added to the stored data structure, along with the implication that rhinos don't have bad breath.

embedding information

A subtle aspect of understanding tree structures is recognizing the relation between the way data is stored and the way that it's retrieved again. This is especially true when a hand-drawn representation of a tree's stored data doesn't (at first glance) show its order or purpose. Consider this tree.

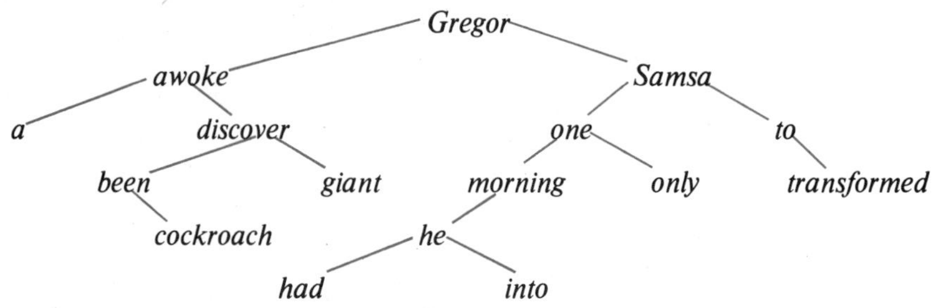

The tree stores the words of this sentence:

> *Gregor Samsa awoke one morning only to discover he had been transformed into a giant cockroach*

in alphabetical order (disregarding capitalization). The first word, 'Gregor', goes to the root of the tree. The second word follows the first alphabetically, so it's stored in the right child. The third word precedes the first alphabetically, so it goes into the left-hand node. The fourth word, 'one', comes after the first, but before the second. It goes to the root's right child's left child. The final resting place of each word is determined by traveling down the tree, turning left or right, or making a new node as necessary.

As you might imagine, we can recursively describe the ordering algorithm.

To Build an Alphabetically Ordered Tree...

binary tree building

1. If the current node is **nil**, store the new word there and stop.
2. If the new word precedes the word in the current node, point to the left child and build an alphabetically ordered tree.
3. If the new word follows the word in the current node, point to the right child and build an alphabetically ordered tree.
4. If the new word is the same as the word in the current node, stop.

In procedure *AddAWord*, below, the final **else** (which represents step 4) isn't necessary, and could be omitted. We've just included it to show you how to touch all the bases.

```
type String = packed array [1..15] of char;
     WordPointer = ↑WordStorage;
     WordStorage = record
                         Word: String;
                         Before, After: WordPointer
                   end;
  ...  {Other definitions and declarations.}
```

binary tree building procedure

```
procedure AddAWord (var Current: WordPointer; NewWord: String);
  {Adds the string NewWord to an alphabetically ordered binary tree.}
  begin
    if Current=nil
      then begin
        new (Current);
        Current↑.Word := NewWord;
        Current↑.Before := nil;
        Current↑.After := nil
      end
      else if NewWord<Current↑.Word
        then AddAWord (Current↑.Before, NewWord)
        else if NewWord>Current↑.Word
          then AddAWord (Current↑.After, NewWord)
          else {The word is a duplicate—NewWord=Current↑.Word.}
  end; {AddAWord}
```

AddAWord is probably the most complicated recursive procedure we'll have to deal with. Note that *AddAWord* is an end recursion—the stack isn't used to store values or pending statements. It could easily be written iteratively.

It will come as a welcome surprise to find that a job that seems complicated (like printing the contents of a tree in alphabetical order), is really pretty easy. It takes an inorder traversal—one of the possible variations on procedure *InspectTree*, which we wrote a few pages back to search an expression tree. The output of *PrintInOrder*, below, assumes that *CurrentWord* currently references the root of the *Gregor Samsa awoke*... tree. (We broke the output into two lines ourselves.)

binary tree inspection procedure

```
procedure PrintInOrder (CurrentWord: WordPointer);
  {Prints the nodes of an alphabetically ordered binary tree in order.}
  begin
    if CurrentWord↑.Before <> nil then
      PrintInOrder (CurrentWord↑.Before);
    write (CurrentWord↑.Word);
    if CurrentWord↑.After <> nil then
      PrintInOrder (CurrentWord↑.After);
    writeln
  end; {PrintInOrder}
```

```
a awoke been cockroach discover giant gregor had
he into morning one only samsa to transformed
```

Self-Check Questions

Q. Suppose that we're creating an alphabetically ordered binary tree using procedure *AddAWord.* What will the trees produced by these sentences look like?

a big cat did everything

zesty young xylophones wed violins

A. A quick perusal shows that the sample sentences are in alphabetical and reverse-alphabetical order. They produce *degenerate* trees—trees that can't be distinguished from ordinary lists.

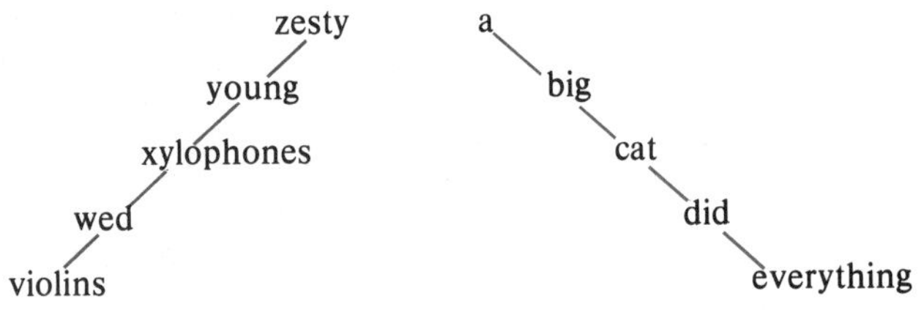

Focus On Programming: Linked Structures 15-3

problem: KWIC

WE'LL END OUR DISCUSSION OF POINTERS with a long example program. It uses some of the linked structures we've just met, and helps demonstrate how simple ideas and techniques can be joined to form long and useful programs. Our problem is:

> Write a program that reads a list of words of interest (keywords), then searches a source file for those words. Each keyword should be printed in its context, e.g. with the four words that come before it and after it.

This is an on-line form of a *KWIC—Key Word In Context—* program. A first appraisal and refinement of the problem presents an obvious program outline.

first refinement

Get the keywords;
Read in the source file one word at a time;
If the current word is a keyword, print it in context;

What should we do with the keywords as they're read in? It's not much trouble to store them in a variety of ways—array, file, linked list, etc. However, step three—*If the current word is a keyword...*—means that we'll want to be able to search through the stored keywords very quickly.

> As we've often found, the choice of an algorithm is intimately tied to the design of a data structure.

It turns out that if keywords are read in at random, then alphabetically ordering them in a binary tree helps minimize the time required to confirm or deny that a given word is present. As a result, 'Get the keywords' is, more or less, procedure *AddAWord* (from the last section). We get the keywords by constructing an alphabetically ordered binary tree.

choosing data structures

The last part of the last step—*print it in context*—presents a more serious problem. Should we look up each word as it's read in, then somehow back up the source file to get the words that came immediately before? Unfortunately, if you know Pascal, you know that we can't back up—we have to reread the entire file. What we really need is a small buffer of some sort that holds the current nine words, and lets us look up the central one. That way, if the central word is in the tree of keywords, we already have the words surrounding it. Any ideas?

ring buffers

The word *buffer* should be a giveaway. A buffer is a queue—the whole point of a buffer is to provide a temporary holding place for data while maintaining its order. In fact, we can represent the queue with a circular list (sometimes called a *ring* buffer). As each new word comes in, it replaces the oldest word in the queue and the 'oldest word' pointer is advanced one place. The current central word (the one we're going to look up) can be accessed with an auxiliary pointer.

Using a ring buffer isn't entirely a bed of roses. We have to establish a context for the first word by pretending to read blank words when initializing the queue. Similarly, pretending to input four blanks at the end of the source file maintains a context through the very last word. This is a small detail, but it's big enough to stump many programmers.

In a second refinement our algorithm becomes:

second refinement

Get the keyword file ready;
Build an alphabetically ordered binary tree;
Get the source file ready;
Initialize a buffer;
Using the buffer, inspect the source file and print its keywords in context;
Inspect the words left in the buffer;

Now, when we begin to write our program, we'll have to address some global concerns that might not seem too urgent, but which could cause trouble. For instance, several of the values the program relies upon may require modification. They should be defined as constants: the length of the longest word, a blank word of that length, and the exact size of a 'context.'

robustness

What about error checking? This means user's errors as well as run-time errors—our program should at least ensure that the keyword and source files aren't blank. A harder sort of robustness involves errors that aren't mistakes at all. Is 'Important' the same word as 'important'? Is a word followed by punctuation identical to the same word followed by a space? Most people would say yes, and a well-written program should agree.

Let's try a third refinement of the *KWIC* algorithm.

third refinement

get the keyword file ready;
get the source file ready;
if *neither of the files is empty*
  then {Make the binary tree of keywords.}
    initialize the tree by creating a root;
    repeat
      get the next word from the keyword file;
      add it to the binary tree of keywords
    until *there aren't any keywords left*;
    initialize the ring buffer with blanks, and the first few source words;
    repeat {Look for the keywords in the source file.}
      get the next word from the source file;
      add it to the ring buffer;
      if *the buffer's center word is found in the keyword file* **then**
        print the contents of the ring buffer
    until *there aren't any source words left*;
    Flush the buffer—take care of the words remaining in the buffer;
  else *Give abnormal termination messages—one of the files was empty*

How can we flush (empty) the buffer without losing the last words it stores? We'll do just what we said a few paragraphs back—add four blank words to the buffer. A jump ahead to a deeper refinement level points the way.

for *the first half of the buffer*
  add a blank to the end of the buffer;
  if *the center word in the buffer is a keyword* **then**
    print the whole buffer;

stub programming

An issue that we won't have to deal with (but which you'll be stuck with in your own programs), is a writing schedule. Sometimes, contradictory programming techniques must be applied at different levels. For example, it's a good idea to omit many refinements and write a program as complicated as *KWIC* in the form of a stub program. A detail as important as searching for the last few words of the source file is, in the final analysis, just a detail. You shouldn't let it delay production of a partially working version.

Our final pseudocode version of *KWIC*, below, leaves out some refinements we brought up ourselves—it doesn't implement upper- to lower-case conversions, or ignore punctuation. Its main purpose is to give names to the program's main procedures, and to help identify the parameters each one will require.

fourth refinement

```
Get file KeyWords ready;
Get file Source ready;
if neither of the files is empty
   then          {Make the binary tree.}
      Root := nil;
      repeat
         InputString (KeyWords, TheWord);
         AddAWord (Root, TheWord)
      until eof (Keywords);
      InitializeTheBuffer (Source, Center, Tail);
      repeat          {Look for the keywords.}
         InputString (Source, TheWord);
         AddItToTheBuffer (Tail, Center, TheWord);
         if ItIsAKeyWord (Root, Center↑.Word) then
            PrintTheContext (Tail);
      until eof (Source)
      FlushTheBuffer (Root, Tail, Center)
   else Give abnormal termination messages.
```

> No matter what programming method you use to develop a program as large as *KWIC*, you shouldn't be afraid of trying to perfect one or more procedures in dummy 'driver' programs.

debugging

If, for example, you're uncertain about your ability to build a binary tree, you should probably write a quick program that builds and traverses binary trees—even if you're using a stub programming approach. A complete tree traversal—which isn't necessarily required in the *KWIC* program—takes only a few lines of code and will confirm that your *AddAWord* procedure was correctly implemented. We've installed an *InspectTheTree* procedure in our *KWIC* that's called only if a global constant called *DEBUGGING* is set to *true*.

testing

Program testing is equally important. By now you should be sophisticated enough to realize that experienced programmers usually find program bugs or shortcomings *not* because they're sharp enough to pick out errors on sight, but by understanding that certain kinds of program input are usually overlooked by novices. Empty keyword or source files shouldn't cause a program crash; neither should blank lines or punctuation. Most potential problems are easy to fix—the hard part is anticipating them.

The actual program is shown over the next few pages. The contents of file *Source* are shown as the program's input. Since *DEBUGGING* is set to *true*, the contents of the alphabetized *KeyWords* tree are shown as well.

KWIC program

```
program KWIC (KeyWords, Source, output);
  {Prints all KeyWords that appear in Source in their context.}
const DEBUGGING = true; {If true, the KeyWords tree is printed.}
     MAXIMUMWORDLENGTH = 20; {Length of the longest string.}
     BLANKWORD = '                    '; {MAXIMUMWORDLENGTH spaces.}
     SIZEOFCONTEXT = 9; {Must be an odd number.}
type String = packed array [1..MAXIMUMWORDLENGTH] of char;
          {Binary tree node definitions.}
    NodePointer = ↑Node;
    Node = record
              Word: String;
              Before, After: NodePointer
           end;
          {Circular list (ring buffer) element definitions.}
    ElementPointer = ↑Element;
    Element = record
                 Word: String;
                 Next: ElementPointer
              end;
var KeyWords,        {File of words we're checking for.}
    Source: text;        {The file we're checking through.}
    Root: NodePointer;        {Accesses the root of the keyword tree.}
    Tail,        {Accesses the oldest element in the buffer.}
    Center: ElementPointer;        {Accesses the 'current' buffer element.}
    TheWord: String;
procedure SkipBlanks (var FromFile: text);
      {Skips leading or trailing blank spaces, including new-lines.}
   var Finished: boolean;
   begin
      Finished := false;
      repeat
         if eof(FromFile)
            then Finished := true
            else if FromFile↑=' '
               then get(FromFile)
               else Finished := true
      until Finished
   end; {SkipBlanks}
```

```
procedure InputString (var FromFile: text; var Word: String);
      {WARNING! Breaks words over MAXIMUMWORDLENGTH characters long.}
      {This version does not modify upper-case letters or punctuation.}
   var Counter: integer;
   begin
      Word := BLANKWORD;
      Counter := 1;
      while (FromFile↑<>' ') and
               (Counter<=MAXIMUMWORDLENGTH) do begin
         {Code to convert upper-case to lower-case and remove
          punctuation will go here at next program refinement.}
         Word [Counter] := FromFile↑;
         get(FromFile);
         Counter := Counter+1
      end;
      SkipBlanks (FromFile)
   end; {InputString}
procedure OutputString (Word: String);
      {Prints the leading nonblank portion of each String array.}
   var Counter: integer;
       Finished: boolean;
   begin
      Counter := 1;
      repeat
         Finished := (Word [Counter]=' ');
         if not Finished then write (Word [Counter]);
         Counter := Counter+1
      until (Counter>MAXIMUMWORDLENGTH) or Finished
   end; {OutputString}
procedure AddAWord (var Current: NodePointer; NewWord: String);
      {Recursively creates an alphabetically-ordered binary tree.}
   begin
      if Current=nil
         then begin
            new (Current);
            Current↑.Word := NewWord;
            Current↑.Before := nil;
            Current↑.After := nil
         end
         else if NewWord<Current↑.Word
            then AddAWord (Current↑.Before, NewWord)
            else if NewWord>Current↑.Word
               then AddAWord (Current↑.After, NewWord)
   end; {AddAWord}
```

```
procedure InspectTheTree (CurrentNode: NodePointer);
      {A recursive debugging procedure that does an inorder search of the binary tree
       of keywords. Only called if the global constant DEBUGGING is true.}
   begin
      if CurrentNode↑.Before <> nil then InspectTheTree (CurrentNode↑.Before);
      writeln (CurrentNode↑.Word);
      if CurrentNode↑.After <> nil then InspectTheTree (CurrentNode↑.After)
   end; {InspectTheTree}
procedure InitializeTheBuffer (var Source: text; var Tail, Center: ElementPointer);
{Creates a ring buffer SIZEOFCONTEXT elements long. Elements older than and
 including Center are initialized as blanks; the rest of the buffer is filled from Source.}
   var TemporaryPointer: ElementPointer;
       Counter: integer;
   begin
      new (TemporaryPointer);
      Tail := TemporaryPointer;          {Locate the oldest element.}
      for Counter := 1 to (SIZEOFCONTEXT div 2) do begin
         TemporaryPointer↑.Word := BLANKWORD;
         new (TemporaryPointer↑.Next);
         TemporaryPointer := TemporaryPointer↑.Next
      end;
      Center := TemporaryPointer;          {Locate the central 'working' element.}
      for Counter := 1 to (SIZEOFCONTEXT div 2) do begin
         new (TemporaryPointer↑.Next);
         TemporaryPointer := TemporaryPointer↑.Next;
         InputString (Source, TemporaryPointer↑.Word)
      end;
      TemporaryPointer↑.Next := Tail          {Make the list circular.}
   end; {InitializeTheBuffer}
procedure AddItToTheBuffer (var Tail, Center: ElementPointer; TheWord: String);
      {Replaces the oldest word in the buffer with the one just input.
       Advances the tail and 'current' pointers.}
   begin
      Tail↑.Word := TheWord;
      Tail := Tail↑.Next;
      Center := Center↑.Next
   end; {AddItToTheBuffer}
```

```
function ItIsAKeyWord (CurrentNode: NodePointer; TheWord: String): boolean;
    {Search the binary tree for a particular word.}
  var ItsFound: boolean;
  begin
    ItsFound := false;
    repeat
      if TheWord<CurrentNode↑.Word
        then CurrentNode := CurrentNode↑.Before
        else if TheWord>CurrentNode↑.Word
          then CurrentNode := CurrentNode↑.After
          else ItsFound := true
    until (CurrentNode=nil) or ItsFound;
    ItIsAKeyWord := ItsFound
  end; {ItIsAKeyWord}
procedure PrintTheContext (Tail: ElementPointer);
    {Prints each word in the buffer (spacing between), then new-lines.}
  var TemporaryPointer: ElementPointer;
  begin
    TemporaryPointer := Tail;
    repeat
      OutputString (TemporaryPointer↑.Word);
      write (' ');
      TemporaryPointer := TemporaryPointer↑.Next
    until TemporaryPointer = Tail;
    writeln
  end; {PrintTheContext}
procedure FlushTheBuffer (Root: NodePointer; var Tail, Center: ElementPointer);
    {Inspects the words remaining in the buffer.}
  var Counter: integer;
  begin
    for Counter := 1 to (SIZEOFCONTEXT div 2) do begin
      AddItToTheBuffer (Tail, Center, BLANKWORD);
      if ItIsAKeyWord(Root, Center↑.Word) then PrintTheContext (Tail)
    end
  end; {FlushTheBuffer}
```

```
begin {KWIC}
  reset (KeyWords);
  SkipBlanks (KeyWords);
  reset (Source);
  SkipBlanks (Source);
  if not eof(KeyWords) and not eof(Source)
    then begin          {KWIC action.}
            {Set up the tree of keywords.}
      Root := nil;
      repeat
        InputString (KeyWords, TheWord);
        AddAWord (Root, TheWord)
      until eof (KeyWords);
      if DEBUGGING then InspectTheTree (Root);
            {Set up the buffer and search for words.}
      InitializeTheBuffer (Source, Tail, Center);
      repeat
        InputString (Source, TheWord);
        AddItToTheBuffer (Tail, Center, TheWord);
        if ItIsAKeyWord(Root, Center↑.Word) then
          PrintTheContext (Tail)
      until eof (Source);
      FlushTheBuffer (Root, Tail, Center)
    end {KWIC then action}
    else begin          {Abnormal termination messages.}
      if eof (KeyWords) then
        writeln ('Abnormal program termination.  KeyWord file empty.');
      if eof (Source) then
        writeln ('Abnormal program termination.  Source file empty.')
    end {else action}
end. {KWIC}
```

↓ ↓ ↓ ↓ ↓

here is a kwic test file that is designed to check special cases of kwic operation. It includes blank lines,

punctuation, and has key words at both the beginning and

end of the file. however, it doesn't include capital letters. the keyword file also contains blank lines. end

```
blank
end
file
here
it
lines
that
    here is a kwic test
is a kwic test file that is designed to
a kwic test file that is designed to check
kwic operation. It includes blank lines, punctuation, and has
both the beginning and end of the file. however,
of the file. however, it doesn't include capital letters.
capital letters. the keyword file also contains blank lines.
keyword file also contains blank lines. end
also contains blank lines. end
```

Antibugging and Debugging 15-4

THE WAY TO UNDERSTAND POINTERS, LIKE the way to Carnegie Hall, is practice, practice, practice. Although pointers aren't an exceptionally hard abstraction, many little rules must be followed when they're used. As a result, not everyone who understands a linked structure can implement it in Pascal. As we mentioned in the introduction, we always have to insist on the highest degree of learning—not 'Do I understand it?' but rather, 'Can I duplicate it?'

The difference between an undefined pointer and a pointer that references an undefined location causes many run-time errors. Suppose that we have these definitions:

```
type ElementPointer = ↑Element;
     Element = record
                 A, B: integer;
                 NextElement: ElementPointer
               end;
var CurrentPosition: ElementPointer;
```

At the start of a program, *CurrentPosition* is undefined (although many Pascal compilers initialize pointer-type variables to **nil**).

> Whether or not *CurrentPosition* has been initialized to **nil**, it does *not* reference a location.

undefined pointer bugs

Programmers usually make the mistake of assuming that *CurrentPosition* references a record of type *Element* whose fields are undefined. Unfortunately, trying to make an assignment results in a run-time crash.

```
CurrentPosition↑.A := 0;        {At run time...}
    ↓        ↓        ↓        ↓
ABNORMAL TERMINATION --
REFERENCE THROUGH NIL POINTER
```

Before a reference can be made through any pointer variable, a location must be allocated (using procedure *new*).

```
new (CurrentPosition);
```

Now *CurrentPosition* references a record whose fields are undefined.

infinite loop bugs

Two varieties of infinite loops are caused by pointers. The first occurs when dynamic allocation runs wild.

```
new (SomeRecord);
repeat
   new (SomeRecord↑.Next);
   SomeRecord := SomeRecord↑.Next
until false        etc.
```

overallocation

This program segment generates a never-ending list. When the computer runs out of new locations to allocate, the program may crash with:

```
ABNORMAL TERMINATION -- HEAP OVERFLOW
```

> Pointer locations are said to be allocated from a *heap* of unused locations in memory.

Heap overflow* crashes are no more serious than 'statement limit exceeded' crashes. They can also occur (rarely) in programs that dynamically allocate many locations without ever using *dispose* to allow reallocation.

endless searches

The second kind of infinite loop results from an endless search, usually through a circular list, for a location or pointer value that isn't there. The fail-safe of running past the end of an array simply doesn't exist. The examples below show **while** loops that are reasonable if and only if we're certain to find pointer *SoughtPosition* or value *SoughtData*.

```
while CurrentPosition <> SoughtPosition do
   CurrentPosition := CurrentPosition↑.Next     etc.
      ⋰
while CurrentPosition↑.Data <> SoughtData do
   CurrentPosition := CurrentPosition↑.Next     etc.
```

* Some systems call these *stack overflows*. We'll see why at the end of this section.

Saving an extra pointer to the starting position and making an additional *boolean* check can be an invaluable antibugging device.

```
Start := CurrentPosition;
while (CurrentPosition <> SoughtPosition)
      and (CurrentPosition↑.Next <> Start) do
   CurrentPosition := CurrentPosition↑.Next     etc.
```

Of course, we're still not in the best of all possible positions—we don't know if we left the loop because we found the location we were looking for, or because we made a complete circuit. Fortunately, that's a minor problem an extra **if** statement can straighten out.

As you might imagine, there are many bugs associated with pointer structures, rather than with pointer types per se. We've just discussed some of the difficulties of using circular lists. Stacks have one very common bug.

stack bugs

> Don't try to pop elements from an empty stack.

A simple check for *TopPointer*=**nil** helps sidestep this problem.

Queues and other structures that use lists also tend to generate boundary errors. When writing procedures that manipulate such structures, it's usually a good idea to remember special (but inevitable) cases. Will the procedure work...

list bugs

...at the beginning of a list?
...at the end of a list?
...if the list is empty?
...if the procedure makes the list empty?

It's easy to make boundary mistakes. For example, the following code is supposed to print a list's contents. Can you spot the bug it contains?

```
CurrentPosition := HeadPointer;
while CurrentPosition↑.Next <> nil do begin
   writeln (CurrentPosition↑.Word);
   CurrentPosition := CurrentPosition↑.Next
end;
```

check boundary conditions

It really holds two bugs. What if the list is empty, and *HeadPointer* is **nil**? The *boolean* expression causes a run-time crash—we're trying to reference the *Next* field of a **nil** pointer. However, a non-empty list has troubles as well. What's the last *Word* field printed? Is it the last element of the list? No—it's the next-to-last. We've made an off-by-one error.

Another common boundary error occurs during list searches. The following bit of code is intended to search a list for a particular *Data* field. We've tried to avoid the error, cited above, of trying to reference the *Next* field of a **nil** pointer.

```
while (CurrentPosition <> nil)
      and (CurrentPosition↑.Data <> SoughtData) do
   CurrentPosition := CurrentPosition↑.Next;
```

Unfortunately, we've forgotten that *boolean* expressions are fully evaluated. When *CurrentPosition* is **nil**, it's clear that the **while** loop's entry condition won't be met. Nonetheless, the second part of the condition (*CurrentPosition↑.Data<>SoughtData*) is still tested. The program crashes making a reference through a **nil** pointer.

A general problem associated with linked structures is the inadvertent loss of individual pointers.

don't lose locations

> It *is* possible to lose locations. When a location *or chain of locations* is lost there's no way to find it again.

A chain of pointers isn't like a ball of string—if the end gets lost, it's really gone. In most operations that involve list insertions or deletion, the order of statements is crucial. Remember that, in making a deletion from a list, pointers must detour around the unnecessary element or elements *before* the deletion takes place.

By their nature, pointers partially deprive the programmer of one of the best debugging tools—the snapshot of current program conditions. The value of a pointer is either **nil**, or the address of a location in memory, and neither value can be printed out.

print the data structure

What we need are procedures that display the contents of a pointer structure. It should be no trouble to pull such routines from 15-2. A list is printed with:

```
CurrentPosition := FirstPointer;
while CurrentPosition <>nil do begin
    writeln (CurrentPosition↑.Word);
    CurrentPosition := CurrentPosition↑.Next
end;
```

Although binary trees can be terrifying, they're easy to search recursively. Here's the code for an *inorder* search of a binary tree.

```
procedure SearchTree (CurrentNode: NodePointer);
    begin
        if CurrentNode↑.Before <> nil then
            SearchTree (CurrentNode↑.Before);
        Inspect (CurrentNode);
        if CurrentNode↑.After <> nil then
            SearchTree (CurrentNode↑.After)
    end;
```

> When in doubt, print the contents of your data structure.

how pointers work

A quick look at a common implementation of pointers may help you understand potential bugs. For all practical purposes, we can imagine that a computer's memory is an extremely long array, like this one:

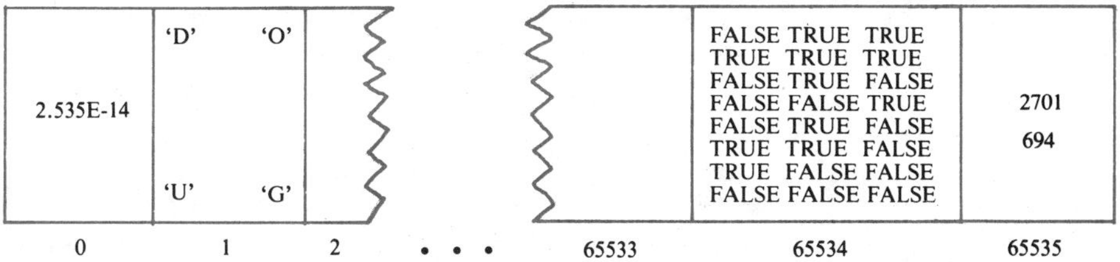

The array's element type is usually called a *word*. It's a basic memory location, usually capable of storing a single *real*, a handful of *char* values, or as many as five or six dozen *boolean* values. (Obviously, a group of two or more words would be required to store larger, structured value types.) The memory array's length is huge—in the tens of thousands.

The value of a pointer variable is essentially a subscript of this large array. As a result, trying to reference a pointer that is undefined (or whose value is **nil**) is much like using an out-of-range array subscript. However, instead of getting a 'subscript out of range' error message, we get a 'reference through **nil** pointer' message.

In terms of the illustration above, the computer's stack is allocated from the left-hand portion of the memory array, while the heap comes from the right-hand side. A run-time error occurs when the stack and heap collide, which is why an error message may refer to a stack overflow, and not a heap overflow.

use auxiliary pointers

The last antibugging comment we'll make involves auxiliary pointers. Very often, bugs are caused because programmers are needlessly stingy when it comes to declaring auxiliary pointers. In the end they have to play musical chairs with the values of the pointers that *are* available. When one pointer serves two purposes, bugs tend to happen.

> Extra pointers are cheap—use them.

Pascal Summary

• pointer type: allows the creation of variables that indirectly access stored values. A pointer is defined as a type that references, or points to, values of another type:

```
type LetterPointer = ↑char;
     DataPointer = ↑DataLocation;
     DataLocation = record
                        a, b, c: integer;
                        d, e, f: char;
                        Next: DataPointer
                    end;
var ThisLetter, ThatLetter: LetterPointer;
                    CurrentRecord, HeadRecord: DataPointer;
```

- dynamic allocation: makes a pointer variable reference a new location:

```
new (ThisLetter);
new (CurrentRecord);
new (CurrentRecord↑.Next);
```

- deallocation: frees the memory location that a pointer references:

```
dispose (ThisLetter);
```

- indirect reference: an assignment to, or inspection of, to the storage location a pointer variable refers to. The pointer variable is followed by an up-arrow or circumflex:

```
ThisLetter↑ := 'L';
CurrentRecord↑.a := 49;
```

- pointer assignment: changes the location that a pointer variable references:

```
ThatLetter := ThisLetter;
CurrentRecord↑.Next := CurrentRecord;
HeadRecord := nil;
```

- element, node: one of the building blocks of a linked data structure. A typical element type will have fields that represent the element's stored data, and one or more fields that store pointers to other elements in the data structure. The element defined below would be happily at home in either a doubly-linked list or binary tree data structure:

```
type ElementPointer = ↑Element;
                      Element = record
                                  Data: ItsType;
                                  Left, Right: ElementPointer
                                end;
```

Important Facts

- The definition of a pointer type may precede the definition of the type it references.
- A pointer variable represents the value stored in a storage location. Pointers can only be compared, for equality or inequality, to each other or to **nil**. The value of a pointer can't be inspected directly.
- A pointer variable is given a value in three ways. It's given a new location with *new*, or can have the current value of another pointer (of the same type) assigned to it, or can be assigned the value **nil**. The *dispose* procedure removes the pointer variable's value.
- The value a pointer variable references (as opposed to the value it represents) can be accessed, for inspection or assignment, using special notation—the name of the pointer variable followed by an up-arrow or circumflex.

- A linked list is a sequence of elements (almost invariably records) that are connected by pointers. A doubly-linked list has pointers connecting in both directions.
- A variety of data structures can be constructed by imposing rules on a simple linked list. In a queue, elements are added to one end, and taken from the other. A deque allows additions or deletions from either end. In a stack, the most recently added element is the first element removed.
- The tree is a recursively defined data structure. Each node of a tree points to one or more distinct sub-trees. In a binary tree, a node can only have two sub-nodes (its children). The topmost node is called the tree's root, while nodes that don't have any children are called leaves.
- A binary tree can be searched in a number of different ways, including preorder (node, then sub-trees), inorder (left sub-tree, node, then right sub-tree), and postorder (leaves, then nodes).
- Losing track of the end of a list or tree is one of the most common pointer-type bugs. Use auxiliary pointers to avoid this problem. Be sure to initialize pointers to **nil** to avoid running past the end of a list or tree.
- When you're dealing with linked structures, the first procedure you write should be a snapshot procedure that prints the data structure's contents.
- The Golden Rule of Pointers: The value of a pointer can't be printed or inspected. It can only be compared (for equality and inequality) to the value of another pointer-variable of the same type, or to **nil**.

Self-test Exercises

15-1 Define pointers to types *integer, char*, and *ListElement*.

15-2 What is a last in, first out data structure? First in, first out? Are they sequential access, or random access structures? Which category (LIFO or FIFO) does Pascal's **file** type fall into? The **array** and **set** types?

15-3 What is the output of this program?

```
program Trial (output);
type Pointer = ↑integer;
var Test: Pointer;
begin
    new (Test);
    Test := nil;
    Test↑ := 1;
    writeln (Test↑)
end.
```

15-4 Write a procedure that determines if two pointer variables of type *Reach* both reference the same location, or indirectly access the same value, or both.

15-5 When is this an illegal assignment?

```
Variable↑ := nil;
```

15-6 In a typical binary tree, each node has pointers to two sub-trees. In consequence, it's possible to travel down a tree (away from the root) but never up a tree (toward the root). Define a pointer-type that overcomes this difficulty.

15-7 Suppose that we have a pointer *Current* to a leaf (a node with no children) of the type defined above. Write statements that give it two children.

15-8 What does function *Mystery* do? Will it ever fail?

```
function Mystery (ThisPosition: ANode): integer;
   var Count: integer;
   begin
      Count := 0;
      while ThisPosition <> nil do begin
         Count := Count + 1;
         ThisPosition := ThisPosition↑.WhoKnows
      end;
      Mystery := Count
   end; {Mystery}
```

15-9 What is the difference between elements of a doubly-linked list, and those of a binary tree?

15-10 Suppose that we have a circular list (or ring buffer) of type *Elements* that stores individual *integer* data items. A *Subsequent* field points the way to the next record. Write a procedure that prints the list's contents. Include a check for an empty or non-circular list.

More Exercises

15-10 When applied to an alphabetically ordered binary tree, an inorder search will print its contents in alphabetical order. How would you write a procedure to print the tree's contents in *reverse* alphabetical order?

15-11 Suppose that *ListPointer* is a pointer type that accesses some record type. What will be the effect of these two statements?

```
writeln (ListPointer);
writeln (ListPointer↑);
```

15-12 Can you think of any uses for pointers to ordinal values? Pointers to pointers?

15-13 An ancient puzzle concerns a ship caught in a terrible storm. Although there were thirty passengers on board, the lifeboats would only hold fifteen. So as not to leave anybody behind, the captain resolved to throw half the passengers overboard before taking to the boats.

As it happens, exactly fifteen of the passengers had slighted the captain by not dining at the Captain's Table during the cruise. The captain, in revenge, arranged all the passengers in a circle, and began to count, throwing every *nth* passenger overboard. As you might imagine, only the passengers he disliked vanished beneath the waves. The captain's fifteen dinner companions were able to use the lifeboats, and the Captain went down with the ship.

What was the number *n*? Use a circular list to simulate the terrible counting process, and find which *n* has the proper result. (Hint: it's less than 30.) Here's the starting order of the passengers—the X's go overboard, and the O's take the lifeboats. The arrow points at the start of the count.

```
→ O O O O O X X X X O O X X O
 X                             X
  X O O X X O X X O X O X O O
```

15-14 Here's a similar problem that's a little harder. Another captain, on a ship with only ten passengers, was in the same position. The passengers were arranged in a circle like this, with five odd numbers representing the losers:

```
              0
        8           1
  9                       2
  6                       3
        7           5
              4
```

Unfortunately, the captain forgot where to begin the count, and what the counting constant was. Write a program to help the captain. For a bonus, find the starting position and counting constant that would help the doomed passengers instead.

15-15 Write a program that will reverse a large text file. In other words, lines that were first shall be last, and the first character of each line will become the last character. Assume that the original file has no more than 80 characters per line.

15-16 Write a program that reads, and evaluates, an *integer* expression given in postfix notation. Simplify the job by not allowing parentheses.

15-17 A bank is trying to decide if it should have separate lines for each teller, or have all customers wait in one 'feeder' line. Write a program that simulates bank operation under both systems. Make the program realistic by having customers arrive at varying intervals, and carry out transactions of different lengths. Naturally, all customers will go to the shortest line available. The program's output should show the total number of customers, the average wait in each system, the average line length, and the longest wait required.

15-18 Marin Motors leases cars in five price ranges: subcompact, compact, midsize, station wagon, luxury. In any one category the price of cars is the same, but their gas mileage may vary. Thus, the last few cars in a cheap category may have poorer mileage than the first few cars that cost more, and a customer going on a long trip would be better off renting the more expensive model. In general, though, mileage drops as the car's size (and rental price) increases.

A customer can request a car in any size, but if that size isn't available, the next larger car is provided at the same cost. A minimum mileage may be requested, and the length of rental must be given in advance, As a service to its customers, Marin Motors will figure out which car they'd be best off renting, given the expected trip mileage, and the stock of cars available.

Write a program that handles bookkeeping and inventory for Marin Motors. You'll have to determine a starting stock of cars, and the prices and mileage of each. The program should rent cars (as detailed above), provide billing information, and show the stock on hand in order of price and mileage when requested. Then, modify the program to simulate Marin Motors' business over a two-week period instead.

15-19 As the penultimate step in defining your alternative high-level programming language, add pointer types. Or, consider the idea of defining binary trees, and lists, as basic data types of the language. What kind of information would have to be provided in the definition of such types? Would they be less useful than Pascal pointers?

Finally, reassess the language you've created. What are its advantages over Pascal? Could you write a program that translates Pascal into the new language? What about vice versa?

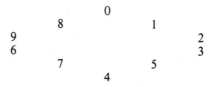

'Now, how long does it take to find something . . .'

16

Advanced Topics: Sorting, Searching, and Matching

One of the more recent additions to the known fundamental constants of nature is Cooper's Constant of Curricular Absorption: 3% per term. This is believed (by Cooper, anyway) to be the rate at a Computer Science course absorbs material from the next course in the sequence. Term after term, there seems to be room left in the last week for harder topics. As a result, every five years or so there's a move to consolidate courses in a two-for-three merger. Each decade or two, by and large, a course suddenly appears from the next higher school—a grad course shows up in the undergraduate catalog, or a college course rears its head in an unsuspecting high school. Obviously, students are getting smarter! In anticipation of a continuation of this trend, we've included a survey of some harder material in this edition of *Oh! Pascal!*

Our survey will cover three topics joined by one theme—the desire to find things. The first, *sorting*, has probably attracted more interest than any other subject in computer science. Suppose that we have a random arrangement of data items—say, an array of numbers, or letters, or records. How can we put them into numerical or alphabetical order? In 16-1 we'll revisit the sorting algorithms we met earlier, and learn about the aptly named *Quicksort* algorithm.

Searching is our second topic. Searching is closely related to sorting, since arranging data in the proper way can make it easier to find what we're looking for. In 16-2 we'll look at two searching algorithms—*binary* search (which takes advantage of data that's already sorted), and *hashing*, which is used for both storing and finding.

String matching is our final topic, in 16-3. Sometimes data is stored in a manner that appears to be totally random, but that actually contains a great deal of meaning. (Take, for instance, the letters that make up this book.) How can we find one word, or sequence of words? We'll look at some ways of finding strings.

If you enjoy this material, you should strongly consider taking a course in Data Structures. This is usually the second or third course in the undergraduate C.S. program, and is one of the most interesting courses in the curriculum. Good luck in your study of Computer Science—we'll be seeing you in the terminal room!

Sorting 16-1

WE HAVE ALREADY SEEN THREE ELEMENTARY sorting methods—selection sort, insertion sort, and bubble sort. Let's reprise their algorithms, in each case sorting an array of *integers* from the least value to the greatest. This simplifies the general sorting problem, in which we have an array of records that we want sorted according to the value of a single field. For convenience, we'll assume the existence of a procedure *Switch* that can exchange the values of two elements of the array we're sorting.

selection sort

Our first algorithm is selection sort. In a selection sort, we find the smallest array element and exchange it with the array's first element, then find the second smallest element and exchange it with the array's second element, etc. In pseudocode, we have:

```
for every 'first' element in the array
    find the largest element in the array;
    exchange it with the 'first' element;
```

analyzing selection sort

The elements to the left of the current 'first' element are always in order, while the 'first' and its right-hand neighbors are random. The outer loop is entered N times, since we have to consider N subarrays. Within the inner loop, we must travel from one end to the other looking for smallest remaining value. This trip takes N steps the first time, $N-1$ the second, $N-2$ the third, etc. On average, it requires $N/2$ steps. Since we ignore constants in big O notation, we'll say that the time required for the algorithm to sort N elements is $O(N^2)$. The code for selection sort is:

selection sort procedure

```
procedure SelectionSort (var Data: TheArrayType);
  {Sorts array Data using selection sort.}
  var First, Current, Least: integer;
  begin
    for First := 1 to ARRAYLIMIT - 1 do begin
      Least := First; {Take a guess that this is the least value.}
      for Current := First+1 to ARRAYLIMIT do
        if Data[Current] < Data[Least] then Least := Current;
        {Look for a smaller value in the remainder of the array.}
      Switch (Data[Least], Data[First])
    end
  end; {SelectionSort}
```

insertion sort

Insertion sort is the second of the simple sorting methods. Now, selection sort kept the array to the left of the current 'first' element sorted. It repeatedly added the smallest remaining element (on the right) to the end of a sorted section (on the left). Insertion sort also keeps the section on the left sorted. However, it takes elements from the right as they come. In contrast to selection sort, it doesn't look for the *smallest* element on the right. Instead, it takes the next element, whatever it is, and inserts it into the proper position on the left. We take a new element from the right, then travel toward the left looking for its correct position. In pseudocode, we have:

insertion sort pseudocode

for *every 'newest' element remaining in the array*
  remove it from the array;
  while *we haven't found a smaller element among elements Newest*−1 . . 1
    slide elements to the right one at a time;
  insert the 'newest' element;

It's easier to picture this if you imagine that the array is already sorted—except for the very last, rightmost element. We remove the last element, then slide its left-hand neighbor to the right. Does the saved element belong in the new 'hole?' If not, slide another element over from the left and check again. Eventually, we make a hole whose left neighbor is smaller than the saved element, and whose right-hand neighbor is bigger. To make sure that we *will* find a smaller element before running off the left end of the array, the data array is defined with one extra element—a 'zeroth' element that's initialized to a very small number.

analyzing insertion sort

This algorithm is also an $O(N^2)$ sorting method. However, we can notice an important difference from selection sort—the *average* time required for insertion sort will probably be less. Indeed, if the list is already nearly sorted, it will approach linear, or $O(N)$ time. For selection sort, in contrast, all elements had to be searched repeatedly regardless of their original order. The code of insertion sort is:

insertion sort procedure

```
procedure InsertionSort (var Data: TheArrayType);
  {Sorts array Data using selection sort.}
  {Assume that Data runs from 0..ARRAYLIMIT}
  var TheNewValue, NewestPos, CurrentPos: integer;
  begin
    Data[0] := -MAXINT;
    for NewestPos := 2 to ARRAYLIMIT do begin
      TheNewValue := Data[NewestPos];
      CurrentPos := NewestPos;
      while Data[CurrentPos-1] > TheNewValue do begin
        Data[CurrentPos] := Data[CurrentPos-1];
        CurrentPos := CurrentPos - 1
      end;
      Data[CurrentPos] := TheNewValue
    end
  end; {InsertionSort}
```

bubble sort

Bubble sort was our third method. To use this algorithm we travel through the entire array, starting from the far right, exchanging adjacent elements if they are out of order. At the end of one pass the smallest element has traveled all the way to the left. The second pass can start from the second element, the third from the third element, etc. By starting each pass on the right, we build an ordered array on the left.

We can imagine that bubble sort combines the techniques of selection sort and insertion sort. Like selection sort, we are repeatedly making exchanges of elements, but like insertion sort, we are sometime inserting elements into the midst of a list that is already ordered. Bubble sort is also an $O(N^2)$ algorithm. Its analysis is like that of selection sort. The outer loop takes N steps, and the inner loop ranges from 1 to N steps, for an average of $N/2$.

analyzing bubble sort

These three methods are all $O(N^2)$ algorithms in the worst case. They share certain characteristics that give a clue to their cost. In each algorithm, we travel down the array, one element at a time, for an outer loop of cost N. For each element, we have to deal with the remainder of the array one element at a time, either looking for a proper element, or looking for the current element's position, again at an average cost of $N/2$.

Note, though, that we said *worst* case. There is a branch of computer science devoted to ignoring Murphy's Law, and estimating the *expected* performance of algorithms. We'll take a closer look at this concept after our next topic—Quicksort.

Quicksort

The algorithms we've seen so far have been stated iteratively, which has made them easy to understand. One of the best sorting algorithms is almost invariably given recursively. It's called *Quicksort*, and was devised by C.A.R. Hoare, who also invented the **case** statement (a question that will probably never appear in *Trivial Pursuit*). At worst, Quicksort is also an $O(N^2)$ algorithm, but in practice, its running time is usually proportional to $N \log_2 N$. Let's reinvent it, and see how and why it works.

The algorithms we've looked at so far have always concentrated on methodically working from one end of an array to the other. Let's try a different approach this time—*divide and conquer*. Suppose that we put all the 'big' numbers in one half of the array, and all the 'small' numbers in the other half. Then, once we have the array neatly divided, we'll take each half, and do the exact same thing. Eventually, we'll get down to subarrays of length one or two, and the array will be sorted.

divide and conquer

Sounds easy, doesn't it? Let's follow one of the stored values. Suppose that the very smallest value (call it a) starts out at the far right end of the array—the place where the biggest value is supposed to be:

We'll take this small value and put it into the left-hand half of the array:

Were we to check the left half—and split *it* in two—we'd move the a again:

Eventually, the a will get to its proper position at the start of the array:

a							

How long did it take the *a* to get to its final resting place? Each time we moved it halfway home. As a general rule about divide and conquer methods...

> An algorithm that works by splitting the remainder in two will take about $\log_2 N$ steps.

Our rule is true because $\log_2 N$ is the maximum number of times we can divide N by 2—$\log_2 N$ of 4 is 2, $\log_2 N$ of 8 is 3, $\log_2 N$ of 32 is 5, etc.

Our algorithm requires that we repeatedly move the *a* into the proper half of the remainder of the array. If the original array is N elements long, $\log_2 N$ steps are required. Since the array has N elements to begin with, we'll have to repeat our basic algorithm N times to sort the entire array. The overall running time of our algorithm, then, will be proportional to N times $\log_2 N$, which is written as $O(N \log_2 N)$.

Now, our algorithm looks good on paper, but we've relied on magic too often to implement it as a program. How do we know what 'big' and 'small' numbers are? How do we know which half of the array to put any given number in? What do we do with the number that was already stored in the element we so cavalierly took over?

This was the problem Hoare faced. Stop reading for a moment and try to imagine how he solved it.

discovering Quicksort

Hoare's solution was very clever. He began by picking a number at random from the array. This lucky value, he claimed, could be considered to be the dividing point between 'big' and 'small.' Then, he searched the left side of the array for a bigger or equal value, and the right side of the array for a smaller value. These values, he said correctly, were in the wrong sides of the array, so he switched them. He started the searches from the ends, going toward the middle, so that eventually the two searches would meet.

One last insight remained. Where would the starting number be when the two searches finished? It would be in its final resting place in the sorted array. As a result, he could ignore this 'middle' value when he repeated the whole process on the left and right sides of the array.

Let's work on the array below. Our wild guess will be that the middle value (3, here) divides the 'big' and 'small' numbers:

9 1 5 7 3 6 4 2 8

a Quicksort example

We exchange the first number greater than or equal to 3 (working from the left) with the first number less than 3 (working from the right):

2 1 5 7 3 6 4 9 8

Now we repeat the step. It is the 3 itself that gets moved this time:

2 1 3 7 5 6 4 9 8

Our left and right searches meet at this point. Note that the 3 is in the correct position for the final sorted array. Each side is unordered, but all the 'small' numbers are on the left, while the 'big' ones are on the right.

What are the differences between Hoare's Quicksort algorithm, and the algorithm we started out with? Our original method relied on neatly dividing the array in half each time, so we know that it's an $N \log_2 N$ algorithm. We were able to do this because we assumed that we would magically know the median value stored in each array segment.

Since Hoare didn't rely on magic, Quicksort might pick a very non-median value to be the basis of the left/right separation of values. In fact, if we somehow pick the very worst value each time—the highest or lowest value in each segment—Quicksort turns out to be an N^2 Slowsort! Fortunately, this would require very bad luck indeed. On the average, we will pick a reasonably median number by chance (even though we were a little bit unlucky in our example, above). Since we'll be roughly splitting the subarrays in half each time, we can expect Quicksort to be an $N \log_2 N$ algorithm.

merge sort

It's interesting to note that Hoare might have taken an entirely different tack. The Quicksort algorithm roughly organizes the array before splitting it in half. However, the opposite approach (splitting, then organizing) is also effective. Suppose that we divide the original array in half, then in half again, and so on, until we have an array of length two. This array can be sorted easily. Then, two ordered arrays of length two can be merged, then two arrays of length four, etc. This is the basis of the recursive algorithm called *merge sort*, which we won't get into.

The final Quicksort algorithm can be described recursively like this:

recursive refinement

to sort an array by Quicksort . . .
    pick some starting element value from the array;
    exchange equal or larger elements (*working from the left*) *with*
            equal or smaller elements (*working from the right*);
    if *it's longer than one element, sort the left-hand array by Quicksort*;
    if *it's longer than one element, sort the right-hand array by Quicksort*;

Let's look at the shaded section more closely. Suppose we begin by picking, as our starting element, some *StarterValue*. We expand the pseudocode above to:

second refinement

repeat
    working from Start to Finish, try to find an element with
                value >= to StarterValue:
    working from Finish to Start, try to find an element with
                value <= to StarterValue;
    switch these two elements;
    move left one, and right one, so that we don't check
                the elements we just exchanged
until *left and right pass*;

After each sorting run, the element that holds *StarterValue* is in its final position—elements to the left are smaller, while elements to the right are larger.

Can you see why the algorithm is stated recursively? Our intention is to 'sort of sort' the array into two sections. Then, we'll sort of sort one of those sections, then one of the new subsections, etc. We can keep track of the *Start* and *Finish* that delimit each subsection by having them declared as value parameters associated with a particular instance of the recursive call.

How do we choose our starting value? As we've formulated the algorithm, we pick the value of the element in the middle of the array segment we're sorting, with:

```
StarterValue := Data [(Start+Finish) div 2)];
```

What information does each call of the Quicksort procedure need? It must have the subscripts of the left and right ends of the array being sorted. The array itself is passed as a **var** parameter, which means that only a single copy of the array ever exists. The completed procedure is shown below:

quicksort procedure

```
procedure Quicksort (Start, Finish: integer; var Data: TheArrayType);
   {Recursively sort array Data, with bounds Start and Finish, using Quicksort}
   var StarterValue, Left, Right, Temp: integer;
   begin
      Left := Start;
      Right := Finish;
      StarterValue := Data [(Start+Finish) div 2]; {Pick a starter.}
      repeat
         while Data[Left] < StarterValue do
            Left := Left + 1; {Find a bigger value on the left.}
         while StarterValue < Data[Right] do
            Right := Right - 1; {Find a smaller value on the right.}
         if Left <= Right then begin {If we haven't gone too far...}
            Temp := Data[Left]; {...switch them.}
            Data[Left] := Data[Right];
            Data[Right] := Temp;
            Left := Left + 1;
            Right := Right - 1
         end {then}
      until Right <= Left;
      if Start < Right then Quicksort (Start, Right, Data);
      if Left < Finish then Quicksort (Left, Finish, Data)
   end; {Quicksort}
```

The procedure's first call is:

```
Quicksort (1, ARRAYLIMIT, Data);
```

performance of algorithms

Earlier we mentioned that the worst-case performance of an algorithm was not the only measure of its suitability. Thinking only in terms of worst-case performance can be misleading, because a particular algorithm's worst case might be very unlikely to occur. A more Panglossian body of computer science research is devoted to calculating an algorithm's *expected* performance, or the behavior it is likely to exhibit most of the time.

When sorting algorithms are compared by expected performance, Quicksort dominates the field. Even though the algorithm's worst case make it no better than the much maligned bubble sort, it is the method of choice for most sorting jobs.

in-place sorting

The sorting methods described here are known as *in-place* algorithms because they do not require additional computer memory for the sort. As a result, any of the methods could be used to sort enormously large arrays—even arrays that came close to the computer's memory limit.* Naturally, very large sorting jobs would probably call for Quicksort. If the array is known to be in close to correct order, though, insertion sort might be used. On occasion, one method will be used to partially sort an array, with another algorithm called to finish the job.

Searching 16-2

WE'VE JUST SPENT SOME TIME DISCUSSING ways of sorting the elements of an array. For some jobs, a sorted array is all we need. For instance, many applications require alphabetically sorted lists. Imagine that a program is supposed to print a dictionary, or the telephone book, or even the index of this text. We start out with a data base, or pool, of values, then we sort the values. Once the values—our names or numbers—are in order, all that's left is printing. The hard computation of the program is finished.

sorting vs. searching

Sometimes, though, the existence of a sorted list can be taken for granted. Instead of *sorting* values, we'll be interested in *finding* individual names or words with a minimum of trouble. Now, how long does it take to find something in a array? Well, the obvious algorithm is:

> **repeat**
>   *look at an array element*
> **until** *we find what we're looking for*;

How long will it take, on average, to an element this way? Suppose that the array contains N elements. Our algorithm takes $O(N)$ steps, since the value of N controls the number of elements we inspect. In the worst case, we'll have to look at all N elements, but on average, inspecting $N/2$ will suffice.

* This is not true for special cases of Quicksort that require close to N recursive calls. However, simple modifications can be made to the algorithm so that there will be no more than $\log_2 N$ recursive calls.

Incidentally, it's interesting to note that sorting the array will only improve our expected performance if the value we're looking for is liable to be absent. In a sorted array, we can cut off the search as soon as we've gone past the position we expect the value to belong in, but an unordered array must be searched all the way to the end.

searching binary trees

It turns out that we already know a much faster way to find things. Do you remember the discussion of binary search trees in Chapter 15? Suppose that we have our values stored in an ordered binary tree instead of an array. Let's assume that it's an exceptionally neat tree (called a *balanced* binary tree) in which most of the non-leaf nodes have two children. In this case, finding a value takes $O(\log_2 N)$ steps. You should try sketching this out on paper to convince yourself that a value can really be found so quickly.

tree disadvantages

Binary trees look like sure winners on paper (since an $O(\log_2 N)$ search is much faster than an $O(N)$ search), but other considerations may rule out their use. In particular, they tend to use considerably more memory than array-based storage methods, and, depending on the values stored, may not be well-balanced without a considerable amount of juggling.

Fortunately, there are some very fast methods we can use to find values in plain old-fashioned arrays. We'll look at two. The first, binary search, relies on an array that is sorted, and will let us find a value in $O(\log_2 N)$ time. It's the array version of the binary tree search algorithm. Since we've already seen the algorithm (in Chapter 11) we'll make binary search interesting by implementing it recursively. The second search method, hashing, is both a means for storing values, and for finding them again. Incredibly, hashing lets us find a value in constant time—the length of the search doesn't depend on N at all. Let's see how they work.

Binary Search

How do you find a number in a phone book? Open it to the middle, and decide if the number is in the lower or upper half of the book. Then, decide which half of the half it's in, then which half of that half, and so on. As a recursively stated solution, *finding a number* is:

> *to find a number in a phone book...*
>
> *decide which half of the book the number is in;*
> *find a number in a phone book;*

dividing the solution space

Once again we return to the the divide and conquer method of problem solving. Note that we aren't so much conquering the problem as wearing it down. We repeatedly divide its solution space until finding the correct solution is trivial. How long will it take? If our solution space is N numbers, then a divide and conquer search takes, at most, $\log_2 N$ steps:

logs grow very slowly

Number	*log_2 of that number (approx.)*
10	3
100	7
1,000	10
10,000	13
10,000	17
1,000,000	20
15,000,000	24
30,000,000	25

According to this table, if New York, Tokyo, and Buenos Aires all shared a single telephone book, a quick-fingered operator would only have to check 25 numbers *at most* before finding the one we want.

Let's apply the binary search idea to finding a number in an array. We've already written code to do this iteratively, so our problem will be coming up with a recursive solution to the problem. A first refinement sheds more heat than light:

first refinement

to find an element by binary search...
   split the array in half;
   find an element by binary search;

Perhaps a reprise of the iterative pseudocode will help:

iterative binary search pseudocode

get the lower and upper bounds;
repeat
   compute a middle;
   if *it's low*
      then *make it* (*plus 1*) *be the new lower bound*
      else *make it* (*minus 1*) *be the new upper bound*
until *we find the number* **or** *decide to stop looking*;
decide why we left the loop;

The shaded sections give us our clue. Suppose that we implement the algorithm as a function. We *get the bounds* as arguments of a call; we can make new bounds simply by changing those arguments. Let's have a second try at a recursive pseudocode:

second recursive refinement

to find an element by binary search (*left and right bounds*)...
   check the middle element;
   if *we've found it, or have searched the whole array*
      then *make the proper assignment to the function*
      else *find an element by binary search* (*with new bounds*);

The completed recursive function is shown below. We're assuming that the array being searched is of type *NumberArray*, with *integer* elements from 1 through *MAX*. A call of *BinarySearch* would be something like:

Position := *BinarySearch* (*Sought, TheArray*, 1, *MAX*);

As before, we'll use a value of 0 to indicate that the sought number could not be found.

recursive binary search function

```
function BinarySearch (Value: integer; Numbers: NumberArray;
                                   Left, Right: integer): integer;
   {Recursive binary search for Value. Returns 0 if it's not found.}
   var Midpoint: integer;
   begin
      Midpoint := (Left + Right) div 2;
      if Left > Right
         then BinarySearch := 0
         else if Value = Numbers[Midpoint]
            then BinarySearch := Midpoint
            else if Value < Numbers[Midpoint]
               then BinarySearch :=
                     BinarySearch (Value, Numbers, Left, Midpoint-1)
               else if Value > Numbers[Midpoint] then
                  BinarySearch :=
                     BinarySearch (Value, Numbers, Midpoint+1, Right)
   end; {BinarySearch}
```

Self-Check Questions

Q. Each time function *BinarySearch* is called, a value parameter copy of the array is created. Can we know how much memory will be required to store all the copies of the array? Will this ever be a problem? What could we do about it?

A. A value parameter will require as much memory as its argument. Fortunately, the function will be called, at most, $\log_2$ *MAX* times. That number, times the size of the array, is the largest amount of memory that will be required. If this is a problem, passing the array as a variable parameter avoids the issue. Only one copy of the array will be extant.

Hashing

We can conclude that when an array of items is sorted, we can employ some pretty clever techniques for finding any particular item. Can we come up with an even better approach? Well, the binary search does about as well as we can expect for an array in 'relative' (e.g. least to greatest) order. To improve on binary search, we'll keep the idea of having the array sorted to begin with, but try to expand our notion of what *sorted to begin with* means.

hashing algorithms

Hashing algorithms compute the location of a particular array element. A hashing algorithm is used both *a*) for originally arranging the array, and *b*) to see if a particular value is present.

Suppose that we sort the values stored in an array according to some consistent rule or formula. We can apply the same rule or formula twice. First, we use it to see where each value is supposed to be stored. Once we've arranged the array according to our method, we apply the same rule or formula in order to *find* a value. We pretend that we're going to *store* the value, then look to see if it's already there.

It's clear that not every rule or formula will give us suitable results. For instance, if our rule is *stick it on the end of the array*, we won't gain any advantage over a simple linear search—the rule is too simple. Since it doesn't take any special characteristic of the value into account, it's not repeatable. However, if our rule is too complicated—*stick it in the proper relative position in the array*—we won't net any gain either.

the hash table

In practice, a good *hash function* will distribute values uniformly throughout a waiting array (called the *hash table*). It will use some unchanging characteristic of the value itself, along with some simple arithmetic, to determine where the value should go.

For example, suppose that we were storing a maximum of one hundred numbers, known to lie in the range 1 through 1,000. We *might* create an array of a thousand elements, and use the actual value as the proper hash table position. This would be wasteful, though, since nine hundred elements will remain unused. Instead, we'd probably declare an array of one hundred elements, and divide each incoming number by 10 to determine its position. This rule—divide by 10, and round up—is our hash function.

It's not hard to imagine a hash function that we could use to distribute string values. Suppose that we want to store one hundred words. If we treat the first two letters as a base 26 number, we'll get a number between 0 (for 'aa') and 675 (for 'zz'). If we **mod** by 100, then add one, we'll have devised a hash function that gives us a hash table position between 1 and 100.

hash table collisions

Now, if a hash function were perfect, it would automatically put every incoming value into a different spot in the hash table. Unfortunately, hash functions tend to be imperfect. Unless we make the hash table excessively large, two or more different values will eventually be sent to the same spot. This is called a *collision*. Every program that uses hashing will have some rule for *collision resolution*—for determining where the value should go if the first choice location is occupied. Stop reading for a moment, and try to think of a rule for resolving collisions.

Programmers take three main approaches. The first is called *probing*. It's simple—stick the value in the next spot. If that's occupied, go one more. If we reach the end of the array, the **mod** operator will let us wrap back to the start of the hash table. Probing is easy to implement, but has the unfortunate side effect of causing problems for values that haven't arrived yet. A new value's proper space may have been taken to resolve an earlier collision, so we've really just robbed Peter to pay Paul. In fact, we'll find that collisions tend to *cluster*, and only make the problem worse.

probing

The second approach to collision resolution is harder to implement, but it avoids the clustering problem. It's called *chaining*. Instead of storing the values themselves in the hash table, we make each table entry the head of a linked list. We store incoming values by adding them to the appropriate linked list. If there's ever a collision, we add a new element to the linked list associated with the particular hash value. Some lists will probably be longer than others (and slow down searches later), but no hash value will interfere with others.

chaining

A third means of collision resolution is probably the neatest. We just rehash, generally using a slightly different hash function. This method is called *double hashing*. This method also avoids problems with clustering, and is a little easier to deal with than chaining algorithms.

double hashing

Hashing, like sorting, is interesting for discussion because there's no 'best' method. Although considerations of efficiency have not weighed heavily on us in this text, tradeoffs between the two computer resources—space, and time—usually determine how and why we choose to implement particular algorithms. If space isn't an issue, we can ensure rapid hashing by declaring extremely large hash tables, ensuring that collisions will never occur. If time isn't an issue, we can declare a minimally-sized hash table, and expect to have to resolve collisions.

In practice, we generally find that optimum results are achieved with a table that's one-and-a-half to two times as large as the number of values that are to be stored. Optimum, in this case, means that time requirements get much worse as we occupy less space, but don't improve greatly when we use a larger hash table.

tradeoffs in hashing

Let's consider some basic hashing code. In each case, we'll assume that we're storing records in an array that's been defined like this:

type definition

```
const LIMIT = 199;

type Data = record
              TheInformation: ItsType;
              Key: integer {this is the search key}
            end;
     HashTable = array [0..LIMIT] of Data;
```

The *HashTable* array index starts with 0 in order to make some calculations further along that involve **mod** easier.

the search key

> The value a hash is based on is called the *search key*. This key is eventually used as the argument of the hash function.

We'll begin by looking at the simplest method of storing a single value:

problem: hashing

> Imagine that we have a hundred records with non-zero *integer* keys, as above. Write a hash function (and related routines) for implementing a hash table.

We can start by initializing the *HashTable*-type variable. If we set each *Key* field to zero, we can easily spot an element that hasn't been used for storage yet.

hash table initialization procedure

```
procedure InitializeTable (var Table: HashTable);
   {Initialize the Key fields of the table elements.}
   var i: integer;
   begin
      for i := 1 to LIMIT do
         Table[i].Key := 0
   end; {InitializeTable}
```

Next, we'll write a routine for inserting an element into the table. Procedure *Insert* using a basic probing algorithm. If the table entry the hash function calls for (element *Position*) is occupied, *Insert* advances to the next location. However, we don't simply increment *Position*. Instead, we increment, and **mod** the sum by the length of the table. This guarantees that we will wrap back to the beginning when we reach the table's end.

hash table insertion procedure

```
procedure Insert (Position: integer; Element: Data;
                                  var Table: HashTable);
   {Insert Element into Table, at or near Position.}
   begin
      while Table[Position].Key <> 0 do
         Position := (Position + 1) mod LIMIT;
      Table[Position] := Element
   end; {Insert}
```

A function that locates an element follows a similar model. We start knowing the *Position* that the element should occupy, based on its key value. The search continues until we find a like key, or until we find a zero-valued key that indicates that the element we're seeking isn't present. If the element isn't found, the function returns a *Position* of *MAXINT*. This time, note that we've taken the trouble of making sure that we don't wind up in an endless loop, searching a full table for a key that isn't there.

hash table search function

```
function Search (Position: integer; Element: Data;
                                   Table: HashTable): integer;
  {Search for Element.Key. Returns MAXINT if not found.}
  var Count: integer;
  begin
    Count := 0;
    while (Table[Position].Key <> Element.Key)
              and (Table[Position].Key <> 0)
                        and (Count <= LIMIT) do begin
      Position := (Position + 1) mod LIMIT;
      Count := Count + 1
    end;
    if Table[Position].Key = Element.Key
      then Search := Position
      else Search := MAXINT
  end; {Search}
```

Finally, let's get to the most interesting part—the hash function. Now, we can write a trivial function like this:

first hash function

```
function EasyHash (Key: integer): integer;
  {Find the proper table entry for Key.}
  begin
    EasyHash := Key mod Limit
  end; {EasyHash}
```

No matter what the *Key* value is, *EasyHash* will return a hash table position between 0 and *LIMIT*. But can you spot the flaw that makes it a poor hash function? To give you a better feel for the problem, imagine that the *Key* value is derived from a name or English word using the method, described earlier, of pretending that the letters represent digits in base 26.

problems with *EasyHash*

EasyHash's weakness lies not with the arithmetic of the function, but with the tendency of names and words to cluster around particular values. In person, for all we know, Mary A. Smith may party hearty, while dull Mary B. Smith takes *Oh! Pascal!* along on dates. To *EasyHash*, though, the keys Smith, Mary A., and Smith, Mary B. will undoubtedly wind up with the same hash table entry.

A quick look at the dictionary will convince you that the clustering problem isn't limited to Smiths and Joneses. The problem we face, then, is to take keys that are very similar, and somehow transform them into hash table positions that are quite different. Stop for a minute and try to think of a method.

Well, one approach is to devise algorithms that avoid characterizing the key by the first few letters of the word. For instance, we might 'add' the first letters to the last letters, or reverse the string, or only consider the middle letters. All these methods have been used, and can be quite successful.

random hashing

A quite different approach provides the basis of more modern hashing algorithms. Instead of trying to create a random number of sorts by jumbling the letter, why not assume that the number *is* random to begin with? Then, use it as the seed of a random number generator! The next number in the generator's pseudo-random sequence (**mod** the length of the hash table, of course) will be the proper hash table position.

The advantage of this method is that, while two keys may be very close to each other numerically, their positions (and hence, the numbers each is followed by) in a pseudo-random sequence are liable to be far apart. Function *RandomHash*, below, employs a random number generator function similar to the one we wrote back in section 5-1. As mentioned, the *Key* value is used as the seed.

a better hash function

```
function RandomHash (Key: integer): integer;
  {Choose a random table entry based on Key.}

  const MODULUS = 65536;
        MULTIPLIER = 25173;
        INCREMENT = 13849;

  begin
    Key := ((MULTIPLIER*Key)+INCREMENT) mod MODULUS;
    RandomHash := Key mod LIMIT
  end; {RandomHash}
```

A test of *RandomHash* with some sample keys shows that an effective distribution can be obtained even when the keys are very close together.

test of *RandomHash*

```
for Seed := 1 to 5 do
   write (Seed:6, ': ', RandomHash (Seed):3);
writeln;
for Seed := 10001 to 10005 do
   write (Seed:6, ': ', RandomHash (Seed):3);
writeln;
```

```
     1:  18      2: 117      3: 151      4:  51      5:  85
 10001:  73  10002: 107  10003:   7  10004: 106  10005: 140
```

As an exercise, you might want to try plotting the output of *RandomHash* for longer runs of close keys—you'll find that, for this particular random number function, some interesting patterns of close calls and collisions develop. How can they be avoided or mitigated?

String Matching 16-3

TEXT EDITORS PROVIDE MOST PEOPLE'S introduction to computing. We think it's only appropriate, then, to close by considering some of the algorithms that make computerized text editors so impressive. In particular, we'll look at the methods text editors use to find individual words in text.

> *String matching* algorithms are used to located a particular subsequence of characters in a much longer file or array.

For our purposes we'll assume that we're always trying to find a string that's located in an array. Does it matter if the array is one or two-dimensional? In most cases, the answer is no. Suppose that we have an algorithm for finding a string in a one-dimensional array of type *Line*. We can usually search a two-dimensional **array of** *Line* by repeating the basic algorithm again and again.

If the string we're looking for contains a blank, matters become more complicated. In ordinary English text, the end of a line implies a space between two words. Fortunately, modifying a *Line*-based algorithm only requires simple arithmetic. Suppose we keep a running count of characters. We can calculate the location *of* the current line with:

(*TotalCount* **div** *length of one line*)+1

and figure out our exact position *on* the current line with:

TotalCount **mod** *length of one line*

To keep matters relatively comprehensible, we'll only deal with the one-dimensional case. Let's assume these definitions:

basic definitions

```
type Source = array [1..MAX] of char;
     String = array [1..LENGTH] of char;
```

We haven't defined either of these as formal string types because we're not going to exploit the special capabilities of Pascal strings. We'll state our problem like this:

problem: string matching

> Assume that an array of type *Source* is filled with characters. Write a procedure or function that tries to find a string *Pattern*, and returns its starting position in the *Source* array.

The Brute Force Approach

The most obvious tack to follow is the direct brute force approach. First, compare the first elements of the source and pattern, then the next two, and so on. Eventually we'll either reach a mismatch (and can start a new set of comparisons one element further further along in the source), or we'll have matched every element, and can announce success. In pseudocode, we have:

refinement

> *initialize the element counters*;
> **repeat**
>   *compare two elements*;
>   **if** *they match*
>   **then** *increment the element counters*
>   **else** *reinitialize the element counters*
> **until** *we're done*;

A few parts of this refinement look suspiciously easy. For instance, the *element counters* keep track of which element of the source and pattern we're comparing. When they're first initialized, each counter will equal one—the very first element of each array. How will they be reinitialized if we find a mismatch?

Well, suppose that *PatPos* gives our current position in the pattern array when a mismatch occurs. Let *SorPos* hold the current position in the source array. If we subtract *PatPos* from *SorPos*, then add one, we'll be back to where we started from. Naturally, *PatPos* itself gets set back to one—the start of the pattern array.

We can expand the *reinitialize the element counters* pseudocode as shown below. As you read, try to decide why *SorPos* has a 'correction' increment of two, rather than one? Also, is the order of assignments important?

second refinement

> *SorPos* := (*SorPos* − *PatPos*) + 2;
> *PatPos* := 1;

The correction factor of two is needed because we don't want to be back where we started from. Rather, we want to be one element further along. The order of the assignments are crucial, since the first assignment uses the original value of *PatPos*.

The **until** *we're done* part of our first refinement also seems to have been tossed off a bit casually. When are we finished? Well, our plan to increment the counters as long as elements keep matching gives us a clue. We'll be finished when *SorPos* exceeds *MAX* (the pattern wasn't there) or when *PatPos* is greater than *LENGTH* (we've found it). A final **if** check lets us know exactly why we left the loop.

The completed code of our brute force algorithm is shown below. Note that the function returns *MAXINT* if the pattern isn't matched.

brute force string matching procedure

```
function StringMatch (Pattern: String; SorText: Source): integer;
  {Brute force pattern-matcher. Returns MAXINT for no match.}
  var PatPos, SorPos: integer;
  begin
    PatPos := 1;
    SorPos := 1;
    repeat
      if Pattern [PatPos] = SorText [SorPos]
        then begin
          SorPos := SorPos + 1;
          PatPos := PatPos + 1
        end {then}
        else begin
          SorPos := (SorPos - PatPos) + 2;
          PatPos := 1
        end {else}
    until (PatPos > LENGTH) or (SorPos > MAX);
    if PatPos > LENGTH
      then StringMatch := SorPos - LENGTH
      else StringMatch := MAXINT
  end; {StringMatch}
```

Self-Check Questions

Q. Suppose that the *Pattern* string were longer than the *SorText* source. Would *StringMatch* still work?

A. Yes. We'd leave the loop because of the **until** exit checks.

Q. What is the worst-case performance of the brute force algorithm? What kind of pattern and source would cause this performance?

A. Suppose there are M elements in the source, and N elements in the pattern. As we travel along the source array, each source element takes a turn at being the first element of a potential match. How many comparisons are associated with each potential match? In the worst of all possible worlds, we'll repeatedly have mismatches on the very last character of the pattern. Thus, the worst case performance of the algorithm is $O(MN)$. There are M (actually $M-N+1$) possible patterns to match, times the N (actually $N-1$) comparisons it takes to establish a mismatch. We assume that *Pattern* is very small compared to the source.

In practice, of course, we'll find mismatches much sooner. The worst possible case would be a source consisting of all zeros, and a pattern of zeros followed by a 1.

Q. In the worst case described above, how long is the pattern in relation to the source?

A. Disregarding the small corrections, the number of element comparisons is $(M-N)*N$, or $MN-N^2$. Using calculus (for the first time in my adult life!), we can determine that the number of comparisons peaks when $M-2N$ equals zero, or when the pattern is about half as long as the source.

Getting Clever: Matching Meets Hashing

An improved pattern matching algorithm (like improved algorithms for sorting and hashing), is computer science's better mousetrap, if not its Fountain of Youth. The last decade or so has seen an explosion of new approaches to finding patterns quickly. Let's look at some of the more successful methods of finding a pattern in a larger source text.

To begin with, can we improve the performance of our brute force algorithm, function *StringMatch*? As we saw above, the worst case comes when a mismatch doesn't occur until the last character of the pattern. If our source and pattern follow the 'worst case form' of a 000...0 source, and a 000...1 pattern, we can make an obvious improvement by checking the last character immediately after we check the first.

This strategy drastically betters the performance of the absolutely worst case, since we won't waste time checking long potential matches that don't fail until the final test. However, it can't be counted as a genuine improvement to our underlying brute force algorithm. What if the pattern we're searching for is 000...10? Just about any special case improvement we can think of can be confounded by a simple counterexample. We've just *tweaked* the algorithm—fine-tuned it without making a real change.

tweaking algorithms

A more fruitful approach was developed in the mid 1970's when researchers considered the problem from a different point of view. What kinds of patterns cause problems that lead to worst-case performance, they asked? Their conclusion was that complicated patterns, like English words, tend not to be especially difficult to match—not because matches came easily, but because *mismatches* showed up right away.

As a simple example, imagine that we're looking up a word in a dictionary. For the vast majority of the search we'll have mismatches on the very first character. Once the first character matches, we'll have many mismatches on the second. Only in a relatively few cases will we have to compare most of the characters of a word. It may take a long time to, say, distinguish a *lightning rod* from a *lightning bug*, but overall, the varieties of lightning are comparatively limited. For the non-difficult patterns, then, the expected search time will usually be proportional to $M+N$—the length of the source plus the pattern.

Now let's consider the uncomplicated patterns, like 000...1, that cause problems. Since even English words are liable to be stored in a binary code, such patterns are not at all unusual. Working independently or in pairs, half a dozen computer scientists had the same clever insight about uncomplicated patterns—*they are repetitious*. As a result, they realized that it might not be necessary to start comparing from the beginning whenever a mismatch was found.

Let's look at an example. Imagine, as source, this repeated sequence:

0101010101 . . .

and, as a pattern, a similar sequence with an exception:

010100

How can we use repetition to speed our search? Suppose that we start to compare the source and pattern, character by character. For five characters all goes well. The sixth is a mismatch—the zero in the pattern doesn't match the one in the source. But must we go back to the first character of the pattern, and compare it to the *second* character of the source? Not if we recognize that we can 'slide' the pattern to the right. The search picks up by comparing the fifth character of the pattern to the seventh character of the source.

We're not going to go into detail here, but the underlying idea isn't complicated. By carefully analyzing the pattern in advance, we can get an idea of how far we must back up in the event of a mismatch. The simpler and more repetitive the pattern and source are, the more effective this approach becomes. There are different aspects to these algorithms (some require backing up in the source, others limit backup to the pattern), but in general, they reduce the number of steps in finding the string to $M+N$ or less.

An entirely different solution to the string-matching problem comes from accepting the fact that computers are just pretty bad at comparing strings. Determining whether or not two sequences of characters (of arbitrary length) are identical has always involved a laborious series of character-by-character comparisons.

Now, if numerical comparisons were as slow as string comparisons, computing as we know it would grind exceeding slow. Fortunately, numbers can be compared very quickly because of one-step operations that are built into the computer hardware. The arithmetic/logic unit, which we discussed way back in the Introduction, can compare two reasonably large (e.g. *MAXINT*-sized) numbers in a single operation.

In developing a quite different approach to the string-finding problem, Richard Karp and M.O. Rabin took advantage of the computer's speed in comparing numbers. They used tools similar to those we explored in 16-2 to develop an algorithm whose performance equals that of the methods described above, and which is a little easier to understand and implement.

Their algorithm, published just five years ago, employs a typically unexpected insight. Now, when we're actually hashing values, we store each value and hope to avoid collisions. Using the Rabin-Karp approach to finding strings, though, we throw the values away—except for the pattern's hash value—and hope that we *have* a collision. If a collision occurs we have a potential match; and if our hash function is really good, the match is almost certain.

The importance of the Rabin-Karp algorithm derives from the technique it uses to avoid collisions due to non-matches.* However, it's not hard to see how the basic algorithm works. We assume that the pattern and source both consist of digits of a base B numbering system, where B is

* In effect, it chooses a hash function at run-time so that a 'malicious' user can't intentionally design a source or pattern that will cause non-match collisions.

the number of different letters used. The pattern, then, is just a number written in base B. We start by counting the number of characters in the pattern. Then we pick a hash function and hash the pattern.

Now, there are two ways to accomplish the hashing. The most obvious method would be to convert the entire pattern from base B into decimal notation, then hash the whole thing at once. However, we can also use an alternative method—hash one character at a time *during* the conversion into decimal. The pseudocode algorithm is:

hashing the pattern

initialize a running total to zero;
for *each 'digit' of the pattern*
  convert the digit to base 10;
  hash it;
  add the hashed value to the original base times the running total;

If you have any difficulty following this algorithm, you should refer back to the hex conversion program in 8-1.

There are two advantages to taking the digit-by-digit route. First, we're able to keep numbers relatively small. Were we to try hashing the entire pattern at once, we might run into *integer*-overflow problems, especially if the random-number-like function we use for hashing employs large primes.

hashing the source

The second advantage comes when we start to hash the source text. Suppose that there are eight letters in the pattern. We'll begin by hashing the first eight letters of the source, and comparing it to the pattern hash. If it doesn't match, we 'subtract' the portion of the source hash due to the first letter, then 'add' a new component to the source hash—the hash of the ninth letter. If the hashes still don't match, we subtract the second letter's hash, and add the tenth's, and so on. In pseudocode:

Rabin-Karp pseudocode

hash the eight digits of the pattern;
hash the first eight digits of the source;
initialize Counter to 8;
while *the source hash and pattern hash aren't equal*
    and *Counter is less than the source length*
  increment Counter;
  reduce SourceHash by the hash of TheSource[*Counter*−8];
  increase SourceHash by the hash of TheSource[*Counter*];

Although the initial hashes take time proportional to the length of the pattern (call that M), travel through the source text (length N) takes place in $O(N)$ steps.

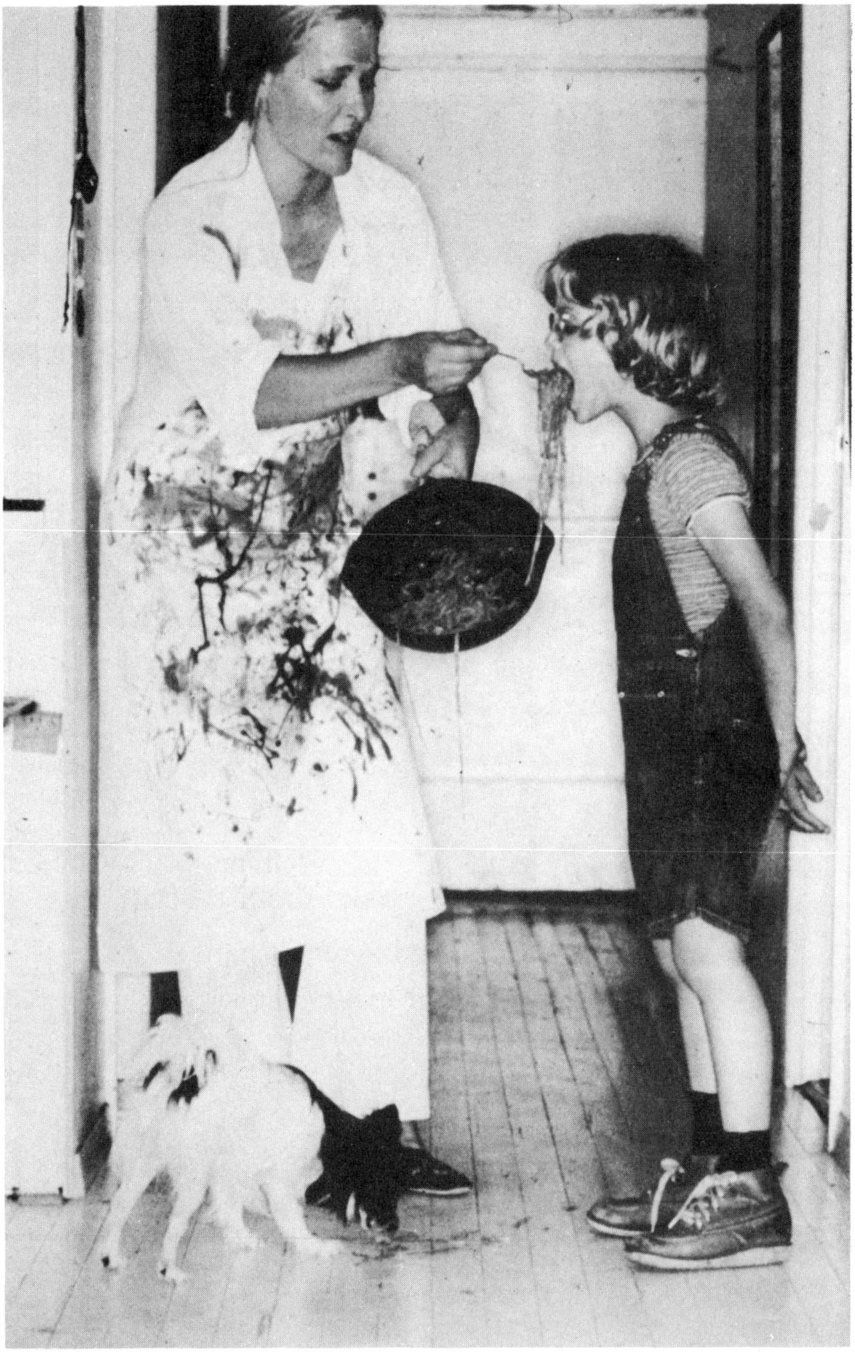

JACKSON POLLACK'S MOTHER

'Programs with many **goto***s are so tangled and difficult to trace through…'*

Appendix: Everything You Wanted to Know About Pascal*

IN THE INTEREST OF MAKING THE LAST sixteen chapters flow a bit more smoothly, a few facts have been obscured in (or even deliberately left out of) our presentation. This appendix briefly explains the areas that were overlooked.

1. The **goto** control statement.
2. A shorthand for type definitions and variable declarations.
3. The standard procedures *pack* and *unpack*.
4. Procedures and functions as parameters.
5. Dynamic allocation of record variants.
6. The standard procedure *page*.

The **goto** Statement

All the programs we've written so far have moved from statement to statement in direct order, except where a procedure or function call caused a temporary detour. However, we can *label* any statement with a number, and explicitly direct the program to *go to* that point. This is arranged by defining *labels* and using the **goto** control statement.

There are three steps to take in using a **goto**. First, the labels used to mark statements must be defined.

labels

> A *label* is a number of one to four digits. The reserved word **label** marks the label definition part. It immediately follows the program (or subprogram) heading.

There are 10,000 possible labels—'0' through '9999'. This segment designates '1', '2', and '3' as labels.

```
         {Program or subprogram heading.}
label 1, 2, 3;            {The label definition part.}
         {Constant definition part.}          etc.
```

The second step is to use the label by putting it, and a colon, in front of a statement.

```
1: writeln ('Abnormal program termination.');
```

> The label is ignored except as an identifying mark. Unless it is skipped over, every labeled statement is executed in the normal course of events. It need not be specifically gone to.

Finally, the **goto** statement tells the computer that program execution should continue from a particular labeled statement. For example:

* . . . but were (justifiably) afraid to ask.

```
if DataIsBad then goto 1;
```

A **goto** can direct program control either forward or backward. Any actions between the **goto** and the labeled statement are skipped.

why have the **goto**?

In a sense the **goto** is a historical anachronism in high-level programming languages. When the first languages were created, their designers (being hopelessly logical) saw that nearly everything a programmer wanted to do could be handled with just two control statements—**if...then**, and **goto**. For example:

```
Count := 1;
Sum := 0;
1: Sum := Sum+Count;
Count := Count+1;
if Count <=100 then goto 1;
writeln ('The sum of the numbers 1 through 100 is ', Sum);
```

We've come to know and love the shaded sequence by its semantic equivalent—the **repeat** statement. As a result, some older languages, like FORTRAN, have fewer control statements than Pascal.

However, Pascal has a much more sophisticated system of controlling program flow—its subprograms and control statements. In fact, we can claim quite correctly that Pascal lets the programmer do just about everything she wants *without* using **goto**s, and that minimizing **goto**s is a virtue. For one thing, most control statment names (like subprogram identifiers) help document what's going on. Statement labels, in contrast, are nondocumenting, or even 'anti'-documenting. As arbitrary numbers, labels aren't the least mnemonic. Their appearance gives no hint of their effect.

structured programming

A more serious problem of using the **goto** is the way it can distort the patterns of a program. In recent years a lot of emphasis has been placed on *structured* programming. Procedures and functions give a program structure by breaking its action into cleanly defined parts, while Pascal's structured statements help clearly delineate cause and effect. We haven't made a big deal about structured programming because we haven't really had non-structured tools—like the **goto**—to work with.

spaghetti programs

> Programs with many **goto**s are so tangled and difficult to trace through that they're often called *spaghetti* programs.

If the **goto** is so bad, why was it included in Pascal? Partly, for sentimental reasons. As we mentioned above, languages like FORTRAN (and even BASIC) depend heavily on the **goto**. People who learned to program in such languages find that **goto**s make it easier for them to implement tricks that we understand better in Pascal.

There are also extraordinary circumstances in which using **goto** s is permissible. Most common is the 'I want to get out of here in a hurry' case. Suppose, for example, that program input is coming from punched cards or tape, and an input checking procedure spots incorrect data. Since we know that there's no point in continuing to process input, we can issue an error message and go to the very end of the program (because it's o.k. to label an **end**).

```
   ∵.         {Assume we're in an input-checking procedure.}
   if DataIsBad then begin
      writeln ('Abnormal program termination -- bad data.');
      goto 1        {Quit program.}
   end;
   ∵.         {Rest of the program.}
1: end. {Main program.}
```

The **goto** is also properly used for beating a hasty retreat from a function whose arguments are determined to be inappropriate. In these cases the desirability of graceful degradation outweighs the stigma attached to using **gotos**.

Incidentally, there are restrictions on where a **goto** can go to. Basically, a **goto** cannot access a relatively internal block or statement. We can't jump from the main program to a procedure, although the reverse is allowed. Likewise, we can't jump into the middle of a structured statement (although we can jump out of one or change our position within one).

Self-Check Questions

Q. What will the output of this program segment be? Assume all labels are validly defined.

```
      goto 2;
         ∵.         {Other statements.}
      1: writeln ('You have been eaten by a troll.  Game over.');
      2: writeln ('You have turned into a vat of glue.  Game over.');
      3: writeln ('A hobgoblin has munched you.  Game over.');
      4: writeln ('Bats flew away with you.  Game over.')
   end. {Main program.}
```

A. As we mentioned earlier, the label is disregarded except as an identifying mark. Each statement from label 2 on is executed.

```
You have turned into a vat of glue.  Game over.
A hobgoblin has munched you.  Game over.
Bats flew away with you.  Game over.
```

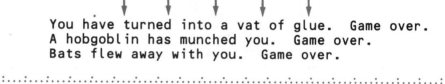

Shorthand Declarations

As we've pointed out a few times, high-level languages are designed mainly for the benefit of people who use them in programming, rather than for the computers such programs ultimately direct. Thus, Wirth named Pascal's control statements **repeat**, **while**, **if**, etc., even though **a**, **b**, **c** and so on are equally convenient from a computer's viewpoint. Although the semantics—the effect—of both meaningful and meaningless reserved words might be the same, their syntax—the actual words and the way they're used—are intended to inhibit errors and help programmers.

human engineering

> Designing a system for the ease and convenience of the people who use it is called *human engineering*. A human-engineered product is created with sympathy for its users, and with an understanding of their problems and of errors they might make.

A subtle aspect of the human engineering of programming languages is the recognition that people are often in a hurry when they write programs. This is reflected in Pascal by an easing of certain syntax rules; or, more accurately, by allowing a simpler alternative syntax in some situations.

> When a structured type is defined, the definition can include descriptions of subtypes.

In the past, we've built up complicated structures by using type identifiers that were already defined. To define an array of records, we'd first define the record type, then use its identifier in defining the array type. However, this step can be skipped. For example:

a two-in-one definition

```
type BoardType = array [1 .. 10] of record
                                      Taken: boolean;
                                      Marker: char
                                    end; {of the record}
```

This shorthand is appropriate in a program that doesn't include any variables (or parameters) of the record type we defined on the fly. The same principle extends to variable declarations.

anonymous types

> When a variable is declared, its type must be given. However, it can be given an *anonymous* type that is described on the spot. The type isn't named, and thus doesn't have to be defined in advance.

We might legally make the following variable declaration:

a shorthand declaration

```
var Board: array [1 .. 10] of record
                                 Taken: boolean;
                                 Marker: char
                               end; {of the record}
```

Board is now an array-type variable, just as though the array and record types used in its declaration had been defined separately. We can make normal assignments to it:

```
Board[3].Taken := true;
Board[3].Marker := 'A';
```

Enumerated ordinal types can also be described rather than defined:

```
var Hue, Color: (Red, Blue, Green);
```

Hue and *Color* are variables of a type with no name.

why do things the long way?

Why didn't we mention these shortcuts earlier? Some of our reasons have to do with programming and teaching style. First of all, the syntax of individually defined types is easier for beginners to debug. Second, individually defined data types are easier to alter (and more likely to be improved) than monolithic definitions. Third, individually defined types are usually better documented than a single large types.

There are also semantic reasons for doing things the long way. These have to do with assignments and the declaration of parameters. Recall that a variable parameter and its argument must be of identical types, as must the variables on both sides of many assignment statements (such as an assignment between two record or array-type variables). However...

restrictions on parameters

> Two variables (or a parameter and its argument) have an identical type only if they're defined with the exact same type identifier. They must have named types, and can't have anonymous types.

This means that a type identifier—and not a shorthand description of the type—must be used in many variable declarations, and in *all* declarations of variable parameters. Other situations require that two variables be *type compatible.*

> Two variables (or a parameter and its argument) are type compatible if they both represent ranges of the same underlying type.

Again, this leads to a frequent requirement that a type be defined, rather than described. For example, we could not even pass *Hue* or *Color* as a value parameter. The type of *Tint* in this heading:

```
procedure Sample (Tint: (Red, Blue, Green));
```

is not compatible with *Hue* and *Color.* According to Pascal's scope rules, *Red, Blue*, and *Green* are being locally redefined. Similarly, the assignment between noncompatible variables in this program segment is illegal:

```
program Trial (input, output);
var Color: (Red, Blue, Green);
procedure Show;
   var Hue: (Red, Blue, Green);
   begin
      Hue := Color;          {This assignment is a type clash.}
        ...   etc.
```

In each case the variable declarations are fine, but the variable types are mismatched.

In summary, the shorthand form of type definition and variable declaration should be confined to small programs or procedures in which the issue of type will not arise. If a program is going to become large or use procedures, the types of its variables should be defined. This makes data structures easier to alter and debug, and allows variables to be passed as parameters and used in assignments.

pack and *unpack*

In Chapter 12 we mentioned the reserved word **packed** in connection with the definition of string types. However, the notion of packing a data structure to minimize the amount of storage it requires within the computer can be applied to any of Pascal's structured types (but usually just to arrays and records).

Although declaring a data structure to be packed saves space in the computer's memory, it generally slows down program execution. This is because the computer has to go through special manipulations to access the component values of packed data. In other words, the computer goes through the time-consuming process of unpacking the stored structure each time one of its fields or elements is altered or inspected.

Now, in the programs we've dealt with in this text the trade-off between program execution speed and data storage space is not a big concern. However, efficiency is something that has to be considered when very large programs are created. Fortunately, Pascal includes some standard procedures that let the programmer take advantage of the space saving aspect of packing the largest common data structure—the array—without sacrificing execution time.

procedure *unpack*

The standard procedure *unpack* assigns the contents of a packed array to a regular array. Its syntax is:

unpack (*PackedArray, NotPackedArray, StartingSubscript*);

where *PackedArray* is a variable of a packed array type, *NotPackedArray* is a variable of a similar (except that it's not packed) array type, and *StartingSubscript* is the position in *NotPackedArray* where the assignment starts.

Let's suppose that we've made the following definitions.

> **type** *PackedType* = **packed array** [*Lower..Upper*] **of** *Data*;
> *OrdinaryType* = **array** [*Minimum..Maximum*] **of** *Data*;
> **var** *PackedArray*: *PackedType*;
> *NotPackedArray*: *OrdinaryType*;
> *StartingSubscript*: *Minimum..Maximum*;

We'll also assume that:

> (*Maximum–Minimum*) >= (*Upper–Lower*)

how *unpack* works

In other words, *PackedArray* is the same size as, or smaller than, *NotPackedArray*. This restriction is necessary because the *StartingSubscript* argument lets us assign a small packed array to part of a larger array that isn't packed.

A call of *unpack*:

> *unpack* (*PackedArray, NotPackedArray, StartingSubscript*);

is equivalent to:

> **for** *i* := *Lower* **to** *Upper* **do**
> *NotPackedArray* [*i–Lower+StartingSubscript*] := *PackedArray* [*i*];

However, *unpack* is usually implemented in a manner that's faster to execute than this **for** statement.

procedure *pack*

The standard procedure *pack* reverses the process. Its syntax is:

> *pack* (*NotPackedArray, StartingSubscript, PackedArray*);

Using the same variables as above, we find that this call:

> *pack* (*NotPackedArray, StartingSubscript, PackedArray*);

how *pack* works

is equivalent to the statement:

> **for** *i* := *Lower* **to** *Upper* **do**
> *PackedArray* [*i*] := *NotPackedArray* [*i–Lower+StartingSubscript*]

Again, we can assume that the procedure is implemented in an optimum manner.

Note, incidentally, that when *PackedArray* and *NotPackedArray* both have the same number of stored components, *StartingSubscript* must equal the first legal subscript of *NotPackedArray*. This is true for both procedures.

Self-Check Questions

Q. Since we can assign their elements one at a time, why couldn't we just make a complete array assignment; i.e.:

PackedArray := *NotPackedArray*;
:

What's the necessity of either *pack* or *unpack*?

A. Once more we've run into the subtle difference between *identical* and *compatible* types. For two arrays to be assignable to each other, they must be of an identical type—declared with the exact same type identifier. Since one array is packed, and the other is not, this is clearly impossible. Thus, *pack* and *unpack* are required to effect the assignment.

Procedures and Functions as Parameters

Procedures and functions may be passed as parameters to other subprograms. This feature is usually taken advantage of in more advanced applications programs, especially when nonstandard library routines are available. As a result, the syntax of procedure and function parameter declarations may be enhanced at your installation, and what we say may be misleading.

At any rate, the general syntax of subprograms as parameters is just about what we would expect—the reserved word **procedure** or **function**, the subprogram's name and parameter list, and its type (if it's a function). For example:

procedure *Graph* (**function** *Compute* (*Limit*):*real*; *OffSet*: *integer*);

When two or more subprograms go in one parameter list, the word **procedure** or **function** must be repeated for each.

function *GreatestResult* (**function** *A* (*ItsArgument*: *real*): *real*;
function *B* (*AnotherArgument*: *real*): *real*;
TheArgument: *real*): *real*;

don't pass the arguments

Now, when a subprogram is passed as a parameter its arguments should *not* be passed along with it. In other words, *GreatestResult* might be called like this:

if *GreatestResult* (*sine, cosine, pi*/4) > *Minimum* **then** etc.

In this call, functions *Sine* and *Cosine* are the arguments of *A* and *B*, while *pi*/4 is their eventual argument. Calls have to be arranged this way to avoid prematurely evaluating argument functions or procedures.

Within *GreatestResult*, *A* and *B* (now representing *Sine* and *Cosine*) are called normally.

```
function GreatestResult (function A (ItsArgument: real): real;
                          function B (AnotherArgument: real): real;
                          TheArgument: real): real;
   {Represents the greater of A and B.}
   var First, Second: real;
   begin
      First := A(TheArgument);
      Second := B(TheArgument);
      if First>Second then GreatestResult := First;
                      else GreatestResult := Second
   end; {GreatestResult}
```

As you might imagine, a procedure or function parameter must be equivalent in type and parameter list to its argument. Because of this restriction, we can only pass *real*-type functions having one *real* argument apiece to *GreatestResult*.

Dynamically Allocating Variants

When a record with variant fields is dynamically allocated, enough space is set aside to store the largest of its variant groups. When each variant group requires about the same amount of storage, this method of storage allocation poses no disadvantages. However, programmers sometimes find themselves in the predicament of dynamically allocating many records of one type, but only requiring the smallest variant group of each. Fortunately, Pascal provides a mechanism for limiting size of each location.

> The dynamic allocation procedure *new* may be given additional arguments, corresponding to relatively nested tag field values. The location that is allocated has enough space to store the record's fixed fields, as well as those of the variant part specified by the stated tag field(s). It is, however, totally undefined.

Suppose that we have this type definition:

```
type LibraryItem = (Book, Magazine, Record);
     Card = ↑CardCatalog;
     CardCatalog = record
                      Available: boolean;
                      Name: packed array [1..50] of char;
                      case Item: LibraryItem of
                         Book: (ISBNNumber: array [1..10] of char);
                         Magazine: (Volume, Issue: integer);
                         Record: (DiscNumber: integer;
                                  ReRelease: boolean)
                   end;
var CurrentCard: Card;
```

The statement:

new (*CurrentCard*);

allocates a complete record large enough the hold the fixed fields, plus any of the variant fields. If we know that we're going to store a magazine, however, the statement:

new (*CurrentCard, Magazine*);

allocates a record whose fields are *Available, Name, Item, Volume*, and *Issue*. Don't forget, though, that *Item* is still undefined.

> A record allocated in this fashion cannot have its variant fields altered, nor can an assignment be made to the entire variable.

A 'complete record' assignment may not be made. Furthermore, changing the value of the tag field won't alter the currently accessible variant fields.

> The deallocation procedure *dispose* must be given additional arguments (representing tag field values) when a record allocated in the manner described above is disposed of.

Disposing of the record we allocated earlier requires this call:

dispose (*CurrentCard, Magazine*);

page We quote from the draft Standard:

> "*page*(*f*) shall cause an implementation-defined effect on the textfile *f*, such that subsequent output to *f* will be on a new page if the textfile is printed on a suitable device, and shall perform an implicit *writeln* . . . the effect of inspecting a textfile to which the page procedure was applied during generation shall be implementation-dependent."

Procedure *page* lets programmers decide when and where page breaks should occur, without requiring them to know exactly how many lines long their paper is. As the quote above states, this is a highly implementation-dependent matter—a call of *page* need not have any effect at all. In any case, *page* is a rarely-used procedure whose effect should be investigated on a case-by-case basis.

Collected Syntax Diagrams

array type

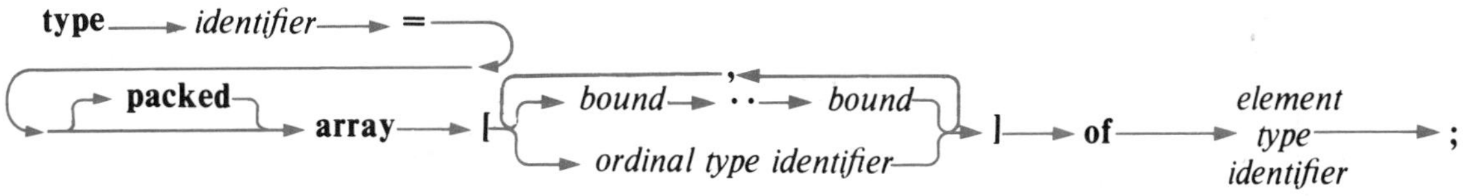

case statement

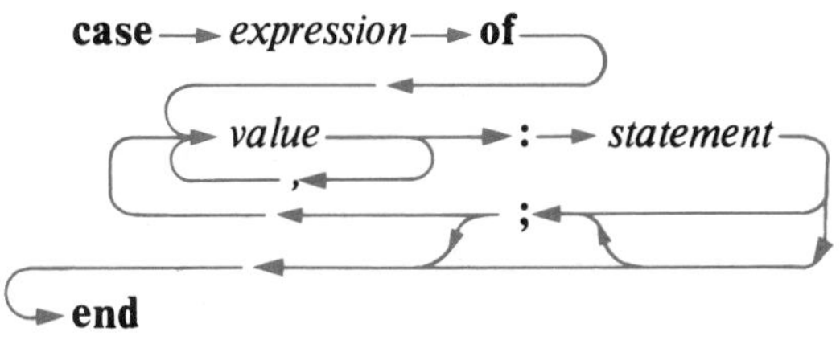

compound statement

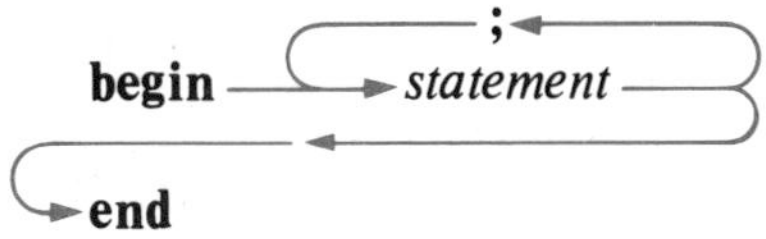

constant definition

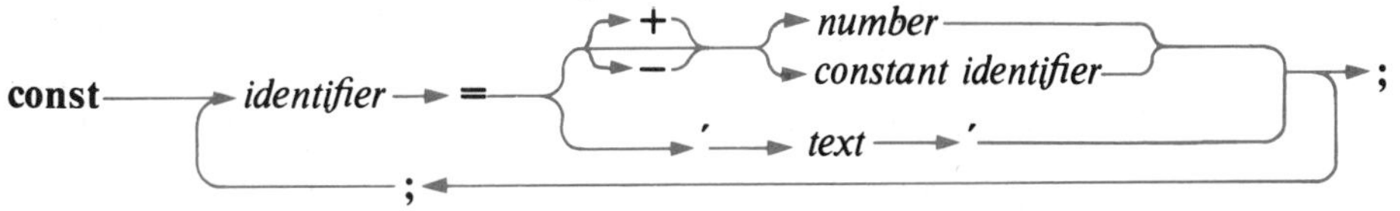

enumerated type definition

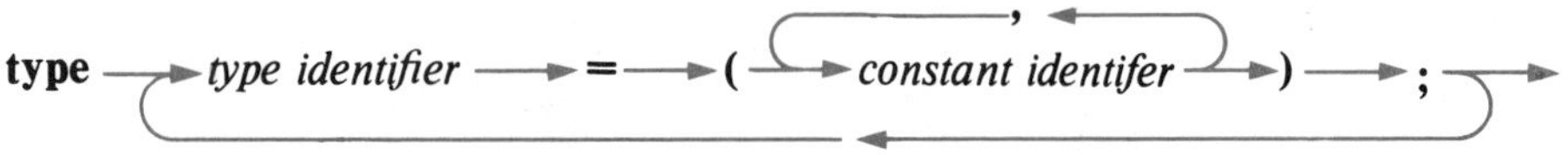

field list

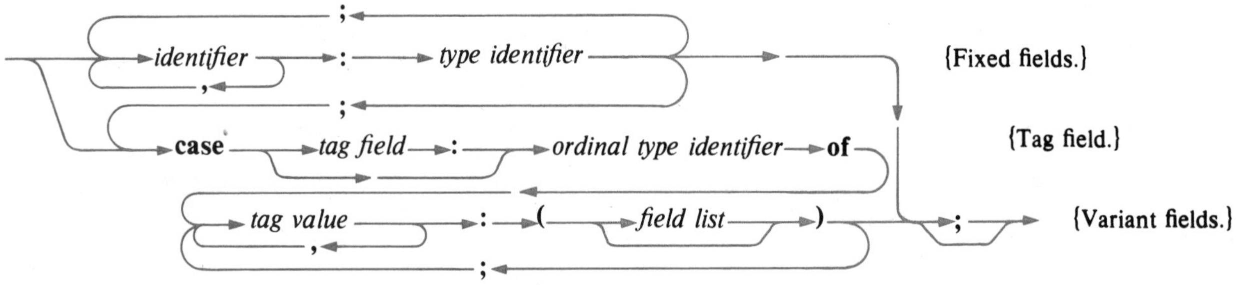

file type

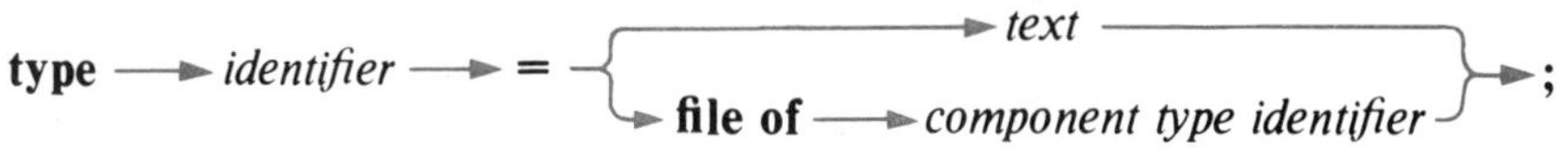

for statement

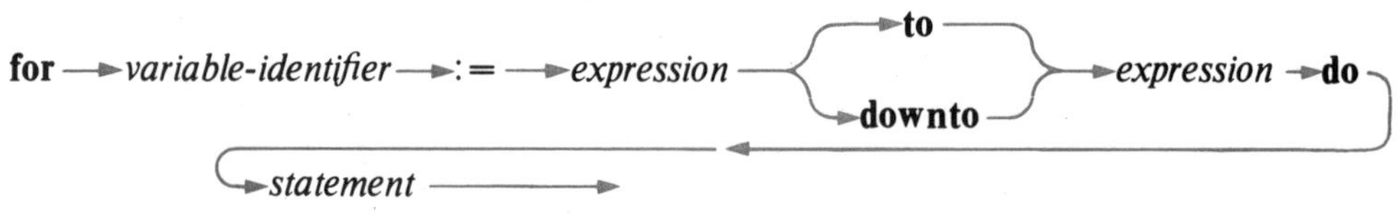

function heading

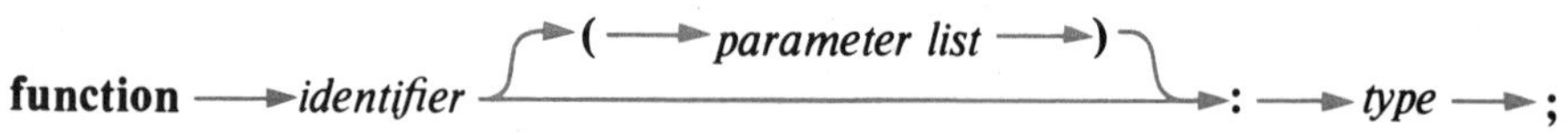

identifier

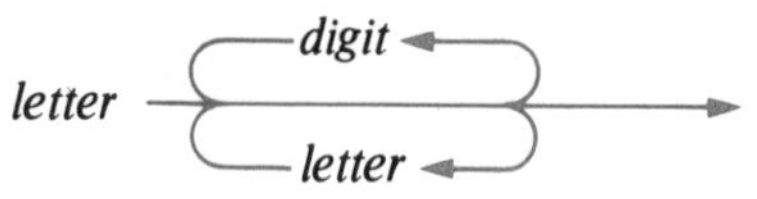

if statement

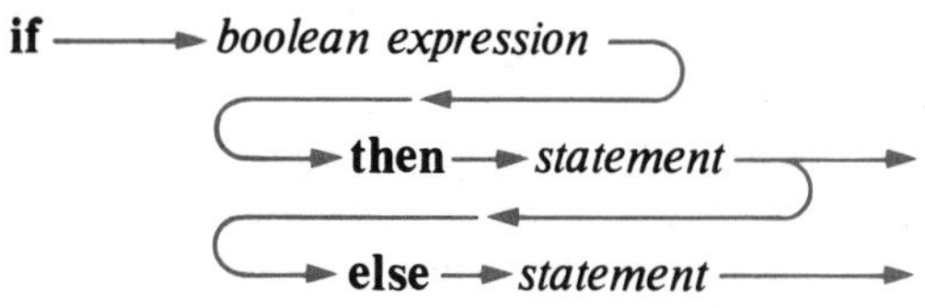

label declaration

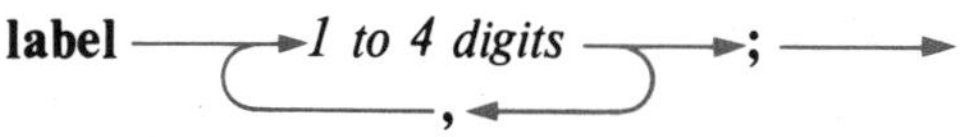

ordinal subrange

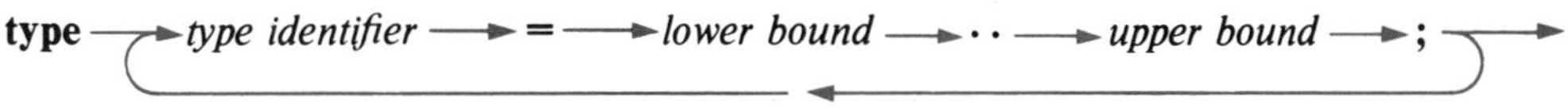

parameter list

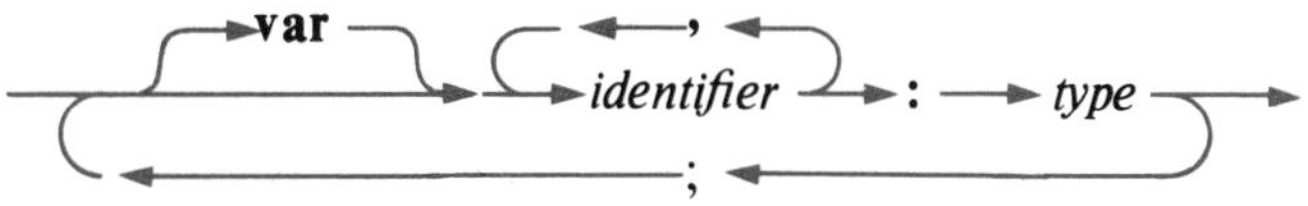

pointer type

procedure heading

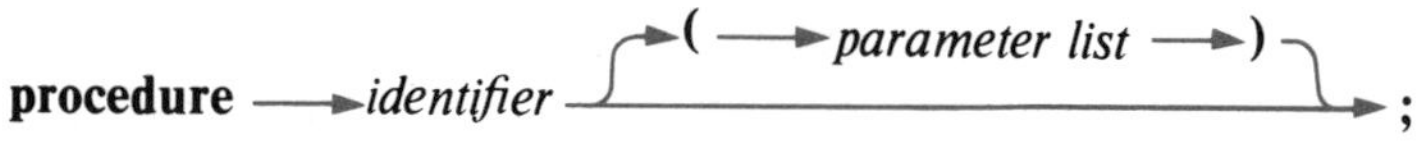

program

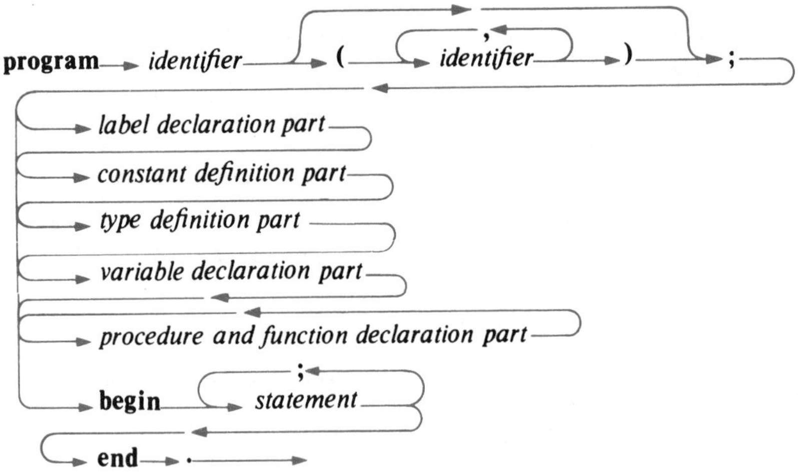

read and readln

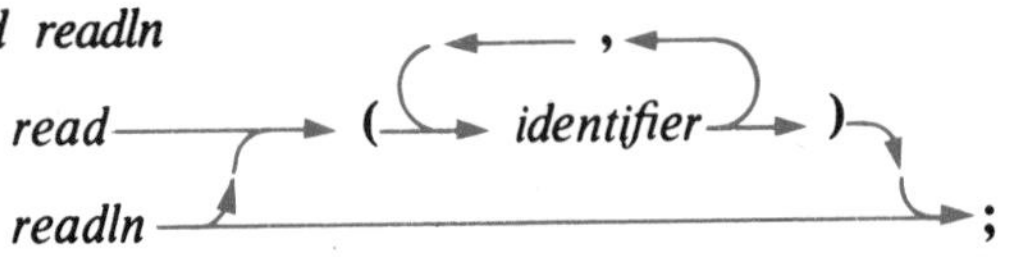

real

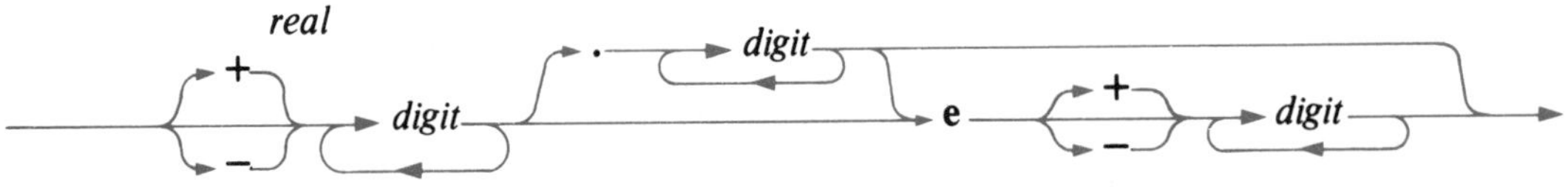

record type

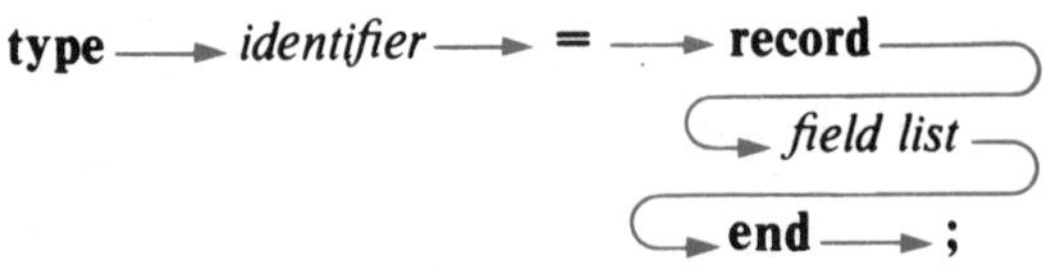

record type (simple)

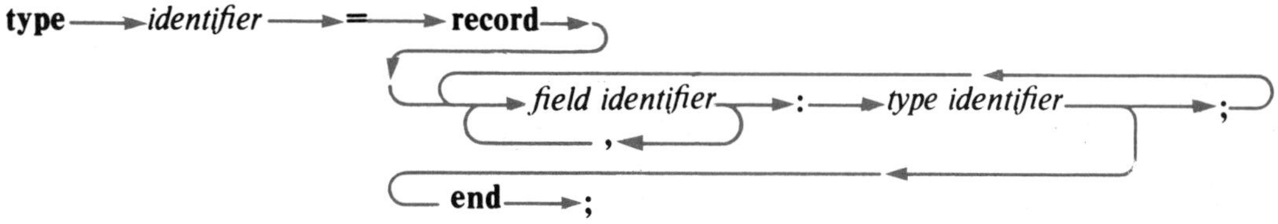

repeat statement

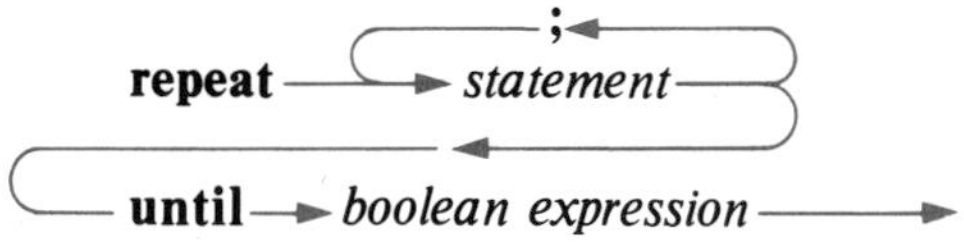

set type

type definition

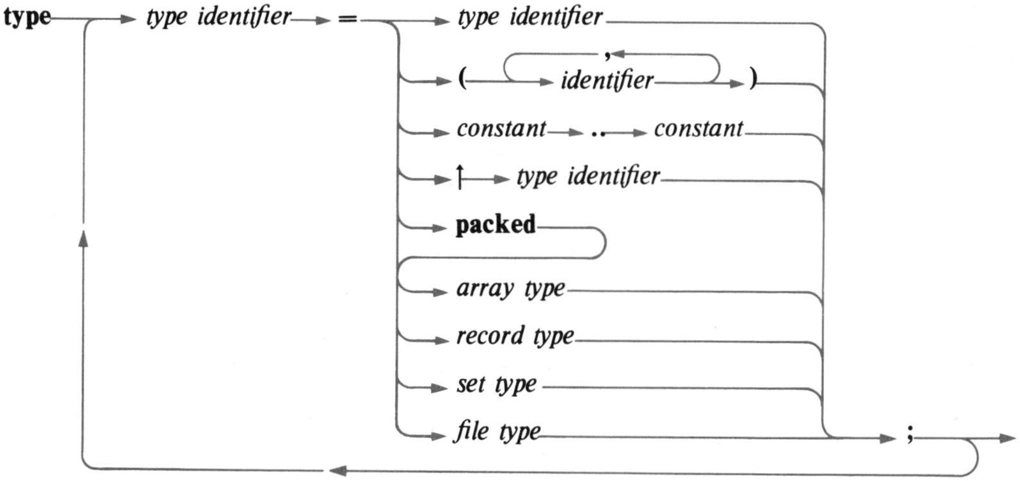

variable declaration

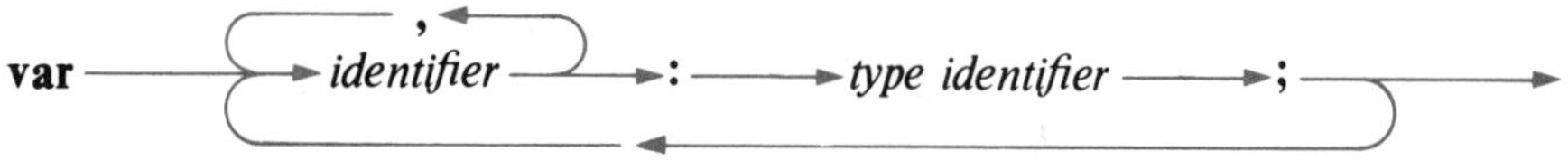

while statement

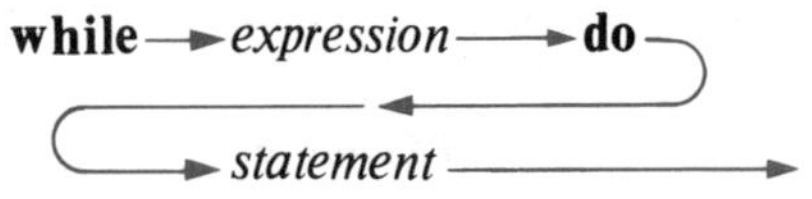

with statement

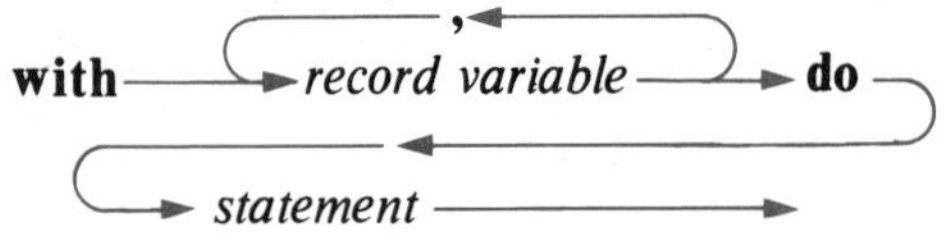

write and writeln

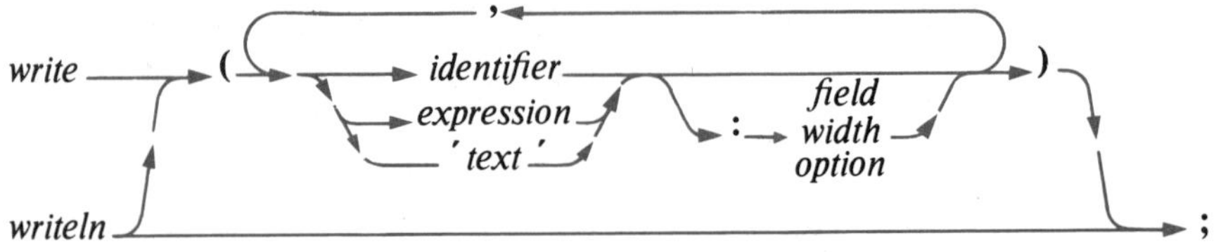

Glossary

access To inspect or alter the contents of a *location.* See *direct access, indirect access.*

action See *statement.*

actual parameter, argument Two phrases that refer to the value or variable actually passed to a subprogram. See also *parameter.*

address The computer's internal name for a location in memory; a location's subscript. A pointer variable represents an address, but it has no external character representation.

algorithm A plan for solving a problem. A program algorithm should be precise enough to allow an accurate coding specification.

allocate Set aside space in the computer's *memory* to hold the values of variables. See *dynamic allocation.*

argument See *parameter.*

array bounds The first and last valid subscripts of an array *dimension.* If a dimension is given by an ordinal type identifier (e.g. **array** [*char*] **of** etc.) the array bounds are the first and last members of the ordinal type.

assignment operator A special Pascal symbol, ':=', used to assign a value to a variable or function identifier.

assignment statement A statement that gives a new value to a variable or function.

base type The values that a set variable potentially represents belong to the set's base type. (Similar to the *component type* of a file.) See also *cardinality.*

batch computer, program A computer that runs programs singly, rather than on a *time-sharing* basis. Batch systems are frequently directed by punched cards, and not from terminals. In this text, batch-oriented programs are those that don't interact with the user. See *interactive.*

binary tree A (usually linked) data structure that is easy to construct and search. See *tree.*

block In Pascal, a *defining block* is the declaration and statement parts of a program or subprogram. The scope of identifiers is limited to the block they're defined or declared in, and to blocks created within that block. Identifiers given meaning in the outermost block are called *global,* while identifiers created (or redefined) in subprograms are said to be *local. Block-structured* is a description of languages (like Pascal) that let a programer put a number of actions into a single, easily-dealt-with unit (like a compound statement or procedure). See also *scope.*

bottom-up A method of analyzing problems or solutions that works from the particular to the general; e.g. from program code to the rationale behind it. *Bottom-up programing* usually involves encoding subprograms in *drivers* to get a better notion of implementation and algorithm difficulties.

boundary condition The situation at the first or last iteration of a loop, or recursive call of a subprogram. See also *entry condition, exit condition.*

brute force A method of programing and problem solving in which a simple partial-solution step is carried out many times. See also *exhaustive search.*

bubble sort An easy but inefficient sorting method in which neighbor values are compared and (possibly) exchanged. The value being sought tends to 'bubble' in the direction of comparison.

buffer A *buffer* is an intermediate holding place. Data is *buffered* if it's stored temporarily en route to its final destination; e.g. interactive computer systems usually buffer input until a carriage return is entered. Similarly, output produced by a call of *write* is frequently buffered until the program encounters a *writeln.*

bug An unintentional program mistake that manifests itself during program compilation or execution. A *syntax bug* is an error in the grammar of using a programing language, while a *semantic bug* is a syntactically correct misuse of the language. See also *feature.*

cardinality The cardinality of an ordinal type is the number of distinct values it contains. *Set cardinality* refers to the number of values (members) a set-type variable represents.

case constant list, case expression An expression of any ordinal type determines which of the actions in a **case** statement's constant list is executed.

```
case (case expression) of
  constant: action;
     : {Constant list}
end;
```

collating sequence The ordering of a computer's character set.

comment An explanatory note about program operation that is ignored by the compiler. See *curly brackets.*

compatible Two variables or expressions are type-compatible if they represent values of (possibly different subranges of) the same *underlying* type. This is a less rigid restriction than the notion of *identical* types, and assignments between compatible variables that pass a compile-time inspection may still cause a run-time error.

compile Convert a program from its English (e.g. Pascal) form into a code the computer can actually execute. A *compiler* is a program that does this automatically.

compile-time error A bug (especially a syntax mistake) that is caught by the compiler, and must be fixed before the program is run.

complete record assignment An assignment between two type-identical record variables:

OneRecord := *TheOther*;

All field-values of one record are assigned to their counterparts in the other.

component The values stored in a file-type variable are its components. Its type is the file's *component type.*

compound statement A series of statements between a **begin** and **end** that form a unit, and are treated semantically like a single statement. In a sense, the statement parts of a program or subprogram are just large compound statements.

computed subscript A fancy way of talking about a subscript that's given as an expression (e.g. *TheArray* [*sqr*(2)]) rather than as a constant value (*TheArray* [4]).

concatenate To join two or more groups of data (especially files and strings) by putting them in sequence. The concatenation of 'Gia' and 'Carangi' is 'GiaCarangi'.

constant A *user-defined constant* is an identifier that's been given a particular ordinal, *real,* or text value. However, the word *constant* is also generally used to refer to the basic representation of any ordinal or *real* value; e.g. '3' is a constant of type *integer,* and *true* is a *boolean* constant.

control character A third 'level' (similar to upper and lower case) of characters. Control characters are generally used internally by the computer, esp. to mark the end of line and end of file.

control statement A statement that controls the execution of an action, forming a *structured statement.* Pascal includes alternative statements, like the **case** statement, and looping statements, such as the **for** statement.

correct A program that can be proven to *always* work is said to be correct.

counter variable An ordinal-type variable that controls the repetition of a **for** loop:

```
for CounterVariable := Lower to Upper
  do      etc.
```

This variable is undefined on exit from the loop.

crash In a large sense, for a computer system to suddenly stop working, usually with disastrous results. See *run-time error* for a description of program crashes.

curly brackets Comment delimiters '{' and '}'; also called *braces.* The alternative symbols '(*' and '*)' may also be used, but not mixed.

data structure A phrase with two levels of meaning. In Pascal, a data structure specifically refers to a structured data type, e.g. a record or array. In general usage, however, a data structure is an abstract way of representing data that is independent of a particular implementation. Thus, trees are data structures as well as records or arrays.

decimal accuracy The number of digits to the right of the decimal in the fixed-point representation of a *real* value. For example, 4.17 has only two digits of decimal accuracy, while 4.1700 has four.

defensive programing Programing in a manner that helps prevent mistakes; using antibugging techniques. See also *robustness.*

definition part The segment of a program or subprogram in which labels (used with the **goto** statement), constants, and ordinal, subrange, pointer, and structured types are defined.

delimiter A word or symbol that marks a boundary. For example, **begin** and **end** are the *delimiters* of a compound statement, and curly brackets *delimit* a comment.

device Usually a piece of equipment (hardware) that is connected to a computer. The predefined identifiers *input* and *output* usually refer to input and output devices. Pascal is often extended by letting other devices be specified (as file parameters) in the program heading.

dimension See *array bounds, subscript.*

direct access Assignment to or inspection of a location using an ordinary variable. See also *indirect access, location.*

directive (Not discussed in the text.) When the Wirth Pascal Standard was revised, it transpired that nobody really knew what category of term the word **forward** was. To clear things up, the idea of a *directive* came into being. A directive is a word that takes the place of a subprogram's definitions, declarations, and statement part, and whose effect is implementation defined. The only standard directive is **forward**, described elsewhere. A presumed directive application might provide a way to include externally written or compiled subprograms.

documentation An explanation of the purpose and operation of a program, usually given by comments. A particularly transparent program is said to be *self-documenting*; its identifiers, format, and algorithm join to clarify the program's action. In a larger sense, documentation is a synonym for 'instruction manual'.

down Computer jargon meaning inoperable, as in 'The system is down.' Frequently the case. To *take down* implies that the system is going down gracefully, instead of crashing. This distinction is often lost on users.

driver A program whose sole purpose is to test the operation of a subprogram.

dynamic allocation Setting aside locations in memory (i.e. creating variables) at run-time, by using procedure *new*. An ordinary variable declaration is a *static allocation* of memory.

echo *v.t.* Output input. *n.* Input output.

efficiency Efficiency is a relative measure of a program's usage of computer resources. From a viewpoint of increasing efficiency, speed in execution and minimization of memory requirements are a program's main virtues.

elegance A measure of the quality of a solution. More precisely, an elegant solution is one that makes you say 'I wish I'd thought of that.'

element The records that make up many linked structures (particularly list-based structures) are called *elements*. The stored values of a set are called elements as well.

empty statement A syntactic 'nonaction', marked by a semicolon. Often used by mistake.

entry condition A *boolean* condition for entering a **while...do** statement:

while (*entry condition*) **do** etc.

The loop will be entered only if this expression is *true*, and its action is repeated only if it remains so. The notion of an entry condition is also used in connection with entering a series of recursive calls.

error check To inspect input for data that would cause a program crash or incorrect results.

evaluate To figure out the value of an expression.

execute To carry out a statement or series of statements.

exhaustive search A programing technique in which all possible answers—the problem's entire *solution space*—are considered in the search for the correct few. See also *brute force.*

exit condition The *boolean* expression given at the end of a **repeat...until** statement:

until (*exit condition*) etc.

The loop is terminated after the exit condition has been evaluated and met. The term is also used to refer to the conditions that cause a series of recursive calls to end.

expression Any representation of a value in Pascal. A variable identifier is a very simple expression; longer expressions may include function calls and operators.

extension A nonstandard addition to Pascal. A common extension is the creation of a character representation for (allowing the output of) user-defined ordinal values.

external An *external file* is a permanently stored file that is either used or created by a Pascal program. On some systems, *external procedures* can be included in a program; however, this is an extension to Pascal. See also *file parameter.*

external character representation Values are usually stored in a coded format within the computer; this is their *internal representation.* Values of types *real, integer, char,* and *boolean,* however, may be entered (and are output) as a sequence of ordinary characters. Thus, they are said to have an *external character representation.*

feature A bug that has been documented.

field list The names and types of the fields (internal variables) of a record structure.

field width In Pascal all output is right-adjusted within a blank *field*—excess space goes to the left of the value. The programer can call for non-standard spacing by following the output value with a colon, and the number of spaces its field should occupy. Default field widths are *system-defined.*

file parameter A program's connections to its environment are given as *file parameters* in the program heading. The standard, predefined file parameters are *input* and *output.* File *output* must usually be included in the heading.

file window An identifier, given by a file name followed by a caret or up-arrow (e.g. *TheFile*↑), whose type is the file's component type. The file window is used for access to files, and holds the value about to be read from, or appended to, any file. The standard procedures *get* and *put* use the file window—*get*(*TheFile*) assigns the next component of *TheFile* to *TheFile*↑, while *put*(*TheFile*) appends the value of *TheFile*↑ to *TheFile.*

fixed part See *record variant.*

fixed-point notation A conventional method of writing real values (optional in Pascal), in which no exponents (or scale factors) are used. Pascal *reals* can be made to print in this notation by following the field width specification with another colon and the number of decimal places desired. For example:

writeln (1.740395E02:6:2)

prints '174.03' in a six-space field, with two digits of *decimal accuracy.*

flakey A description usually applied to computer systems. Not generally reliable because of hardware problems, prone to glitches.

floating-point notation A method of writing *real* values, sometimes called *scientific notation.* In Pascal, it means that *reals* are written with only one digit to the left of the decimal point and raised to an appropriate power of ten by a *scale factor.* For example, '470.1' is shown as '4.701E02', and read '4.701 times 10 to the 2*nd* power'

forward declaration The specification of a subprogram's name and parameters in advance of the actual declaration (sometimes to allow recursive calls). The word **function** or **procedure**, and the subprogram's name and parameter list (and type, if a function) are followed by the word **forward**. When the subprogram is eventually declared, its parameter list (and type) are omitted. See also *directive.*

function In Pascal, a function is a subprogram that computes and represents a value. See also *subprogram.*

function heading The first line of a function declaration. It includes the function's name, its parameters (if any), and its type.

garbage collection Returning to memory (with *dispose*) or simply saving (for reassignment) dynamically allocated memory locations that are no longer required. Garbage collection is necessary in programs that use very large numbers of dynamically allocated variables.

get(f) See *file window.*

gets A euphemism for 'is assigned the value,' as in '*Age* gets 14.'

glitch A transient, inconsistent bug that isn't your fault. See *flakey.*

global identifier See *block.*

guru A frequently surly person who knows all the answers. May be preceded by a noun indicating area of expertise; e.g. *system guru.*

hack As a noun, a *hack* is a segment of code that is either very clever or awfully stupid, but works. To *hack* on or at something means to work on it without any great hope of success: 'I'll hack on my program for a few more hours.' Simply *hacking* something means to explore it for no particular reason, usually late at night. One who does this becomes a *hacker.* The term also describes someone who is a guru in a particular field; e.g. a *system hacker.*

handwave To gloss over a complex point by saying many words that don't really have anything to do with the subject. Often used in explaining why your program (which you plagiarized but don't understand) works.

heap The portion of computer memory from whence dynamically allocated variables spring.

identical Two variables have identical types if they are declared with the exact same type identifier. This notion is especially important when passing arguments to variable-parameters—they must be of an identical type. In general, two types are not identical if they are defined separately, even if the definitions are letter-for-letter the same.

identifier A word whose meaning is defined or declared by the programer. Pascal identifiers must begin with a letter, and may contain any number of letters or digits. However, the number of significant characters is implementation-defined.

implement, implementation To *implement* something is to bring it into being; algorithms are *implemented* by being written as programs. An *implementation*, however, is usually intended to refer to a particular computer system, e.g. the Berkeley or Minneapolis Pascal implementation.

implementation-defined A value that may vary from Pascal system to Pascal system, but which *must* be defined. The values of type *char* are implementation defined.

in A relational operator associated with sets. Its left operand is a value of any set type, its right operand is a value of the set's base type, and its result is *boolean.*

increment In general a value is *incremented* by increasing it a little bit. In programing the *increment*, or amount added, is usually one (or its equivalent in ordinal types other than *integer*).

index Often used as a synonym for *subscript*, or more generally to indicate a particular position in a sequence (file, linked list, array, etc.).

indirect access Inspecting (or making a change to) the value stored in a memory location by using a pointer type variable. The variable's identifier must be followed by an up-arrow or caret. See also *direct access, location.*

initialize To give a starting value to. Some systems may automatically initialize variables and pointers, but it's poor programing practice to rely on this.

inorder search See *tree searching.*

input *Program input* is the data a program acquires from any external source. The identifier *input* can appear in the program heading as a standard file parameter; it is equivalent to a textfile, and usually refers to a terminal keyboard or card reader.

interactive computer, program A computer system that is usually directed from video terminals, and shares its resources among many users simultaneously. In this text, interactive programs require user-interaction during program execution.

internal An *internal file* is defined and declared within a program, and lasts only for the duration of a program. Compare to *external.*

iteration Repetition, looping.

kludge The Rube Goldberg device of programing. A kludge is usually a clever (but not always transparent) programing trick intended to get around a shortcoming in a programing language, or a bug in a program.

lateral thinking A technique of problem solving that involves looking at many brief solution sketches before exploring any of them in depth.

library In computer jargon, a collection of nonstandard procedures that are available to every programer. Not every Pascal system supports a program library.

lineprinter A glorified typewriter that is attached to, and run by, a computer. So named because it can print an entire line at once. Most systems have some way of sending program listings and results to a lineprinter for perusal at leisure.

linked structure A pointer-based data structure. A series, or *list*, of records is linked together by pointer fields—each record contains a pointer field that accesses at least one other record of the same type. See also *queue, stack, tree.*

list disposal Returning the elements of a dynamically allocated linked list to memory. See *garbage collection.*

listing *See lineprinter.*

local identifier See *block.*

location A storage place in the computer's memory. In Pascal, locations are restricted to storing values of one particular type.

loop action The action executed by any loop statement. Under normal circumstances loop actions in Pascal are unbreakable units—a loop cannot be exited in the middle of its action.

main program As we've used it, the statement part of a program (as opposed to the statement part of any subprogram).

massage Something done to a problem to make it friendlier. To massage a problem is to restate it in the hope that a solution method will show itself, or that previously hidden information will become visible.

matrix A loose synonym for a two-dimensional array.
memory Where the computer stores information (variables, pending statements, etc.) about a currently running program.
mnemonic Literally, a memory aid. A mnemonic identifier is one that is easy to remember, and which explains the identifier's purpose. See also *documentation.*
modularity A program virtue. A *modular* program is divided into self-contained, independent subprograms (*modules*) whose connections to the main program are generally specified as parameters. See also *side effect.*
name list An internal accounting of identifiers for the benefit of the computer. Each record's field list has its own name list, thus these names don't conflict with other variables declared in the same block.
nesting A structured statement that is the action of a like-structured statement is said to be *nested*; e.g. nested **for** loops. Data structures are also nested if one structure contains another; e.g. a record variant that has a variant part itself.
nil *pointer* A pointer variable whose value is **nil**. It does not access a location in memory.
node See *tree.*
number crunching Using a computer to analyze mathematical or scientific data. Generally applied as a term of derision to engineering programs.
object In the context of programing languages, an *object* is an allocated portion of computer memory, esp. for the storage of variables and user-defined constants.
one-dimensional, two-dimensional The number of dimensions an array has is equivalent to the number of subscripts required to access a particular storage location.
operand, operator An *operator* is a symbol (like '+' or '*') or word-symbol (like **div**). Operators can be joined with *operands*, or representations of values, to form expressions. Most operators are *binary*, which means that they require two operands, e.g. 2+2. A few operators, however, are *unary* and only need a single operand, e.g. **not** *Finished.*
operator hierarchy A scheme that helps determine the order in which operations in an expression are carried out. Pascal operators are divided into four levels of precedence. First are the *unary* operators (see above) plus, minus, and **not**. Subexpressions containing these operators are evaluated first. Next come the *multiplying* operators *, /, **div**, **mod**, and **and**, then the *adding* operators +, −, and **or**. The last group contains the *relational* operators =, <>, <, >, <=, >=, and **in**. Parentheses can be used to change the order of evaluation imposed by the operator hierarchy.
ordinal type In Pascal, an *ordinal type* is an ordered range of values. Because the number of values in *real* may vary, type *real* is excluded from the ordinal types (although it is a *simple* type). There are three standard ordinal types—*integer, boolean,* and *char*—and others may be defined by the programer. The standard functions *pred, succ,* and *ord* may be given arguments of any ordinal type. See also *subrange, user-defined ordinal type.*
output *Program output* is the results produced by a program. The predefined identifier *output* can appear in the program heading as a standard file parameter; it is equivalent to a textfile, and usually refers to a terminal screen or lineprinter.
parameter In general, a particular value that is substituted for a general term. In Pascal, a parameter is a variable created in the *parameter list* portion of a subprogram: a *value-parameter* is a local variable whose starting value is *passed* as an *argument* to the subprogram, and a *variable-parameter* is a local re-naming of a (relatively) global variable. These are also called *formal parameters.* The *actual parameter* (argument) of a value-parameter may be any *compatible* value, while that of a variable-parameter must be a *type-identical* variable.
parameter list The portion of a subprogram heading in which value- and variable-parameters are declared.
paren A quick way of referring to either left or right parentheses (usually clarified by context). '(4*5)' can be read aloud as 'Paren four star five paren'.
passed Given as an argument. See *actual parameter.*
period notation See *individual field access.*
pop Remove the topmost element of a stack.
postorder, preorder Binary tree inspection schemes. See *tree searching.*

precedence The notion of *operator precedence* lets rules be established for determining the order in which expressions are evaluated. (See *operator hierarchy.*) *Name precedence* describes Pascal's convention for re-using identifiers—the most locally defined or declared identifier takes precedence over a like-named (but relatively global) identifier. See also *block.*

predefined identifier A constant, type, file, or subprogram identifier that is accessible without being defined or declared by the programer. Predefining additional identifiers is a common *extension* to Pascal.

procedure A subprogram that handles part of the job of a larger program. Syntactically, a Pascal *procedure declaration* is nearly identical to a program. However, the procedure heading includes a *parameter list,* and the declaration is followed by a semicolon rather than a period. See also *subprogram, function.*

procedure call The invocation of a procedure. The procedure's name, along with any arguments it requires, is a statement that serves to activate the procedure.

program heading The first noncomment line of a program. It includes the program's name and its file parameters. The predefined file *output* must usually be included. See also *file parameter.*

prompt A line of output that informs the program user that input is expected.

pseudocode A hybrid language for describing algorithms that contains enough English to be understandable, and enough Pascal to point the way to program implementation. See also *stepwise refinement.*

pseudorandom A sequence of numbers that contains a random distribution of digits, but which isn't really random because a known, repeatable algorithm controls its generation.

push Add an element to the top of a stack.

put(f) See *file window.*

queue A (usually linked) data structure. Items are added to one end of the queue, and removed from the other. Hence, a queue is a *first in, first out* structure.

radian A unit of measure of angles. 2π radians is 360°, so one radian is about 57.3°.

random access A data structure in which the particular order of stored elements has no effect on retrieval. The array is a random access structure; a file or list isn't. See *sequential access.*

real world In programing, institutions or companies at which 'programing' is used in the same sentence as 'COBOL', 'FORTRAN', etc. Usually used pejoratively by those not there. Talking about someone who has entered the real world is not unlike mentioning a deceased person.

record variant A **record** structure may have two distinct sections—a *fixed* part, and a *variant* part. The fixed part specifies fields common to all variables of that record type. The variant part declares groups of fields that co-exist in the space allotted to the variable. The value of a common *tag* field indicates which group of variant fields is being used at any time.

recursion, recursive A *recursive data structure* is defined in terms of itself; pointer types are recursively defined. *Recursion,* as a programing method, relies on calls of subprograms that are *recursive*—they call themselves.

reference Informally, *reference* and *access* are synonyms. Pointer-type variables reference, or access, or point to, variables of their reference type.

reference type The type of variable accessed by a pointer-type variable.

relational operator One of the operators =, <>, <, >, <=, >=, and **in**. Used in forming *boolean*-valued expressions.

representation 'Way of showing,' as in 'A function call is the representation of a value.'

reserved word Part of the basic vocabulary of Pascal. Reserved words may not be redefined. Generally printed in **bold face type.**

result A math word that means 'answer'. When an expression is evaluated, the answer is called a *result.*

right thing Whatever good programing practice calls for. For example, a robust program will *do the right thing* when it encounters bad input.

ring buffer A circular list that queues a fixed number of values. Whenever a new value arrives, the oldest one is removed. Used to preserve a 'current' sequence of data values.

robustness A desirable program quality. Robust programs are resistant to user errors, they *error-check* input and they degrade gracefully.

root The topmost node of a tree. See *tree.*

run-time check An automatic check the computer

makes during program execution (as opposed to a *compile-time* check, made when a program is first compiled). For example, type-checking of input is done at run-time.
run-time error A mistake that occurs during program execution, causing the program to *crash* (halt).
scale factor See *floating-point notation.*
scientific notation See *floating-point notation.*
scope The *scope* of an identifier is its range of meaning within a program. See *block, precedence.*
selection sort A simple sorting method. The largest (or smallest) value is found, then the next so, etc. Thus, the most desirable value is always being 'selected' from the remaining values.
sentinel As we use it, a *sentinel* is a special value used to mark the end of input. However, sentinels can be used to denote the end of any search area; e.g. the last value stored in an array might be a sentinel.
sequential access A data structure whose stored data must be retrieved in order, rather than at random. Files are sequential access structures, as are most *linked* structures.
set operator An operator that can be used with set-type operands. In Pascal, three set operators have set-type results—*union* ('+'), *difference* ('−'), and *intersection* ('*'). However, the relational operators can also be used in set expressions and produce *boolean* result values—*equality* ('='), *inequality* ('<>'), *includes* ('>='), *is included by* ('<='), and **in**.
side effect The change of a (relatively) global variable from within a subprogram, except when it is passed as a variable-parameter. Side effects are harmful because they make programs confusing, and disrupt their *modularity.*
simple type One of the standard types *real, boolean, char,* and *integer,* or any user-defined ordinal or subrange type. Basically, the simple types establish categories of value, while *structured* types provide different means of storage and access.
solution space See *exhaustive search.*
spaghetti programs Programs whose flow of control is difficult to follow, typically due to unconstrained use of the **goto** statement.
sparse matrix An two-dimensional array whose elements are largely identical.
square brackets These brackets [] are used to access stored array values, and in forming set expressions.
stack The computer's stack stores partially executed subprograms and their current variables—the local variables created in a series of recursive calls are 'put on the stack'. As a (usually linked) data structure, a stack stores values in *last in, first out* order. See also *pop, push.*
standard function, standard procedure Subprograms that are predefined in all Pascal implementations, although an individual system might define others as well. The identifier of a standard procedure or function may be usurped for another purpose, but this is usually inadvisable.
standard input, standard output See *input, output.*
Standard Pascal The official Pascal language. Programs written in Standard Pascal should run, without error, on any Pascal compiler. Our reference in this text is the (Draft) ANSI/IEEE Pascal Standard, X3J9/81-093.
state To phrase an expression. Also, the current condition of something, e.g. 'What's the state of your terminal?' 'Wedged!'
state variable A variable that represents the present condition of input, output, or program computation. *Ordinal* types are often defined to provide values for state variables.
statement Pascal's unit of activity. Statements are generally separated by a semicolon, and can be broadly characterized—see *assignment statement, compound statement, control statement, empty statement, procedure call.*
statement part The final portion of a program or subprogram. It contains a series of statements to be executed.
stepwise refinement A method of programing in which an abstract algorithm is stated, then successively refined and restated until it can be implemented. A progressively more Pascal-like pseudocode usually describes the solution at each step along the way.
string In general, a sequence of characters (much like *text*). In Pascal, a *string type* is often taken to be a packed array of *char* values.
structured type One of the standard types **array**, **set**, **record**, or **file**. Structured types provide different means of storage and access to *simple* values or other structures. See also *simple type.*
structured walkthrough A guided tour, on paper,

of a program. A structured walkthrough tries to find errors in design or implementation by exposing a program to comments by other programers.

stub program A working shell of a program, intended to test the basic ideas behind the program's design. Although a stub program's main data structures are defined and its main subprograms declared, it only approximates the action of a final version. See also *top-down debugging.*

subprogram A procedure or function, similar to a *subroutine.* Subprograms are intended to divide the work of a large program into small segments that are more easily written and debugged.

subrange A user-defined type that contains a continuous sequence of the values of any ordinal type, but which need not include the *entire* range of that type. For example:

type *SmallInteger* = 1..500; {A subrange of *integer.*}

Subrange types are usually used as a preventive antibugging measure, ensuring that the value of a variable or function does not fall outside some reasonable range. See also *compatible.*

subscript In Pascal, a subscript (given between square brackets) is required to access any particular element of an array-type variable.

syntax chart A diagram that illustrates the legal construction of Pascal programs, or portions of programs.

system defined A value that varies from system to system, but which must be defined; e.g. *maxint.*

system dependent A feature or value that is not required on all Pascal implementations, but which can be locally specified; e.g. the wording (and in fact, the existence) of error messages.

tag field See *record variant.*

terminated Finished, particularly in regard to loop statement.

text The predefined identifier *text* is equivalent to the definition **file of** *char*; it defines *textfiles.* In general usage, *text* refers to a sequence of characters between single quotes; e.g.:

writeln ('This is text');

A user-defined *text constant* or *string* is a special instance of the above:

const *NAME* = 'Patti'

However, in Pascal any series of two or more characters between single quotes can be called a text constant. (A single character between quotes is a constant of type *char.*) See also *string.*

text processing Working with characters; a generalized way of describing nonnumerical programing. See *number crunching.*

top-down debugging Spreading debugging and testing throughout the entire programing process. The general idea is to find major bugs caused by poorly defined data structures or badly conceived subprograms first, and worry about syntax and other local concerns later. Thus, abstract bugs are dealt with before concrete ones. Usually used in conjunction with *stub programing.*

top-down method An approach to problem solving and programing. The 'top' of a problem is an abstract English statement, while its 'bottom' is a detailed solution. For example, a top-down explanation of a program demonstrates how the final program was arrived at and implemented, instead of just telling how the code works. See also *stepwise refinement.*

transfer function A function that represents a value of one Pascal simple type as a value of a different type. Typically, values of an ordinal type will be represented as *integers* to allow arithmetic-like operations on them.

transparency An interesting word with opposite meanings. *Transparent code* is code whose purpose and effect is easily seen; it is clear. A *transparent process*, on the other hand, is neither seen nor necessarily understood. For example, a computer's storage allocation is transparent; it is hidden from the user.

tree A (usually linked) data structure. Each *node* of the tree stores data, and points to zero or more distinct subtrees. A tree's first node is its *root*, every node is a *parent* that may have *children*, and a node with no children is a *leaf.* In a *binary tree* each node is limited to a maximum of two children.

tree searching Inspecting the nodes of a tree. There are three strategies for searching binary trees—*inorder* search, in which the left subtree is inspected, then the root, and finally the right subtree; *postorder* search, in which we inspect the left subtree, then the right subtree, and finally the root; and *preorder* search, which first visits the root, then the left subtree, and then the right subtree.

truth table A table that shows the operands and result values of *boolean* expressions; usually, the table contains all possible evaluations of a particular expression.

type clash A mismatch of types in an expression, assignment, or subprogram call that causes a program crash. See also *compatible, identical.*

type definition The specification and naming of a class of values (see *ordinal type* or *subrange) or a variable structure (see structured type*). The *type definition part* is an optional portion of every program and subprogram.

undefined A variable, function, or pointer that has not explicitly been given a value is said to be *undefined.* The counter variable of a **for** loop is also undefined on exit from the loop.

underlying type When a standard or user-defined ordinal type is the basis of an ordinal subrange, it is said to *underly* the subrange type. See also *compatible.*

user Someone who uses programs, especially those you've written. Generally assumed to be a total ignoramus.

user-defined ordinal type A unique group of values whose identifiers and relative order are specified by the programer. User-defined ordinal values may be used wherever standard ordinal values are appropriate. However, they have no *external character representation,* and cannot be input or output as character sequences. (Some extended Pascals do allow input and output of user-defined ordinal values.)

value parameter, variable parameter See *parameter.*

variant field, variant part, variant record See *record variant.*

wedged Stuck. 'My program gets wedged doing *integer* reads.'

window See *file window.*

Answers to Exercises

Self-Test Answers: 1

1-1 When the program doesn't receive input from the keyboard or punched cards.
1-2 Absolutely nothing—the insertion is just a comment.
1-3 The statement's output is:

```
No,no, you can't take that awayfrom me.
```

Sometimes blanks have to be inserted before words to make spacing correct.
1-4 There are 172 ways of spelling the word.

```
program Palindrome (input, output);
var Char1, Char2, Char3, Char4, Char5: char;
begin
    writeln ('Please enter a five-letter palindrome.');
    readln (Char1, Char2, Char3, Char4, Char5);
    writeln (Char1, Char2, Char3, Char4, Char5);
    writeln (Char2, Char3, Char4, Char5, Char2);
    writeln (Char3, Char4, Char5, Char2, Char3);
    writeln (Char4, Char5, Char2, Char3, Char4);
    writeln (Char1, Char2, Char3, Char4, Char5)
end.
```

1-5 The standard types are *real, integer, char*, and *boolean.* A type clash occurs when we try to give a variable of one type a value of a different type. It causes a program crash (except when we give a *real* variable an *integer* value).

1-6 The value of unassigned or undefined variables is system dependent. Although some systems will *initialize* or automatically give the value 0 to *integer* or *real* variables, or ' ' to *char* variables, others won't—and trying to print the value of an undefined variable might cause a program crash.

1-7 When a thing is system defined, everybody's Pascal has it in one form or other. System dependent rules or values, on the other hand, are usually extensions of some sort. Not every implementation (version) of Pascal will contain them.

1-8 The syntax errors are easy to spot—*b* is obviously punctuated wrong, and *e* contains a split infinitive. The semantic errors are much harder—*a, c*, and *f* are all correct, meaningful English as stated. However, they should probably be rewritten as:

What is this thing called love?
I should say not!
Woman: without her, man is nothing.

The weirdest example, *d*, was deliberately devised by Noam Chomsky to show a sentence that is syntactically perfect, but semantically nonsensical.

1-9 Remember that *readln* gets a value for its variables (if it is given any), then discards the rest of the line. All examples below are correct.

readln (*Onions*);
read (*LettuceHeads*);
readln;
readln (*GarlicCloves*); etc.

1-10 Field widths may be given as expressions. The fields below are 1, 5, 3, and 4 spaces.

```
A    5   6   D
```

1-11 Two kinds of errors can't be caught at compile time—mistakes in the program's algorithm (what it figures out, and how it goes about it), and mistakes in the program's input that might cause type clashes. An error that the computer could *never* spot is:

writeln ('The sum of two and two is', 2+3);

1-12 A blank line may *not* be inserted between the lines of input—it would be a mistake.

0 17
= 0.618

1-13 *readln* (*Month, JunkChar, Date, AnotherJunkChar, Year*);

Self-Test Answers: 2

2-1 Yes. Blank spaces and carriage returns are disregarded except as separators of values, reserved words, and identifiers.

2-2 *a*) *integer*, *b*) *real*, *c*) This is an invalid expression—there is a clash between the types of 10.0 (*real*) and **div** (an *integer* operator).

2-3 In this segment, *Temporary* is an *integer* variable, while *Remainder* is *real*.

Temporary := *trunc* (55.55);
Remainder := (*Temporary* **mod** 7) + (55.55 − *Temporary*);

2-4 Yes, both assignments are valid. The value of *Opposite* is −77 after the assignment. It would be 99 if *Whole* were initialized to −99.

2-5 Two. Addition and subtraction have the lowest precedence.

2-6 The result is *real* in both cases.

2-7 The only predefined constant in standard Pascal is *MAXINT*, the value of the largest allowed *integer* value. However, your system might have other predefined constants.

2-8 Pascal has no exponentiation operator. The expression *exp*(*b***ln*(*a*)) represents *a* raised to the *b* power.

2-9 By using the expression above, substituting 1/3 for *b*. In general, 1/*n* is substituted.

2-10 Negative.

2-11 If *chr*(*ord*('A')+25) equals 'Z', the characters are contiguous.

2-12 *Text* or *string* constants.

2-13 *Width* is an arbitrary field width specification.

writeln ('Product is ', *Product*:*Width*:1);

2-14 Five—one for each assignment.

2-15 Note that there can't be a blank space between the two values.

73T

Self-Test Answers: 3

3-1 There are no restrictions.

3-2 By the context the identifier is used in. If the identifier is used in a procedure or function, it refers to the local variable. If the identifier appears in the outside program, it refers to the global variable.

3-3
```
procedure Reverse;
    var Temporary: char;
    begin
        Temporary := First;
        First := Fourth;
        Fourth := Temporary;
        Temporary := Second;
        Second := Third;
        Third := Temporary
    end; {Reverse}
```

3-4 Just as you'd do it by hand—in effect, by finding the number of hundreds, tens, and ones.

```
procedure ReverseTheNumber;
    var Hundreds, Tens, Ones: integer;
    begin
        Hundreds := TheNumber div 100;
        Tens := (TheNumber mod 100) div 10;
        Ones := (TheNumber mod 10);
        ReversedNumber := (100*Ones) + (10*Tens) + Hundreds;
    end; {ReverseTheNumber}
```

3-5 Only from their context. A procedure identifier always appears on a line by itself, as a statement. A constant identifier never appears on the left-hand side of an assignment statement. Constant and variable identifiers are always used as part of an assignment statement, or as arguments to procedures (like *write*) or functions.

3-6 About twenty lines—one screenful (or pageful) of code.

3-7

```
PrintNumbers (1, 1);
PrintNumbers (3, 5);
PrintNumbers (13, 21);
writeln;
```

3-8 *Parameter* usually refers to the value or variable parameter formally declared in a subprogram heading, while an *argument* is generally the actual value or variable passed to it.

3-9 A side effect is an assignment to a global variable identifier from within a subprogram. Side effects make the implicit documentation of procedure or function calls misleading—we expect that only the arguments of variable parameters will be altered within the procedure.

3-10 *Time* must have been defined as a value or variable parameter in *Clock's* heading, like this:

```
procedure Clock (Time: integer);
    var Time: integer;          etc.
```

3-11 The program's output is '   2   4   5'.

3-12 **procedure** *Separate* (*Argument*: *real*; **var** *WholePart, FractionalPart*: *integer*);

```
begin
  WholePart := trunc(Argument);
  FractionalPart := trunc(10000*(Argument-WholePart))
end; {Separate}
```

3-13 A variable parameter really *is* just a renaming of its global argument variable. Thus, the output of *HardToBelieve* is '   7' and '   8'.

3-14 Any ordinal type, or *real*.

3-15 Only when we make an assignment to the function—within the body of the function itself. This is usually the last statement of the function.

3-16 No. The types of both the function and its parameters must be known and specified when the function is written. Thus, there's no way we could write the equivalent of the standard function *sqr* (which defies this rule).

3-17 In bottom-up testing and debugging, the programmer views her program as a collection of individually written and tested subprograms. If each of these modules works when it's attached to a 'driver' program, she feels confident that the completed program will also work. The program as a whole is not tested until it's complete.

A top-down approach aims at testing and debugging the entire program, even if (at first) it mainly consists of dummy subprograms. Major program connections and ideas can be tried out before the programmer is committed to a particular design. As modules are completed and added to the program, the programmer can assure herself that her program still works.

Whether or not one approach is better than the other depends on your job and aims. Small programs, in which the job of each module is well-defined, are usually better tested by a bottom-up method. Large programs, however, fare better from the top-down approach, especially if several people are working on a single project. Testing and debugging are distributed throughout the programming process, and specific operation goals are easy to establish.

3-18 Function *SluggingPercentage* contains an inadvertent recursive call of itself. We should have used a temporary variable in the first assignment to avoid this problem.

```
function SluggingPercentage (AtBats, Singles, Doubles, Triples, Homers: integer): real;
  var NumberOfBases: integer;
  begin
    NumberOfBases := Singles+(2*Doubles)+(3*Triples)+(4*Homers);
    SluggingPercentage := NumberOfBases/AtBats
  end; {SluggingPercentage}
```

Self-Test Answers: 4

4-1 The first loop will execute one statement; the second, none.

4-2 The internal assignment to *Limit* doesn't affect the number of times the loop iterates.

```
11  7  8  9 10 11 12 13 14 15
```

4-3
```
for Counter := 1 to 12 do
   writeln (2*Counter);
```

4-4 The *real* type, because it's not an ordinal type—there's no standard 'next' *real*.

4-5 Its value is unknown—the counter variable is undefined on exit from the loop.

4-6
```
for LineCount := 1 to Last do begin
   for LetterCount := 1 to LineCount do
      read (TheNextLetter);
   write (TheNextLetter);
   readln         {Get rid of the rest of the input line.}
end;
writeln;
```

4-7 Twenty seven and ten, respectively.

4-8 In effect, we're maintaining a moving window of input numbers.

```
procedure PrintDifference;
   var FirstNumber, SecondNumber, Counter: integer:
   begin
      read (SecondNumber);
      for Counter := 1 to 9 do begin
         FirstNumber := SecondNumber;
         read (SecondNumber);
         writeln (SecondNumber - FirstNumber)
      end {for}
   end; {PrintDifference}
```

4-9 Note that this procedure has no protection against an incorrect *Length* value.

```
procedure Average (Length: integer; var Average: real);
   var Total, NextNumber, Count: integer;
   begin
      Total := 0;
      for Count := 1 to Length do begin
         read (NextNumber);
         Total := Total+NextNumber
      end;
      Average := Total/Length
   end; {Average}
```

4-10 A procedure that prints the current values of all program variables. It's used as an aid in program debugging.

Self-Test Answers: 5

5-1 Three—**case**, **of**, and **end**.

5-2 Only five values can appear—-4, -3, -2, -1, and 0.

5-3 Try printing the output of different values of *n*—1st, 2nd, 3rd, etc.

5-4
```
case ItemNumber of
   0, 3, 5: writeln ('Hats');
   1, 4: writeln ('Bats and Cats');
   2: writeln ('Slats')
end;
```

5-5 Note that input for *FindQuadrant* must be prompted before its call.

```
procedure FindQuadrant;
   var Angle: real;
   begin
      readln (Angle);
      write ('An angle of ', Angle:3:2, ' degrees falls in the ');
      case trunc(Angle/90) mod 4 of
         0: writeln ('first quadrant.');
         1: writeln ('second quadrant.');
         2: writeln ('third quadrant.');
         3: writeln ('fourth quadrant.')
      end {case}
   end; {FindQuadrant}
```

5-6 There's no shorthand for giving the values in a **case** constant list. The constants must be given one-by-one:

```
case Grade of
   'A', 'B', 'C', 'D': writeln ('Passing');
   'F': writeln ('Failing')
end;
```

5-7

Input	*Output*
AA	It
AB	is
BA	an Ancient
BB	an Mariner

5-8 Because he stoppeth one in three.

5-9 In procedure *Count*, input values are either digits or blanks.

```
procedure Count;
   var Character: char;
      LoopCounter, DigitCounter: integer;
   begin
      DigitCounter := 0;
      for LoopCounter := 1 to 40 do begin
         read (Character);
         case Character of
            ' ', '1', '2', '3', '5', '6', '7', '0': ;
            '4', '8', '9': DigitCounter := DigitCounter+1
         end {case}
      end; {for}
      writeln ('The number of fours, eights, and nines is ', DigitCounter)
   end; {Count}
```

5-10 What is not is often What is not is

5-11 The constant list of a **case** statement must contain the actual constants (the literal representations) of the counter variable's type. Since parameters are variables (and couldn't go in the value list), it wouldn't do us any good to pass 2, 3, and 6 as parameters.

```
procedure CountDigits (SizeOfInput: integer; var Occurrences: integer);
  var NextCharacter: char;
      LoopCounter: integer;
  begin
    Occurrences := 0;
    for LoopCounter := 1 to SizeOfInput do begin
      read (NextCharacter);
      case NextCharacter of
        '1', '4', '5', '7', '8', '9', '0': ;
        '2', '3', '6': Occurrences := Occurrences+1
      end {case}
    end {for}
  end; {CountDigits}
```

5-12 Test data can only show the presence of program bugs, rather than their absence. However, good test data demonstrates specific conditions for which a program will work.

Self-Test Answers: 6

6-1 Because *boolean* operators have higher precedence than the relational operators. The terms that use only relational operators must go in parentheses.

6-2 *a* and *c*.

6-3 When *StillSearching* and *Found* are both either *true* or *false*.

6-4 Certainly.

6-5

```
function ReturnNegative (Argument: real): real;
  begin
    if Argument < 0
      then ReturnNegative := Argument
      else ReturnNegative := -Argument
  end; {ReturnNegative}
```

6-6

```
function IsADigit (PotentialDigit: char): boolean;
  begin
    IsADigit := PotentialDigit in ['0'..'9']
  end; {IsADigit}
```

6-7 In pseudocode, we have:

```
Pick a random number between 1 and 100;
if the number is 1..35 then Pick := 4
  else if the number is 36..50 then Pick := 5
    else if the number is 51..69 then Pick := 6
      else if the number is 70..100 then Pick := 7;
```

6-8

```
function Divisible (First, Second: integer): boolean;
  begin
    Divisible := (First mod Second) = 0
  end; {Divisible}
```

6-9 Note that reversing the actions makes our job easy—the *writeln* doesn't change any of the variables in the *boolean* expression.

```
if (2*X) <= Y then
    writeln ('Able was I ere I saw Elba.');
if (2*X) > Y then begin
    Y := 2*Y; X := X/2
end;
```

6-10 *false true false*

6-11 Both program segments have the same ultimate effect—the smallest of *a*, *b*, and *c* is assigned to *Smallest*. However, they approach the problem in different ways. The first method makes every possible test before making an assignment. The second method, in contrast, makes an assignment—*Smallest* := *a*—then tests its correctness. Thus, the second method takes advantage of the insight that one of the values *must* be the smallest to simplify the Pascal code.

6-12 Both program segments have the same effect—they take an action that depends on the value of *Amount*. (We're assuming that none of the procedure calls alter this value.) The code on the left, though, is less efficient. Very often, unnecessary *boolean* checks will be made long after we've taken the appropriate action. The right-hand code, however, forms a **case** statement of sorts. After an action is taken, the rest of the *boolean* checks (the rest of the indented statements) are skipped.

6-13
```
procedure CheckDivisibility (Divisor, Dividend: integer);
  begin
   if (Dividend mod Divisor) = 0
    then writeln (Divisor:1, ' divides ', Dividend:1, ' evenly.')
    else writeln (Divisor:1, ' doesn't divide ', Dividend:1, ' evenly.')
  end; {CheckDivisibility}
```

6-14 Note the use of 0 and 501 as *sentinel* values for initializing *LargestEven* and *SmallestOdd*. If *LargestEven* and *SmallestOdd* still have these values (which are outside the range of valid entries) at the end of the loop, we know that no even or odd values were read in. Why is the **then** action stated as a compound statement?

```
LargestEven := 0;
SmallestOdd := 501;
for Counter := 1 to 100 do begin
    read (Number);
    if odd (Number)
        then begin if Number<SmallestOdd then SmallestOdd := Number end
        else if Number>LargestEven then LargestEven := Number
end;
```

6-15
```
if n>=2 then n := (3*n)-6;
```

6-16

```
a) ['A', 'E', 'I', 'O', 'U']
b) ['B'..'D', 'F'..'H', 'J'..'N', 'P'..'T', 'V'..'Z']
```

6-17 Note the nested **if** statements:

```
DigitCount := 0;
PunctuationCount := 0;
for Counter := 1 to 250 do begin
    read (Character);
    if Character in ['0'..'9']
        then DigitCount := DigitCount+1
        else if Character in ['.', ';', ',', ':', '!', '?'] then
            PunctuationCount := PunctuationCount+1
    end; {for}
```

6-18 Example 1 is the most obvious and straightforward solution to the problem. The code is correct, and easy to follow. In example 2, we make the insight that neither 1 nor 5 are even, and reduce the amount of work the computer does. Example 3 takes the next logical step—the programmer figures out the answer, and makes the assignment herself. However, example 4 illustrates the problem with being *too* clever—a dumb mistake is just as wrong as a hard mistake. We conclude that straightforwardness, cleverness, simplicity, and correctness all have to be considered in writing code.

Self-Test Answers: 7

7-1 *f, g*: neither **while** nor **repeat**.
b, c, d: **repeat** only.
e: **while** and **repeat**.
a: **while** only.

7-2 Error check input; give the user a chance to correct mistaken input; run it for three sets of ten, resting two minutes between each set.

7-3 It contains a bug. To correct it, initialize *Count* to 0 instead of 1.

7-4 The *boolean* condition in the **if** statement is misstated—it should be <>, rather than =. We incorrectly enter the loop if the first character read is a blank.

7-5 No. It, too, contains a bug—the first pair of values is lost. The statements inside the **while** loop should be reversed.

7-6 Note that the sense of each condition must be reversed:

```
repeat
    read (First, Last)
until (First <> Start) or (Finish = Last)
```

7-7 Again, we have to reverse the sense of the condition. However, we must also initialize *Number* so that the loop can be entered at all.

```
Count := -1;
Number := 0;
while Number >= 0 do begin
    read (Number);
    Count := Count + 1
end;
```

7-8

```
for i := 4 downto 0 do
  writeln (i * 5);
```

7-9

```
Power := 0;
TwoToThatPower := 1;
read (LimitNumber);        {The number we want to exceed.}
while TwoToThatPower < LimitNumber do begin
  Power := Power + 1;
  TwoToThatPower := TwoToThatPower * 2
end;
writeln ('Two to the ', Power:1, ' power is greater than or equal to ', LimitNumber:1);
```

7-10

```
StartingPopulation := NumberOfFish;
NumberOfYears := 0;
repeat
   NumberOfFish := 0.977 * NumberOfFish;
   NumberOfYears := 1 + NumberOfYears
until NumberOfFish <= (StartingPopulation/10);
writeln (StartingPopulation:1, ' will decrease by 90% within ', NumberOfYears:1, ' years.');
```

7-11 *a*) Sue, while Patti had had 'had', had had 'had had'. 'Had had' had had a better effect on the teacher.
b) Zero, of course.
c) This is the classic boundary problem. Eleven posts are required.

7-12 Function *LargestFactor* implements an easy algorithm for finding the greatest common divisor.

```
function LargestFactor (First, Second: integer): integer;
   var ProposedFactor: integer;
   begin
      if First < Second
         then ProposedFactor := First
         else ProposedFactor := Second;
      while ((First mod ProposedFactor)<>0) or ((Second mod ProposedFactor)<>0) do
         ProposedFactor := ProposedFactor-1;
      LargestFactor := ProposedFactor
   end; {LargestFactor}
```

Self-Test Answers: 8

8-1 The character representation of the end-of-line character is a blank space. If it's echoed, it prints as an ordinary blank—there's no line-feed.

8-2 The code below prevents confusing the end-of-line character with a plain blank.

```
if eof
   then writeln ('At the end of the file.')
   else if eoln
      then writeln ('At the end of the line.')
      else begin
         read (NextCharacter);
         if NextCharacter=' '
            then writeln ('The next character is an ordinary space.')
            else writeln ('The next character is a non-blank.')
      end;
```

8-3 Procedure *readln* may be called at *eoln*. The call's effect is to discard the end-of-line character, and set *eof* to *true*. However, it is a run-time error to call *readln* at *eof*.

8-4 It reads and echoes characters until it encounters an empty line. Remember this one!

8-5 How robust is this procedure? What is the final value of *NextLetter* if there aren't any letters?

```
procedure GetNextLetter (var NextLetter: char);
    var NextCharacter: char;
    begin
        NextCharacter := ' ';          {A 'dummy' initialization.}
        while not eof and not (NextCharacter in ['a'..'z', 'A'..'Z']) do
            read (NextCharacter);
        if eof
            then writeln ('At end-of-file. No letters found.')
            else NextLetter := NextCharacter
    end; {GetNextLetter}
```

8-6 Can't be done. We can read the end-of-line character, but it's stored as a space. It may, however, be possible to assign its value to a variable (by using the *chr* function) if you know its ordinal position in the computer's character set.

8-7 It's removed. Where it goes, nobody knows.

8-8 As always, a check for *eof* must start the procedure.

```
procedure LetterSearch (var Largest, Smallest: char);
    var CurrentCharacter: char;
    begin
        Largest := chr(ord('a')-1);
        Smallest := chr(ord('z')+1);
        if eof then writeln ('Empty input file. Results will be incorrect.');
        while not eof do begin
            read (CurrentCharacter);
            if CurrentCharacter in ['a'..'z'] then begin
                if CurrentCharacter>Largest then Largest := CurrentCharacter;
                if CurrentCharacter<Smallest then Smallest := CurrentCharacter
            end {CurrentCharacter is lower-case.}
        end {while}
    end; {LetterSearch}
```

8-9 All the letters in the file are identical.

8-10 Again, we have to check for *eof* before reading any character.

```
procedure ReadAndEcho (Sentinel: char; LookingForSentinel: boolean);
    var Finished: boolean;
        Current: char;
    begin
        if not eof then begin
            read (Current);
            if LookingForSentinel
                then Finished := Current=Sentinel
                else Finished := false;
            while not Finished and not eof do begin
                write (Current);
                read (Current);
                if LookingForSentinel then Finished := Current=Sentinel
            end;
            writeln
        end
    end; {ReadAndEcho}
```

Self-Test Answers: 9

9-1 Both types are *simple* types, which means that they're ordered groups of indivisible values. Ordinal types, however, are *enumerable*. It's possible to list, in order, every value of an ordinal type. The values of type *real*, in contrast, can't be enumerated. There's just no notion of of a 'next' *real* in either mathematics or Pascal.

9-2 The identifiers *Green* and *Yellow* can't be used both as constants of type *Hue*, and as variable identifiers.

9-3 The definitions of *GradePoints* (subranges of *real* aren't allowed) and *Alphabet* (the lower bound exceeds the upper bound) are both illegal.

9-4 If a Pascal processor only uses the first eight characters of an identifier, the constants *Straight* and *StraightFlush* will appear to be identical. This isn't standard Pascal, but it's a common shortcoming.

9-5 No—it's illegal Pascal. The bounds of a subrange must be set before the program is compiled.

9-6 *a*) Any of the variables.
b) Any variable as long as its value is in the range *Infrared..Blue*.
c) None of them—the variable parameter and its argument must have identical type names.
d) None of the variables. *Hue* must be defined with a type identifier—it's illegal to define it on the spot as we've done.

9-7 Only if the type is a subrange (or renaming) of one of the standard types. The enumerated types have no external character representation.

9-8 The function call represents the *char* value *chr*(5), and not the *Weather* value *Plague*.

9-9 First, *Sunday* is 'greater' than *Monday*, so the the loop limits are ineffective. Second, '*writeln* (*Today*);' is illegal—enumerated ordinal values can't be printed. Finally, the assignment to *Today* is illegal because *Today* is the **for** loop counter variable.

9-10 Looking at the type definition is the only way.

9-11
```
while ord (NewType) <> 0 do
    NewType := pred (NewType);
```

Self-Test Answers: 11

11-1 In two ways—by specifying array bounds, or by giving the name of an ordinal type (besides *integer*) or subrange.

11-2 The elements of an array can be arrays themselves. The first two definitions define a type equivalent to (but not the same as) the third definition.

```
type StoredArray = array [1..10] of integer;
    StoringArray = array [1..10] of StoredArray;
    TheEquivalent = array [1..10, 1..10] of integer;
```

11-3 Both assignments are correct. The second is just a simplified version of the first.

11-4 Only *a* and *d* should be solved using arrays.

11-5 Packed arrays of type *char* can be compared using any of the relational operators. They need not be of identical types; however, each array must have the same number of stored elements.

11-6
```
type Word = packed array [1..8] of char;
    ProgramData = array [1..100] of Word;
```

11-7 Ordering *a* will require the greatest number of updates: 25. Arrangement *c*, which begins with only 1 element out of place, requires the fewest: 9.

11-8

```
for Counter := 1 to 25 do begin
   List [(Counter*2) - 1] := 'O';
   List [Counter*2] := 'E'
end;
```

11-9 When the segment is executed, *AlsoOccupied* will always be *true* because we always inspect *Board* [*Row, Column*] (which we know is occupied). The **if** statements should contain an additional check to prevent inspection of this square.

11-10 Note that the locally defined array is of the largest potential size. Its actual required dimensions can't be passed as parameters, because variables can't appear in a type definition.

```
function IsMagic (Square: SquareType; Side: integer): boolean;
   type CheckArray = array [1..100] of boolean;
   var Check: CheckArray;
      Row, Column, Counter: integer;
   begin
      for Counter := 1 to sqr (Side) do
         Check [Counter] := false;
      {Initialize as much of the Check array as we'll need.}
      for Row := 1 to Side do
         for Column := 1 to Side do
            Check [Square [Row, Column]] := true;
         {Check off all the numbers in Square.}
      IsMagic := true;
      for Counter := 1 to sqr(Side) do
         if not Check [Counter] then IsMagic := false
      {If any numbers between 1 and Side squared weren't}
      {checked off, Square must contain an illegal number.}
   end; {IsMagic}
```

Self-Test Answers: 12

12-1 False, true, and false.

12-2 It's illegal. *Style* must be defined before it can be used in the *Unit* record definition.

12-3 The computer would be unable to distinguish between an identifier containing a period, and an access of one field of a record. For example, imagine a record with a field called *Price*, a variable *Item* of that type, and an ordinary variable named *Item.Price*. When the identifier *Item.Price* appears in a program does it refer to the record, or to the ordinary variable? This is one reason that periods can't appear in Pascal identifiers.

12-4 Only the two *Period*-type variables. Although *SnowsOfYesteryear* might appear to be of the same type, it is not.

12-5

```
type Owner = (Red, Black);
     Checker = record
                  Row, Column: 1..8;
                  Color: Owner
               end;
```

12-6 **with** *City* **do begin**

```
    Latitude.Degrees := 22;
    Latitude.Minutes := 17;
    Latitude.Seconds := 34;
    Latitude.Direction := North;
    Longitude.Degrees := 53;
    Longitude.Minutes := 41;
    Longitude.Seconds := 9;
    Longitude.Direction := West
end;
```

12-7 There is no way to distinguish between the sub-fields of *Latitude* and *Longitude*.

12-8

```
if (Home.Prefix = Office.Prefix) and (Home.Number = Office.Number) then
  writeln ('Home and office numbers are identical.');
if Office.AreaCode = Car.AreaCode then writeln ('Same area code.');
Car.Prefix := Home.Prefix;
```

12-9 Once.

12-10 The value of the tag field tells us which variant group of fields is currently in use.

12-11 The output is 'B'. The record accessed in the **with** statement is the one located by *Series* [*Current*] when the statement is first entered.

Self-Test Answers: 13

13-1 The files *input* and *output*.

13-2 It must be the argument of a variable parameter.

13-3 Put the instructions in an external file, then have your program read and echo the instructions file.

13-4 Assume that function *IntegerEquivalent* finds the *integer* equivalent of its *char* argument, according to the telephone dial—'a', 'b', and 'c' equal 2, etc.

```
if not (input↑ in ['A'..'Y'])
   then read (PhoneNumber)          {Read it as a integer.}
   else begin
      PhoneNumber := 1000000*IntegerEquivalent (input↑);
      get (input);
      PhoneNumber := PhoneNumber+(100000*IntegerEquivalent (input↑));
      get (input);
      read (TheRestOfTheNumber);
      PhoneNumber := PhoneNumber + TheRestOfTheNumber
   end;
```

13-5 It counts the number of blank lines in file *TheSource*.

13-6

```
reset (TheFile);
NumberOfComponents := 0;
while not eof(TheFile) do begin
   NumberOfComponents := NumberOfComponents + 1;
   get (TheFile)
end;
```

13-7 Begin with a line-counter variable initialized to 1, and have the statement *write*(*LineCounter*) appear at the start of the procedure. Then, after the *writeln* that flushes the current line from the output buffer, increment *LineCounter*, and (if it's not *eof*) *write* it again.

13-8 The procedure call *read*(*FileName, Value*) can be restated as:

```
Value := FileName↑;
get (FileName);
```

The call *write*(*FileName, Value*) is equivalent to:

```
FileName↑ := Value;
put (FileName);
```

13-9 We wrote this solution using a **repeat** rather than a **while**. Does it make any difference?

```
reset (TheDeck);
repeat
   if not eof(TheDeck) then begin
      writeln (TheDeck↑.Number, TheDeck↑.Suit, TheDeck↑.Found);
      get (TheDeck)
   end
until eof(TheDeck)
```

13-10 It can't. One file has to be copied onto the other one component at a time.

13-11

```
reset (F);
for Counter := 1 to (X-1) do readln (F);
while not eoln(F) do begin
   read (F, CurrentCharacter);
   write (F, CurrentCharacter)
end;
writeln;
```

13-12 The program will crash as it attempts to read past the end of file *Data*. Why? Recall that blank spaces and end-of-lines are ignored except as value separators. However, they're skipped over *before* each new value is read. Since every textfile ends with at least one blank (the final end-of-line character), procedure *read* bravely throws it away, looks for the next integer value, and runs past end of file.

13-13 When *eof* is *true*, the file window (*TheFile*↑ here) is undefined. Thus, our code is in the awkward position of using an undefined value in a *boolean* expression.

Self-Test Answers: 14

14-1 Don't forget that *all* months have 28 days, and most of them have 30!

```
type Months = (Jan, Feb, Mar, Apr, May, June, July, Aug, Sep, Oct, Nov, Dec);
     SetOfMonths = set of Months;
var ShortMonths, MediumMonths, LongMonths: SetOfMonths;
begin
   ShortMonths := [Jan..Dec];
   MediumMonths := [Jan, Mar..Dec];
   LongMonths := [Jan, Mar, May, July, Aug, Oct, Dec];
         ... etc.
```

14-2

[]	[*Rock*]	[*Roll*]	[*Reggae*]
[*Rock, Roll*]	[*Rock, Reggae*]	[*Roll, Reggae*]	[*Rock..Reggae*]

14-3 Expressions *a* and *c* are *true*. The others are *false*.

14-4 *Movers + Groovers + Shakers + Quakers + Lovers + Fighters*
Lovers + Fighters
Movers − Groovers
*(Shakers * Quakers) − Lovers*
(Movers + Shakers + Lovers + Fighters) − (Groovers + Quakers)

14-5 It is not an error to try to remove elements of an empty set. *SomeSet* is empty after the assignment.

14-6 It would certainly be convenient to have a predefined function that represented the number of members in its set-valued argument.

```
function SetCount (LetterGroup: CapitalSet): integer;
   var Count: integer;
      Letter: char;
   begin
      Count := 0;
      for Letter := 'A' to 'Z' do
         if Letter in LetterGroup then Count := Count+1;
      SetCount := Count;
   end; {SetCount}
```

14-7
```
Letter := 'Z';
while not (Letter in LetterGroup) do
  Letter := pred(Letter);
```

14-8 What happens if *LetterGroup* is an empty set? The entry condition should be restated as:

```
(not (Letter in LetterGroup)) and (Letter <= 'Z')
```

14-9 The symbols +, −, and * are special because they're each used to represent several different operations. For example, the symbol * may be used as the *real* multiplication, *integer* multiplication, or set intersection operator. Its effect is determined from its context: the compiler inspects the types of the symbol's operands, then translate the operator to an appropriate action.

14-10 Two to the *n*th power values.

Self-Test Answers: 15

15-1
```
type IntPointer = ↑integer;
PointToChar = ↑char;
ReferenceListElement = ↑ListElement;
```

15-2 A stack is a last in, first out structure, because the last element pushed onto the stack is the first one popped off. A queue is first in, first out because its elements are added to one end, and taken from the other. The earliest element to go on is the first to come off. Both are sequential access structures—neither stack or queue elements can be accessed at random. A file-type variable has a first in, first out structure (although it isn't a queue). Since arrays and sets are random access types, the notion of LIFO and FIFO doesn't make sense in reference to them.

15-3 *Trial* has no output, because it crashes during execution. When *Test* is assigned the value **nil**, it no longer accesses a location. Any attempted assignment to *Test*↑ is an illegal reference through a **nil** pointer.

15-4
```
procedure CheckIdentity (First, Second: Reach);
  begin
    write ('The pointers reference ');
    if First=Second
      then write ('the same location, ')
      else write ('different locations, ');
    write ('and indirectly access ');
    if First↑=Second↑
      then write ('the same value.')
      else write ('different values.')
  end; {CheckIdentity}
```

15-5 The assignment is only valid when *Variable* is a pointer type. If *Variable* is a file-type variable, the assignment's illegal.

15-6
```
type SuperPointer = ↑SuperNode;
  SuperNode = record
                Data: TheDataType;
                Left, Right, Previous: SuperPointer
              end;
```

15-7
```
new (Current↑.Left);
new (Current↑.Right);
Current↑.Left↑.Previous := Current;
Current↑.Left↑.Left := nil;
Current↑.Left↑.Right := nil;
Current↑.Right↑.Previous := Current;
Current↑.Right↑.Right := nil;
Current↑.Right↑.Left := nil;
```

15-8 *Mystery* follows a sequence of pointers (stored in field *WhoKnows*), and represents the number of elements found. It fails if the sequence is circular. To avoid this problem, a local copy of the original *ThisPosition* should be maintained.

15-9 For all practical purposes, they're identical as defined, since each requires the exact same number of pointer fields.

15-10 Note the use of *Start* to remember our starting position.

```
procedure PrintCircle (Current: Elements);
  var Start: Elements;
  begin
    if Current<>nil then begin
      Start := Current;
      repeat
        writeln (Current↑.Data);
        Current := Current↑.Subsequent
      until (Current=Start) or (Current=nil)
    end
  end; {PrintCircle}
```

Index to Programs and Subprograms

Chapter 1 Getting Acquainted with Programs

Chapter 2 Programming Calculations

Chapter 3 Procedures and Functions

Chapter 4 The **for** Statement

Chapter 5 The **case** Statement

Chapter 6 The **if** Statement

Chapter 7 The Conditional Loops

Chapter 8 Text Processing

Chapter 9 Enumerated Ordinal Types

Chapter 11 Arrays

Chapter 12 Records

Chapter 13 Files

Chapter 14 Sets

Chapter 15 Pointers

Chapter 16 Sorting, Searching, Matching

Index

Model Program

```
program SoTypical (input, output);                       {heading}

const  LIMIT=10;                                         {integer constant}
       POUNDSIGN='#';                                    {char constant}
       AMORCITA='Ilana';                                 {string constant}

type  Hues=(Red, Blue, Green, Orange, Violet);           {enumerated ordinal type}
      Shades=Blue..Orange;                               {subrange}
      SmallNumbers=1..10;                                {subrange}
      String=packed array [1..LIMIT] of char;            {string}
      Class=record
              Name: String;
              Units: integer;
              Grade: char
            end;                                         {record-type}
      Grades=array [SmallNumbers] of Class;              {array type}
      ColorCount=array [1..10, 'A'..'Z'] of Hues;        {array type}
      ClassFile=file of Class;                           {file type}
      Pastels=set of Shades;                             {set type}
      NextWord=↑Sentence;                                {pointer}
      Sentence=record                                    {dynamically allocable Record}
                 CurrentWord: String;
                 ComingWord: NextWord
               end;

var  High, Low, Counter: integer;                        {integer}
     First, Last: char;                                  {char}
     Height, Weight: real;                               {real}
     Testing, DeBugging: boolean;                        {boolean}
     Colors: Hues;                                       {enumerated type}
     Shorts: SmallNumbers;                               {subrange}
     Name: String;                                       {string}
     OneCourse: Class;                                   {record}
     Curriculum: Grades;                                 {array}
     ColorSquares: ColorCount;                           {array}
     Schedule: ClassFile;                                {file}
     Source, Results: text;                              {textfile}
     Crayons: Pastels                                    {set}
     List, Pointer: NextWord                             {pointer}

procedure VeryBusy (Incoming: integer; var Outgoing: integer);     {procedure declaration}
  {A procedure with value and variable parameters.}
  var Local: integer;
  begin
    readln (Local);
    Outgoing := Incoming * Local
  end; {VeryBusy}
```